NON SANZ DROICT.

William Shakespeare

Pericles, Prince of Tyre

Edited by Ernest Schanzer

Cymbeline

Edited by Richard Hosley

The Two Noble Kinsmen

(with John Fletcher)

Edited by Clifford Leech

With New and Updated Critical Essays and a Revised Bibliography

THE SIGNET CLASSICS SHAKESPEARE
General Editor: Sylvan Barnet

SIGNET CLASSICS

SIGNET CLASSICS
Published by New American Library, a division of
Penguin Group (USA) Inc., 375 Hudson Street,
New York, New York 10014, USA
Penguin Group (Canada), 90 Eglinton Avenue East, Suite 700, Toronto,
Ontario M4P 2Y3, Canada (a division of Pearson Penguin Canada Inc.)
Penguin Books Ltd., 80 Strand, London WC2R 0RL, England
Penguin Ireland, 25 St. Stephen's Green, Dublin 2,
Ireland (a division of Penguin Books Ltd.)
Penguin Group (Australia), 250 Camberwell Road, Camberwell, Victoria 3124,
Australia (a division of Pearson Australia Group Pty. Ltd.)
Penguin Books India Pvt. Ltd., 11 Community Centre, Panchsheel Park,
New Delhi - 110 017, India
Penguin Group (NZ), cnr Airborne and Rosedale Roads, Albany,
Auckland 1310, New Zealand (a division of Pearson New Zealand Ltd.)
Penguin Books (South Africa) (Pty.) Ltd., 24 Sturdee Avenue,
Rosebank, Johannesburg 2196, South Africa

Penguin Books Ltd., Registered Offices:
80 Strand, London WC2R 0RL, England

Published by Signet Classics, an imprint of New American Library,
a division of Penguin Group (USA) Inc.

First Signet Classics Printing (Second Revised Edition), November 2006
10 9 8 7 6 5 4 3 2

Pericles, Prince of Tyre
Copyright © Ernest Schanzer, 1965
Copyright © Sylvan Barnet, 1963, 1988, 2006

Cymbeline
Copyright © Richard Hosley, 1968, 1988, 2006
Copyright © Sylvan Barnet, 1963, 1988, 2006

The Two Noble Kinsmen
Copyright © Clifford Leech, 1966
Copyright © Sylvan Barnet, 1963, 1988, 2006
All rights reserved

Contents

Shakespeare: An Overview
Biographical Sketch vii / *A Note on the Anti-Stratfordians, Especially Baconians and Oxfordians* xi / The Shakespeare Canon xv / Shakespeare's English xviii / Shakespeare's Theater xxv / *A Note on the Use of Boy Actors in Female Roles* xxxii / Shakespeare's Dramatic Language: Costumes, Gestures and Silences; Prose and Poetry xxxv / The Play Text as a Collaboration xlii / Editing Texts xlviii / Shakespeare on the Stage lii

Shakespeare: An Overview

Biographical Sketch

Between the record of his baptism in Stratford on 26 April 1564 and the record of his burial in Stratford on 25 April 1616, some forty official documents name Shakespeare, and many others name his parents, his children, and his grandchildren. Further, there are at least fifty literary references to him in the works of his contemporaries. More facts are known about William Shakespeare than about any other playwright of the period except Ben Jonson. The facts should, however, be distinguished from the legends. The latter, inevitably more engaging and better known, tell us that the Stratford boy killed a calf in high style, poached deer and rabbits, and was forced to flee to London, where he held horses outside a playhouse. These traditions are only traditions; they may be true, but no evidence supports them, and it is well to stick to the facts.

Mary Arden, the dramatist's mother, was the daughter of a substantial landowner; about 1557 she married John Shakespeare, a tanner, glove maker, and trader in wool, grain, and other farm commodities. In 1557 John Shakespeare was a member of the council (the governing body of Stratford), in 1558 a constable of the borough, in 1561 one of the two town chamberlains, in 1565 an alderman (entitling him to the appellation of "Mr."), in 1568 high bailiff—the town's highest political office, equivalent to mayor. After 1577, for an unknown reason he drops out of local politics. What *is* known is that he had to mortgage his wife's property, and that he was involved in serious litigation.

The birthday of William Shakespeare, the third child and the eldest son of this locally prominent man, is unrecorded, but the Stratford parish register records that the infant was baptized on

26 April 1564. (It is quite possible that he was born on 23 April, but this date has probably been assigned by tradition because it is the date on which, fifty-two years later, he died, and perhaps because it is the feast day of St. George, patron saint of England.) The attendance records of the Stratford grammar school of the period are not extant, but it is reasonable to assume that the son of a prominent local official attended the free school— it had been established for the purpose of educating males precisely of his class—and received substantial training in Latin. The masters of the school from Shakespeare's seventh to fifteenth years held Oxford degrees; the Elizabethan curriculum excluded mathematics and the natural sciences but taught a good deal of Latin rhetoric, logic, and literature, including plays by Plautus, Terence, and Seneca.

On 27 November 1582 a marriage license was issued for the marriage of Shakespeare and Anne Hathaway, eight years his senior. The couple had a daughter, Susanna, in May 1583. Perhaps the marriage was necessary, but perhaps the couple had earlier engaged, in the presence of witnesses, in a formal "troth plight," which would render their children legitimate even if no further ceremony were performed. In February 1585, Anne Hathaway bore Shakespeare twins, Hamnet and Judith.

That Shakespeare was born is excellent; that he married and had children is pleasant; but that we know nothing about his departure from Stratford to London or about the beginning of his theatrical career is lamentable and must be admitted. We would gladly sacrifice details about his children's baptism for details about his earliest days in the theater. Perhaps the poaching episode is true (but it is first reported almost a century after Shakespeare's death), or perhaps he left Stratford to be a schoolmaster, as another tradition holds; perhaps he was moved (like Petruchio in *The Taming of the Shrew*) by

> Such wind as scatters young men through the world,
> To seek their fortunes farther than at home
> Where small experience grows.   (1.2.49–51)

In 1592, thanks to the cantankerousness of Robert Greene, we have our first reference, a snarling one, to Shakespeare as an actor and playwright. Greene, a graduate of St. John's College, Cambridge, had become a playwright and a pamphleteer in

London, and in one of his pamphlets he warns three university-educated playwrights against an actor who has presumed to turn playwright:

> There is an upstart crow, beautified with our feathers, that with his *tiger's heart wrapped in a player's hide* supposes he is as well able to bombast out a blank verse as the best of you, and being an absolute Johannes-factotum [i.e., jack-of-all-trades] is in his own conceit the only Shake-scene in a country.

The reference to the player, as well as the allusion to Aesop's crow (who strutted in borrowed plumage, as an actor struts in fine words not his own), makes it clear that by this date Shakespeare had both acted and written. That Shakespeare is meant is indicated not only by *Shake-scene* but also by the parody of a line from one of Shakespeare's plays, *3 Henry VI*: "O, tiger's heart wrapped in a woman's hide" (1.4.137). If in 1592 Shakespeare was prominent enough to be attacked by an envious dramatist, he probably had served an apprenticeship in the theater for at least a few years.

In any case, although there are no extant references to Shakespeare between the record of the baptism of his twins in 1585 and Greene's hostile comment about "Shake-scene" in 1592, it is evident that during some of these "dark years" or "lost years" Shakespeare had acted and written. There are a number of subsequent references to him as an actor. Documents indicate that in 1598 he is a "principal comedian," in 1603 a "principal tragedian," in 1608 he is one of the "men players." (We do not have, however, any solid information about which roles he may have played; later traditions say he played Adam in *As You Like It* and the ghost in *Hamlet,* but nothing supports the assertions. Probably his role as dramatist came to supersede his role as actor.) The profession of actor was not for a gentleman, and it occasionally drew the scorn of university men like Greene, who resented writing speeches for persons less educated than themselves, but it was respectable enough; players, if prosperous, were in effect members of the bourgeoisie, and there is nothing to suggest that Stratford considered William Shakespeare less than a solid citizen. When, in 1596, the Shakespeares were granted a coat of arms—i.e., the right to be considered gentlemen—the grant was made to Shakespeare's father, but probably William Shakespeare had arranged the matter on his own behalf. In subsequent transactions he is occasionally styled a gentleman.

Although in 1593 and 1594 Shakespeare published two narrative poems dedicated to the Earl of Southampton, *Venus and Adonis* and *The Rape of Lucrece,* and may well have written most or all of his sonnets in the middle nineties, Shakespeare's literary activity seems to have been almost entirely devoted to the theater. (It may be significant that the two narrative poems were written in years when the plague closed the theaters for several months.) In 1594 he was a charter member of a theatrical company called the Chamberlain's Men, which in 1603 became the royal company, the King's Men, making Shakespeare the king's playwright. Until he retired to Stratford (about 1611, apparently), he was with this remarkably stable company. From 1599 the company acted primarily at the Globe theater, in which Shakespeare held a one-tenth interest. Other Elizabethan dramatists are known to have acted, but no other is known also to have been entitled to a share of the profits.

Shakespeare's first eight published plays did not have his name on them, but this is not remarkable; the most popular play of the period, Thomas Kyd's *The Spanish Tragedy,* went through many editions without naming Kyd, and Kyd's authorship is known only because a book on the profession of acting happens to quote (and attribute to Kyd) some lines on the interest of Roman emperors in the drama. What is remarkable is that after 1598 Shakespeare's name commonly appears on printed plays—some of which are not his. Presumably his name was a drawing card, and publishers used it to attract potential buyers. Another indication of his popularity comes from Francis Meres, author of *Palladis Tamia: Wit's Treasury* (1598). In this anthology of snippets accompanied by an essay on literature, many playwrights are mentioned, but Shakespeare's name occurs more often than any other, and Shakespeare is the only playwright whose plays are listed.

From his acting, his playwriting, and his share in a playhouse, Shakespeare seems to have made considerable money. He put it to work, making substantial investments in Stratford real estate. As early as 1597 he bought New Place, the second-largest house in Stratford. His family moved in soon afterward, and the house remained in the family until a granddaughter died in 1670. When Shakespeare made his will in 1616, less than a month before he died, he sought to leave his property intact to his descendants. Of small bequests to relatives and to friends (including three actors, Richard Burbage, John Heminges, and Henry Condell), that to his wife of the second-best bed has provoked the most comment. It has sometimes been taken as a sign of an unhappy marriage (other supposed signs are the apparently hasty marriage, his wife's seniority of eight years, and his residence in London without his family). Perhaps the second-best bed was the bed the couple had slept in, the best bed being reserved for visitors. In any case, had Shakespeare not excepted it, the bed would have gone (with the rest of his household possessions) to his daughter and her husband.

On 25 April 1616 Shakespeare was buried within the chancel of the church at Stratford. An unattractive monument to his memory, placed on a wall near the grave, says that he died on 23 April. Over the grave itself are the lines, perhaps by Shakespeare, that (more than his literary fame) have kept his bones undisturbed in the crowded burial ground, where old bones were often dislodged to make way for new:

> Good friend, for Jesus' sake forbear
> To dig the dust enclosed here.
> Blessed be the man that spares these stones
> And cursed be he that moves my bones.

A Note on the Anti-Stratfordians, Especially Baconians and Oxfordians

Not until 1769—more than a hundred and fifty years after Shakespeare's death—is there any record of anyone expressing doubt about Shakespeare's authorship of the plays and poems. In 1769, however, Herbert Lawrence nominated Francis Bacon (1561–1626) in *The Life and Adventures of Common Sense*. Since then, at least two dozen other nominees have been offered, including Christopher Marlowe, Sir Walter Raleigh, Queen Elizabeth I, and Edward de Vere, 17th earl of Oxford. The impulse behind all anti-Stratfordian movements is the scarcely concealed snobbish opinion that "the man from Stratford" simply could not have written the plays because he was a country fellow without a university education and without access to high society. Anyone, the argument goes, who used so many legal terms, medical terms, nautical terms, and so forth, and who showed some familiarity with classical writing, must have attended a university, and anyone who knew so much about courtly elegance and courtly deceit must himself have moved among courtiers. The plays do indeed reveal an author whose interests were exceptionally broad, but specialists in any given field—law, medicine, arms and armor, and so on—soon find that the plays do not reveal deep knowledge in specialized matters; indeed, the playwright often gets technical details wrong.

The claim on behalf of Bacon, forgotten almost as soon as it was put forth in 1769, was independently reasserted by Joseph C. Hart in 1848. In 1856 it was reaffirmed by W. H. Smith in a book, and also by Delia Bacon in an article; in 1857 Delia Bacon published a book, arguing that Francis Bacon had directed a group of intellectuals who wrote the plays.

Francis Bacon's claim has largely faded, perhaps because it was advanced with such evident craziness by Ignatius Donnelly, who in *The Great Cryptogram* (1888) claimed to break a code in the plays that proved Bacon had written not only the plays attributed to Shakespeare but also other Renaissance works, for instance the plays of Christopher Marlowe and the essays of Montaigne.

Consider the last two lines of the Epilogue in *The Tempest*:

As you from crimes would pardoned be,
Let your indulgence set me free.

What was Shakespeare—sorry, Francis Bacon, Baron Verulam—*really* saying in these two lines? According to Baconians, the lines are an anagram reading, "Tempest of Francis Bacon, Lord Verulam; do ye ne'er divulge me, ye words." Ingenious, and it is a pity that in the quotation the letter *a* appears only twice in the cryptogram, whereas in the deciphered message it appears three times. Oh, no problem; just alter "Verulam" to "Verul'm" and it works out very nicely.

Most people understand that with sufficient ingenuity one can torture any text and find in it what one wishes. For instance: Did Shakespeare have a hand in the King James Version of the Bible? It was nearing completion in 1610, when

Shakespeare was forty-six years old. If you look at the 46th Psalm and count forward for forty-six words, you will find the word *shake*. Now if you go to the end of the psalm and count backward forty-six words, you will find the word *spear*. Clear evidence, according to some, that Shakespeare slyly left his mark in the book.

Bacon's candidacy has largely been replaced in the twentieth century by the candidacy of Edward de Vere (1550–1604), 17th earl of Oxford. The basic ideas behind the Oxford theory, advanced at greatest length by Dorothy and Charlton Ogburn in *This Star of England* (1952, rev. 1955), a book of 1297 pages, and by Charlton Ogburn in *The Mysterious William Shakespeare* (1984), a book of 892 pages, are these: (1) The man from Stratford could not possibly have had the mental equipment and the experience to have written the plays—only a courtier could have written them; (2) Oxford had the requisite background (social position, education, years at Queen Elizabeth's court); (3) Oxford did not wish his authorship to be known for two basic reasons: writing for the public theater was a vulgar pursuit, and the plays show so much courtly and royal disreputable behavior that they would have compromised Oxford's position at court. Oxfordians offer countless details to support the claim. For example, Hamlet's phrase "that ever I was born to set it right" (1.5.89) barely conceals "E. Ver, I was born to set it right," an unambiguous announcement of de Vere's authorship, according to *This Star of England* (p. 654). A second example: Consider Ben Jonson's poem entitled "To the Memory of My Beloved Master William Shakespeare," prefixed to the first collected edition of Shakespeare's plays in 1623. According to Oxfordians, when Jonson in this poem speaks of the author of the plays as the "swan of Avon," he is alluding not to William Shakespeare, who was born and died in Stratford-on-Avon and who throughout his adult life owned property there; rather, he is alluding to Oxford, who, the Ogburns say, used "William Shakespeare" as his pen name, and whose manor at Bilton was on the Avon River. Oxfordians do not offer any evidence that Oxford took a pen name, and they do not care that Oxford had sold the manor in 1581, forty-two years before Jonson wrote his poem. Surely a reference to the Shakespeare who was born in Stratford, who had returned to Stratford, and who had died there only seven years before Jonson wrote the poem is more plausible. And exactly why Jonson, who elsewhere also spoke of Shakespeare as a playwright, and why Heminges and Condell, who had acted with Shakespeare for about twenty years, should speak of Shakespeare as the author in their dedication in the 1623 volume of collected plays is never adequately explained by Oxfordians. Either Jonson, Heminges and Condell, and numerous others were in on the conspiracy, or they were all duped—equally unlikely alternatives. Another difficulty in the Oxford theory is that Oxford died in 1604, and some of the plays are clearly indebted to works and events later than 1604. Among the Oxfordian responses are: At his death Oxford left some plays, and in later years these were touched up by hacks, who added the material that points to later dates. *The Tempest,* almost universally regarded as one of Shakespeare's greatest plays and pretty clearly dated to 1611, does indeed date from a period after the death of Oxford, but it is a crude piece of work that should not be included in the canon of works by Oxford.

The anti-Stratfordians, in addition to assuming that the author must have been a man of rank and a university man, usually assume two conspiracies: (1) a conspiracy in Elizabethan and Jacobean times, in which a surprisingly large number of persons connected with the theater knew that the actor Shakespeare did not write the plays attributed to him but for some reason or other pretended that he did; (2) a conspiracy of today's Stratfordians, the professors who teach Shakespeare in the colleges and universities, who are said to have a vested interest in preserving Shakespeare as the author of the plays they teach. In fact, (1) it is inconceivable that the secret of Shakespeare's nonauthorship could have been preserved by all of the people who supposedly were in on the conspiracy, and (2) academic fame awaits any scholar today who can disprove Shakespeare's authorship.

The Stratfordian case is convincing not only because hundreds or even thousands of anti-Stratford arguments—of the sort that say "ever I was born" has the secret double meaning "E. Ver, I was born"—add up to nothing at all but also because irrefutable evidence connects the man from Stratford with the London theater and with the authorship of particular plays. The anti-Stratfordians do not seem to understand that it is not enough to dismiss the Stratford case by saying that a fellow from the provinces simply couldn't have written the plays. Nor do they understand that it is not enough to dismiss all of the evidence connecting Shakespeare with the plays by asserting that it is perjured.

The Shakespeare Canon

We return to William Shakespeare. Thirty-seven plays as well as some nondramatic poems are generally held to constitute the Shakespeare canon, the body of authentic works. The exact dates of composition of most of the works are highly uncertain, but evidence of a starting point and/or of a final limiting point often provides a framework for informed guessing. For example, *Richard II* cannot be earlier than 1595, the publication date of some material to which it is indebted; *The Merchant of Venice* cannot be later than 1598, the year Francis Meres mentioned it. Sometimes arguments for a date hang on an alleged topical allusion, such as the lines about the unseasonable weather in *A Midsummer Night's Dream,* 2.1.81–117, but such an allusion, if indeed it is an allusion to an event in the real world, can be variously interpreted, and in any case there is always the possibility that a topical allusion was inserted years later, to bring the play up-to-date. (The issue of alterations in a text between the time that Shakespeare drafted it and the time that it was printed—alterations due to censorship or playhouse practice or Shakespeare's own second thoughts—will be discussed in "The Play Text as a Collaboration" later in this overview.) Dates are often attributed on the basis of style, and although conjectures about style usually rest on other conjectures (such as Shakespeare's development as a playwright, or the appropriateness of lines to character), sooner or later one must rely on one's literary sense. There is no documentary proof, for example, that *Othello* is not as early as *Romeo and Juliet,* but one feels that *Othello* is a later, more mature work, and because the first record of its performance is 1604, one is glad enough to set its composition at that date and not push it back into Shakespeare's early years. (*Romeo and Juliet* was first published in 1597, but evidence suggests that it was written a little earlier.) The following chronology, then, is indebted not only to facts but also to informed guesswork and sensitivity. The dates, necessarily imprecise for some works, indicate something like a scholarly consensus concerning the time of original composition. Some plays show evidence of later revision.

Plays. The first collected edition of Shakespeare, published in 1623, included thirty-six plays. These are all accepted as Shakespeare's, though for one of them, *Henry VIII,* he is thought to have had a collaborator. A thirty-seventh play, *Pericles,* published in 1609 and attributed to Shakespeare on the title page, is also widely accepted as being partly by Shakespeare even though it is not included in the 1623 volume. Still another play not in the 1623 volume, *The Two Noble Kinsmen,* was first published in 1634, with a title page attributing it to John Fletcher and Shakespeare. Probably most students of the subject now believe that Shakespeare did indeed have a hand in it. Of the remaining plays attributed at one time or another to Shakespeare, only one, *Edward III,* anonymously published in 1596, is now regarded by some scholars as a serious candidate. The prevailing opinion, however, is that this rather simpleminded play is not Shakespeare's; at most he may have revised some passages, chiefly scenes with the Countess of Salisbury. We include *The Two Noble Kinsmen* but do not include *Edward III* in the following list.

1588–94	*The Comedy of Errors*
1588–94	*Love's Labor's Lost*
1589–91	*2 Henry VI*
1590–91	*3 Henry VI*
1589–92	*1 Henry VI*
1592–93	*Richard III*
1589–94	*Titus Andronicus*
1593–94	*The Taming of the Shrew*
1592–94	*The Two Gentlemen of Verona*
1594–96	*Romeo and Juliet*
1594–96	*The Merchant of Venice*
1595	*Richard II*
1595–96	*A Midsummer Night's Dream*
1596–97	*King John*
1596–97	*1 Henry IV*
1597	*The Merry Wives of Windsor*
1597–98	*2 Henry IV*

Poems. In 1989 Donald W. Foster published a book in which he argued that "A Funeral Elegy for Master William Peter," published in 1612, ascribed only to the initials W.S., *may* be by Shakespeare. Foster later published an article in a scholarly journal, *PMLA* 111 (1996), in which he asserted the claim more positively. The evidence begins with the initials, and includes the fact that the publisher and the printer of the elegy had published Shakespeare's *Sonnets* in 1609. But such facts add up to rather little, especially because no one has found any connection between Shakespeare and William Peter (an Oxford graduate about whom little is known, who was murdered at the age of twenty-nine). The argument is based chiefly on statistical examinations of word patterns, which are said to correlate with Shakespeare's known work. Despite such correlations, however, many readers feel that the poem does not sound like Shakespeare. True, Shakespeare has a great range of styles, but his work is consistently imaginative and interesting. Many readers find neither of these qualities in "A Funeral Elegy." The poem is now attributed to John Ford.

Shakespeare's English

1. Spelling and Pronunciation. From the philologist's point of view, Shakespeare's English is modern English. It requires footnotes, but the inexperienced reader can comprehend substantial passages with very little help, whereas for the same reader Chaucer's Middle English is a foreign language. By the beginning of the fifteenth century the chief grammatical changes in English had taken place, and the final unaccented *-e* of Middle English had been lost (though it survives even today in spelling, as in *name*); during the fifteenth century the dialect of London, the commercial and political center, gradually displaced the provincial dialects, at least in writing; by the end of the century, printing had helped to regularize and stabilize the language, especially spelling. Elizabethan spelling may seem erratic to us (there were dozens of spellings of *Shakespeare,* and a simple word like *been* was also spelled *beene* and *bin*), but it had much in common with our spelling. Elizabethan spelling was conservative in that for the most part it reflected an older pronunciation (Middle English) rather than the sound of the language as it was then spoken, just as our spelling continues to reflect medieval pronunciation— most obviously in the now silent but formerly pronounced letters in a word such as *knight.* Elizabethan pronunciation, though not identical with ours, was much closer to ours than to that of the Middle Ages. Incidentally, though no one can be certain about what Elizabethan English sounded like, specialists tend to believe it was rather like the speech of a modern stage Irishman (*time* apparently was pronounced *toime, old* pronounced *awld, day* pronounced *die,* and *join* pronounced *jine*) and not at all like the Oxford speech that most of us think it was.

An awareness of the difference between our pronunciation and Shakespeare's is crucial in three areas—in accent, or number of syllables (many metrically regular lines may look irregular to us); in rhymes (which may not look like rhymes); and in puns (which may not look like puns). Examples will be useful. Some words that were at least on occasion stressed differently from today are *aspèct, còmplete, fòrlorn, revènue,* and *sepùlcher.* Words that sometimes had an additional syllable are *emp[e]ress, Hen[e]ry, mon[e]th,* and *villain* (three syllables, *vil-lay-in*). An additional syllable is often found in possessives, like *moon's* (pronounced *moones*), and in words ending in *-tion* or *-sion.* Words that had one less syllable than they now have are *needle* (pronounced *neel*) and *violet* (pronounced *vilet*). Among rhymes now lost are *one* with *loan, love* with *prove, beast* with *jest, eat* with *great.* (In reading, trust your sense of metrics and your ear, more than your eye.) An example of a pun that has become obliterated by a change in pronunciation is Falstaff's reply to Prince Hal's "Come, tell us your reason" in *1 Henry IV*: "Give you a reason on compulsion? If reasons were as plentiful as blackberries, I would give no man a reason upon compulsion, I" (2.4.237–40). The *ea* in *reason* was pronounced rather like a long *a,* like the *ai* in *raisin,* hence the comparison with blackberries.

Puns are not merely attempts to be funny; like metaphors they often involve bringing into a meaningful relationship areas of experience normally seen as remote. In *2 Henry IV,* when Feeble is conscripted, he stoically says, "I care not. A man can die but once. We owe God a death" (3.2.242–43), punning on *debt,* which was the way *death* was pronounced. Here an enormously significant fact of life is put into simple commercial imagery, suggesting its commonplace quality. Shakespeare used the same pun earlier in *1 Henry IV,* when Prince Hal says to Falstaff, "Why, thou owest God a death," and Falstaff replies, " 'Tis not due yet: I would be loath to pay him before his day. What need I be so forward with him that calls not on me?" (5.1.126–29).

Sometimes the puns reveal a delightful playfulness; sometimes they reveal aggressiveness, as when, replying to Claudius's "But now, my cousin Hamlet, and my son," Hamlet says, "A little more than kin, and less than kind!" (1.2.64–65). These are Hamlet's first words in the play, and we already hear him warring verbally against Claudius. Hamlet's "less than kind" probably means (1) Hamlet is not of Claudius's family or nature, *kind* having the sense it still has in our word *mankind;*

(2) Hamlet is not kindly (affectionately) disposed toward Claudius; (3) Claudius is not naturally (but rather unnaturally, in a legal sense incestuously) Hamlet's father. The puns evidently were not put in as sops to the groundlings; they are an important way of communicating a complex meaning.

2. *Vocabulary.* A conspicuous difficulty in reading Shakespeare is rooted in the fact that some of his words are no longer in common use—for example, words concerned with armor, astrology, clothing, coinage, hawking, horsemanship, law, medicine, sailing, and war. Shakespeare had a large vocabulary—something near thirty thousand words—but it was not so much a vocabulary of big words as a vocabulary drawn from a wide range of life, and it is partly his ability to call upon a great body of concrete language that gives his plays the sense of being in close contact with life. When the right word did not already exist, he made it up. Among words thought to be his coinages are *accommodation, all-knowing, amazement, bare-faced, countless, dexterously, dislocate, dwindle, fancy-free, frugal, indistinguishable, lackluster, laughable, overawe, premeditated, sea change, star-crossed.* Among those that have not survived are the verb *convive,* meaning to feast together, and *smilet,* a little smile.

Less overtly troublesome than the technical words but more treacherous are the words that seem readily intelligible to us but whose Elizabethan meanings differ from their modern ones. When Horatio describes the Ghost as an "erring spirit," he is saying not that the ghost has sinned or made an error but that it is wandering. Here is a short list of some of the most common words in Shakespeare's plays that often (but not always) have a meaning other than their most usual modern meaning:

'a	he
abuse	deceive
accident	occurrence
advertise	inform
an, and	if
annoy	harm
appeal	accuse
artificial	skillful

brave	fine, splendid
censure	opinion
cheer	(1) face (2) frame of mind
chorus	a single person who comments on the events
closet	small private room
competitor	partner
conceit	idea, imagination
cousin	kinsman
cunning	skillful
disaster	evil astrological influence
doom	judgment
entertain	receive into service
envy	malice
event	outcome
excrement	outgrowth (of hair)
fact	evil deed
fancy	(1) love (2) imagination
fell	cruel
fellow	(1) companion (2) low person (often an insulting term if addressed to someone of approximately equal rank)
fond	foolish
free	(1) innocent (2) generous
glass	mirror
hap, haply	chance, by chance
head	army
humor	(1) mood (2) bodily fluid thought to control one's psychology
imp	child
intelligence	news
kind	natural, acting according to nature
let	hinder
lewd	base
mere(ly)	utter(ly)
modern	commonplace
natural	a fool, an idiot

naughty	(1) wicked (2) worthless
next	nearest
nice	(1) trivial (2) fussy
noise	music
policy	(1) prudence (2) stratagem
presently	immediately
prevent	anticipate
proper	handsome
prove	test
quick	alive
sad	serious
saw	proverb
secure	without care, incautious
silly	innocent
sensible	capable of being perceived by the senses
shrewd	sharp
so	provided that
starve	die
still	always
success	that which follows
tall	brave
tell	count
tonight	last night
wanton	playful, careless
watch	keep awake
will	lust
wink	close both eyes
wit	mind, intelligence

All glosses, of course, are mere approximations; sometimes one of Shakespeare's words may hover between an older meaning and a modern one, and as we have seen, his words often have multiple meanings.

3. *Grammar.* A few matters of grammar may be surveyed, though it should be noted at the outset that Shakespeare sometimes made up his own grammar. As E. A. Abbott says in *A Shakespearian Grammar*, "Almost any part of speech can be used as any other part of speech": a noun as a verb ("he childed as I fathered"); a verb as a noun ("She hath made compare"); or

an adverb as an adjective ("a seldom pleasure"). There are hundreds, perhaps thousands, of such instances in the plays, many of which at first glance would not seem at all irregular and would trouble only a pedant. Here are a few broad matters.

Nouns: The Elizabethans thought the *-s* genitive ending for nouns (as in *man's*) derived from *his*; thus the line "'gainst the count his galleys I did some service," for "the count's galleys."

Adjectives: By Shakespeare's time adjectives had lost the endings that once indicated gender, number, and case. About the only difference between Shakespeare's adjectives and ours is the use of the now redundant *more* or *most* with the comparative ("some more fitter place") or superlative ("This was the most unkindest cut of all"). Like double comparatives and double superlatives, double negatives were acceptable; Mercutio "will not budge for no man's pleasure."

Pronouns: The greatest change was in pronouns. In Middle English *thou, thy,* and *thee* were used among familiars and in speaking to children and inferiors; *ye, your,* and *you* were used in speaking to superiors (servants to masters, nobles to the king) or to equals with whom the speaker was not familiar. Increasingly the "polite" forms were used in all direct address, regardless of rank, and the accusative *you* displaced the nominative *ye.* Shakespeare sometimes uses *ye* instead of *you,* but even in Shakespeare's day *ye* was archaic, and it occurs mostly in rhetorical appeals.

Thou, thy, and *thee* were not completely displaced, however, and Shakespeare occasionally makes significant use of them, sometimes to connote familiarity or intimacy and sometimes to connote contempt. In *Twelfth Night* Sir Toby advises Sir Andrew to insult Cesario by addressing him as *thou*: "If thou thou'st him some thrice, it shall not be amiss" (3.2.46–47). In *Othello* when Brabantio is addressing an unidentified voice in the dark he says, "What are you?" (1.1.91), but when the voice identifies itself as the foolish suitor Roderigo, Brabantio uses the contemptuous form, saying, "I have charged thee not to haunt about my doors" (93). He uses this form for a while, but later in the scene, when he comes to regard Roderigo as an ally, he shifts back to the polite *you,* beginning in line 163, "What said she to you?" and on to the end of the scene. For reasons not yet satisfactorily explained, Elizabethans used *thou* in addresses to God—"O God, thy arm was here," the king says in *Henry V* (4.8.108)—and to supernatural characters such as ghosts and witches. A subtle variation occurs in *Hamlet*. When Hamlet first talks with the Ghost in 1.5, he uses *thou,* but when he sees the Ghost in his mother's room, in 3.4, he uses *you,* presumably because he is now convinced that the Ghost is not a counterfeit but is his father.

Perhaps the most unusual use of pronouns, from our point of view, is the neuter singular. In place of our *its, his* was often used, as in "How far that little candle throws *his* beams." But the use of a masculine pronoun for a neuter noun came to seem unnatural, and so *it* was used for the possessive as well as the nominative: "The hedge-sparrow fed the cuckoo so long / That it had it head bit off by it young." In the late sixteenth century the possessive form *its* developed, apparently by analogy with the *-s* ending used to indicate a genitive noun, as in *book*'s, but *its* was not yet common usage in Shakespeare's day. He seems to have used *its* only ten times, mostly in his later plays. Other usages, such as "you have seen Cassio and she together" or the substitution of *who* for *whom,* cause little problem even when noticed.

Verbs, Adverbs, and Prepositions: Verbs cause almost no difficulty: The third person singular present form commonly ends in *-s,* as in modern English (e.g., "He blesses"), but sometimes in *-eth* (Portia explains to Shylock that mercy "blesseth him that gives and him that takes"). Broadly speaking, the *-eth* ending was old-fashioned or dignified or "literary" rather than colloquial, except for the words *doth, hath,* and *saith.* The *-eth* ending (regularly used in the King James Bible, 1611) is very rare in Shakespeare's dramatic prose, though not surprisingly it occurs twice in the rather formal prose summary of the narrative poem *Lucrece.* Sometimes a plural subject, especially if it has collective force, takes a verb ending in *-s,* as in "My old bones aches." Some of our strong or irregular preterites (such as *broke*) have a different form in Shakespeare (*brake*); some verbs that now have a weak or regular preterite (such as *helped*) in Shakespeare have a strong or irregular preterite (*holp*). Some adverbs that today end in *-ly* were not inflected: "grievous sick," "wondrous strange." Finally, prepositions often are not the ones we expect: "We are such stuff as dreams are made on," "I have a king here to my flatterer."

Again, none of the differences (except meanings that have substantially changed or been lost) will cause much difficulty. But it must be confessed that for some elliptical passages there is no widespread agreement on meaning. Wise editors resist saying more than they know, and when they are uncertain they add a question mark to their gloss.

Shakespeare's Theater

In Shakespeare's infancy, Elizabethan actors performed wherever they could—in great halls, at court, in the courtyards of inns. These venues implied not only different audiences but also different playing conditions. The innyards must have made rather unsatisfactory theaters: on some days they were unavailable because carters bringing goods to London used them as depots; when available, they had to be rented from the innkeeper. In 1567, presumably to avoid such difficulties, and also to avoid regulation by the Common Council of London, which was not well disposed toward theatricals, one John Brayne, brother-in-law of the carpenter turned actor James Burbage, built the Red Lion in an eastern suburb of London. We know nothing about its shape or its capacity; we can say only that it may have been the first building in Europe constructed for the purpose of giving plays since the end of antiquity, a thousand years earlier. Even after the building of the Red Lion, theatrical activity continued in London in makeshift circumstances, in marketplaces and inns, and always uneasily. In 1574 the Common Council required that plays and playing places in London be licensed because

> sundry great disorders and inconveniences have been found to ensue to this city by the inordinate haunting of great multitudes of people, specially youth, to plays, interludes, and shows, namely occasion of frays and quarrels, evil practices of incontinency in great inns having chambers and secret places adjoining to their open stages and galleries.

The Common Council ordered that innkeepers who wished licenses to hold performance put up a bond and make contributions to the poor.

The requirement that plays and innyard theaters be licensed, along with the other drawbacks of playing at inns and presumably along with the success of the Red Lion, led James Burbage to rent a plot of land northeast of the city walls, on property outside the jurisdiction of the city. Here he built England's second playhouse, called simply the Theatre. About all that is known of its construction is that it was wood. It soon had imitators, the most famous being the Globe (1599), essentially an amphitheater built across the Thames (again outside the city's jurisdiction), constructed with timbers of the Theatre, which had been dismantled when Burbage's lease ran out.

Admission to the theater was one penny, which allowed spectators to stand at the sides and front of the stage that jutted into the yard. An additional penny bought a seat in a covered part of the theater, and a third penny bought a more comfortable seat and a better location. It is notoriously difficult to translate prices into today's money, since some things that are inexpensive today would have been expensive in the past and vice versa—a pipeful of tobacco (imported, of course) cost a lot of money, about three pennies, and an orange (also imported) cost two or three times what a chicken cost—but perhaps we can get some idea of the low cost of the penny admission when we realize that a penny could also buy a pot of ale. An unskilled laborer made about five or sixpence a day, an artisan about twelve pence a day, and the hired actors (as opposed to the sharers in the company, such as Shakespeare) made about ten pence a performance. A printed play cost five or sixpence. Of course a visit to the theater (like a visit to a baseball game today) usually cost more than the admission since the spectator probably would also buy food and drink. Still, the low entrance fee meant that the theater was available to all except the very poorest people, rather as movies and most athletic events are today. Evidence indicates that the audience ranged from apprentices who somehow managed to scrape together the minimum entrance fee and to escape from their masters for a few hours, to prosperous members of the middle class and aristocrats who paid the additional fee for admission to the galleries. The exact proportion of men to women cannot be determined, but women of all classes certainly were present. Theaters were open every afternoon but Sundays for much of the year, except in times of plague, when they were closed because of fear of infection. By the way, no evidence suggests the presence of toilet facilities. Presumably the patrons relieved themselves by making a quick trip to the fields surrounding the playhouses.

There are four important sources of information about the structure of Elizabethan public playhouses—drawings, a contract, recent excavations, and stage directions in the plays. Of drawings, only the so-called de Witt drawing (c. 1596) of the Swan—really his friend Aernout van Buchell's copy of

Johannes de Witt, a Continental visitor to London, made a drawing of the Swan theater in about the year 1596. The original drawing is lost; this is Aernout van Buchell's copy of it.

Johannes de Witt's drawing—is of much significance. The drawing, the only extant representation of the interior of an Elizabethan theater, shows an amphitheater of three tiers, with a stage jutting from a wall into the yard or center of the building. The tiers are roofed, and part of the stage is covered by a roof that projects from the rear and is supported at its front on two posts, but the groundlings, who paid a penny to stand in front of the stage or at its sides, were exposed to the sky. (Performances in such a playhouse were held only in the daytime; artificial illumination was not used.) At the rear of the stage are two massive doors; above the stage is a gallery.

The second major source of information, the contract for the Fortune (built in 1600), specifies that although the Globe (built in 1599) is to be the model, the Fortune is to be square, eighty feet outside and fifty-five inside. The stage is to be forty-three feet broad, and is to extend into the middle of the yard, i.e., it is twenty-seven and a half feet deep.

The third source of information, the 1989 excavations of the Rose (built in 1587), indicate that the Rose was fourteen-sided, about seventy-two feet in diameter with an inner yard almost fifty feet in diameter. The stage at the Rose was about sixteen feet deep, thirty-seven feet wide at the rear, and twenty-seven feet wide downstage. The relatively small dimensions and the tapering stage, in contrast to the rectangular stage in the Swan drawing, surprised theater historians and have made them more cautious in generalizing about the Elizabethan theater. Excavations at the Globe have not yielded much information, though some historians believe that the fragmentary evidence suggests a larger theater, perhaps one hundred feet in diameter.

From the fourth chief source, stage directions in the plays, one learns that entrance to the stage was by the doors at the rear (*"Enter one citizen at one door, and another at the other"*). A curtain hanging across the doorway—or a curtain hanging between the two doorways—could provide a place where a character could conceal himself, as Polonius does, when he wishes to overhear the conversation between Hamlet and Gertrude. Similarly, withdrawing a curtain from the doorway could "discover" (reveal) a character or two. Such discovery scenes are very rare in Elizabethan drama, but a good example occurs in *The Tempest*

(5.1.171), where a stage direction tells us, *"Here Prospero discovers Ferdinand and Miranda playing at chess."* There was also some sort of playing space "aloft" or "above" to represent, for instance, the top of a city's walls or a room above the street. Doubtless each theater had its own peculiarities, but perhaps we can talk about a "typical" Elizabethan theater if we realize that no theater need exactly fit the description, just as no mother is the average mother with 2.7 children.

This hypothetical theater is wooden, round, or polygonal (in *Henry V* Shakespeare calls it a "wooden *O*"), capable of holding some eight hundred spectators who stood in the yard around the projecting elevated stage—these spectators were the "groundlings"—and some fifteen hundred additional spectators who sat in the three roofed galleries. The stage, protected by a "shadow" or "heavens" or roof, is entered from two doors; behind the doors is the "tiring house" (attiring house, i.e., dressing room), and above the stage is some sort of gallery that may sometimes hold spectators but can be used (for example) as the bedroom from which Romeo—according to a stage direction in one text—"goeth down." Some evidence suggests that a throne can be lowered onto the platform stage, perhaps from the "shadow"; certainly characters can descend from the stage through a trap or traps into the cellar or "hell." Sometimes this space beneath the stage accommodates a sound-effects man or musician (in *Antony and Cleopatra "music of the hautboys* [oboes] *is under the stage"*) or an actor (in *Hamlet* the *"Ghost cries under the stage"*). Most characters simply walk on and off through the doors, but because there is no curtain in front of the platform, corpses will have to be carried off (Hamlet obligingly clears the stage of Polonius's corpse, when he says, "I'll lug the guts into the neighbor room"). Other characters may have fallen at the rear, where a curtain on a doorway could be drawn to conceal them.

Such may have been the "public theater," so called because its inexpensive admission made it available to a wide range of the populace. Another kind of theater has been called the "private theater" because its much greater admission charge (sixpence versus the penny for general admission at the public theater) limited its audience to the wealthy or the prodigal. The private theater was basically a large room, entirely roofed and therefore artificially illuminated, with a stage at one end. The theaters thus were distinct in two ways: One was essentially an amphitheater that catered to the general public; the other was a hall that catered to the wealthy. In 1576 a hall theater was established in Blackfriars, a Dominican priory in London that had been suppressed in 1538 and confiscated by the Crown and thus was not under the city's jurisdiction. All the actors in this Blackfriars theater were boys about eight to thirteen years old (in the public theaters similar boys played female parts; a boy Lady Macbeth played to a man Macbeth). Near the end of this section on Shakespeare's theater we will talk at some length about possible implications in this convention of using boys to play female roles, but for the moment we should say that it doubtless accounts for the relative lack of female roles in Elizabethan drama. Thus, in *A Midsummer Night's Dream,* out of twenty-one named roles, only four are female; in *Hamlet,* out of twenty-four, only two (Gertrude and Ophelia) are female. Many of Shakespeare's characters have fathers but no mothers—for instance, King Lear's daughters. We need not bring in Freud to explain the disparity; a dramatic company had only a few boys in it.

To return to the private theaters, in some of which all of the performers were children—the "eyrie of . . . little eyases" (nest of unfledged hawks—2.2.347–48) which Rosencrantz mentions when he and Guildenstern talk with Hamlet. The theater in Blackfriars had a precarious existence, and ceased operations in 1584. In 1596 James Burbage, who had already made theatrical history by building the Theatre, began to construct a second Blackfriars theater. He died in 1597, and for several years this second Blackfriars theater was used by a troupe of boys, but in 1608 two of Burbage's sons and five other actors (including Shakespeare) became joint operators of the theater, using it in the winter when the open-air Globe was unsuitable. Perhaps such a smaller theater, roofed, artificially illuminated, and with a tradition of a wealthy audience, exerted an influence in Shakespeare's late plays.

Performances in the private theaters may well have had intermissions during which music was played, but in the public theaters the action was probably uninterrupted, flowing from scene to scene almost without a break. Actors would enter, speak, exit, and others would immediately enter and establish (if necessary) the new locale by a few properties and by words and gestures. To indicate that the scene took place at night, a player or two would carry a torch. Here are some samples of Shakespeare establishing the scene:

This is Illyria, lady.   (*Twelfth Night*, 1.2.2)

Well, this is the Forest of Arden.   (*As You Like It*, 2.4.14)

This castle has a pleasant seat; the air
Nimbly and sweetly recommends itself
Unto our gentle senses.   (*Macbeth*, 1.6.1–3)

The west yet glimmers with some streaks of day.
                                                                          (*Macbeth*, 3.3.5)

Sometimes a speech will go far beyond evoking the minimal setting of place and time, and will, so to speak, evoke the social world in which the characters move. For instance, early in the first scene of *The Merchant of Venice* Salerio suggests an explanation for Antonio's melancholy. (In the following passage, *pageants* are decorated wagons, floats, and *cursy* is the verb "to curtsy," or "to bow.")

Your mind is tossing on the ocean,
There where your argosies with portly sail—
Like signiors and rich burghers on the flood,
Or as it were the pageants of the sea—
Do overpeer the petty traffickers
That cursy to them, do them reverence,
As they fly by them with their woven wings.   (1.1.8–14)

Late in the nineteenth century, when Henry Irving produced the play with elaborate illusionistic sets, the first scene showed a ship moored in the harbor, with fruit vendors and dock laborers, in an effort to evoke the bustling and exotic life of Venice. But Shakespeare's words give us this exotic, rich world of commerce in his highly descriptive language when Salerio speaks of "argosies with portly sail" that fly with "woven wings"; equally important, through Salerio Shakespeare conveys a sense of the orderly, hierarchical society in which the lesser ships, "the petty traffickers," curtsy and thereby "do . . . reverence" to their superiors, the merchant prince's ships, which are "Like signiors and rich burghers."

On the other hand, it is a mistake to think that except for verbal pictures the Elizabethan stage was bare. Although Shakespeare's Chorus in *Henry V* calls the stage an "unworthy scaffold" (Prologue 1.10) and urges the spectators to "eke out our performance with your mind" (Prologue 3.35), there was considerable spectacle. The last act of *Macbeth,* for instance, has five stage directions calling for *"drum and colors,"* and another sort of appeal to the eye is indicated by the stage direction *"Enter Macduff, with Macbeth's head."* Some scenery and properties may have been substantial; doubtless a throne was used, but the pillars supporting the roof would have served for the trees on which Orlando pins his poems in *As You Like It.*

Having talked about the public theater—"this wooden *O*"— at some length, we should mention again that Shakespeare's plays were performed also in other locales. Alvin Kernan, in *Shakespeare, the King's Playwright: Theater in the Stuart Court 1603–1613* (1995), points out that "several of [Shakespeare's] plays contain brief theatrical performances, set always in a court or some noble house. When Shakespeare portrayed a theater, he did not, except for the choruses in *Henry V,* imagine a public theater" (p. 195). (Examples include episodes in *The Taming of the Shrew, A Midsummer Night's Dream, Hamlet,* and *The Tempest.*)

A Note on the Use of Boy Actors in Female Roles

Until fairly recently, scholars were content to mention that the convention existed; they sometimes also mentioned that it continued the medieval practice of using males in female roles, and that other theaters, notably in ancient Greece and in China and Japan, also used males in female roles. (In classical Noh drama in Japan, males still play the female roles.) Prudery may have been at the root of the academic failure to talk much about the use of boy actors, or maybe there really is not much more to say than that it was a convention of a male-centered culture (Stephen Greenblatt's view, in *Shakespearean Negotiations* [1988]). Further, the very nature of a convention is that it is not thought about: Hamlet is a Dane and Julius Caesar is a Roman, but in Shakespeare's plays they speak English, and we in the audience never give this odd fact a thought. Similarly, a character may speak in the presence of others and we understand, again without thinking about it, that he or she is not heard by the figures on the stage (the aside); a character alone on the stage may speak (the soliloquy), and we do not take the character to be unhinged; in a realistic (box) set, the fourth wall, which allows us to see what is going on, is miraculously missing. The no-nonsense view, then, is that the boy actor was an accepted convention, accepted unthinkingly—just as today we know that Kenneth Branagh is not Hamlet, Al Pacino is not Richard III, and Denzel Washington is not the Prince of Aragon. In this view, the audience takes the performer for the role, and that is that; such is the argument we now make for race-free casting, in which African-Americans and Asians can play roles of persons who lived in medieval Denmark and ancient Rome. But gender perhaps is different, at least today. It is a matter of abundant academic study: The Elizabethan theater is now sometimes called a transvestite theater, and we hear much about cross-dressing.

Shakespeare himself in a very few passages calls attention to the use of boys in female roles. At the end of *As You Like It* the boy who played Rosalind addresses the audience, and says, "O men, . . . if I were a woman, I would kiss as many of you as had beards that pleased me." But this is in the Epilogue; the plot is over, and the actor is stepping out of the play and into the audience's everyday world. A second reference to the practice of boys playing female roles occurs in *Antony and Cleopatra,* when Cleopatra imagines that she and Antony will be the subject of crude plays, her role being performed by a boy:

> The quick comedians
> Extemporally will stage us, and present
> Our Alexandrian revels: Antony
> Shall be brought drunken forth, and I shall see
> Some squeaking Cleopatra boy my greatness.   (5.2.216–20)

In a few other passages, Shakespeare is more indirect. For instance, in *Twelfth Night* Viola, played of course by a boy, disguises herself as a young man and seeks service in the house of a lord. She enlists the help of a Captain, and (by way of explaining away her voice and her beardlessness) says,

> I'll serve this duke
> Thou shalt present me as an eunuch to him.   (1.2.55–56)

In *Hamlet,* when the players arrive in 2.2, Hamlet jokes with the boy who plays a female role. The boy has grown since Hamlet last saw him: "By'r Lady, your ladyship is nearer to heaven than when I saw you last by the altitude of a chopine" (a lady's thick-soled shoe). He goes on: "Pray God your voice . . . be not cracked" (434–38).

Exactly how sexual, how erotic, this material was and is, is now much disputed. Again, the use of boys may have been unnoticed, or rather not thought about—an unexamined convention—by most or all spectators most of the time, perhaps *all* of the time, except when Shakespeare calls the convention to the attention of the audience, as in the passages just quoted. Still, an occasional bit seems to invite erotic thoughts. The clearest example is the name that Rosalind takes in *As You Like It,* Ganymede—the beautiful youth whom Zeus abducted. Did boys dressed to play female roles carry homoerotic appeal for straight men (Lisa Jardine's view, in *Still Harping on Daughters* [1983]), or for gay men, or for some or all women in the audience? Further, when the boy actor played a woman who (for the purposes of the plot) disguised herself as a male, as Rosalind, Viola, and Portia do—so we get a boy playing a woman playing a man—what sort of appeal was generated, and for what sort of spectator?

Some scholars have argued that the convention empowered women by letting female characters display a freedom unavailable in Renaissance patriarchal society; the convention, it is said, undermined rigid gender distinctions. In this view, the convention (along with plots in which female characters for a while disguised themselves as young men) allowed Shakespeare to say what some modern gender critics say: Gender is a constructed role rather than a biological given, something we make, rather than a fixed binary opposition of male and female (see Juliet Dusinberre, in *Shakespeare and the Nature of Women* [1975]). On the other hand, some scholars have maintained that the male disguise assumed by some female characters serves only to reaffirm traditional social distinctions since female characters who don male garb (notably Portia in *The Merchant of Venice* and Rosalind in *As You Like It*) return to their female garb and at least implicitly (these critics say) reaffirm the status quo. (For this last view, see Clara Claiborne Park, in an essay in *The Woman's Part*, ed. Carolyn Ruth Swift Lenz et al. [1980].) Perhaps no one answer is right for all plays; in *As You Like It* cross-dressing empowers Rosalind, but in *Twelfth Night* cross-dressing comically traps Viola.

Shakespeare's Dramatic Language: Costumes, Gestures and Silences; Prose and Poetry

Because Shakespeare was a dramatist, not merely a poet, he worked not only with language but also with costume, sound effects, gestures, and even silences. We have already discussed some kinds of spectacle in the preceding section, and now we will begin with other aspects of visual language; a theater, after all, is literally a "place for seeing." Consider the opening stage direction in *The Tempest*, the first play in the first published collection of Shakespeare's plays: *"A tempestuous noise of thunder and Lightning heard: Enter a Ship-master, and a Boteswain."*

Costumes: What did that shipmaster and that boatswain wear? Doubtless they wore something that identified them as men of the sea. Not much is known about the costumes that Elizabethan actors wore, but at least three points are clear: (1) many of the costumes were splendid versions of contemporary Elizabethan dress; (2) some attempts were made to approximate the dress of certain occupations and of antique or exotic characters such as Romans, Turks, and Jews; (3) some costumes indicated that the wearer was supernatural. Evidence for elaborate Elizabethan clothing can be found in the plays themselves and in contemporary comments about the "sumptuous" players who wore the discarded clothing of noblemen, as well as in account books that itemize such things as "a scarlet cloak with two broad gold laces, with gold buttons down the sides."

The attempts at approximation of the dress of certain occupations and nationalities also can be documented from the plays themselves, and it derives additional confirmation from a drawing of the first scene of Shakespeare's *Titus Andronicus*—the only extant Elizabethan picture of an identifiable episode in a play. (See pp. xxxviii–xxxix.) The drawing, probably done in 1594 or 1595, shows Queen Tamora pleading for mercy. She wears a somewhat medieval-looking robe and a crown; Titus wears a toga and a wreath, but two soldiers behind him wear costumes fairly close to Elizabethan dress. We do not know, however, if the drawing represents an actual stage production in the public theater, or perhaps a private production, or maybe only a reader's visualization of an episode. Further, there is some conflicting evidence: In *Julius Caesar* a reference is made to Caesar's doublet (a close-fitting jacket), which, if taken literally, suggests that even the protagonist did not wear Roman clothing; and certainly the lesser characters, who are said to wear hats, did not wear Roman garb.

It should be mentioned, too, that even ordinary clothing can be symbolic: Hamlet's "inky cloak," for example, sets him apart from the brightly dressed members of Claudius's court and symbolizes his mourning; the fresh clothes that are put on King Lear partly symbolize his return to sanity. Consider, too, the removal of disguises near the end of some plays. For instance, Rosalind in *As You Like It* and Portia and Nerissa in *The Merchant of Venice* remove their male attire, thus again becoming fully themselves.

Gestures and Silences: Gestures are an important part of a dramatist's language. King Lear kneels before his daughter Cordelia for a benediction (4.7.57–59), an act of humility that contrasts with his earlier speeches banishing her and that contrasts also with a comparable gesture, his ironic kneeling before Regan (2.4.153–55). Northumberland's failure to kneel before King Richard II (3.3.71–72) speaks volumes. As for silences, consider a moment in *Coriolanus*: Before the protagonist yields to his mother's entreaties (5.3.182), there is this stage direction: *"Holds her by the hand, silent."* Another example of "speech in dumbness" occurs in *Macbeth,* when Macduff learns that his wife and children have been murdered. He is silent at first, as Malcolm's speech indicates: "What, man! Ne'er pull your hat upon your brows. Give sorrow words" (4.3.208–9). (For a discussion of such moments, see Philip C.

McGuire's *Speechless Dialect: Shakespeare's Open Silences* [1985].)

Of course when we think of Shakespeare's work, we think primarily of his language, both the poetry and the prose.

Prose: Although two of his plays (*Richard II* and *King John*) have no prose at all, about half the others have at least one quarter of the dialogue in prose, and some have notably more: *1 Henry IV* and *2 Henry IV,* about half; *As You Like It* and *Twelfth Night,* a little more than half; *Much Ado About Nothing,* more than three quarters; and *The Merry Wives of Windsor,* a little more than five-sixths. We should remember that despite Molière's joke about M. Jourdain, who was amazed to learn that he spoke prose, most of us do not speak prose. Rather, we normally utter repetitive, shapeless, and often ungrammatical torrents; prose is something very different—a sort of literary imitation of speech at its most coherent.

Today we may think of prose as "natural" for drama; or even if we think that poetry is appropriate for high tragedy we may still think that prose is the right medium for comedy. Greek, Roman, and early English comedies, however, were written in verse. In fact, prose was not generally considered a literary medium in England until the late fifteenth century; Chaucer tells even his bawdy stories in verse. By the end of the 1580s, however, prose had established itself on the English comic stage. In tragedy, Marlowe made some use of prose, not simply in the speeches of clownish servants but even in the speech of a tragic hero, Doctor Faustus. Still, before Shakespeare, prose normally was used in the theater only for special circumstances: (1) letters and proclamations, to set them off from the poetic dialogue; (2) mad characters, to indicate that normal thinking has become disordered; and (3) low comedy, or speeches uttered by clowns even when they are not being comic. Shakespeare made use of these conventions, but he also went far beyond them. Sometimes he begins a scene in prose and then shifts into verse as the emotion is heightened; or conversely, he may shift from verse to prose when a speaker is lowering the emotional level, as when Brutus speaks in the Forum.

Shakespeare's prose usually is not prosaic. Hamlet's prose includes not only small talk with Rosencrantz and Guildenstern

but also princely reflections on "What a piece of work is a man" (2.2.312). In conversation with Ophelia, he shifts from light talk in verse to a passionate prose denunciation of women (3.1.103), though the shift to prose here is perhaps also intended to suggest the possibility of madness. (Consult Brian Vickers, *The Artistry of Shakespeare's Prose* [1968].)

Poetry: Drama in rhyme in England goes back to the Middle Ages, but by Shakespeare's day rhyme no longer dominated poetic drama; a finer medium, blank verse (strictly speaking, unrhymed lines of ten syllables, with the stress on every second syllable), had been adopted. But before looking at unrhymed poetry, a few things should be said about the chief uses of rhyme in Shakespeare's plays. (1) A couplet (a pair of rhyming lines) is sometimes used to convey emotional heightening at the end of a blank verse speech; (2) characters sometimes speak a couplet as they leave the stage, suggesting closure; (3) except in the latest plays, scenes fairly often conclude with a couplet, and sometimes, as in *Richard II,*

2.1.145–46, the entrance of a new character within a scene is preceded by a couplet, which wraps up the earlier portion of that scene; (4) speeches of two characters occasionally are linked by rhyme, most notably in *Romeo and Juliet*, 1.5.95–108, where the lovers speak a sonnet between them; elsewhere a taunting reply occasionally rhymes with the previous speaker's last line; (5) speeches with sententious or gnomic remarks are sometimes in rhyme, as in the duke's speech in *Othello* (1.3.199–206); (6) speeches of sardonic mockery are sometimes in rhyme—for example, Iago's speech on women in *Othello* (2.1.146–58)—and they sometimes conclude with an emphatic couplet, as in Bolingbroke's speech on comforting words in *Richard II* (1.3.301–2); (7) some characters are associated with rhyme, such as the fairies in *A Midsummer Night's Dream*; (8) in the early plays, especially *The Comedy of Errors* and *The Taming of the Shrew*, comic scenes that in later plays would be in prose are in jingling rhymes; (9) prologues, choruses, plays-within-the-play, inscriptions, vows, epilogues, and so on are often in rhyme, and the songs in the plays are rhymed.

Neither prose nor rhyme immediately comes to mind when we first think of Shakespeare's medium: It is blank verse, unrhymed iambic pentameter. (In a mechanically exact line there are five iambic feet. An iambic foot consists of two syllables, the second accented, as in *away*; five feet make a pentameter line. Thus, a strict line of iambic pentameter contains ten syllables, the even syllables being stressed more heavily than the odd syllables. Fortunately, Shakespeare usually varies the line somewhat.) The first speech in *A Midsummer Night's Dream,* spoken by Duke Theseus to his betrothed, is an example of blank verse:

> Now, fair Hippolyta, our nuptial hour
> Draws on apace. Four happy days bring in
> Another moon; but, O, methinks, how slow
> This old moon wanes! She lingers my desires,
> Like to a stepdame, or a dowager,
> Long withering out a young man's revenue.   (1.1.1–6)

As this passage shows, Shakespeare's blank verse is not mechanically unvarying. Though the predominant foot is the iamb (as in *apace* or *desires*), there are numerous variations. In the first line the stress can be placed on "fair," as the regular metrical pattern suggests, but it is likely that "Now" gets almost as much emphasis; probably in the second line "Draws" is more heavily emphasized than "on," giving us a trochee (a stressed syllable followed by an unstressed one); and in the fourth line each word in the phrase "This old moon wanes" is probably stressed fairly heavily, conveying by two spondees (two feet, each of two stresses) the oppressive tedium that Theseus feels.

In Shakespeare's early plays much of the blank verse is endstopped (that is, it has a heavy pause at the end of each line), but he later developed the ability to write iambic pentameter verse paragraphs (rather than lines) that give the illusion of speech. His chief techniques are (1) enjambing, i.e., running the thought beyond the single line, as in the first three lines of the speech just quoted; (2) occasionally replacing an iamb with another foot; (3) varying the position of the chief pause (the caesura) within a line; (4) adding an occasional unstressed syllable at the end of a line, traditionally called a feminine ending; and (5) beginning or ending a speech with a half line.

Shakespeare's mature blank verse has much of the rhythmic flexibility of his prose; both the language, though richly figurative and sometimes dense, and the syntax seem natural. It is also often highly appropriate to a particular character. Consider, for instance, this speech from _Hamlet,_ in which Claudius, King of Denmark ("the Dane"), speaks to Laertes:

> And now, Laertes, what's the news with you?
> You told us of some suit. What is't, Laertes?
> You cannot speak of reason to the Dane
> And lose your voice. What wouldst thou beg, Laertes,
> That shall not be my offer, not thy asking? (1.2.42–46)

Notice the short sentences and the repetition of the name "Laertes," to whom the speech is addressed. Notice, too, the shift from the royal "us" in the second line to the more intimate "my" in the last line, and from "you" in the first three lines to the more intimate "thou" and "thy" in the last two lines. Claudius knows how to ingratiate himself with Laertes.

For a second example of the flexibility of Shakespeare's blank verse, consider a passage from _Macbeth._ Distressed by the doctor's inability to cure Lady Macbeth and by the imminent battle, Macbeth addresses some of his remarks to the doctor and others to the servant who is arming him. The entire speech, with its pauses, interruptions, and irresolution (in "Pull't off, I say," Macbeth orders the servant to remove the armor that the servant has been putting on him), catches Macbeth's disintegration. (In the first line, _physic_ means "medicine," and in the fourth and fifth lines, _cast the water_ means "analyze the urine.")

> Throw physic to the dogs, I'll none of it.
> Come, put mine armor on. Give me my staff.
> Seyton, send out.—Doctor, the thanes fly from me.—
> Come, sir, dispatch. If thou couldst, doctor, cast
> The water of my land, find her disease
> And purge it to a sound and pristine health,
> I would applaud thee to the very echo,
> That should applaud again.—Pull't off, I say.—

What rhubarb, senna, or what purgative drug,
Would scour these English hence? Hear'st thou of them?

(5.3.47–56)

Blank verse, then, can be much more than unrhymed iambic
pentameter, and even within a single play Shakespeare's blank
verse often consists of several styles, depending on the speaker
and on the speaker's emotion at the moment.

The Play Text as a Collaboration

Shakespeare's fellow dramatist Ben Jonson reported that the
actors said of Shakespeare, "In his writing, whatsoever he
penned, he never blotted out line," i.e., never crossed out material
and revised his work while composing. None of Shakespeare's
plays survives in manuscript (with the possible exception of a
scene in *Sir Thomas More*), so we cannot fully evaluate the
comment, but in a few instances the published work clearly
shows that he revised his manuscript. Consider the following
passage (shown here in facsimile) from the best early text of
Romeo and Juliet, the Second Quarto (1599):

Ro. Would I were fleepe and peace fo fweet to reft
The grey eyde morne fmiles on the frowning night,
Checking the Eafterne Clouds with ftreaks of light,
And darkneffe fleckted like a drunkard reeles,
From forth daies pathway, made by *Tytans* wheeles.
Hence will I to my ghoftly Friers clofe cell,
His helpe to craue, and my deare hap to tell.

Exit.

Enter Frier alone with a basket. (night,
Fri. The grey-eyed morne fmiles on the frowning
Checking the Eafterne clowdes with ftreaks of light:
And fleckeld darkneffe like a drunkard reeles,
From forth daies path, and *Tytans* burning wheeles:
Now ere the fun aduance his burning eie,

Romeo rather elaborately tells us that the sun at dawn is dis-pelling the night (morning is smiling, the eastern clouds are checked with light, and the sun's chariot—Titan's wheels—advances), and he will seek out his spiritual father, the Friar. He exits and, oddly, the Friar enters and says pretty much the same thing about the sun. Both speakers say that "the gray-eyed morn smiles on the frowning night," but there are small differences, perhaps having more to do with the business of printing the book than with the author's composition: For Romeo's "check-ring," "fleckted," and "pathway," we get the Friar's "checking," "fleckeld," and "path." (Notice, by the way, the inconsistency in Elizabethan spelling: Romeo's "clouds" become the Friar's "clowdes.")

Both versions must have been in the printer's copy, and it seems safe to assume that both were in Shakespeare's manu-script. He must have written one version—let's say he first wrote Romeo's closing lines for this scene—and then he de-cided, no, it's better to give this lyrical passage to the Friar, as the opening of a new scene, but he neglected to delete the first version. Editors must make a choice, and they may feel that the reasonable thing to do is to print the text as Shakespeare in-tended it. But how can we know what he intended? Almost all modern editors delete the lines from Romeo's speech, and re-tain the Friar's lines. They don't do this because they know Shakespeare's intention, however. They give the lines to the Friar because the first published version (1597) of *Romeo and Juliet* gives only the Friar's version, and this text (though in many ways inferior to the 1599 text) is thought to derive from the memory of some actors, that is, it is thought to represent a performance, not just a script. Maybe during the course of re-hearsals Shakespeare—an actor as well as an author—unilater-ally decided that the Friar should speak the lines; if so (remember that we don't know this to be a fact) his final inten-tion was to give the speech to the Friar. Maybe, however, the ac-tors talked it over and settled on the Friar, with or without Shakespeare's approval. On the other hand, despite the 1597 version, one might argue (if only weakly) on behalf of giving the lines to Romeo rather than to the Friar, thus: (1) Romeo's comment on the coming of the daylight emphasizes his separa-tion from Juliet, and (2) the figurative language seems more ap-propriate to Romeo than to the Friar. Having said this, in the Signet edition we have decided in this instance to draw on the evidence provided by earlier text and to give the lines to the Friar, on the grounds that since Q1 reflects a production, in the theater (at least on one occasion) the lines were spoken by the Friar.

A playwright sold a script to a theatrical company. The script thus belonged to the company, not the author, and author and company alike must have regarded this script not as a literary work but as the basis for a play that the actors would create on the stage. We speak of Shakespeare as the author of the plays, but readers should bear in mind that the texts they read, even when derived from a single text, such as the First Folio (1623), are inevitably the collaborative work not simply of Shakespeare with his company—doubtless during rehearsals the actors would suggest alterations—but also with other forces of the age. One force was governmental censorship. In 1606 parliament passed "an Act to restrain abuses of players," prohibiting the utterance of oaths and the name of God. So where the earliest text of *Othello* gives us "By heaven" (3.3.106), the First Folio gives "Alas," presumably reflecting the compliance of stage practice with the law. Similarly, the 1623 version of *King Lear* omits the oath "Fut" (probably from "By God's foot") at 1.2.142, again presumably reflecting the line as it was spoken on the stage. Editors who seek to give the reader the play that Shakespeare initially conceived—the "authentic" play conceived by the solitary Shakespeare—probably will restore the missing oaths and references to God. Other editors, who see the play as a collaborative work, a construction made not only by Shakespeare but also by actors and compositors and even government censors, may claim that what counts is the play as it was actually performed. Such editors regard the censored text as legitimate, since it is the play that was (presumably) finally put on. A performed text, they argue, has more historical reality than a text produced by an editor who has sought to get at what Shakespeare initially wrote. In this view, the text of a play is rather like the script of a film; the script is not the film, and the play text is not the performed play. Even if we want to talk about the play that Shakespeare "intended," we will find ourselves talking about a script that he handed over to a company with the intention that it be implemented by actors. The "intended" play is the one that the actors—we might almost say "society"—would help to construct.

Further, it is now widely held that a play is also the work of readers and spectators, who do not simply receive meaning, but who create it when they respond to the play. This idea is fully in accord with contemporary poststructuralist critical thinking, notably Roland Barthes's "The Death of the Author," in *Image-Music-Text* (1977), and Michel Foucault's "What Is an Author?", in *The Foucault Reader* (1984). The gist of the idea is that an author is not an isolated genius; rather, authors are subject to the politics and other social structures of their age. A dramatist especially is a worker in a collaborative project, working most obviously with actors—parts may be written for particular actors—but working also with the audience. Consider the words of Samuel Johnson, written to be spoken by the actor David Garrick at the opening of a theater in 1747:

> The stage but echoes back the public voice;
> The drama's laws, the drama's patrons give,
> For we that live to please, must please to live.

The audience—the public taste as understood by the playwright—helps to determine what the play is. Moreover, even members of the public who are not part of the playwright's immediate audience may exert an influence through censorship. We have already glanced at governmental censorship, but there are also other kinds. Take one of Shakespeare's most beloved characters, Falstaff, who appears in three of Shakespeare's plays, the two parts of *Henry IV* and *The Merry Wives of Windsor*. He appears with this name in the earliest printed version of the first of these plays, *1 Henry IV,* but we know that Shakespeare originally called him (after an historical figure) Sir John Oldcastle. Oldcastle appears in Shakespeare's source (partly reprinted in the Signet edition of *1 Henry IV*), and a trace of the name survives in Shakespeare's play, 1.2.43–44, where Prince Hal punningly addresses Falstaff as "my old lad of the castle." But for some reason—perhaps because the family of the historical Oldcastle complained—Shakespeare had to change the name. In short, the play as we have it was (at least in this detail) subject to some sort of censorship. If we think that a text should present what we take to be the author's intention, we probably will want to replace *Falstaff*

with *Oldcastle*. But if we recognize that a play is a collaboration, we may welcome the change, even if it was forced on
Shakespeare. Somehow *Falstaff,* with its hint of *false-staff,* i.e.,
inadequate prop, seems just right for this fat knight who, to our
delight, entertains the young prince with untruths. We can go as
far as saying that, at least so far as a play is concerned, an insistence on the author's original intention (even if we could know
it) can sometimes impoverish the text.

The tiny example of Falstaff's name illustrates the point that
the text we read is inevitably only a version—something in effect
produced by the collaboration of the playwright with his actors,
audiences, compositors, and editors—of a fluid text that Shakespeare once wrote, just as the *Hamlet* that we see on the screen
starring Kenneth Branagh is not the *Hamlet* that Shakespeare saw
in an open-air playhouse starring Richard Burbage. *Hamlet* itself,
as we shall note in a moment, also exists in several versions. It is
not surprising that there is now much talk about the *instability* of
Shakespeare's texts.

Because he was not only a playwright but was also an actor
and a shareholder in a theatrical company, Shakespeare probably was much involved with the translation of the play from
a manuscript to a stage production. He may or may not have
done some rewriting during rehearsals, and he may or may not
have been happy with cuts that were made. Some plays, notably *Hamlet* and *King Lear,* are so long that it is most unlikely that the texts we read were acted in their entirety.
Further, for both of these plays we have more than one early
text that demands consideration. In *Hamlet,* the Second
Quarto (1604) includes some two hundred lines not found in
the Folio (1623). Among the passages missing from the Folio
are two of Hamlet's reflective speeches, the "dram of evil"
speech (1.4.13–38) and "How all occasions do inform against
me" (4.4.32–66). Since the Folio has more numerous and often fuller stage directions, it certainly looks as though in the
Folio we get a theatrical version of the play, a text whose cuts
were probably made—this is only a hunch, of course—not because Shakespeare was changing his conception of Hamlet
but because the playhouse demanded a modified play. (The
problem is complicated, since the Folio not only cuts some of
the Quarto but adds some material. Various explanations have
been offered.)

Or take an example from *King Lear*. In the First and Second Quarto (1608, 1619), the final speech of the play is given to Albany, Lear's surviving son-in-law, but in the First Folio version (1623), the speech is given to Edgar. The Quarto version is in accord with tradition—usually the highest-ranking character in a tragedy speaks the final words. Why does the Folio give the speech to Edgar? One possible answer is this: The Folio version omits some of Albany's speeches in earlier scenes, so perhaps it was decided (by Shakespeare? by the players?) not to give the final lines to so pale a character. In fact, the discrepancies are so many between the two texts, that some scholars argue we do not simply have texts showing different theatrical productions. Rather, these scholars say, Shakespeare substantially revised the play, and we really have two versions of *King Lear* (and of *Othello* also, say some)—two different plays—not simply two texts, each of which is in some ways imperfect.

In this view, the 1608 version of *Lear* may derive from Shakespeare's manuscript, and the 1623 version may derive from his later revision. The Quartos have almost three hundred lines not in the Folio, and the Folio has about a hundred lines not in the Quartos. It used to be held that all the texts were imperfect in various ways and from various causes—some passages in the Quartos were thought to have been set from a manuscript that was not entirely legible, other passages were thought to have been set by a compositor who was new to setting plays, and still other passages were thought to have been provided by an actor who misremembered some of the lines. This traditional view held that an editor must draw on the Quartos and the Folio in order to get Shakespeare's "real" play. The new argument holds (although not without considerable strain) that we have two authentic plays, Shakespeare's early version (in the Quarto) and Shakespeare's—or his theatrical company's—revised version (in the Folio). Not only theatrical demands but also Shakespeare's own artistic sense, it is argued, called for extensive revisions. Even the titles vary: Q1 is called *True Chronicle Historie of the life and death of King Lear and his three Daughters*, whereas the Folio text is called *The Tragedie of King Lear*. To combine the two texts in order to produce what the editor thinks is the play that Shakespeare intended to write is, according to this view, to produce a text that is false to the history of the play. If the new view is correct, and we do have texts of two distinct versions of *Lear* rather than two imperfect versions of one play, it supports in a textual way the poststructuralist view that we cannot possibly have an unmediated vision of (in this case) a play by Shakespeare; we can only recognize a plurality of visions.

Editing Texts

Though eighteen of his plays were published during his lifetime, Shakespeare seems never to have supervised their publication. There is nothing unusual here; when a playwright sold a play to a theatrical company he surrendered his ownership to it. Normally a company would not publish the play, because to publish it meant to allow competitors to acquire the piece. Some plays did get published: Apparently hard-up actors sometimes pieced together a play for a publisher; sometimes a company in need of money sold a play; and sometimes a company allowed publication of a play that no longer drew audiences. That Shakespeare did not concern himself with publication is not remarkable; of his contemporaries, only Ben Jonson carefully supervised the publication of his own plays.

In 1623, seven years after Shakespeare's death, John Heminges and Henry Condell (two senior members of Shakespeare's company, who had worked with him for about twenty years) collected his plays—published and unpublished—into a large volume, of a kind called a folio. (A folio is a volume consisting of large sheets that have been folded once, each sheet thus making two leaves, or four pages. The size of the page of course depends on the size of the sheet—a folio can range in height from twelve to sixteen inches, and in width from eight to eleven; the pages in the 1623 edition of Shakespeare, commonly called the First Folio, are approximately thirteen inches tall and eight inches wide.) The eighteen plays published during Shakespeare's lifetime had been issued one play per volume in small formats called quartos. (Each sheet in a quarto has been folded twice, making four leaves, or eight pages, each page being about nine inches tall and seven inches wide, roughly the size of a large paperback.)

Heminges and Condell suggest in an address "To the great variety of readers" that the republished plays are presented in better form than in the quartos:

> Before you were abused with diverse stolen and surreptitious copies, maimed and deformed by the frauds and stealths of injurious impostors that exposed them; even those, are now offered to your view cured and perfect of their limbs, and all the rest absolute in their numbers, as he [i.e., Shakespeare] conceived them.

There is a good deal of truth to this statement, but some of the quarto versions are better than others; some are in fact preferable to the Folio text.

Whoever was assigned to prepare the texts for publication in the First Folio seems to have taken the job seriously and yet not to have performed it with uniform care. The sources of the texts seem to have been, in general, good unpublished copies or the best published copies. The first play in the collection, *The Tempest,* is divided into acts and scenes, has unusually full stage directions and descriptions of spectacle, and concludes with a list of the characters, but the editor was not able (or willing) to present all of the succeeding texts so fully dressed. Later texts occasionally show signs of carelessness: in one scene of *Much Ado About Nothing* the names of actors, instead of characters, appear as speech prefixes, as they had in the Quarto, which the Folio reprints; proofreading throughout the Folio is spotty and apparently was done without reference to the printer's copy; the pagination of *Hamlet* jumps from 156 to 257. Further, the proofreading was done while the presses continued to print, so that each play in each volume contains a mix of corrected and uncorrected pages.

Modern editors of Shakespeare must first select their copy; no problem if the play exists only in the Folio, but a considerable problem if the relationship between a Quarto and the Folio—or an early Quarto and a later one—is unclear. In the case of *Romeo and Juliet,* the First Quarto (Q1), published in 1597, is vastly inferior to the Second (Q2), published in 1599. The basis of Q1 apparently is a version put together from memory by some actors. Not surprisingly, it garbles many passages and is much shorter than Q2. On the other hand, occasionally Q1 makes better sense than Q2. For instance, near the end of the play, when the parents have assembled and learned of the deaths of Romeo and Juliet, in Q2 the Prince says (5.3.208–9),

> Come, *Montague;* for thou art early vp
> To see thy sonne and heire, now earling downe.

The last three words of this speech surely do not make sense, and many editors turn to Q1, which instead of "now earling downe" has "more early downe." Some modern editors take only "early" from Q1, and print "now early down"; others take "more early," and print "more early down." Further, Q1 (though, again, quite clearly a garbled and abbreviated text) includes some stage directions that are not found in Q2, and today many editors who base their text on Q2 are glad to add these stage directions, because the directions help to give us a sense of what the play looked like on Shakespeare's stage. Thus, in 4.3.58, after Juliet drinks the potion, Q1 gives us this stage direction, not in Q2: *"She falls upon her bed within the curtains."*

In short, an editor's decisions do not end with the choice of a single copy text. First of all, editors must reckon with Elizabethan spelling. If they are not producing a facsimile, they probably modernize the spelling, but ought they to preserve the old forms of words that apparently were pronounced quite unlike their modern forms—*lanthorn, alablaster*? If they preserve these forms are they really preserving Shakespeare's forms or perhaps those of a compositor in the printing house? What is one to do when one finds *lanthorn* and *lantern* in adjacent lines? (The editors of this series in general, but not invariably, assume that words should be spelled in their modern form, unless, for instance, a rhyme is involved.) Elizabethan punctuation, too, presents problems. For example, in the First Folio, the only text for the play, Macbeth rejects his wife's idea that he can wash the blood from his hand (2.2.60–62):

> No: this my Hand will rather
> The multitudinous Seas incarnardine,
> Making the Greene one, Red.

Obviously an editor will remove the superfluous capitals, and will probably alter the spelling to "incarnadine," but what about the comma before "Red"? If we retain the comma, Macbeth is calling the sea "the green one." If we drop the comma, Macbeth is saying that his bloody hand will make the sea ("the Green") *uniformly* red.

An editor will sometimes have to change more than spelling and punctuation. Macbeth says to his wife (1.7.46–47):

I dare do all that may become a man,
Who dares no more, is none.

For two centuries editors have agreed that the second line is unsatisfactory, and have emended "no" to "do": "Who dares do more is none." But when in the same play (4.2.21–22) Ross says that fearful persons

Floate upon a wilde and violent Sea
Each way, and moue,

need we emend the passage? On the assumption that the compositor misread the manuscript, some editors emend "each way, and move" to "and move each way"; others emend "move" to "none" (i.e., "Each way and none"). Other editors, however, let the passage stand as in the original. The editors of the Signet Classics Shakespeare have restrained themselves from making abundant emendations. In their minds they hear Samuel Johnson on the dangers of emendation: "I have adopted the Roman sentiment, that it is more honorable to save a citizen than to kill an enemy." Some departures (in addition to spelling, punctuation, and lineation) from the copy text have of course been made, but the original readings are listed in a note following the play, so that readers can evaluate the changes for themselves.

Following tradition, the editors of the Signet Classics Shakespeare have prefaced each play with a list of characters, and throughout the play have regularized the names of the speakers. Thus, in our text of *Romeo and Juliet,* all speeches by Juliet's mother are prefixed "Lady Capulet," although the 1599 Quarto of the play, which provides our copy text, uses at various points seven speech tags for this one character: *Capu. Wi.* (i.e., Capulet's wife), *Ca. Wi., Wi., Wife, Old La.* (i.e., Old Lady), *La.,* and *Mo.* (i.e., Mother). Similarly, in *All's Well That Ends Well,* the character whom we regularly call "Countess" is in the Folio (the copy text) variously identified as *Mother, Countess, Old Countess, Lady,* and *Old Lady.* Admittedly there is some loss in regularizing, since the various prefixes may give us a hint of the way Shakespeare (or a scribe who copied Shakespeare's manuscript) was thinking of the character in a particular scene—for instance, as a mother, or as an old lady. But too much can be made of these differing prefixes, since the social relationships implied are *not* always relevant to the given scene.

We have also added line numbers and in many cases act and scene divisions as well as indications of locale at the beginning of scenes. The Folio divided most of the plays into acts and some into scenes. Early eighteenth-century editors increased the divisions. These divisions, which provide a convenient way of referring to passages in the plays, have been retained, but when not in the text chosen as the basis for the Signet Classics text they are enclosed within square brackets, [ ], to indicate that they are editorial additions. Similarly, though no play of Shakespeare's was equipped with indications of the locale at the heads of scene divisions, locales have here been added in square brackets for the convenience of readers, who lack the information that costumes, properties, gestures, and scenery afford to spectators. Spectators can tell at a glance they are in the throne room, but without an editorial indication the reader may be puzzled for a while. It should be mentioned, incidentally, that there are a few authentic stage directions—perhaps Shakespeare's, perhaps a prompter's—that suggest locales, such as *"Enter Brutus in his orchard,"* and *"They go up into the Senate house."* It is hoped that the bracketed additions in the Signet text will provide readers with the sort of help provided by these two authentic directions, but it is equally hoped that the reader will remember that the stage was not loaded with scenery.

Shakespeare on the Stage

Each volume in the Signet Classics Shakespeare includes a brief stage (and sometimes film) history of the play. When we read about earlier productions, we are likely to find them eccentric, obviously wrongheaded—for instance, Nahum Tate's version of *King Lear,* with a happy ending, which held the stage for about a century and a half, from the late seventeenth century until the end of the first quarter of the nineteenth. We see engravings of David Garrick, the greatest actor of the eighteenth century, in eighteenth-century garb as King Lear, and we smile, thinking how absurd the production must have been. If we are more thoughtful, we say, with the English novelist L. P. Hartley, "The past is a foreign country: they do things differently there." But if the eighteenth-century staging is a foreign country, what of the plays of the late sixteenth and seventeenth centuries? A foreign language, a foreign theater, a foreign audience.

Probably all viewers of Shakespeare's plays, beginning with Shakespeare himself, at times have been unhappy with the plays on the stage. Consider three comments about production that we find in the plays themselves, which suggest Shakespeare's concerns. The Chorus in *Henry V* complains that the heroic story cannot possibly be adequately staged:

> But pardon, gentles all,
> The flat unraisèd spirits that hath dared
> On this unworthy scaffold to bring forth
> So great an object. Can this cockpit hold
> The vasty fields of France? Or may we cram
> Within this wooden *O* the very casques
> That did affright the air at Agincourt?
> . . . .
> Piece out our imperfections with your thoughts.
>
> (Prologue 1.8–14, 23)

Second, here are a few sentences (which may or may not represent Shakespeare's own views) from Hamlet's longish lecture to the players:

> Speak the speech, I pray you, as I pronounced it to you, trippingly on the tongue. But if you mouth it, as many of our players do, I had as lief the town crier spoke my lines. . . . O, it offends me to the soul to hear a robustious periwig-pated fellow tear a passion to tatters, to very rags, to split the ears of the groundlings. . . . And let those that play your clowns speak no more than is set down for them, for there be of them that will themselves laugh, to set on some quantity of barren spectators

to laugh too, though in the meantime some necessary question of the play be then to be considered. That's villainous and shows a most pitiful ambition in the fool that uses it.

(3.2.1–47)

Finally, we can quote again from the passage cited earlier in this introduction, concerning the boy actors who played the female roles. Cleopatra imagines with horror a theatrical version of her activities with Antony:

> The quick comedians
> Extemporally will stage us, and present
> Our Alexandrian revels: Antony
> Shall be brought drunken forth, and I shall see
> Some squeaking Cleopatra boy my greatness
> I' th' posture of a whore.   (5.2.216–21)

It is impossible to know how much weight to put on such passages—perhaps Shakespeare was just being modest about his theater's abilities—but it is easy enough to think that he was unhappy with some aspects of Elizabethan production. Probably no production can fully satisfy a playwright, and for that matter, few productions can fully satisfy *us*; we regret this or that cut, this or that way of costuming the play, this or that bit of business.

One's first thought may be this: Why don't they just do "authentic" Shakespeare, "straight" Shakespeare, the play as Shakespeare wrote it? But as we read the plays—words written to be performed—it sometimes becomes clear that we do not know *how* to perform them. For instance, in *Antony and Cleopatra* Antony, the Roman general who has succumbed to Cleopatra and to Egyptian ways, says, "The nobleness of life / Is to do thus" (1.1.36–37). But what is "thus"? Does Antony at this point embrace Cleopatra? Does he embrace and kiss her? (There are, by the way, very few scenes of kissing on Shakespeare's stage, possibly because boys played the female roles.) Or does he make a sweeping gesture, indicating the Egyptian way of life?

This is not an isolated example; the plays are filled with lines that call for gestures, but we are not sure what the gestures should be. *Interpretation* is inevitable. Consider a passage in *Hamlet*. In 3.1, Polonius persuades his daughter, Ophelia, to talk to Hamlet while Polonius and Claudius eavesdrop. The two men conceal themselves, and Hamlet encounters Ophelia. At 3.1.131 Hamlet suddenly says to her, "Where's your father?" Why does Hamlet, apparently out of nowhere—they have not been talking about Polonius—ask this question? Is this an example of the "antic disposition" (fantastic behavior) that Hamlet earlier (1.5.172) had told Horatio and others—including us—he would display? That is, is the question about the whereabouts of her father a seemingly irrational one, like his earlier question (3.1.103) to Ophelia, "Ha, ha! Are you honest?" Or, on the other hand, has Hamlet (as in many productions) suddenly glimpsed Polonius's foot protruding from beneath a drapery at the rear? That is, does Hamlet ask the question because he has suddenly seen something suspicious and now is testing Ophelia? (By the way, in productions that do give Hamlet a physical cue, it is almost always Polonius rather than Claudius who provides the clue. This itself is an act of interpretation on the part of the director.) Or (a third possibility) does Hamlet get a clue from Ophelia, who inadvertently betrays the spies by nervously glancing at their place of hiding? This is the interpretation used in the BBC television version, where Ophelia glances in fear toward the hiding place just after Hamlet says "Why wouldst thou be a breeder of sinners?" (121–22). Hamlet, realizing that he is being observed, glances here and there *before* he asks "Where's your father?" The question thus is a climax to what he has been doing while speaking the preceding lines. Or (a fourth interpretation) does Hamlet suddenly, without the aid of any clue whatsoever, intuitively (insightfully, mysteriously, wonderfully) sense that someone is spying? Directors must decide, of course—and so must readers.

Recall, too, the preceding discussion of the texts of the plays, which argued that the texts—though they seem to be before us in permanent black on white—are unstable. The Signet text of *Hamlet*, which draws on the Second Quarto (1604) and the First Folio (1623), is considerably longer than any version staged in Shakespeare's time. Our version, even if spoken very briskly and played without any intermission, would take close to four hours, far beyond "the two hours' traffic of our stage" mentioned in the Prologue to *Romeo and Juliet*. (There are a few contemporary references to the duration of a play, but none mentions more than three hours.) Of Shakespeare's plays, only *The Comedy of Errors, Macbeth,* and *The Tempest* can be done in less than three hours without cutting. And even if we take a play that exists only in a short text, *Macbeth,* we cannot claim that we are experiencing the very play that Shakespeare conceived, partly because some of the Witches' songs almost surely are non-Shakespearian additions, and partly because we are not willing to watch the play performed without an intermission and with boys in the female roles.

Further, as the earlier discussion of costumes mentioned, the plays apparently were given chiefly in contemporary, that is, in Elizabethan dress. If today we give them in the costumes that Shakespeare probably saw, the plays seem not contemporary but curiously dated. Yet if we use our own dress, we find lines of dialogue that are at odds with what we see; we may feel that the language, so clearly not our own, is inappropriate coming out of people in today's dress. A common solution, incidentally, has been to set the plays in the nineteenth century, on the grounds that this attractively distances the plays (gives them a degree of foreignness, allowing for interesting costumes) and yet doesn't put them into a museum world of Elizabethan England.

Inevitably our productions are adaptations, *our* adaptations, and inevitably they will look dated, not in a century but in twenty years, or perhaps even in a decade. Still, we cannot escape from our own conceptions. As the director Peter Brook has said, in *The Empty Space* (1968):

> It is not only the hair-styles, costumes and make-ups that look dated. All the different elements of staging—the shorthands of behavior that stand for emotions; gestures, gesticulations and tones of voice—are all fluctuating on an invisible stock exchange all the time. . . . A living theatre that thinks it can stand aloof from anything as trivial as fashion will wilt. (p. 16)

As Brook indicates, it is through today's hairstyles, costumes, makeup, gestures, gesticulations, tones of voice—this includes our *conception* of earlier hairstyles, costumes, and so forth if we stage the play in a period other than our own—that we inevitably stage the plays.

It is a truism that every age invents its own Shakespeare, just as, for instance, every age has invented its own classical world. Our view of ancient Greece, a slave-holding society in which even free Athenian women were severely circumscribed, does not much resemble the Victorians' view of ancient Greece as a glorious democracy, just as, perhaps, our view of Victorianism itself does not much resemble theirs. We cannot claim that the Shakespeare on our stage is the true Shakespeare, but in our stage productions we find a Shakespeare that speaks to us, a Shakespeare that our ancestors doubtless did not know but one that seems to us to be the true Shakespeare—at least for a while.

Our age is remarkable for the wide variety of kinds of staging that it uses for Shakespeare, but one development deserves special mention. This is the now common practice of race-blind or color-blind or nontraditional casting, which allows persons who are not white to play in Shakespeare. Previously blacks performing in Shakespeare were limited to a mere three roles, Othello, Aaron (in *Titus Andronicus*), and the Prince of Morocco (in *The Merchant of Venice*), and there were no roles at all for Asians. Indeed, African-Americans rarely could play even one of these three roles, since they were not welcome in white companies. Ira Aldridge (c. 1806–67), a black actor of undoubted talent, was forced to make his living by performing Shakespeare in England and in Europe, where he could play not only Othello but also—in whiteface—other tragic roles such as King Lear. Paul Robeson (1898–1976) made theatrical history when he played Othello in London in 1930, and there was some talk about bringing the production to the United States, but there was more talk about whether American audiences would tolerate the sight of a black man—a real black man, not a white man in blackface—kissing and then killing a white woman. The idea was tried out in summer stock in 1942, the reviews were enthusiastic, and in the following year Robeson opened on Broadway in a production that ran an astounding 296 performances. An occasional all-black company sometimes performed Shakespeare's plays, but otherwise blacks (and other minority members) were in effect shut out from performing Shakespeare. Only since about 1970 has it been common for nonwhites to play major roles along with whites. Thus, in a 1996–97 production of *Antony and Cleopatra,* a white Cleopatra, Vanessa Redgrave, played opposite a black Antony, Dorian Harewood. Multiracial casting is now especially common at the New York Shakespeare Festival, founded in 1954 by Joseph Papp, and in England, where even siblings such as Claudio and Isabella in *Measure for Measure* or Lear's three daughters may be of different races. Probably most viewers today soon stop worrying about the lack of realism, and move beyond the color of the performers' skin to the quality of the performance.

Nontraditional casting is not only a matter of color or race; it includes sex. In the past, occasionally a distinguished woman of the theater has taken on a male role—Sarah Bernhardt (1844–1923) as Hamlet is perhaps the most famous example—but such performances were widely regarded as eccentric. Although today there have been some performances involving cross-dressing (a drag *As You Like It* staged by the National Theatre in England in 1966 and in the United States in 1974 has achieved considerable fame in the annals of stage history), what is more interesting is the casting of women in roles that traditionally are male but that need not be. Thus, a 1993–94 English production of *Henry V* used a woman—*not* cross-dressed—in the role of the governor of Harfleur. According to Peter Holland, who reviewed the production in *Shakespeare Survey* 48 (1995), "having a female Governor of Harfleur feminized the city and provided a direct response to the horrendous threat of rape and murder that Henry had offered, his language and her body in direct connection and opposition" (p. 210). Ten years from now the device may not play so effectively, but today it speaks to us. Shakespeare, born in the Elizabethan Age, has been dead nearly four hundred years, yet he is, as Ben Jonson said, "not of an age but for all time." We must understand, however, that he is "for all time" precisely because each age finds in his abundance something for itself and something of itself.

And here we come back to two issues discussed earlier in this introduction—the instability of the text and, curiously, the Bacon/Oxford heresy concerning the authorship of the plays. *Of course* Shakespeare wrote the plays, and we should daily fall on our knees to thank him for them—and yet there is something to the idea that he is not their only author. Every editor, every director and actor, and every reader to some degree shapes them, too, for when we edit, direct, act, or read, we inevitably become Shakespeare's collaborator and re-create the plays. The plays, one might say, are so cunningly contrived that they guide our responses, tell us how we ought to feel, and make a mark on us, but (for better or for worse) we also make a mark on them.

—SYLVAN BARNET
Tufts University

Pericles, Prince of Tyre

THE LATE,

And much admired Play,

Called

Pericles, Prince
of Tyre

With the true Relation of the whole Historie,
aduentures, and fortunes of the said Prince:

As also,

The no lesse strange, and worthy accidents,
in the Birth and Life, of his Daughter
MARIANA.

As it hath been diuers and sundry times acted by
his Maiesties Seruants, at the Globe on
the Banck-side.

By William ⚜ Shakespeare.

Imprinted at London for *Henry Gosson*, and are
to be sold at the signe of the Sunne in
Pater-noster row, &c.
1 6 0 9.

Title page of the First Quarto of *Pericles* (1609).

Introduction

Pericles presents several unique problems. Most critics are agreed that, while Acts 3, 4, and 5 are substantially Shakespeare's, Acts 1 and 2 are not. The questions to be asked, therefore, are: Who is the author of Acts 1 and 2? And, further, how did the non-Shakespearian first two acts come to be joined to the Shakespearian last three acts? As to this there are two main possibilities: 1) that Shakespeare collaborated with another playwright, as he did a few years later with John Fletcher in *Henry VIII, Two Noble Kinsmen,* and the lost *Cardenio;* 2) that Shakespeare came across a complete play on the subject of *Pericles* and began to rewrite it at the point where the subject matter caught his imagination, the point at which Pericles, during a storm at sea, is suddenly confronted with the death of his wife and the birth of his daughter. According to this hypothesis, Shakespeare, being an extremely busy man, did not bother to rewrite the first two acts, except, perhaps, to add a few touches here and there.

Of these two possibilities the latter seems to me by far the more likely. That Shakespeare should have collaborated with the author of the first two acts seems very improbable. To collaborate with John Fletcher is one thing; to collaborate with the exceedingly mediocre talent that could produce Acts 1 and 2 of *Pericles,* quite another. It is true that these first two acts must have been a good deal better than they are in the text in which they have come down to us. For the Quarto text—and this adds greatly to the intricate problems presented by the play—is very corrupt, not only in Acts 1 and 2, but in the Shakespearian part as well. Whole lines are missing, others are garbled, verse is frequently set out as prose, and occasionally prose as verse. It is, most scholars are agreed, a text based on a report made from visits to the theater, and bears the usual marks of such a reported text—above all, a large number of auditory errors and mislineation of Shakespeare's blank verse.

The Quarto of *Pericles*, then, is, in many ways, very imperfect. But where for other Shakespeare plays with bad Quarto texts we also have a good text, for *Pericles* we have only the one text, published for the first time in 1609, in what was, no doubt, a pirated edition (i.e., it was printed without the permission of Shakespeare and his company). The problem of the authorship of the first two acts is therefore made much more difficult by the absence of any good text of the play, and scholars have not been able to agree on the probable identity of the author, though various candidates, such as Thomas Heywood, George Wilkins, and, most recently, John Day, have been put forward.

The whole matter is further complicated by the publication in 1608 of a prose narrative by George Wilkins, entitled *The Painfull Aduentures of Pericles Prince of Tyre*, "being," we are assured on the title page, "the true History of the Play of *Pericles*, as it was lately presented by the worthy and ancient Poet *Iohn Gower*." And in *The Argument of the whole Historie* the reader is entreated "to receiue this Historie in the same maner as it was vnder the habite of ancient *Gower* the famous English Poet, by the Kings Maiesties Players [i.e., Shakespeare's company] excellently presented." There is every indication that Wilkins' claim is trustworthy: that he had witnessed one or more performances of Shakespeare's play and had based his novel on this, while also drawing freely (and without acknowledgment) on Laurence Twine's prose version of the same story, *The Patterne of Painefull Aduentures*, which had been reprinted in 1607, and is one of the two chief sources of *Pericles*. In publishing his novel in 1608 Wilkins, no doubt, attempted to exploit the great popularity which the play, according to all indications, enjoyed from the outset.

Wilkins' novel is of great interest and value since, next to the Quarto text, it provides the only clue about the nature of the play as performed by Shakespeare's company that we possess. Not only can editors of *Pericles* draw on it in devising their stage directions (as has been done in this edition, for instance, at 2.2.16, where the s.d. "As each Knight passes, his page, who goes before him, presents his shield to the Princess" is based on Wilkins' "their Pages before them bearing their Deuices on their shields . . . which being by the knights Page deliuered to the Lady"), but they can find support in it for emendations of

corrupt readings in the Quarto text. For example, the change of
the Quarto's certainly corrupt "untimely" to "uncomely" at
1.1.129 is strongly supported by Wilkins' "hee was become
both father, sonne, and husband by his vncomely and abhorred
actions with his owne child." At one point in the text of this edition (3.2.84–87) even a whole sentence, which in the Quarto is
manifestly corrupt, Cerimon's

> I heard of an Egyptian
> That had nine hours lien dead,
> Who was by good appliance recoverèd

has been replaced by the corresponding sentence in Wilkins'
narrative, which, with the words in parentheses omitted, sounds
very much like Shakespeare's verse and thus may well repro-
duce what he had written: "I haue read of some Egyptians, who
after foure houres death (if man may call it so) haue raised im-
pouerished bodies, like to this, vnto their former health."

Lastly, there is one scene where the Quarto text is undoubtedly deficient, and where Wilkins' novel, even if we cannot
draw on it for emendations, affords us glimpses of what the
main outline of the Shakespearian original appears to have
been. It is the scene between Marina and Lysimachus in the
brothel (4.6.70–122). In Wilkins' novel, as in the play, Lysimachus is depicted as an old client of the bawd, led to the
brothel by lust. But in the novel, as the result of Marina's passionate pleas and reproaches, he undergoes a reformation, declaring: "I hither came with thoughtes intemperate, foule and
deformed, the which your paines so well hath laued, that they
are now white." It is here that the novel diverges most sharply
from the play, where, at the corresponding point, Lysimachus is
made to declare:

> For me, be you thoughten
> That I came with no ill intent; for to me
> The very doors and windows savor vilely.

This stands, of course, in complete contradiction to what we
have been shown in the first part of the scene, where Lysimachus is presented as an old and favorite client. This contradiction has led some scholars to suggest that Lysimachus' later
claims reflect a change of mind on Shakespeare's part, a belated

attempt to make him a more acceptable husband for Marina. But it seems incredible that Shakespeare should not have bothered to bring the earlier part of the scene into line with this new conception. Furthermore, the writing, which is for the most part Shakespearian up to line 110, ceases to be so at precisely the point at which Lysimachus protests his innocence, and we get such wretched un-Shakespearian stuff as his "For me, be you thoughten. . . ." I believe, then, that lines 110–22 represent the reporter's attempt to reconstruct an only dimly remembered passage, which, for some reason, was missing in his report, and that in doing so he turned Lysimachus from a character somewhat like that of Bertram in *All's Well* into one closer to the Duke in *Measure for Measure*. The great value of Wilkins' account of this scene is not only that he preserved for us what I believe to be Shakespeare's version of it, which had been distorted by the reporter, but that he incidentally seems to have kept a good many of Shakespeare's lines which are missing in the Quarto text, as the following extract from the dialogue between Marina and Lysimachus will show. The lines which seem to me Shakespearian have been italicized and the blank verse line-division has been indicated.

If you take from mee mine honour, *you are like him,/that makes a gappe into forbidden ground,* after whome too many enter, and you are guiltie of all their euilles: my life is yet vnspotted, my chastitie vnstained in thought. *Then if your violence deface this building,/the workemanship of heauen, made vp for good,* and not to be the exercise of sinnes intemperaunce, you do kill your owne honour, abuse your owne iustice, and impouerish me. Why quoth *Lysimachus, this house wherein thou liuest,/is euen the receptacle of all mens sinnes,/and nurse of wickednesse,* and how canst thou then be otherwise then naught, that liuest in it? It is not good, answered *Marina,* when you that are the Gouernour, who should liue well, *the better to be bolde to punish euill,* doe knowe that there is such a roofe, and yet come vnder it. Is there a necessitie (my yet good Lord) if there be fire before me, that I must strait then thither flie and burne my selfe? Or if suppose this house, (*which too too many feele such houses are)/should be the Doctors patrimony, and Surgeons feeding;* folowes it therefore, that I must needs infect my self to giue them maintenance? O my good Lord, kill me, but not deflower me, punish me how you please, so you spare my chastitie, and since it is all the dowry that both the Gods haue giuen, and men haue left to me, do not you take it from me; make me your seruant, I will willingly obey you; make mee your bondwoman, *I will accompt it freedome; let me be/the worst that is called vile, so I may still/liue honest, I am content:* or if you thinke it is too blessed a happinesse to haue me so, *let me euen now, now in this minute die,* and Ile accompt my death more happy than my birth. With which wordes (being spoken vpon her knees) while her eyes were the glasses that carried the water of her mishap, the good Gentlewoman being mooued, hee lift her vp with his hands, and euen then imbraced her in his hart, saying aside: *Now surely this is Virtues image,/or rather, Vertues selfe, sent downe, from heauen,/a while to raigne on earth,* to teach vs what we should be. So in steede of willing her to drie her eyes, he wiped the wet himselfe off, and could haue found in his heart, with modest thoughts to haue kissed her, but that hee feared the offer would offend her. This onely hee sayde, Lady, for such your vertues are, *a furre more worthy stile your beuty challenges,* and no way lesse your beauty can promise me that you are, *I hither came/with thoughtes intemperate, foule and deformed,* the which your paines so well hath laued, that they are now white, continue still to all so, and for my parte, *who hither came but to haue payd the price,/a peece of golde for your virginitie,* now giue you twenty to releeue your honesty. *It shall become you still/to be euen as you are, a peece of goodnesse,/the best wrought vppe, that euer Nature made,* and if that any shall inforce you ill, if you but send to me, I am your friend. With which promise, leauing her presence, she most humbly thanked the Gods for the preseruation of of her chastitie, and the reformation of his mind.

I should mention at this point a hypothesis which attempts to account for the stylistic differences between the first two and the last three acts of the play in a radically different way from those mentioned so far. In an important article (*Shakespeare Survey* 5, pp. 25–49) Professor Philip Edwards has suggested that Shakespeare may have been responsible for the entire play, and that the difference in style between the two parts may be due to the different methods adopted by two reporters: the one reporting Acts 1 and 2, the other Acts 3–5. The former "welds into mediocre verse the words, phrases and general sense of the original so far as he can remember them. He is at his best in prose, where remodeling is not attempted. The second reporter, perhaps giving the original very much more faithfully than his predecessor, makes no attempt at rewriting, and after the first scene does not make more than desultory attempts to write down the verse in lines." This hypothesis is in many ways attractive. For instance, it accounts better than any other for the intermittent occurrence in the first two acts of lines that are manifestly Shakespearian. But there are several grave objections to it, which make it in my view untenable: 1. It seems hard to believe that two men should be willing to adopt such utterly different methods of reporting in order to achieve a composite text. 2. If the first two acts were really by Shakespeare, then those lines in the Quarto text which are identical with passages in Wilkins' novel ought to be acceptable Shakespearian verse. But this is clearly not so. For example:

> A gentleman of Tyre; my name Pericles;
> My education been in arts and arms;
> Who, looking for adventures in the world,
> Was by the rough seas reft of ships and men,
> And after shipwrack driven upon this shore
>
> (2.3.83–87)

agrees almost word for word with the corresponding passage in Wilkins' narrative, but is plainly not Shakespearian. 3. If the report of the last three acts of the play is so much more faithful than that of the first two acts, we ought to find more verbal echoes of the Quarto in the part of Wilkins' narrative corresponding to the last three acts than in that corresponding to the first two. In fact, rather the reverse is the case.*

The likeliest hypothesis seems to me, then, that late in 1607 or early in 1608, at about the time he was writing *Antony and Cleopatra*, Shakespeare came across a manuscript play on the subject of *Pericles* (which may or may not have been performed on the stage), written by some very minor playwright; that he rewrote entirely the last three acts, and had it performed by his

---

*Two recent studies offer what seems to be irrefutable evidence that George Wilkins was the author of the non-Shakespearian passages. See Brian Vickers, *Shakespeare, Co-Author* (2002), and MacD. Jackson, *Defining Shakespeare: "Pericles" as Test Case* (2003).

company at the Globe theater in the spring of 1608.* But it seems that Shakespeare rewrote not only the last three acts, but also occasional lines in the first two acts and, I believe, one whole scene, 2.1.

As we read through the wooden, jog-trot, largely end-stopped verse of the first two acts, we come across lines which are late Shakespearian in diction and movement. The most notable example of this occurs in the play's opening scene, in Pericles' speech to King Antiochus after he has solved the riddle. It begins with the mediocre verse typical of the author of the first two acts:

> Great King,
> Few love to hear the sins they love to act;
> 'Twould braid yourself too near for me to tell it.
> Who has a book of all that monarchs do,
> He's more secure to keep it shut than shown;
> For vice repeated is like the wand'ring wind
> Blows dust in others' eyes to spread itself;
> And yet the end of all is bought thus dear:
> The breath is gone, and the sore eyes see clear
> To stop the air would hurt them.
>
> (1.1.92–101)

Then come a few lines which are unmistakably Shakespearian:

> The blind mole casts
> Copped hills towards heaven, to tell the earth is thronged
> By man's oppression; and the poor worm doth die for't.
>
> (101–03)

And then the former verse continues on its jog-trot way.

As for the opening scene of Act 2, consisting of a mixture of verse and prose, few commentators have been bold enough to assign it to Shakespeare. But if it is not his work, it is remarkably like it, both in its verse and prose; and it certainly cannot be by the author of the remainder of the first two acts, for it is utterly different in style and manner. If we make allowance for

---

*The latest date of composition of the Shakespearian part of *Pericles*, May 1608, seems provided by the play's entry in the Stationers' Register in that month. Its earliest date seems determined chiefly by the style of the verse, which cannot be much earlier than 1607.

the corruption of the text, there is nothing in the scene which one needs deny to Shakespeare. Pericles' opening speech is quite Shakespearian, though it deteriorates towards the end:

> Yet cease your ire, you angry stars of heaven!
> Wind, rain, and thunder, remember, earthly man
> Is but a substance that must yield to you. . . .
>
> (2.1.1–3)

There enter three fishermen, and the ways in which they are made instantly real and vivid with the greatest economy of means, and in which they dispense their worldly wisdom and witticisms, bear the mark of Shakespeare. The fishermen's prose is counterpointed by Pericles' verse, and some of this is undoubtedly Shakespearian, e.g.,

> What I have been I have forgot to know;
> But what I am want teaches me to think on:
> A man thronged up with cold.
>
> (70–72)

and two lines towards the end of the scene, which no one but Shakespeare could have written:

> And spite of all the rapture of the sea,
> This jewel holds his building on my arm.
>
> (54–55)

There remains still the problem of the authorship of the choruses. This is made much more difficult by the fact that they are written in a purposely archaic idiom, to suit their speaker, the poet Gower, a contemporary of Chaucer, whose version of the story in his *Confessio Amantis* served as the play's main source. Most of the choruses are clearly written in imitation of the octosyllabic couplets in which Gower had told his story. And their archaic idiom also suits the old tale which is the play's subject matter. Ben Jonson referred to *Pericles* contemptuously as a "moldy tale," but the appearance of the mold of antiquity is clearly just what its authors wished to achieve. This is vividly brought home to us by the opening lines of Gower's first chorus (1–10). From the first, the story's antiquity is emphasized as one of its chief virtues.

Which of the choruses are by Shakespeare, and which by the author of Acts 1 and 2? All the indications are that the Shakespearian choruses start precisely where we would expect—at the beginning of Act 3. Shakespeare tries to maintain a certain continuity with the earlier choruses in the play by using archaic diction and octosyllabic couplets (though he abandons these for decasyllables after the opening chorus of Act 4). But though written purposely in a naive and simple idiom, the Shakespearian choruses are quite devoid of the clumsy, empty, elliptic diction and lame rhythm of the earlier choruses. The juxtaposition of a few lines from each will make the difference manifest. Here are the opening lines of the chorus at the beginning of Act 2:

> Here have you seen a mighty king
> His child iwis to incest bring;
> A better prince and benign lord
> That will prove awful both in deed and word.
> Be quiet, then, as men should be,
> Till he hath passed necessity.
> I'll show you those in trouble's reign
> Losing a mite, a mountain gain.
> The good in conversation,
> To whom I give my benison,
> Is still at Tharsus, where each man
> Thinks all is writ he spoken can;
> And, to remember what he does,
> Build his statue to make him glorious.
> But tidings to the contrary
> Are brought your eyes; what need speak I?

And here, by contrast, are the opening lines of the chorus at the beginning of Act 3:

> Now sleep y-slackèd hath the rout;
> No din but snores the house about,
> Made louder by the o'erfed breast
> Of this most pompous marriage feast.
> The cat, with eyne of burning coal,
> Now couches 'fore the mouse's hole;
> And crickets sing at the oven's mouth
> All the blither for their drouth.
> Hymen hath brought the bride to bed,

> Where by the loss of maidenhead
> A babe is molded. Be attent,
> And time that is so briefly spent
> With your fine fancies quaintly eche.
> What's dumb in show I'll plain with speech.

We still have archaisms (y-slackèd, eyne), but the verse is incomparably more vivid, vigorous, and accomplished. Moreover, into these Shakespearian choruses enters an element not found in those of Acts 1 and 2, but familiar to us from the choruses in *Henry V:* the audience is repeatedly asked to use its imagination to eke out what is being presented on the stage (e.g., "And time that is so briefly spent/With your fine fancies quaintly eche"; "In your supposing once more put your sight:/Of heavy Pericles think this his bark").

The story of Pericles, or Apollonius of Tyre, as he was called previous to Shakespeare's play, had been one of the most popular tales in the Middle Ages and the Renaissance. Probably it goes back to Hellenistic times, having its origin in some lost Greek romance. Not only the story's names and settings point to this (Pentapolis is located in the play as somewhere in Greece, while Tyre, Ephesus, Tharsus, and Mytilene, where the rest of the action takes place, are all on or near the coast of Asia Minor), but the outline of the story is typical of the Greek romances. These are tales of marvelous adventures, marked by an abundance of shipwrecks; hairbreadth escapes from wild beasts, bandits, or pirates; innocent maidens, who preserve their virtue in spite of all assaults; and ending in miraculous reunions of parents and children, brothers and sisters, husbands and wives, long believed dead. The main emotion which the Greek romances set out to arouse in the reader is a sense of wonder at the strange incidents which they describe. And a sense of wonder is also one of the main emotions aroused by Shakespeare's Last Plays; "rare," "strange," "wonderful," "like an old tale," are expressions which characters in these plays use again and again to voice their response to the events they witness, and this response is also shared by the audience.

In the English drama written before Shakespeare there is one type of play which sets out to evoke this response, and which is linked with the Greek romances: the miracle play or dramatized saint's legend, a form of drama highly popular beginning with the twelfth century, and still performed in Shakespeare's youth. Unfortunately few of these plays have survived, but from these and extant French miracle plays one can infer their nature. Like the Greek romances, they are tales of strange adventures, separations, wanderings across seas and lands, rescues miraculously effected, dangers overcome and trials passed, until the final triumph of reunion with loved relatives or the triumph of martyrdom. It has been claimed—justly, I think—that these miracle plays had a much profounder influence on the development of English Renaissance drama than had the medieval mystery plays. And the editor of the New Arden *Pericles* has suggested that it was from such miracle plays that the broad structural features of the play may be derived.

In its structure *Pericles* is unlike any of Shakespeare's earlier comedies. This can be seen most readily if we compare the handling of time. In the comedies before *Pericles* Shakespeare either observed the most rigorous unity of time, as in *The Comedy of Errors,* or he contained the action within a few days, as in *A Midsummer Night's Dream,* or at most within a few months, as in *All's Well*. But nowhere had he used a time scheme similar to that of *Pericles*, where between Acts 3 and 4 there is a time gap of fourteen years. This time scheme is used once more in *The Winter's Tale,* where between Acts 3 and 4 there is an interval of sixteen years. And in both plays, while in the first three acts our attention centers on the royal father (Pericles, Leontes), in the fourth act his place is taken by his daughter (Marina, Perdita), while the fifth act is given over to the reunion of father and daughter, followed by the reunion of husband and wife. In consequence we have in these two plays a kind of double focus, upon father and daughter, which is quite unlike anything found in Shakespeare's other plays.* In the earlier comedies our attention is sometimes divided between different pairs of lovers, as in *Two Gentlemen, Love's Labor's Lost,* or *The Taming of the Shrew;* or between different groups of characters, as in *A Midsummer Night's Dream, As You Like It,* and *Twelfth Night*. But nowhere else do we have this shift of focus from father to daughter, and the great gap of time in the middle of the play.

*This double focus is well brought out by the Quarto's title page: "The late, And much admired Play, Called Pericles, Prince of Tyre. With the true Relation of the whole Historie, aduentures, and fortunes of the said Prince: As also, The no lesse strange, and worthy accidents, in the Birth and Life, of his Daughter Mariana."

In *The Winter's Tale* this structure is all-important as a vehicle of the play's significances by contrasting the images of wintry barrenness and desolation centering on Leontes with images of spring and fertility centering on Perdita. In *Pericles* the function of the double focus is less immediately obvious. The parallels between the misfortunes that befall father and daughter—in both cases their afflictions begin with a plot to murder them, which they escape, only to be overtaken by further calamities—have a similar effect to the parallels between main plot and subplot in *King Lear* and *Timon of Athens*. The sudden and violent blows of fortune which strike Marina, as they had struck her father, deepen and widen the play's image of the world as a lasting storm, whirring us from our friends (4.1.19). But to this parallel Shakespeare adds a contrast, found in the way in which father and daughter respond to these afflictions.

A number of critics in recent years have claimed that Pericles, as Shakespeare depicts him, is an embodiment of patience in adversity, a kind of male Griselda-figure, and that the play presents an *exemplum* of this virtue of patience that leads to restoration and happiness. Now it is true that, compared to his prototypes in the sources, Pericles behaves under the earlier blows of fortune with much moderation and restraint. For instance, in his reception of the news of his wife's death, wherein Gower and Twine he indulges in the most frantic display of grief, in Shakespeare's scene he expresses it much less vehemently. Yet nothing suggests to me here that he is meant to be seen as an embodiment of patience in adversity. The nurse, Lychorida, repeatedly calls upon him to be patient: "Patience, good sir; do not assist the storm" (assist, that is, by his loud cries of grief); "Patience, good sir,/Even for this charge." (3.1.19,26–27). It would be odd to be preaching patience to a figure embodying that virtue. His reception of the news of Marina's death, as described in dumb show and chorus, suggests even less that Shakespeare thought of Pericles as preeminently a patient man. "Cleon shows Pericles the tomb," we are told, "whereat Pericles makes lamentation, puts on sackcloth, and in a mighty passion departs." And Gower comments:

> And Pericles, in sorrow all devoured,
> With sighs shot through and biggest tears o'ershowered,
> Leaves Tharsus and again embarks. He swears
> Never to wash his face, nor cut his hairs.
> He puts on sackcloth, and to sea. He bears

> A tempest, which his mortal vessel tears,
> And yet he rides it out.
>
> (4.4.25–31)

The "tempest, which his mortal vessel tears" is, of course, the storm of his "mighty passion" that ravages his mortal body. He does not die ("And yet he rides it out"). But he shuts himself away from all human society, and when Marina visits him, he has not spoken to a living soul for three months. Can Shakespeare really have thought that this is the way in which exemplars of patience accept the blows of fortune? Wilkins certainly thought otherwise, and makes clear his view of Pericles' action of shutting himself away from his fellowmen by making Lysimachus declare that "though his misfortunes haue beene great, and by which he hath great cause for this sorrow, it is great pitty he should continue thus peruerse and obstinate, or so noble a gentleman come to so dishonorable a death," and having Marina tell her father that "hee was borne a Prince, whose dignity being to gouerne others, it was most foule in him to misgouerne himselfe."

Neither can I believe in the suggestion made by one of the proponents of this view (J. M. S. Tompkins in *Review of English Studies*, 1952, 315 ff.)—a suggestion which has been widely accepted—that Shakespeare called his hero "Pericles" after the Athenian statesman, whose life he could have read in Plutarch, who stresses the patience of his hero at the beginning and end of the "Life." I can perceive no resemblance between the two, apart from the fact that they are both excellent fellows. Previously it had been held—and, I think, rightly—that the name has been derived from the *Arcadia,* Sir Philip Sidney's great prose romance, which is full of incidents like those described in *Pericles*. One of its two heroes, called Pyrocles, is depicted as a pattern of all princely virtues. That Shakespeare had Sidney's hero in mind while writing his play seems proved by the fact that Marina's description of her father's behavior during the storm at sea in which she was born closely follows. Sidney's account of Pyrocles' behavior during the storm at sea which precedes his shipwreck (see below, "The Sources of *Pericles.*").* Like Sidney's hero, Pericles is depicted as an exem-

---

*That the author of the first two acts also had Pyrocles in mind when writing of his hero's adventures seems indicated by 2.1. and 2.2. As J. C. Maxwell has pointed out, there is nothing in previous versions of the story about the fishing up of the rusty armor, or about the hero's participation and

plar not of patience but of all princely excellences. The episodes in the first two acts—often claimed, I believe unjustly, to be insufficiently integrated with the rest of the play—serve not only to present instances of the many blows of fortune that strike Pericles, but also to exhibit his various excellences: his perspicacity in solving Antiochus' riddle (even if it does not seem to *us* a particularly hard one); his loving care of his subjects, which makes him grieve over the danger to which he has unwittingly exposed them; his surpassing excellence in the tournament; his accomplishment in ballroom dancing in full armor (in the *Arcadia* it is the other hero, Musidorus, who dances featly in armor); his supreme skill as a musician; and his modesty, courtesy, and graceful bearing throughout these scenes. Only in his response to the blows of fortune does he fall short of the princely ideal, most signally in his self-seclusion from all human society after being falsely persuaded of the death of Marina. In this he again resembles Pyrocles, whose only discernible fault is a lack of patience in adversity, which culminates in the episode in which he attempts to brain himself by running his head against the wall, after being falsely persuaded of the death of his beloved Philoclea. (The parallel is increased by the resemblance between Dionyza and Sidney's Cecropia, which has been noted by commentators.)

Just as Pericles is depicted as the pattern of all princely excellences, so Marina is shown to be the pattern of all excellences becoming to a princess. This is made manifest both in the action and in Gower's commentary upon it, above all in his opening choruses in Acts 4 and 5. If we are looking for a figure in the play exemplifying patience in adversity, it is here that it is to be found. This is emphasized in the great recognition scene, when Pericles exclaims:

---

victory in a tournament. In Gower he takes part and excels in athletic games held in the presence of the King; in Twine he gains the King's favor by his expertise in playing tennis with him and washing him in his bath. The idea of Pericles entering the lists anonymously, in an old, rusty armor inherited from his father, with a pair of bases made from a fisherman's cloak, and proving victorious over all rivals, would seem to have been suggested by Sidney's description of how Pyrocles, in mean attire, entered the lists and defeated the champion at a tournament at the court of King Basilius: "For he had neither picture, nor device; his armor of as old a fashion (besides the rusty poorness) that it might better seem a monument of his grandfather's courage; about his middle he had, instead of bases, a long cloak of silk, which, as unhandsomely as it needs must, became the wearer. . . ." (*Arcadia,* 1.17.5).

> Tell thy story.
> If thine, considered, prove the thousandth part
> Of my endurance, thou art a man, and I
> Have suffered like a girl; yet thou dost look
> Like Patience gazing on kings' graves, and smiling
> Extremity out of act.
>
> (5.1.137–42)

Her endurance has, in fact, proved much greater than his. Instead of shutting herself up in her grief, after suffering a series of afflictions which more than equal his, this fourteen-year-old girl becomes the admired teacher of many skills to pupils of noble race. She then endures Pericles' initial rough reception of her, yet continues to look "Like Patience gazing on kings' graves, and smiling/Extremity out of act."

We have seen, then, that the play's double focus on father and daughter serves to bring out a contrast as well as a parallel between them, both of which are important to the play's full effect. Elsewhere, too, in *Pericles* such basic parallels and contrasts are to be found. In the non-Shakespearian part there is above all the extended parallel and contrast between the main action of Act 1 and Act 2. Having presented in Act 1 the wicked king with his wicked daughter, whose hand Pericles tries to gain by solving a riddle, the playwright presents in Act 2 the good king with his good daughter, whose hand Pericles tries to gain by winning a tournament. Just as he was successful in solving the riddle, he is successful in winning the tournament. And where the wicked king, Antiochus, pretended friendship towards him, while actually planning his death, the good king, Simonides, pretends enmity towards him, while actually planning to make him his son-in-law.

In the Shakespearian part there is the extended parallel between Pericles' mistaken belief in the death of his wife and his mistaken belief in the death of his daughter, and his final reunion with each. Less obvious is the contrast between the monstrous incest of father and daughter in Act 1, brought out in such lines of the riddle as

> He's father, son, and husband mild;
> I mother, wife, and yet his child
>
> (1.1.69–70)

and the blessed "incest" of father and daughter in Act 5, suggested by Pericles' words to Marina, "Thou that beget'st him that did thee beget" (5.1.198).

It is such parallels and contrasts—which are typical both of Sidney's *Arcadia* and of Shakespeare's previous plays—that help to give shape and coherence to the episodic and formless romance material on which *Pericles* is based.

I have taken issue with the view that Pericles is an exemplar of the virtue of patience in adversity. Even more misleading I find the common assertion that Shakespeare presents the main events of the play, both the misfortunes and the reunions, as the work of divine Providence. The whole pattern of Pericles' painful adventures, as these critics see it, is a pattern imposed by the gods. But the notion of a divine Providence that persecutes wholly virtuous characters so cruelly and for so long is repugnant, and so several of these critics are driven to discover some offense in the protagonists for which they are punished. Such an attempt to find a pattern of sin, punishment, expiation, and restoration in the play seems to me to violate and distort its whole spirit. It is to assimilate *Pericles* to *The Winter's Tale* and *The Tempest*, where sin and expiation do play an important part. In *Pericles*, as in the miracle plays, we are confronted with the *undeserved* sufferings of the wholly innocent and entirely virtuous—of Pericles, Thaisa, and Marina. And both their misfortunes and their restoration are shown to be mainly due to accident, to chance. The goddess who presides over the play is not Diana but Fortuna. It is by accident that the waves throw up the coffin containing Thaisa at Ephesus near the house of Cerimon, just the person who possesses the rare medical knowledge and skill needed to restore her to life. It is accident that brings Pericles' ship to Mytilene and Marina on board this ship, thus enabling father and daughter to be reunited. To see in all this the hand of Providence is indeed to take away from our sense of wonder. Only once in the play is there any clear evidence of supernatural intervention: in 5.1., where the Goddess Diana appears to Pericles in a vision. Without this vision the final reunion of Thaisa with her husband and daughter would have been difficult to bring about. In both of Shakespeare's sources this vision is found, though only in Shakespeare is it the goddess Diana that appears to Pericles. Gower speaks of a vision sent by "the high god," while in Twine's version an angel appears to Pericles in his sleep. But I can find no suggestion in the play that Diana had any other part in its events.

It is true that, like all Shakespeare's virtuous and noble characters, Pericles sees the hand of heaven behind all the accidents that befall him. At the news of Thaisa's death he cries out,

> O you gods!
> Why do you make us love your goodly gifts,
> And snatch them straight away?
>
> (3.1.22–24)

And at the reunion with Thaisa he exclaims:

> You gods, your present kindness
> Makes my past miseries sports.
>
> (5.3.39–40)

But, as with Shakespeare's great tragedies, this view is not imposed by the play upon the audience. It is above all contradicted by the choruses (except for the final moralistic one, of doubtful authorship), for Gower insists repeatedly upon Fortune's responsibility for the events. It is Fortune, he tells us, at the beginning of Act 2, that threw Pericles ashore near Pentapolis. It is "Fortune's mood," he remarks at the beginning of Act 3, that conjures up the storm during which Marina is born.

> Let Pericles believe his daughter's dead,
> And bear his courses to be orderèd
> By Lady Fortune;
>
> (4.4.46–48)

he comments in Act 4. But Lady Fortune is merely the personification of the power of accident in human affairs.

I have spoken of the sense of wonder and amazement which Shakespeare's Last Plays seek to evoke in both characters and audience. It vents itself in a language which is characteristic of these plays, and which has appeared only fitfully before, chiefly in Shakespeare's late tragedies. It is a simple, translucent language, melodious in sound, slow in pace, remote and dreamlike in its effect. Certain images tend to recur, above all images of precious objects: pearls, jewels, silver, and gold. Here are two examples of it from our play:

> She is alive! Behold,
> Her eyelids, cases to those heavenly jewels
> Which Pericles hath lost, begin to part
> Their fringes of bright gold; the diamonds
> Of a most praisèd water doth appear
> To make the world twice rich. Live,
> And make us weep to hear your fate, fair creature,
> Rare as you seem to be.
>
> (3.2.99–106)

> I am great with woe, and shall deliver weeping.
> My dearest wife was like this maid, and such
> My daughter might have been: my queen's square brows;
> Her stature to an inch; as wandlike straight;
> As silver-voiced; her eyes as jewellike
> And cased as richly; in pace another Juno;
> Who starves the ears she feeds, and makes them hungry
> The more she gives them speech.
>
> (5.1.108–15)

Apart from the more powerful evocation of a sense of wonder, and the style in which it expresses itself, what is it that chiefly marks off *Pericles* from Shakespeare's preceding comedies, and that points forward to the other Last Plays?

Closely related to this increased sense of wonder is a greater predominance of fairy-tale motifs and fairy-tale atmosphere. *Pericles* is full of such motifs, from the opening scene, in which the young Prince has to solve a riddle in order to gain the hand of the beautiful princess, to the play's epilogue, which announces, in the manner of fairy tales, the reward of the virtuous and the cruel punishment of the wicked. This fairy-tale atmosphere makes it easier to accept the improbabilities in the play's action: Pericles' failure to visit his daughter for fourteen years after leaving her with Cleon and Dionyza; Thaisa's decision to lead the life of a vestal because, unaccountably, she will never see her husband again. (This could easily have been motivated, as it is in Gower and Wilkins, by her mistaken belief that her husband was drowned during the storm at sea. Perhaps some lines to this effect have dropped out of the text.)

Allied to the increased predominance of the fairy-tale atmosphere is the intrusion of the supernatural, which does not enter into the earlier comedies, with the single exception of *A*

Midsummer Night's Dream. In *Pericles* Diana appears to the hero in a vision; in *Cymbeline* Jupiter descends on his eagle and prophesies; in *The Winter's Tale* we have the oracle of Apollo; and in *The Tempest* Ariel and his fellow-spirits.

I have already spoken of the difference of structure which marks off *Pericles* and *The Winter's Tale* from all of Shakespeare's other plays. Next, there is the difference in the young heroine. It is partly a difference in age: Marina is fourteen years old, Miranda fifteen, Perdita sixteen, while the young heroines of the preceding comedies, such as Beatrice, Portia, Rosalind, and Viola, seem a good deal older. For a heroine in a previous play who is of Marina's age we have to turn not to a comedy but to an early tragedy. Juliet, too, is fourteen years old. In personality also Marina is more like Juliet, or like Cordelia, than she is like Portia, or Beatrice, or Rosalind, who dazzle us above all by their wit. And unlike all the heroines of the preceding comedies, Marina exists primarily not in relation to a lover but to her father. She is given a husband at the end, but in a most perfunctory way, and we are never even told whether she loves him. Shakespeare is clearly not at all interested in the Marina-Lysimachus relationship. In the other Last Plays there is no parallel to this. While the relation of father and daughter is also of some importance in them, it is the relation of the daughter to her lover, of Perdita to Florizel, of Miranda to Ferdinand, of Imogen to Posthumus, that mainly concerns us.

Finally, these Last Plays differ from the preceding comedies in the weight and scope given to the scenes depicting the reunion of loved relatives long separated and believed dead. This motif is dominant in *Pericles, Cymbeline,* and *The Winter's Tale*— much less so in *The Tempest.* It had also occurred in some of Shakespeare's earlier comedies. In *Twelfth Night* and *Measure for Measure* a loved brother, firmly believed dead, suddenly appears alive before his sister. In *Much Ado* and *All's Well* a bride believed dead appears alive before her bridegroom or husband. In the final scene of *The Comedy of Errors* Shakespeare staged the biggest reunion of them all: not only two pairs of twin brothers, who had been separated since babyhood, are reunited, but the parents of the one pair with each other as well as with their sons, all after some thirty-three years of separation. It is the perfunctory manner in which these reunions are dramatized, the absence of any expression of their emotional experience, which makes these scenes in the earlier comedies (with the exception of *Twelfth Night*) so different in impact from the reunion scenes especially of *Pericles* and *The Winter's Tale*.

Till the closing of the theaters in 1642 *Pericles* seems to have been one of Shakespeare's greatest stage successes. The fact that the Quarto text was reprinted five times between 1609 and 1635 alone bears witness to its popularity. At the Restoration it was the first of Shakespeare's plays to be revived, with Betterton in the title role. But in the two hundred and fifty years from then until the beginning of this century the play fell into disrepute, receiving only a handful of performances, and even these giving the play in a radically altered or mutilated form. Only in the last few decades has it begun again to receive the attention it deserves from producers and critics, who have come to see that, as well as being full of highly effective scenes for the stage, it contains some of Shakespeare's loveliest and most haunting verse.

ERNEST SCHANZER

Pericles, Prince of Tyre

[ACT 1]

*Before the king's palace at Antioch, with heads
displayed upon its walls.]*

Enter Gower.°*

Gower. To sing a song that old° was sung,
    From ashes ancient Gower is come,
    Assuming man's infirmities,°
    To glad your ear, and please your eyes.
    It hath been sung at festivals,   5
    On ember-eves° and holidays,
    And lords and ladies in their lives
    Have read it for restoratives.
    The purchase° is to make men glorious;
    Et bonum quo antiquius eo melius.°   10
    If you, born in those latter times,
    When wit's more ripe, accept my rhymes,
    And that to hear an old man sing
    May to your wishes pleasure bring,
    I life would wish, and that I might   15
    Waste it for you, like taper-light.

---

*The degree sign (°) indicates a footnote, which is keyed to the text
by the line number. Text references are printed in **boldface** type; the
annotation follows in roman type.
1.s.d. **Gower** John Gower, fourteenth-century poet   **1 old** of old   **3
Assuming man's infirmities** putting on man's infirm body   **6 ember-
eves** evenings before the fasts known as "ember days"   **9 purchase**
gain   **10 Et ... melius** and the more ancient a good thing is the better
it is (Latin)

25

This Antioch,° then; Antiochus the great
Built up this city for his chiefest seat,
The fairest in all Syria—
20   I tell you what mine authors say.
This king unto him took a peer,°
Who died, and left a female heir,
So buxom,° blithe, and full of face,°
As heaven had lent her all his grace;
25   With whom the father liking took,
And her to incest did provoke.
Bad child, worse father, to entice his own
To evil should° be done by none.
But custom° what they did begin
30   Was with long use accounted no sin.
The beauty of this sinful dame
Made many princes thither frame,°
To seek her as a bedfellow,
In marriage pleasures playfellow;
35   Which to prevent he made a law,
To keep her still, and men in awe:°
That whoso asked her for his wife,
His riddle told° not, lost his life.
So for her many a wight did die,
40   As yon grim looks do testify. [*Points to the heads.*]
What now ensues, to the judgment of your eye
I give my cause, who best can justify.°   *Exit.*

[Scene 1. *Before the palace of Antioch.*]

Enter Antiochus, Prince Pericles, and followers.

Antiochus. Young Prince of Tyre, you have at large
   received°
The danger of the task you undertake.

17 **This Antioch** this is Antioch   21 **peer** companion, consort   23
buxom gay, lively   23 **full of face** beautiful (?) with a round face (?)
28 **should** which should   29 **custom** through custom   32 **frame** direct their course   36 **To . . . awe** to keep her always to himself, and to
keep others from demanding her in marriage   38 **told** expounded
41–42 **What . . . justify** in what now ensues I submit my case to the
judgment of your eye, as you are best able to acquit me (of the charge of
having told an incredible tale)   1.1.1 **at large received** learned fully

Pericles. I have, Antiochus, and, with a soul
    Embold'ned with the glory of her praise,
    Think death no hazard in this enterprise.   5

Antiochus. Music!   [*Music sounds.*]
    Bring in our daughter, clothèd like a bride,
    For the embracements even of Jove himself;
    At whose conception, till Lucina reigned,°
    Nature this dowry° gave to glad her presence.°   10
    The senate house of planets all did sit,
    To knit in her their best perfections.

Enter Antiochus' daughter.

Pericles. See where she comes, appareled like the spring,
    Graces her subjects, and her thoughts the king
    Of every virtue gives° renown to men!   15
    Her face the book of praises, where is read
    Nothing but curious° pleasures, as from thence
    Sorrow were ever razed,° and testy wrath
    Could never be her mild companion.°
    You gods that made me man, and sway in love;°   20
    That have enflamed desire in my breast
    To taste the fruit of yon celestial tree
    Or die in th' adventure, be my helps,
    As° I am son and servant to your will,
    To compass such a boundless happiness!   25

Antiochus. Prince Pericles—

Pericles. That would be son to great Antiochus.

Antiochus. Before thee stands this fair Hesperides,°
    With golden fruit, but dangerous to be touched;
    For deathlike dragons here affright thee hard.   30
    Her face like heaven enticeth thee to view
    Her countless glory, which desert must gain;

9 **till Lucina reigned** i.e., before her birth (Lucina is the goddess of childbirth)   10 **this dowry** i.e., her beauty   10 **to glad her presence** to make her presence delightful (?)   15 **gives** which gives   17 **curious** exquisite   18 **razed** erased   19 **her mild companion** the companion of her mildness   20 **and sway in love** and who govern in love   24 **As** as surely as   28 **Hesperides** the daughters of Hesperus, the evening star (but here, by confusion, the garden containing the golden apples, which, with the aid of a dragon, they were appointed to watch)

And which without desert, because thine eye
Presumes to reach, all the whole heap° must die.
35   Yon sometimes° famous princes, like thyself,
Drawn by report, advent'rous by desire,
Tell thee, with speechless tongues and semblance pale,
That without covering, save yon field of stars,
Here they stand martyrs slain in Cupid's wars;
40   And with dead cheeks advise thee to desist
For° going on death's net, whom none resist.

Pericles. Antiochus, I thank thee, who hath taught
My frail mortality to know itself,
And by those fearful objects to prepare
45   This body, like to them, to what I must;
For death remembered should be like a mirror,
Who tells us life's but breath, to trust it error.
I'll make my will, then; and, as sick men do,
Who know the world, see heaven, but, feeling woe,
50   Gripe° not at earthly joys as erst they did,
So I bequeath a happy peace to you
And all good men, as every prince should do;
My riches to the earth from whence they came;
[*To the Princess*] But my unspotted fire of love to
you.
55   Thus, ready for the way of life or death,
I wait the sharpest blow, Antiochus.

Antiochus. Scorning advice, read the conclusion° then:
[*He throws down the riddle.*]
Which read and not expounded, 'tis decreed,
As these before thee thou thyself shalt bleed.

60   *Daughter.* Of all 'sayed yet,° mayst thou prove prosperous!
Of all 'sayed yet, I wish thee happiness.

Pericles. Like a bold champion I assume the lists,°
Nor ask advice of any other thought
But faithfulness and courage.

34 **the whole heap** the whole body   35 **sometimes** once   41 **For**
for fear of   50 **Gripe** grasp   57 **conclusion** riddle   60 **'sayed yet**
who have yet assayed   62 **assume the lists** undertake the contest

[He reads] the riddle.

I am no viper,° yet I feed   65
On mother's flesh, which did me breed.
I sought a husband, in which labor
I found that kindness° in a father.
He's father, son, and husband mild;
I mother, wife, and yet his child.   70
How they may be, and yet in two,°
As you will live, resolve it you.

[Aside] Sharp physic is the last.° But O, you powers,
That gives° heaven countless eyes to view men's acts:
Why cloud they not their sights perpetually,   75
If this be true which makes me pale to read it?
Fair glass of light,° I loved you, and could still,
Were not this glorious casket stored with ill.
But I must tell you, now my thoughts revolt;
For he's no man on whom perfections wait   80
That, knowing sin within, will touch the gate.
You are a fair viol, and your sense° the strings;
Who, fingered to make man his lawful music,
Would draw heaven down, and all the gods to hearken;
But being played upon before your time,   85
Hell only danceth at so harsh a chime.
Good sooth,° I care not for you.

[He turns towards the Princess.]

Antiochus. Prince Pericles, touch not, upon thy life,
For that's an article within our law
As dangerous° as the rest. Your time's expired.   90
Either expound now, or receive your sentence.

Pericles. Great King,
Few love to hear the sins they love to act;
'Twould braid° yourself too near° for me to tell it.

---

65 **I am no viper** (vipers were believed to be born by eating their
way out of the mother's body)   68 **kindness** (1) kinship (2) affection
71 **How . . . two** how these things may be, and yet all be found in two
persons   73 **Sharp physic is the last** the last condition of the riddle
is an unpleasant medicine   74 **gives** give (the third person plural in *s*
is not unusual)   77 **glass of light** i.e., one who reflects light, as does
a mirror, but does not contain it   82 **sense** senses (?)   87 **Good
sooth** truly   90 **dangerous** rigorous   94 **braid** upbraid   94 **too
near** touching you too closely

95   Who has a book of all that monarchs do,
        He's more secure to keep it shut than shown;
        For vice repeated° is like the wand'ring wind
        Blows° dust in others' eyes to spread° itself;
        And yet the end of all is bought thus dear:
100   The breath is gone, and the sore eyes see clear
        To stop the air would hurt them. The blind mole casts
        Copped° hills towards heaven, to tell the earth is throngèd°
        By man's oppression; and the poor worm° doth die for't.
        Kings are earth's gods; in vice their law's their will;
105   And if Jove stray, who dares say Jove doth ill?
        It is enough you know; and it is fit,
        What being more known grows worse, to smother it.
        All love the womb that their first being bred;
        Then give my tongue like leave to love my head.

Antiochus. [_Aside_] Heaven, that I had thy head! He has
110   found the meaning.
        But I will gloze° with him. [_Aloud_] Young Prince of Tyre,
        Though by the tenor of our strict edict,
        Your exposition misinterpreting,
        We might proceed to cancel of° your days,
115   Yet hope, succeeding° from so fair a tree
        As your fair self, doth tune us otherwise.
        Forty days longer we do respite you;
        If by which time our secret be undone,°
        This mercy shows we'll joy in such a son.
120   And until then your entertain° shall be
        As doth befit our honor and your worth.
                            [_Exeunt all but Pericles._]

Pericles. How courtesy would seem° to cover sin,
        When what is done is like an hypocrite,
        The which is good in nothing but in sight!°

---

97 **repeated** talked about   98 **Blows** which blows   98 **to spread** in spreading   102 **Copped** peaked   102 **throngèd** crushed   103 **worm** creature   111 **gloze** talk speciously   114 **cancel of** the canceling of   115 **succeeding** resulting   118 **secret be undone** riddle be solved   120 **entertain** entertainment, reception   122 **seem** make a specious appearance   124 **sight** outward appearance

If it be true that I interpret false,   125
Then were it certain you were not so bad
As with foul incest to abuse your soul;
Where now you're both a father and a son
By your uncomely° claspings with your child,
Which pleasures fits a husband, not a father;   130
And she an eater of her mother's flesh
By the defiling of her parents' bed;
And both like serpents are, who though they feed
On sweetest flowers, yet they poison breed.
Antioch, farewell, for wisdom sees, those men   135
Blush° not in actions blacker than the night,
Will 'schew° no course to keep them from the light.
One sin, I know, another doth provoke;
Murder's as near to lust as flame to smoke.
Poison and treason are the hands of sin,   140
Ay, and the targets,° to put off° the shame.
Then, lest my life be cropped to keep you clear,
By flight I'll shun the danger which I fear.   *Exit.*

Enter Antiochus.

Antiochus. He hath found the meaning,
For which we mean to have his head. He must   145
Not live to trumpet forth my infamy,
Nor tell the world Antiochus doth sin
In such a loathèd manner.
And therefore instantly this prince must die;
For by his fall my honor must keep high.   150
Who attends us there?

Enter Thaliard.

Thaliard.   Doth your Highness call?

Antiochus. Thaliard,
     You are of our chamber,° Thaliard, and our mind
          partakes°
     Her private actions to your secrecy;
     And for your faithfulness we will advance you.   155

---

129 **uncomely** improper (see Introduction, p. 5)   136 **Blush** who
blush   137 **'schew** eschew, avoid   141 **targets** shields   141 **put
off** avert   153 **of our chamber** our chamberlain   153 **partakes**
imparts

Thaliard, behold, here's poison, and here's gold!
We hate the Prince of Tyre, and thou must kill him.
It fits thee not to ask the reason why.
Because we bid it. Say, is it done?

Thaliard. My lord, 'tis done.

160 *Antiochus.*   Enough.

Enter a Messenger.

Let your breath cool yourself telling your haste.

Messenger. My lord, Prince Pericles is fled.   [*Exit.*]

Antiochus. As thou wilt live, fly after; and like an arrow
     shot from a well-experienced archer hits the mark his
165 eye doth level° at, so thou never return unless thou say
     Prince Pericles is dead.

Thaliard. My lord, if I can get him within my pistol's
     length, I'll make him sure° enough. So farewell to your
     Highness.

Antiochus. Thaliard, adieu! [*Exit Thaliard.*] Till Pericles be
170   dead
     My heart can lend no succor to my head.   [*Exit.*]

[Scene 2. *Tyre. A room in the palace.*]

Enter Pericles.

Pericles. [*To Servants without*] Let none disturb us.
     Why should this change of thoughts,
     The sad companion, dull-eyed melancholy,
     Be my so used° a guest as not an hour
5   In the day's glorious walk or peaceful night,
     The tomb where grief should sleep, can breed me
         quiet?
     Here pleasures court mine eyes, and mine eyes shun
         them,
     And danger, which I feared, is at Antioch,

165 **level** aim   168 **sure** unable to do harm   1.2.4 **used** customary

Whose arm seems far too short to hit me here;
Yet neither pleasure's art can joy° my spirits,   10
Nor yet the other's distance comfort me.
Then it is thus: the passions of the mind,
That have their first conception by misdread,°
Have after-nourishment and life by care;
And what was first but fear what might be done,   15
Grows elder now and cares° it be not done.
And so with me: the great Antiochus,
'Gainst whom I am too little to contend,
Since he's so great can° make his will his act,
Will think me speaking, though I swear to silence;   20
Nor boots it me° to say I honor him,
If he suspect I may dishonor him.
And what may make him blush in being known°
He'll stop the course by which it might be known.
With hostile forces he'll o'erspread the land,   25
And with th' ostent° of war will look so huge,
Amazement° shall drive courage from the state,
Our men be vanquished ere they do resist,
And subjects punished that ne'er thought offense;
Which care of them, not pity of myself,   30
Who am no more but as the tops of trees
Which fence° the roots they grow by and defend them,
Makes both my body pine and soul to languish,
And punish that before that he would punish.

*Enter [Helicanus and] all the Lords to
Pericles.*

First Lord. Joy and all comfort in your sacred breast!   35

Second Lord. And keep your mind, till you return to us,
    Peaceful and comfortable!°

10 **joy** give joy to   13 **misdread** dread of evil   16 **cares** is anxious that   19 **can** that he can   21 **boots it me** does it avail me   23
in being known if it were known   26 **th' ostent** the display   27
Amazement consternation   32 **fence** protect   36–37 **And keep . . .
comfortable** (these lines must be either corrupt or misplaced, as
Pericles' decision to leave Tyre is not taken till the end of the scene)
37 **comfortable** cheerful (a passage in which Helicanus reproves
Pericles for wasting "his body there with pining sorrow, upon whose
safety depended the lives and prosperity of a whole kingdom"
[Wilkins] and is sternly rebuked by him for his presumption, must
have preceded the next speech, but is missing from the text)

Helicanus. Peace, peace, and give experience tongue.°
    They do abuse° the King that flatter him,
40   For flattery is the bellows blows up° sin;
    The thing the which is flattered but a spark
    To which that blast gives heat and stronger glowing;
    Whereas reproof, obedient and in order,
    Fits kings, as they are men, for they may err.
45   When Signor Sooth° here does proclaim a peace
    He flatters you, makes war upon your life.
    Prince, pardon me, or strike me, if you please;
    I cannot be much lower than my knees.
                             [He kneels.]

Pericles. All leave us else!° But let your cares o'erlook°
50   What shipping and what lading's° in our haven,
    And then return to us.   *[Exeunt Lords.]*
                  Helicanus,
    Thou hast moved us. What seest thou in our looks?

Helicanus. An angry brow, dread lord.

Pericles. If there be such a dart in princes' frowns,
55   How durst thy tongue move anger to our face?

Helicanus. How dares the plants look up to heaven, from
       whence
    They have their nourishment?

Pericles.   Thou knowest I have power
    To take thy life from thee.

Helicanus.   I have ground the ax myself;
    Do but you strike the blow.

Pericles.   Rise, prithee, rise.
                           [He raises him.]
60   Sit down. Thou art no flatterer.
    I thank thee for't; and heaven forbid
    That kings should let their ears hear their faults hid!°

---

38 **give experience tongue** allow experience to speak   39 **abuse** ill-use   40 **blows up** which fans into flame   45 **Signor Sooth** Sir Flattery   49 **All leave us else** everybody else leave us   49 **o'er-look** look into   50 **lading** cargo   62 **hear their faults hid** i.e., hear the flattery which hides their faults

Fit counselor and servant for a prince,
Who by thy wisdom makes a prince thy servant,
What wouldst thou have me do?

Helicanus.　　　　　　　　　　　To bear with patience　*65*
Such griefs as you do lay upon yourself.

Pericles. Thou speak'st like a physician, Helicanus,
That ministers a potion unto me
That thou wouldst tremble to receive thyself.
Attend° me then: I went to Antioch,　　　　　*70*
Where, as thou know'st, against the face of death
I sought the purchase° of a glorious beauty,
From whence an issue I might propagate
Are arms° to princes and bring joys to subjects.
Her face was to mine eye beyond all wonder;　*75*
The rest—hark in thine ear—as black as incest;
Which by my knowledge found, the sinful father
Seemed° not to strike, but smooth;° but thou know'st
　　this:
'Tis time to fear when tyrants seems to kiss.
Which fear so grew in me, I hither fled,　　　*80*
Under the covering of a careful° night,
Who seemed my good protector; and, being here,
Bethought me what was past, what might succeed.
I knew him tyrannous; and tyrants' fears
Decrease not, but grow faster than the years;　*85*
And should he doubt, as no doubt he doth,°
That I should open° to the list'ning air
How many worthy princes' bloods were shed
To keep his bed of blackness unlaid ope,°
To lop that doubt,° he'll fill this land with arms,　*90*
And make pretense of wrong that I have done him;
When all for mine, if I may call, offense
Must feel war's blow, who° spares not innocence;
Which love to all, of which thyself art one,
Who now° reprovedst me for't—

---

70 **Attend** listen to　72 **purchase** acquisition　74 **Are arms**
which are arms　78 **Seemed** pretended　78 **smooth** flatter　81
careful taking good care　86 **And should . . . he doth** (the first
"doubt," meaning "fear," is pronounced as a disyllable)　87 **open**
reveal　89 **unlaid ope** undisclosed　90 **doubt** dread, fear　93
who which　95 **now** just now

95 *Helicanus.*   Alas, sir!

Pericles. Drew sleep out of mine eyes, blood from my
      cheeks,
    Musings into my mind, with thousand doubts
    How I might stop this tempest ere it came;
    And finding little comfort to relieve them,
100   I thought it princely charity to grieve them.°

Helicanus. Well, my lord, since you have given me leave
      to speak,
    Freely will I speak. Antiochus you fear,
    And justly, too, I think, you fear the tyrant
    Who either by public war or private treason
105   Will take away your life.
    Therefore, my lord, go travel for a while,
    Till that his rage and anger be forgot,
    Or till the Destinies do cut his thread of life.
    Your rule direct° to any; if to me,
110   Day serves not light more faithful° than I'll be.

Pericles. I do not doubt thy faith.
    But should he wrong my liberties° in my absence?

Helicanus. We'll mingle our bloods together in the earth,
    From whence we had our being and our birth.

115 *Pericles.* Tyre, I now look from thee then, and to Tharsus
    Intend° my travel, where I'll hear from thee,
    And by whose letters I'll dispose myself.°
    The care I had and have of subjects' good
    On thee I lay, whose wisdom's strength can bear it.
120   I'll take thy word for faith, not ask thine oath:
    Who shuns not to break one° will crack both.
    But in our orbs we'll live so round° and safe,°
    That time of both this truth shall ne'er convince:°

---

100 **grieve them** grieve for them   109 **direct** assign   110 **Day . . .
faithful** day is not served by light more faithfully   112 **liberties**
prerogatives   116 **Intend** direct   117 **dispose myself** direct my
actions   121 **one** (pronounced as a disyllable)   122 **we'll live so
round** (1) we'll live so honestly (2) we'll move in such a perfect circle
122 **safe** trustworthily   123 **of both . . . convince** shall never con-
fute this truth regarding both of us

Thou showed'st a subject's shine, I a true prince.°
                              Exit [with Helicanus].

                    [Scene 3. *The palace at Tyre.*]

                      Enter Thaliard solus.°

Thaliard. So this is Tyre, and this the court. Here must I
    kill King Pericles; and if I do it not, I am sure to be
    hanged at home. 'Tis dangerous. Well, I perceive he was
    a wise fellow and had good discretion that, being bid to
    ask what he would of the King, desired he might know   5
    none of his secrets. Now do I see he had some reason
    for't: for if a king bid a man be a villain, he's bound by
    the indenture° of his oath to be one. Husht, here comes
    the lords of Tyre.

          Enter Helicanus, Escanes, with other Lords.

Helicanus. You shall not need, my fellow peers of Tyre,   10
    Further to question me of your king's departure.
    His sealed commission left in trust with me
    Does speak sufficiently he's gone to travel.

Thaliard. [*Aside*] How? The King gone?

Helicanus. If further yet you will be satisfied   15
    Why, as it were, unlicensed of your loves°
    He would depart, I'll give some light unto you.
    Being at Antioch—

Thaliard. [*Aside*]   What from Antioch?

Helicanus. Royal Antiochus—on what cause I know not—
    Took some displeasure at him; at least he judged so;   20
    And doubting lest° he had erred or sinned,
    To show his sorrow, he'd correct° himself;

---

124 **Thou . . . prince** you showed a subject's luster, I showed myself
a true prince 1.3.s.d. **solus** alone (Latin)   8 **indenture** contract binding servant to master   16 **unlicensed of your loves** without your
loving assent   21 **doubting lest** fearing that ("doubting" is here trisyllabic)   22 **he'd correct** he wanted to punish

So puts himself unto the shipman's toil,
With whom each minute threatens life or death.

Thaliard. [*Aside*] Well, I perceive I shall not be hanged
25   now
Although I would.
But since he's gone, the King's ears it must please
He scaped the land, to perish at the seas.
I'll present myself. [*Aloud*] Peace to the lords of Tyre!

30 *Helicanus.* Lord Thaliard from Antiochus is welcome.

Thaliard. From him I come
With message unto princely Pericles.
But since my landing I have understood
Your lord has betook himself to unknown travels.
35   Now message must return from whence it came.

Helicanus. We have no reason to desire it,
Commended° to our master, not to us.
Yet, ere you shall depart, this we desire:
As friends to Antioch we may feast in Tyre.
                                        Exit [*with the rest*].

[Scene 4. *Tharsus*.]

Enter Cleon, the Governor of Tharsus, with his wife
[*Dionyza*] *and others.*

Cleon. My Dionyza, shall we rest us here,
And by relating tales of others' griefs,
See if 'twill teach us to forget our own?

Dionyza. That were to blow at fire in hope to quench it;
5   For who digs° hills because they do aspire
Throws down one mountain to cast up a higher.
O my distressed lord, even such our griefs are;
Here they are but felt and seen with mischief 's° eyes,
But like to groves, being topped, they higher rise.

37 **Commended** since it is commended   1.4.5 **digs** digs down   8
mischief 's misfortune's

Cleon. O Dionyza,   10
    Who wanteth food and will not say he wants it,
    Or can conceal his hunger till he famish?
    Our tongues and sorrows cease not to sound deep
    Our woes into the air, our eyes to weep,°
    Till tongues fetch breath that may proclaim them
       louder,   15
    That, if heaven slumber while their creatures want,
    They may awake their helps to comfort them.
    I'll then discourse our woes, felt several years,
    And wanting breath to speak help me° with tears.

Dionyza. I'll do my best, sir.   20

Cleon. This Tharsus, o'er which I have the government,
    A city on° whom plenty held full hand,
    For riches strewed herself° even in her streets;
    Whose towers bore heads so high they kissed the clouds,
    And strangers ne'er beheld but wond'red at;   25
    Whose men and dames so jetted and adorned,°
    Like one another's glass to trim them by;°
    Their tables were stored full, to glad the sight,
    And not so much to feed on as delight;
    All poverty was scorned, and pride so great,   30
    The name of help grew odious to repeat.°

Dionyza. O, 'tis too true!

Cleon. But see what heaven can do by this our change:
    These mouths who but of late earth, sea, and air
    Were all too little to content and please,   35
    Although they gave their creatures in abundance,
    As houses are defiled for want of use,
    They are now starved for want of exercise;
    Those palates who, not yet two summers younger,
    Must have inventions° to delight the taste,   40

13–14 **Our tongues . . . to weep** let our sorrowful tongues (hendi-
adys) not cease to . . . , let our eyes not cease to weep   19 **help me**
do you help me   22 **on** over   23 **riches strewed herself** ("riches"
is a feminine singular)   26 **jetted and adorned** strutted and dressed
themselves up   27 **glass to trim them by** pattern according to
which to array themselves   31 **repeat** mention   40 **inventions** ingenious novelties

Would now be glad of bread, and beg for it;
Those mothers who, to nuzzle up° their babes,
Thought nought too curious,° are ready now
To eat those little darlings whom they loved.
45 So sharp are hunger's teeth that man and wife
Draw lots who first shall die to lengthen life.
Here stands a lord, and there a lady weeping;
Here many sink, yet those which see them fall
Have scarce strength left to give them burial.
50 Is not this true?

Dionyza. Our cheeks and hollow eyes do witness it.

Cleon. O, let those cities that of plenty's cup
And her prosperities so largely taste,
With their superfluous riots,° hear these tears!
55 The misery of Tharsus may be theirs.

Enter a Lord.

Lord. Where's the Lord Governor?

Cleon. Here.
Speak out thy sorrows which thou bring'st in haste,
For comfort is too far for us to expect.

60 *Lord.* We have descried, upon our neighboring shore,
A portly sail° of ships make hitherward.

Cleon. I thought as much.
One sorrow never comes but brings an heir
That may succeed as his inheritor;
65 And so in ours: some neighboring nation,
Taking advantage of our misery,
Hath stuffed the hollow vessels with their power,°
To beat us down, the which are down already,
And make a conquest of unhappy me,
70 Whereas° no glory's got to overcome.

Lord. That's the least fear; for, by the semblance
Of their white flags displayed, they bring us peace,
And come to us as favorers, not as foes.

---

42 **nuzzle up** bring up   43 **curious** exquisite   54 **superfluous riots** inordinate revels   61 **portly sail** stately fleet   67 **power** armed force   70 **Whereas** where

Cleon. Thou speak'st like him's untutored to repeat:°
    Who makes the fairest show means most deceit.   75
    But bring they what they will, what need we fear?
    On ground's the lowest,° and we are halfway there.
    Go tell their general we attend° him here,
    To know for what he comes, and whence he comes,
    And what he craves.°   80

Lord. I go, my lord.   [*Exit.*]

Cleon. Welcome is peace, if he on peace consist;°
    If wars, we are unable to resist.

                Enter Pericles, with Attendants.

Pericles. Lord Governor, for so we hear you are,
    Let not our ships and number of our men   85
    Be like a beacon fired t' amaze your eyes.
    We have heard your miseries as far as Tyre,
    And seen the desolation of your streets;
    Nor come we to add sorrow to your tears,
    But to relieve them of their heavy load;   90
    And these our ships you happily may think°
    Are like the Trojan horse was° stuffed within
    With bloody veins expecting overthrow,°
    Are stored with corn to make your needy bread,°
    And give them life whom hunger starved half dead.   95

All. The gods of Greece protect you!
    And we'll pray for you.   [*They kneel.*]

Pericles.   Arise, I pray you, rise;
    We do not look for reverence but for love,
    And harborage for ourself, our ships, and men.

Cleon. The which when any shall not gratify,°   100
    Or pay you with unthankfulness in thought,
    Be it our wives, our children, or ourselves,

---

74 **him's untutored to repeat** him who has never been taught to re-
cite   77 **On ground's the lowest** i.e., he that lies upon the ground
can fall no lower   78 **attend** await   80 **craves** desires   82 **on
peace consist** stands on peace   91 **you happily may think** you may
perhaps think   92 **was** which was   93 **With . . . overthrow** i.e.,
with bloodthirsty warriors waiting for the overthrow (of Troy)   94
your needy bread bread for your needy citizens   100 **gratify** show
gratitude for

The curse of heaven and men succeed their evils!
Till when—the which I hope shall ne'er be seen—
105 Your Grace is welcome to our town and us.

Pericles. Which welcome we'll accept; feast here awhile,
Until our stars that frown lend us a smile.   *Exeunt.*

[ACT 2]

Enter Gower.

Gower. Here have you seen a mighty king
   His child iwis° to incest bring;
   A better prince and benign lord
   That will prove awful° both in deed and word.
   Be quiet, then, as men should be,   5
   Till he hath passed necessity.°
   I'll show you those in trouble's reign°
   Losing a mite, a mountain gain.
   The good in conversation,°
   To whom I give my benison,   10
   Is still at Tharsus, where each man
   Thinks all is writ he spoken can;°
   And, to remember° what he does,
   Build his statue to make him glorious.
   But tidings to the contrary   15
   Are brought your eyes; what need speak I?

Dumb Show

*Enter at one door Pericles, talking with Cleon; all the
train with them. Enter at another door a Gentleman with
a letter to Pericles; Pericles shows the letter to Cleon.
Pericles gives the Messenger a reward and knights him.
Exit Pericles at one door, and Cleon at another.*

   Good Helicane, that stayed at home,
   Not to eat honey like a drone

2.2 **iwis** assuredly 4 **awful** commanding profound respect 6
passed necessity experienced extreme hardship 7 **those in trouble's reign** those who under the dominion of trouble 9 **conversation** conduct, way of life 12 **all . . . can** all his words are holy writ
13 **remember** commemorate

From others' labors, for he strives
20   To killen bad, keep good alive,
And to fulfill his prince' desire,
Sends word of all that haps in Tyre:
How Thaliard came full bent with° sin
And hid intent° to murder him;
25   And that in Tharsus was not best
Longer for him to make his rest.
He, doing so,° put forth to seas,
Where when men been there's seldom ease;
For now the wind begins to blow;
30   Thunder above and deeps below
Makes such unquiet that the ship
Should° house him safe is wracked and split;
And he, good prince, having all lost,
By waves from coast to coast is tossed.
35   All perishen of man, of pelf,°
Ne aught escapend° but himself;
Till fortune, tired with doing bad,
Threw him ashore, to give him glad.°
And here he comes. What shall be next,
40   Pardon old Gower—this 'longs° the text.   [*Exit.*]

[Scene 1. *Pentapolis, at the seashore*.]

Enter Pericles, wet.

Pericles. Yet cease your ire, you angry stars of heaven!
Wind, rain, and thunder, remember, earthly man
Is but a substance that must yield to you;
And I, as fits my nature, do obey you.
5   Alas, the seas hath cast me on the rocks,
Washed me from shore to shore, and left me breath
Nothing to think on but ensuing death.
Let it suffice the greatness of your powers
To have bereft a prince of all his fortunes;

---

23 **bent with** intent upon   24 **And hid intent** and with hidden intent   27 **doing so** i.e., acting as advised   32 **Should** which should
35 **pelf** possessions   36 **escapend** escaping   38 **glad** gladness
40 **'longs** belongs to

And having thrown him from your wat'ry grave,   10
Here to have death in peace is all he'll crave.

Enter three Fishermen.

First Fisherman. What ho, Pilch!°

Second Fisherman. Ha, come and bring away° the nets!

First Fisherman. What, Patchbreech, I say!

Third Fisherman. What say you, master?   15

First Fisherman. Look how thou stirr'st now!° Come away,° or I'll fetch thee with a wanion.°

Third Fisherman. Faith, master, I am thinking of the poor men that were cast away before us even now.

First Fisherman. Alas, poor souls, it grieved my heart   20
to hear what pitiful cries they made to us to help them, when, well-a-day,° we could scarce help ourselves.

Third Fisherman. Nay, master, said not I as much when I saw the porpoise how he bounced and tumbled? They say they're half fish, half flesh. A plague on them! They   25
ne'er come but I look to be washed. Master, I marvel how the fishes live in the sea.

First Fisherman. Why, as men do a-land: the great ones eat up the little ones. I can compare our rich misers to nothing so fitly as to a whale; 'a° plays and tumbles, driving   30
the poor fry before him, and at last devours them all at a mouthful: Such whales have I heard on a' th' land,° who never leave gaping till they swallowed the whole parish, church, steeple, bells, and all.

Pericles. [*Aside*] A pretty moral.°   35

Third Fisherman. But, master, if I had been the sexton, I would have been that day in the belfry.

Second Fisherman. Why, man?

2.1.12 **Pilch** (a coarse outer garment made of leather or skin, here used, like Patchbreech, jestingly as a name) 13 **bring away** bring here without delay 16 **how thou stirr'st now!** what a stock you are! 16–17 **Come away** come here right away 17 **with a wanion** with a vengeance 22 **well-a-day** alas 30 **'a** he 32 **heard on a' th' land** heard of on land 35 **moral** tale conveying a moral lesson

Third Fisherman. Because he should have swallowed me
40   too; and when I had been in his belly, I would have kept
      such a jangling of the bells that he should never have left
      till he cast bells, steeple, church, and parish up again.
      But if the good King Simonides were of my mind—

Pericles. [*Aside*] Simonides!

45   *Third Fisherman.* We would purge the land of these drones
      that rob the bee of her honey.

Pericles. [*Aside*] How from the finny subject° of the sea
      These fishers tell the infirmities of men;
      And from their wat'ry empire recollect°
50   All that may men approve° or men detect!°
      [*Aloud*] Peace be at your labor, honest fishermen!

Second Fisherman. Honest good fellow, what's that? If it
      be a day fits you, scratch it out of the calendar, and no-
      body look after it.°

55   *Pericles.* May° see the sea hath cast upon your coast—

Second Fisherman. What a drunken knave was the sea to
      cast° thee in our way!

Pericles. A man whom both the waters and the wind
      In that vast tennis court hath made the ball
60   For them to play upon entreats you pity him.
      He asks of you that never used to beg.

First Fisherman. No, friend, cannot you beg? Here's them
      in our country of Greece gets more with begging than
      we can do with working.

65   *Second Fisherman.* Canst thou catch any fishes, then?

Pericles. I never practiced it.

---

47 **subject** subjects, citizens   49 **recollect** gather up   50 **approve**
commend   50 **detect** expose (in wrongdoing)   52–54 **Honest . . .
after it** (a lost line in which Pericles wishes the fishermen a good day
appears to have preceded this passage. The fisherman rudely replies
that if the day fitted Pericles' wretched appearance it ought to be removed from the calendar)   55 **May** you may   57 **cast** (1) cast up,
vomit (2) throw

Second Fisherman. Nay, then, thou wilt starve, sure; for
    here's nothing to be got nowadays unless thou canst
    fish for't.

Pericles. What I have been I have forgot to know;   70
    But what I am want teaches me to think on:
    A man thronged up° with cold. My veins are chill,
    And have no more of life than may suffice
    To give my tongue that heat to ask your help;
    Which if you shall refuse, when I am dead,   75
    For that° I am a man, pray you see me burièd.

First Fisherman. Die, quoth-a?° Now gods forbid't! And I
    have a gown here! Come, put it on; keep thee warm.
    Now, afore me,° a handsome fellow! Come, thou shalt
    go home, and we'll have flesh for holidays, fish for fast-   80
    ing days, and moreo'er puddings and flapjacks,° and
    thou shalt be welcome.

Pericles. I thank you, sir.

Second Fisherman. Hark you, my friend: you said you
    could not beg.   85

Pericles. I did but crave.

Second Fisherman. But crave? Then I'll turn craver too,
    and so I shall 'scape whipping.°

Pericles. Why, are your beggars whipped, then?

Second Fisherman. O, not all, my friend, not all! For if   90
    all your beggars were whipped, I would wish no better
    office than to be beadle. But, master, I'll go draw up the
    net.   [*Exit with Third Fisherman.*]

Pericles. [*Aside*] How well this honest mirth becomes°
    their labor!   95

First Fisherman. Hark you, sir, do you know where ye are?

---

72 **thronged up** overwhelmed   76 **For that** because   77 **quoth-a**
did he say   79 **afore me** upon my word   81 **flapjacks** pancakes
87–88 **Then I'll . . . whipping** i.e., through not calling himself a beggar (whipping, administered by the beadle, was the regular punishment of beggars in Shakespeare's day)   94 **becomes** suits with

Pericles. Not well.

First Fisherman. Why, I'll tell you: this is called Pentapolis, and our king the good Simonides.

100 *Pericles.* The good Simonides do you call him?

First Fisherman. Ay, sir; and he deserves so to be called,
for his peaceable reign and good government.

Pericles. He is a happy king, since he gains from his subjects the name of good by his government. How far is
105 his court distant from this shore?

First Fisherman. Marry,° sir, half a day's journey. And I'll
tell you, he hath a fair daughter, and tomorrow is her
birthday; and there are princes and knights come from
all parts of the world to joust and tourney for her love.

110 *Pericles.* Were my fortunes equal to my desires, I could
wish to make one there.

First Fisherman. O, sir, things must be as they may; and
what a man cannot get he may lawfully deal for his
wife's soul.°

Enter the two Fishermen, drawing up a net.

115 *Second Fisherman.* Help, master, help! Here's a fish hangs
in the net like a poor man's right° in the law: 'twill
hardly come out. Ha, bots on't,° 'tis come at last; and
'tis turned to a rusty armor.

Pericles. An armor, friends! I pray you, let me see it.
120   Thanks, Fortune, yet, that after all thy crosses
         Thou givest me somewhat to repair° myself;
         And though it was mine own, part of my heritage
         Which my dead father did bequeath to me,
         With this strict charge, even as he left his life:
125   "Keep it, my Pericles; it hath been a shield

---

106 **Marry** why (a mild oath, from "By the Virgin Mary") 113–14
he may ... wife's soul (no sense can be made of the text as it stands,
nor has it been plausibly emended) 116 **right** just claim 117 **bots
on't** a plague upon it 121 **repair** renew, restore

'Twixt me and death"—and pointed to this brace°—
"For that it saved me, keep it; in like necessity—
The which the gods protect thee from!—may't defend
  thee."
It kept where I kept, I so dearly loved it;
Till the rough seas, that spares not any man,   130
Took it in rage, though calmed have given't again.
I thank thee for't. My shipwrack now's no ill,
Since I have here my father gave° in his will.

First Fisherman. What mean you, sir?

Pericles. To beg of you, kind friends, this coat of worth,   135
  For it was sometime target° to a king;
  I know it by this mark. He loved me dearly,
  And for his sake I wish the having of it;
  And that you'd guide me to your sovereign's court,
  Where with it I may appear a gentleman.   140
  And if that ever my low fortune's better,
  I'll pay your bounties; till then rest your debtor.

First Fisherman. Why, wilt thou tourney for the lady?

Pericles. I'll show the virtue° I have borne in arms.

First Fisherman. Why, d' ye take it, and the gods give thee   145
  good on't!

Second Fisherman. Ay, but hark you, my friend: 'twas we
  that made up this garment through the rough seams of
  the waters. There are certain condolements,° certain
  vails.° I hope, sir, if you thrive, you'll remember from   150
  whence you had them.°

Pericles. Believe't, I will!
  By your furtherance I am clothed in steel;
  And spite of all the rapture° of the sea,

---

126 **brace** armor covering the arms   133 **my father gave** that
which my father gave   136 **target** literally, light shield, hence protection   144 **virtue** valor   149 **condolements** (probably a mala-
propism through confusion with "dole" meaning "distribution of
gifts")   150 **vails** perquisites, tips   151 **them** i.e., the armor   154
rapture act of plunder, seizure

155   This jewel holds his building° on my arm.
Unto thy value° I will mount myself
Upon a courser, whose delightful steps
Shall make the gazer joy to see him tread.
Only, my friend, I yet am unprovided
160   Of a pair of bases.°

Second Fisherman. We'll sure provide. Thou shalt have my
best gown to make thee a pair; and I'll bring thee to the
court myself.

Pericles. Then honor be but equal to my will,
165   This day I'll rise, or else add ill to ill.   [*Exeunt.*]

[Scene 2. *Pentapolis. The court of Simonides. A public
way leading to the lists. A pavilion near it.*]

*Enter Simonides, with [Lords,] Attendants, and
Thaisa.*

Simonides. Are the knights ready to begin the triumph?°

First Lord. They are, my liege,
And stay your coming to present themselves.

Simonides. Return° them we are ready; and our daughter,
5   In honor of whose birth these triumphs are,
Sits here like Beauty's child, whom Nature gat°
For men to see and seeing wonder at.   [*Exit a Lord.*]

Thaisa. It pleaseth you, my royal father, to express
My commendations great, whose merit's less.

10   *Simonides.* It's fit it should be so; for princes are
A model° which heaven makes like to itself:
As jewels lose their glory if neglected,
So princes their renowns if not respected.

---

155 **building** fixed place 156 **Unto thy value** to as high a value (as
the jewel will fetch) 160 **bases** pleated skirt, worn by knights on
horseback 2.2.1 **triumph** festivity, here tournament 4 **Return**
tell by way of answer 6 **gat** begat 11 **model** likeness in little

'Tis now your honor,° daughter, to entertain°
The labor of each knight in his device.°   15

Thaisa. Which, to preserve mine honor, I'll perform.

[*Simonides and Thaisa take seats in the pavilion.*]
The first Knight passes by. [*As each Knight passes, his
page, who goes before him, presents his shield to the
Princess.*]

Simonides. Who is the first that doth prefer° himself?

Thaisa. A knight of Sparta, my renownèd father;
  And the device he bears upon his shield
  Is a black Ethiop reaching at the sun.   20
  The word,° *Lux tua vita mihi.*°

Simonides. He loves you well that holds his life of you.

                    The second Knight [*passes*].

  Who is the second that presents himself?

Thaisa. A prince of Macedon, my royal father;
  And the device he bears upon his shield
  Is an armed knight that's conquered by a lady;   25
  The motto thus, in Spanish, *Più per dolcezza che per
  forza.*°

                    [*The*] *third Knight* [*passes*].

Simonides. And what's the third?

Thaisa.   The third of Antioch;
  And his device a wreath of chivalry.°
  The word, *Me pompae provexit apex.*°   30

                    [*The*] *fourth Knight* [*passes*].

Simonides. What is the fourth?

---

14 **honor** honorable duty   14 **entertain** receive   15 **device** emblematic figure, accompanied by a motto, inscribed on the shield   17 **prefer** present   21 **word** motto   21 **Lux tua vita mihi** thy light is life to me (Latin)   27 **Più . . . forza** more by gentleness than by force (Italian)   29 **wreath of chivalry** the twisted band by which, in heraldry, the crest is joined to the knight's helmet   30 **Me pompae provexit apex** the crown of the triumph has led me on (Latin)

Thaisa. A burning torch that's turnèd upside down.
     The word, *Qui me alit me extinguit.*°

Simonides. Which shows that beauty hath his° power and
     will,
35   Which can as well inflame as it can kill.

               [*The*] *fifth Knight* [*passes*].

Thaisa. The fifth, an hand environèd with clouds,
     Holding out gold that's by the touchstone tried.
     The motto thus, *Sic spectanda fides.*°

               [*The*] *sixth Knight* [*, Pericles, passes, without page*].

Simonides. And what's the sixth and last, the which the
     knight himself
40   With such a graceful courtesy delivered?°

Thaisa. He seems to be a stranger; but his present° is
     A withered branch, that's only green at top;
     The motto, *In hac spe vivo.*°

Simonides. A pretty moral.
45   From the dejected state wherein he is,
     He hopes by you his fortunes yet may flourish.

First Lord. He had need mean better than his outward
     show
     Can any way speak in his just commend;°
     For by his rusty outside he appears
50   To have practiced more the whipstock° than the lance.

Second Lord. He well may be a stranger, for he comes
     To an honored triumph strangely furnishèd.

Third Lord. And on set purpose let his armor rust
     Until this day to scour it in the dust.

55   *Simonides.* Opinion's° but a fool that makes us scan°
     The outward habit for the inward man.

33 **Qui ... extinguit** who feeds me puts me out (Latin) 34 **his** its
38 **Sic spectanda fides** thus is faithfulness to be tried (Latin) 40
delivered presented 41 **present** object presented 43 **In hac spe
vivo** in this hope I live (Latin) 48 **commend** commendation 50
To have practiced more the whipstock to have wielded more the
handle of a whip, i.e., worked as a carter 55 **Opinion** public opinion 55 **scan** scrutinize, examine

But stay, the knights are coming!
We will withdraw into the gallery.   [*Exeunt.*]
                              Great shouts [*within*], *and all cry*
                                    "*The mean° Knight!*"

[*Scene 3. Pentapolis. A hall of state.*]

Enter the King [, *Thaisa, Marshal, Lords, Ladies,*] *and*
     Knights from tilting, [*and Attendants*].

Simonides. Knights,
     To say you're welcome were superfluous.
     To place upon the volume of your deeds,
     As in a title page, your worth in arms,°
     Were more than you expect, or more than's fit,   5
     Since every worth in show commends itself.
     Prepare for mirth, for mirth becomes a feast.
     You are princes and my guests.

Thaisa. But you my knight and guest;
     To whom this wreath of victory I give,
     And crown you king of this day's happiness.   10

Pericles. 'Tis more by fortune, lady, than my merit.

Simonides. Call it by what you will, the day is yours;
     And here, I hope, is none that envies it.
     In framing° an artist, art hath thus decreed: 15
     To make some good, but others to exceed;
     And you are her labored scholar.° Come, queen o' th'
          feast—
     For, daughter, so you are—here take your place.
     Marshal, the rest as they deserve their grace.°

Knights. We are honored much by good Simonides.   20

Simonides. Your presence glads our days. Honor we love;
     For who hates honor hates the gods above.

Marshal. Sir, yonder is your place.

58s.d. **mean** shabby   2.3.4 **As . . . arms** (title pages of early printed
books often proclaimed the excellence of their contents)   15 **fram-
ing** molding   17 **her labored scholar** the scholar over whom art
took special pains   19 **grace** favor

Pericles.   Some other is more fit.

First Knight. Contend not, sir; for we are gentlemen
25   Have° neither in our hearts nor outward eyes
       Envied the great, nor shall the low despise.

Pericles. You are right courteous knights.

Simonides.   Sit, sir, sit.
       [*Aside*] By Jove I wonder, that is king of thoughts,
       These cates° resist me, he but thought upon.°

30   *Thaisa.* [*Aside*] By Juno, that is queen of marriage,
       All viands that I eat
       Do seem unsavory, wishing him my meat.
       [*To Simonides*] Sure he's a gallant gentleman.

Simonides. He's but a country gentleman;
35   Has done no more than other knights have done;
       Has broken a staff or so; so let it pass.

Thaisa. [*Aside*] To me he seems like diamond to glass.

Pericles. [*Aside*] Yon king's to me like to my father's
           picture,
       Which tells me in that glory once he was;
40   Had princes sit like stars about his throne,
       And he the sun for them to reverence;
       None that beheld him but, like lesser lights,
       Did vail° their crowns to his supremacy;
       Where now his son's a glowworm in the night,
45   The which hath fire in darkness, none in light.
       Whereby I see that Time's the king of men;
       He's both their parent and he is their grave,
       And gives them what he will, not what they crave.

Simonides. What, are you merry, knights?

50   *Knights.* Who can be other in this royal presence?

Simonides. Here, with a cup that's stored unto the brim—
       As you do love, fill to° your mistress' lips—
       We drink this health to you.

Knights.   We thank your Grace.

25 **Have** that have   29 **cates** delicacies   29 **resist . . . upon** repel
me (?) when I but think of him   43 **vail** lower   52 **to** in honor of

Simonides. Yet pause awhile.
    Yon knight doth sit too melancholy,   55
    As if the entertainment in our court
    Had not a show might countervail° his worth.
    Note it not you, Thaisa?

Thaisa. What is't to me, my father?

Simonides. O, attend, my daughter: 60
    Princes, in this, should live like gods above,
    Who freely give to everyone that come
    To honor them.
    And princes not doing so are like to gnats,
    Which make a sound, but killed are wond'red at.°   65
    Therefore, to make his entrance° more sweet,
    Here, say we drink this standing-bowl° of wine to him.

Thaisa. Alas, my father, it befits not me
    Unto a stranger knight to be so bold:
    He may my proffer take for an offense,   70
    Since men take women's gifts for impudence.

Simonides. How?
    Do as I bid you, or you'll move me else!

Thaisa. [*Aside*] Now, by the gods, he could not please me
    better.

Simonides. And furthermore tell him we desire to know
    of him   75
    Of whence he is, his name and parentage.

Thaisa. The King my father, sir, has drunk to you.

Pericles. I thank him.

Thaisa. Wishing it so much blood unto your life.

Pericles. I thank both him and you, and pledge him freely.   80

Thaisa. And further he desires to know of you
    Of whence you are, your name and parentage.

---

57 **countervail** be equal to   65 **but killed are wond'red at** i.e., when they are found to be such small animals, after making so great a noise   66 **entrance** (trisyllabic)   67 **standing-bowl** bowl resting on a foot

Pericles. A gentleman of Tyre; my name Pericles;
   My education been° in arts and arms;
85   Who, looking for adventures in the world,
   Was by the rough seas reft of ships and men,
   And after shipwrack driven upon this shore.

Thaisa. He thanks your Grace; names himself Pericles,
   A gentleman of Tyre,
90   Who only by misfortune of the seas,
   Bereft of ships and men, cast on this shore.

Simonides. Now, by the gods, I pity his misfortune,
   And will awake him from his melancholy.
   Come, gentlemen, we sit too long on trifles,
95   And waste the time which looks for other revels.
   Even in your armors, as you are addressed,°
   Will well° become a soldier's dance.
   I will not have excuse with saying this:
   Loud music° is too harsh for ladies' heads,
100   Since they love men in arms° as well as beds.

They dance.°

So, this was well asked, 'twas so well performed.
   Come, sir, here's a lady that wants breathing° too;
   And I have heard you knights of Tyre
   Are excellent in making ladies trip,°
105   And that their measures° are as excellent.

Pericles. In those that practice them they are, my lord.

Simonides. O, that's as much as you would be denied
   Of your fair courtesy.°

84 **been** has been   96 **addressed** accoutered   97 **Will well** (two
such words as "your steps" must have originally preceded this)   99
Loud music i.e., the loud noise made by the clashing of their armor
(?)   100 **arms** (a pun is presumably intended)   100s.d. **They
dance** (most editors assume that the first dance is performed by the
Knights alone, the second by the Knights and Ladies. The text, especially line 102, suggests rather that both dances are mixed. In the first
dance Thaisa and, perhaps, Pericles do not participate; in the second
they dance together)   102 **breathing** exercise   104 **trip** dance a
light dance (with a *double entendre*)   105 **measures** dances   107–08
denied/Of your fair courtesy refused permission to show your courtesy (by dancing with Thaisa) (?)

They dance.

                    Unclasp, unclasp!
Thanks, gentlemen, to all; all have done well,
[*To Pericles*] But you the best. Pages and lights, to
    conduct   110
These knights unto their several lodgings! Yours, sir,
We have given order be next our own.

Pericles. I am at your Grace's pleasure.

Simonides. Princes, it is too late to talk of love,
    And that's the mark I know you level° at.   115
    Therefore each one betake him to his rest;
    Tomorrow all for speeding° do their best.   [*Exeunt.*]

[Scene 4. *Tyre.*]

Enter Helicanus and Escanes.

Helicanus. No, Escanes, know this of me:
    Antiochus from incest lived not free;
    For which, the most high gods not minding° longer
    To withhold the vengeance that they had in store,
    Due to this heinous capital offense,   5
    Even in the height and pride of all his glory,
    When he was seated in a chariot
    Of an inestimable value, and
    His daughter with him, a fire from heaven came,
    And shriveled up their bodies, even to loathing.   10
    For they so stunk
    That all those eyes adored° them ere their fall
    Scorn now their hand should give them burial.

Escanes. 'Twas very strange.

Helicanus. And yet but justice; for though this king were
    great,   15

115 **level** aim 117 **speeding** success 2.4.3 **minding** being inclined 12 **adored** that adored

His greatness was no guard to bar heaven's shaft,
But sin had his° reward.

Escanes.   'Tis very true.

Enter two or three Lords.

First Lord. See, not a man in private conference
    Or council has respect with him but he.

20 *Second Lord.* It shall no longer grieve° without reproof.

Third Lord. And cursed be he that will not second it.

First Lord. Follow me then. Lord Helicane, a word.

Helicanus. With me? And welcome. Happy day, my lords!

First Lord. Know that our griefs° are risen to the top,
25   And now at length they overflow their banks.

Helicanus. Your griefs, for what? Wrong not your prince
    you love.

First Lord. Wrong not yourself, then, noble Helicane;
    But if the Prince do live, let us salute him,
    Or know what ground's made happy by his breath.
30   If in the world he live, we'll seek him out;
    If in his grave he rest, we'll find him there;
    And be resolved° he lives to govern us,
    Or, dead, gives cause to mourn his funeral,
    And leaves us to our free election.

Second Lord. Whose death's indeed the strongest in our
35   censure.°
    And knowing this: kingdoms without a head,
    Like goodly buildings left without a roof
    Soon fall to ruin, your noble self,
    That best know how to rule and how to reign,
40   We thus submit unto—our sovereign.

All. Live, noble Helicane!

17 **his** its   20 **grieve** be a grievance   24 **griefs** grievances   32
resolved satisfied   35 **the strongest in our censure** the more likely
supposition in our judgment

Helicanus. For honor's cause, forbear your suffrages.
　If that you love Prince Pericles, forbear.
　Take I° your wish, I leap into the seas
　Where's hourly trouble for a minute's ease.   45
　A twelvemonth longer let me entreat you
　To forbear° the absence of your king;
　If in which time expired he not return,
　I shall with agèd patience bear your yoke.
　But if I cannot win you to this love,°   50
　Go search like nobles, like noble subjects,
　And in your search spend your adventurous worth;
　Whom if you find, and win unto return,
　You shall like diamonds sit about his crown.

First Lord. To wisdom he's a fool that will not yield;   55
　And since Lord Helicane enjoineth us,
　We with our travels will endeavor it.

Helicanus. Then you love us, we you, and we'll clasp
　hands:
　When peers thus knit, a kingdom ever stands.

　　　　　　　　　　　　　　　　　　　[*Exeunt.*]

[*Scene 5. Pentapolis. A room in the palace.*]

*Enter the King reading of a letter at one door; the
　　　　　Knights meet him.*

First Knight. Good morrow to the good Simonides.

Simonides. Knights, from my daughter this I let you
　know:
　That for this twelvemonth she'll not undertake
　A married life.
　Her reason to herself is only known,   5
　Which from her by no means° can I get.

Second Knight. May we not get access to her, my lord?

---

44 **Take I** if I should accept   47 **forbear** tolerate, endure   50 **love**
act of kindness   2.5.6 **means** (here pronounced as a disyllable)

Simonides. Faith, by no means. She hath so strictly tied her
    To her chamber that 'tis impossible.
10   One twelve moons° more she'll wear Diana's livery.°
    This by the eye of Cynthia° hath she vowed,
    And on her virgin honor will not break it.

Third Knight. Loath° to bid farewell, we take our leaves.
                         [Exeunt Knights.]

Simonides. So, they are well dispatched.
15   Now to my daughter's letter:
    She tells me here she'll wed the stranger knight,
    Or never more to view nor day nor light.
    'Tis well, mistress; your choice agrees with mine.
    I like that well! Nay, how absolute° she's in't,
20   Not minding whether I dislike or no!
    Well, I do commend her choice,
    And will no longer have it be delayed.
    Soft,° here he comes! I must dissemble it.

Enter Pericles.

Pericles. All fortune to the good Simonides!

25 *Simonides.* To you as much. Sir, I am beholding° to you
    For your sweet music this last night. I do
    Protest my ears were never better fed
    With such delightful pleasing harmony.

Pericles. It is your Grace's pleasure to commend;
    Not my desert.

30 *Simonides.*   Sir, you are music's master.

Pericles. The worst of all her scholars, my good lord.

Simonides. Let me ask you one thing: What do you
    think of
    My daughter, sir?

___

10 **One twelve moons** one year   10 **wear Diana's livery** i.e., remain a virgin   11 **Cynthia** the moon   13 **Loath** (here pronounced
as a disyllable)   19 **absolute** positive, decided   23 **Soft** hold (an
interjection)   25 **beholding** indebted

Pericles.   A most virtuous princess.

Simonides. And she is fair too, is she not?

Pericles. As a fair day in summer, wondrous fair.   35

Simonides. Sir, my daughter thinks very well of you;
    Ay, so well that you must be her master,
    And she will be your scholar: therefore look to it.

Pericles. I am unworthy for her schoolmaster.

Simonides. She thinks not so; peruse this writing else.°   40

Pericles. [*Aside*] What's here?
    A letter that she loves the knight of Tyre!
    'Tis the King's subtlety to have my life.
    [*Kneels*] O, seek not to entrap me, gracious lord,
    A stranger and distressèd gentleman,   45
    That never aimed so high to° love your daughter,
    But bent all offices° to honor her.

Simonides. Thou hast bewitched my daughter, and thou
    art
    A villain!

Pericles.   By the gods, I have not.
    Never did thought of mine levy° offense;   50
    Nor never did my actions yet commence
    A deed might° gain her love or your displeasure.

Simonides. Traitor, thou liest!

Pericles.   Traitor?

Simonides.   Ay, traitor!

Pericles. Even in his throat—unless it be the King—
    That calls me traitor I return the lie.   55

Simonides. [*Aside*] Now, by the gods, I do applaud his
    courage.

Pericles. My actions are as noble as my thoughts,

---

40 **else** if you do not believe it   46 **to** as to   47 **bent all offices**
turned all my services   50 **levy** (apparently misused for "level," i.e.,
aim)   52 **might** that might

That never relished of° a base descent.
I came unto your court for honor's cause,
60   And not to be a rebel to her state;°
And he that otherwise accounts of me,
This sword shall prove he's honor's enemy.

Simonides. No?
Here comes my daughter, she can witness it.

Enter Thaisa.

65   *Pericles.* Then, as you are as virtuous as fair,
Resolve° your angry father if my tongue
Did e'er solicit, or my hand subscribe
To any syllable that made love to you.

Thaisa. Why, sir, say if you had,
70   Who takes offense at that would° make me glad?

Simonides. Yea, mistress, are you so peremptory?°
(*Aside*) I am glad on't with all my heart.—
I'll tame you; I'll bring you in subjection!
Will you, not having my consent,
75   Bestow your love and your affections
Upon a stranger?—(*aside*) who, for aught I know,
May be, nor can I think the contrary,
As great in blood as I myself—
Therefore hear you, mistress: either frame
80   Your will to mine—and you, sir, hear you:
Either be ruled by me, or I'll make you—
Man and wife.
Nay, come, your hands and lips must seal it too!
And being joined, I'll thus your hopes destroy;
85   And for further grief—God give you joy!
What, are you both pleased?

Thaisa.   Yes, if you love me, sir.

Pericles. Even as my life my blood° that fosters it.

Simonides. What, are you both agreed?

---

58 **relished of** had a trace of   60 **her state** honor's domain   66
Resolve inform   70 **would** which would   71 **peremptory** determined   87 **my blood** i.e., loves my blood

Both. Yes, if 't please your Majesty.

Simonides. It pleaseth me so well that I will see you
    wed;   90
  And then, with what haste you can, get you to bed.

                                     Exeunt.

[ACT 3]

Enter Gower.

Gower. Now sleep y-slackèd° hath the rout;°
  No din but snores the house about,
  Made louder by the o'erfed breast
  Of this most pompous° marriage feast.
5 The cat, with eyne° of burning coal,
  Now couches 'fore the mouse's hole;
  And crickets sing at the oven's mouth
  All the blither for their drouth.°
  Hymen° hath brought the bride to bed,
10 Where by the loss of maidenhead
  A babe is molded. Be attent,°
  And time that is so briefly° spent
  With your fine fancies° quaintly° eche.°
  What's dumb in show I'll plain° with speech.

[Dumb Show]

*Enter Pericles and Simonides at one door, with Atten-
dants; a Messenger meets them, kneels, and gives Pericles
a letter; Pericles shows it Simonides; the Lords kneel to
him. Then enter Thaisa with child, with Lychorida, a
nurse; the King shows her the letter; she rejoices; she
and Pericles take leave of her father, and depart [with Lychorida and their Attendants. Then exeunt Simonides and
the rest].*

3.1 **y-slackèd** reduced to inactivity   1 **rout** company of revelers   4
pompous magnificent   5 **eyne** eyes (archaic plural)   8 **drouth**
dryness   9 **Hymen** the god of marriage   11 **attent** attentive   12
briefly quickly   13 **fancies** imaginings   13 **quaintly** skillfully
13 **eche** augment (old spelling of "eke")   14 **plain** explain

By many a dern° and painful° perch°   15
Of Pericles the careful search
By the four opposing coigns°
Which the world together joins
Is made with all due diligence
That horse and sail and high expense   20
Can stead° the quest. At last from Tyre,
Fame answering the most strange inquire,°
To th' court of King Simonides
Are letters brought, the tenor these:
Antiochus and his daughter dead,   25
The men of Tyrus on the head
Of Helicanus would set on
The crown of Tyre, but he will none.
The mutiny he there hastes t' appease;
Says to 'em, if King Pericles   30
Come not home in twice six moons,
He, obedient to their dooms,°
Will take the crown. The sum° of this,
Brought hither to Pentapolis,
Y-ravishèd° the regions round,   35
And everyone with claps can° sound,°
"Our heir-apparent is a king!
Who dreamt, who thought of such a thing?"
Brief,° he must hence depart to Tyre.
His queen with child makes her desire—   40
Which who shall cross?—along to go.
Omit we all their dole° and woe.
Lychorida, her nurse, she takes,
And so to sea. Their vessel shakes
On Neptune's billow; half the flood   45
Hath their keel cut;° but Fortune's mood
Varies again: the grislèd° north
Disgorges such a tempest forth
That, as a duck for life that dives,

15 **dern** wild, drear   15 **painful** toilsome   15 **perch** measure of land   17 **opposing coigns** opposite corners   21 **stead** be of use to   22 **Fame . . . inquire** Rumor having responded to inquiries in the most distant regions (?)   32 **dooms** judgments   33 **sum** gist   35 **Y-ravishèd** enraptured   36 **can** began (a Middle English variant of "gan")   36 **sound** proclaim, declare   39 **Brief** in short   42 **dole** grief   45–46 **half . . . cut** i.e., half the voyage has been completed   47 **grislèd** horrible, grisly

50   So up and down the poor ship drives.
        The lady shrieks and, well-a-near,°
        Does fall in travail with her fear;
        And what ensues in this fell storm
        Shall for itself itself perform.
55   I nill° relate, action° may
        Conveniently the rest convey;
        Which might not what by me is told.
        In your imagination hold
        This stage the ship, upon whose deck
60   The sea-tossed Pericles appears to speak.   [*Exit.*]

                    [Scene 1.]

                Enter Pericles, a-shipboard.

Pericles. The god of this great vast° rebuke these surges,
        Which wash both heaven and hell; and thou that hast
        Upon the winds command, bind them in brass,
        Having called them from the deep! O, still
5   Thy deaf'ning dreadful thunders; gently quench
        Thy nimble° sulphurous flashes! O, how, Lychorida,
        How does my queen? Thou stormest venomously;
        Wilt thou spit all thyself? The seaman's whistle
        Is as a whisper in the ears of death,
10   Unheard. Lychorida!—Lucina,° O
        Divinest patroness and midwife gentle
        To those that cry by night, convey thy deity
        Aboard our dancing boat; make swift the pangs
        Of my queen's travails! Now, Lychorida!

                Enter Lychorida [with an infant].

15 *Lychorida.* Here is a thing too young for such a place,
        Who, if it had conceit,° would die, as I
        Am like to do. Take in your arms this piece
        Of your dead queen.

        Pericles.   How? How, Lychorida?

51 **well-a-near** alas   55 **nill** will not (Middle English)   55 **action**
(here pronounced as a trisyllable)   3.1.1 **vast** boundless expanse   6
nimble swift   10 **Lucina** the goddess of childbirth   16 **conceit** capacity to understand

Lychorida. Patience, good sir; do not assist the storm.
  Here's all that is left living of your queen—   20
  A little daughter. For the sake of it
  Be manly, and take comfort.

Pericles.   O you gods!
  Why do you make us love your goodly gifts,
  And snatch them straight away? We here below
  Recall not what we give, and therein may   25
  Vie honor with you.°

Lychorida.   Patience, good sir,
  Even for this charge.°

Pericles.   Now, mild may be thy life!
  For a more blusterous birth had never babe;
  Quiet and gentle thy conditions! For
  Thou art the rudeliest welcome to this world   30
  That ever was prince's child. Happy what follows!
  Thou hast as chiding a nativity
  As fire, air, water, earth and heaven can make,
  To herald thee from the womb. Even at the first
  Thy loss is more than can thy portage quit,°   35
  With all thou canst find here. Now the good gods
  Throw their best eyes upon't!

Enter two Sailors.

First Sailor. What courage, sir? God save you!

Pericles. Courage enough. I do not fear the flaw:°
  It hath done to me the worst. Yet, for the love   40
  Of this poor infant, this fresh,° new seafarer,
  I would it would be quiet.

First Sailor. Slack the bolins° there! Thou wilt not, wilt
  thou? Blow, and split thyself!

Second Sailor. But sea-room, and° the brine and cloudy   45
  billow kiss the moon, I care not.

26 **Vie honor with you** compete with you in respect of honor   27
Even for this charge for the sake of the babe left in your care   35
than can thy portage quit than your cargo (i.e., all that you are going
to possess in the course of the voyage of life) can compensate for (?)
39 **flaw** gust of wind   41 **fresh** raw, inexperienced   43 **bolins**
ropes from weather-side of square sail to bow   45 **and** if

First Sailor. Sir, your queen must overboard; the sea
works° high, the wind is loud, and will not lie° till the
ship be cleared of the dead.

50 *Pericles.* That's your superstition.

First Sailor. Pardon us, sir; with us at sea it hath been
still° observed; and we are strong in custom.° Therefore
briefly° yield her; for she must overboard straight.

Pericles. As you think meet. Most wretched queen!

55 *Lychorida.* Here she lies, sir.

Pericles. A terrible childbed hast thou had, my dear;
No light, no fire. Th' unfriendly elements
Forgot thee utterly; nor have I time
To give thee hallowed to thy grave, but straight
60 Must cast thee, scarcely coffined, in the ooze;
Where, for° a monument upon thy bones,
And e'er-remaining lamps, the belching whale
And humming water must o'erwhelm thy corpse,
Lying with simple shells. O Lychorida,
65 Bid Nestor bring me spices, ink and paper,
My casket and my jewels; and bid Nicander
Bring me the satin coffin.° Lay the babe
Upon the pillow. Hie thee, whiles I say
A priestly farewell to her. Suddenly,° woman!
                              [*Exit Lychorida.*]

70 *Second Sailor.* Sir, we have a chest beneath the hatches,
Caulked and bitumèd° ready.

Pericles. I thank thee. Mariner, say, what coast is this?

Second Sailor. We are near Tharsus.

Pericles.   Thither, gentle mariner,
Alter thy course for Tyre. When canst thou reach it?

75 *Second Sailor.* By break of day, if the wind cease.

---

48 **works** rages   48 **lie** subside   52 **still** always   52 **strong in
custom** steadfast in observing customs   53 **briefly** quickly   61 **for**
instead of   67 **coffin** case, box   69 **Suddenly** at once   71 **bi-
tumèd** made watertight with bitumen

Pericles. O make for Tharsus!
  There will I visit Cleon, for the babe
  Cannot hold out to Tyrus. There I'll leave it
  At careful° nursing. Go thy ways,° good mariner.
  I'll bring the body presently.°   *Exit* [*with Sailors*].   80

[*Scene 2. Ephesus. A room in Cerimon's house.*]

Enter Lord Cerimon with a Servant.

Cerimon. Philemon, ho!

Enter Philemon.

Philemon. Doth my lord call?

Cerimon. Get fire and meat for those poor men:
  'T 'as been a turbulent and stormy night.
                     [*Exit Philemon.*]

Servant. I have been in many; but such a night as this   5
  Till now I ne'er endured.

Cerimon. Your master will be dead ere you return.
  There's nothing can be minist'red to nature
  That can recover him. Give this to the 'pothecary,
  And tell me how it works.°   [*Exit Servant.*]

Enter two Gentlemen.

First Gentleman.   Good morrow.   10

Second Gentleman. Good morrow to your lordship.

Cerimon.   Gentlemen,
  Why do you stir so early?

First Gentleman. Sir,
  Our lodgings, standing bleak upon the sea,
  Shook as the earth did quake;   15
  The very principals° did seem to rend

79 **careful** full of good care   79 **Go thy ways** come along   80 **presently** immediately   3.2.8–9 **Give . . . works** (this prescription must be intended for someone other than the servant's master)   16 **principals** chief rafters of a house

And all to topple. Pure surprise and fear
Made me to quit the house.

Second Gentleman. That is the cause we trouble you so
    early;
'Tis not our husbandry.°

20 *Cerimon.*   O, you say well.

First Gentleman. But I much marvel that your lordship,
    having
Rich tire° about you, should at these early hours
Shake off the golden slumber of repose.
'Tis most strange,
25 Nature should be so conversant with pain,°
Being thereto not compelled.

Cerimon.   I held it ever
Virtue and cunning° were endowments greater
Than nobleness° and riches: careless heirs
May the two latter darken and expend,
30 But immortality attends° the former,
Making a man a god. 'Tis known, I ever
Have studied physic, through which secret art,
By turning o'er authorities, I have,
Together with my practice, made familiar
35 To me and to my aid° the blest infusions
That dwells in vegetives,° in metals, stones;
And I can speak of the disturbances
That nature works, and of her cures; which gives me
A more° content in course of true delight
40 Than to be thirsty after tottering honor,
Or tie my treasure up in silken bags,
To please the Fool and Death.°

Second Gentleman. Your honor has through Ephesus
    poured forth

---

20 **husbandry** zeal for work 22 **tire** belongings 25 **pain** trouble, labor 27 **cunning** skill 28 **nobleness** nobility (i.e., social rank) 30 **attends** awaits 35 **my aid** my assistant (?) 36 **vegetives** vegetables, herbs 39 **more** greater 42 **the Fool and Death** (probably an allusion to the Dance of Death, in which these two figures often appeared as companions)

Your charity, and hundreds call themselves
Your creatures, who by you have been restored; 45
And not° your knowledge, your personal pain,° but even
Your purse, still° open, hath built Lord Cerimon
Such strong renown as time shall never raze.

Enter two or three [Servants] with a chest.

First Servant. So; lift there!

Cerimon. What's that?

First Servant. Sir, even now
Did the sea toss up upon our shore this chest. 50
'Tis of some wrack.

Cerimon. Set't down, let's look upon't.

Second Gentleman. 'Tis like a coffin, sir.

Cerimon. Whate'er it be,
'Tis wondrous heavy. Wrench it open straight.°
If the sea's stomach be o'ercharged with gold,
'Tis a good constraint of fortune 55
It belches upon us.°

Second Gentleman. 'Tis so, my lord.

Cerimon. How close 'tis caulked and bitumed!
Did the sea cast it up?

First Servant. I never saw so huge a billow, sir,
As tossed it upon shore.

Cerimon. Wrench it open: soft! It smells 60
Most sweetly in my sense.

Second Gentleman. A delicate odor.

Cerimon. As ever hit my nostril. So; up with it!
O you most potent gods! What's here, a corse!

Second Gentleman. Most strange!

Cerimon. Shrouded in cloth of state;°

46 **not** not only 46 **pain** trouble 47 **still** always 53 **straight**
immediately 56 **It belches upon us** that it belches this chest upon
us 64 **cloth of state** magnificent fabric

65   Balmed,° and entreasured with full bags of spices!
      A passport too! Apollo, perfect me°
      In the characters!°   [*Reads from a scroll.*]

         Here I give to understand,
         If e'er this coffin drives a-land,
70   I, King Pericles, have lost
         This queen, worth all our mundane cost.°
         Who finds her, give her burying;
         She was the daughter of a king.
         Besides this treasure for a fee,
75   The gods requite his charity!

      If thou livest, Pericles, thou hast a heart
      That even cracks for woe! This chanced tonight.°

Second Gentleman. Most likely, sir.

Cerimon.   Nay, certainly tonight;
      For look how fresh she looks! They were too rough
80   That threw her in the sea. Make a fire within.
      Fetch hither all my boxes in my closet.
                                        [*Exit Servant.*]
      Death may usurp on nature° many hours,
      And yet the fire of life kindle again
      The o'erpressed spirits. [I have read
85   Of some Egyptians, who after four hours' death
      Have raised impoverished° bodies, like to this,
      Unto their former health.]°

         Enter one [*Servant*] *with napkins and fire.*

                                  Well said,° well said;
      The fire and cloths.°
      The still and woeful music that we have,
90   Cause it to sound, beseech you. [*Music.*]
      The viol once more! How thou stirr'st,° thou block!

65 **Balmed** anointed with fragrant oil   66 **perfect me** instruct me
fully   67 **characters** writing (the stress falls here on the second syllable)   71 **mundane cost** worldly riches   77 **tonight** last night
82 **nature** man's physical constitution   84–87 (see Introduction,
p. 5)   86 **impoverished** deprived of their native strength   87 **Well
said** well done   88 **cloths** napkins   91 **How thou stirr'st** how
quick you are (used ironically)

The music there! [*Music.*] I pray you, give her air.
Gentlemen,
This queen will live: nature° awakes; a warmth
Breathes out of her. She hath not been entranced°   *95*
Above five hours. See how she 'gins to blow°
Into life's flower again!

First Gentleman.   The heavens
Through you increase our wonder, and sets up
Your fame forever.

Cerimon.   She is alive! Behold,
Her eyelids, cases to those heavenly jewels   *100*
Which Pericles hath lost, begin to part
Their fringes of bright gold; the diamonds
Of a most praisèd water° doth appear
To make the world twice rich. Live,
And make us weep to hear your fate, fair creature,   *105*
Rare as you seem to be.   *She moves.*

Thaisa.   O dear Diana,
Where am I? Where's my lord? What world is this?

Second Gentleman. Is not this strange?

First Gentleman.   Most rare!

Cerimon.   Hush, my gentle neighbors!
Lend me your hands; to the next chamber bear her.
Get linen. Now this matter must be looked to,   *110*
For her relapse is mortal.° Come, come;
And Aesculapius° guide us!
      They carry her away. Exeunt Omnes.°

---

94 **nature** the vital powers 95 **entranced** in a swoon 96 **blow**
bloom 103 **water** luster 111 **is mortal** would be fatal 112
Aesculapius Greek god of medicine 112s.d. **Omnes** all (Latin)

[Scene 3. *Tharsus.*]

Enter Pericles at Tharsus with Cleon and Dionyza
[, and Lychorida with Marina in her arms].

Pericles. Most honored Cleon, I must needs be gone:
My twelve months are expired, and Tyrus stands
In a litigious° peace. You and your lady,
Take from my heart all thankfulness! The gods
Make up the rest upon you!

5   *Cleon.*   Your shafts of fortune,
Though they hurt you mortally, yet glance
Full° woundingly on us.

Dionyza.   O your sweet queen!
That the strict fates had pleased you had brought her
        hither
To have blest mine eyes with her!

Pericles.   We cannot but
10 Obey the powers above us. Could I rage
And roar as doth the sea she lies in, yet
The end must be as 'tis. My gentle babe,
Marina, whom, for° she was born at sea,
I have named so, here I charge
15 Your charity withal,° leaving her
The infant of your care; beseeching you
To give her princely training, that she may
Be mannered as she is born.

Cleon.   Fear not, my lord, but think
Your Grace, that fed my country with your corn,
20 For which the people's prayers still fall upon you,
Must in your child be thought on. If neglection°
Should therein make me vile, the common body,°
By you relieved, would force me to my duty.

3.3.3 **litigious** productive of contention   7 **Full** very   13 **for** because
15 **withal** with   21 **neglection** neglect   22 **common body** common
people

But if to that my nature need a spur,
The gods revenge it upon me and mine,   25
To the end of generation!°

Pericles.   I believe you.
Your honor and your goodness teach me to't,
Without your vows. Till she be married, madam,
By bright Diana, whom we honor all,
Unscissored shall this hair of mine remain,   30
Though I show ill in't. So I take my leave.
Good madam, make me blessèd in your care
In bringing up my child.

Dionyza.   I have one myself,
Who shall not be more dear to my respect°
Than yours, my lord.

Pericles.   Madam, my thanks and prayers.   35

Cleon. We'll bring your Grace e'en to the edge o' th' shore,
Then give you up to the masked° Neptune and
The gentlest winds of heaven.

Pericles.   I will embrace
Your offer. Come, dearest madam. O, no tears,
Lychorida, no tears!   40
Look to your little mistress, on whose grace°
You may depend hereafter. Come, my lord.   [*Exeunt.*]

[Scene 4. *Ephesus.*]

Enter Cerimon and Thaisa.

Cerimon. Madam, this letter, and some certain jewels,
Lay with you in your coffer; which are
At your command. Know you the character?°

Thaisa. It is my lord's. That I was shipped at sea
I well remember, even on my eaning time;°   5

_____

26 **To the end of generation** i.e., until the human race ceases to
procreate (?)   34 **respect** care   37 **masked** deceptively calm (?)
41 **grace** favor   3.4.3 **character** handwriting   5 **eaning time** time
of childbirth

But whether there delivered, by the holy gods,
I cannot rightly say. But since King Pericles,
My wedded lord, I ne'er shall see again,
A vestal livery will I take me to,°
10   And never more have joy.

Cerimon. Madam, if this you purpose as ye speak,
Diana's temple is not distant far,
Where you may abide till your date° expire.
Moreover, if you please, a niece of mine
15   Shall there attend you.

Thaisa. My recompense is thanks, that's all;
Yet my good will is great, though the gift small.
                                        Exit [*with Cerimon*].

9 **A vestal ... to** i.e., I will live the life of a vestal virgin   13 **date**
term of life

[ACT 4]

Enter Gower.

Gower. Imagine Pericles arrived at Tyre,
  Welcomed and settled to his own desire.
  His woeful queen we leave at Ephesus,
  Unto Diana there's° a votaress.
  Now to Marina bend your mind,   5
  Whom our fast-growing scene must find
  At Tharsus, and by Cleon trained
  In music's letters;° who hath gained
  Of education all the grace,
  Which makes her both the heart and place°   10
  Of general wonder. But, alack,
  That monster, Envy, oft the wrack°
  Of earnèd praise, Marina's life
  Seeks to take off by treason's° knife.
  And in this kind:° Our Cleon hath   15
  One daughter, and a full grown wench,
  Even ripe for marriage rite. This maid
  Hight° Philoten; and it is said
  For certain in our story, she
  Would ever with Marina be.   20
  Be't when she weaved the sleided° silk
  With fingers long, small,° white as milk;
  Or when she would with sharp needle° wound
  The cambric, which she made more sound
  By hurting it; or when to th' lute   25

4.4 **there's** there as   8 **music's letters** the study of music   10 **place** dwelling   12 **wrack** ruin   14 **treason's** treachery's   15 **in this kind** in the following way   18 **Hight** is named   21 **sleided** (a variant of "sleaved," i.e., divided into filaments)   22 **small** slender   23 **needle** (here pronounced as a monosyllable)

77

She sung, and made the night-bird° mute,
That still records with moan;° or when
She would with rich and constant pen
Vail° to her mistress Dian; still
30 This Philoten contends in skill
With absolute° Marina: so
With dove of Paphos° might the crow
Vie° feathers white. Marina gets
All praises, which are paid as debts,
35 And not as given. This so darks°
In Philoten all graceful marks
That Cleon's wife, with envy rare,
A present° murderer does prepare°
For good Marina, that her daughter
40 Might stand peerless by this slaughter.
The sooner her vile thoughts to stead,°
Lychorida, our nurse, is dead;
And cursèd Dionyza hath
The pregnant° instrument of wrath
45 Prest° for this blow. The unborn event°
I do commend to your content;°
Only I carry wingèd time
Post° on the lame feet of my rhyme;
Which never could I so convey
50 Unless your thoughts went on my way.
Dionyza does appear,
With Leonine, a murderer.   *Exit.*

[Scene 1. *Tharsus, near the seashore.*]

Enter Dionyza with Leonine.

Dionyza. Thy oath remember; thou hast sworn to do't.
'Tis but a blow, which never shall be known.

---

26 **night-bird** nightingale   27 **still records with moan** ever sings
dolefully   29 **Vail** do homage   31 **absolute** free from imperfection
32 **dove of Paphos** Venus' dove   33 **Vie** compete in respect of   35
darks darkens, puts in the shade   38 **present** speedy   38 **prepare**
provide   41 **stead** aid   44 **pregnant** disposed, inclined   45 **Prest**
ready   45 **event** outcome   46 **commend to your content** commend to you, hoping that it will please you   48 **Post** in post haste

Thou canst not do a thing in the world so soon
To yield thee so much profit. Let not conscience,
Which is but cold, or flaming love thy bosom
Enslave too nicely;° nor let pity, which   5
Even women have cast off, melt thee, but be
A soldier to° thy purpose.

Leonine. I will do't. But yet she is a goodly creature!

Dionyza. The fitter then the gods should have her.   10
Here she comes weeping° her old nurse's death!
Thou art resolved?

Leonine.   I am resolved.

Enter Marina with a basket of flowers.

Marina. No, I will rob Tellus° of her weed°
To strew thy green° with flowers; the yellows, blues,
The purple violets, and marigolds,   15
Shall as a carpet° hang upon thy grave,
While summer days doth last. Ay me, poor maid,
Born in a tempest, when my mother died,
This world to me is as a lasting storm,
Whirring° me from my friends.°   20

Dionyza. How now, Marina, why do you keep alone?
How chance my daughter is not with you?
Do not consume your blood with sorrowing.°
Have you a nurse of me! Lord, how your favor°
Is changed with this unprofitable woe!   25
Come, give me your flowers.
On the sea margent walk with Leonine.
The air is quick° there and it pierces, and
Sharpens the stomach. Come, Leonine, take
Her by the arm, walk with her.

Marina.   No, I pray you.   30
I'll not bereave you of your servant.

4.1.6 **nicely** scrupulously   8 **A soldier to** wholly devoted to   11
weeping lamenting   13 **Tellus** the earth   13 **weed** garment (of
flowers)   14 **green** i.e., the green turf of Lychorida's grave   16
carpet piece of tapestry   20 **Whirring** whirling, hurrying along
20 **friends** relations   23 **Do ... sorrowing** (alluding to the ancient
notion that each sigh takes a drop of blood from the heart)   24 **favor**
face, looks   28 **quick** sharp

Dionyza.   Come, come!
    I love the King your father and yourself
    With more than foreign° heart. We every day
    Expect him here. When he shall come, and find
35 Our paragon to all reports° thus blasted,
    He will repent the breadth° of his great voyage;
    Blame both my lord and me, that we have taken
    No care to your best courses.° Go, I pray you,
    Walk, and be cheerful once again; reserve°
40 That excellent complexion, which did steal
    The eyes of young and old. Care not for me;
    I can go home alone.

Marina.   Well, I will go;
    But yet I have no desire to it.

Dionyza.   Come, come,
    I know 'tis good for you.
45 Walk half an hour, Leonine, at the least.
    Remember what I have said.

Leonine.   I warrant° you, madam.

Dionyza. I'll leave you, my sweet lady, for a while.
    Pray, walk softly,° do not heat your blood.
    What! I must have care of you.

Marina.   My thanks, sweet madam.

                                    [*Exit Dionyza.*]
    Is this wind westerly that blows?

50 *Leonine.*   Southwest.

Marina. When I was born the wind was north.

Leonine.   Was't so?

Marina. My father, as nurse says, did never fear,
    But cried "Good seamen!" to the sailors, galling°
    His kingly hands haling ropes;
55 And, clasping° to the mast, endured a sea
    That almost burst the deck.

33 **foreign** not of one's family   35 **to all reports** according to all
reports   36 **breadth** extent   38 **to your best courses** to what was
best for you   39 **reserve** preserve, guard   46 **warrant** promise
48 **softly** slowly   53 **galling** making sore by chafing   55 **clasping**
clinging

Leonine. When was this?

Marina. When I was born.
  Never was waves nor wind more violent;
  And from the ladder-tackle washes off
  A canvas-climber.° "Ha!" says one, "wolt° out?"   60
  And with a dropping° industry they skip
  From stem to stern; the boatswain whistles, and
  The master calls and trebles their confusion.

Leonine. Come, say your prayers!

Marina. What mean you?   65

Leonine. If you require a little space for prayer,
  I grant it. Pray; but be not tedious, for
  The gods are quick of ear, and I am sworn
  To do my work with haste.

Marina. Why will you kill me?

Leonine. To satisfy my lady.   70

Marina. Why would she have me killed?
  Now, as° I can remember, by my troth,
  I never did her hurt in all my life.
  I never spake bad word nor did ill turn
  To any living creature. Believe me, la,°   75
  I never killed a mouse, nor hurt a fly;
  I trod upon a worm against my will,
  But I wept for't. How have I offended,
  Wherein my death might yield her any profit,
  Or my life imply her any danger?   80

Leonine. My commission
  Is not to reason of the deed, but do't.

Marina. You will not do't for all the world, I hope.
  You are well-favored,° and your looks foreshow
  You have a gentle heart. I saw you lately,   85
  When you caught hurt in parting two that fought.

---

60 **canvas-climber** sailor climbing aloft to trim sails   60 **wolt** wilt
61 **dropping** dripping wet   72 **as** as far as   75 **la** (exclamation to
emphasize a statement)   84 **well-favored** good-looking

Good sooth,° it showed well in you. Do so now.
Your lady seeks my life: come you between,
And save poor me, the weaker!

Leonine.   I am sworn,
And will dispatch.   [*Seizes her.*]

Enter Pirates.

First Pirate.   Hold, villain!
                              [*Leonine runs away.*]

90 *Second Pirate.*   A prize! A prize!

Third Pirate. Half-part,° mates, half-part! Come, let's have
    her aboard suddenly.°   [*They carry off Marina.*]

Enter Leonine.

Leonine. These roguing° thieves serve the great pirate
    Valdes,
    And they have seized Marina. Let her go;
95 There's no hope° she'll return. I'll swear she's dead,
    And thrown into the sea. But I'll see further:
    Perhaps they will but please themselves upon her,
    Not carry her aboard. If she remain,
    Whom they have ravished must by me be slain.   *Exit.*

[Scene 2. *Mytilene. In front of a brothel.*]

Enter the three Bawds [*i.e., a Pander, his servant Boult,
and a Bawd*].

Pander. Boult!

Boult. Sir?

Pander. Search the market narrowly! Mytilene is full of
    gallants. We lost too much money this mart° by being
5   too wenchless.

Bawd. We were never so much out of creatures. We have

87 **Good sooth** truly   91 **Half-part** go shares   92 **suddenly** at
once   93 **roguing** vagrant   95 **hope** i.e., fear   4.2.4 **mart** market-
time

but poor three, and they can do no more than they can do; and they with continual action are even as good as rotten.

Pander. Therefore let's have fresh ones, whate'er we pay for them. If there be not a conscience to be used in every trade, we shall never prosper. 10

Bawd. Thou say'st true: 'tis not our bringing up of poor bastards—as, I think, I have brought up some eleven—

Boult. Ay, to eleven;° and brought them down again.° But shall I search the market? 15

Bawd. What else, man? The stuff° we have, a strong wind will blow it to pieces, they are so pitifully sodden.°

Pander. Thou sayest true; they're too unwholesome, o' conscience.° The poor Transylvanian is dead that lay with the little baggage. 20

Boult. Ay, she quickly pooped° him; she made him roast meat for worms. But I'll go search the market.   *Exit.*

Pander. Three or four thousand chequins° were as pretty a proportion° to live quietly, and so give over.° 25

Bawd. Why to give over, I pray you? Is it a shame to get° when we are old?

Pander. O, our credit° comes not in like the commodity,° nor the commodity wages not° with the danger. Therefore, if in our youths we could pick up some pretty 30 estate, 'twere not amiss to keep our door hatched.° Besides, the sore terms we stand upon with the gods will be strong with us for giving o'er.

---

15 **to eleven** up to the age of eleven   15 **brought them down again** i.e., by prostituting them   17 **stuff** goods for sale   18 **sodden** grown rotten by soaking (referring to the treatment of venereal disease by means of the sweating tub)   19–20 **o' conscience** on my conscience   22 **pooped** foundered (?)   24 **chequins** sequins, Italian gold coins   25 **proportion** portion, share   25 **give over** give up, retire   26 **get** acquire money   28 **credit** reputation   28 **commodity** profit   29 **wages not** is not commensurate   31 **hatched** with the hatch (the lower half of a divided door) shut

Bawd. Come, other sorts° offend as well as we.

35 *Pander.* As well as we? Ay, and better too; we offend worse.
Neither is our profession any trade;° it's no calling. But
here comes Boult.

Enter Boult, with the Pirates and Marina.

Boult. Come your ways,° my masters! You say she's
a virgin?

40 *First Pirate.* O, sir, we doubt it not.

Boult. Master, I have gone through° for this piece° you see.
If you like her, so; if not, I have lost my earnest.°

Bawd. Boult, has she any qualities?°

Boult. She has a good face, speaks well, and has excellent
45 good clothes. There's no farther necessity of qualities
can° make her be refused.

Bawd. What's her price, Boult?

Boult. It cannot be bated° one doit° of a thousand
pieces.

50 *Pander.* Well, follow me, my masters; you shall have
your money presently.° Wife, take her in. Instruct her
what she has to do, that she may not be raw° in her
entertainment.°   [*Exeunt Pander and Pirates.*]

Bawd. Boult, take you the marks of her, the color of her
55 hair, complexion, height, her age, with warrant of her
virginity; and cry "He that will give most shall have
her first!" Such a maidenhead were no cheap thing, if
men were as they have been. Get this done as I command you.

---

34 **sorts** classes of people 36 **trade** recognized business 38
Come your ways come along 41 **gone through** completed the process of bargaining (?) 41 **piece** girl 42 **earnest** money given as a
deposit 43 **qualities** accomplishments 46 **can** that can 48
bated reduced 48 **doit** smallest coin, worth half a farthing 51
presently immediately 52 **raw** inexperienced 53 **entertainment**
manner of reception

Boult. Performance shall follow.   *Exit.*   60

Marina. Alack that Leonine was so slack, so slow!
  He should have struck, not spoke; or that these pirates,
  Not enough barbarous, had not o'erboard
  Thrown me to seek my mother!

Bawd. Why lament you, pretty one?   65

Marina. That I am pretty.

Bawd. Come, the gods have done their part in you.

Marina. I accuse them not.

Bawd. You are light° into my hands, where you are like
  to live.   70

Marina. The more my fault
  To 'scape his hands where I was like to die.

Bawd. Ay, and you shall live in pleasure.

Marina. No.

Bawd. Yes, indeed shall you, and taste gentlemen of all   75
  fashions. You shall fare well: you shall have the dif-
  ference° of all complexions.° What° do you stop your
  ears?

Marina. Are you a woman?

Bawd. What would you have me be, and° I be not a   80
  woman?

Marina. An honest° woman, or not a woman.

Bawd. Marry,° whip thee, gosling!° I think I shall have
  something to do with you.° Come, you're a young
  foolish sapling, and must be bowed as I would have   85
  you.

---

69 **are light** have fallen   76–77 **difference** variety   77 **complexions** colors of skin, i.e., men of every race   77 **What** why   80 **and
if**   82 **honest** chaste   83 **Marry** (interjection expressing indignation)   83 **whip thee, gosling** hang thee, greenhorn   83–84 **have . . .
you** have trouble with you

Marina. The gods defend me!

Bawd. If it please the gods to defend you by men, then men
must comfort you, men must feed you, men stir you up.°
90   Boult's returned.

[*Enter Boult.*]

Now, sir, hast thou cried° her through the market?

Boult. I have cried her almost to the number of her
hairs;° I have drawn her picture with my voice.

Bawd. And I prithee tell me, how dost thou find the inclina-
95   tion of the people, especially of the younger sort?

Boult. Faith, they listened to me as they would have
hearkened to their father's testament. There was a
Spaniard's mouth wat'red and° he went to bed to her
very description.

100 *Bawd.* We shall have him here tomorrow with his best
ruff on.

Boult. Tonight, tonight. But, mistress, do you know
the French knight that cowers i' the hams?

Bawd. Who, Monsieur Veroles?°

105 *Boult.* Ay, he: he offered° to cut a caper at the proclama-
tion; but he made a groan at it, and swore he would see
her tomorrow.

Bawd. Well, well; as for him, he brought his disease hither.
Here he does but repair° it. I know he will come in our
110   shadow,° to scatter his crowns of the sun.°

Boult. Well, if we had of every nation a traveler, we
should lodge them with this sign.°

Bawd. [*To Marina*] Pray you, come hither awhile. You have
fortunes coming upon you. Mark me: you must seem to

---

89 **stir you up** excite you   91 **cried** (1) advertised by loud cries (2)
extolled   92–93 **almost . . . hairs** any number of times   98 **and** as if
104 **Veroles** (from French *vérole*=pox)   105 **offered** attempted
109 **repair** renew   110 **shadow** shelter   110 **crowns of the sun**
French gold coins   112 **this sign** i.e., Marina's charms

do that fearfully which you commit willingly; despise   115
profit where you have most gain. To weep that you live
as ye do makes pity in your lovers: seldom but that
pity begets you a good opinion, and that opinion a
mere° profit.

Marina. I understand you not.   120

Boult. O, take her home,° mistress, take her home! These
blushes of hers must be quenched with some present°
practice.

Bawd. Thou sayest true, i' faith, so they must. For your
bride goes to that with shame which is her way to go   125
with warrant.°

Boult. Faith, some do, and some do not. But, mistress, if I
have bargained for the joint—

Bawd. Thou mayest cut a morsel off the spit.

Boult. I may so?   130

Bawd. Who should deny it? Come, young one, I like the
manner of your garments well.

Boult. Ay, by my faith, they shall not be changed yet.

Bawd. Boult, spend thou that in the town. Report what a
sojourner we have: you'll lose nothing by custom.°   135
When nature framed° this piece, she meant thee a good
turn. Therefore say what a paragon she is, and thou hast
the harvest out of thine own report.

Boult. I warrant you, mistress, thunder shall not so
awake the beds of eels° as my giving out her beauty   140
stirs up the lewdly inclined. I'll bring home some tonight.

Bawd. Come your ways! Follow me.

119 **mere** downright   121 **take her home** tell her your mind (?)
122 **present** immediate   125–26 **which … warrant** to which she
is entitled to go   135 **by custom** i.e., by our getting customers   136
framed shaped   139–40 **thunder … eels** (thunder was supposed to
rouse eels from the mud)

Marina. If fires be hot, knives sharp, or waters deep, Un-
145 tied I still my virgin knot will keep.
       Diana aid my purpose!

Bawd. What have we to do with Diana? Pray you, will you
       go with us?   *Exit [with the rest].*

[Scene 3. *Tharsus.*]

Enter Cleon and Dionyza.

Dionyza. Why are you foolish? Can it be undone?

Cleon. O Dionyza, such a piece of slaughter
       The sun and moon ne'er looked upon!

Dionyza. I think you'll turn a child again.

5   *Cleon.* Were I chief lord of all this spacious world,
       I'd give it to undo the deed. A lady
       Much less in blood than virtue,° yet a princess
       To equal any single crown o' th' earth
       I' th' justice of compare!° O villain Leonine!
10   Whom thou hast pois'ned too.
       If thou hadst drunk to him,° 't had been a kindness°
       Becoming° well thy fact.° What canst thou say
       When noble Pericles shall demand his child?

Dionyza. That she is dead. Nurses are not the fates°
15   To foster it, not ever to preserve.
       She died at night. I'll say so. Who can cross° it?
       Unless you play the pious innocent,
       And for an honest attribute° cry out
       "She died by foul play."

Cleon.   O, go to.° Well, well.

4.3.7 **Much ... virtue** even more so in point of virtue than of descent   9 **I' th' justice of compare** in a just comparison   11 **If ...
him** i.e., if thou hadst poisoned thyself in pledging him   11 **a kindness** (1) a kind action (2) an appropriate action   12 **Becoming** befit-
ting   12 **fact** deed   14 **fates** (a line seems to have dropped out
here, to the effect that the nurse's power over human life is merely "To
foster it ...")   16 **cross** contradict   18 **an honest attribute** the
reputation of honesty   19 **go to** (an expression of disapproval)

Of all the faults beneath the heavens the gods   20
Do like this worst.

Dionyza.   Be one of those that thinks
The petty wrens of Tharsus will fly hence
And open this to Pericles.° I do shame
To think of what a noble strain you are,
And of how coward a spirit.

Cleon.   To such proceeding   25
Whoever but his approbation added,
Though not his prime° consent, he did not flow°
From honorable sources.

Dionyza.   Be it so, then.
Yet none does know but you how she came dead,
Nor none can know, Leonine being gone.   30
She did distain° my child, and stood between
Her and her fortunes: none would look on her,
But cast their gazes on Marina's face;
Whilst ours was blurted at,° and held a malkin,°
Not worth the time of day.° It pierced me thorough;   35
And though you call my course unnatural,
You not your child well loving, yet I find
It greets me° as an enterprise of kindness°
Performed to your sole daughter.

Cleon.   Heavens forgive it!

Dionyza. And as for Pericles, what should he say?   40
We wept after her hearse, and yet we mourn.
Her monument°
Is almost finished, and her epitaphs
In glitt'ring golden characters° express
A general praise to her, and care in us   45
At whose expense 'tis done.

22–23 **The petty . . . Pericles** (an allusion to the popular belief in the
revelation of hidden murders by a telltale bird)   27 **prime** initial
27 **flow** issue   31 **distain** cast a slur on   34 **blurted at** treated
with scorn   34 **malkin** slut   35 **the time of day** a greeting   38
greets me presents itself to me   38 **kindness** love   42 **monument**
(probably a few words, such as "which stands i' the market-place,"
have here dropped out)   44 **characters** letters

Cleon.   Thou art like the harpy,
    Which, to betray, dost, with thine angel's face,
    Seize with thine eagle's talents.°

Dionyza. Ye're like one that superstitiously
50   Do swear to th' gods that winter kills the flies.°
    But yet I know you'll do as I advise.   *[Exeunt.]*

[Scene 4. *Before Marina's monument at Tharsus.*

Enter Gower.]

Gower. Thus time we waste,° and long leagues make short;
    Sail seas in cockles,° have and wish but for't;°
    Making,° to take° our imagination,
    From bourn to bourn,° region to region.
5   By you being pardoned, we commit no crime
    To use one language in each several clime
    Where our scene° seems to live. I do beseech you
    To learn of me, who stand i' th' gaps to teach you
    The stages of our story. Pericles
10   Is now again thwarting° the wayward seas,
    Attended on by many a lord and knight,
    To see his daughter, all his life's delight.
    Old Helicanus goes along. Behind
    Is left to govern it, you bear in mind,
15   Old Escanes, whom Helicanus late°
    Advanced in Tyre to great and high estate.
    Well-sailing ships and bounteous winds have brought
    This king to Tharsus—think his pilot thought;°
    So with his steerage° shall your thoughts go on—

47–48 **dost . . . talents** i.e., dost, while smiling at thy victim with
thine angel's face, seize it with thine eagle's talents (a common variant of "talons")   49–50 **Ye're . . . flies** i.e., you are so much afraid
of divine vengeance that you even swear to the gods that it is not you
but winter which is guilty of the death of flies   4.4.1 **waste** annihi-
late   2 **cockles** cockleshells   2 **have . . . for't** have by merely
wishing for it   3 **Making** making our way   3 **take** captivate, delight   4 **bourn** frontier   7 **scene** dramatic performance   10
thwarting crossing   15 **late** recently   18 **think his pilot thought**
think that his pilot is thought   19 **with his steerage** with the course
held by Pericles

To fetch his daughter home, who first° is gone.   20
Like motes and shadows see them move awhile.
Your ears unto your eyes I'll reconcile.

[*Dumb Show*]

*Enter Pericles at one door, with all his train; Cleon
and Dionyza at the other. Cleon shows Pericles the
tomb; whereat Pericles makes lamentation, puts on
sackcloth, and in a mighty passion departs. [Then
Cleon, Dionyza, and the rest go also.*]

See how belief may suffer by foul show!°
This borrowed passion° stands for true-owed° woe.
And Pericles, in sorrow all devoured,   25
With sighs shot through and biggest tears o'ershowered,
Leaves Tharsus and again embarks. He swears
Never to wash his face, nor cut his hairs.
He puts on sackcloth, and to sea. He bears
A tempest, which his mortal vessel° tears,   30
And yet he rides it out.° Now please you wit°
The epitaph is° for Marina writ
By wicked Dionyza.
        [*Reads the inscription on Marina's monument.*]

"The fairest, sweetest, and best lies here,
Who withered in her spring of year.   35
She was of Tyrus the King's daughter,°
On whom foul death hath made this slaughter.
Marina was she called; and at her birth
Thetis,° being proud, swallowed some part o' th'
        earth.
Therefore the earth, fearing to be o'erflowed,   40
Hath Thetis' birth-child° on the heavens bestowed;
Wherefore she° does—and swears she'll never
        stint—

20 **first** before him   23 **suffer by foul show** be abused by hypocrisy
24 **borrowed passion** counterfeit grief   24 **true-owed** sincerely
owned   30 **vessel** i.e., his body   31 **he rides it out** i.e., he survives
it   31 **wit** know   32 **is** that is   36 **of Tyrus the King's daughter**
daughter of the King of Tyrus   39 **Thetis** a sea nymph (here, as
commonly in Elizabethan literature, confused with Tethys, wife of
Oceanus, hence the sea personified)   41 **birth-child** person born in
a particular place   42 **she** i.e., the sea

Make raging battery upon shores of flint."

No visor° does become black villainy
45 So well as soft and tender flattery.
Let Pericles believe his daughter's dead,
And bear his courses to be orderèd°
By Lady Fortune; while our scene° must play
His daughter's woe and heavy well-a-day°
50 In her unholy service. Patience, then,
And think you now are all in Mytilen.   *Exit.*

[Scene 5. *Mytilene. A street before the brothel.*]

Enter [, from the brothel,] two Gentlemen.

First Gentleman. Did you ever hear the like?

Second Gentleman. No, nor never shall do in such a place
as this, she being once gone.

First Gentleman. But to have divinity preached there! Did
5 you ever dream of such a thing?

Second Gentleman. No, no. Come, I am for no more
bawdy houses. Shall's go hear the vestals° sing?

First Gentleman. I'll do anything now that is virtuous; but
I am out of the road of rutting° forever.
          Exit [with the other].

[Scene 6. *Mytilene. A room in the brothel.*

Enter Pander, Bawd, and Boult.]

Pander. Well, I had rather than twice the worth of her she
had ne'er come here.

Bawd. Fie, fie upon her! She's able to freeze the god

44 **visor** mask, disguise 47 **bear ... orderèd** suffer his actions to
be regulated 48 **scene** performance 49 **well-a-day** grief 4.5.7
vestals virgin priestesses 9 **rutting** fornication

　　　Priapus,° and undo a whole generation. We must either
　　　get her ravished or be rid of her. When she should do　　　5
　　　for clients her fitment° and do me the kindness of our
　　　profession, she has me° her quirks, her reasons, her
　　　master-reasons, her prayers, her knees; that she would
　　　make a puritan of the devil, if he should cheapen° a
　　　kiss of her.　　　　10

Boult. Faith, I must ravish her, or she'll disfurnish° us of all
　　　our cavalleria° and make our swearers priests.

Pander. Now, the pox upon her green-sickness° for me!°

Bawd. Faith, there's no way to be rid on't but by the way to
　　　the pox.° Here comes the Lord Lysimachus disguised.　　　15

Boult. We should have both lord and lown,° if the peevish
　　　baggage would but give way to customers.

　　　　　　　Enter Lysimachus.

Lysimachus. How now! How° a dozen of virginities?

Bawd. Now, the gods to-bless° your Honor!

Boult. I am glad to see your Honor in good health.　　　20

Lysimachus. You may so; 'tis the better for you that your
　　　resorters stand upon sound legs. How now, wholesome°
　　　iniquity, have you that° a man may deal withal° and
　　　defy the surgeon?

Bawd. We have here one, sir, if she would—but there　　　25
　　　never came her like in Mytilene.

Lysimachus. If she'd do the deeds of darkness, thou
　　　wouldst say.

4.6.4 **Priapus** the classical god of fertility　6 **fitment** duty　6–7
do me . . . has me (the "ethical dative," frequently used in narrative
by Shakespeare)　9 **cheapen** bargain for　11 **disfurnish** deprive
12 **cavalleria** body of gentlemen (Italian)　13 **green-sickness**
squeamishness　13 **for me** say I　15 **pox** syphilis　16 **lown** loon,
lowborn fellow　18 **How** at what price　19 **to-bless** bless entirely
("to" is an intensive prefix)　22 **wholesome** health-giving (used
ironically)　23 **that** that which　23 **deal withal** have sexual relations with

Bawd. Your Honor knows what 'tis to say° well enough.

30   *Lysimachus.* Well, call forth, call forth.

Boult. For flesh and blood, sir, white and red, you shall
see a rose; and she were a rose indeed, if she had
but—

Lysimachus. What, prithee?

35   *Boult.* O, sir, I can be modest.

Lysimachus. That dignifies the renown of a bawd no less
than it gives a good report to a punk to be chaste.°
                                                    [*Exit Boult.*]

Bawd. Here comes that which grows to° the stalk—never
plucked yet, I can assure you.

                    [*Enter Boult with Marina.*]

40   Is she not a fair creature?

Lysimachus. Faith, she would serve after a long voyage at
sea. Well, there's for you. Leave us.

Bawd. I beseech your Honor, give me leave: a word, and
I'll have done presently.°

45   *Lysimachus.* I beseech you, do.

Bawd. [*To Marina*] First, I would have you note, this is an
honorable man.

Marina. I desire to find him so, that I may worthily note°
him.

50   *Bawd.* Next, he's the governor of this country, and a man
whom I am bound to.

Marina. If he govern the country, you are bound° to him
indeed; but how honorable he is in that I know not.

---

29 **what 'tis to say** how to express my meaning   37 **it gives . . .
chaste** to be chaste gives a good reputation to a prostitute (the whole
speech is ironic)   38 **grows to** is an integral part of   44 **presently**
at once   48 **note** respect   52 **bound** subject (another example of
Marina's "quirks" of which the bawd complained)

Bawd. Pray you, without any more virginal fencing, will   55
  you use him kindly? He will line your apron with
  gold.

Marina. What he will do graciously, I will thankfully
  receive.

Lysimachus. Ha' you done?

Bawd. My lord, she's not paced° yet; you must take some   60
  pains to work her to your manage.° Come, we will leave
  his Honor and her together. Go thy ways.°
                   [*Exeunt Bawd, Pander, and Boult.*]

Lysimachus. Now, pretty one, how long have you been at
  this trade?

Marina. What trade, sir?   65

Lysimachus. Why, I cannot name't but I shall offend.

Marina. I cannot be offended with my trade. Please you to
  name it.

Lysimachus. How long have you been of this profession?

Marina. E'er since I can remember.   70

Lysimachus. Did you go to't° so young? Were you a
  gamester° at five or at seven?

Marina. Earlier too, sir, if now I be one.

Lysimachus. Why, the house you dwell in proclaims
  you to be a creature of sale.   75

Marina. Do you know this house to be a place of such
  resort, and will come into't? I hear say you're of honorable parts and are the governor of this place.

Lysimachus. Why, hath your principal° made known unto
  you who I am?   80

Marina. Who is my principal?

---

60 **paced** taught her paces   61 **manage** action and paces to which a
horse is trained   62 **Go thy ways** come along   71 **go to't** copu-
late   72 **gamester** one addicted to amorous sport   79 **principal**
employer

Lysimachus. Why, your herb-woman; she that sets seeds
    and roots of shame and iniquity. O, you have heard
    something of my power, and so stand aloof for more
85   serious wooing. But I protest to thee, pretty one, my au-
    thority shall not see thee, or else look friendly upon
    thee. Come, bring me to some private place. Come,
    come.

Marina. If you were born to honor, show it now;
90   If put upon you,° make the judgment good
    That thought you worthy of it.

Lysimachus. How's this? How's this? Some more; be
    sage.

Marina.   For me,
    That am a maid, though most ungentle fortune
    Have placed me in this sty, where, since I came,
95   Diseases have been sold dearer than physic—
    That the gods
    Would set me free from this unhallowed place,
    Though they did change me to the meanest bird
    That flies i' th' purer air!

Lysimachus.   I did not think
    Thou couldst have spoke so well; ne'er dreamt thou
100   couldst.
    Had I brought hither a corrupted mind,
    Thy speech had altered it. Hold, here's gold for thee:
    Persever in that clear° way thou goest,
    And the gods strengthen thee!

Marina.   The good gods preserve you!

105 *Lysimachus.* For me, be you thoughten°
    That I came with no ill intent; for to me
    The very doors and windows savor° vilely.
    Fare thee well. Thou art a piece of virtue, and
    I doubt not but thy training hath been noble.

---

90 **If put upon you** if honor was bestowed upon you   103 **clear**
free from blame   105 **For me, be you thoughten** (this line,
like much else in this scene, is undoubtedly corrupt, but the true
reading seems irrecoverable; see Introduction, pp. 5–7)   107 **savor**
smell

Hold, here's more gold for thee. 110
A curse upon him, die he like a thief,
That robs thee of thy goodness! If thou dost
Hear from me, it shall be for thy good.

[*Enter Boult.*]

Boult. I beseech your Honor, one piece for me.

Lysimachus. Avaunt,° thou damned doorkeeper!° 115
Your house, but for this virgin that doth prop it,
Would sink, and overwhelm you. Away!   [*Exit.*]

Boult. How's this? We must take another course with you.
If your peevish° chastity, which is not worth a breakfast
in the cheapest country under the cope,° shall undo a 120
whole household, let me be gelded like a spaniel. Come
your ways.

Marina. Whither would you have me?

Boult. I must have your maidenhead taken off, or the
common hangman shall execute it.° Come your ways. 125
We'll have no more gentlemen driven away. Come your
ways, I say.

Enter Bawd.

Bawd. How now! What's the matter?

Boult. Worse and worse, mistress: she has here spoken
holy words to the Lord Lysimachus. 130

Bawd. O abominable!

Boult. She makes our profession as it were to stink
afore the face of the gods.

Bawd. Marry, hang her up forever!

Boult. The nobleman would have dealt with her like 135
a nobleman, and she sent him away as cold as a snow-
ball; saying his prayers too.

---

115 **Avaunt** be off   115 **doorkeeper** pander   119 **peevish** refrac-
tory   120 **cope** sky   124–25 **or the . . . execute it** (with a play on
the "head" of "maidenhead")

Bawd. Boult, take her away! Use her at thy pleasure.
Crack the glass of her virginity, and make the rest
140   malleable.

Boult. And if° she were a thornier piece of ground than she
is, she shall be ploughed.

Marina. Hark, hark, you gods!

Bawd. She conjures!° Away with her! Would she had never
145   come within my doors! Marry, hang you! She's born
to undo us. Will you not go the way of womenkind?
Marry come up,° my dish of chastity with rosemary and
bays!°   [*Exit.*]

Boult. Come, mistress; come your ways with me.

150 *Marina.* Whither wilt thou have me?

Boult. To take from you the jewel you hold so dear.

Marina. Prithee, tell me one thing first.

Boult. Come now, your one thing.

Marina. What canst thou wish thine enemy to be?

155 *Boult.* Why, I could wish him to be my master, or, rather,
my mistress.

Marina. Neither of these are so bad as thou art,
Since they do better thee in their command.°
Thou hold'st a place for which the painèd'st° fiend
160   Of hell would not in reputation change.
Thou art the damnèd doorkeeper to every
Coistrel° that comes inquiring for his Tib;°
To the choleric fisting° of every rogue

---

141 **And if** even if   144 **conjures** invokes supernatural aid (with
the suggestion of black magic)   147 **Marry come up** (an expression
of contempt akin to our "hoity-toity")   147–48 **dish . . . bays**
(a gibe at Marina's ostentatious virtue; dishes at Christmas were
thus garnished)   158 **do better . . . command** are superior to
you through their position of authority   159 **painèd'st** most tormented   162 **Coistrel** base fellow   162 **Tib** strumpet   163 **fisting**
punching

    Thy ear is liable; thy food is such
    As hath been belched on by infected lungs.   165

Boult. What would you have me do? Go to the wars, would
    you? Where a man may serve seven years for the loss of
    a leg, and have not money enough in the end to buy him
    a wooden one?

Marina. Do any thing but this thou doest.° Empty   170
    Old receptacles,° or common shores,° of filth;
    Serve by indenture° to the common hangman.
    Any of these ways are yet better than this.
    For what thou professest° a baboon, could he speak,
    Would own a name too dear.° That the gods   175
    Would safely deliver me from this place!
    Here, here's gold for thee.
    If that thy master would gain by me,
    Proclaim that I can sing, weave, sew, and dance,
    With other virtues° which I'll keep from boast;   180
    And I will undertake all these to teach.
    I doubt not but this populous city will
    Yield many scholars.

Boult. But can you teach all this you speak of?

Marina. Prove that I cannot, take me home again,   185
    And prostitute me to the basest groom°
    That doth frequent your house.

Boult. Well, I will see what I can do for thee. If I can place
    thee, I will.

Marina. But amongst honest women?   190

Boult. Faith, my acquaintance lies little amongst them. But
    since my master and mistress hath bought you, there's

---

170 **doest** (pronounced as a disyllable)   171 **receptacles** (the stress
here falls on the first syllable)   171 **common shores** i.e., the no-
man's-land by the sea, where filth was allowed to be deposited for the
tide to wash away   172 **by indenture** i.e., as apprentice   174 **thou
professest** you have as an occupation   175 **Would ... dear** would
claim to possess too high a reputation   180 **virtues** accomplishments   186 **groom** menial

no going but by their consent. Therefore I will make
them acquainted with your purpose,° and I doubt not but
195 I shall find them tractable enough. Come, I'll do for thee
what I can; come your ways. *Exeunt.*

[ACT 5]

Enter Gower.

Gower. Marina thus the brothel 'scapes, and chances
 Into an honest house, our story says.
 She sings like one immortal, and she dances
 As goddesslike to her admired lays;
 Deep clerks° she dumbs, and with her neele° composes 5
 Nature's own shape of bud, bird, branch, or berry,
 That even her art sisters° the natural roses;
 Her inkle,° silk, twin with the rubied cherry;
 That pupils lacks she none of noble race,
 Who pour their bounty on her; and her gain 10
 She gives the cursèd bawd. Here we her place;
 And to her father turn our thoughts again,
 Where we left him on the sea. We there him lost;
 Whence, driven before the winds, he is arrived
 Here where his daughter dwells; and on this coast 15
 Suppose him now at anchor. The city's hived°
 God Neptune's annual feast to keep; from whence
 Lysimachus our Tyrian ship espies,
 His banners sable, trimmed with rich expense;
 And to him° in his barge with fervor hies. 20
 In your supposing° once more put your sight:
 Of heavy° Pericles think this his bark;
 Where what is done in action, more, if might,°
 Shall be discovered.° Please you, sit and hark. *Exit.*

5.5 **Deep clerks** men of profound learning 5 **neele** needle 7 **sisters** is exactly like 8 **inkle** linen thread 16 **The city's hived** i.e., the citizens are gathered like bees in a hive 19–20 **His . . . him** its . . . it 21 **In your supposing** under the guidance of your imagination 22 **heavy** sorrowful 23 **more, if might** and more if it were possible 24 **discovered** disclosed

[Scene 1. *On board Pericles' ship, off Mytilene. A pavilion on deck, with a curtain before it; Pericles within, unkempt and clad in sackcloth, reclining on a couch.*]

Enter Helicanus, to him two Sailors [, one belonging to the Tyrian vessel, the other of Mytilene].

Tyrian Sailor. Where is Lord Helicanus?
　　He can resolve° you. O, here he is.
　　Sir, there is a barge put off from Mytilene,
　　And in it is Lysimachus, the Governor,
5　　Who craves to come aboard. What is your will?

Helicanus. That he have his. Call up some gentlemen.

Tyrian Sailor. Ho, gentlemen! my lord calls.

Enter two or three Gentlemen.

First Gentleman. Doth your lordship call?

Helicanus. Gentlemen, there is some° of worth would
　　come aboard.
10　　I pray, greet him fairly.°　　　　[*Exeunt the Gentlemen.*]

Enter Lysimachus [and Lords, with the Gentlemen].

Mytilenian Sailor. [*To Lysimachus*] Sir,
　　This is the man that can, in aught you would,
　　Resolve you.

Lysimachus. Hail, reverend sir! The gods preserve you!

15　*Helicanus.* And you, sir, to outlive the age I am,
　　And die as I would do.

5.1.2 **resolve** free from uncertainty　9 **some** someone　10 **fairly** courteously

Lysimachus.   You wish me well.
  Being on shore, honoring of Neptune's triumphs,°
  Seeing this goodly vessel ride before us,
  I made to it, to know of whence you are.

Helicanus. First, what is your place?°

Lysimachus.   I am the Governor of   20
  This place you lie before.

Helicanus. Sir,
  Our vessel is of Tyre, in it the King;
  A man who for this three months hath not spoken
  To anyone, nor taken sustenance   25
  But to prorogue° his grief.

Lysimachus. Upon what ground is his distemperature?°

Helicanus. 'Twould be too tedious to repeat;
  But the main grief springs from the loss
  Of a belovèd daughter and a wife.   30

Lysimachus. May we not see him?

Helicanus. You may;
  But bootless° is your sight; he will not speak
  To any.

Lysimachus.   Yet let me obtain my wish.

Helicanus. [*Draws back the curtain*] Behold him. This
  was a goodly person   35
  Till the disaster that, one mortal° night,
  Drove him to this.

Lysimachus. Sir King, all hail! The gods preserve you!
  Hail, royal sir!

Helicanus. It is in vain; he will not speak to you.   40

Lord. Sir,
  We have a maid in Mytilene, I durst wager,
  Would win some words of him.

---

17 **triumphs** festivities   20 **place** official position   26 **prorogue**
prolong   27 **distemperature** mental disturbance   33 **bootless** un-
availing   36 **mortal** fatal

Lysimachus.   'Tis well bethought.
 She questionless, with her sweet harmony,
45 And other chosen° attractions, would allure,
 And make a batt'ry through his deafened ports,°
 Which now are midway stopped.
 She is all happy as the fairest of all,
 And with her fellow maid is now upon
50 The leafy shelter that abuts against
 The island's side.

          [*He whispers to a Lord, who leaves.*]

Helicanus. Sure, all° effectless; yet nothing we'll omit
 That bears recovery's name. But since your kindness
 We have stretched thus far, let us beseech you
55 That for our gold we may provision have,
 Wherein we are not destitute for want,
 But weary for the staleness.

Lysimachus.   O sir, a courtesy
 Which if we should deny, the most just God
 For every graff° would send a caterpillar,
60 And so inflict° our province. Yet once more
 Let me entreat to know at large° the cause
 Of your king's sorrow.

Helicanus. Sit, sir, I will recount it to you.
 But see, I am prevented.°

          [*Enter Lord with Marina and another girl.*]

65 *Lysimachus.* O, here's the lady that I sent for.
 Welcome, fair one! Is't not a goodly presence?°

Helicanus. She's a gallant° lady.

Lysimachus. She's such a one that, were I well assured
 Came° of a gentle kind° and noble stock,
70 I'd wish no better choice, and think me rarely° wed.

---

45 **chosen** choice   46 **ports** inlets   52 **all** entirely   59 **graff**
graft, grafted plant   60 **inflict** afflict   61 **at large** in full   64 **prevented** forestalled   66 **presence** person   67 **gallant** excellent   69
Came she came   69 **kind** family   70 **rarely** splendidly

[*To Marina*] Fair one, all goodness that consists in°
  bounty
Expect even here, where is a kingly patient.
If that thy prosperous° and artificial° feat
Can draw him but to answer thee in aught,
Thy sacred physic shall receive such pay   75
As thy desires can wish.

Marina.   Sir, I will use
My utmost skill in his recovery,
Provided
That none but I and my companion maid
Be suffered to come near him.

Lysimachus.   Come, let us leave her;   80
And the gods make her prosperous!

          [*They withdraw. Marina sings.*]

Lysimachus. Marked he your music?

Marina.   No, nor looked on us.

Lysimachus. See, she will speak to him.

Marina. Hail, sir! My lord, lend ear.

Pericles. Hum, ha!   [*He pushes her back.*]   85

Marina. I am a maid,
My lord, that ne'er before invited eyes,°
But have been gazed on like a comet. She speaks,
My lord, that, may be, hath endured a grief
Might equal yours, if both were justly weighed.   90
Though wayward fortune did malign° my state,
My derivation was from ancestors
Who stood equivalent with mighty kings:
But time hath rooted out my parentage,
And to the world and awkward casualties°   95
Bound me in servitude. [*Aside*] I will desist.

---

71 **goodness that consists in** good things that inhere in   73 **prosperous** successful   73 **artificial** skillful   87 **invited eyes** i.e., invited anyone to look at her   91 **malign** treat malignantly   95 **awkward casualties** adverse chances

But there is something glows upon my cheek,
And whispers in mine ear "Go not till he speak."

Pericles. My fortunes—parentage—good parentage—
100   To equal mine—was it not thus? What say you?

Marina. I said, my lord, if you did know my parentage,
You would not do me violence.

Pericles.   I do think so.
Pray you, turn your eyes upon me.
You're like something that—what countrywoman?°
Here of these shores?

105 *Marina.*   No, nor of any shores.
Yet I was mortally° brought forth, and am
No other than I appear.

Pericles. I am great° with woe, and shall deliver° weeping.
My dearest wife was like this maid, and such
My daughter might have been: my queen's square
110   brows;
Her stature to an inch; as wandlike straight;
As silver-voiced; her eyes as jewellike
And cased° as richly; in pace° another Juno;
Who starves the ears she feeds, and makes them hungry
115   The more she gives them speech. Where do you live?

Marina. Where I am but a stranger: from the deck
You may discern the place.

Pericles.   Where were you bred?
And how achieved you these endowments, which
You make more rich to owe?°

120 *Marina.* If I
Should tell my history, it would seem like lies
Disdained in the reporting.°

Pericles.   Prithee, speak.
Falseness cannot come from thee; for thou lookest

---

104 **what countrywoman?** of what country?   106 **mortally** humanly   108 **great** pregnant   108 **deliver** give birth to   113 **cased** encased   113 **pace** gait   119 **to owe** by owning them   122 **in the reporting** in the very act of utterance

Modest as Justice, and thou seemest a palace
For the crowned Truth to dwell in. I will believe thee,   *125*
And make my senses credit thy relation
To points that seem impossible; for thou lookest
Like one I loved indeed. What were thy friends?°
Didst thou not say when I did push thee back—
Which was when I perceived thee—that thou cam'st   *130*
From good descending?°

Marina.   So indeed I did.

Pericles. Report thy parentage. I think thou said'st
Thou hadst been tossed from wrong to injury,
And that thou thought'st thy griefs might equal mine,
If both were opened.°

Marina.   Some such thing I said,   *135*
And said no more but what my thoughts
Did warrant me was likely.

Pericles.   Tell thy story.
If thine, considered, prove the thousandth part
Of my endurance,° thou art a man, and I
Have suffered like a girl; yet thou dost look   *140*
Like Patience gazing on kings' graves, and smiling
Extremity out of act.° What were thy friends?°
How lost thou them? Thy name, my most kind virgin?
Recount, I do beseech thee: come, sit by me.

Marina. My name is Marina.

Pericles.   O, I am mocked,   *145*
And thou by some incensèd god sent hither
To make the world to laugh at me.

Marina.   Patience, good sir,
Or here I'll cease.

Pericles.   Nay, I'll be patient.
Thou little know'st how thou dost startle me
To call thyself Marina.

---

128 **friends** relations   131 **descending** lineage   135 **opened** disclosed   139 **my endurance** what I have endured   142 **Extremity
out of act** extreme calamity out of striking (?) extreme despair out of
committing suicide (?)   142 **friends** relations

150 *Marina.*   The name
   Was given me by one that had some power:
   My father, and a king.

   Pericles.   How, a king's daughter?
   And called Marina?

   Marina.   You said you would believe me;
   But, not to be a troubler of your peace,
   I will end here.

155 *Pericles.*   But are you flesh and blood?
   Have you a working pulse, and are no fairy?
   Motion° as well? Speak on. Where were you born?
   And wherefore called Marina?

   Marina.   Called Marina
   For I was born at sea.

   Pericles.   At sea! What mother?

160 *Marina.* My mother was the daughter of a king;
   Who died the minute I was born,
   As my good nurse Lychorida hath oft
   Delivered° weeping.

   Pericles.   O, stop there a little!
   This is the rarest dream that e'er dulled sleep
165 Did mock sad fools withal.° This cannot be:
   My daughter's buried. Well, where were you bred?
   I'll hear you more, to th' bottom of your story,
   And never interrupt you.

   Marina. You scorn. Believe me, 'twere best I did give o'er.

170 *Pericles.* I will believe you by the syllable
   Of what you shall deliver. Yet, give me leave:
   How came you in these parts? Where were you bred?

   Marina. The King my father did in Tharsus leave me;
   Till cruel Cleon, with his wicked wife,
175 Did seek to murder me;
   And having wooed a villain to attempt it,

157 **Motion** i.e., the movement of the blood and spirits through the
body   163 **Delivered** reported   165 **withal** with

Who having drawn to do't,
A crew of pirates came and rescued me;
Brought me to Mytilene.° But, good sir,
Whither will you have me? Why do you weep? It
    may be   *180*
You think me an impostor: no, good faith!
I am the daughter to King Pericles,
If good King Pericles be.°

Pericles.   Ho, Helicanus!

Helicanus. Calls my lord?

Pericles. Thou art a grave and noble counselor,   *185*
Most wise in general. Tell me, if thou canst,
What this maid is, or what is like° to be,
That thus hath made me weep?

Helicanus.   I know not;
But here's the regent, sir, of Mytilene
Speaks° nobly of her.

Lysimachus.   She never would tell   *190*
Her parentage; being demanded that,
She would sit still° and weep.

Pericles. O Helicanus, strike me, honored sir!
Give me a gash, put me to present pain;
Lest this great sea of joys rushing upon me   *195*
O'erbear° the shores of my mortality,
And drown me with their sweetness. O, come hither,
Thou that beget'st° him that did thee beget;
Thou that wast born at sea, buried at Tharsus,
And found at sea again! O Helicanus,   *200*
Down on thy knees; thank the holy gods as loud
As thunder threatens us: this is Marina!
What was thy mother's name? Tell me but that,
For truth can never be confirmed enough,
Though doubts did ever sleep.

---

179 **Mytilene** (the final syllable is here sounded)   183 **be** i.e., be
alive   187 **like** likely   190 **Speaks** that speaks   192 **still** always
196 **O'erbear** overwhelm   198 **beget'st** i.e., gives new life to

205 *Marina.*   First, sir, I pray,
      What is your title?

Pericles. I am Pericles of Tyre: but tell me now
      My drowned queen's name, as in the rest you said
      Thou hast been godlike perfect, and thou art°
210   The heir of kingdoms and another life
      To Pericles, thy father.

Marina. [*Kneels*] Is it no more to be your daughter than
      To say my mother's name was Thaisa?
      Thaisa was my mother, who did end
215   The minute I began.

Pericles. Now blessing on thee! Rise; thou art my child.
      Give me fresh garments. [*To Marina*] Mine own!
         Helicanus,
      She is not dead at Tharsus, as she should have been°
      By° savage Cleon. She shall tell thee all;
220   When thou shalt kneel, and justify in knowledge°
      She is thy very princess. Who is this?

Helicanus. Sir, 'tis the Governor of Mytilene,
      Who, hearing of your melancholy state,
      Did come to see you.

Pericles.   I embrace you.
225   Give me my robes. I am wild in my beholding.°
      O heavens bless my girl! [*Music.*] But hark, what
         music?
      Tell Helicanus, my Marina, tell him
      O'er, point by point, for yet he seems to doubt,
      How sure you are my daughter. But what music?

230 *Helicanus.* My lord, I hear none.

Pericles. None?
      The music of the spheres! List, my Marina.

Lysimachus. It is not good to cross him; give him way.

---

209 **and thou art** (these words are missing in the text)   218 **should
have been** was said to be   219 **By** at the hands of   220 **justify in
knowledge** affirm in recognition of her claim   225 **beholding** appearance, looks (?)

Pericles. Rarest sounds! Do ye not hear?

Lysimachus.   Music, my lord?

Pericles. I hear most heavenly music.   235
   It nips me unto° list'ning, and thick slumber
   Hangs upon mine eyes. Let me rest.   [*He sleeps.*]

Lysimachus. A pillow for his head. So leave him all.
   Well, my companion friends,
   If this but answer to my just belief,   240
   I'll well remember you.°   [*Exeunt all but Pericles.*]

   Diana [*appears to Pericles in a vision*].

Diana. My temple stands in Ephesus. Hie thee thither,
   And do upon mine altar sacrifice.
   There, when my maiden priests are met together,
   Before the people all,   245
   Reveal how thou at sea didst lose thy wife.
   To mourn thy crosses,° with thy daughter's, call,
   And give them repetition to the life.°
   Perform my bidding, or thou livest in woe;
   Do't, and happy,° by my silver bow!   250
   Awake, and tell thy dream.   [*She vanishes.*]

Pericles. Celestial Dian, goddess argentine,°
   I will obey thee. Helicanus!

   [*Enter Helicanus, Lysimachus, and Marina.*]

Helicanus.   Sir?

Pericles. My purpose was for Tharsus, there to strike
   The inhospitable Cleon; but I am   255
   For other service first: toward Ephesus
   Turn our blown° sails; eftsoons° I'll tell thee why.
   [*To Lysimachus*] Shall we refresh us, sir, upon your
      shore,

---

236 **nips me unto** compels me to   240–41 **If this ... you** i.e., if
Marina is really a princess (and therefore a fit match for me) I shall
well reward you (?) (lines 239–41 read like the reporter's addition and
ought, probably, to be omitted)   247 **crosses** misfortunes   248
repetition to the life lifelike recital   250 **happy** i.e., thou livest
happy   252 **argentine** silvery   257 **blown** inflated by the wind
257 **eftsoons** afterwards, shortly

And give you gold for such provision as
260 Our intents° will need?

Lysimachus. Sir,
With all my heart; and when you come ashore
I have another suit.

Pericles.   You shall prevail,
Were it to woo my daughter; for it seems
265 You have been noble towards her.

Lysimachus. Sir, lend me your arm.

Pericles.   Come, my Marina.
                        Exeunt.

[Scene 2. *The temple of Diana at Ephesus; Thaisa and several maidens standing near the altar, all appareled as priestesses; Cerimon and other inhabitants of Ephesus attending.*

Enter Gower.]

Gower. Now our sands are almost run;
More a little, and then dumb.
This, my last boon, give me—
For such kindness must relieve me—
5 That you aptly° will suppose
What pageantry, what feats, what shows,
What minstrelsy and pretty° din,
The regent made in Mytilin
To greet the King. So he thrived
10 That he is promised to be wived
To fair Marina; but in no wise
Till he° had done his sacrifice,
As Dian bade: whereto being bound,°
The interim, pray you, all confound.°
15 In feathered briefness° sails are filled,

---

260 **intents** purposes   5.2.5 **aptly** readily   7 **pretty** pleasing   12
he i.e., Pericles, whereas in lines 9–10 Lysimachus is referred to   13
bound on his way   14 **all confound** entirely consume   15 **In feathered briefness** with winged speed

And wishes fall out as they're willed.
At Ephesus the temple° see
Our king and all his company.
That he can hither come so soon
Is by your fancies' thankful doom.°   [*Exit.*]   20

[*Scene 3. The temple of Diana. Enter Pericles, with
    Lysimachus, Helicanus, and Marina.*]

Pericles. Hail, Dian! To perform thy just command,
    I here confess myself the King of Tyre;
    Who, frighted from my country, did wed
    At Pentapolis the fair Thaisa.
    At sea in childbed died she, but brought forth   5
    A maid-child called Marina; who, O goddess,
    Wears yet thy silver livery.° She at Tharsus
    Was nursed with Cleon;° whom at fourteen years
    He sought to murder; but her better stars
    Brought her to Mytilene; 'gainst whose shore   10
    Riding,° her fortunes brought the maid aboard us,
    Where, by her own most clear remembrance, she
    Made known herself my daughter.

Thaisa.   Voice and favor!°
    You are, you are—O royal Pericles!   [*Swoons.*]

Pericles. What means the nun? She dies! Help, gentlemen!   15

Cerimon. Noble sir,
    If you have told Diana's altar true,°
    This is your wife.

Pericles.   Reverend appearer,° no.
    I threw her overboard with these very arms.

Cerimon. Upon this coast, I warrant you.

Pericles.   'Tis most certain.   20

17 **Ephesus the temple** the temple of Ephesus   20 **your fancies'
thankful doom** the thanks-deserving verdict of your imaginations
5.3.7 **Wears yet thy silver livery** i.e., is still a virgin   8 **with Cleon**
in Cleon's family   11 **Riding** as we rode at anchor   13 **favor**
looks, face   17 **true** the truth   18 **appearer** one who appears

Cerimon. Look to the lady. O, she's but overjoyed.
    Early one blustering morn this lady
    Was thrown upon this shore. I oped the coffin,
    Found there rich jewels; recovered her,° and placed
      her
    Here in Diana's temple.

25 *Pericles.*   May we see them?

Cerimon. Great sir, they shall be brought you to my house,
    Whither I invite you. Look, Thaisa is
    Recoverèd.

Thaisa.   O, let me look!
    If he be none of mine, my sanctity
30   Will to my sense bend no licentious ear,°
    But curb it, spite of seeing. O, my lord,
    Are you not Pericles? Like him you spake,
    Like him you are. Did you not name a tempest,
    A birth and death?

Pericles.   The voice of dead Thaisa!

35 *Thaisa.* That Thaisa am I, supposèd dead and drowned.

Pericles. Immortal Dian!

Thaisa.   Now I know you better.
    When we with tears parted° Pentapolis,
    The King my father gave you such a ring.
                     [*Points to his ring.*]

Pericles. This, this! No more.° You gods, your present
      kindness
40   Makes my past miseries sports. You shall do well
    That° on the touching of her lips I may
    Melt and no more be seen. O come, be buried
    A second time within these arms.

---

24 **recovered her** restored her to consciousness   29–30 **If he . . . licentious ear** if he is not my husband, my holiness will not listen licentiously to my desire   37 **parted** departed from   39 **No more** i.e., no more confirmation is needed that you are Thaisa (alternatively one could punctuate "No more, you gods!" and interpret: give me no greater happiness, you gods!)   40–41 **You shall do well/That** you would do well if

Marina.   My heart
  Leaps to be gone into my mother's bosom.
                                [*Kneels to Thaisa.*]

Pericles. Look who kneels here: flesh of thy flesh, Thaisa;   *45*
  Thy burden at the sea, and called Marina,
  For she was yielded° there.

Thaisa.   Blest, and mine own!

Helicanus. Hail, madam, and my queen!

Thaisa.   I know you not.

Pericles. You have heard me say, when I did fly from Tyre
  I left behind an ancient substitute.   *50*
  Can you remember what I called the man?
  I have named him oft.

Thaisa.   'Twas Helicanus then.

Pericles. Still confirmation.
  Embrace him, dear Thaisa; this is he.
  Now do I long to hear how you were found;   *55*
  How possibly preserved; and who to thank,
  Besides the gods, for this great miracle.

Thaisa. Lord Cerimon, my lord: this man,
  Through whom the gods have shown their power; that
    can
  From first to last resolve you.°

Pericles.   Reverend sir,   *60*
  The gods can have no mortal officer
  More like a god than you. Will you deliver°
  How this dead queen re-lives?

Cerimon.   I will, my lord.
  Beseech you first, go with me to my house,
  Where shall be shown you all was found with her;   *65*
  How she came placed here in the temple;
  No needful thing omitted.

---

47 **yielded** brought forth   60 **resolve you** free you from doubt   62
deliver relate

Pericles.   Pure Dian,
 I bless thee for thy vision, and will offer
 Nightly oblations to thee. Thaisa,
70   This Prince, the fair betrothèd of your daughter,
 Shall marry her at Pentapolis. And now,
 This ornament
 Makes° me look dismal will I clip to form;°
 And what this fourteen years no razor touched,
75   To grace thy marriage-day I'll beautify.

Thaisa. Lord Cerimon hath letters of good credit,° sir,
 My father's dead.

Pericles. Heavens make a star of him! Yet there, my queen,
 We'll celebrate their nuptials, and ourselves
80   Will in that kingdom spend our following days.
 Our son and daughter shall in Tyrus reign.
 Lord Cerimon, we do our longing stay°
 To hear the rest untold.° Sir, lead's the way.

                                        [*Exeunt.*]

                [*Enter*] *Gower.*

[*Gower.*] In Antiochus and his daughter you have heard
85   Of monstrous lust the due and just reward.
 In Pericles, his queen and daughter, seen,
 Although assailed with fortune fierce and keen,
 Virtue preserved from fell destruction's blast,°
 Led on by heaven, and crowned with joy at last.
90   In Helicanus may you well descry
 A figure of truth, of faith, of loyalty.
 In reverent Cerimon there well appears
 The worth that learnèd charity aye wears.
 For wicked Cleon and his wife, when fame°
95   Had spread his cursèd deed, the honored name
 Of Pericles to rage the city turn,°

---

73 **Makes** which makes 73 **form** proper shape 76 **credit**
trustworthiness 82 **stay** delay 83 **untold** i.e., that is yet untold
88 **blast** blowing up (?) stroke of lightning (?) blight (?) 94 **fame**
report 94–96 **when fame . . . city turn** i.e., holding Pericles' name
in such honor, the citizens are enraged by the report of the murder of
his child

That him and his° they in his palace burn;
The gods for murder seemèd so content
To punish them, although not done but meant.°
So, on your patience evermore attending,   *100*
New joy wait on you! Here our play has ending.

                                        [*Exit.*]

                        FINIS

---

97 **his** i.e., his family   99 **although not done but meant** although
the murder was not carried out but merely intended

Textual Note

The booke of Pericles Prynce of Tyre (i.e., presumably, the promptbook) was entered, together with *Antony and Cleopatra,* in the Stationers' Register on May 20, 1608. Both plays were entered to Edward Blount, and, as neither of them was published by him, it has been supposed that these were "blocking entries," designed to prevent piracy. If so, this proved unsuccessful in the case of *Pericles,* for what is certainly a pirated version of the play was brought out in 1609 by another publisher, Henry Gosson. It proved so popular that a second quarto edition of the play was published by him in the same year, a third appeared in 1611, a fourth in 1619, a fifth in 1630, and a sixth in 1635 (Q2–Q6). As all of these are merely reprints of each other, they have no independent textual authority. *Pericles* was not included in the first collected edition of Shakespeare's plays, the First Folio of 1623, and was not added to any collected edition until the second impression of the Third Folio, in 1664, where it was reprinted from Q6. Varying explanations of the reason for the play's exclusion from the First Folio have been put forward: copyright difficulties; the absence of a good text available to the editors; the fact that the play is only partly Shakespeare's. The last would seem the most probable reason, and is only weakened by the inclusion in the Folio of *Henry VIII.*

The only authoritative text of *Pericles* is therefore that of the First Quarto of 1609 (Q). It is unfortunately a very poor text, as the list below of some hundred and eighty corrupt readings makes immediately apparent. At least some twenty of these would seem to be auditory errors, due to a mishearing by the reporter of the words spoken on the stage (apparent instances of this are found at 1.1.114; 1.2.86; 2.2.30; 4 Chorus 26; 4.4.24; 5.1.228). Most scholars are agreed that the text derives from a report of the play as performed by Shakespeare's company. It is the degree of badness of the report about which they are divided. Some would group it with the "bad" Quartos, such as those of *Romeo and Juliet* and *Hamlet;* others insist that, in spite of numerous corruptions, many of them due to the compositors, the text is basically a good one. My own view is that the Quarto of *Pericles* stands somewhere between the good and the bad Quartos: too faithful to its original to be classed as a "bad" Quarto; too full of errors (both graphic and auditory), of omissions, and additions, to be accounted a good one.

Next to the errors due to mishearing, the reporter seems responsible for a variety of other deficiencies in the text:

1) In the Shakespearian part, after—for the most part impeccably—setting out the verse of 3.1, he apparently found the task too demanding, and wrote out the remaining blank verse as prose; and that is how most of it was set by the compositors. 2) He occasionally seems to have added words, or even whole lines, that can scarcely have been in the Shakespearian original (e.g. 5.1.240–41). 3) There are two scenes in the play in which an evident gap in the report is to be found: in 1.2, where some dialogue between Pericles and Helicanus is evidently missing (before line 38. See gloss on lines 38–48); and in 4.6, where some dialogue between Marina and Lysimachus appears to have been lost (after line 109). In the first case the reporter seems to have made little attempt to fill the gap; in the second case he apparently tried to fill it by reconstructing the missing lines from memory—a memory which must have been exceedingly dim (see Introduction).

But apart from this instance, there is no indication in the text that—as in all the "bad" Quartos proper—the report was a memorial reconstruction. On the contrary—at least in the Shakespearian part—the report must have been made at the theater, probably during repeated visits to performances of the play. Long scenes such as 3.1 and 5.1, in which the text has every appearance of adhering faithfully to the Shakespearian original, cannot have been reported from memory.* In the non-Shakespearian part it is much more difficult to be sure of this, and there are some grounds for supposing that its fidelity to the original text is not as great (notably in 2.1).

The majority of the corrupt readings in Q seem, in fact, to have been introduced not by the reporter but by the compositors

---

*I do not share Philip Edwards' pessimistic view that "we have in these later acts only the *disjecta membra* of once powerful verse," that "we lose sight, presumably forever, of the genuine version of the last three acts, from the opening of III.ii." (*Shakespeare Survey* 5, 1952, 38.)

(Philip Edwards has shown them to have been three in number), who were uniformly slovenly and careless at their task (except in 2.5, which seems to be free from compositorial errors). They misread words, misassigned speeches, occasionally omitted speech prefixes, sometimes set prose as verse, and made only sporadic—and then quite inept—attempts to reestablish Shakespeare's blank verse division. The occasional omission of words within a line (as at 1.4.13), or of a whole line (as, apparently, after line 14 in 4.3 and probably after line 122 in 1.2), would also seem to be attributable to them rather than to the reporter.

The text of this edition diverges on a number of points from preceding ones: 1) Where the Quarto text is manifestly corrupt and we are left with nonsense, I have not hesitated to emend, even when we cannot be sure that the chosen emendation is necessarily the right one and when previous modern editors have retained the original reading. Instances of this are found at 1.4.13; 3.2.84–87; 4.1.11; and 5.1.209. On the other hand, Q readings have, on a very few occasions, been retained where previous editors have emended, e.g. at 3.1.67, where editors have unnecessarily emended Q's "coffin" to "coffer," since the two words were used interchangeably in Shakespeare's day.

2) Like other editors, I have for the most part followed Malone's relineation of Shakespeare's blank verse in the passages where it was set as prose. But occasionally, where better and more Shakespearian verse seemed to result, I have introduced line divisions not found in previous editions, e.g., at 3.3.9–15; 4.1.27–30; 5.1.20–21.

3) Sometimes I have departed from the punctuation adopted by previous editors, and thereby imposed a different meaning on the text. An example of this is found at 1.1.7–12:

> Bring in our daughter, clothèd like a bride,
> For the embracements even of Jove himself;
> At whose conception, till Lucina reigned,
> Nature this dowry gave to glad her presence.
> The senate house of planets all did sit,
> To knit in her their best perfections.

The last four lines are a major crux in the play, and have been much emended and discussed. Most editors put a colon in 1.10, either after "gave" or after "presence" (Q puts a semicolon after "gave" and a comma after "presence"), thus making the planetary influence itself Nature's dowry. But this does not make astrological sense, as a) beauty was considered the gift of Nature, not of the planets; b) planetary influence would be thought of as exerted at birth, not between conception and birth; c) such planetary influence would not be believed to be in the gift of Nature. By punctuating as above, I have separated Nature's gift from that of the planets, interpreting: "between conception and birth Nature gave her her beauty as dowry ('this dowry': the beauty you are about to behold); then, at her birth, the planets bestowed upon her, other, non-physical, perfections over which they have control." The change in punctuation thus restores sense to the passage, and to Nature and the stars what is the due of each.

4) Not infrequently the explanations given in the glosses differ from those of previous editors. For example at 1 Chorus 42 the word "justify," instead of having its modern meaning, is, I believe, one of a series of legal metaphors, and has the archaic meaning of "acquit, absolve" (*Oxford English Dictionary* 4); while at 5.1.220 I believe it has another archaic meaning, that of "affirm" (*Oxford English Dictionary* 5b).

5) I have parted company from previous editors over several stage directions, which they have taken over from Malone's edition, and which seem quite unjustified. There are two chief instances of this. At the opening of 3.2 Q's direction reads, *Enter Lord Cerymon with a seruant.* Malone, followed by most subsequent editors, added to this *and some Persons who have been shipwrecked,* because of Cerimon's line, "Get fire and meat for these poor men" (line 3). But to march several characters onto the stage, only to march them off again a few lines later (line 10) without their having uttered a word, would be a most un-Shakespearian piece of dramaturgy. I have, therefore, adhered to Q's direction, and emended "these" in line 3 to "those," so that Cerimon is speaking of some poor men—there is not the slightest indication that they are shipwrecked—who are never brought on stage, but are merely mentioned in order to display Cerimon in his role of benefactor. The other instance occurs at the opening of 5.1. We are on board Pericles' ship, having just been told by Gower:

> In your supposing once more put your sight:
> Of heavy Pericles think this his bark. (5. Chorus 21–22)

Malone, with evidently little faith in the audience's capacity for supposing, has added to the required direction (*"On board Pericles' Ship,"* etc.), "A Barge lying beside the Tyrian Vessel." At line 10 he introduced the direction, *The Gentlemen and the Two Sailors descend, and go on board the Barge. Enter, from thence, Lysimachus and Lords;* at line 51, *Exit Lord, in the Barge of Lysimachus;* and at line 64, *Enter, from the Barge, Lord, Marina, and a young Lady.* And all these directions have been taken over by subsequent editors. It is not clear how Malone envisaged the staging of this, but he evidently imagined the barge—by means of some piece of stage machinery—departing, and returning a few minutes later with Marina, all in full view of the audience. There is neither need nor warrant for all this, and in the present edition Malone's barge has been silently dropped.

In the Quartos of *Pericles* the text is not divided into acts and scenes. The act division was introduced by the Third Folio, and the scene division by Malone. In the present text spelling and punctuation have been modernized, and speech prefixes expanded and regularized. All additions to Q's stage directions are indicated by square brackets. Purely typographical errors have been silently corrected. All other departures from the Quarto text are listed below, with the adopted reading, in italics, given first, followed by Q's reading, in roman.

1 Chorus   39 *a* of

1.1.8 *For the embracements* For embracements   18 *razed* racte   57 *Antiochus* [Q omits]   112 *our* your   114 *cancel* counsell   121s.d. *Exeunt . . . Pericles* Manet Pericles solus   128 *you're* you   129 *uncomely* vntimley   170 *Antiochus* [Q omits]

1.2.s.d. *Enter Pericles* Enter Pericles with his Lords   4 *Be my* By me   21 *honor him* honour   26 *th' ostent* the stint   31 *am* once   42 *blast* sparke   45 *a peace* peace   66 *you* you yourselfe   83 *Bethought me* Bethought   84 *fears* feare   86 *doubt* doo't   100 *grieve them* griue for them   122 *we'll* will

1.3.1 *Thaliard* [Q omits]   27 *ears it* seas   28 *seas* Sea   30 *Helicanus* [Q omits]   34 *betook* betake

1.4.13 *sorrows cease not* sorrowes   17 *helps* helpers   36 *they* thy   39 *two summers* too sauers   58 *thou* thee   67 *Hath* That   74 *him's* himnes   76–77 *will, what need we fear?/On ground's the lowest,* will, and what they can,/What need wee leaue our grounds the lowest?

2 Chorus   11 *Tharsus* Tharstill   19 *for he strives* for though he striue

22 *Sends word* Sau'd one   24 *hid intent to murder* hid in Tent to murdred [changed in some copies of Q to "had intent to murder"]

2.1.6 *me breath* my breath   12 *What ho, Pilch!* What, to pelch?   17 *fetch thee* fetch'th   31 *devours* deuowre   39 *Third Fisherman.* I. 53 *scratch it* Search   77 *quoth-a* ke-tha   80 *holidays* all day   81 *moreo'er* more; or   89 *your* you   98–99 *is called Pentapolis* I cald Pantapoles   120 *thy crosses* crosses   128 *thee from!—may't* thee, Fame may   154 *rapture* rupture   157 *delightful* delight   164 *equal* a Goale

2.2.4 *daughter* daughter heere   27 *Più per dolcezza che per forza* Pue Per doleera kee per forsa   28 *what's* with   29 *chivalry* Chiually   30 *pompae* Pompey   56 *for* by

2.3.3 *To* I   13 *yours* your   26 *Envied* Enuies   29 *but* not   38 *Yon* You   39 *tells me* tels   44 *son's* sonne like   51 *stored* stur'd   52 *you do* do you   114 *Simonides* [Q omits]

2.4.10 *their* those   33 *gives* giue's   34 *leaves* leaue   35 *death's indeed* death in deed,   36 *this: kingdoms* this Kingdome is   42 *For* Try   57 *endeavor it* endeauour

3 Chorus   2 *the house about* about the house   6 *'fore* from   7 *crickets* Cricket   8 *All* Are   17 *coigns* Crignes   29 *t' appease* t'oppresse   35 *Y-ravishèd* Iranyshed   46 *fortune's mood* fortune mou'd   60 *sea-tossed* seas tost

3.1.7 *Thou stormest* then storme   11 *midwife* my wife   26 *Vie* Vse   52 *custom* easterne   53 *for . . . straight* [In Q this is printed after "meet" in the next line]   60 *in the ooze* in oare   63 *And* The   65 *paper* Taper

3.2.3 *those* these   26 *held* hold   37 *And I can* and can   38 *gives* doth giue   41 *treasure* pleasure   48 *never raze* neuer   57 *bitumed* bottomed   77 *even* euer   84–87 *I have read/Of some Egyptians, who after four hours' death/Have raised impoverished bodies, like to this,/Unto their former health* I heard of an Egiptian that had 9 howers lien dead,/Who was by good applyaunce recouered   89 *still* rough   95 *Breathes* breath

3.3.5 *shafts* shakes   6 *hurt* hant   7 *woundingly* wondringly   29–30 *honor all,/Unscissored* honour,/All vnsisterd   31 *ill* will

3.4.5 *eaning* learning

4 Chorus   10 *her* hie   10 *heart* art   14 *Seeks* Seeke   17 *ripe* right   17 *rite* sight   21 *she* they   26 *night-bird* night bed   32 *With dove of Paphos might the crow* The Doue of Paphos might with the crow   47 *carry* carried

4.1.5–6 *or flaming love thy bosom/Enslave* in flaming, thy loue bosome, enflame   11 *weeping her old nurse's* weeping for her onely Mistresse   19 *is as a* is a   24–25 *favor/Is* fauours   27 *On the sea margent* ere the sea marre it   62 *stem* sterne   92 s.d. *They . . . Marina* Exit   95 *she'll* shee will

4.2.4 *much* much much   19 *they're too* ther's two   48 *It* I   64 *me to* me, for to   72 *was like to* was to   103 *i' the* ethe   110 *crowns of* crownes in 124 *Bawd.* Mari.

4.3.1 *are* ere   6 *A* O   12 *fact* face   17 *pious* impious   27 *prime* prince 28 *sources* courses   31 *distain* disdaine   33 *Marina's* Marianas

4.4.7 *scene* sceanes   8 *i' th' gaps* with gappes   10 *the* thy   12 *life's* liues 16 *Tyre* time   18 *his* this   19 *go on* grone   24 *true-owed* true olde   29 *puts* put   48 *scene* Steare

4.6.s.d. *Enter . . . Boult* Enter Bawdes 3 36 *dignifies* dignities   37 *punk* number   66 *name't* name   84 *aloof* aloft   125 *ways* way   132 *She* He 149 *ways* way   181 *I will* will   190 *women* woman

5 Chorus   8 *silk, twin* Silke Twine,   13 *lost* left   14 *Whence* Where   16 *city's hived* Citie striu'de

5.1.11 *Mytilenian Sailor.* Hell. [changed in some copies of Q to *1. Say.*] 15 *you, sir, to* you to   34–36 *Lys. Yet . . . wish./Hel. Behold . . . Till* yet . . . wish./Lys. Behold . . . person./Hell. Till   36 *night* wight   46 *ports* parts   49 *And with her fellow maid is now* and her fellow maides, now   66 *presence* present   70 *I'd* I do   70 *rarely wed* rarely to wed   71 *Fair one, all* Faire on all   71 *bounty* beautie   73 *feat* fate   81s.d. *They . . . sings* The Song   82 *Marked* Marke   104 *countrywoman* Countrey women 105 *shores? . . . shores* shewes? . . . shewes   109 *such* sucha one   126 *make my senses* make senses   129 *say* stay   143 *thou them? Thy* thou thy 157 *Motion as well?* Motion well,   165–66 *be: My daughter's buried.* be my daughter, buried;   183 *Pericles* Hell.   209–10 *perfect, and thou art/The* perfit, the   210 *life* like   216 *thou art* th' art   228 *doubt* doat 235 *Pericles. I hear most heavenly music* Lys. I heare./Per. Most heauenly Musicke   248–49 *life./Perform* like, or performe   263 *suit* sleight

5.3.6 *who* whom   8 *whom* who   15 *nun* mum   22 *one* in   49 *Pericles.* Hell.   68 *I bless* blesse   69 *Nightly* night   83 [Q has *FINIS* after this line, as well as after line 101]   88 *preserved* preferd   99 *punish them* punish

The Sources of *Pericles*

The chief literary influence discernible in *Pericles* is Sir Philip Sidney's *Arcadia*. It extends not only to structure, action, treatment of character, themes, and atmosphere (see Introduction, pp. 15 ff.), but also to a number of verbal echoes in both parts of the play. In the non-Shakespearian part we find such echoes at 1.1.11–12 ("The senate house of the planets was at no time so set, for the decreeing of perfection in a man"), and 1.1.63–64 ("asking no advise of no thought, but of faithfulnes and courage"); in the Shakespearian part the echoes at 3.2.100–04 ("Her faire liddes then hiding her fairer eyes, seemed unto him sweete boxes of mother of pearle, riche in themselves, but contaning in them farre richer Jewells") and at 4 Ch. 23–25 ("the cloth loking with many eies upon her, & lovingly embracing the wounds she gave it") are less close but still manifest. The most extensive detailed parallel also belongs to Shakespeare's part: Marina's description of her father's behavior during the storm at sea in which she was born,

> My father, as nurse says, did never fear,
> But cried "Good seamen!" to the sailors, galling
> His kingly hands haling ropes
>
> (4.1.52–54)

was closely influenced by the great storm scene in the *Arcadia* (which also seems to have left its mark on the opening scene of *The Tempest*), where we are told of the Princes that they "did in their countenances accuse no point of feare, but encouraging them [the sailors] to doo what might be done (putting their handes to everie most painefull office). . . ." While Shakespeare, as was his wont, has made the description far more vivid and dramatic, he retains the order in which the three ingredients—fearlessness, encouragement, painful office—are mentioned in Sidney's account.

The play has two main sources: Book VIII of John Gower's *Confessio Amantis,* written towards the end of the fourteenth century and printed in 1532 and 1554; and Laurence Twine's prose narrative *The Patterne of Painefull Aduentures,* registered in 1576, and extant in an undated edition and a reprint in 1607. Though both sources were drawn upon throughout the play, the influence of Gower greatly predominates, so that his spirit is fitly chosen to act as the play's presenter. Not only does it usually follow Gower rather than Twine at points in the plot where the two diverge, but it is also much more under the verbal influence of Gower than of Twine. I have been able to find only one clear verbal echo of Twine (at 1 Ch. 18), while there are many such echoes of Gower; at 3.2.107 the whole line is taken over from Gower (lines 1206–07, "Ha, wher am I?/Where is my Lord, what world is this?"), and other verbal echoes are found, for instance, at 1.1.156; 5 Ch. 14; and 5.1.86.

The names, too, are mainly derived from Gower: Dionyza (*Dionise* in Gower, *Dionisiades* in Twine); Lychorida (*Lichorida* in Gower, *Ligozides* in Twine); Thaisa (derived from *Thaise,* Gower's name for Pericles' daughter, called Tharsia in Twine; Pericles' wife is there called *Lucina* and left nameless in Gower); Leonine (in Gower the name of the pander); Helicanus (from a Tyrian messenger called *Hellican* in Gower's text, but *Helicanus* in one of the Latin glosses; *Elinatus* in Twine); Philoten (*Philomacia* in Twine); Thaliard (*Taliart* in Gower, *Taliarchus* in Twine). Cerimon's name is found in both Gower and Twine. The names Pericles, Marina, Simonides, Lysimachus, Cleon, Escanes, Boult are not found in any of the sources. They may have been Shakespeare's inventions, or may have been taken over by him from the old play.

The only exception to the predominance of Gower as a source is found in three scenes in Act 4, where Twine is principally drawn on. In 4.1. Marina's mourning for her dead nurse, and her intended visit to her grave, are entirely based on Twine, there being no mention of this in Gower; the intervention of the pirates is also much closer to Twine. Act 4, scene 3 is entirely based on Twine. There is nothing in Gower to suggest that Cleon in any way disapproves of the murder. In 4.6 the play follows Twine in making Lysimachus visit the brothel as a client, whereas in Gower he is free from any stain, never visits the brothel, and encounters Marina for the first time on board her father's ship.

Readers wishing to study Gower and Twine's share in each scene of the play should consult the headnotes in J. C. Maxwell's edition. Whether Shakespeare went directly to these sources or depended entirely on the old play which he rewrote—if this is, in fact, what happened—is a moot point. But his use of sources elsewhere suggests that he would not have shunned the labor of reading Gower, Twine, and whatever other version of the story came his way; and it seems probable that the verbal echoes of Gower were derived at first hand. The only indication that any other version of the story has been made use of is the word "bitumed" at 3.1.71 and 3.2.57. This word, which is found neither in Gower nor Twine—nor anywhere else in Shakespeare—occurs in its Latin form ("cum bitumine liniri"), in the same context, in the story as told in the *Gesta Romanorum,* the Latin collection of tales, probably compiled around the turn of the thirteenth century, from which Twine's novel, by way of a French translation, is derived.

The Shakespearian part of *Pericles* follows the narrative outline of the sources with a fidelity not found elsewhere in the poet's dramatization of romance material, and this may be taken as a further indication that the scenario is not of his devising. Oddly, the non-Shakespearian part of the play adds more that is not in Gower and Twine than the Shakespearian part. No suggestion in any of the sources is provided for the figure of Helicanus, and his scene with Pericles (1.2) and with the Tyrian Lords (2.4); nor for the tournament scene (2.2; see Introduction, pp. 15–16n.), or for Simonides' faked anger with Pericles (2.5). As G. A. Barker has pointed out in an important article in *English Studies* 44 (1963), the main concern of the author of the first two acts seems to have been with political ideas—with what constitutes the good ruler. But this theme is of little importance in Shakespeare's part of the play. And neither he nor the author of the first two acts betrays much concern with what was Gower's avowed purpose in telling the Apollonius story: to make men see that unlawful love, like Antiochus', leads to disaster, whereas lawful, honorable love, like Apollonius', leads eventually to happiness (lines 1993–2019). Much closer to the heart of Shakespeare's presentation seems Twine's view of the story's events; it is well expressed by the title page of his novel, "The Patterne of painefull Aduentures: Containing the most excellent, pleasant and variable Historie of the strange accidents that befell vnto Prince Apollonius, the Lady Lucina his wife, and Tharsia his daughter. Wherein the vncertaintie of this world, and the fickle state of mans life are liuely described." To this Shakespeare adds a concern with the way in which men endure the blows of Fortune, expressed by means of the parallels and contrasts discussed in the Introduction.

To provide some indication of how Shakespeare dramatized the narrative material of his sources, I have selected for reprinting the lines from Gower corresponding to Act 5, and the chapters in Twine's novel corresponding to Act 4 of the play (where Twine's influence is strongest). In both extracts the spelling and punctuation have been modernized, and typographical errors have been silently corrected. In the lines from Gower I have also modernized some of the word forms (e.g., "their" and "them" for "her" and "hem," "then" for "tho"), except where the demands of the rhyme made this impossible. To prevent the meter from collapsing, I have retained the letter "e" whenever it is sounded (as indicated by a dot placed above it). For the extract from Gower I have followed the text in the 1554 edition, since this is the one the playwright is most likely to have used. Words in square brackets in defective lines have been taken from the MS readings in Macaulay's edition (1901). The text used for the extract from Twine is that of the 1607 reprint.

JOHN GOWER

From Confessio Amantis, Book VIII (1554)

And thus tofore° the wind they drive,	
Till long° and latè they arrive	
With great distress, as it was seen,	
Upon the town of *Mytilene*,	1610
Which was a noble city tho.°	
And happens thilkè° timè so	
The lordès both and the commune°	
The highè feastès of *Neptune*	
Upon the strand at [the] rivage,°	1615
As it was custom and usage,	
Solemnèlichè they besigh.°	
When they this strangè vessel sigh°	
Come in, and has his sail avaled,°	
The town thereof has spoke and taled.°	1620
The lord which of the city was,	
Whose name is *Athenagoras,*	
Was there, and said he woudè see	
What ship it is, and who they be	
That been therein. And after soon,	1625
When that he sigh it was to-doon,	
His bargè was for him arrayed,°	
And he goes forth, and has assayed.°	
He found the ship of great array;°	
But what thing it amountè may?°	1630

1607 **tofore** before   1608 **long** at length   1611 **tho** then   1612
thilke at that very   1613 **commune** common people   1615 **rivage**
shore   1617 **Solemneliche they besigh** they solemnly attended to
1618 **sigh** saw   1619 **avaled** lowered   1620 **taled** talked   1626–27
to-doon,/His barge . . . arrayed all done—that his barge was prepared
for him   1628 **assayed** ventured   1629 **of great array** splendidly
appointed   1630 **it amounte may** may it mean

He sigh they maden heavy cheer;°
But well him thinks by the manner°
That they been° worthy men of blood,
And asketh of them how it stood.
1635   And they him tellen all the case:
How that their lord fordrivè° was,
And what a sorrow that he made,
Of which there may no man him glad.°
He prays that he their lord may see.
1640   But they him told it may not be,
For he lies in so dark a place
That there may no wight° see his face.
But for all that, though them be loath,°
He found the ladder, and down he goth,
1645   And to him spoke, but none answer
Again of him ne° might he hear,
For aught that he can do or sain:
And thus he goes him up again.
      Then was there spoke in many wise
1650   Amongès them that weren wise
Now this, now that, but at the last
The wisdom of the town thus cast:°
That young *Thaisè* was a-sent.°
For if there be amendèment
1655   To gladè with° this woeful king,
She can° so much of every thing
That she shall gladen him anon.
      A messenger for her is gone,
And she came with her harp in hand,
1660   And said them that she wouldè fond°
By all the wayès that she can
To gladè with this sorry° man.
But what he was she wistè nought,°
But all the ship her has besought

1631 **heavy cheer** sad faces 1632 **him . . . manner** it seems to
him by their deportment 1633 **been** are   1636 **fordrive**
driven about 1638 **glad** comfort 1642 **wight** man 1643
them be loath they are unwilling 1645–46 **none . . . ne** no
1652 **cast** determined 1653 **a-sent** sent for 1654–55 **if there
be amendement/To glade with** if there were a way to comfort
1656 **can** understands 1660 **fond** endeavor 1662 **sorry** sorrowful 1663 **wiste nought** knew not at all

That she her wit on him dispend,°   1665
In aunter if° he might amend,
And say it shall be well acquit.°
    When she has understanden it,
She goes her down there as° he lay,
Where that she harpeth many a lay,   1670
And like an angel sang withal.
But he no morè than the wall
Took heed of anything he heard.
    And when she saw that he so fared,°
She falleth with him into words,   1675
And telleth him of sundry bords,°
And asketh him demandès° strange,
Whereof° she made his heartè change,
And to her speech his ear he laid,°
And has marvel of that° she said.   1680
For in proverb and in problem
She spoke, and bade he shouldè deem°
In many a subtle question.
But he for no suggestion
Which toward him she couldè steer°   1685
He wouldè not one word answer;
But, as a madman, at the last
His head weeping away he cast,°
And half in wrath he bade her go.
But yet she wouldè not do so,   1690
But in the darkè forth she goth
Till she him toucheth, and he wroth,°
And after herè with his hand
He smote.° And thus, when she him found
Diseasèd,° courteously she said: 1695
"Avoi,° my lord, I am a maid!
And if ye wistè what I am,
And out of what lineage I came,

1665 **dispend** expend   1666 **In aunter if** on the chance that   1667
acquit requited   1669 **there as** where   1674 **fared** behaved
1676 **bords** jests   1677 **demandes** questions   1678 **Whereof**
whereby   1679 **laid** lent   1680 **has marvel of that** marvels at
what   1682 **deem** judge   1684–85 **for no suggestion . . . steer** despite any suggestion she could put to him   1688 **cast** turned   1692
wroth becomes angry   1693–94 **after . . . smote** thereupon smote
her with his hand   1695 **Diseasèd** vexed   1696 **Avoi** fie

Ye wouldè not be so salvage."°

1700 With that he sobers his courage°
And put away his heavy cheer.°
But of them two° a man may lere°
What is to be so sib° of blood:
None wist of other how it stood,°

1705 And yet the father at the last
His heart upon this maidè cast,
That° he her loveth kindèly°—
And yet he wistè never why,
But all was known ere that° they went.

1710 For God, [which] wot° their whole intent,
Their heartès both anon discloseth.
This king unto this maid opposeth,°
And asketh first what was her name,
And where she learnèd all this game,

1715 And of what kin [that] she was come.
And she, that has her wordès nome,°
Answers and says: "My name is Thaise,
That was some time° well at ease.
In Tharse I was forthdrawn and fed,°

1720 There I learnèd, till I was sped,°
Of that I can.° My father eke°
I not° where that I should him seek;
He was a king, men toldè me.
My mother dreint° [was] in the sea."

1725 From point to point all she him told
That she has long in heartè hold,
And never durstè make her moan
But only to this lord alone,
To whom her heartè can nought hele,°

1730 Turn it to woe, turn it to weal,

1699 **salvage** barbarous   1700 **sobers his courage** calms down
1701 **heavy cheer** sad looks   1702 **of them two** from these two
1702 **lere** learn   1703 **sib** related   1704 **None wist . . . stood**
neither knew who the other was   1707 **That** so that   1707
kindely (1) in accordance with Nature (2) affectionately   1709
ere that before   1710 **wot** knows   1712 **opposeth** asks questions   1716 **his wordes nome** taken in his words   1718 **some
time** formerly   1719 **forthdrawn and fed** brought up and bred
1720 **was sped** reached the desired end   1721 **Of that I can** that
which I know   1721 **eke** moreover   1722 **not** know not   1724
dreint drowned   1729 **hele** conceal

Turn it to good, turn it to harm.
 And he then took her in his arm,
But such a joy as he then made
Was never seen; thus been they glad
That sorry hadden be toforn.°   1735
From this day [forth] Fortune has sworn
To set them upward on the wheel.
So goes the world, now woe, now weal.
 This king has foundè newè grace,°
So that out of his darkè place   1740
He goes him up into the light,
And with him came that sweetè wight,°
His daughter *Thaise,* and forth anon
They both into the cabin gon
Which was ordainèd° for the king.   1745
And there he did off all his thing,°
And was arrayèd royally.
And out he came all openly,
Where *Athenagoras* he found,
[The] which was lord of all the land.   1750
He prays the king to come and see
His castle both and his city—
And thus they go forth all in fere,°
This king, this lord, this maiden dear.
This lord then made them richè feast,   1755
With everything which was honest,°
To pleasè with this worthy king:
There lacketh him no manner thing.°
By yet, for all his noble array,°
Wifeless he was unto that day,   1760
As he that yet was° of young age.
 So fell there into his courage°
The lusty° woe, the gladè pain
Of lovè, which no man restrain
Yet never might as now tofore.°   1765

1735 **That sorry hadden be toforn** that had been sorrowful before
1739 **newe grace** renewed good fortune 1742 **wight** creature
1745 **ordainèd** set aside 1746 **did off all his thing** removed all his
apparel 1753 **in fere** together 1756 **honest** honorable 1758 **no
manner thing** nothing of any kind 1759 **array** state 1761 **As he
that yet was** being yet 1762 **courage** heart 1763 **lusty** pleasant
1765 **as now tofore** up to now

This lordè thinks all this world lore°
But if° the king will do him grace.
He waiteth time, he waiteth place,
Him thought° his heartè would to-break°
1770 Till he may to this maidè speak
And to her father eke also
For marriage. And it fell so
That all was done right as he thought.
His purpose to an end he brought.
1775 She wedded him as for her lord—
Thus been they all of one accord.
When all was done right as they would,
The king unto his sonnè told
Of *Tharsè* thilkè traitery;°
1780 And said how in his company
His daughter and himselven eke
Shall go vengeancè for to seek.
    The shippès werè ready soon,
And when they saw it was to-doon,°
1785 Withoutè let of any went,°
With sail updrawè° forth they went
Towardè *Tharse* upon the tide.
But he that wot what shall betide,
The highè God, which would him keep,°
1790 When that this king was fast asleep
By nightès time, he has him bid
To sail into another stead:°
To *Ephesum* he bade him draw,
And, as it was that timè law,
1795 He shall do there his sacrifice.
And eke he bade in allè wise°
That in the temple, amongst all,
His fortune, as it is befall,°
Touching his daughter and his wife,
1800 He shall beknowe,° upon his life.

1766 **lore** lost   1767 **But if** unless   1769 **Him thought** it
seemed to him   1769 **to-break** break utterly   1779 **Of Tharse
thilke traitery** of that treachery at Tharsus   1784 **to-doon** completely done   1785 **Withoute let of any** went without any hindrance in their passage   1786 **updrawe** hoist   1789 **keep**
preserve   1792 **stead** place   1796 **in alle wise** fully   1798 **is
befall** has happened   1800 **beknowe** make known

    The king of this avision°
Has great imagination°
What thing it signifyè may;
And natheless,° when it was day,
He bade cast anchor and abode;°   *1805*
And while that he on anchor rode,
The wind, that was toforè strange,°
Upon the point began to change,
And turneth thither as° it should.
Then knew he well that God it would,°   *1810*
And bade the master make him yare,°
Tofore the wind for he would fare°
To *Ephesum,* and so he did.
And when he came into the stead
Where as he shouldè land, he landeth   *1815*
With all the haste he may, and fondeth
To shapen him° in such a wise
That he may by the morrow arise
And do after the mandèment°
Of him which has him thither sent.   *1820*
And, in the wisè that he thought,°
Upon the morrow so he wrought.
His daughter and his son he nom,°
And forth unto the temple he com
With a great rout in company,°   *1825*
His giftès for to sacrify.°
    The citizens then hearden say
Of such a king that came to pray
Unto *Dianè,* the goddess,
And, left° all other business,   *1830*
They comen thither for to see
The king and the solemnity.

1801 **avision** vision 1802 **Has great imagination** speculates
much 1804 **natheless** nevertheless 1805 **abode** waited 1807
tofore strange before unfriendly 1809 **thither as** in the direction
in which 1810 **it would** wanted it 1811 **make him yare** make
himself ready 1812 **Tofore . . . fare** for he wanted to sail before the
wind 1816–17 **fondeth/To shapen him** endeavors to dispose himself 1819 **mandement** command 1821 **in the wise that he
thought** in the way he intended 1823 **nom** took 1825 **With a
great rout in company** accompanied by a great troop 1826 **His
giftes for to sacrify** in order to offer up his gifts 1830 **left** having
left

    With worthy knightès environed,
    The king himself has abandoned°
1835   To the temple in good intent.°
    The door is up, and in he went;
    Whereas° with great devotion°
    Of holy contemplation
    Within his heart he made his shrift.
1840   And after that a richè gift
    He offers with great reverence;
    And there, in open audience°
    Of them that stooden then about,
    He told them, and declareth out,°
1845   His hap,° such as him is befall;
    There was nothing forgot of all.
    His wife, as it was God's grace,
    Which was professèd° in the place,
    As she that was° abessè there,
1850   Unto his tale has laid° her ear.
    She knew the voice and the visage:
    For pure joy as in a rage
    She straught° [un]to him all at ones,
    And fell a-swoon upon the stones
1855   Whereof the temple floor was paved.
    She was anon with water layed,
    Till she came to herself again,
    And thennè she began to sain:
    "Ah, blessèd be the highè sond°
1860   That I may see my husèband,
    Which whilom° he and I were one!"
    The king with that knew her anon,
    And took her in his arm and kissed;
    And all the town this soon it wist.
1865   Then was there joyè manifold,
    For every man this tale has told
    As for miracle,° and were glad.

1834 **himself has abandoned** has betaken himself   1835 **in good intent** for a worthy purpose   1837 **Whereas** where   1837 **devotion** devoutness, reverence   1842 **audience** hearing   1844 **out** fully   1845 **hap** fortunes   1848 **was professèd** had been received into the religious order   1849 **As she that was** being   1850 **laid** lent   1853 **straught** went   1859 **sond** decree   1861 **whilom** once   1867 **As for miracle** as being a miracle

But never man such joyè made
As does the king, which has his wife.
And when men heard how that her life   *1870*
Was savèd, and by whom it was,
They wondered all of such a case:°
Through all the land arose the speech°
Of Master *Cerimon,* the leech,
And of the curè which he did.   *1875*
The king himself then has [him] bid,
And eke his queenè forth with him,
That he the town of *Ephesim*
Will leave and go where as they be:
For never man of his degree   *1880*
Has done to them so muchel° good.
And he his profit understood,
And granteth with them for to wend.°
And thus they maden there an end,
And tooken leave, and go to ship   *1885*
With all the wholè fellowship.°

1872 **They wondered . . . case** they were all amazed by such a happening   1873 **speech** talk   1881 **muchel** much   1883 **with them
for to wend** to go with them   1886 **fellowship** company

LAURENCE TWINE

From The Pattern of Painful Adventures, Chapters XI–XV (1607)

CHAPTER XI

How after the death of Ligozides, the nurse, Dionisiades, envying at the beauty of Tharsia, conspired her death, which should have been accomplished by a villain of the country.

Tharsia much lamented the death of Ligozides, her nurse, and caused her body to be solemnly buried not far off, in a field without the walls of the city, and mourned for her a whole year following. But when the year was expired, she put off her mourning attire, and put on her other apparel, and frequented the schools, and the study of liberal sciences as before. And whensoever she returned from school, she would receive no meat before she had visited her nurse's sepulcher, which she did daily, entering thereunto, and carrying a flagon of wine with her; where she used to abide a space, and to call upon her father and mother. Now on a day it fortuned that, as she passed through the street with Dionisiades and her companion Philomacia, the people, beholding the beauty and comeliness of Tharsia, said: "Happy is that father that hath Tharsia to his daughter, but her companion that goeth with her is foul and evil favored." When Dionisiades heard Tharsia commended, and her own daughter Philomacia so dispraised, she returned home wonderful wroth, and, withdrawing herself into a solitary place, began thus secretly to discourse of the matter: "It is now fourteen years since Apollonius, this foolish girl's father, departed from hence, and he never sendeth letters for her, nor any remembrance unto her; whereby I conjecture that he is dead. Ligozides, her nurse, is departed, and there is nobody now of whom I should stand in fear. And therefore I will now slay her, and dress up mine own daughter in her apparel and jewels." When she had thus resolved herself upon this wicked purpose, in the meanwhile there came home one of their country villains, called Theophilus, whom she called, and said thus unto him: "Theophilus, my trusty friend, if ever thou look for liberty, or that I should do thee pleasure, do so much for me as to slay Tharsia." Then said Theophilus: "Alas, mistress, wherein hath that innocent maiden offended, that she should be slain?" Dionisiades answered: "She innocent? Nay, she is a wicked wretch, and therefore thou shalt not deny to fulfill my request, but do as I command thee, or else I swear, by the gods, thou shalt dearly repent it." "But how shall I best do it, mistress?" said the villain. She answered: "She hath a custom, as soon as she returneth home from school, not to eat meat before that she have gone into her nurse's sepulcher, where I would have thee stand ready, with a dagger drawn in thine hand, and when she is come in, gripe her by the hair of the head, and so slay her. Then take her body and cast it into the sea, and when thou hast so done, I will make thee free, and besides reward thee liberally." Then took the villain a dagger, and girded himself therewith, and with an heavy heart and weeping eyes went forth toward the grave, saying within himself: "Alas, poor wretch that I am, alas, poor Theophilus, that canst not deserve thy liberty but by shedding of innocent blood." And with that he went into the grave, and drew his dagger, and made him ready for the deed. Tharsia was now come from school, and made haste unto the grave with a flagon of wine, as she was wont to do, and entered within the vault. Then the villain rushed violently upon her, and caught her by the hair of the head, and threw her to the ground. And while he was now ready to stab her with the dagger, poor, silly Tharsia, all amazed casting up her eyes upon him, knew the villain, and, holding up her hands, said thus unto him: "O Theophilus, against whom have I so grievously offended that I must die therefore?" The villain answered: "Thou hast not offended, but thy father hath, which left thee behind him in Stranguilio's house with so great a treasure in money and princely ornaments." "O," said the maiden, "would God he had not done so! But I pray thee, Theophilus, since there is no hope for me to escape my life, give me licence to say my prayers before I die." "I give thee licence," said the villain. "And I take God to record that I am constrained to murder thee against my will."

CHAPTER XII

How certain pirates rescued Tharsia when she should have been slain, and carried her unto the city Machilenta, to be sold among other bondslaves.

As fortune, or rather the providence of God, served, while Tharsia was devoutly making her prayers, certain pirates, which were come aland and stood under the side of an hill, watching for some prey, beholding an armed man offering violence unto a maiden, cried unto him and said: "Thou cruel tyrant, that maiden is our prey and not thy victory, and therefore hold thine hands from her, as thou lovest thyself!" When the villain heard that, he ran away as fast as he could, and hid himself behind the sepulcher. Then came the pirates and rescued Tharsia, and carried her away to their ships, and hoist sails and departed. And the villain returned home to his mistress, and said unto her: "That which you commanded me to do is dispatched, and therefore now I think it good that you put on a mourning garment, and I also, and let us counterfeit great sorrow and heaviness in the sight of all the people, and say that she died of some grievous disease." But Stranguilio himself consented not to this treason, but so soon as he heard of the foul mischance, being as it were all amort, and mazed with heaviness and grief, he clad himself in mourning array, and lamented that woeful case, saying: "Alas, in what mischief am I wrapped, what might I do or say herein? The father of this maiden delivered this city from the peril of death; for this city's sake he suffered shipwreck, lost his goods, and endured penury. And now he is requited with evil for good. His daughter, which he committed unto me to be brought up, is now devoured by a most cruel lioness. Thus I am deprived, as it were, of mine own eyes, and forced to bewail the death of an innocent, and am utterly spoiled through the fierce biting of a most venomous serpent." Then casting his eyes up towards heaven, "O God," said he, "thou knowest that I am innocent from the blood of silly Tharsia, which thou hast to require at Dionisiades' hands." And therewithal he looked towards his wife, saying: "Thou wicked woman, tell me, how hast thou made away Prince Apollonius' daughter? Thou that livest both to the slander of God and man." Dionisiades answered in many words, evermore excusing herself, and moderating the wrath of Stranguilio, she counterfeited a feigned sorrow by attiring herself and her daughter in mourning apparel, and in dissembling tears before the people of the city, to whom she said: "Dearly beloved friends and citizens of Tharsus: for this cause we do weep and mourn in your sight, because the joy of our eyes, and staff of our old age, the maiden Tharsia is dead, leaving unto us bitter tears and sorrowful hearts. Yet have we already taken order for her funerals, and buried her according to her degree." These words were right grievous unto the people, and there was almost none that let not [fall] some tears for sorrow. And they went with one accord unto the marketplace, whereas her father's image stood, made of brass, and erected also another unto her there, with this inscription: *Unto the virgin Tharsia in lieu of her father's benefits, the citizens of Tharsus have erected this monument.*

CHAPTER XIII

How the pirates which stole away Tharsia brought her to the city Machilenta, and sold her to a common bawd, and how she preserved her virginity.

The meantime, while these troubles were at Tharsus, the pirates, being in their course upon the sea, by benefit of a happy wind arrived at Machilenta, and came into the city. Now had they taken many more men and women besides Tharsia, whom they brought all ashore, and set them to sell as slaves for money. Then came there sundry to buy such as they lacked for their purposes, amongst whom a most vile man-bawd, beholding the beauty and tender years of Tharsia, offered money largely for her. Howbeit Athanagoras, who was prince of the same city, beholding likewise the noble countenance and regarding the great discretion of the maiden in communication, outbid the bawd, and offered for her ten sestercies of gold. But the bawd, being loath to lose so commodious a prey, offered twenty. "And I will give thirty," said Athanagoras. "Nay, I will give forty," said the bawd. "And I fifty," quoth Athanagoras. And so they continued in outbidding one another until the bawd offered an hundred sestercies of gold, to be payed ready down. "And whosoever will give more," said he, "I will yet give ten sestercies more than he." Then Prince Athanagoras thus bethought him secretly in his mind: "If I should contend with the bawd to buy her at so high a price, I must needs sell other slaves to pay for her, which

were both loss and shame unto me. Wherefore I will suffer him
to buy her, and when he setteth her to hire, I will be the first
man that shall come unto her, and I will gather the flower of her
virginity; which shall stand me in as great stead as if I had
bought her." Then the bawd paid the money, and took the
maiden and departed home. And when he came into his house,
he brought her into a certain chapel, where stood the idol of Priapus, made of gold, and garnished with pearls and precious
stones. This idol was made after the shape of a man, with a
mighty member, unproportionable to the body, always erected,
whom bawds and lechers do adore, making him their god, and
worshipping him. Before this filthy idol he commanded Tharsia
with reverence to fall down. But she answered: "God forbid,
master, that I should worship such an idol. But sir," said she,
"are you a Lapsatenian?" "Why askest thou?" said the bawd. "I
ask," quoth she, "because the Lapsatenians do worship Priapus." This spake she of simplicity, not knowing what he was.
"Ah, wretch," answered he, "knowest thou not that thou art
come into the house of a covetous bawd?" When Tharsia heard
that, she fell down at his feet and wept, saying: "O master, take
compassion upon my virginity, and do not hire out my body for
so vile a gain!" The bawd answered: "Knowest thou not that
neither bawd nor hangman do regard tears or prayers?" Then
called he unto him a certain villain, which was governor over
his maids, and said unto him: "Let this maiden be decked in virgin's apparel, precious and costly, and write this title upon her:
whosoever deflow'reth Tharsia shall pay ten pieces of gold; and
afterward she shall be common unto the people for one piece at
a time." The villain fulfilled his master's commandment, and
the third day after that she was bought she was with great
solemnity conducted through the street with music, the bawd
himself with a great multitude going before, and so conveyed
unto the brothel house. When she was come thither, Athanagoras, the prince, disguising his head and face because he would
not be known, came first in unto her. Whom when Tharsia saw,
she threw herself down at his feet and said unto him: "For the
love of God, gentleman, take pity on me, and by the name of
God I adjure and charge you that you do no violence unto me,
but bridle your lust, and hearken unto my unhappy estate, and
consider diligently from whence I am sprung. My father was
poor Apollonius, Prince of Tyrus; whom force constrained to
forsake his own country. My mother was daughter to Altistrates,

King of Pentapolis, who died in the birth of me, poor wretch, upon the sea. My father also is dead, as was supposed, which caused Dionisiades, wife to Stranguilio of Tharsus—to whom my father committed me, of special trust, to be brought up, being but an infant—envying mine estate, and thirsting after my wealth, to seek my death by the hands of a villain; which had been accomplished—and I would to God it had before I had seen this day—but that I was suddenly taken away by the pirates, which sold me unto this filthy bawd." With these or suchlike words declared she her heavy fortune, eftsoons sobbing and bursting out into streams of tears, that for extreme grief she could scarcely speak. When she had in this manner uttered her sorrow, the good Prince, being astonished, and moved with compassion, said unto her: "Be of good cheer, Tharsia, for surely I rue thy case; and I myself have also a daughter at home, to whom I doubt that the like chances may befall."

And when he had so said, he gave her twenty pieces of gold, saying: "Hold here a greater price or reward for thy virginity than thy master appointed. And say as much unto others that come unto thee as thou hast done unto me, and thou shalt withstand them." Then Tharsia fell on her knees, and weeping said unto him: "Sir, I give you most hearty thanks for your great compassion and courtesy, and most heartily I beseech you upon my knees not to descry unto any that which I have said unto you." "No, surely," answered Athanagoras, "unless I tell it unto my daughter, that she may take heed, when she cometh unto the like years, that she fall not into the like mishap." And when he had so said, he let fall a few tears and departed. Now as he was going, he met with another pilgrim that with like devotion came for to seek the same saint; who demanded of him how he liked of the maiden's company. "Truly," answered Athanagoras, "never better of any." Then the young man, whose name was Aportatus, entered into the chamber, and the maiden, after the manner, shut the door to, and Athanagoras listened at the window. Then said Aportatus unto Tharsia: "How much did the Prince give unto thee?" She answered: "Forty pieces of gold." Then said he: "Receive here of me an whole pound weight of gold." The Prince, which heard this talk, thought then in his mind: "The more that you do give her, the more she will weep, as thinking that you would look for recompense, the which she meaneth not to perform."

The maiden received the money, and fell down on her knees at his feet, and declared unto him all her estate with tears, as is before showed. When Aportatus heard that, he was moved with compassion, and he took her up from the ground, saying: "Arise, Lady Tharsia, we are all men, and subject to the like chances." And therewithal he departed. And when he came forth, he found Prince Athanagoras before the door, laughing at him, to whom he said: "Is it well done, my liege, thus to delude a poor gentleman? Was there none to whom you might begin in tears but unto me only?" Then communed they further of the matter, and sware an oath between themselves that they would not bewray these words unto any. And they withdrew themselves aside into a secret place, to see the going in and coming forth of other, and they saw many which went in and gave their money, and came forth again weeping. Thus Tharsia, through the grace of God, and fair persuasions, preserved her body undefiled.

CHAPTER XIV

How Tharsia withstood a second assault of her virginity, and by what means she was preserved.

When night was come, the master bawd used always to receive the money which his women had got by the use of their bodies the day before. And when it was demanded of Tharsia, she brought him the money, as the price and hire of her virginity. Then said the bawd unto her: "It is well done, Tharsia. Use diligence henceforth, and see that you bring me thus much money every day." When the next day was passed also, and the bawd understood that she remained a virgin still, he was offended, and called unto him the villain that had charge over the maids, and said unto him: "Sirrah, how chanceth it that Tharsia remaineth a virgin still? Take her unto thee, and spoil her of her maidenhead, or be sure thou shalt be whipped." Then said the villain unto Tharsia: "Tell me, art thou yet a virgin?" She answered: "I am, and shall be as long as God will suffer me." "How, then," said he, "hast thou gotten all this money?" She answered, with tears, falling down upon her knees: "I have declared mine estate, humbly requesting all men to take compassion on my virginity." And now likewise, falling then down at his feet also, "Take pity on me, good friend, which am a poor captive, and the daughter of a king, and do not defile me!" The villain answered: "Our master the bawd is very covetous and greedy of money, and therefore I see no means for thee to continue a virgin." Whereunto Tharsia replied: "I am skillful in the liberal sciences, and well exercised in all studies, and no man singeth or playeth on instruments better than I. Wherefore, bring me into the marketplace of the city, that men may hear my cunning. Or let the people propound any manner of questions, and I will resolve them. And I doubt not but by this practice I shall get store of money daily." When the villain heard this device, and bewailed the maiden's mishap, he willingly gave consent thereto, and brake with the bawd, his master, touching that matter, who, hearing of her skill, and hoping for the gain, was easily persuaded.

Now when she was brought into the marketplace, all the people came thronging to see and hear so learned a virgin, before whom she uttered her cunning in music, and her eloquence in speaking, and answered manifestly unto all such questions as were propounded unto her with such perspicuity that all confessed themselves fully satisfied, and she won great fame thereby, and gained great sums of money. But as for Prince Athanagoras, he had evermore a special regard in the preservation of her virginity, none otherwise than if she had been his own daughter, and rewarded the villain very liberally for his diligent care over her.

CHAPTER XV

How Apollonius, coming to Tharsus and not finding his daughter, lamented her supposed death; and, taking ship again, was driven by a tempest to Machilenta, where Tharsia was.

Return we now again unto Prince Apollonius, who, while these things were doing at Machilenta, when the fourteenth year was expired, arrived at Tharsus, and came into the city unto the house of Stranguilio and Dionisiades, with whom he had left his young daughter Tharsia. Whom when Stranguilio beheld and knew, he ran hastily unto his wife Dionisiades and said: "Thou reportedst that Prince Apollonius was dead, and lo now, where he is come to require his daughter! What shall we now do, or say unto him?" Then cried she out: "Alas, wretched husband and wife that we are! Let us quickly put on our mourning attire, and shed forth tears, and he will believe us that his daughter died a natural death." And when they had appareled themselves, they came forth unto Apollonius, who, seeing them in mourning attire, said unto them: "My trusty friends Stranguilio and Dionisiades, why weep ye thus at my coming? And tell me, I pray you—which I rather believe—whether these tears be not rather mine than yours." "Not so, my lord Apollonius," answered the wicked woman. "And I would to God some other body and not mine husband or I were enforced to tell you these heavy tidings, that your dear daughter Tharsia is dead." When Apollonius heard that word, he was suddenly cut to the heart, and his flesh trembled that he could scarce stand on his legs. And long time he stood amazed, with his eyes intentively fixed on the ground. But at length, recovering himself and taking fresh breath, he cast up his eyes upon her and said: "O woman, if my daughter be dead, as thou sayest she is, is the money also and apparel perished with her?" She answered: "Some is, and some yet remaineth. And as for your daughter, my lord, we were always in good hope that when you came you should have found her alive and merry. But to the intent you may the better believe us concerning her death, we have a sufficient witness. For our citizens, being mindful of your benefits bestowed upon them, have erected unto her a monument of brass by yours, which you may go see if you please." And when she had so said, she brought forth such money, jewels, and apparel which it pleased her to say were remaining of Tharsia's store. And Apollonius, believing indeed that she was dead, said unto his servants: "Take up this stuff and bear it away unto the ships, and I will go walk unto my daughter's monument." And when he came there, he read the superscription in manner as above written, and he fell suddenly, as it were, into an outrageous affection, and cursed his own eyes, saying: "O, most cruel eyes, why can you not yield forth sufficient tears, and worthily bewail the death of my dear daughter?" And with that word, with grief and extreme sorrow, he fell into a swoon; from which so soon as ever he was once revived, immediately he went unto the ships unto his servants, unto whom he said: "Cast me, I beseech you, into the very bottom of the sea. For I have no joy of my life, and my desire is to yield up my ghost in the water." But his servants used great persuasions with him to assuage his sorrow, wherein presently they some deal prevailed, as they might in so woeful a case. And partly the time, which is a curer of all cares, continually mitigated some part of the grief. And he, espying the wind to serve well for their departure, hoist up sail and bid the land adieu. They had not thus sailed long in their course but the wind came about to a contrary quarter, and blew so stiffly that it troubled both sea and ships. The rain fell fiercely overhead, the sea wrought wondrously under the ship, and, to be short, the tempest was terrible for the time. It was then thought best in that extremity to strike sail and let the helm go, and to suffer the ship to drive with the tide, whither it should please God to direct it. But as joy evermore followeth heaviness, so was this sharp storm occasion of a sweet meeting of the father with the daughter, as in process hereafter it shall appear. For while Apollonius' ship runneth thus at random, it striketh upon the shore of the city Machilenta, where at that present his daughter Tharsia remained.

Commentaries

G. WILSON KNIGHT

From The Crown of Life

Pericles might be called a Shakespearian morality play. The epilogue asserts as much, though it does no justice to the more important scenes, which so tower above the rest and which it would be a great error to relate too sharply to any known type of drama. These, whatever we think of them, are spontaneous, new creations. And yet, in spite of their superiority, they cannot be isolated: *Pericles* is too thoroughly organic a play for that, with all its running coherences of idea, image, and event. These demand a short retrospective comment.

There are the continual references to "fortune" personified at 4.4.48 as "Lady Fortune" (cp. *Timon of Athens*, 1.1.64), variously entwined with the sequence of sad and happy adventures and used rather as in *Antony and Cleopatra* with strong suggestion of "chance." The gods are referred to as in *King Lear*, though with a greater sense of their reality, beneficence, and intervention; as in "you most potent gods" (3.2.63); the "powers that gives heaven countless eyes to view men's acts" (1.1.73–74); "we cannot but obey the powers above us" (3.3.9–10). The "most high gods" quickly punish, with "heaven's shaft," the wicked (2.4.3,

From *The Crown of Life* by G. Wilson Knight. 2nd ed. London: Methuen & Co., Ltd., 1948. Reprinted by permission of Methuen & Co., Ltd., and Barnes & Noble, Inc.

16), but are otherwise conceived as kindly (2.3.61). Such deities counter the chancelike concept of "fortune." Somewhat sterner are the Destinies, conventionally supposed as cutting the thread of life (1.2.108), and also the typically Shakespearian conception:

> Time's the king of men;
> He's both their parent and he is their grave.   (2.3.46–47)

Religious reverence crystallizes into the personal deities of Neptune and Diana; the first to be related to our voyages and tempests, the latter of high importance at the end.

To pass to the more human essences. There are a number of variations concerning true and false value played on riches (gold, silver and jewels) following, as we have noted, the use of riches in *The Merchant of Venice* and *Timon of Athens*. Now in *Timon of Athens* the gold of the later action may be related to the aristocratic essence, the spiritual fineness of Timon himself; and something similar happens in *Pericles*. For our glitter of jewels and other riches blends naturally into the play's royalism, where again we have a divergence of directions, with distinctions drawn between the wicked and good princes (Antiochus, Cleon and Dionyza against Pericles and Simonides); the former tyrannous (1.2.103) and regarding conscience as unworthy of noble blood (4.3.23–25); the others, chivalrous and relating princely honor to charity (1.4.85–95; 2.3.24–26; 61–63).

Here we may approach a new subtlety creeping into Shakespeare's royalism: his emphasis on the discovery (by the owner or someone else) of a child's royal birth (in Marina,* Perdita, Guiderius, Arviragus, Miranda). Royal blood is felt mystically, spiritually, with Marina as a palace "for the crowned Truth to dwell in" (5.1.125). We are reminded of Wordsworth's child forgetting "the glories he hath known and that imperial palace whence he came" (in the *Ode on Intimations of Immortality*); and of Coleridge's remarkable play *Zapolya,* specifically written on the pattern of Shakespeare's last plays, where the spiritual connotations of the discovery of royal blood are vividly felt. Where the later poets witness a "spiritual" reality, Shakespeare

---

*Professor D. G. James, in *Scepticism & Poetry,* has written interestingly on the discovery of Marina's royal birth.

works from firmer basis of Tudor royalism; but he invariably develops that, as in his manipulation of Timon's innate aristocracy, into something more spiritual, chivalric, or Christian, with stress on generosity and humility (as with Theseus in *A Midsummer Night's Dream*). This development reaches its finest results in his semi-mystic approach to the royal children from *Pericles* to *Henry VIII;* and may delicately be referred to some yet more universal intimation concerning the royal birth and destinies of the individual human soul, widely understood; for the royal protagonist of drama is always primarily an objectification of the spectator's individual self; his "I"; and certainly in *Pericles* the greatest moments are weighted by a sense of man's universal destiny. So, whatever our political principles, we find the royalistic image radiating its lines of force; and it is precisely this princeliness that renders the rich, kindly and even humorous (3.2.54–56) Lord Cerimon, on whom sits the aristocratic luster of Timon, more attractive than his great descendant Prospero, who, though of ducal status, is more coldly conceived. Indeed, both *Pericles* and *The Winter's Tale* hold a certain freshness that the later, more coherent, play lacks. Something is lost as miracle becomes assured.

These imaginative strands are all Shakespearian favorites; but their use is new. They are newly actualized: what was formerly imagery becomes dramatic fact. The old image of storm gives us "enter Pericles, wet"; that of bark-in-storm becomes a stage-setting, with Pericles "on shipboard"; the old association love=jewel is built into a personal sense of Thaisa's and Marina's jewel-like worth; the love-image of jewel-thrown-into-the-sea (see *The Shakespearian Tempest,* pp. 64–69; 222–23) becomes Thaisa in her jewel-stored coffin (like Portia's picture in the casket) thrown overboard. Shakespeare's continual reference to pagan deities works up to the "feast of Neptune" and actual appearance of Diana. Finally, music, for so long a dramatic accompaniment to scenes of love and reunion, becomes an active force in Cerimon's magic and explicitly mystical in Pericles' "music of the spheres" (5.1.232). A similar process develops the Friars of *Romeo and Juliet* and *Much Ado about Nothing,* both plot manipulators within their dramas with a tendency to arrange false appearances of death, into the miracle-working Cerimon taking on the plot manipulation of life itself and restoring the dead. *Pericles* is the result of no sudden vision; it is Shakespeare's total poetry on the brink of self-knowledge.

It is accordingly not strange that art, as such, should be given greater emphasis than hitherto; in stage direction, ceremonious procession (as of the tourneying knights) and ritual setting; in dumb show; in monumental inscriptions, and metaphors; in musical accomplishment (Pericles' and Marina's); in Marina's dancing and decorative needlework. The arts least emphasized in Shakespeare, the static arts of design, assume a new prominence, giving us the exquisite descriptions of Marina in monumental terms. Shakespeare's drama is aspiring towards the eternal harmony and the eternal pattern.

The new excellences are bought at a cost. Pericles himself is a passive figure, quite unlike Shakespeare's usual dynamic protagonists. He himself does nothing crucial; his fall is purely an awareness of evil, like Hamlet's, his good acts are perfunctorily set down, his repentance in sackcloth and unshaven hair a repentance for no guilt of his own but rather for the fact of mortality in a harsh universe. He is here for things to happen to and forges little or nothing for himself; his most original actions are a series of escapes or departures; he is too humble to press his suit for Thaisa. He is, indeed, less a realized person than man, almost "every man," in the morality sense, as the epilogue suggests. We can, however, improve on the epilogue by seeing the whole as a panorama of life from adolescent fantasy and a consequent fall, through good works to a sensible and fruitful marriage, and thence into tragedy, with a reemergence beyond mortal appearances into some higher recognition and rehabilitation. The medium is myth or parable, supposedly, of course, realistic: we must not expect death to be totally negated; Thaisa's father dies (5.3.77); Cerimon cannot restore everyone (3.2.7). But, as in parable always, it is the central person, or persons, that count; and here the deaths of Thaisa and Marina are shown, in the fiction, as false, though with an intensity surpassing fiction.

JOHN F. DANBY

From Poets on Fortune's Hill

Shakespeare's late verse is a poetry of feeling. For all its richness it is simpler than the verse of the middle period:

> A terrible child-bed hast thou had, my dear;
> No light, no fire; the unfriendly elements
> Forgot thee utterly; nor have I time
> To give thee hallow'd to thy grave, but straight
> Must cast thee, scarcely coffin'd, to the ooze,
> Where, for a monument upon thy bones,
> And aye-remaining lamps, the belching whale
> And humming water must o'erwhelm thy corpse,
> Lying with simple shells.

(3.1.56–64)

Dr. Tillyard has referred to "that simple, yet strained, remote and magical note that sounds from time to time in the last plays." The note is sounded, though, very often, together with others—others that are strained and violent, strained in the suddenness of their contrasts. "Lying with simple shells" gives one note: the adjective dissolving disdain in nostalgic envy. "Belching whale" gives another—the monstrous, indifferent, and bestial life, and yet the mindless, contented coarseness of the creature. "Humming water" gives yet another—the dizzying depths through which we sink to the "simple shells," the loss of consciousness, the sound of the distant storm confused to a blind murmur, then the water itself humming as it spins in its vortices, humming like a top, still yet swirling: and as one consciousness is lost we adopt the consciousness of the sea, and

From *Poets on Fortune's Hill* by John F. Danby. London: Faber and Faber, Ltd., 1952. Reprinted by permission of Faber and Faber, Ltd.

death is a sleep and the sound of humming as restful as a lull-aby, until we are "lying with simple shells" in the absolute "Ap-athie" we both long for and disdain.

But in addition to notes like this there is also that of a baroque self-consciousness, the manner daring of "aye-remaining lamps." This intrudes, too, between the intimate immediacy and natural-ism of the opening lines and the imaginative moment of the closing ones. Something of self-consciousness has to be counted in to complete the description of the late-Shakespearian style: a distance to which Shakespeare projects his creation, a lack of emotional *engagement*, and yet a rich appreciation—an almost indulgent exaggeration—of the opportunity for stance any mo-ment can bring along.

Passages such as this tempt us further than Shakespeare him-self seems inclined to go. The immensely suggestive moments can lead out beyond the frame of character and beyond the frame of the theme: into the realm of "humming water" and "belching whale." But Shakespeare had a frame to support him and to keep the moments coherently together. In the case of the last three acts of *Pericles* the frame is supplied by the romance world which had also served the writer of the first two acts.

For *Pericles* is a study of the prince in misfortune. The first two acts show a good man embroiled, swept from security by the tempest of another's wickedness. The misfortunes are ex-ternal, the loss is the loss of a throne. The second part begins with the more inward loss of a wife, a loss however which brings the gain of a daughter, for Fortune always has a "doutous or double visage." Shakespeare is supported by what he has himself learned about the inner structure of this world as well as guided by what he knows of it from others who have also explored it.

Act 3 begins with the tempest and ends with Pericles making provision for his daughter, the "fresh-new seafarer," and bid-ding "a priestly farewell" to his wife. Scene 1 is a lyrical Shake-spearian handling of the matter of Patience. In his opening speech Pericles addresses the "god of this great vast"—a deity higher than Fortune. In the first shock of his grief at hearing of Thaisa's death he is in danger of being overthrown. "Patience, good sir," the nurse calls to him, "do not assist the storm,"—

Be manly and take comfort.

(3.1.19, 22)

The force of Lychorida's last words is apt to be lost on a post-Renaissance audience. "Manly" implies the summoning up of the full fortitude manhood implies, but also assumes in this context the creaturely dependence of that manhood; virtue cannot be self-sufficient however far it exerts itself, and even though it is asserted to the full. Pericles calls out against the gods, but it is a human bewilderment rather than a passionate revolt. Again Lychorida cries, "Patience, good sir." Pericles recovers himself and turns to the child. The overflow of compassion is a good augury. Only those can take comfort who can give comfort, and there is immense tenderness in Pericles' words. By the time he is finished he has found a new balance. His reply to the sailor indicates the firm hold he now has on his reestablished manliness:

> FIRST SAILOR. *What courage, sir? God save you!*
> PERICLES. *Courage enough. I do not fear the flaw:*
> *It hath done to me the worst.*

> (38–40)

When the sailors tell him his wife must be cast overboard he submits to the necessity. In the great speech we have already analyzed he fully realizes death's final "apathie"—away from the storm, on the sea's floor, "lying with simple shells": an apathy which is the opposite of patience as death is the opposite of life. He bids Thaisa "a priestly farewell."

The difference between the first and the second parts of *Pericles* can now be more clearly seen. Instead of reporting moral precepts Shakespeare is presenting moral occasions. The audience not only has a map to the territory, it can also see the movements of the protagonist across the countryside. In taking over or resuming the play Shakespeare judged rightly that what it needed was a "voice"—the impression of a living personality, and that personality a center of sensitive moral consciousness. The unit of communication now is the whole scene. Inside that scene we can see the complete turn or rotation of a person responding to a completely given moral occasion. Lyrically evocative as the scene is, the lyrical imagery would not be sufficient, however, without the clearly mapped territory behind it—which Shakespeare shared both with his audience and his collaborator. "Belching whale" and "humming water," overpoweringly suggestive as they are, are not as illuminatingly definitive as the interchange between the sailor and the bereaved husband. "Imagery" is a deceptive word to use in connection with occasions such as this. Imagery includes more than metaphor, more even than is usually included in the phrase "verbal texture." Shakespeare's main controlling image is the image of a man in certain circumstances speaking from the midst of his situation to another man (Shakespeare, again, gives the Sailor a "voice"). The flow of meaning that then takes place only has significance within the moral situation that has been presented. The emotive aura of the separable "images" (what Aristotle called "diction") is large and maybe vague. The total moral reference of the scene, however, is specific and precise. And the references in this case fall within the field covered by "patience in adversity."

The two explaining systems which have been applied recently to the interpretation of the Last Plays miss, I think, the essentially Elizabethan—and for that matter the more deeply human—inwardness of the romance scheme. The first of these has been based on the *Golden Bough* and the fertility cycle and rebirth. The second has been similarly based on the Christian conception of regeneration and resurrection. Neither, I think, is as satisfactory as the contemporary and conventional scheme which Shakespeare used. Anthropology does not take us far enough. By its insidious precipitations it tends to silt over the clear and sharp contours of the Renaissance moral world. The second explaining system errs in the opposite direction. It carries us too far and too fast. It particularizes in a field of meaning beyond Shakespeare's intention—though Shakespeare, I have no doubt, would know St. Paul and the burial service, and accepted the New Testament. To theologize the last plays, however, is to distort them. Though patience as Shakespeare conceives it implies St. Paul and the New Testament, patience as Shakespeare realizes it in the Last Plays is a familiar and well-walked parish in a wider diocese. Nor is the parish presided over by the Fisher King, and in it St. Paul is taken for granted but not allegorized in every Whitsun pastoral. And this brings us to a further distortion which over-anxiety about the greatness of Shakespeare's final plays is sometimes responsible for—a distortion of their tone. Shakespeare's last plays are not conceived at the same level of seriousness as Dante's *Paradiso*. They have an *ironia* of their own. Shakespeare during the last period is comparatively relaxed. He makes a toy of thought. Drawing on the full richness of his inner life, sporadically, as they do, executed with the unanxious brilliance of the maestro who has never lost his flair for improvisation, as they are, the final plays are for all that adjusted to the level of entertainment, controlled by an intention "which was to please."

The "resurrection" scene in *Pericles,* for example, follows immediately on the storm and Thaisa's committal to the sea. The casket in which Thaisa has been placed is washed ashore near the house of Cerimon. Cerimon, as the Epilogue says, is a "reverend" example of "learned charity": as Mr. Wilson Knight has pointed out, Shakespeare's first sketch for Prospero. Cerimon prefers the power which wisdom gives to that which the mere governor can exercise:

> I held it ever,
> Virtue and cunning were endowments greater
> Than nobleness and riches: careless heirs
> May the two latter darken and expend;
> But immortality attends the former,
> Making a man a god. 'Tis known I ever
> Have studied physic.

(3.2.26–32)

With a kind of endearing *pietas* Shakespeare builds up his scene along lines slightly old-fashioned. We are shown Cerimon first in actual fact helping "some Persons who have been shipwrecked." We then see him being greeted by two gentlemen who announce his character:

> Your honor hath through Ephesus pour'd forth
> Your charity, and hundreds call themselves
> Your creatures, who by you have been restor'd.

(43–45)

Finally Thaisa's coffin is brought in and opened, and the moment of her resuscitation occurs. Again the lyrical note is struck. The verse quickens and pants with wonder:

> Gentlemen,
> This queen will live: nature awakes; a warmth
> Breathes out of her . . . see how she 'gins to blow
> Into life's flower again . . .
> . . . She is alive; behold
> Her eyelids, cases to those heavenly jewels

Which Pericles hath lost,
Begins to part their fringes of bright gold;
And diamonds of a most praised water
Do appear, to make the world twice rich. Live,
And make us weep to hear your fate, fair creature,
Rare as you seem to be!
Thaisa.   O dear Diana!
Where am I? Where's my lord? What world is this?
                                                      (93–107)

When thinking of symbolism we must remember that one of the
most important things an apple can mean is simply itself.
Thaisa's reawakening feels to her like a rebirth—and also like a
loss. To the spectators it is wonder enough, the more so that
Thaisa is a miracle of beauty. But the moment attains its highest
significance, I think, when it is brought into relation with Pericles' great speech before the committal, and into the general
romance frame of "doutous fortune" and the Providence that
smiles while it seems to frown. We do not need to make it more
important than that—nor less. And indeed, while there is a
restoration of the seeming dead to breathing warmth, it is still a
world of trial and of separation to which Thaisa is brought back.
Cut off from Pericles, she must retire to Diana's temple and endure her exile in patience.

KENNETH MUIR

From Shakespeare as Collaborator

In the restoration scene,* tempest imagery is again used, but
now no longer expressing hatred and discord—

> Lest this great sea of joys rushing upon me
> O'erbear the shores of my mortality,
> And drown me with their sweetness.

> (5.1.195–97)

Once again, as in *King Lear,* the restoration is accompanied by
music, first by Marina's lost song, and then by the music of the
spheres; it is followed by Pericles' demand for fresh garments
and by the appearance of Diana in a vision—the first theophany
in Shakespeare's works.[†]

The quality of the scene may be illustrated by a single image.
In *Twelfth Night* Viola speaks of the love-sick maid who

> sat like Patience on a monument,
> Smiling at grief.

> (2.4.114–15)

A similar image is used in this scene in *Pericles* with even
greater dramatic force. The hero, meeting his daughter after
many years of suffering, sees in her face the signs of her suffer-

From *Shakespeare as Collaborator* by Kenneth Muir. London: Methuen
& Co., Ltd., 1960. Reprinted by permission of Methuen & Co., Ltd., and
Barnes & Noble, Inc.
*The reader may be referred to the chapter in Derek Traversi's *Shake-
speare's Last Period* and to the masterly analysis by G. Wilson Knight in
The Crown of Life.
[†]The appearance of Hymen in *As You Like It* is in a masque performed by
human actors.

ing and of ordeals bravely borne. He then uses the following image:

> yet thou dost look
> Like Patience gazing on kings' graves, and smiling
> Extremity out of act.

(140–42)

This wonderful image suggests all that Marina has undergone and all that Pericles himself has endured. It suggests that Marina is a king's daughter; it suggests her courage and patience in adversity—pursued by a murderer, captured by pirates, and sold to a brothel. Pericles is to be reborn; Thaisa is to be restored to him from the sea; and the whole family is to be reunited in an earthly resurrection. This is the situation in the play, and the image is exquisitely appropriate to it. The theme of the play is the restoration of the lost and the conquest of death by love—in so far as the theme of one of Shakespeare's plays can be expressed in abstract terms. This theme, this particular scene, its antecedents and its sequel, and the face of the girl imagined by the poet called up the inevitable image which is not merely a symbolic description of Marina but also helps to create the vision of the play.

Journeys that end in lovers' meeting, scenes in which brother and sister, husband and wife, or parents and children meet again after long separation, when each believed the other dead, were frequent episodes in Elizabethan fiction—and in the Greek Romances on which they were sometimes based—and they have always been effective on the stage, whether in Greek tragedy or Latin comedy. Two of Euripides' most effective scenes are the meeting of Iphigenia and Orestes in Tauris and the restoration of Alcestis to her husband. Even the reunion of Egeon and his wife in *The Comedy of Errors* is a moving scene in a play which is largely farcical; the silent reunion of Isabella and Claudio is a little-recognized masterstroke in *Measure for Measure;* and the meeting of Viola and Sebastian in *Twelfth Night* is a touching climax to that play. The meeting of Pericles and Marina surpasses all these. Its effectiveness, and the effectiveness of the whole play, is due partly to Shakespeare's creation of a kind of myth which he could set up against the changes and chances of this mortal life. He is calling in a new world to redress the balance of the old, a new world in which the designs of evil men are frustrated and in which everything comes right in the end—the beautiful queen is not really dead, the beautiful princess is saved from murder and rape and the contamination of the brothel, and the hero, after more trials and tribulations than are normally the lot of man, is rewarded with unforeseen and unimagined happiness. Shakespeare is aware that his story is too good to be true, but such fables are a criticism of life as it is, and (as some think) a statement of faith. In a pagan setting he creates what is virtually an immortality myth.

The misfortunes that befall Pericles are undeserved, and the restoration to him of his wife and child is due to the inscrutable workings of Providence. In the plays which followed Shakespeare set out to eliminate accident, and to infuse the restoration theme with ethical meaning. This could be done only by replacing the workings of an arbitrary providence by the operations of sin and forgiveness. Leontes' jealousy causes the death of Mamillius, and apparently of Hermione also, the loss of Perdita, and estrangement from Polixenes. But the two kings are reconciled through the marriage of their children; and when Leontes by his penitence has earned forgiveness, Hermione is restored to him. In *Pericles* Shakespeare had dealt at length with the finding of the lost daughter and only cursorily with the reunion of husband and wife. In *The Winter's Tale* the emphasis is reversed. The father-daughter recognition takes place offstage, and Shakespeare concentrates on the reunion of Leontes and Hermione—because Leontes has sinned chiefly against her and needs her forgiveness before the play can end in reconciliation. In *Cymbeline* Imogen forgives Posthumus for his attempted murder, and their reconciliation does not require a marriage of children to cement it. In *The Tempest* Shakespeare concentrates on the act of forgiveness itself. In *The Winter's Tale* and *Cymbeline* the hero is the sinner; in *The Tempest* the hero is sinned against, and the betrayal had taken place sixteen years before. By this means Shakespeare eliminated the break of sixteen years which occurs in both *Pericles* and *The Winter's Tale*. The advantages are not all on one side; and the French critic who remarked that Shakespeare finally succeeded in obeying the unity of time by eliminating action altogether was not without some justification. The looser structure of *The Winter's Tale* is necessary to the particular effects at which Shakespeare was aiming; and the yet looser structure of *Pericles* is the only way by which the story of Apollonius could be put on the stage.

In recent years there has been a revival of interest in the play, heralded by T. S. Eliot's exquisite *Marina* and by Wilson Knight's eloquent reassessment in *The Crown of Life,* and exemplified by productions at the Old Vic and Birmingham and by two at Stratford. One Stratford production omitted the first act, and the liberties taken in the other seemed to indicate a lack of confidence in the play's ability to appeal to a modern audience. But at Birmingham the audience was captivated throughout the performance; and this was yet another indication that Shakespeare knew better than his critics, and better even than modish producers, that he had hit on precisely the right form for the material he was dramatizing, and that we have no right to deplore the taste of the groundlings who were enthusiastic when the play was first performed.

CAROL THOMAS NEELY

Pericles: Incest, Birth, and the Death of Mothers

In Shakespeare's late romances—*Pericles*, *Cymbeline*, *The Winter's Tale*, and *The Tempest*—nuptials, families, and states are shattered. In their tour-de-force denouements, marriage, the family, and the state are restored together, assuring sexual health, procreative fertility, and political order. The structure of these plays works toward thematic resolutions and comfortably happy endings. The excessive power of the men is expressed, blunted, and transmuted into benign forms, while threatening female sexuality is chastened through women's defended chastity, disguise, separation, confinement, or death. These transformations are made possible by the birth of children, the absence or death of mothers, the deemphasis on marriage, and the alternative focus on the father-daughter bond—a relationship which, while allowing the father to exercise his power, also enables him to learn its limits. Antiochus's incest opens *Pericles* with a graphic emblem of paternal tyranny. The blessings that the romance fathers eventually bestow on their daughters' nuptials embody the tempering of paternal power.

The incest shockingly encountered at the beginning of *Pericles* and decisively eschewed at the conclusion of *The Tempest* is the antithesis of this healthy father-daughter union and of the other relations flowing from it. The incest of Antiochus and his daughter is an emblem of extreme and interconnected perversions of patriarchal control. Antiochus, a husband, father, and "mighty king" (2.Cho.1), abuses his marital, paternal, sexual, and political power. He defiles his marriage vows and the memory of his dead

From *Broken Nuptials in Shakespeare's Plays* (New Haven: Yale University Press, 1985), pp. 167–77, abridged by author.

wife. He "provoke[s]" (1.Cho.26–27) his daughter to eat "her mother's flesh" and to corrupt her own. The riddle itself—

> I am no viper, yet I feed
> On mother's flesh, which did me breed.
> I sought a husband, in which labor
> I found that kindness in a father.
> He's father, son, and husband mild;
> I mother, wife, and yet his child.
> How they may be, and yet in two,
> As you will live, resolve it you—
>
> (1.1.65–72)

also emphasizes the daughter's seductiveness and complicity. It embodies the confusion of generations and kinship roles, the perversion of sexuality, and the destructive collapse of the family that are the consequences of incest. Because the father contrives to keep her "still" (1.Cho.36), the daughter is deprived of growth, normal sexuality, and her place in the scheme of generations. So is Antiochus himself who is left essentially wifeless, daughterless, and heirless. His "law" (35) to enable him to retain possession of his daughter and behead her suitors is a tyrannical exercise of his political power: "Kings are earth's gods; in vice their law's their will" (1.1.104). Further, in "pride of all his glory" (2.4.6), Antiochus arrogantly flaunts his crime, soliciting suitors and deliberately revealing his secret through the obvious riddle and presentation of his daughter, "clothèd like a bride,/For the embracements even of Jove himself" (1.1.7–8). Antiochus's perverse assumption of Jove's power and the resulting contamination and collapse of the family are fittingly avenged by the "fire from heaven" that consumes the pair "shrivel[ing] up their bodies, even to loathing" (2.4.9,10).

These characteristics of incest revealed in *Pericles* and the other romances are compatible with Claude Lévi-Strauss's well-known analysis of the incest prohibition as a means to ensure the exchange of women in marriage and in this way create social bonds and extend social cohesion. Lévi-Strauss's discussion illuminates the possessiveness that characterizes incest in the plays: "incest, in the broadest sense of the word, consists in obtaining by oneself, and for oneself, instead of by another, and for another." Incest, he shows, is a dream "that one could gain without losing, enjoy without sharing," is the myth "eternally denied to social man, of a world in which one might *keep to oneself*."* I use *incestuous* in such an extended sense to refer to literal incest and to nonsexual but similarly possessive, exclusive, and static bonds between friends, fathers and children, siblings, and I analyze the patriarchal underpinnings of this myth, which are as apparent in Shakespeare as in Lévi-Strauss and Freud.

Shakespeare altered the incest riddle he found in his sources, making it both easier and harder to answer; his changes, like his unique inclusion of the daughter onstage when Pericles is tested, emphasize its effects on her. In earlier versions of the riddle such as the one in Laurence Twine's *The Patterne of Painefull Adventures*—"I am carried with mischief, I eat my mother's flesh; I seek my brother my mother's husband and I cannot find him"—the riddle's hidden referent and correct answer is Antiochus himself.† He can be said to eat his mother's flesh because the incest makes his daughter his "mother" (i.e., mother-in-law): "As wife, she becomes the mother-in-law of her husband as daughter."‡ The riddle's second hidden referent is the suitor, the daughter's potential husband who would become as a result of the incest both "brother" (i.e., his brother-in-law) to Antiochus (since his daughter is also his wife) and "husband" to Antiochus's "mother" (i.e., his mother-in-law, since his daughter is also his mother). The father cannot "find" this future husband because he prohibits his daughter's marriage. The focus of this very difficult riddle is on the father and on his rivalry with his daughter's suitors. In Shakespeare's altered riddle the answer is the daughter: its focus is on her acquiescence in corruption (it is now she who "feed[s] on mother's flesh") and on the confusion of her roles as well as her father's: "He's father, son, and husband mild; I mother, wife, and yet his

---

*Claude Lévi-Strauss, *The Elementary Structures of Kinship,* trans, J. H. Bell, J. R. von Sturmer, and R. Needham (Boston: Beacon Press, 1969): 489, 497. I am indebted in a general way to Stanley Cavell's analysis of the connections between incest, romance, marriage, and remarriage in *Pursuits of Happiness: The Hollywood Comedy of Remarriage* (Cambridge, MA: Harvard University Press, 1981).

†In Geoffrey Bullough, ed. *Narrative and Dramatic Sources of Shakespeare* (New York: Columbia University Press, 1977), 6:428.

‡P. Goolden, "Antiochus's Riddle in Gower and Shakespeare," *Review of English Studies,* n.s. 6 (1955): 246. This article lucidly untangles the meaning of various versions of the riddle and shows how Shakespeare altered its traditional form.

child." The *Pericles* riddle unlike that in the sources is technically unanswerable, since Antiochus's daughter has no name
and has been deprived of a clear-cut role by which she can be
designated.* In Shakespeare's version Antiochus's destruction
of his daughter is at the heart of his tyranny.

The vicious potentials of male power that Antiochus's incest
manifests—violent aggression, sexual degradation, possessiveness, jealousy, tyranny—are released and then mitigated, dis-
pelled or transmuted in the subsequent action of *Pericles* and of
the other romances. Incest's two-tiered disruption of marriage
and family relations is reiterated in modified ways in the other
plays when nuptials or marriage are impeded or broken in two
generations. The incest of Antiochus grotesquely caricatures
the concatenation of marital, familial, and political ties and
their potential for mutual corruption. But the potential for mutual restoration is also present. In *Pericles* it is embodied in Pericles himself, the "benign lord" (2.Cho.3), who is the antithesis
of Antiochus and who undoes the tyrant's incest. Losing wife
and daughter, he regains them by his withdrawal into patient,
passive mourning.

In this play, Marina's resemblance to her mother becomes
the catalyst, not to incest, but to a recognition scene which,
much altered from the sources, reverses the dynamics of the
play's opening. Marina's riddling remarks, which suggest her
mysterious birth and submerged identity—"No, nor of any
shores./Yet I was mortally brought forth, and am/No other than
I appear" (5.1.105–07) *can* be explicated; they lead to wondrous clarification for her and Pericles. This is possible because
Marina knows her identity—her name and her parentage—can
announce that she is "Called Marina/For I was born at sea"
(158–59), that she is "the daughter to King Pericles" (182), and
that her "mother's name was Thaisa" (213). Marina's answer-
able riddles enable her to become Pericles' mother—"Thou that
beget'st him"—not through the verbal and sexual confusions of
the incest riddle but through her father's symbolic regaining of
his identity, his symbolic rejuvenation. In *Cymbeline, The Winter's Tale*, and *The Tempest*, the protagonists themselves, like
Pericles' antithesis, Antiochus, exercise their power to corrupt

---

*Phyllis Gorfain, "Puzzle and Artifice: The Riddle as Metapoetry in *Per-
icles*," *Shakespeare Survey* 29 (1976):11–20 shows how the *Pericles* riddle,
because unanswerable, confounds the ordinary structural and cultural functions of riddles.

family or social bonds. But instead of being destroyed, they are preserved, like Pericles, to cooperate in the restoration of the bonds that they themselves have helped to shatter.

In *Pericles* as in the other romances, childbirth makes possible incest and is its antithesis. It is present in the romances in dramatic episodes and pervasive metaphors—as a psychological crisis and as a resonant symbol. The moment of birth alters the family constellation, extending it and anticipating its division and proliferation instead of consuming it. Childbirth is ultimately regenerative but at first traumatic for mother, child, and father. As wife becomes mother in the romances, her power and vulnerability are heightened; she is both fulfilled and divided, and the sexuality that is confirmed by the birth of her child seems to require nullification. When husband becomes father, he gains an emblem of his potency and an extension of his powers. But he is also made to confront his wife's sexual power and his own decline and mortality. The child, "freed and enfranchised" (*WT*, 2.2.60) from the womb, experiences violent separation from parents and is threatened with confinement, banishment, or death. These subsequent painful separations, reiterating that of parturition, permit growth and lead to the reformation of the old family and the creation of a new one.

The puzzling absence of mothers in many Shakespeare plays (where, as in *The Taming of the Shrew, Love's Labor's Lost, Midsummer Night's Dream, The Merchant of Venice, Much Ado About Nothing, As You Like It, Troilus and Cressida, Othello, King Lear, Cymbeline, The Tempest,* there are children with fathers but no mothers present or accounted for) has often been noted, and a variety of explanations offered. The rarity of mothers may reflect or confirm demographic data showing that Renaissance women frequently died in childbirth. The scarcity of older women in the plays contrasts sharply, however, with the concern for widows in the period and in Shakespeare's family in Stratford, where his mother, wife, sister, one or both daughters, and some of his aunts outlived their husbands.* It may embody the social reality that patriarchal culture vested all authority in the male parent, making it both logical and fitting that he alone should represent that authority in the drama. It

---

*See my "Shakespeare's Women: Historical Facts and Dramatic Representations," in *Shakespeare's Personality,* ed. Norman Holland, Sidney Homan, and Bernard J. Paris (Berkeley: University of California Press, 1988) for a discussion of the women in Shakespeare's family.

may result from a scarcity of boy actors capable of playing mature women in Shakespeare's company, although the playwright's creation of Lady Macbeth, Cleopatra, and Volumnia not long before the romances suggests that he had actors he could count on to play such roles. It may derive not from the restraints of the actors but those of dramatic genre: the uncommonness of mature women as protagonists in comedy, history play, and tragedy.

The nature of the phenomenon and the relative significance of the factors accounting for it vary from genre to genre or even from play to play. The scarcity of mothers in comedy, which probably derives from the father's authority to negotiate marriages in the period, serves to highlight the Oedipal conflicts that are traditional to the genre. In the romances, however, mothers are not merely absent but are explicitly dead or else die or apparently die in the course of the play. If the death occurs before the play's action, it is noted and remembered. These deaths and mock deaths are prominent determinants of plot and theme. The absence of mothers in the romances causes broken nuptials in the older generation, allows female sexuality to be represented by the chaste innocence of young daughters, and shifts emotional and dramatic emphasis to father-daughter bonds. Mock deaths in the romances symbolize separation and engender reconciliation not only in the heterosexual bond but in the mother-child bond as well.

Like Titania's votress in *Midsummer Night's Dream,* who, "being mortal, of that boy did die" (2.1.135), Thaisa in *Pericles* and other mothers in the romances die in childbirth or closely following the birth of a child. These concomitant births and deaths exaggerate the trauma of birth and manifest its physical and psychological consequences for the mother. The frighteningly liminal nature of childbirth is dramatized in Thaisa's "blusterous" (3.1.28) delivery in a tempest at sea exactly midway between her father's and her husband's kingdoms: "Their vessel shakes/On Neptune's billow; half the flood/Hath their keel cut" (3.Cho.44–46). The mother experiences physical and emotional division and transformation of role and identity. The location of Thaisa's delivery symbolizes how her position as daughter becomes attenuated as she takes on the new role of mother to a child who is first connected to her, then violently separated from her. The vulnerability of the mother and the violence of this separation of one body into two are implied when Marina is seen as "this piece/Of [the] dead queen" (3.1.17–18), Posthumus is "ripped" (*Cym*, 5.4.37) from the dead body of his mother, and Perdita is from Hermione's "breast,/The innocent milk in its most innocent mouth,/Haled out to murder" (*WT*, 3.2.97–99). These three mothers die or seem to die in childbirth or immediately afterward. Miranda's mother also seems to have died soon after her birth, since the daughter, two when she was exiled from Milan, remembers her waiting woman but not her mother.

When they survive the physical division of childbirth, mothers remain emotionally bound to their children and fatally vulnerable to the loss of them. In the tragedies mothers, for example Lady Montague, Lady Capulet, and Gertrude, die ambiguously in connection with the loss or death of children. In the romances, too, mothers' deaths are connected with or a consequence of the loss of children. Thaisa "dies" at sea in childbirth. Posthumus's mother's death in childbirth results from grief at the death of her two sons. Hermione, already grieving over violent separation from Perdita, "dies" at the announcement of Mamillius's death; his name connotes the intimate physical bond between mother and child, which extends beyond birth and makes the loss of a child a kind of death. Even the wicked queen in *Cymbeline* develops "a fever with the absence of her son,/A madness, of which her life's in danger" (*Cym*, 4.3.2–3) and dies, although unaware that Cloten has died arrogantly identifying himself as "the queen's son" (*Cym*, 4.2.93).

Birth and the fierce bonds between mother and child can be destructive for children and stepchildren as well as for mothers. In *Pericles*, Marina's stormy birth is imaged as an assault; it prefigures other assaults and losses that the children of romance must endure:

> Thou hast as chiding a nativity
> As fire, air, water, earth, and heaven can make
> To herald thee from the womb. Even at the first
> Thy loss is more than can thy portage quit,
> With all thou canst find here.
>
> (3.1.32–36)

After Marina's abrupt separation from her mother's womb and subsequent loss of her mother, her father abandons her; later

Dionyza, the stepmother who has raised her, plots her death. The Queen in *Cymbeline* likewise plots Imogen's death. Both stepmothers act out of their love for their own children. Perdita is taken away from her mother, and Mamillius dies of grief at his mother's loss of honor and his separation from her. Cloten dies in consequence of the arrogance bred in him by his aggressive mother. Even Euriphile is accused, at the end of *Cymbeline*, of stealing the King's sons. The destructive potential in mothers' and surrogate mothers' intimate bonds with their children, dramatized in the margins of the romances, is embodied in two grotesque images in *Pericles*. Cleon attacks Dionyza, who has apparently murdered Marina, the child in her care, as "like the harpy/Which, to betray, dost, with thine angel's face,/Seize with thine eagle's talents" (4.3.46–48), and describes as one of the consequences of famine, "Those mothers who, to nuzzle up their babes,/Thought nought too curious, [and] are ready now/To eat those little darlings whom they loved" (1.4.42–44).

In the romances, the death of bad mothers protects fathers and children from their destructive power. The death of good mothers allows their sexual and procreative power to be appropriated and idealized. Idealization is effected when dead mothers are ritually buried and mourned and their memory cherished. Thaisa's sea burial associates her with a nature which, in contrast to that of the storm, is benign. She receives a "priestly farewell" (3.1.69); in her sea grave, where "e'er-remaining lamps, the belching whale/And humming water must o'erwhelm thy corpse,/Lying with simple shells" (62–64), she is absorbed into the tranquil rhythms of nature in preparation for her regeneration within its cycles: "nature awakes; a warmth/Breathes out of her . . . See how she 'gins to blow/Into life's flower again!" (3.2.94–97). Euriphile, the surrogate mother to Cymbeline's sons, is buried with a beautiful dirge that imagines her similarly removed from nature's destructive excesses—"Fear no more the heat o' th' sun/Nor the furious winter's rages" (4.2.258–59)—and that imagines death as protection and consummation. Her grave is honored daily by Guiderius and Arviragus as Hermione's "grave" is visited daily by Leontes.

Through their deaths into nature and the cherishing of their memory, the desexualization and sanctification of good mothers is achieved. It is achieved also by mothers' mock deaths—by the long, chaste seclusion of Thaisa as a vestal virgin in the Temple of Diana (a curious denial of her sexual initiation and motherhood) and of Hermione as, in effect, a statue in the house of Paulina. Through these deaths, the mothers' sexuality, necessary for conception and childbirth, is eliminated from the romances until the moment when they can bequeath it to marriageable daughters. Thaisa and Hermione are reborn into sexual roles again only at the moment of their daughters' betrothals, and Miranda is not told of her mother or family history until she becomes marriageable, and a suitor is at hand.

As a result of mothers' deaths and their other losses, fathers, too, withdraw, deny their sexuality, and, in the absence of wives, learn to take on nurturing roles. The fathers' sexuality and their part in generation are minimized—most explicitly when Gower deftly and comfortably removes Pericles entirely from his idealized description of defloration and conception: "Hymen hath brought the bride to bed,/Where by loss of maidenhead/A babe is molded" (3.Cho.9–11). The fathers endure withdrawals that parallel in some ways the seclusion of wives. Pericles, after the death of Thaisa, vows not to shave his hair until his daughter's marriage, and after Marina's apparent death, he suffers a deathlike mourning. Leontes also withdraws from life, eschewing the possibility of heirs who might revive his kingdom. Prospero's involuntary seclusion is likewise characterized by sexual abstinence, penance, and transformation. He, Belarius in *Cymbeline*, and the old Shepherd in *Winter's Tale* nurture children and surrogate children, taking them up "for pity" (*WT*, 3.3.75), educating or trying to educate them, and preparing for the moment when they will reach maturity.*

In each of the plays, it is the children's becoming "ripe for marriage" (*Per*, 4.Cho.17) that ends the father's withdrawal and leads to the revival of the wife and to other reunions. The reestablishment of the bond between parent and child and the acknowledgment of the powerful physical connection between them overshadows in the romances the sexual union— or reunion—of husband and wife, who are "one flesh" only

---

*Marianne Novy, *Love's Argument: Gender Relations in Shakespeare* (Chapel Hill: University of North Carolina Press, 1984), pp. 164–87, shows how men in the romances take on conventionally feminine nurturing roles.

symbolically and by means of their children. Pericles's recovery of his wife gives way to Thaisa's acknowledgment of the daughter whose existence she only now realizes.

Marina.   My heart
     Leaps to be gone into my mother's bosom.
     (Kneels)
Pericles. Look who kneels here: flesh of thy flesh, Thaisa;
     Thy burden at the sea, and called Marina,
     For she was yielded there.
Thaisa.   Blest, and mine own!
              (5.3.43–47)

In Cymbeline, Imogen's and Posthumus's reunion embrace is likewise interrupted—by Cymbeline's desire for recognition by his daughter:

Cymbeline. How now, my flesh, my child?
     What, mak'st thou me a dullard in this act?
     Wilt thou not speak to me?
Imogen. (Kneeling)   Your blessing, sir.
              (5.5.264–66)

At the conclusion of The Winter's Tale, Hermione is called from her embrace of Leontes to bless the daughter for whom she has preserved herself:

Paulina.   kneel,
     And pray your mother's blessing; turn, good lady,
     Our Perdita is found.
Hermione.   You gods look down,
     And from your sacred vials pour your graces
     Upon my daughter's head! Tell me, mine own,
     Where hast thou been preserved?
              (5.3.119–24)

Even in The Tempest, where the central family is not reunited—where the mother remains absent, and Prospero's and Miranda's separation is yet to come—the final reunion of the play, that of Alonso with the son he believes dead, recapitulates the earlier parent/child reunions:

Ferdinand. Though the seas threaten, they are merciful
          I have cursed them without cause. (*Kneels*)
Alonso.   Now all the blessings
          Of a glad father compass thee about.

                                          (5.1.178–80)

In *Pericles*, the opening incest is transformed, through marriage, birth, and Marina's independence into a concluding celebration of the reunion of Pericles and Thaisa, the promised nuptials of Marina and Lysimachus, and the rule of Pericles in Pentapolis, his wife's inherited kingdom, and of the younger couple in Tyre, Pericles's kingdom. This canceling of incest through the extension of the family in time and space is implicit in Gower's concluding Chorus:

> In Antiochus and his daughter you have heard
> Of monstrous lust the due and just reward.
> In Pericles, his queen and daughter seen,
> Although assailed with fortune fierce and keen,
> Virtue preserved from fell destruction's blast,
> Led on by heaven, and crowned with joy at last.

                                          (5.3.84–89)

MICHAEL DOBSON

Adrian Noble's *Pericles*, 2002

There was nothing very new about this *Pericles*, no mistaking it for anything other than a fine and typical specimen of Noble's late manner: here again were the quantities of windblown silk, the bright plain pastel nursery colors, the unspecifically and inoffensively orientalist costume designs, the large, graceful, storytelling gestures. Here too was Noble's tendency to present Shakespeare as if alongside Charles and Mary Lamb, through the lens of classic children's literature, an aspect of his recent work, which produced such an interesting *Midsummer Night's Dream* and such a disastrous *Twelfth Night*. The difference here was that all of these mannerisms fitted *Pericles* like a glove in a way that they didn't quite fit either of the other romances which Noble has directed in recent seasons, *Cymbeline* and *The Tempest*. The overall conceit, such as it was, was to have Peter McKintosh design *Pericles* as if it were a tale from Edmund Dulac's illustrated edition of the *Arabian Nights*—and, efficiently and undistractingly, it just worked. The notion of this being a "promenade" production in any very developed sense, never really achieved by its two predecessors, was largely abandoned: most of the action took place on a flat circular island in the middle of the arena, reached by a single ramp, rather than directly among any of the audience. (As a result, incidentally, this production transferred rather more successfully to the end-on RST [Royal Shakespeare Theatre] than did its two fellows.)

This raised acting area, coupled with some elegant aerial work, proved more than adequate to the needs of this deliberately faux-naive, mock-medieval play: a single billowing sheet

From *Shakespeare Survey* 55 (2003): 271–73. Reprinted with the permission of Cambridge University Press. The title is the editor's.

of silk, for example, easily transformed it into a ship for the great storm scene, without any of the noisy fairground machinery which Boyd's *Tempest* had employed to simulate a heavy swell. The happy combination of this play's willingly childish storytelling method and Noble's correspondingly arch simplicity of method was beautifully exemplified at the end of this scene by the handling of Thaisa's funeral at sea. Once she had been placed in her coffin, that coffin was simply slid backward out of the way along the ramp below and beyond the billowing sail; then at the scene's close the sail fell onto it, rippling like the sea; then in the next scene, where Thaisa is washed ashore, the coffin was simply drawn forward back into the acting area from under the sail by Cerimon's helpers. There was no straining aftereffect, no overdone real rainfall, just exactly what was needed to tell the story and to remind the audience to be in the mood to be told such a story. The decor, similarly, gave just enough information about the settings of scenes and about the pleasures of its own elegant tact without intruding: hanging Byzantine lamps to suggest eastern Mediterranean palaces; cushions; turbans; colored robes; scimitars.

The performances, meanwhile, perverse as it sounds to say it, were just perfectly not too good, worlds away from the suspect slick perfection on display in Doran's *Much Ado*. [Ray] Fearon was beautiful, and fit, and human, and you could understand every word he said, and he was the protagonist, and you wanted very much to see what happened to him next: anything much more than that would have thrown the whole show out of kilter. If the problem of psychological motivation even arises with *Pericles,* something has gone wrong, and here it didn't. Lauren Ward's Thaisa was dignified and lovely. Kananu Kirimi's Marina was waiflike and affecting. Olwen May's Bawd was twisted and nasty and human; and that's all that was needed. (Sirine Saba—a conspicuously good Mopsa in *The Winter's Tale*, part schoolmarm, part vixen—characteristically and enjoyably gave slightly more than was needed to her series of cameos as Antiochus's daughter, Lychorida, and "the little baggage," 4.2.21, at the Mytilene brothel.) As Gower, Brian Protheroe told the story without ever getting in its way or appearing to think that the play was really about either him or the harmless moralizing with which he punctuated it. Such showy touches as this production did display were exactly where they should have been, in the inset spectacular set pieces: a good display of severed heads in Antioch, mockingly kissed by Geoff Francis's Antiochus; a very enjoyable and agile martial arts contest for Thaisa's birthday; above all, a stunning effect for Pericles's dream vision after the reunion with Marina, when a tiny scrap of white cloth fluttering rapidly down toward the stage from what seemed like miles above his head suddenly turned out to be Fiona Lait as a white-robed Diana, tumbling delicately down a rope—a benign, supernatural revision of the earlier swash-buckling descent on ropes made by the Sinbad-like pirates who abducted Marina from Tharsus. A sometimes excessive use of incidental music (including a sadly banal song, used both for Pericles's serenade to Thaisa and Marina's initial attempt to revive him in the reunion scene) seemed typical of the failure of nerve which the RSC has been suffering about productions for large spaces since even before *Les Misérables*, but this was otherwise an exquisitely judged account of an unfairly neglected and mysteriously powerful play.

SYLVAN BARNET

Pericles on Stage and Screen

After reading a dozen or so reviews of productions of *Pericles* in the past two decades, almost all of which begin by speaking of *Pericles* as "one of Shakespeare's least-produced plays," one realizes that *Pericles* has established itself firmly in the Shakespeare canon, even though it was not included in the 1623 First Folio edition of Shakespeare's plays.

We are likely to think that our age has discovered this play, but in fact it was highly popular in its own day. When *Pericles* was first published in 1609, the text said that the play was "diverse and sundry times acted by his Majesty's servants at the Globe on the Bankside." Between 1609 and 1635 *Pericles* was published six times, a sign of considerable popularity. Its popularity is further attested by Ben Jonson's complaint in 1629 that audiences instead of attending *his* plays went to see "some mouldy tale like *Pericles*." Documents refer to four specific performances of *Pericles* before the puritans closed the theaters in 1642. Two of these documents mention performances for courtly audiences—the Venetian ambassador in 1607 or 1608, and the French ambassador in 1619—so it is evident that despite Jonson's grumbling the play was not popular simply with persons of uneducated taste. We know that court productions were often highly spectacular, and the opportunity that *Pericles* affords for splendid display (Gower, serving as the chorus, says the play will "please your eyes") and for music doubtless was and still is part of the reason for its appeal. In addition to stage directions that call for masques and dumb shows, some of Gower's choric lines almost invite an accompanying display in pantomime.

From 1642 until 1660 the theaters in England were closed, but when they reopened in the spring of 1660, in the days just before the restoration of Charles II, thirteen plays were staged at the old Cockpit Theatre. Of these, *Pericles* was the only one by Shakespeare. Thomas Betterton, then about twenty-five, was "highly applauded" for his performance in the title role. He and most of his fellow-actors at the Cockpit soon joined with Sir William Davenant to become the Duke's Company, which on December 12, 1660, was awarded the exclusive acting rights to *Pericles* for two months. The play was almost surely performed, therefore, early in 1661, but then it vanished from the stage for more than three quarters of a century; and when it appeared again, in 1738, it was in the shape of George Lillo's adaptation *Marina*, a three-act play based chiefly on the last two acts of *Pericles*, with substantial additions by Lillo.

After Lillo's *Marina*, more than a century elapsed before there was a significant production of *Pericles*. This was Samuel Phelps's version at Sadler's Wells in 1854, with Phelps as Pericles. He omitted the chorus (Gower), combined 1.2 and 1.3, 2.3 and 2.5, and 4.2 and 4.6 (the brothel in Mytilene), and he heavily censored the brothel scenes. Of the bowdlerization, Douglas Jerrold wrote in *Lloyd's Weekly London News*:

> The fourth act, so dangerous to represent, has been disinfected of its impurities in a manner that would win the praise of the most fastidious member of the most moral Board of Health that ever held its sittings within the camphored precincts of Exeter Hall. The greatest theatrical purist need not be afraid to visit that foul room at Mytilene, since it has been whitewashed and purified by the pen of Mr. Phelps.

A single example of the laundering will suffice: for Shakespeare's "And prostitute me to the basest groom," Phelps substituted, "And sacrifice me to the basest groom." Curiously, Phelps kept the first scene of the play but suppressed its riddling material about the incestuous relation of the princess and her father, so the scene lost its point. The production, acclaimed by critics and the public, ran for fifty-five performances, a record for Sadler's Wells. Doubtless much of the success was due to the awe-inspiring spectacle with which the play was staged, since Phelps had decided to compete with Kean's opulent *Sardanapalus*, which was then playing at the Princess's. (The decision was not characteristic of Phelps; his *Pericles* was his only spectacular production.) Because the scenery was unusually elaborate, it could not easily be taken down and then set up again, so while *Pericles* was being produced, Phelps suspended repertory playing. Although he was especially successful in conveying the rolling billows and the tossing ship, he also paid attention to banquets, trains of courtiers, and dances, all of which aroused much comment. The *Times*, on October 16, 1854, called attention to some of the effects:

> Certainly, as a spectacle, the play of *Pericles*, as produced at Sadler's Wells, is a marvel. . . . When Pericles is thrown on the sands, it is with the very best of rolling seas, the waves advancing and receding as when governed by Mr. Macready in *Acis and Galatea* at Drury Lane. In the palace of Pentapolis he finds costumes of a kind with which we have been familiarized by *Sardanapalus* at the Princess's. When the storm afterwards rocks his vessel, it rocks in real earnest, and spectators of delicate stomachs may have uneasy reminiscences of Folkestone and Boulogne. But all this is as nothing to the wonders that take place when Pericles has discovered his daughter, and sets sail for Ephesus. An admirably equipped Diana, with her car in the clouds, orders his course to her sacred city, to which he is conducted by a moving panorama of excellently-painted coast scenery. The interior of the temple, where the colossal figure of the many-breasted goddess stands in all its glory amid gorgeously-attired votaries, is the last "bang" of the general magnificence.

John Coleman, friend and admirer and biographer of Phelps, in turn devised an adaptation of *Pericles*, which in 1900 Frank Benson's company performed at Stratford-upon-Avon. Coleman omitted Gower and most of the first act, made minor changes in the second and third acts, bowdlerized the brothel scenes in the fourth act, but left the fifth act largely as it was. The result was received fairly coolly. In 1921 Robert Atkins produced an unexpurgated version at the Old Vic, with Atkins as Gower, Rupert Harvey as Pericles, and Mary Sumner as Marina. This production, done in what was thought to be an Elizabethan manner, seems to have stimulated other directors in the 1920s, including Nugent Monck, who in 1929 produced *Pericles* at the Maddermarket Theatre in Norwich, where he used an Elizabethan (apron) stage. The 1930s also saw some productions, including a second production by Robert Atkins, in the open air in Regents Park in 1939. Stratford-upon-Avon, in 1900 the site of Coleman's mangled version, staged the play again in 1947, when Nugent Monck put on his second version, this time omitting much of Gower and the whole of the first act but retaining most of the remainder. Monck's production, with Paul Scofield as Pericles and Daphne Slater as Marina, ran for about an hour and a half and was highly praised. In 1950 Scofield and Slater played it again, this time uncut. In 1954 Douglas Seale directed a nearly uncut *Pericles* for the Birmingham Repertory Theatre, with Richard Pasco as Pericles and Doreen Aris as Marina. Gower's lines were delivered in a singsong fashion, though without accompaniment by a lute. A permanent set was used, helping the action to flow swiftly, without delays for changes. Some passages were also made more comprehensible by the addition of lines from George Wilkins's *The Painful Adventures of Pericles*, a prose tale that is indebted both to Shakespeare's play and to Shakespeare's source.

In 1958 Tony Richardson directed the play at Stratford-upon-Avon, with Richard Johnson as Pericles, Geraldine McEwan as Marina, and Edric Connor as Gower. Connor, a West Indian calypso singer and actor, sang Gower's lines, addressing not the audience in the theater but the seamen on the stage. Kenneth Tynan reported that in this production "the action flows like a stream over rapids, accompanied by music that twangles and bubbles, disguising the bad bits and enlivening the good." The play opened in darkness, with exotic music and flickers of light; the darkness dissolved, revealing (against a background of cordage and sails) that the flickers came from six great oars, three rowers on each side of the stage, rowing to the rhythm of a sea chantey, though the only intelligible words at first were "Roll and go." Thus, the play became a nautical yarn told by an old spinner of tales to an enthralled audience. Muriel St. Clare Byrne, reviewing the production in *Shakespeare Quarterly*, Autumn 1958, wrote,

> As the story-teller weaves his spell, out of the background of ship and sky his magic summons the figures of his tale; and as they materialize he retires downstage, and when an episode ends he steps back into the scene, sometimes before the beings his fancy has evoked have all departed. . . . The characters have no dimensional quality, no more depth than folktale heroes and

villains. In this world of good and evil, vice and virtue are as flatly personified as in a morality, and visual impact is the important thing.

St. Clare Byrne goes on to indicate something of the visual aspect of this impressive production:

> The opening episode—incest at Antioch—catches the right note of barbaric violence and lust, all in brilliant blues, greens, purple and silver against a lurid red background. Antiochus and his men seem made of spikes and fantastic scythed spears, and there is a grim reminder of the fate that lies behind the riddle that the hero must read to win the hand of the King's daughter, when the heads of the suitors who have preceded him are borne in impaled on tall spears. Thence to Tarsus, where the starving populace, in dulled grays and greens and black, look almost incandescent with decay; and so to Pentapolis, red and gold for the triumphs and feasting. . . .

Handsome spectacle and excellent acting also characterized Nagle Jackson's production in Oregon in 1967, but in 1969 Terry Hands chose a different approach when he staged the play with the Royal Shakespeare Company at Stratford-upon-Avon, putting it on in what was essentially a white box that focused attention on the actors. The acting, like the set, was highly stylized; one might almost say the play was choreographed. Costumes ranged from a full robe for the medieval Gower to lizard leggings and scanty covering for others. It was said that the seminudity was supposed to evoke thoughts of Botticelli's *Three Graces*, i.e., a world of allegorized fleshly beauty, but on the whole the reviewers were unenthusiastic. One reviewer couldn't see the point of doing the play at all: "Apart from the opportunity of dressing the entire cast in jock straps— irrespective of their dubious sex—one fails to see the reason for dragging up this dire piece of business."

Nineteen seventy-three saw a rather gimmicky production directed by Toby Robertson in Edinburgh and later in Stratford-upon-Avon. Revealing a debt to Jean Genet's *The Balcony*, Robertson set the play in a 1930s eastern Mediterranean brothel, with female and transvestite male prostitutes, where the customers and residents performed *Pericles* for their own entertainment, doubling or tripling small parts, using improvised props, and creating sets out of nothing, in the manner of Bertolt Brecht. Thus, the ship in the storm was represented by a swaying oval of actors who held aloft one performer as a figurehead. The doubling caused some confusion, especially because of some uncertain sexual identification. For instance, the male madam, in corsets and silk stockings, took on the role of the heterosexual and incestuous King of Antioch, whose daughter was played by a man. In the great reunion scene between Pericles and his daughter Marina, the brothel was mercifully blacked out and the lines were allowed their full force. One effective touch must be mentioned: Pericles (Derek Jacobi) was the only figure to wear a Renaissance costume. Robertson directed a similar production in New York in 1980 for the Jean Cocteau Repertory company.

A New York production in 1974, directed by Edward Berkeley, also used a gimmick: the play was presented by a troupe of traveling players who entered and exited from two covered wagons at the sides of the stage. Before the play began, the performers entertained the audience with juggling, tumbling, and some distressing clowning, including a parody of Cinderella, in which the clown-prince entered the audience and, attempting to fit the slipper to the feet of members of the audience, grimaced at the smells. Much fun was had by the cast, who improvised a storm with tin plates and a thunder sheet, scratched their groins, and sometimes deliberately missed their cues. Despite this sort of thing, Randall Duk Kim as Pericles and Mary Beth Hurt as Marina were effective, but otherwise the play indeed seemed to be Ben Jonson's "mouldy tale."

A relatively straightforward production at Stratford-upon-Avon in 1979, directed by Ron Daniels, with Peter McEnery as Pericles and Julie Peasgood as Marina, was uneven but nevertheless was more satisfactory. Some cuts were made, but (as in Douglas Seale's version of 1954) there were also some additions from George Wilkins's *The Painful Adventures of Pericles*, and the play ran for some two and a half hours. There was no set, only a black background and a circle marked on the floor to indicate the acting area and to suggest cosmic doings. A few simple properties were used, for instance a wooden post against which Gower could lean before starting his tale. Later, the fishermen hung their nets from the post, and during the storm, actors clung to a rope stretching diagonally across the stage and fastened to the post. Roger Warren, reviewing the production in

Shakespeare Survey 33, commented on the especially effective staging of Marina's conversion of Lysimachus in the brothel:

> A double mattress was placed center stage, upon which they both knelt; Marina seemed very vulnerable, both because of her fragile slightness and because of her close proximity to Lysimachus on a bed. She seemed to win him over, not only by her pleading (strengthened with additions from Wilkins's version of the scene), but also by her enchanting tenderness and unaffected innocence; you felt that their love was born in the process.

Although the properties were simple, vaguely Oriental costumes (turbans, baggy trousers) lent an exotic touch, and the action as a whole moved from the barbarous Antioch to the purity of Diana's shrine.

In 1983 Peter Sellars, furnished with a tiny budget—eleven actors took all of the parts—produced a brilliant *Pericles* as his first production for the Boston Shakespeare Company. Sellars, though only in his mid-twenties at the time, had already established a reputation both for brilliance and for his cavalier treatment of texts. *Pericles,* then, probably was the ideal vehicle; since the play exists only in a highly corrupt text, Sellars could stage it as imaginatively as he wished without the danger that he would be charged with mutilating a classic. In a note in the program, Sellars wrote that *Pericles* fuses "the classical blaze of Shakespeare's late tragedies with the hard, bright glare of contemporary comedy and the flickering pageantry of the Renaissance masque, and the special illumination of the Christian mystery play." This rather stuffy statement allowed him to costume the play in a variety of styles. Robes of no particular period were mixed with modern dress; when Pericles met with his Tyrian council, the councillors wore three-piece suits and carried briefcases, but their faces were covered with bland plastic masks. The masks that Sellars used throughout the play were themselves of several sorts, ranging from elaborate creations to joke-store masks such as (for Boult, the brothel keeper) a little pig's snout held on by a rubber band. Sometimes performers took on other roles, switching wigs and masks onstage. In the first scene, where Pericles guesses the secret of Antiochus and his daughter—the two have an incestuous relation—the father and daughter, both masked, were dressed like figures in a porno show, he in S & M leather, she in white bra and panties. In this production, only Pericles, Thaisa, and Marina did not wear masks; and when Lysimachus repented he removed his mask.

If one had to name an influence operating on Sellars, one would name Brecht, but the production was only intermittently Brechtian, and much of it was characterized by the "pageantry" and "mystery" that Sellars talked of in the program. Since he had little money, he had to make his spectacle out of almost nothing, and he succeeded brilliantly. The storm, during which Marina is born and Thaisa is thought to die, was created in part by actors at the sides of the stage shaking bits of metal but chiefly by a light bulb wildly swinging here and there across a darkened stage. The effect was to turn the theater, miraculously, into a rolling ship. It must be said, however, that since many of the performers were very weak, the evening seemed very long (in fact it *was* long, since the production took three and a half hours), and the interest was almost entirely in Sellars' direction. On the other hand, as other productions have also shown, some of the scenes, especially the brothel scenes and the great reunion between Pericles and Marina, are almost actor-proof.

Also in 1983 a production at the Theatre Royal, Stratford East, directed by David Utz, conveyed something of a fairy-tale quality, with Cerimon as a wizard wearing a conical hat. Countries were differentiated by color: Antioch was bloodred, Tharsus yellow, Pentapolis green, Ephesus blue, and Mytilene purple. The set was largely huge crates. Thus, Pericles delivered his speech to "the god of this great vast" from the top of a crate carried around the stage by sailors. There was a lot of doubling; a single actor played all the tyrants (Antiochus, Cleon, Simonides, and Lysimachus). As Ralph Berry points out in *Shakespeare in Performance*, doubling is fairly common in modern productions of *Pericles*, and it is of various sorts. Thus, Terry Hands in his 1969 Royal Shakespeare Company production emphasized similarities by doubling Dionyza and the bawd— both villains—and Antiochus and Boult (villains again), but directors who have aimed for a contrast have doubled (for instance) Dionyza and Diana, and, similarly for contrast, Antiochus's daughter and Marina. Either way, the doubling helped to reveal the mythic aspects of the play.

Another exceptionally interesting *Pericles* was done at the Shakespeare festival at Stratford, Ontario, in 1986, where Richard Ouzounian, like Robertson in 1973 and Sellars in 1983, adopted a somewhat Brechtian manner. For instance, to indicate a ship under sail, men agitated a sail. Gower was a black singer, as in the Stratford-upon-Avon production of 1958, but the Ontario Gower was a female rock singer who used too much mike to suit most of the critics. What was perhaps especially significant about the production was that it made substantial use of Wilkins's *Painful Adventures of Pericles*, thus clarifying many passages that are puzzling in the text of the play. Perhaps this *Pericles* made more sense, line by line, than any other production since the early seventeenth century.

In 1989–90 David Thacker directed a production of the Royal Shakespeare Company, first at the Swan at Stratford-upon-Avon and then in London. Gower, played by a West Indian, remained onstage even when his role was not called for, reading a book while seated in an armchair at the edge of the stage. The text was (as usual) trimmed here and there but it was also amplified with some additions drawn from George Wilkins's prose narrative, *The Painfull Adventures of Pericles Prince of Tyre* (1608). The production was sometimes realistic, sometimes stylized—thus, the storm was represented by a man struggling with a representation of the tiller, while other performers slid around on ropes and ladders—and the costumes were eclectic, but on the whole the production was true to the play.

Phyllida Lloyd in 1993–94 directed a production—perhaps better called an adaptation—for the Royal National Theatre. Seeing the play as a dream, a fantastic journey, Lloyd emphasized spectacle, aural effects, and stage machinery—at least one reviewer spoke of it as *Pericles, The Musical*. Thus, the revolve of the stage was almost always in motion, tilting and turning to represent the agitated sea, but unfortunately sometimes the stage elevators were noisy and did not always work, and the flying apparatus sometimes malfunctioned. The attempt was characterized as "total theatre" and "postmodern theatre," but reviews were cool, most reviewers agreeing that the activity obscured the play, which, despite some obscure passages and some looseness of construction, nevertheless is surely about loss and restoration, and the survival of innocence in a corrupt world.

Adrian Noble in 2002 directed the Royal Shakespeare Company at the Roundhouse (a former locomotive shed north of London) and also at Stratford-upon-Avon. Because we reprint, above, Michael Dobson's comment on the multiethnic production (a black Pericles, a white Thaisa, a mixed-race Marina), it is enough here to say that this highly stylized version was on the whole reviewed favorably.

Although in the nineteenth century the play was staged chiefly as a spectacle, with seemingly realistic sets showing beautiful exotic places, productions from the middle of the twentieth century up to the present have emphasized certain themes, treating the play almost as an allegory, and they therefore use symbolic rather than realistic sets. These productions probably are influenced by the writings of G. Wilson Knight, who in the selection that we reprint in this volume begins by saying "*Pericles* might be called a Shakespearian morality play," i.e., a play like those late medieval plays such as *Everyman*, in which allegorical elements representing good and evil engage in a contest for the protagonist's soul. Following this line, Andrei Serban, who staged *Pericles* in 2003–04 in Cambridge, Massachusetts, said in an interview, "I see *Pericles* as an allegory, with the hero functioning as an Everyman who must journey through the world until he reaches maturity." Serban, asserting that "The incest [Pericles] uncovers in Antioch obsesses him for the rest of his life," went on to describe the play as "Pericles' attempt to expiate the sin he found in Antioch." The characters reflect his "psychic state" and the sea reflects "the emotional peaks and troughs of Pericles' voyage." Given such a view of the play, a realistic presentation will not work. Serban in some scenes went so far as to use video and film— nude shots of the incestuous King Antiochus and his daughter (these were repeatedly shown, to the annoyance of many viewers)—and strange costumes. The production was not favorably received, the costumes especially provoking the reviewers. One reviewer said, "Thaisa, looking . . . like Minnie Mouse, must seduce Pericles garbed in what seems an orange bell, with approximations of cantaloupes on her shoulders, nevertheless making lyrical, vaguely Asian music as she dances with bells about her ankles." This reviewer (Carolyn Clay) went on to say that the use of film footage suggested that Serban was "more interested in all the overlay than he is in the transporting powers of the play's famed reconciliation scenes. . . . In the end, the director does as much as his wind and weather to sink Pericles."

Although Mary Zimmerman's production at the Shakespeare Theater in Washington, D.C., in 2003, repeated at the Goodman Theatre in Chicago in 2005–06, was somewhat like Serban's in that it was stylized rather than realistic, it was infinitely more successful. Zimmerman, who had achieved fame with highly imaginative productions of such mythic material as *The Odyssey*, *The Arabian Nights*, and *Metamorphoses*, presented the audience first with a stage curtain showing a sail. When the curtain went up, the audience saw a minimal white box set with a large window and a balcony, but this space became magical, a place not where character was psychoanalyzed but where billowing blue cloth represented the sea, where male players carrying sticks tipped with sailing vessels became a fleet, and where women carrying the moon and stars became the heavens. But it was not overly pretty and it was not lacking in down-to-earth comic bits: When Marina was about to be destroyed by the wicked Leonine (the evil Queen Dionyza's instrument), a narrator walked across the stage and read, to great comic effect, "Enter pirates." Romance shared the stage with bawdry, epic motifs with low comedy. This highly imaginative production conveyed a sense of the miraculous. The "truth" of the play, such as it is, here was the truth of fairy tales, of dreams, of poetry.

2002–03 was a strong time for productions of *Pericles:*

> To sing a song that old was sung,
> From ashes ancient Gower is come,
> Assuming man's infirmities,
> To glad your ear, and please your eyes.

In this period ancient Gower sang his song (i.e., told his tale) not only in the productions by Noble, Serban, Zimmerman, and (not here discussed) Neil Bartlett's London production at the Hammersmith (2003) but also in a superb Japanese production staged at the Olivier Theatre in London, directed by Yukio Ninagawa. English surtitles were used, and because the play was performed in Japanese the Anglophone audience was spared the creaky language of some portions. The production began with the sounds of gunfire and of exploding bombs while weary limping refugees, lugging battered suitcases, hobbled onto the stage. Gower was played by two street performers (one with a lute) in a locale that suggested burned-out Hiroshima. Here indeed were "man's infirmities," but in the midst of this wretchedness and violence, some water trickling out of pipes offered nourishment to the refugees and suggested renewed life. Later, when Thaisa was resurrected, the taps spouted water. Theatrical effects that may in this report sound unconvincing were movingly effective. Locales were given distinct colors: white for Tharsus, blue for Pentapolis, purple for Mytilene. Dumb show scenes were performed by puppets; waves were represented by billowing silk; Thaisa, brought back to life, levitated above her coffin. It was unreal and yet it was somehow connected with real life, thoroughly appropriate to a play that traces a movement from death to rebirth. Words of Thornton Wilder come to mind: "The theatre is supremely fitted to say: 'Behold! These things are.'" Or we can quote Antonin Artaud: "We need above all a theater that wakes us up: nerves and heart." Ninagawa's production, in short, did what most people hope an experience in the theater will do: It revitalized its audience.

In speaking about *Pericles* on the stage, it is also worth mentioning that in recent years colleges and universities have occasionally produced the play, not very often, of course, but still with a frequency that is remarkable. For instance, at the University of Arizona, ART (Arizona Repertory Theatre), Brent Gibbs directed a production in 2005. Like some of the most successful recent professional productions, much of it was highly stylized. For instance, the joust—always a problem—was presented not as a combat but as a dance in which Pericles triumphed by a single gesture, and the waves to which Marina's coffin was consigned were represented by performers dressed in white.

Finally, a few words about the BBC TV version (1983), directed by David Jones, with Mike Gwilym as Pericles. Jones gives us almost the full text of the play, with some additional passages from George Wilkins's prose narrative adapted into blank verse. The sets are fairly realistic, though some locales are given a predominant color, purple for Mytilene, yellow for Ephesus, and red for Antioch. The costumes are tunics and loose trousers, suggestive of North Africa, but they are also sometimes symbolic: The incestuous King Antiochus wears a bloodred cloak, and the "good king Simonides" wears a white tunic. A number of shots of sandy places appropriately suggest Pericles's wanderings. When Gower speaks of "Neptune's billows" in the third act, we see waves superimposed on his face, but otherwise the ocean is not shown, though we do see Pericles on the rocking deck of a ship. On the whole, film techniques such as this superimposition are not used, but we do get a fade-out in Gower's first speech: When he says, "This, Antioch then," his face is gradually replaced by Antiochus's garden. Some viewers may wish that the director had made more use of cinematic techniques—or for that matter of theatrical techniques such as are associated with Brecht and his followers—but the presentation is thoroughly respectable and provides a useful introduction to the play.

Even when eked out with passages from Wilkins, much of the play remains obscure, and much else remains creaky. But much is splendid. There is, however, another important aspect of the play, one that perhaps readers may skim over but that becomes highly apparent when the play is staged. This is what, for want of a better word, we can call the realism of the brothel scenes, scenes whose dark, unnerving wit rivals the dark scenes of *Measure for Measure*. When we think of *Pericles* as a play that belongs to a group we call "the last plays," or the "romances"—we may forget that it includes such an incisively drawn character as the brothel keeper, who says, "The poor Transylvanian is dead that lay with the little baggage." This is not to assert that the scenes in the brothel give us "real" life while the other scenes—let's say the reconciliation between Pericles and Marina—give us fantasy. When we see the reconciliation, and listen to the words, the speeches seem miraculously close to our own feelings. However much we may talk abstractly about the mythlike qualities of Shakespeare's last plays, a production of any of them, including *Pericles*, reminds us that the works are in close contact with life as we feel it.

Bibliographic note: Brief histories of *Pericles* on the stage can be found in the editions of the play by Roger Warren (1990), Doreen Del Vecchio and Antony Hammond (1998), and Suzanne Gossett (2004). The title of David Skeele's *Thwarting the Wayward Seas: A Critical and Theatrical History of Shakespeare's "Pericles" in the Nineteenth and Twentieth Centuries* (1998) indicates its coverage, but for more about Phelps's production of 1854, see John Forbes-Robertson's *The Life and Life-Work of Samuel Phelps* (1886) and John Coleman's *Memoirs of Phelps* (1888), and also a modern study, Shirley S. Allen's *Samuel Phelps and Sadler's Wells* (1971). On productions since the middle of the twentieth century, see *Shakespeare Survey* (an annual) and *Shakespeare Quarterly*. Some reviews (especially those with an academic slant) are reprinted in volumes of *Shakespearean Criticism*, and many journalistic reviews are reprinted in *Theatre Record*. The following have been especially helpful: On David Thacker's 1989–90 production, Peter Holland in *Shakespeare Survey* 44 (1992): 166–70; on Phyllida Lloyd's 1993–94 production, Peter Holland in *Shakespeare Survey* 48 (1995): 223–24, and especially Melissa Gibson in *Pericles: Critical Essays,* ed. David Skeele (2000), 332–38; on Ninagawa's 2003 production, Richard Wilson in *The Times Literary Supplement,* April 11, 2003, p. 21. Recent productions are announced and are sometimes reviewed on Google. The BBC TV version is discussed briefly by Susan Willis in *The BBC Shakespeare* (1991), and at length by Paul Nelsen in David Skeele's *"Pericles": Critical Essays* (2000).

Cymbeline

The Tragedy of CYMBELINE.

Headband from the first printing of *Cymbeline*, in the First Folio (1623).

Introduction

In *Cymbeline* Shakespeare combines three stories which originate at three different points in space (so to speak) and gradually converge toward the end of the play. The first story is of a wife who is separated from and eventually reunited with her husband: Imogen and Posthumus. This constitutes the primary action of the play. It fills the first two acts to the exclusion of all else, and, though subordinated to a secondary and a tertiary action in Acts 3 and 4, it dominates the last act. Thus it is the major structural entity of the play, giving shape to the whole from beginning to end. The second story is of two sons who have been separated from their father in infancy and who eventually are reunited with him: Guiderius and Arviragus. This constitutes the secondary action of the play. It does not begin, however, in the first act and run in parallel with the primary action, as do the secondary actions of *Twelfth Night*, *The Merchant of Venice*, and *King Lear*. Rather, it begins in the middle of the play (3.3), is partly joined to the primary action through the sojourn of Imogen with the sons in her assumed identity of Fidele (3.6–4.2), and is fully joined to the primary action in the long last scene of the play (5.5). In this respect it bears a general resemblance to the secondary actions of *Pericles* and *The Winter's Tale* (where the subject is again the reunion of child with parent), the chief difference being that in those plays Shakespeare, having chosen to present the early story of the mother and father together with the story of the loss of the infant child, employed a mid-play lapse of many years during which the child might grow to marriageable age. The third story is of a king who successfully defends his country against invasion: Cymbeline. This, despite the emphasis given it by the play's title and by Cymbeline's presence in the primary action from the start in his role as Imogen's father, constitutes a tertiary action, beginning, like the secondary action, not in the first act but in the middle of the play, when the Roman ambassador Lucius demands tribute of Cymbeline (3.1). Gradually the tertiary action approaches the other actions of the play, joining first the primary action when Lucius accepts Fidele as his page (4.2), then the secondary when Guiderius and Arviragus decide to take up arms against the Romans (4.4). In the last scene the three actions are fused in a brilliant denouement in which no less than twenty-five plot complications are untied.

Each of the three stories of which *Cymbeline* is composed is itself a combination of various literary elements. The Imogen-Posthumus story is by all odds the most complex of the three. The basic source of this story is the ninth novella of the Second Day of Boccaccio's *Decameron* (see The Sources of *Cymbeline*, page 344). (Shakespeare also made some use of a German variant of the Boccaccio novella which had been translated into English under the title of *Frederick of Jennen* early in the sixteenth century.) In the first half of his story Shakespeare is generally faithful to the first half of Boccaccio's story. Like Boccaccio, he presents the husband's wager on the wife's chastity, the villain's stratagem of the trunk, the consequent winning of the wager, and the servant's failure to carry out the husband's order to kill the wife. A significant variation in this part of the story is that Shakespeare's villain actually attempts the seduction of the wife; Boccaccio's villain becomes by common report so convinced of the wife's chastity that he gives up all thought of winning the wager without guile and proceeds immediately to the stratagem of the trunk. Another significant variation is Shakespeare's providing a father for the heroine—and, in fact, a father who is a king. Accordingly the heroine is raised in rank from merchant's wife to princess, the initial separation on which the whole story turns being due not to the husband's casual absence on commerce but to his political exile. Thus a subsequent connection with the political story of Cymbeline is provided for.

For the first half of the Imogen-Posthumus story (and for the second as well) Shakespeare used also as source an anonymous dramatic romance entitled *The Rare Triumphs of Love and Fortune* (acted 1582). (In *Cymbeline* the two sources may be thought of as superimposed one upon the other.) In *Love and Fortune* a princess named Fidelia (compare Imogen's pseudonym Fidele) is in love with a supposed orphan who, like

Posthumus, has been brought up as the King's ward. Fidelia's brother secures the banishment of the lover, who thereupon sends word to Fidelia to run away from court and meet him at a cave. (The plan miscarries and Fidelia, like Imogen, wanders about until she meets an old man who, like Belarius, had been a courtier until unjustly banished by the King and who now lives as a hermit in a cave.) To the basic situation of *Love and Fortune* Shakespeare added the folk-tale motif of the Wicked Stepmother, a significant difference from the usual situation being that Shakespeare's stepmother wishes not to substitute her own child for the father's child but to advance her son by marrying him to the father's daughter, who, in the absence of surviving male issue, is heir to the kingdom. (The Queen's motivation becomes more conventional at 3.5.64.) Thus a political motive for the banishment of Posthumus is provided. The Physician is an added character required by the plot device of the potion, which Shakespeare made use of later in the play.

In the second half of the Imogen-Posthumus story Shakespeare departed more widely from Boccaccio's story, but he retained its essential framework. In Boccaccio, the wife adopts male disguise, takes service with a merchant, travels with him to Alexandria, passes into the service of the Sultan (whose especial favor she comes to enjoy), meets the villain in a shop, and succeeds in bringing him to judgment before the Sultan and her husband. The villain is forced to confess, the husband repents of his error, husband and wife are reunited, and the villain is executed. In Shakespeare, the wife adopts male disguise, travels to Wales (where she lives for a time with rustic outlaws), takes service with the general of an invading army, is captured along with the invaders by the King (whose especial favor she comes to enjoy), recognizes the villain among the captives, and succeeds in bringing him to judgment before the King and her husband. The villain repents and confesses, the husband repents of his error, husband and wife are reunited, and the villain is forgiven.

Two variations in this part of the Imogen-Posthumus story have the effect of unifying divergent strands of the triple-action plot. The disguised wife's sojourn with rustic outlaws in the mountains of Wales (apparently suggested by Fidelia's experience in *Love and Fortune* but perhaps also reflective of Erminia's pastoral sojourn in Book VII of Tasso's *Jerusalem Delivered*) connects the primary action with the secondary action involving Cymbeline's lost sons; and Imogen's acceptance of service with the Roman general Lucius (which is essentially present in Boccaccio) connects the primary action with the tertiary action of the invasion of Britain. Two further variations are of interest. The first, a structural matter, involves the point at which the author begins his story. Boccaccio begins his story at the point of the wager, Shakespeare his at a point shortly after the marriage that will make the wager possible. It is as though *Cymbeline* were the second part of an Elizabethan two-part play of which the first part, a comedy, has ended, as by convention a comedy should, with the marriage of lovers who have succeeded in overcoming all obstacles (parental opposition among them) to their union. In *Othello* Shakespeare had already used this particular starting point for a story of jealousy in marriage, beginning the action with a confrontation of angry father and successful wooer in presence of the newly married daughter. In *Cymbeline* there is the same initial confrontation, the chief difference being that the father (unlike Brabantio) does not suggest to the husband the possibility of the daughter's infidelity. Another variation from Boccaccio is the strong emphasis which Shakespeare gives to the reciprocal themes of repentance and forgiveness. Posthumus, long before he learns he has been deceived by Iachimo, sincerely repents of, and wishes to die in expiation for, the crime which he supposes he has committed against Imogen; and, as he freely repents, so Imogen freely forgives him. Again, Iachimo, when his plot is exposed, undergoes a "conversion" which may be compared with the conversion of Edmund in *King Lear* ("some good I mean to do, Despite of mine own nature") and contrasted with the defiant persistence in evil of Iago in *Othello* ("Demand me nothing. What you know, you know"). The sincerity of Iachimo's conversion is proved by his willingness to accept the punishment of death; and, as he freely repents, so Posthumus freely forgives him. Here, as in *The Winter's Tale* and *The Tempest,* Shakespeare echoes themes he had treated more fully in *The Merchant of Venice* and *Measure for Measure.*

In addition to these variations, Shakespeare made four important additions to the latter half of Boccaccio's story: the killing of Cloten, the supposed death of Imogen, Imogen's mistaking Cloten's body for that of Posthumus, and the Vision of Posthumus.

Since there is no character in Boccaccio corresponding to Cloten, his essential character may well have been suggested by

Fidelia's villainous brother in *Love and Fortune*. The killing of Cloten by Guiderius is closely connected with Cloten's intention to rape Imogen. This intention makes Cloten an example of lust and villainy to be compared with the example afforded by Iachimo: the one lecherous villain is stupid and boorish, the other subtle and Italianate. The intention also "justifies" the killing of Cloten, for in effect Guiderius, even though unaware of Cloten's intention and Fidele's true identity, acts to protect his sister from rape. The manner of the killing—decapitation, with the severed head being thrown into a stream which will carry it to the sea—appears to echo a folk ritual of some sort. There is a patent allusion to the death of Orpheus, whose severed head was thrown into the river Hebrus, down which it was carried to the sea and eventually to Lesbos; and there was an analogous ritual connected with the worship of Adonis at Alexandria, where "a Head, of papyrus, representing the god, was, with every show of mourning, committed to the waves, and borne within seven days by a current . . . to Byblos . . ." (Jessie L. Weston, *From Ritual to Romance,* ed. 1957, p. 47). (These allusions, mock-epic or mock-mythic in relation to Cloten himself, may carry serious meaning in relation to Cloten as a surrogate for Posthumus.) The killing of Cloten may be compared also with the killing of Antigonus in *The Winter's Tale:* in each case a vicious or a flawed character is punished for attempted violence against the heroine, and in each case there seems to be operative a tradition of tragicomedy which goes back ultimately to what Aristotle called "tragedy with a double issue"—that is to say, a play threatening death which provides a happy ending for "good" characters but the reward of death for "bad." This tradition is involved also in the death of the Queen at the end of the play.

The general plot device of the supposed death of a beloved woman (a staple of Greek romance) was one that Shakespeare had already used in *Romeo and Juliet, Much Ado About Nothing,* and *Pericles,* and that he was to use again in *The Winter's Tale;* and the particular device of the potion that brings about the supposed death he had used in *Romeo and Juliet.* In *Cymbeline* (4.2) the supposed death of Imogen symbolizes the death which Posthumus had commanded, separates Imogen from the rustic outlaws, and emphasizes the operation of Providence in the accident of the malevolent Queen's having requested poison of a physician who, because of his wisdom and benevolence, supplied her instead with a harmless sleeping potion.

The killing of Cloten and the supposed death of Imogen lead to the Elizabethan-Gothic grotesquerie of Imogen's mistaking the headless body of Cloten for that of Posthumus. Through this theatrically sensational mistake (so embarrassing to modern audiences) Shakespeare makes the interesting point that Imogen, like Posthumus, can be victimized by circumstance and deceived by appearance—and in a situation outwardly suggestive of sexual compromise, for unwittingly the paragon of virtue lies beside and lovingly embraces the body of a man who is not her husband but her would-have-been rapist. (Even so she has earlier unwittingly spent the night with her would-be seducer Iachimo.) A possible source of this episode exists in an anonymous dramatic romance entitled *Clyomon and Clamydes,* dating from the 1580's. Here the heroine, Neronis, who has left the court in the disguise of a boy and taken service with a shepherd, comes upon a coffin containing the body of the King of Norway, earlier slain in combat by Neronis's lover Clyomon. Since Clyomon has left his emblazoned shield beside the coffin, Neronis mistakes the body of the King of Norway for that of Clyomon, grieves, despairs, and is on the point of committing suicide. At this moment the personification of Providence descends from heaven, gives Neronis a paper informing her that Clyomon is alive, and returns to heaven. Another possible source of this episode is afforded by the *Ethiopica* of Heliodorus, in which Theagenes embraces the body of a dead woman which he mistakes for that of his beloved, Charicleia.

The Vision of Posthumus (5.4), in which Jupiter descends from heaven, may have been suggested by the descent of Providence in *Clyomon and Clamydes.* In any case, the Vision involves a literary tradition deriving ultimately from the appearance-of-a-god-in-a-dream of classical epic. Shakespeare had used such a dream theophany in *Pericles,* where the goddess Diana appears to the protagonist in a dream; and he had used the closely allied convention of the appearance-of-a-ghost-in-a-dream in *Richard III,* where the Ghosts of Richard's victims appear successively to the dreaming Richard and Richmond. A native stage tradition may also be influential, for the great fifteenth-century scriptural cycles frequently employ the appearance-of-an-angel-in-a-dream. An Elizabethan stage convention is certainly operative, the god who descends from stage cover to stage by means of suspension-gear: Juno in *The Tem-*

pest, Venus in Greene's *Alphonsus King of Aragon,* Providence in the anonymous *Clyomon and Clamydes,* perhaps Diana in *Pericles.* In *Cymbeline,* as Bertrand Evans has pointed out (see Commentaries), Jupiter is not a *deus ex machina* in the sense that he resolves a complication of the plot; rather, the theophany focuses our growing awareness that God's providence is indeed at work, even though for a time (during the long and frightening absence of Iachimo, the only person who, by confessing his slander against Imogen, can resolve the major complication of the plot) we may have seen little visible evidence of it. It should be added that the authenticity of the Vision, frequently called in question by critics of the nineteenth and early twentieth centuries, is now (together with the authenticity of the rest of the play) generally accepted, perhaps largely because of the cogent demonstration by G. Wilson Knight in *The Crown of Life* (1948; see Commentaries).

At least one other influence on the Imogen-Posthumus story can be discerned: that of Greek romance. The influence was already present in Boccaccio's story, for Greek romance characteristically involves a separation of lover from beloved (or of husband from wife), consequent wanderings over great distances and for long periods of time, and an eventual reunion of the lovers. *Apollonius of Tyre,* which Shakespeare had dramatized in *Pericles,* is a good example of the type, but an example of specific relevance to *Cymbeline* is afforded by the *Ethiopica* of Heliodorus, of which an Elizabethan translation (the first of three) appeared in 1567. From the *Ethiopica* (to which he had alluded in *Twelfth Night,* 5.1.118) Shakespeare apparently took a suggestion for the striking of the disguised Imogen by Posthumus (5.5). Charicleia, who has been separated from her lover, Theagenes, comes to Memphis and recognizes him. Since she is disguised as a beggar, however, Theagenes does not recognize her.

Frantically, as if sight of him had stung her, she ran to him, clasped him close, hung upon his neck, and caressed him with inarticulate sighs and tears. When he saw her face, begrimed and purposely discolored, and her torn and tattered garments, he took her for a shameless beggar. He pulled her off and thrust her away, and when she would not let go he struck her for troubling him and blocking his view of Calasiris and his sons. She said to him softly, "Pythias, have you forgotten the lamp?" The words struck Theagenes like a bolt. He remembered that the lamp was a token they had agreed upon and gazed into Charicleia's eyes, whose brilliance broke upon him like the sun's rays through a cloud. He threw his arms about her and embraced her.

(translation by Moses Hadas)

The striking of Imogen by Posthumus may also reflect a device of the romantic epics, the individual combat between two knights in which the lover, ignorant of his opponent's sex and true identity, fights with and sometimes kills his beloved in male disguise. Romantic-epic examples include the combat between Tancred and Clorinda in Book XII of Tasso's *Jerusalem Delivered* and that between Arthegal and Britomart in Book III of Spenser's *Fairy Queen;* and dramatic examples in the same tradition include the combat between the title characters of Kyd's *Soliman and Perseda* and between Amintor and Aspatia in *The Maid's Tragedy* by Beaumont and Fletcher.

The secondary action of the play—consisting of the story of Guiderius and Arviragus—begins in 3.3, although we are warned early to expect it by a reference to Cymbeline's lost sons at 1.1.57. The Guiderius-Arviragus story employs that standard device of romance tradition, the "lost child." This is Shakespeare's most important innovation in the "historical" materials available to him. Usually—because of the characteristic concern of romance with love—the lost child is a girl, apparently of low degree, who is enabled to marry her lover of high degree when it is revealed that she also is of gentle birth. This is the situation of the heroine in many of the comedies of Plautus and Terence, and it is a common situation in pastoral romance. (Examples are afforded by Glycerium in the *Andria* of Terence, Pastorella in Book VI of *The Fairy Queen,* and Perdita in *The Winter's Tale.*) Sometimes the lost child is a boy, but in such cases the story does not usually involve a love situation, presumably because the mobility required of the wanderer who comes to the environment of the lost child is unsuited to the decorum of a girl. (Compare the convenience, if not the necessity, of Imogen's male disguise.) Sometimes the lost male child is involved ultimately in a situation in which he unwittingly takes or threatens the life of his father (for example, the *Oedipus* of Sophocles) or in which the father unwittingly takes or threatens the life of his son (for example, *The Captives* of Plautus).

Cymbeline's threat to execute the confessed homicide Guiderius, who is actually his own son, seems to echo the oedipal situation of *The Captives,* in which the father, Hegio, threatens to execute the supposed slave, Tyndarus, who is actually his own son.

The Guiderius-Arviragus story includes the corollary story of Belarius: as they are lost children, so he is their supposed father. Belarius is primarily the "rusticated courtier" of pastoral romance: the educated and civilized gentleman or nobleman who lives in isolation or among shepherds and with whom the protagonist passes some time during his wanderings. Sometimes the rusticated courtier's exile is voluntary, the result of an unhappy love affair or some other disillusionment. An example is Philisides in Sidney's *Arcadia.* More frequently the rusticated courtier's exile is enforced, the result of banishment for political reasons. An example is the Duke Senior in *As You Like It.* Belarius, an example of the latter type, has an apparent source in Bomelio, the unjustly exiled courtier of *Love and Fortune* who lives in a cave and whom Fidelia meets after running away from court.

Belarius, however, is not only the rusticated courtier, he is also the "shepherd father" of pastoral romance. Usually the shepherd father is only a foster father and the lost child that he rears as his own is a girl. Examples are Melibee, supposed father of Pastorella in Book VI of *The Fairy Queen,* and the Shepherd, supposed father of Perdita in *The Winter's Tale.* Shakespeare makes Belarius not a shepherd but a hunter, because Guiderius and Arviragus must have had the sort of training with weapons that will fit them to fight effectively in defense of their country; and he makes Belarius a mountaineer in order to emphasize the danger of his position as a political outlaw. (Thus Shakespeare, through discarding sheep and shepherds, emphasizes the basic primitivism which is at the core of most pastoralism.) Nevertheless, it is convenient briefly to regard Belarius as a "shepherd" father in order to understand his relation to tradition. Since the rusticated courtier is rarely a father, Shakespeare seems, in Belarius, to have combined the pastoral character-types of the courtier rusticated for political reasons and the shepherd father. He was to make the same significant combination in amplified and most original form in *The Tempest,* where the only essential departure from the combined traditions (aside from the omission of sheep and shepherds) is that Prospero is not the foster father but the true father of Miranda.

The Guiderius-Arviragus story is amplified and linked to the tertiary action of the play by Shakespeare's use of material from Holinshed's *Chronicles of England, Scotland, and Ireland* (1587): specifically the Scottish victory over Danish invaders at the Battle of Luncarty (near Perth) in 976, which was achieved through the stalwart fighting of the husbandman Hay and his two sons (see *The History of Scotland,* in The Sources of *Cymbeline,* page 361). This joining of the Guiderius-Arviragus story to the Cymbeline story (4.4, 5.2–3) leads to its further joining, in the final scene of the play, to the Imogen-Posthumus story.

The tertiary action of the play—consisting of the Cymbeline story—begins in 3.1 with the appearance of the Roman ambassador Lucius, although we are warned to expect this action by a reference to Lucius at 2.3.55 and by another to the payment of Roman tribute at 2.4.13. The basic source is *The History of England* in Holinshed's *Chronicles,* but particular details have been traced to other sources. Since Holinshed attributes the denial of tribute to Cymbeline's son Guiderius, Shakespeare may well have followed Spenser (*The Fairy Queen,* II.x.50) in attributing the denial to Cymbeline. Moreover, a number of Shakespearian details appear to derive from Thomas Blenerhasset's "Guidericus" in the 1578 edition of the Second Part of *The Mirror for Magistrates* and from John Higgins's "Guiderius" in the 1587 edition of *The Mirror.* Perhaps the most interesting are the disguising of Posthumus as a British soldier and his fighting against the Romans. These details were apparently suggested by Higgins's account of the Roman captain Hamonius, who disguises himself as a British soldier and pretends to fight against the Romans in order to gain the opportunity of killing Guiderius. One other influence on the Cymbeline story is Shakespeare's own tradition of depicting the invasion of Britain or England, as in *King Lear, Richard III, 3 Henry VI,* and *King John.* In each of these cases, as in *Cymbeline,* the invasion is represented as partly or entirely beneficial to the island kingdom.

The foregoing account stresses the abundance of sources and traditions which Shakespeare characteristically blended into an organic whole in writing *Cymbeline.* The play is extremely complex in its relation to tradition. It is also complex in other respects, posing a number of problems both real and imaginary. The critics have reacted very differently to *Cymbeline.* At one extreme are the Rationalists, chief among them Dr. Johnson (1765):

> To remark the folly of the fiction, the absurdity of the conduct, the confusion of the names and manners of different times, and the impossibility of the events in any system of life, were to waste criticism upon unresisting imbecility, upon faults too evident for detection, and too gross for exaggeration.

At the other extreme are the Imogenolaters, of whom perhaps the best example is Swinburne (1880):

> The very crown and flower of all her father's daughters—I do not speak here of her human father but her divine—woman above all Shakespeare's women is Imogen. As in Cleopatra we found the incarnate sex, the woman everlasting, so in Imogen we find half-glorified already the immortal godhead of womanhood.

Neither critic need now be taken seriously, although it may be observed that Johnson's aversion to the violent yoking together of Roman Britain and Renaissance Rome reveals a characteristic blindness to the essence of romance.

Many other problems once posed by *Cymbeline* have been solved by recent criticism and scholarship. One such problem has already been mentioned: doubt of the authenticity of certain parts of the play, in particular the Vision of Posthumus. No one now denies that the play is entirely the work of Shakespeare. Another problem has been posed by the suggestion of a lost source-play. The theory, however, is both unnecessary and unsupported by evidence, and it seems to be at variance with what we know of Shakespeare's originality in the handling of multiple sources in such plays as *King Lear, The Merchant of Venice,* and *The Taming of the Shrew.* Another problem has been posed by A. H. Thorndike's suggestion that *Cymbeline* reveals the influence of Beaumont and Fletcher's *Philaster.* This theory has now been effectively disposed of by the late Harold S. Wilson in his English Institute lecture of 1951. Another problem has been posed by the complexity of the plot, which, entailing as it does some two dozen separate denouements, prompted Shaw, in *Cymbeline Refinished,* to rewrite the last act at half the length of the original for a production of 1937. Here Shakespeare's technical virtuosity and its relation to themes of the play have been well expounded by Bertrand Evans (see Commentaries, page 374). Still another problem has been posed by the character of Posthumus and particularly his motivation in accepting Iachimo's wager. Here W. W. Lawrence has enlightened us by setting Posthumus's action in an appropriate context of Renaissance conceptions of a wife's chastity and her husband's honor. And yet another difficulty is posed by the play's characteristic style, which is heavily metaphorical, often perverse in syntax, and sometimes so elliptical as to raise the question whether we are dealing with a metaphysical toughness of thought and angularity of expression comparable to Donne's, or simply with a corrupt text. In the large majority of cases, surely, the former interpretation is to be preferred, for the style of *Cymbeline* can be paralleled in such near-contemporary plays as *Antony and Cleopatra, Coriolanus,* and *The Winter's Tale.*

One teasing problem remains. Modern editors classify *Cymbeline* as a comedy. Why then was the play classified as a tragedy in the Shakespeare Folio of 1623? The classification could be simply an error, Heminges and Condell having forgotten that the play does not end with the death of the title character. Or, as has been suggested, the classification could be due to late receipt of copy in the printing-house, after the comedies (the first of the three genres of the Folio) had been printed off. Neither explanation is very satisfactory. On balance it seems more reasonable to assume that the classification resulted from a deliberate decision on the part of Heminges and Condell. The problem can perhaps be solved by considering two other Folio plays now classified as comedies: *The Winter's Tale* and *Troilus and Cressida.* (All three plays are tragicomedies, the first two of traditional type, the third of nontraditional.) What is the difference between, on the one hand, *The Winter's Tale* (classified as a comedy in the Folio) and, on the other, *Cymbeline* and *Troilus and Cressida* (classified as tragedies in the Folio)? Simply that the first play does not include war in its action, whereas the two latter plays do. In this respect *The Winter's Tale* is like the thirteen other "comedies" of the Folio classification, and *Cymbeline* and *Troilus and Cressida* are like the ten other "tragedies" of the Folio classification. (The distinction does not, to be sure, hold exactly in the case of *All's Well That Ends Well* and *Romeo and Juliet:* in the former play, however, war is not a political matter but a device to expose the braggart soldier

Parolles; and in the latter play war is represented by the feud between the rival houses of Capulet and Montague.) Having denied themselves the convenient classification of tragicomedy, Heminges and Condell seem to have made the best of an imperfect bargain by associating *The Winter's Tale* with that Shakespearian genre (comedy) which usually excludes war from the action, *Cymbeline* and *Troilus and Cressida* with that Shakespearian genre (tragedy) which (like history) usually includes war in the action. Some uncertainty about their decision may be reflected in the fact that in the Folio *The Winter's Tale* stands as the very last of the comedies, *Cymbeline* as the very last of the tragedies. *Troilus and Cressida,* for reasons connected with the printing of the Folio, stands by itself between the histories and the tragedies.

Cymbeline is generally dated during the theatrical season of 1609–10. It was seen by Simon Forman, presumably at the Globe, sometime before September 12, 1611, when Forman died. (Unfortunately his account of the play merely names the characters and summarizes the plot.) *Cymbeline* may have been designed for original production by the King's Men at their indoor theater, the Blackfriars, or at their outdoor theater, the Globe. The issue is relatively unimportant, however, since the same plays were frequently performed at both kinds of playhouse, public and private. On January 1, 1634, *Cymbeline* was acted "at Court by the King's Players," being "well-liked by the King." Probably the theater was the Cockpit-in-Court at Whitehall, though it may have been the Great Hall of Whitehall Palace. In original production *Cymbeline* was presumably performed on a stage generally similar to the one that appears in the well-known De Witt drawing of the Swan Playhouse—that is to say, without benefit of an "inner stage." The present text has been annotated in accordance with this assumption.

RICHARD HOSLEY

[*Dramatis Personae*

Cymbeline, King of Britain
Imogen, daughter to Cymbeline by a former wife, later
    disguised under the name of Fidele
Posthumus Leonatus, a gentleman, husband to Imogen
Guiderius } sons to Cymbeline, disguised under
Arviragus } the names of Polydore and Cadwal,
          } supposed sons to Morgan
Belarius, a banished lord, disguised under the name of
    Morgan
The Queen, wife to Cymbeline
Cloten, son to the Queen by a former husband
Cornelius, a physician employed by the Queen
Pisanio, servant to Posthumus
Lords attending on Cymbeline
Ladies attending on the Queen
Helen, a lady attending on Imogen
Two Lords, friends to Cloten
Two Gentlemen of Cymbeline's court
Two Briton Captains
Musicians employed by Cloten
Messengers
Two Jailers

Caius Lucius, Roman ambassador, later general of the
    Roman forces
Two Roman Senators
Roman Tribunes
Roman Captains
A Soothsayer, named Philharmonus
Philario, an Italian friend to Posthumus
Iachimo, an Italian friend to Philario
A Frenchman, friend to Philario

Jupiter
Ghost of Sicilius Leonatus, father to Posthumus

Ghost of the Mother to Posthumus
Ghosts of the two young Brothers to Posthumus, called
    Leonati

Briton Soldiers, Roman Soldiers, Attendants, a Dutchman,
    and a Spaniard (friends to Philario)

Scene: Britain, Rome, Wales]

Cymbeline

ACT 1

Scene 1. [*Britain*.]

Enter two Gentlemen.

First Gentleman. You do not meet a man but frowns. Our bloods°*
  No more obey the heavens than our courtiers
  Still seem as does the King's.°

Second Gentleman.   But what's the matter?

First Gentleman. His daughter, and the heir of's kingdom, whom
  He purposed to his wife's sole son—a widow   5
  That late he married—hath referred° herself
  Unto a poor but worthy gentleman. She's wedded,
  Her husband banished, she imprisoned. All
  Is outward sorrow, though I think the King
  Be touched at very heart.

Second Gentleman.   None but the King?   10

First Gentleman. He that hath lost her too. So is the Queen,

---

*The degree sign (°) indicates a footnote, which is keyed to the text by line number. Text references are printed in **boldface** type; the annotation follows in roman type.
1.1.1 **bloods** moods 3 **seem as does the King's** wear expressions like the King's 6 **referred** given

211

That most desired the match. But not a courtier,
Although they wear their faces to the bent°
Of the King's looks, hath a heart that is not
Glad at the thing they scowl at.

15 *Second Gentleman.*   And why so?

First Gentleman. He that hath missed the Princess is a
        thing
    Too bad for bad report, and he that hath her—
    I mean, that married her, alack good man,
    And therefore banished—is a creature such
20 As, to seek through the regions of the earth
    For one his like, there would be something failing
    In him that should compare. I do not think
    So fair an outward and such stuff within
    Endows a man but he.

Second Gentleman.   You speak him far.°

25 *First Gentleman.* I do extend him, sir, within himself,°
    Crush him together rather than unfold
    His measure duly.

Second Gentleman. What's his name and birth?

First Gentleman. I cannot delve him to the root. His father
    Was called Sicilius, who did join his honor°
30 Against the Romans with Cassibelan,
    But had his titles by Tenantius, whom
    He served with glory and admired° success,
    So gained the sur-addition° Leonatus;
    And had, besides this gentleman in question,
35 Two other sons, who in the wars o' th' time
    Died with their swords in hand; for which their father,
    Then old and fond of issue,° took such sorrow
    That he quit being, and his gentle lady,
    Big of this gentleman our theme, deceased

---

13 **bent** inclination   24 **speak him far** praise him much   25 **do
extend . . . himself** i.e., do not exaggerate his real merit   29 **honor**
reputation (as a soldier)   32 **admired** wondered at   33 **sur-
addition** additional title   37 **fond of issue** doting on children

As he was born. The King he takes the babe 40
To his protection, calls him Posthumus Leonatus,
Breeds him and makes him of his bedchamber,°
Puts to him° all the learnings that his time°
Could make him the receiver of, which he took
As we do air, fast as 'twas minist'red, 45
And in's spring became a harvest, lived in court—
Which rare it is to do—most praised, most loved,
A sample to the youngest, to th' more mature
A glass that feated them,° and to the graver
A child that guided dotards. To his mistress, 50
For whom he now is banished—her own price°
Proclaims how she esteemed him and his virtue.
By her election° may be truly read
What kind of man he is.

Second Gentleman.   I honor him
Even out of° your report. But pray you tell me, 55
Is she sole child to th' King?

First Gentleman.   His only child.
He had two sons—if this be worth your hearing,
Mark it—the eldest of them at three years old,
I' th' swathing clothes the other, from their nursery
Were stol'n, and to this hour no guess in knowledge 60
Which way they went.

Second Gentleman.   How long is this ago?

First Gentleman. Some twenty years.

Second Gentleman. That a king's children should be so
    conveyed,°
So slackly guarded, and the search so slow
That could not trace them!

First Gentleman.   Howsoe'er 'tis strange, 65
Or that the negligence may well be laughed at,
Yet is it true, sir.

---

42 **of his bedchamber** i.e., a chamberlain   43 **Puts to him** sets him
to work at   43 **time** age   49 **glass that feated them** mirror that reflected their features   51 **price** what she is willing to undergo for his
sake   53 **election** choice   55 **out of** beyond   63 **conveyed** stolen

Second Gentleman.   I do well believe you.

First Gentleman. We must forbear.° Here comes° the gentleman,
 The Queen, and Princess.   *Exeunt*

   Enter the Queen, Posthumus, and Imogen.

70 *Queen.* No, be assured you shall not find me, daughter,
 After the slander° of most stepmothers,
 Evil-eyed unto you. You're my prisoner, but
 Your jailer shall deliver you the keys
 That lock up your restraint. For you, Posthumus,
75 So soon as I can win th' offended King,
 I will be known your advocate. Marry,° yet
 The fire of rage is in him, and 'twere good
 You leaned unto° his sentence with what patience
 Your wisdom may inform you.

Posthumus.   Please your Highness,
 I will from hence today.

80 *Queen.*   You know the peril.
 I'll fetch a turn about the garden, pitying
 The pangs of barred affections, though the King
 Hath charged you should not speak together.   *Exit.*

Imogen.   O
 Dissembling courtesy! How fine this tyrant
85 Can tickle° where she wounds! My dearest husband,
 I something fear my father's wrath, but nothing—
 Always reserved° my holy duty°—what
 His rage can do on me. You must be gone,
 And I shall here abide the hourly shot
90 Of angry eyes, not comforted to live

68 **forbear** withdraw   68 **Here comes** (this entrance-announcement
shows that, though the stage is technically "clear" at line 69 [at which
point F marks a new scene], the oncoming players enter before the off-
going ones have completed their exit)   71 **slander** ill repute   76
Marry indeed (by the Virgin Mary)   78 **leaned unto** deferred to
85 **tickle** (pretend to) please   87 **reserved** excepting   87 **duty** i.e.,
of child to parent

But that there is this jewel in the world
That I may see again.

Posthumus.   My queen, my mistress.
O lady, weep no more, lest I give cause
To be suspected of more tenderness
Than doth become a man. I will remain   95
The loyal'st husband that did e'er plight troth;
My residence, in Rome at one Philario's,
Who to my father was a friend, to me
Known but by letter. Thither write, my queen,
And with mine eyes I'll drink the words you send,   100
Though ink be made of gall.

                    Enter Queen.

Queen.   Be brief, I pray you.
If the King come, I shall incur I know not
How much of his displeasure. [*Aside*] Yet I'll move him
To walk this way. I never do him wrong
But he does buy° my injuries, to be friends;   105
Pays dear for my offenses.   [*Exit.*]

Posthumus.   Should we be taking leave
As long a term as yet we have to live,
The loathness to depart would grow. Adieu.

Imogen. Nay, stay a little.
Were you but riding forth to air yourself,   110
Such parting were too petty. Look here, love;
This diamond was my mother's. [*Giving a ring*] Take it,
        heart,
But° keep it till you woo another wife,
When Imogen is dead.

Posthumus.   How, how? Another?
You gentle gods, give me but this I have,   115
And cere up° my embracements from a next
With bonds of death! Remain, remain thou here
While sense can keep it on. And, sweetest, fairest,
As I my poor self did exchange for you

---

105 **buy** i.e., gladly accept   113 **But** only   116 **cere up** shroud

120   To your so infinite loss, so in our trifles
       I still win of you. For my sake wear this.

                              [*Giving a bracelet*]

       It is a manacle of love; I'll place it
       Upon this fairest prisoner.

Imogen.   O the gods!
       When shall we see again?

                    Enter Cymbeline and Lords.

Posthumus.   Alack, the King!

Cymbeline. Thou basest thing, avoid° hence, from my
125   sight!
       If after this command thou fraught° the court
       With thy unworthiness, thou diest. Away!
       Thou'rt poison to my blood.

Posthumus.   The gods protect you,
       And bless the good remainders of° the court.
       I am gone.   *Exit.*

130 *Imogen.*   There cannot be a pinch in death
       More sharp than this is.

Cymbeline.   O disloyal thing
       That shouldst repair° my youth, thou heap'st
       A year's age on me.

Imogen.   I beseech you, sir,
       Harm not yourself with your vexation.
135   I am senseless of° your wrath; a touch more rare°
       Subdues all pangs, all fears.

Cymbeline.   Past grace? obedience?

Imogen. Past hope, and in despair; that way, past grace.

Cymbeline. That mightst have had the sole son of my
       queen.

Imogen. O blessed that I might not! I chose an eagle
140   And did avoid a puttock.°

125 **avoid** go   126 **fraught** freight, burden   129 **remainders of**
those who remain at   132 **repair** renew   135 **am senseless of** do
not feel   135 **touch more rare** finer anxiety   140 **puttock** kite
(bird of prey)

Cymbeline. Thou took'st a beggar, wouldst have made my
        throne
    A seat for baseness.

Imogen.   No, I rather added
    A luster to it.

Cymbeline.   O thou vile one!

Imogen.   Sir,
    It is your fault that I have loved Posthumus.
    You bred him as my playfellow, and he is   145
    A man worth any woman; overbuys me
    Almost the sum he pays.°

Cymbeline.   What, art thou mad?

Imogen. Almost, sir. Heaven restore me! Would I were
    A neatherd's° daughter, and my Leonatus
    Our neighbor shepherd's son.

                    Enter Queen.

Cymbeline.   Thou foolish thing!   150
    [*To Queen*] They were again together. You have done
    Not after our command. Away with her
    And pen her up.

Queen.   Beseech° your patience. Peace,
    Dear lady daughter, peace! Sweet sovereign,
    Leave us to ourselves, and make yourself some
        comfort   155
    Out of your best advice.°

Cymbeline.   Nay, let her languish
    A drop of blood a day and, being aged,
    Die of this folly.

                    Exeunt [*Cymbeline and Lords*].

_____

146–47 **overbuys me . . . pays** he exceeds me in worth by almost the
price which he is now called upon to pay, i.e., banishment (J. M. Nosworthy)   149 **neatherd's** cowherd's   153 **Beseech** I beseech   156
advice consideration

Enter Pisanio.

Queen.   Fie, you must give way.—
   Here is your servant. How now, sir? What news?

Pisanio. My lord your son drew on my master.

160 *Queen.*   Ha!
   No harm, I trust, is done?

Pisanio.   There might have been
   But that my master rather played than fought
   And had no help of anger. They were parted
   By gentlemen at hand.

   Queen.   I am very glad on't.

165 *Imogen.* Your son's my father's friend; he takes his part°
   To draw upon an exile. O brave sir!
   I would they were in Afric both together,
   Myself by with a needle° that I might prick
   The goer-back. Why came you from your master?

170 *Pisanio.* On his command. He would not suffer me
   To bring him to the haven, left these notes
   Of what commands I should be subject to
   When't pleased you to employ me.

   Queen.   This hath been
   Your faithful servant. I dare lay° mine honor
   He will remain so.

175 *Pisanio.*   I humbly thank your Highness.

Queen. Pray walk awhile.   [*Exit Queen.*]

Imogen. About some half-hour hence, pray you speak
      with me.
   You shall at least go see my lord aboard.
   For this time leave me.   *Exeunt* [*severally°*].

---

165 **takes his part** plays his usual role   168 **needle** (pronounced
"neel")   174 **lay** stake   179s.d. **severally** by different tiring-house
doors (Imogen follows the Queen offstage while Pisanio exits by the
other door)

Scene 2. [*Britain.*]

Enter Cloten° and two Lords.

First Lord. Sir, I would advise you to shift a shirt; the
violence of action hath made you reek° as a sacrifice. Where air comes out, air comes in; there's
none abroad so wholesome as that you vent.°

Cloten. If my shirt were bloody, then to shift it. Have I hurt   5
him?

Second Lord. [*Aside*] No, faith, not so much as his patience.

First Lord. Hurt him? His body's a passable° carcass if he
be not hurt. It is a throughfare for steel if it be not hurt.

Second Lord. [*Aside*] His steel was in debt. It went o' th'   10
backside the town.°

Cloten. The villain would not stand° me.

Second Lord. [*Aside*] No, but he fled forward still, toward
your face.

First Lord. Stand you? You have land enough of your own,   15
but he added to your having, gave you some ground.

Second Lord. [*Aside*] As many inches as you have oceans.
Puppies!

Cloten. I would they had not come between us.

Second Lord. [*Aside*] So would I, till you had measured   20
how long a fool you were upon the ground.

Cloten. And that she should love this fellow and refuse me!

Second Lord. [*Aside*] If it be a sin to make a true election,° she is damned.

1.2.s.d. **Cloten** (rhymes with "rotten"; cf. "Cloten's clotpoll,"
4.2.184) 2 **reek** give off vapors   4 **vent** give off   8 **passable** af-
fording passage (quibble on "tolerable")   10–11 **It went . . . the
town** like a debtor avoiding a creditor by taking a back street (i.e., his
rapier missed)   12 **stand** confront   23–24 **election** choice

25   *First Lord.* Sir, as I told you always, her beauty and her
        brain go not together. She's° a good sign,° but I have
        seen small reflection of her wit.

     Second Lord. [*Aside*] She shines not upon fools, lest the
        reflection should hurt her.

30   *Cloten.* Come, I'll to my chamber. Would there had been
        some hurt done!

     Second Lord. [*Aside*] I wish not so—unless it had been the
        fall of an ass, which is no great hurt.

     Cloten. You'll go with us?

35   *First Lord.* I'll attend your lordship.

     Cloten. Nay, come, let's go together.

     Second Lord. Well, my lord.   *Exeunt.*

                    Scene 3. [*Britain.*]

                 Enter Imogen and Pisanio.

     Imogen. I would thou grew'st unto the shores o' th' haven
        And questioned'st every sail. If he should write,
        And I not have it, 'twere a paper lost
        As offered mercy is.° What was the last
        That he spake to thee?

5   *Pisanio.*   It was his queen, his queen.

     Imogen. Then waved his handkerchief?

     Pisanio.   And kissed it, madam.

     Imogen. Senseless° linen, happier therein than I!
        And that was all?

10   *Pisanio.*   No, madam. For so long
        As he could make me with this eye or ear
        Distinguish him from others, he did keep
        The deck, with glove or hat or handkerchief

26 **She's** she has   26 **sign** appearance   1.3.3–4 **'twere ... mercy
is** i.e., a letter gone astray would be as great a loss as mercy that fails
to reach its object   7 **Senseless** without feeling

Still waving, as° the fits and stirs of 's mind
Could best express how slow his soul sailed on,
How swift his ship.

Imogen.   Thou shouldst have made him
   As little as a crow or less, ere left   15
   To after-eye° him.

Pisanio.   Madam, so I did.

Imogen. I would have broke mine eyestrings, cracked
      them but
   To look upon him till the diminution
   Of space° had pointed him sharp as my needle;
   Nay, followed him till he had melted from   20
   The smallness of a gnat to air, and then
   Have turned mine eye and wept. But, good Pisanio,
   When shall we hear from him?

Pisanio.   Be assured, madam,
   With his next vantage.°

Imogen. I did not take my leave of him, but had   25
   Most pretty things to say. Ere I could tell him
   How I would think on him at certain hours
   Such thoughts and such; or I could make him swear
   The shes of Italy should not betray
   Mine interest and his honor; or have charged him   30
   At the sixth hour of morn, at noon, at midnight,
   T'encounter me with orisons,° for then
   I am in heaven for him; or ere I could
   Give him that parting kiss which I had set
   Betwixt two charming° words—comes in my father,   35
   And like the tyrannous breathing of the north
   Shakes all our buds from growing.

                    Enter a Lady.°

Lady.   The Queen, madam,
   Desires your Highness' company.

─────────────────────────────

12 **as** as if   15–16 **ere . . . after-eye** before you stopped looking
after   19 **space** i.e., distance   24 **vantage** opportunity   32 **T'encounter . . . orisons** join me in prayers   35 **charming** protecting
from evil   37s.d. (the Lady's message has the theatrical function of
motivating Imogen's exit)

Imogen. Those things I bid you do, get them dispatched.
I will attend the Queen.

40 *Pisanio.*   Madam, I shall.   *Exeunt.*

Scene 4. [*Rome.*]

*Enter Philario, Iachimo,° a Frenchman, a Dutchman, and
a Spaniard.*

Iachimo. Believe it, sir, I have seen him in Britain. He was
then of a crescent note,° expected to prove so worthy as
since he hath been allowed the name of. But I could then
have looked on him without the help of admiration,°
5 though the catalogue of his endowments had been
tabled° by his side and I to peruse him by items.

Philario. You speak of him when he was less furnished
than now he is with that which makes° him both without
and within.

10 *Frenchman.* I have seen him in France. We had very many
there could behold the sun° with as firm eyes as he.

Iachimo. This matter of marrying his king's daughter,
wherein he must be weighed rather by her value than his
own, words him, I doubt not, a great deal from the matter.°

15 *Frenchman.* And then his banishment.

Iachimo. Ay, and the approbation of those that weep this
lamentable divorce under her colors° are wonderfully to
extend him,° be it but to fortify her judgment, which
else an easy battery might lay flat for taking a beggar
20 without less° quality.° But how comes it he is to sojourn
with you? How creeps acquaintance?

1.4.s.d. **Iachimo** (probably pronounced "Yákimo"; cf. "yellow
Iachimo," 2.5.14; but possibly pronounced "Jáckimo" since the name
is a variant of the Italian *Giacomo*) 2 **crescent note** growing reputation 4 **admiration** wonder 6 **tabled** tabulated 8 **makes** is
the making of 11 **behold the sun** (as the eagle—noblest of birds—
was thought to do) 14 **words him . . . matter** makes him out better
than he truly is 17 **colors** banner 18 **extend him** enlarge his reputation 20 **without less** i.e., with less (double negative) 20 **quality** inherent worth

Philario. His father and I were soldiers together, to whom
    I have been often bound for no less than my life.

                Enter Posthumus.

    Here comes the Briton. Let him be so entertained°
    amongst you as suits, with gentlemen of your knowing, to   25
    a stranger° of his quality.° I beseech you all be better
    known to this gentleman, whom I commend to you as a
    noble friend of mine. How worthy he is I will leave to ap-
    pear hereafter, rather than story him in his own hearing.

Frenchman. Sir, we have known together° in Orleans.   30

Posthumus. Since when I have been debtor to you for cour-
    tesies which I will be ever to pay and yet pay still.

Frenchman. Sir, you o'errate my poor kindness. I was glad
    I did atone° my countryman and you. It had been pity
    you should have been put together° with so mortal a   35
    purpose as then each bore, upon importance° of so
    slight and trivial a nature.

Posthumus. By your pardon, sir, I was then a young trav-
    eler; rather shunned to go even° with what I heard than
    in my every action to be guided by others' experiences.   40
    But upon my mended judgment, if I offend not to say it
    is mended, my quarrel was not altogether slight.

Frenchman. Faith, yes, to be put to the arbitrament of
    swords, and by such two that would by all likelihood
    have confounded° one the other or have fall'n both.   45

Iachimo. Can we with manners ask what was the difference?

Frenchman. Safely, I think. 'Twas a contention in public,
    which may without contradiction° suffer the report. It
    was much like an argument that fell out last night, where
    each of us fell in praise of our country° mistresses; this   50
    gentleman at that time vouching—and upon warrant of

---

24 **entertained** welcomed   26 **stranger** foreigner   26 **quality**
rank   30 **known together** been acquainted   34 **atone** reconcile
35 **put together** i.e., in a duel   36 **importance** a matter   39
shunned . . . even refused to agree   45 **confounded** destroyed   48
contradiction objection   50 **country** i.e., of our own countries
(with bawdy quibble)

bloody affirmation°—his to be more fair, virtuous, wise, chaste, constant, qualified,° and less attemptable than any the rarest of our ladies in France.

55 *Iachimo.* That lady is not now living, or this gentleman's opinion, by this,° worn out.

Posthumus. She holds her virtue still, and I my mind.

Iachimo. You must not so far prefer her 'fore ours of Italy.

60 *Posthumus.* Being so far provoked as I was in France, I would abate° her nothing, though I profess myself her adorer, not her friend.°

Iachimo. As fair and as good—a kind of hand-in-hand° comparison—had been something too fair and too good
65 for any lady in Britain. If she went before° others I have seen, as that diamond of yours outlusters many I have beheld, I could not but believe she excelled many; but I have not seen the most precious diamond that is, nor you the lady.

70 *Posthumus.* I praised her as I rated her. So do I my stone.

Iachimo. What do you esteem it at?

Posthumus. More than the world enjoys.°

Iachimo. Either your unparagoned mistress is dead, or she's outprized° by a trifle.

75 *Posthumus.* You are mistaken. The one may be sold or given, or° if there were wealth enough for the purchase or merit for the gift. The other is not a thing for sale, and only the gift of the gods.

Iachimo. Which the gods have given you?

80 *Posthumus.* Which by their graces I will keep.

51–52 **warrant ... affirmation** pledge to support by shedding blood (R. B. Heilman) 53 **qualified** endowed with good qualities 56 **by this** by this time 61 **abate** depreciate 62 **friend** paramour 63 **hand-in-hand** claiming equality 65 **went before** excelled 72 **enjoys** possesses 74 **outprized** exceeded in value 76 **or** either

Iachimo. You may wear her in title yours, but you know strange fowl light upon neighboring ponds. Your ring may be stol'n too. So your brace of unprizable estimations,° the one is but frail and the other casual.° A cunning thief, or a that-way-accomplished courtier, would hazard the winning both of first and last. 85

Posthumus. Your Italy contains none so accomplished a courtier to convince the honor° of my mistress, if, in the holding or loss of that, you term her frail. I do nothing doubt you have store of thieves; notwithstanding, I fear not my ring. 90

Philario. Let us leave° here, gentlemen.

Posthumus. Sir, with all my heart. This worthy signior, I thank him, makes no stranger of me; we are familiar at first.° 95

Iachimo. With five times so much conversation I should get ground of° your fair mistress, make her go back even to the yielding, had I admittance, and opportunity to° friend.

Posthumus. No, no. 100

Iachimo. I dare thereupon pawn the moiety° of my estate to your ring, which in my opinion o'ervalues it something. But I make my wager rather against your confidence than her reputation; and, to bar your offense herein too, I durst attempt it against any lady in the world. 105

Posthumus. You are a great deal abused° in too bold a persuasion,° and I doubt not you sustain what y'are worthy of by your attempt.

Iachimo. What's that?

Posthumus. A repulse—though your attempt, as you call it, 110 deserve more: a punishment too.

83–84 **unprizable estimations** inestimable values   84 **casual** liable to accident   88 **convince the honor** conquer the chastity   92 **leave** leave off   94–95 **at first** from the first   96–97 **get ground of** gain an advantage over (a dueling metaphor followed by bawdy quibbles on "go back" and "yielding")   98 **to** as a   101 **moiety** half   106 **abused** deceived   106–07 **persuasion** opinion

Philario. Gentlemen, enough of this. It came in too suddenly; let it die as it was born, and I pray you be better
acquainted.

115 *Iachimo.* Would I had put my estate and my neighbor's on
th' approbation° of what I have spoke!

Posthumus. What lady would you choose to assail?

Iachimo. Yours, whom in constancy you think stands
so safe. I will lay you ten thousand ducats to your ring
120 that, commend me to the court where your lady is, with
no more advantage than the opportunity of a second
conference, and I will bring from thence that honor of
hers which you imagine so reserved.

Posthumus. I will wage° against your gold, gold to it. My
125 ring I hold dear as my finger; 'tis part of it.

Iachimo. You are a friend, and therein the wiser. If you buy
ladies' flesh at a million a dram, you cannot preserve it
from tainting. But I see you have some religion in you,
that° you fear.

130 *Posthumus.* This° is but a custom in your tongue. You bear
a graver purpose, I hope.

Iachimo. I am the master of my speeches, and would
undergo° what's spoken, I swear.

Posthumus. Will you? I shall but lend my diamond till your
135 return. Let there be covenants° drawn between's. My
mistress exceeds in goodness the hugeness of your
unworthy thinking. I dare you to this match: here's my
ring.

Philario. I will have it no lay.°

140 *Iachimo.* By the gods, it is one. If I bring you no sufficient
testimony that I have enjoyed the dearest bodily part of
your mistress, my ten thousand ducats are yours; so is
your diamond too. If I come off and leave her in such
honor as you have trust in, she your jewel, this your

116 **approbation** proof   124 **wage** wager   129 **that** since   130 **This**
i.e., what you say   133 **undergo** undertake   135 **covenants** a legal
agreement   139 **lay** wager

jewel, and my gold are yours—provided I have your 145
commendation° for my more free entertainment.°

Posthumus. I embrace these conditions. Let us have articles betwixt us. Only, thus far you shall answer: if you
make your voyage upon her and give me directly° to
understand you have prevailed, I am no further your 150
enemy; she is not worth our debate. If she remain unse-
duced, you not making it appear otherwise, for your ill
opinion and th' assault you have made to her chastity
you shall answer me with your sword.

Iachimo. Your hand; a covenant. We will have these things 155
set down by lawful counsel, and straight away° for
Britain, lest the bargain should catch cold and starve.° I
will fetch my gold and have our two wagers recorded.

Posthumus. Agreed.	[*Exeunt Posthumus and Iachimo.*]

Frenchman. Will this hold, think you?	160

Philario. Signior Iachimo will not from it. Pray let us fol-
low 'em.	*Exeunt.*

Scene 5. [*Britain.*]

Enter Queen, Ladies, and Cornelius.

Queen. Whiles yet the dew's on ground, gather those
flowers.
Make haste. Who has the note° of them?

Lady.	I, madam.

Queen. Dispatch.°	*Exeunt Ladies.*
Now, Master Doctor, have you brought those drugs?

Cornelius. Pleaseth your Highness, ay. Here they are,
madam.	[*Presenting a box*]	5
But I beseech your Grace, without offense—
My conscience bids me ask—wherefore you have

---

146 **commendation** introduction to her   146 **entertainment** welcome   149 **directly** plainly   156 **straight away** immediately   I
shall leave   157 **starve** die   1.5.2 **note** list   3 **Dispatch** make haste

Commanded of me these most poisonous compounds,°
Which are the movers of a languishing death,
But, though slow, deadly.

10 *Queen.*   I wonder, Doctor,
Thou ask'st me such a question. Have I not been
Thy pupil long? Hast thou not learned° me how
To make perfumes? distil? preserve? yea, so
That our great king himself doth woo me oft
15 For my confections?° Having thus far proceeded—
Unless thou think'st me devilish—is't not meet
That I did amplify my judgment° in
Other conclusions?° I will try the forces
Of these thy compounds on such creatures as
20 We count not worth the hanging—but none human—
To try the vigor of them and apply
Allayments to their act,° and by them° gather
Their° several virtues and effects.

Cornelius.   Your Highness
Shall from this practice but make hard your heart.
25 Besides, the seeing these effects will be
Both noisome and infectious.

Queen.   O, content thee.

Enter Pisanio.

[*Aside*] Here comes a flattering rascal. Upon him
Will I first work. He's for his master,
And enemy to my son.—How now, Pisanio?—
30 Doctor, your service for this time is ended;
Take your own way.

Cornelius. [*Aside*]   I do suspect you, madam,
But you shall do no harm.

Queen. [*To Pisanio*]   Hark thee, a word.

Cornelius. [*Aside*] I do not like her. She doth think she
    has

---

8 **compounds** drugs   12 **learned** taught   15 **confections** drugs
17 **judgment** knowledge   18 **conclusions** experiments   22 **Allayments to their act** antidotes to their action   22 **them** i.e., the experiments   23 **Their** i.e., of the compounds

Strange ling'ring poisons. I do know her spirit
And will not trust one of her malice with   35
A drug of such damned nature. Those she has
Will stupefy and dull the sense awhile,
Which first perchance she'll prove° on cats and dogs,
Then afterward up higher; but there is
No danger in what show of death it makes,   40
More than the locking up the spirits a time,
To be more fresh, reviving. She is fooled
With a most false effect, and I the truer
So to be false with her.

Queen.   No further service, Doctor,
Until I send for thee.

Cornelius.   I humbly take my leave.   *Exit.*   45

Queen. Weeps she still, say'st thou? Dost thou think in
time
She will not quench° and let instructions enter
Where folly now possesses? Do thou work.
When thou shalt bring me word she loves my son,
I'll tell thee on the instant thou art then   50
As great as is thy master; greater, for
His fortunes all lie speechless and his name
Is at last gasp. Return he cannot nor
Continue where he is. To shift his being°
Is to exchange one misery with another,   55
And every day that comes comes to decay°
A day's work in him. What shalt thou expect
To be depender on a thing that leans,
Who cannot be new built, nor has no friends
So much as but to prop him?
          [*Dropping the box; Pisanio picks it up.*]
                            Thou tak'st up   60
Thou know'st not what, but take it for thy labor.
It is a thing I made which hath the King
Five times redeemed from death. I do not know
What is more cordial.° Nay, I prithee take it.
It is an earnest° of a farther good   65
That I mean to thee. Tell thy mistress how

38 **prove** test   47 **quench** cool down   54 **being** location   56 **de-cay** destroy   64 **cordial** restorative   65 **earnest** pledge

The case stands with her; do't as from thyself.
Think what a chance thou changest on,° but think
Thou hast thy mistress still—to boot, my son,
70 Who shall take notice of thee. I'll move the King
To any shape of thy preferment° such
As thou'lt desire; and then myself, I chiefly,
That set thee on to this desert,° am bound
To load thy merit richly. Call my women.
Think on my words.   *Exit Pisanio.*
75   A sly and constant knave,
Not to be shaked; the agent for his master,
And the remembrancer° of her to hold
The handfast° to her lord. I have given him that
Which, if he take, shall quite unpeople her
80 Of liegers° for her sweet,° and which she after,
Except she bend her humor,° shall be assured
To taste of too.

                    Enter Pisanio and Ladies.

                    So, so. Well done, well done.
The violets, cowslips, and the primroses
Bear to my closet.° Fare thee well, Pisanio.
Think on my words.   *Exeunt Queen and Ladies.*

85 *Pisanio.*   And shall do.
But when to my good lord I prove untrue,
I'll choke myself. There's all I'll do for you.   *Exit.*

                    Scene 6. [*Britain.*]

                    Enter Imogen alone.

Imogen. A father cruel and a stepdame false,
A foolish suitor to a wedded lady
That hath her husband banished. O, that husband,
My supreme crown of grief, and those repeated°

---

68 **chance thou changest on** i.e., opportunity you have to change service (?)   71 **preferment** advancement   73 **desert** action meriting reward   77 **remembrancer** person employed to remind someone (legal term)   78 **handfast** marriage contract   80 **liegers** ambassadors   80 **sweet** lover   81 **bend her humor** change her mind   84 **closet** private room   1.6.4 **repeated** (already) enumerated

Vexations of it! Had I been thief-stol'n,   5
As my two brothers, happy; but most miserable
Is the desire that's glorious.° Blessed be those,
How mean° soe'er, that have their honest wills,°
Which seasons° comfort. Who may this be? Fie!

Enter Pisanio and Iachimo.

Pisanio. Madam, a noble gentleman of Rome,   10
Comes° from my lord with letters.

Iachimo.   Change you,° madam:
The worthy Leonatus is in safety
And greets your Highness dearly.

                                        [*Presenting a letter*]

Imogen.   Thanks, good sir.
You're kindly welcome.

Iachimo. [*Aside*] All of her that is out of door° most rich!   15
If she be furnished with a mind so rare,
She is alone th' Arabian bird,° and I
Have lost the wager. Boldness be my friend!
Arm me, audacity, from head to foot,
Or like the Parthian° I shall flying fight—   20
Rather, directly fly.

Imogen. (*Reads*) "He is one of the noblest note,° to whose
kindnesses I am most infinitely tied. Reflect° upon him
accordingly, as you value your trust—

                                    Leonatus."   25
So far I read aloud.
But even the very middle of my heart
Is warmed by th' rest and takes it thankfully.
You are as welcome, worthy sir, as I
Have words to bid you, and shall find it so   30
In all that I can do.

---

7 **desire that's glorious** i.e., unfulfilled longing that aspires to great
things (Nosworthy) 8 **mean** low-ranking 8 **honest wills** plain
desires 9 **seasons** give relish to 11 **Comes** who comes 11 **you**
i.e., your expression 15 **out of door** external, visible 17 **Arabian
bird** phoenix (of which species only one example existed at a time)
20 **Parthian** mounted archer who shot arrows behind him while in
flight (Iachimo will resort to indirect methods) 22 **note** reputation
23 **Reflect** bestow attention

Iachimo.   Thanks, fairest lady.
What, are men mad? Hath nature given them eyes
To see this vaulted arch and the rich crop°
Of sea and land, which can distinguish 'twixt
35   The fiery orbs above and the twinned° stones
Upon the numbered° beach, and can we not
Partition° make with spectacles so precious°
'Twixt fair and foul?

Imogen.   What makes your admiration?°

Iachimo. It cannot be i' th' eye, for apes and monkeys,
40   'Twixt two such shes, would chatter this way° and
Contemn with mows° the other; nor i' th' judgment,
For idiots, in this case of favor,° would
Be wisely definite;° nor i' th' appetite°—
Sluttery, to such neat excellence opposed,
45   Should make desire vomit emptiness,°
Not so allured to feed.

Imogen. What is the matter, trow?°

Iachimo.   The cloyèd will°—
That satiate yet unsatisfied desire, that tub
Both filled and running—ravening first the lamb,
Longs after for the garbage.

50   *Imogen.*   What, dear sir,
Thus raps° you? Are you well?

Iachimo.   Thanks, madam, well.
[*To Pisanio*] Beseech you, sir, desire
My man's abode° where I did leave him.
He's strange and peevish.°

Pisanio.   I was going, sir,

---

33 **crop** harvest 35 **twinned** exactly alike 36 **numbered**
abounding (in stones) 37 **Partition** distinction 37 **spectacles so
precious** i.e., eyesight 38 **admiration** wonder 40 **this way** towards Imogen 41 **mows** grimaces 42 **case of favor** question of
beauty 43 **definite** decisive 43 **appetite** physical desire 45
make . . . emptiness i.e., destroy desire 47 **What . . . trow** what
are you talking about, I wonder 47 **will** sexual desire 51 **raps**
transports 52–53 **desire . . . abode** request that my servant remain
54 **strange and peevish** a foreigner and skittish

    To give him welcome.   *Exit.*   55

Imogen. Continues well my lord? His health, beseech you?

Iachimo. Well, madam.

Imogen. Is he disposed to mirth? I hope he is.

Iachimo. Exceeding pleasant; none a stranger° there
    So merry and so gamesome. He is called   60
    The Briton reveler.

Imogen.   When he was here
    He did incline to sadness,° and ofttimes
    Not knowing why.

Iachimo.   I never saw him sad.
    There is a Frenchman his companion, one
    An eminent monsieur that, it seems, much loves   65
    A Gallian° girl at home. He furnaces°
    The thick° sighs from him, whiles the jolly Briton—
    Your lord, I mean—laughs from's free lungs, cries "O,
    Can my sides hold to think that man who knows
    By history, report, or his own proof°   70
    What woman is, yea, what she cannot choose
    But must be, will's free hours languish° for
    Assurèd bondage?"

Imogen.   Will my lord say so?

Iachimo. Ay, madam, with his eyes in flood with laughter.
    It is a recreation to be by   75
    And hear him mock the Frenchman. But heavens know
    Some men are much to blame.

Imogen.   Not he, I hope.

Iachimo. Not he—but yet heaven's bounty towards him
    might
    Be used more thankfully. In himself 'tis° much;
    In you, which I account his, beyond all talents.°   80

---

59 **none a stranger** there is no foreigner   62 **sadness** seriousness
66 **Gallian** French   66 **furnaces** exhales like a furnace   67 **thick**
frequent   70 **proof** experience   72 **languish** pass in languishing
79 **'tis** i.e., heaven's bounty is   80 **beyond all talents** beyond all
natural endowments, i.e., inestimable

Whilst I am bound to wonder, I am bound
　　To pity too.

Imogen.　　　　What do you pity, sir?

Iachimo. Two creatures heartily.

Imogen.　　　　　　　　Am I one, sir?
　　You look on me. What wrack° discern you in me
　　Deserves your pity?

85　*Iachimo.*　　　　　　Lamentable! What,
　　To hide me from the radiant sun and solace°
　　I' th' dungeon by a snuff!°

Imogen.　　　　　　　　I pray you, sir,
　　Deliver with more openness your answers
　　To my demands. Why do you pity me?

90　*Iachimo.* That others do,
　　I was about to say, enjoy your—but
　　It is an office° of the gods to venge it,
　　Not mine to speak on't.

Imogen.　　　　　　You do seem to know
　　Something of me or what concerns me. Pray you,
95　Since doubting° things go ill often hurts more
　　Than to be sure they do—for certainties
　　Either are past remedies, or, timely knowing,°
　　The remedy then born—discover° to me
　　What° both you spur and stop.

Iachimo.　　　　　　　Had I this cheek
100　To bathe my lips upon; this hand, whose touch,
　　Whose every touch, would force the feeler's soul
　　To th' oath of loyalty; this object, which
　　Takes prisoner the wild motion of mine eye,
　　Fixing it only here; should I, damned then,
105　Slaver with lips as common as the stairs
　　That mount the Capitol; join gripes° with hands
　　Made hard with hourly falsehood (falsehood, as
　　With labor); then bye-peeping° in an eye

84 **wrack** disaster　86 **solace** find pleasure　87 **snuff** candle-end
92 **office** duty　95 **doubting** fearing　97 **timely knowing** if one
knows in time　98 **discover** reveal　99 **What** why　106 **gripes**
grips　108 **bye-peeping** peeping sidelong

Base and illustrous° as the smoky light
That's fed with stinking tallow—it were fit   110
That all the plagues of hell should at one time
Encounter° such revolt.°

Imogen.   My lord, I fear,
Has forgot Britain.

Iachimo.   And himself. Not I
Inclined to this intelligence pronounce°
The beggary° of his change, but 'tis your graces   115
That from my mutest conscience° to my tongue
Charms this report out.

Imogen.   Let me hear no more.

Iachimo. O dearest soul, your cause doth strike my heart
With pity that doth make me sick. A lady
So fair, and fastened to an empery°   120
Would° make the great'st king double, to be partnered
With tomboys° hired with that self exhibition°
Which your own coffers yield; with diseased ventures°
That play with all infirmities for gold
Which rottenness can lend nature; such boiled stuff°   125
As well might poison poison! Be revenged,
Or she that bore you was no queen, and you
Recoil° from your great stock.

Imogen.   Revenged?
How should I be revenged? If this be true—
As I have such a heart that both mine ears   130
Must not in haste abuse—if it be true,
How should I be revenged?

Iachimo.   Should he make me
Live like Diana's priest betwixt cold sheets,
Whiles he is vaulting variable ramps,°

---

109 **illustrous** lackluster 112 **Encounter** confront 112 **revolt**
inconstancy 113–14 **Not I . . . pronounce** I, though disinclined to
bring this news, report 115 **beggary** meanness 116 **conscience**
knowledge 120 **empery** empire 121 **Would** which would 122
tomboys whores 122 **self exhibition** self-same allowance 123
ventures whores 125 **boiled stuff** i.e., women who have been
"sweated" for venereal disease 128 **Recoil** decline 134 **variable
ramps** fickle whores

135   In your despite, upon your purse? Revenge it.
       I dedicate myself to your sweet pleasure,
       More noble than that runagate° to your bed,
       And will continue fast to your affection,
       Still close° as sure.

       Imogen.   What ho, Pisanio!

140   *Iachimo.* Let me my service tender on your lips.

       Imogen. Away, I do condemn mine ears that have
       So long attended thee.° If thou wert honorable,
       Thou wouldst have told this tale for virtue, not
       For such an end thou seek'st, as base as strange.
145   Thou wrong'st a gentleman who is as far
       From thy report as thou from honor, and
       Solicits here a lady that disdains
       Thee and the devil alike. What ho, Pisanio!
       The King my father shall be made acquainted
150   Of thy assault. If he shall think it fit
       A saucy stranger in his court to mart°
       As in a Romish stew° and to expound
       His beastly mind to us, he hath a court
       He little cares for and a daughter who
155   He not respects at all. What ho, Pisanio!

       Iachimo. O happy Leonatus! I may say
       The credit° that thy lady hath of° thee
       Deserves thy trust, and thy most perfect goodness
       Her assured credit. Blessèd live you long,
160   A lady to the worthiest sir that ever
       Country called his,° and you his mistress, only
       For the most worthiest fit. Give me your pardon.
       I have spoke this to know if your affiance°
       Were deeply rooted, and shall make your lord
165   That which he is, new o'er; and he is one°
       The truest mannered,° such a holy witch°

       137 **runagate** traitor   139 **close** secret   142 **attended thee** lis-
       tened to you (in anger Imogen shifts from formal "you" to familiar
       "thee," thus treating Iachimo as an inferior; at line 168 she reverts to
       "you")   151 **to mart** should do business   152 **Romish stew** Ro-
       man bawdyhouse   157 **credit** trust   157 **of** in   161 **his** its own
       163 **affiance** faith   165 **one** above all   166 **truest mannered**
       most honestly behaved   166 **witch** charmer

That he enchants societies into° him.
Half all men's hearts are his.

Imogen.   You make amends.

Iachimo. He sits 'mongst men like a descended god.
He hath a kind of honor sets him off   *170*
More than a mortal seeming.° Be not angry,
Most mighty Princess, that I have adventured
To try your taking° of a false report, which hath
Honored with confirmation your great judgment
In the election of a sir so rare,   *175*
Which° you know cannot err. The love I bear him
Made me to fan° you thus, but the gods made you,
Unlike all others, chaffless. Pray your pardon.

Imogen. All's well, sir. Take my pow'r i' th' court for yours.

Iachimo. My humble thanks. I had almost forgot   *180*
T' entreat your grace but in a small request,
And yet of moment too, for it concerns
Your lord, myself, and other noble friends
Are° partners in the business.

Imogen.   Pray what is't?

Iachimo. Some dozen Romans of us and your lord—   *185*
The best feather of our wing—have mingled sums
To buy a present for the Emperor;
Which I, the factor° for the rest, have done
In France. 'Tis plate of rare device, and jewels
Of rich and exquisite form, their values great,   *190*
And I am something curious,° being strange,°
To have them in safe stowage. May it please you
To take them in protection?

Imogen.   Willingly;
And pawn mine honor for their safety. Since
My lord hath interest in them, I will keep them   *195*
In my bedchamber.

---

167 **into** to   171 **mortal seeming** human appearance   173 **try your taking** test your reception   176 **Which** who   177 **fan** winnow   184 **Are** i.e., who are   188 **factor** agent   191 **curious** anxious   191 **strange** a foreigner

Iachimo.   They are in a trunk
    Attended by my men. I will make bold
    To send them to you, only for this night.
    I must aboard tomorrow.

Imogen.   O, no, no.

200 *Iachimo.* Yes, I beseech, or I shall short° my word
    By length'ning my return. From Gallia°
    I crossed the seas on purpose and on promise
    To see your grace.

Imogen.   I thank you for your pains.
    But not away tomorrow!

Iachimo.   O, I must, madam.

205   Therefore I shall beseech you, if you please
    To greet your lord with writing, do't tonight.
    I have outstood my time, which is material
    To th' tender° of our present.

Imogen.   I will write.
    Send your trunk to me; it shall safe be kept
210   And truly yielded you. You're very welcome.

                           Exeunt [severally°].

---

200 **short** fall short of   201 **Gallia** France   208 **tender** giving
210s.d. **severally** by different tiring-house doors

ACT 2

Scene 1. [*Britain.*]

Enter Cloten and the two Lords.

Cloten. Was there ever man had such luck? When I kissed
the jack,° upon an upcast° to be hit away! I had a hundred pound on't. And then a whoreson jackanapes must
take me up° for swearing, as if I borrowed mine oaths of
him and might not spend them at my pleasure.   5

First Lord. What got he by that? You have broke his pate
with your bowl.

Second Lord. [*Aside*] If his wit had been like him that broke
it, it would have run all out.

Cloten. When a gentleman is disposed to swear, it is   10
not for any standers-by to curtail his oaths. Ha?

Second Lord. No, my lord—[*Aside*] nor crop the ears of
them.

Cloten. Whoreson dog, I gave him satisfaction! Would he
had been one of my rank.°   15

Second Lord. [*Aside*] To have smelled like a fool.

Cloten. I am not vexed more at anything in th' earth. A pox
on't! I had rather not be so noble as I am. They dare not
fight with me because of the Queen my mother. Every
jack-slave° hath his bellyful of fighting, and I must go   20
up and down like a cock that nobody can match.

2.1.1–2 **kissed the jack** came close to the target ball (in the game of
bowls) 2 **upcast** chance 4 **take me up** rebuke me 15 **of my
rank** i.e., so I might have challenged him to a duel (the Second Lord
quibbles) 20 **jack-slave** lout

239

Second Lord. [*Aside*] You are cock and capon too, and°
you crow, cock, with your comb on.

Cloten. Sayest thou?

25 *Second Lord.* It is not fit your lordship should undertake°
every companion° that you give offense to.

Cloten. No, I know that, but it is fit I should commit
offense° to my inferiors.

Second Lord. Ay, it is fit for your lordship only.

30 *Cloten.* Why, so I say.

First Lord. Did you hear of a stranger° that's come to
court tonight?

Cloten. A stranger, and I not know on't?

Second Lord. [*Aside*] He's a strange fellow himself, and
35 knows it not.

First Lord. There's an Italian come, and, 'tis thought, one
of Leonatus' friends.

Cloten. Leonatus? A banished rascal, and he's another,
whatsoever he be. Who told you of this stranger?

40 *First Lord.* One of your lordship's pages.

Cloten. Is it fit I went to look upon him? Is there no dero-
gation° in't?

Second Lord. You cannot derogate,° my lord.

Cloten. Not easily, I think.

45 *Second Lord.* [*Aside*] You are a fool, granted; therefore
your issues,° being foolish, do not derogate.

Cloten. Come, I'll go see this Italian. What I have lost
today at bowls I'll win tonight of him. Come, go.

Second Lord. I'll attend your lordship.

                                                 Exeunt [*Cloten and First Lord*].

---

22 **and** if 25 **undertake** take on 26 **companion** low fellow
27–28 **commit offense** offer battle 31 **stranger** foreigner 41–42
derogation loss of dignity 43 **cannot derogate** do anything
derogatory to your rank (with quibble on "have no dignity to lose")
46 **issues** deeds

That such a crafty devil as is his mother　　　　　　50
Should yield the world this ass! A woman that
Bears all down° with her brain, and this her son
Cannot take two from twenty, for his heart,°
And leave eighteen. Alas, poor princess,
Thou divine Imogen, what thou endur'st,　　　　　　55
Betwixt a father by thy stepdame governed,
A mother hourly coining plots, a wooer
More hateful than the foul expulsion is
Of thy dear husband, than that horrid act
Of the divorce he'ld make. The heavens hold firm　　60
The walls of thy dear honor, keep unshaked
That temple, thy fair mind, that thou mayst stand,
T' enjoy thy banished lord and this great land! *Exit.*

Scene 2. [*Britain.*]

Enter Imogen in her bed,° and a Lady.

Imogen. Who's there? My woman Helen?

Lady.　　　　　　　　　　　　　Please you, madam.

Imogen. What hour is it?

Lady.　　　　　　　　　　　Almost midnight, madam.

Imogen. I have read three hours then. Mine eyes are
　weak.
Fold down the leaf where I have left. To bed.
Take not away the taper, leave it burning;　　　　　　5
And if thou canst awake by four o' th' clock,
I prithee call me. Sleep hath seized me wholly.
　　　　　　　　　　　　　　　　　[*Exit Lady.*]
To your protection I commend me, gods.
From fairies° and the tempters of the night
Guard me, beseech ye!　　　　　　　　　　　　　10

---

52 **Bears all down** overcomes everything　53 **for his heart** to save
his life　2.2.s.d. **Enter ... bed** (in Elizabethan open-stage production the bed is "thrust out" upon the stage by attendants and the trunk
is carried on; in modern proscenium-arch production the bed and trunk
are usually "discovered" by raising the front curtain)　9 **fairies** i.e.,
malignant fairies

Sleeps. Iachimo [comes] from the trunk.

Iachimo. The crickets sing, and man's o'erlabored sense
    Repairs itself by rest. Our Tarquin° thus
    Did softly press the rushes° ere he wakened
    The chastity he wounded. Cytherea,°
15   How bravely° thou becom'st thy bed, fresh lily,°
    And whiter than the sheets! That I might touch!
    But kiss, one kiss! Rubies unparagoned,
    How dearly they do't! 'Tis her breathing that
    Perfumes the chamber thus. The flame o' th' taper
20   Bows toward her and would underpeep her lids
    To see th' enclosèd lights, now canopied
    Under these windows,° white and azure-laced
    With blue of heaven's own tinct. But my design:
    To note the chamber. I will write all down:
25   Such and such pictures; there the window; such
    Th' adornment of her bed; the arras, figures,
    Why, such and such; and the contents o' th' story.°
    Ah, but some natural notes° about her body
    Above ten thousand meaner movables°
30   Would testify, t' enrich mine inventory.
    O sleep, thou ape° of death, lie dull° upon her.
    And be her sense but as a monument,°
    Thus in a chapel lying. Come off, come off—
                     [Removing her bracelet]
    As slippery as the Gordian knot was hard.
35   'Tis mine, and this will witness outwardly,
    As strongly as the conscience° does within,
    To th' madding of her lord. On her left breast
    A mole cinque-spotted,° like the crimson drops
    I' th' bottom of a cowslip. Here's a voucher°
40   Stronger than ever law could make. This secret
    Will force him think I have picked the lock and ta'en
    The treasure of her honor. No more. To what end?

---

12 **Tarquin** (who raped Lucrece) 13 **rushes** Elizabethan floor-covering 14 **Cytherea** Venus 15 **bravely** magnificently 15 **lily** emblem of chastity 22 **windows** shutters, i.e., eyelids 27 **th' story** i.e., the story depicted on the arras (cf. 2.4.69) 28 **notes** marks 29 **meaner movables** lesser furnishings 31 **ape** mimic 31 **dull** heavy 32 **monument** recumbent effigy on a tomb 36 **conscience** knowledge 38 **cinque-spotted** having five spots 39 **voucher** guarantee

Why should I write this down that's riveted,
Screwed to my memory? She hath been reading late
The tale of Tereus.° Here the leaf 's turned down   45
Where Philomel gave up. I have enough.
To th' trunk again, and shut the spring of it.
Swift, swift, you dragons of the night, that dawning
May bare the raven's eye.° I lodge in fear.
Though this a heavenly angel, hell is here.   50
                                              Clock strikes.
One, two, three. Time, time!   [*Goes into the trunk.*]
                                              Exeunt.°

Scene 3. [*Britain.*]

Enter Cloten and Lords.

First Lord. Your lordship is the most patient man in loss,
the most coldest° that ever turned up ace.°

Cloten. It would make any man cold° to lose.

First Lord. But not every man patient after the noble temper of your lordship. You are most hot and furious when   5
you win.

Cloten. Winning will put any man into courage. If I could
get this foolish Imogen, I should have gold enough. It's
almost morning, is't not?

First Lord. Day, my lord.   10

Cloten. I would this music would come. I am advised to
give her music a-mornings; they say it will penetrate.°

Enter Musicians.

Come on, tune. If you can penetrate° her with your
fingering, so; we'll try with tongue too. If none will do,   15
let her remain, but I'll never give o'er.° First, a very

---

45 **Tereus** (who raped Philomela; apparently the book is Ovid's
Metamorphoses)   49 **bare the raven's eye** (the raven supposedly
being an early bird)   51s.d. **Exeunt** (the bed and trunk are carried
offstage or concealed by dropping the front curtain)   2.3.2 **coldest**
calmest   2 **ace** one, the lowest throw at dice (pun on "ass")   3 **cold**
gloomy   12-13 **penetrate** affect emotionally (with bawdy quibble)
15 **give o'er** give up

excellent good-conceited° thing; after, a wonderful
sweet air with admirable rich words to it—and then let
her consider.

Song.

Hark, hark, the lark at heaven's gate sings,
20   And Phoebus gins° arise,
His steeds to water at those springs
    On chaliced flowers that lies;
And winking Mary-buds° begin
    To ope their golden eyes.
25   With every thing that pretty is,
        My lady sweet, arise,
            Arise, arise!

Cloten. So, get you gone. If this penetrate, I will consider°
your music the better; if it do not, it is a vice° in her ears
30   which horsehairs° and calves' guts,° nor the voice of
unpaved° eunuch to boot, can never amend.

                              [*Exeunt Musicians.*]

            Enter Cymbeline and Queen.

Second Lord. Here comes the King.

Cloten. I am glad I was up so late, for that's the reason I
was up so early. He cannot choose but take this service
35   I have done fatherly. Good morrow to your Majesty and
to my gracious mother.

Cymbeline. Attend you here the door of our stern daughter? Will she not forth?

Cloten. I have assailed her with musics, but she vouchsafes
40   no notice.

Cymbeline. The exile of her minion° is too new;
She hath not yet forgot him. Some more time
Must wear the print of his remembrance out,
And then she's yours.

16 **good-conceited** well-devised 20 **Phoebus gins** Apollo (the
sun) begins to 23 **winking Mary-buds** closed marigold buds 28
consider reward 29 **vice** flaw 30 **horsehairs** bowstrings 30
calves' guts fiddle-strings 31 **unpaved** unstoned (i.e., castrated)
41 **minion** darling

Queen.   You are most bound to th' King,
  Who lets go by no vantages° that may   45
  Prefer° you to his daughter. Frame° yourself
  To orderly solicits,° and be friended
  With aptness of the season. Make denials
  Increase your services. So seem as if
  You were inspired to do those duties which   50
  You tender to her; that you in all obey her,
  Save when command to your dismission° tends,
  And therein you are senseless.°

Cloten.   Senseless? Not so.

[*Enter a Messenger.*]

Messenger. So like you,° sir, ambassadors from Rome.
  The one is Caius Lucius.

Cymbeline.   A worthy fellow,   55
  Albeit he comes on angry purpose now.
  But that's no fault of his. We must receive him
  According to the honor of his sender,
  And towards himself, his goodness forespent° on us,
  We must extend our notice. Our dear son,   60
  When you have given good morning to your mistress,
  Attend the Queen and us. We shall have need
  T' employ you towards this Roman. Come, our
    queen.   *Exeunt* [*all but Cloten*].

Cloten. If she be up, I'll speak with her; if not,
  Let her lie still and dream. By your leave, ho!   65

[*Knocks.*]

  I know her women are about her. What
  If I do line° one of their hands? 'Tis gold
  Which buys admittance—oft it doth—yea, and
    makes
  Diana's rangers° false° themselves, yield up
  Their deer to th' stand o' th' stealer;° and 'tis gold 70

---

45 **vantages** opportunities 46 **Prefer** recommend 46 **Frame**
prepare 47 **solicits** solicitations 52 **dismission** rejection 53
senseless insensible 54 **So like you** if you please 59 **forespent**
having earlier been spent 67 **line** i.e., with money 69 **rangers**
gamekeepers 69 **false** betray 70 **stand o' th' stealer** standing-
place of the hunter (quibble on "erection of the phallus")

Which makes the true man killed and saves the thief,
Nay, sometime hangs both thief and true man. What
Can it not do and undo? I will make
One of her women lawyer to° me, for
75   I yet not understand° the case myself.
By your leave.   *Knocks.*

                    Enter a Lady.

Lady. Who's there that knocks?

Cloten.   A gentleman.

Lady.   No more?

Cloten. Yes, and a gentlewoman's son.

Lady.   That's more
Than some whose tailors are as dear as yours
80   Can justly boast of. What's your lordship's pleasure?

Cloten. Your lady's person. Is she ready?°

Lady.   Ay,
To keep her chamber.

Cloten.   There is gold for you.
Sell me your good report.

Lady. How? My good name? Or to report of you
85   What I shall think is good? The Princess!

                    Enter Imogen. [Exit Lady.]

Cloten. Good morrow, fairest sister. Your sweet hand.

Imogen. Good morrow, sir. You lay out too much pains
For purchasing but trouble. The thanks I give
Is telling you that I am poor of thanks
And scarce can spare them.

90   *Cloten.*   Still I swear I love you.

Imogen. If you but said so, 'twere as deep° with me.
If you swear still,° your recompense is still
That I regard it not.

74 **lawyer to** quibble on "lower to," i.e., lie down for   75 **understand** quibble on "stand under," i.e., penetrate   81 **ready** dressed
91 **deep** effective   92 **still** continually

Cloten.   This is no answer.

Imogen. But° that you shall not say I yield, being silent,
  I would not speak. I pray you spare me. Faith,   95
  I shall unfold° equal discourtesy°
  To your best kindness. One of your great knowing°
  Should learn, being taught, forbearance.

Cloten. To leave you in your madness, 'twere my sin.
  I will not.   100

Imogen. Fools are not mad folks.

Cloten.   Do you call me fool?

Imogen. As I am mad, I do.
  If you'll be patient, I'll no more be mad;
  That cures us both. I am much sorry, sir,
  You put me to forget a lady's manners   105
  By being so verbal;° and learn now for all
  That I, which know my heart, do here pronounce
  By th' very truth of it, I care not for you,
  And am so near the lack of charity
  To accuse myself I hate° you—which I had rather   110
  You felt than make't my boast.

Cloten.   You sin against
  Obedience, which you owe your father. For
  The contract you pretend° with that base wretch,
  One bred of alms and fostered with cold dishes,
  With scraps o' th' court—it is no contract, none.   115
  And though it be allowed in meaner° parties—
  Yet who than he more mean?—to knit their souls,
  On whom there is no more dependency°
  But brats and beggary, in self-figured° knot;
  Yet you are curbed from that enlargement° by   120
  The consequence° o' th' crown, and must not foil°
  The precious note° of it with a base slave,

94 **But** so   96 **unfold** display   96 **equal discourtesy** i.e., discourtesy equal   97 **knowing** knowledge   106 **verbal** talkative   110 **To accuse . . . hate** that I accuse myself of hating   112–13 **For . . . pretend** as for the marriage contract you claim   116 **meaner** lowerranking   118 **dependency** retinue   119 **self-figured** shaped by one's self   120 **enlargement** freedom   121 **consequence** importance   121 **foil** defile   122 **note** eminence, importance

A hilding for° a livery, a squire's cloth,
A pantler°—not so eminent.

Imogen.   Profane fellow!
125 Wert thou the son of Jupiter, and no more
But what thou art besides, thou wert too base
To be his groom. Thou wert dignified° enough,
Even to the point of envy, if 'twere made
Comparative for your virtues to be styled
130 The under-hangman of his kingdom,° and hated
For being preferred° so well.

Cloten.   The south fog° rot him!

Imogen. He never can meet more mischance than come
To be but named of thee. His meanest garment
That ever hath but clipped° his body is dearer
135 In my respect° than all the hairs above thee,
Were they all made such men. How now, Pisanio?

Enter Pisanio.

Cloten. "His garment"? Now the devil—

Imogen. To Dorothy my woman hie thee presently.°

Cloten. "His garment"?

Imogen.   I am sprited° with a fool,
140 Frighted, and angered worse. Go bid my woman
Search for a jewel that too casually
Hath left mine arm. It was thy master's. Shrew° me
If I would lose it for a revenue
Of any king's in Europe. I do think
145 I saw't this morning; confident I am
Last night 'twas on mine arm; I kissed it.
I hope it be not gone to tell my lord
That I kiss aught but he.

Pisanio.   'Twill not be lost.

123 **hilding for** good-for-nothing fit only for   124 **pantler** pantry-servant   127 **dignified** given honor   128–30 **if 'twere ... king-dom** if, according to the virtue of each of you, you were made under-hangman and he king (Heilman)   131 **preferred** advanced   131 **The south fog** the damp, supposedly unhealthy, south wind   134 **clipped** embraced   135 **respect** regard   138 **presently** im-mediately   139 **sprited** haunted   142 **Shrew** curse

Imogen. I hope so.° Go and search.   [*Exit Pisanio.*]

Cloten.   You have abused me.
    "His meanest garment"?

Imogen.   Ay, I said so, sir.   150
    If you will make't an action,° call witness to't.

Cloten. I will inform your father.

Imogen.   Your mother too.
    She's my good lady and will conceive,° I hope,
    But the worst of me. So I leave you, sir,
    To th' worst of discontent.   *Exit.*

Cloten.   I'll be revenged.   155
    "His meanest garment"? Well.   *Exit.*°

Scene 4. [*Rome.*]

Enter Posthumus and Philario.

Posthumus. Fear it not, sir. I would I were so sure
    To win the King as I am bold° her honor
    Will remain hers.

Philario.   What means° do you make to him?

Posthumus. Not any, but abide the change of time,
    Quake in the present winter's state, and wish   5
    That warmer days would come. In these feared° hopes
    I barely gratify° your love; they failing,
    I must die much your debtor.

Philario. Your very goodness and your company
    O'erpays all I can do. By this,° your king   10
    Hath heard of great Augustus; Caius Lucius
    Will do's commission throughly. And I think
    He'll grant the tribute, send th' arrearages,
    Or look upon our Romans, whose remembrance
    Is yet fresh in their grief.

149 **so** i.e., not   151 **action** lawsuit   153 **conceive** come to believe
156s.d. **Exit** (by the other door)   2.4.2 **bold** confident   3 **means**
overtures   6 **feared** fear-laden   7 **gratify** repay   10 **this** this time

15 *Posthumus.*   I do believe,
    Statist° though I am none, nor like to be,
    That this will prove a war; and you shall hear
    The legions now in Gallia sooner landed
    In our not-fearing Britain than have tidings
20 Of any penny tribute paid. Our countrymen
    Are men more ordered than when Julius Caesar
    Smiled at their lack of skill but found their courage
    Worthy his frowning at. Their discipline,
    Now mingled with their courages, will make known
25 To their approvers° they are people such
    That mend upon° the world.

                    Enter Iachimo.

Philario.   See, Iachimo!

Posthumus. The swiftest harts have posted° you by land,
    And winds of all the corners° kissed your sails
    To make your vessel nimble.

Philario.   Welcome, sir.

30 *Posthumus.* I hope the briefness of your answer° made
    The speediness of your return.

Iachimo.   Your lady
    Is one of the fairest that I have looked upon.

Posthumus. And therewithal the best, or let her beauty
    Look through a casement to allure false hearts
    And be false with them.

35 *Iachimo.*   Here are letters° for you.

Posthumus. Their tenor good, I trust.

Iachimo.   'Tis very like.

Posthumus. Was Caius Lucius in the Briton court
    When you were there?

Iachimo.   He was expected then,
    But not approached.

16 **Statist** politician   25 **approvers** testers   26 **That mend upon**
whose reputation grows with   27 **have posted** must have sped   28
corners i.e., of the earth   30 **your answer** the answer you received
35 **are letters** is a letter

Posthumus.   All is well yet.
Sparkles this stone as it was wont, or is't not   40
Too dull for your good wearing?

Iachimo.   If I have lost it,
I should have lost the worth of it in gold.
I'll make a journey twice as far t' enjoy
A second night of such sweet shortness which
Was mine in Britain—for the ring is won.   45

Posthumus. The stone's too hard to come by.

Iachimo.   Not a whit,
Your lady being so easy.

Posthumus.   Make not, sir,
Your loss your sport. I hope you know that we
Must not continue friends.

Iachimo.   Good sir, we must,
If you keep covenant. Had I not brought   50
The knowledge° of your mistress home, I grant
We were to question° farther, but I now
Profess myself the winner of her honor,
Together with your ring, and not the wronger
Of her or you, having proceeded but   55
By both your wills.

Posthumus.   If you can make't apparent
That you have tasted her in bed, my hand
And ring is yours. If not, the foul opinion
You had of her pure honor gains or loses
Your sword or mine, or masterless leave° both   60
To who shall find them.

Iachimo.   Sir, my circumstances,°
Being so near the truth as I will make them,
Must first induce you to believe; whose strength
I will confirm with oath, which I doubt not
You'll give me leave to spare° when you shall find   65
You need it not.

Posthumus.   Proceed.

_____

51 **knowledge** carnal knowledge   52 **question** dispute (as in a duel)
60 **leave** let it leave   61 **circumstances** details   65 **spare** omit

Iachimo.   First, her bedchamber—
Where I confess I slept not, but profess
Had that was well worth watching°—it was hanged
With tapestry of silk and silver; the story
70 Proud Cleopatra, when she met her Roman°
And Cydnus swelled above the banks, or° for
The press of boats or pride: a piece of work
So bravely° done, so rich, that it did strive
In workmanship and value;° which I wondered
75 Could be so rarely and exactly wrought,
Since the true life on't was—

Posthumus.   This is true,
And this you might have heard of here, by me
Or by some other.

Iachimo.   More particulars
Must justify° my knowledge.

Posthumus.   So they must,
Or do your honor injury.

80 *Iachimo.*   The chimney°
Is south the chamber, and the chimney-piece°
Chaste Dian bathing. Never saw I figures
So likely to report° themselves. The cutter°
Was as another Nature, dumb;° outwent° her,
Motion and breath left out.

85 *Posthumus.*   This is a thing
Which you might from relation° likewise reap,
Being, as it is, much spoke of.

Iachimo.   The roof o' th' chamber
With golden cherubins is fretted.° Her andirons—
I had forgot them—were two winking° Cupids

---

68 **watching** remaining awake for   70 **Roman** Antony   71 **or** either   73 **bravely** finely   73–74 **it did strive . . . value** it was
doubtful whether the workmanship or the intrinsic value was greater
79 **justify** prove   80 **chimney** fireplace   81 **chimney-piece** sculpture placed over the fireplace   83 **likely to report** apt to identify
83 **cutter** sculptor   84 **as . . . dumb** like Nature in creative power
although unable to make the sculpture speak   84 **outwent** surpassed
86 **relation** report   88 **fretted** carved   89 **winking** with closed
eyes, i.e., blind

Of silver, each on one foot standing, nicely   90
Depending on their brands.°

Posthumus.   This is her honor!
Let it be granted you have seen all this—and praise
Be given to your remembrance—the description
Of what is in her chamber nothing saves
The wager you have laid.

Iachimo.   Then, if you can   95
                    [*Showing the bracelet*]
Be pale,° I beg but leave to air this jewel. See!
And now 'tis up° again. It must be married
To that your diamond; I'll keep them.

Posthumus.   Jove!
Once more let me behold it. Is it that
Which I left with her?

Iachimo.   Sir, I thank her, that.   100
She stripped it from her arm; I see her yet.
Her pretty action did outsell° her gift,
And yet enriched it too. She gave it me and said
She prized it once.

Posthumus.   May be she plucked it off
To send it me.

Iachimo.   She writes so to you, doth she?   105

Posthumus. O, no, no, no, 'tis true. Here, take this too.
                    [*Giving the ring*]
It is a basilisk° unto mine eye,
Kills me to look on't. Let there be no honor
Where there is beauty; truth, where semblance; love,
Where there's another man. The vows of women   110
Of no more bondage be to where they are made
Than they are to their virtues, which is nothing.°
O, above measure false!

---

91 **Depending on their brands** leaning on their torches   96 **Be
pale** remain unflushed, i.e., calm   97 **up** put up, pocketed   102
outsell exceed in value   107 **basilisk** monster supposedly capable
of killing by look   110–12 **The vows . . . nothing** let the vows of
women be no more binding to the recipients of them than women are
bound to their own virtues—which is not at all (Nosworthy)

Philario.   Have patience, sir,
And take your ring again; 'tis not yet won.
115   It may be probable° she lost it, or
Who knows if one° her women, being corrupted,
Hath stol'n it from her?

Posthumus.   Very true,
And so I hope he came by't. Back my ring;
Render to me some corporal sign about her
120   More evident° than this, for this was stol'n.

Iachimo. By Jupiter, I had it from her arm.

Posthumus. Hark you, he swears; by Jupiter he swears.
'Tis true—nay, keep the ring—'tis true. I am sure
She would not lose it. Her attendants are
125   All sworn° and honorable. They induced to steal it?
And by a stranger? No, he hath enjoyed her.
The cognizance° of her incontinency
Is this.° She hath bought the name of whore thus dearly.
There, take thy hire,° and all the fiends of hell
Divide themselves between you!

130   *Philario.*   Sir, be patient.
This is not strong enough to be believed
Of one persuaded° well of.

Posthumus.   Never talk on't.
She hath been colted° by him.

Iachimo.   If you seek
For further satisfying, under her breast—
135   Worthy the pressing—lies a mole, right proud
Of that most delicate lodging. By my life,
I kissed it, and it gave me present° hunger
To feed again, though full. You do remember
This stain° upon her?

Posthumus.   Ay, and it doth confirm

---

115 **probable** provable   116 **one** one of   120 **evident** conclusive
125 **sworn** i.e., to loyalty   127 **cognizance** badge   128 **this** the
bracelet   129 **hire** reward   132 **persuaded** that we are persuaded
to think   133 **colted** possessed sexually   137 **present** immediate
139 **stain** mark

Another stain,° as big as hell can hold,   140
Were there no more but it.

Iachimo.   Will you hear more?

Posthumus. Spare your arithmetic; never count the turns.
Once, and a million!

Iachimo.   I'll be sworn.

Posthumus.   No swearing.
If you will swear you have not done't, you lie,
And I will kill thee if thou dost deny   145
Thou'st made me cuckold.

Iachimo.   I'll deny nothing.

Posthumus. O that I had her here, to tear her limb-meal!°
I will go there and do't i' th' court, before
Her father. I'll do something.   *Exit.*

Philario.   Quite besides
The government° of patience! You have won.   150
Let's follow him and pervert° the present wrath
He hath against himself.

Iachimo.   With all my heart.   *Exeunt.*

[Scene 5. *Rome.*]

Enter Posthumus.

Posthumus. Is there no way for men to be,° but women
Must be half-workers?° We are all bastards,
And that most venerable man which I
Did call my father was I know not where
When I was stamped.° Some coiner° with his tools   5
Made me a counterfeit; yet my mother seemed
The Dian° of that time. So doth my wife
The nonpareil° of this. O, vengeance, vengeance!

---

140 **stain** corruption   147 **limb-meal** limb from limb   150 **government** control   151 **pervert** divert   2.5.1 **be** exist   2 **half-
workers** i.e., in   begetting   5 **stamped** minted   5 **coiner**
counterfeiter   7 **Dian** Diana (goddess of chastity)   8 **nonpareil**
one without equal

Me of my lawful pleasure she restrained

10 And prayed me oft forbearance—did it with
A pudency° so rosy, the sweet view on't°
Might well have warmed old Saturn°—that I thought her
As chaste as unsunned snow. O, all the devils!
This yellow° Iachimo in an hour, was't not?

15 Or less? At first?° Perchance he spoke not, but,
Like a full-acorned° boar, a German one,
Cried "O!" and mounted; found no opposition
But what he looked for should oppose and she
Should from encounter guard. Could I find out

20 The woman's part in me! For there's no motion°
That tends to vice in man but I affirm
It is the woman's part. Be it lying, note it,
The woman's; flattering, hers; deceiving, hers;
Lust and rank° thoughts; hers, hers; revenges, hers;

25 Ambitions, covetings, change of prides,° disdain,
Nice° longing, slanders, mutability,°
All faults that have a name, nay, that hell knows,
Why, hers, in part or all, but rather all.
For even to vice

30 They are not constant, but are changing still
One vice but of a minute old for one
Not half so old as that. I'll write against them,
Detest them, curse them. Yet 'tis greater skill°
In a true hate to pray they have their will;

35 The very devils cannot plague them better.   *Exit.*

---

11 **pudency** modesty   11 **on't** of it   12 **Saturn** (considered to be cold and gloomy)   14 **yellow** i.e., of complexion   15 **At first** immediately   16 **full-acorned** fed full with acorns   20 **motion** impulse   24 **rank** lascivious   25 **change of prides** varying extravagances   26 **Nice** wanton   26 **mutability** inconstancy   33 **skill** reason

ACT 3

Scene 1. [*Britain.*]

*Enter in state Cymbeline, Queen, Cloten, and Lords at one
door and, at another, Caius Lucius and Attendants.*

Cymbeline. Now say, what would Augustus Caesar with us?

Lucius. When Julius Caesar, whose remembrance yet
Lives in men's eyes and will to ears and tongues
Be theme and hearing ever, was in this Britain
And conquered it, Cassibelan thine uncle,   5
Famous in Caesar's praises no whit less
Than in his feats deserving it, for him
And his succession granted Rome a tribute,
Yearly three thousand pounds, which by thee lately
Is left untendered.

Queen.   And, to kill the marvel,°   10
Shall be so ever.

Cloten.   There be many Caesars
Ere such another Julius. Britain's a world
By itself, and we will nothing pay
For wearing our own noses.

Queen.   That opportunity
Which then they had to take from's, to resume   15
We have again. Remember, sir, my liege,
The kings your ancestors, together with
The natural bravery of your isle, which stands
As Neptune's park, ribbèd° and palèd° in
With rocks unscalable and roaring waters,   20

3.1.10 **kill the marvel** end the astonishment (caused by nonpayment)
19 **ribbèd** enclosed   19 **palèd** fenced

257

With sands that will not bear your enemies' boats
But suck them up to th' topmast. A kind of conquest
Caesar made here, but made not here his brag
Of "Came and saw and overcame." With shame,
25   The first that ever touched him, he was carried
From off our coast, twice beaten; and his shipping,
Poor ignorant° baubles on our terrible seas,
Like eggshells moved upon their surges, cracked
As easily 'gainst our rocks. For joy whereof
30   The famed Cassibelan, who was once at point°—
O giglot° Fortune!—to master° Caesar's sword,
Made Lud's Town° with rejoicing fires bright
And Britons strut with courage.

Cloten. Come, there's no more tribute to be paid. Our king-
35   dom is stronger than it was at that time, and, as I said,
there is no moe such Caesars. Other of them may have
crooked° noses, but to owe° such straight arms, none.

Cymbeline. Son, let your mother end.

Cloten. We have yet many among us can gripe° as hard as
40   Cassibelan. I do not say I am one, but I have a hand.
Why tribute? Why should we pay tribute? If Caesar can
hide the sun from us with a blanket or put the moon in
his pocket, we will pay him tribute for light; else, sir, no
more tribute, pray you now.

45   *Cymbeline.* You must know,
Till the injurious° Romans did extort
This tribute from us, we were free. Caesar's ambition,
Which swelled so much that it did almost stretch
The sides o' th' world, against all color° here
50   Did put the yoke upon's; which to shake off
Becomes a warlike people, whom we reckon
Ourselves to be. We do say then to Caesar,
Our ancestor was that Mulmutius which
Ordained our laws, whose use the sword of Caesar
55   Hath too much mangled, whose repair and franchise°

---

27 **ignorant** inexperienced   30 **at point** at the point   31 **giglot**
wanton   31 **to master** of mastering   32 **Lud's Town** London   37
crooked i.e., Roman   37 **owe** own   39 **gripe** grasp   46 **injurious**
insulting   49 **against all color** without any right   55 **franchise**
free exercise

Shall, by the power we hold, be our good deed,
Though Rome be therefore angry. Mulmutius made our
    laws,
Who was the first of Britain which did put
His brows within a golden crown and called
Himself a king.

Lucius.   I am sorry, Cymbeline,   60
That I am to pronounce Augustus Caesar—
Caesar, that hath moe kings his° servants than
Thyself domestic officers—thine enemy.
Receive it from me then: war and confusion°
In Caesar's name pronounce I 'gainst thee. Look   65
For fury not to be resisted. Thus defied,
I thank thee for myself.

Cymbeline.   Thou art welcome, Caius.
Thy Caesar knighted me; my youth I spent
Much under him; of him I gathered honor,
Which he to seek° of me again, perforce,   70
Behooves me keep at utterance.° I am perfect°
That the Pannonians and Dalmatians° for
Their liberties are now in arms, a precedent
Which not to read would show the Britons cold.°
So Caesar shall not find them.

Lucius.   Let proof° speak.   75

Cloten. His Majesty bids you welcome. Make pastime with
us a day or two, or longer. If you seek us afterwards in
other terms, you shall find us in our saltwater girdle; if
you beat us out of it, it is yours. If you fall in the adventure, our crows shall fare the better for you, and there's   80
an end.

Lucius. So, sir.

Cymbeline. I know your master's pleasure, and he mine.
All the remain° is, welcome.   *Exeunt.*

---

62 **his** as his   64 **confusion** destruction   70 **he to seek** his seeking
71 **keep at utterance** defend to the last ditch   71 **perfect** well
aware   72 **Pannonians and Dalmatians** inhabitants of present-day
Hungary and Yugoslavia   74 **cold** deficient in spirit   75 **proof** experience   84 **the remain** that remains

Scene 2. [*Britain.*]

Enter Pisanio reading of a letter.

Pisanio. How? of adultery? Wherefore write you not
    What monsters her accuse? Leonatus,
    O master, what a strange° infection
    Is fall'n into thy ear! What false Italian,
5   As poisonous-tongued as handed, hath prevailed
    On thy too ready hearing? Disloyal? No.
    She's punished for her truth° and undergoes,°
    More goddesslike than wifelike, such assaults
    As would take in° some virtue. O my master,
10   Thy mind to° her is now as low as were
    Thy fortunes. How? That I should murder her,
    Upon the love and truth and vows which I
    Have made to thy command? I her? Her blood?
    If it be so to do good service, never
15   Let me be counted serviceable. How look I
    That I should seem to lack humanity
    So much as this fact° comes to? [*Reading*] "Do't! The letter
    That I have sent her, by her own command
    Shall give thee opportunity." O damned paper,
20   Black as the ink that's on thee! Senseless° bauble,
    Art thou a fedary for° this act, and look'st
    So virginlike without? Lo, here she comes.

Enter Imogen.

    I am ignorant in° what I am commanded.

Imogen. How now, Pisanio?

25 *Pisanio.* Madam, here is a letter from my lord.

Imogen. Who, thy lord? That is my lord Leonatus?

3.2.3 **strange** foreign   7 **truth** fidelity   7 **undergoes** endures   9 **take in** conquer   10 **to** compared with   17 **fact** crime   20 **Senseless** inanimate   21 **fedary for** accomplice in   23 **am ignorant in** will pretend ignorance of

O, learn'd indeed were that astronomer°
That knew the stars as I his characters;°
He'ld lay the future open. You good gods,
Let what is here contained relish of love,   30
Of my lord's health, of his content—yet not°
That we two are asunder; let that grieve him.
Some griefs are med'cinable;° that is one of them,
For it doth physic love°—of his content
All but in that. Good wax, thy leave. Blest be   35
You bees that make these locks of counsel.° Lovers
And men in dangerous bonds° pray not alike;
Though forfeiters° you cast in prison, yet
You clasp young Cupid's tables.° Good news, gods!
                                                    [*Reading*]
  "Justice and your father's wrath, should he take me in   40
his dominion, could not be so cruel to me as° you, O the
dearest of creatures, would even renew me with your
eyes. Take notice that I am in Cambria° at Milford
Haven. What your own love will out of this advise you,
follow. So he wishes you all happiness, that remains   45
loyal to his vow, and your increasing in love.
                                        Leonatus Posthumus."
O, for a horse with wings! Hear'st thou, Pisanio?
He is at Milford Haven. Read, and tell me
How far 'tis thither. If one of mean affairs°   50
May plod it in a week, why may not I
Glide thither in a day? Then, true Pisanio,
Who long'st like me to see thy lord, who long'st—
O, let me bate°—but not like me, yet long'st,
But in a fainter kind—O, not like me!   55
For mine's beyond beyond: say, and speak thick°—
Love's counselor should fill the bores of hearing,°
To th' smothering of the sense—how far it is
To this same blessèd Milford. And by th' way°

---

27 **astronomer** astrologer   28 **characters** handwriting   31 **not**
not content   33 **med'cinable** curative   34 **physic love** keep love
healthy   36 **locks of counsel** waxen seals   37 **in dangerous bonds**
under contracts imposing penalties   38 **forfeiters** contract-violators
39 **tables** notebooks   41 **as** but that   43 **Cambria** Wales   50
mean affairs ordinary business   54 **bate** abate, modify (the statement)   56 **thick** profusely   57 **bores of hearing** ears   59 **by th'
way** on the way

60   Tell me how Wales was made so happy as
        T' inherit such a haven. But first of all,
        How we may steal from hence, and for the gap
        That we shall make in time from our hence-going
        And our return, to excuse. But first, how get hence?
65   Why should excuse be born or ere begot?°
        We'll talk of that hereafter. Prithee speak,
        How many score of miles may we well rid°
        'Twixt hour and hour?

Pisanio.   One score 'twixt sun and sun,
        Madam, 's enough for you, and too much too.

70 *Imogen.* Why, one that rode to's execution, man,
        Could never go so slow. I have heard of riding wagers
        Where horses have been nimbler than the sands
        That run i' th' clock's behalf.° But this is fool'ry.
        Go bid my woman feign a sickness, say
75   She'll home to her father; and provide me presently°
        A riding suit, no costlier than would fit
        A franklin's° housewife.°

Pisanio.   Madam, you're best consider.

    Imogen. I see before me,° man. Nor here, nor here,°
        Nor what ensues,° but have a fog in them
80   That I cannot look through. Away, I prithee;
        Do as I bid thee. There's no more to say.
        Accessible is none but Milford way.

                                        Exeunt [severally].

---

65 **or ere begot** i.e., before conception (of the deed which makes excuse necessary)   67 **rid** cover   73 **i' th' clock's behalf** in place of
a clock   75 **presently** immediately   77 **franklin** small landowner
77 **housewife** (pronounced "huzzif")   78 **before me** i.e., what is
immediately ahead   78 **Nor here, nor here** neither to this side nor
that   79 **what ensues** the eventual outcome

Scene 3. [*Wales.*]

Enter Belarius, Guiderius, and Arviragus.

Belarius. A goodly day not to keep house with such
    Whose roof 's as low as ours! Stoop, boys. This gate°
    Instructs you how t' adore the heavens and bows you°
    To a morning's holy office. The gates of monarchs
    Are arched so high that giants may jet° through   5
    And keep their impious turbans on without
    Good morrow to the sun. Hail, thou fair heaven!
    We house i' th' rock, yet use thee not so hardly°
    As prouder livers do.

Guiderius.   Hail, heaven!

Arviragus.   Hail, heaven!

Belarius. Now for our mountain sport. Up to yond hill;   10
    Your legs are young. I'll tread these flats. Consider,
    When you above perceive me like a crow,
    That it is place° which lessens and sets off,°
    And you may then revolve what tales I have told you
    Of courts, of princes, of the tricks in war.   15
    This° service is not service, so being done,
    But being so allowed.° To apprehend thus
    Draws us a profit from all things we see,
    And often, to our comfort, shall we find
    The sharded° beetle in a safer hold°   20
    Than is the full-winged eagle. O, this life
    Is nobler than attending for a check,°
    Richer than doing nothing for a bribe,
    Prouder than rustling in unpaid-for silk:

3.3.2 **This gate** one of the tiring-house doors (representing the
"cave") 3 **bows you** makes you bow 5 **jet** strut 8 **hardly** badly
13 **place** position 13 **sets off** displays to advantage 16 **This** any
particular 17 **allowed** approved 20 **sharded** provided with wing-
cases 20 **hold** stronghold 22 **attending for a check** doing service at court only to receive a rebuke

25   Such gain the cap° of him that makes him fine°
        Yet keeps his book uncrossed.° No life to ours.

        Guiderius. Out of your proof° you speak. We poor
            unfledged
        Have never winged from view o' th' nest, nor know not
        What air's from home. Haply this life is best
30   If quiet life be best, sweeter to you
        That have a sharper known, well corresponding
        With your stiff age; but unto us it is
        A cell of ignorance, traveling abed,°
        A prison, or a debtor that not dares
        To stride a limit.°

35   *Arviragus.*   What should we speak of
        When we are old as you? When we shall hear
        The rain and wind beat dark December, how
        In this our pinching° cave shall we discourse
        The freezing hours away? We have seen nothing.
40   We are beastly:° subtle as the fox for prey,
        Like° warlike as the wolf for what we eat.
        Our valor is to chase what flies. Our cage
        We make a choir, as doth the prisoned bird,
        And sing our bondage freely.

        Belarius.   How you speak!
45   Did you but know the city's usuries
        And felt them knowingly; the art o' th' court,
        As hard to leave as keep,° whose top to climb
        Is certain falling, or so slipp'ry that
        The fear's as bad as falling; the toil o' th' war,
50   A pain° that only seems to seek out danger
        I' th' name of fame and honor, which dies i' th' search
        And hath as oft a sland'rous epitaph
        As record of fair act; nay, many times
        Doth ill deserve° by doing well; what's worse,
55   Must curtsy at the censure. O boys, this story

---

25 **gain the cap** win approval   25 **makes him fine** dresses
elegantly   26 **keeps...uncrossed** does not cancel the debts
in his account book   27 **proof** experience   33 **abed** i.e., in
imagination   35 **stride a limit** step over a boundary   38
pinching distressingly cold   40 **beastly** beastlike   41 **Like**
as   47 **keep** remain at   50 **pain** labor   54 **deserve** earn

The world may read in me. My body's marked
With Roman swords, and my report° was once
First with the best of note.° Cymbeline loved me,
And when a soldier was the theme, my name
Was not far off. Then was I as a tree   60
Whose boughs did bend with fruit. But in one night
A storm or robbery, call it what you will,
Shook down my mellow hangings,° nay, my leaves,
And left me bare to weather.

Guiderius.   Uncertain favor!

Belarius. My fault being nothing, as I have told you oft,   65
But that two villains, whose false oaths prevailed
Before my perfect honor, swore to Cymbeline
I was confederate with the Romans. So
Followed my banishment, and this twenty years
This rock and these demesnes have been my world,   70
Where I have lived at honest freedom, paid
More pious debts to heaven than in all
The fore-end° of my time. But up to th' mountains!
This is not hunters' language. He that strikes
The venison first shall be the lord o' th' feast;   75
To him the other two shall minister,
And we will fear no poison, which attends°
In place of greater state. I'll meet you in the valleys.
                    Exeunt [Guiderius and Arviragus].
How hard it is to hide the sparks of nature!
These boys know little they are sons to th' King,   80
Nor Cymbeline dreams that they are alive.
They think they are mine, and though trained up thus
     meanly
I' th' cave wherein they bow, their thoughts do hit
The roofs of palaces, and Nature prompts them
In simple and low things to prince it much   85
Beyond the trick° of others. This Polydore,
The heir of Cymbeline and Britain, who
The King his father called Guiderius—Jove!
When on my three-foot stool I sit and tell
The warlike feats I have done, his spirits fly out   90

---

57 **report** reputation 58 **note** reputation 63 **hangings** fruit
73 **fore-end** early part 77 **attends** is present 86 **trick** capacity

Into my story; say "Thus mine enemy fell,
And thus I set my foot on's neck," even then
The princely blood flows in his cheek, he sweats,
Strains his young nerves,° and puts himself in posture
95 That acts my words. The younger brother Cadwal,
Once Arviragus, in as like a figure°
Strikes life into my speech and shows much more
His own conceiving.° [*Horn.*] Hark, the game is roused!
O Cymbeline, heaven and my conscience knows
100 Thou didst unjustly banish me; whereon,
At three and two years old, I stole these babes,
Thinking to bar thee of succession as
Thou refts° me of my lands. Euriphile,
Thou wast their nurse; they took thee for their mother,
105 And every day do honor to her grave.
Myself, Belarius, that am Morgan called,
They take for natural father. The game is up.°   *Exit.*

Scene 4. [*Wales.*]

Enter Pisanio and Imogen.

Imogen. Thou told'st me, when we came from horse, the
          place
Was near at hand. Ne'er longed my mother so
To see me first as I have° now. Pisanio, man,
5 Where is Posthumus? What is in thy mind
That makes thee stare thus? Wherefore breaks that sigh
From th' inward of thee? One but painted thus
Would be interpreted a thing perplexed°
Beyond self-explication. Put thyself
10 Into a havior° of less fear, ere wildness°
Vanquish my staider senses. What's the matter?°
Why tender'st thou that paper to me with
A look untender? If 't be summer news,

---

94 **nerves** sinews   96 **in … figure** playing his part equally well   98
conceiving interpretation   103 **refts** robbed   107 **up** roused   3.4.3
have i.e., have longing (to see Posthumus)   7 **perplexed** troubled   9
havior appearance   9 **wildness** panic   10 **matter** business

Smile to't before; if winterly, thou need'st
But keep that count'nance still. My husband's hand?
That drug-damned Italy hath outcraftied° him,   15
And he's at some hard point.° Speak, man! Thy tongue
May take off some extremity,° which to read
Would be even mortal to me.

Pisanio.   Please you read,
And you shall find me, wretched man, a thing
The most disdained of fortune.   20

Imogen. (Reads) "Thy mistress, Pisanio, hath played the
strumpet in my bed, the testimonies whereof lies bleeding in me. I speak not out of weak surmises, but from
proof as strong as my grief and as certain as I expect my
revenge. That part thou, Pisanio, must act for me, if thy   25
faith be not tainted with the breach of hers. Let thine
own hands take away her life. I shall give thee opportunity at Milford Haven—she hath my letter for the
purpose—where, if thou fear to strike and to make me
certain it is done, thou art the pander to her dishonor   30
and equally to me disloyal."

Pisanio. What shall I need to draw my sword? The paper
Hath cut her throat already. No, 'tis slander,
Whose edge is sharper than the sword, whose tongue
Outvenoms all the worms° of Nile, whose breath   35
Rides on the posting° winds and doth belie°
All corners of the world. Kings, queens, and states,°
Maids, matrons, nay, the secrets of the grave
This viperous slander enters. What cheer, madam?

Imogen. False to his bed? What is it to be false?   40
To lie in watch° there and to think on him?
To weep 'twixt clock and clock?° If sleep charge°
  nature,
To break it with a fearful° dream of him
And cry myself awake? That's false to's bed, is it?

15 **outcraftied** outwitted   16 **at some hard point** in some difficult
situation   17 **take ... extremity** lessen the shock   35 **worms** serpents   36 **posting** speeding   36 **belie** fill with lies   37 **states**
lords   41 **in watch** awake   42 **'twixt clock and clock** from hour to
hour   42 **charge** burden   43 **fearful** frightening

45 *Pisanio.* Alas, good lady!

    Imogen. I false? Thy° conscience witness! Iachimo,
        Thou didst accuse him of incontinency.
        Thou then looked'st like a villain; now, methinks,
        Thy favor's° good enough. Some jay° of Italy,
50   Whose mother was her painting,° hath betrayed him.
        Poor I am stale, a garment out of fashion,
        And, for I am richer than to hang by th' walls,°
        I must be ripped. To pieces with me! O,
        Men's vows are women's traitors! All good seeming,°
55   By thy revolt,° O husband, shall be thought
        Put on for villainy, not born where't grows,°
        But worn a bait for ladies.

    Pisanio.   Good madam, hear me.

    Imogen. True honest men, being heard° like false Aeneas,°
        Were in his time thought false, and Sinon's° weeping
60   Did scandal° many a holy tear, took pity
        From most true wretchedness. So thou, Posthumus,
        Wilt lay the leaven on all proper men;°
        Goodly° and gallant shall be false and perjured
        From thy great fail.° Come, fellow, be thou honest;
65   Do thou thy master's bidding. When thou seest him,
        A little witness my obedience. Look,
        I draw the sword myself. Take it, and hit
        The innocent mansion of my love, my heart.
        Fear not, 'tis empty of all things but grief.
70   Thy master is not there, who was indeed
        The riches of it. Do his bidding, strike!
        Thou mayst be valiant in a better cause,
        But now thou seem'st a coward.

    Pisanio.   Hence, vile instrument!
        Thou shalt not damn my hand.

---

46 **Thy** i.e., Posthumus'   49 **favor** appearance   49 **jay** whore   50
Whose . . . painting i.e., dependent upon make-up   52 **for . . . walls**
i.e., since I am too valuable to be set aside   54 **seeming** appearance
55 **revolt** turning away   56 **not . . . grows** i.e., transplanted (hence
assumed)   58 **heard** heard to speak   58 **Aeneas** (who jilted Dido)
59 **Sinon** (who persuaded Troy to admit the Trojan Horse)   60 **scandal** make disreputable   62 **lay . . . men** cause all honorable men to be
thought corrupt   63 **Goodly** handsome   64 **fail** failure

Imogen.　　　　　　　　　　　　Why, I must die,
And if I do not by thy hand, thou art　　　　　　　　*75*
No servant of thy master's. Against self-slaughter
There is a prohibition so divine
That cravens° my weak hand. Come, here's my heart—
Something's° afore't; soft,° soft, we'll no defense—
Obedient° as the scabbard. What is here?　　　　　　*80*
The scriptures° of the loyal Leonatus
All turned to heresy? Away, away,
Corrupters of my faith! You shall no more
Be stomachers° to my heart. Thus may poor fools
Believe false teachers. Though those that are betrayed　*85*
Do feel the treason sharply, yet the traitor
Stands in worse case of woe.
And thou, Posthumus, that didst set up
My disobedience 'gainst the King my father
And make me put into contempt the suits　　　　　　*90*
Of princely fellows, shalt hereafter find
It is no act of common passage, but
A strain of rareness;° and I grieve myself
To think, when thou shalt be disedged° by her
That now thou tirest° on, how thy memory　　　　　　*95*
Will then be panged° by me. Prithee dispatch,
The lamb entreats the butcher. Where's thy knife?
Thou art too slow to do thy master's bidding
When I desire it too.

Pisanio.　　　　　　　　　　O gracious lady,
Since I received command to do this business　　　　*100*
I have not slept one wink.

Imogen.　　　　　　　　　　Do't, and to bed then.

Pisanio. I'll wake mine eyeballs out° first.

---

78 **cravens** makes cowardly　79 **Something** Posthumus' letter　79
soft wait　80 **Obedient** i.e., as ready to receive the sword　81
scriptures writings　84 **stomachers** ornamental cloth worn under
lacing of the bodice (she has been holding the letter against her
breast)　92–93 **It ... rareness** i.e., my choice of you was not an
everyday matter but resulted from rare qualities　94 **be disedged**
have lost the edge (of appetite)　95 **tirest** feedest ravenously (hawking term)　96 **panged** tormented　102 **wake ... out** remain awake
till my eyes drop out

Imogen.   Wherefore then
        Didst undertake it? Why hast thou abused
        So many miles with a pretense? This place?
105   Mine action and thine own? Our horses' labor?
        The time inviting thee? The perturbed court
        For my being absent? whereunto I never
        Purpose return. Why hast thou gone so far,
        To be unbent° when thou hast ta'en thy stand,°
110   Th' elected° deer before thee?

Pisanio.   But to win time
        To lose so bad employment, in the which
        I have considered of a course. Good lady,
        Hear me with patience.

Imogen.   Talk thy tongue weary, speak.
        I have heard I am a strumpet, and mine ear,
115   Therein false struck, can take no greater wound,
        Nor tent to bottom that.° But speak.

Pisanio.   Then, madam,
        I thought you would not back° again.

Imogen.   Most like,
        Bringing me here to kill me.

Pisanio.   Not so, neither.
        But if I were as wise as honest, then
120   My purpose would prove well. It cannot be
        But that my master is abused.° Some villain,
        Ay, and singular° in his art, hath done you both
        This cursèd injury.

Imogen. Some Roman courtesan.°

Pisanio.   No, on my life:
125   I'll give but notice you are dead, and send him
        Some bloody sign of it,° for 'tis commanded
        I should do so. You shall be missed at court,
        And that will well confirm it.

---

109 **unbent** with bow unbent, unprepared   109 **stand** hunting station   110 **elected** chosen   116 **tent . . . that** probe reaching to bottom of the wound   117 **back** go back   121 **abused** deceived   122
singular unique   124 **courtesan** courtier   126 **it** your death

Imogen.   Why, good fellow,
What shall I do the while? Where bide? How live?
Or in my life what comfort when I am   130
Dead to my husband?

Pisanio.   If you'll back to th' court—

Imogen. No court, no father, nor no more ado
With that harsh, noble, simple nothing,
That Cloten, whose love suit hath been to me
As fearful as a siege.

Pisanio.   If not at court,   135
Then not in Britain must you bide.

Imogen.   Where then?
Hath Britain all the sun that shines? Day, night,
Are they not but° in Britain? I' th' world's volume
Our Britain seems as of it, but not in't;°
In a great pool a swan's nest. Prithee think   140
There's livers out of Britain.

Pisanio.   I am most glad
You think of other place. Th' ambassador,
Lucius the Roman, comes to Milford Haven
Tomorrow. Now if you could wear a mind
Dark° as your fortune is, and but disguise   145
That° which, t' appear itself,° must not yet be
But by self-danger, you should tread a course
Pretty and full of view;° yea, haply,° near
The residence of Posthumus, so nigh, at least,
That though his actions were not visible, yet   150
Report should render° him hourly to your ear
As truly as he moves.

Imogen.   O, for such means,
Though peril to my modesty,° not death on't,
I would adventure.

Pisanio.   Well then, here's the point:

138 **not but** only   139 **of it . . . in't** i.e., part of the world yet separated from it   145 **Dark** inscrutable   146 **That** her sex   146 **itself** i.e., as itself   148 **full of view** with good prospects   148 **haply**
perhaps   151 **render** describe   153 **modesty** chastity

155   You must forget to be a woman; change
       Command° into obedience, fear and niceness°—
       The handmaids of all women, or more truly
       Woman it° pretty self—into a waggish courage;
       Ready in gibes, quick-answered,° saucy, and
160   As quarrelous° as the weasel. Nay, you must
       Forget that rarest treasure of your cheek,
       Exposing it—but O, the harder° heart!
       Alack, no remedy—to the greedy touch
       Of common-kissing Titan,° and forget
165   Your laborsome° and dainty trims,° wherein
       You made great Juno angry.°

Imogen.   Nay, be brief.
       I see into thy end° and am almost
       A man already.

Pisanio.   First, make yourself but like one.
       Forethinking° this, I have already fit°—
170   'Tis in my cloak-bag—doublet, hat, hose, all
       That answer° to them. Would you, in their serving,°
       And with what imitation you can borrow
       From youth of such a season,° 'fore noble Lucius
       Present yourself, desire his service,° tell him
175   Wherein you're happy,° which will make him know,°
       If that his head have ear in music; doubtless
       With joy he will embrace° you, for he's honorable,
       And, doubling that, most holy. Your means° abroad—
       You have me, rich, and I will never fail
       Beginning nor supplyment.

180 *Imogen.*   Thou art all the comfort
       The gods will diet me with. Prithee away.

---

156 **Command** habit of commanding (as a person of rank) 156
niceness fastidiousness 158 **it** its 159 **quick-answered** quick-
answering 160 **quarrelous** quarrelsome 162 **harder** too hard
164 **common-kissing Titan** the sun which kisses everything alike
165 **laborsome** elaborate 165 **trims** apparel 166 **angry** i.e.,
with jealousy 167 **end** purpose 169 **Forethinking** planning in
advance for 169 **fit** prepared 171 **answer** correspond 171 **in
their serving** with their aid 173 **season** age 174 **his service** em-
ployment as his servant 175 **happy** accomplished 175 **make
him know** satisfy him 177 **embrace** welcome 178 **means** i.e., of
subsistence

There's more to be considered, but we'll even°
All that good time will give us. This attempt
I am soldier to,° and will abide° it with
A prince's courage. Away, I prithee.   *185*

Pisanio. Well, madam, we must take a short farewell,
Lest, being missed, I be suspected of
Your carriage° from the court. My noble mistress,
Here is a box; I had it from the Queen.
What's in't is precious. If you are sick at sea   *190*
Or stomach-qualmed at land, a dram of this
Will drive away distemper.° To some shade,
And fit you to your manhood. May the gods
Direct you to the best.

Imogen.   Amen. I thank thee.
                                       Exeunt [severally].

Scene 5. [*Britain.*]

*Enter Cymbeline, Queen, Cloten, Lucius, [a Messenger,
                Attendants,] and Lords.*

Cymbeline. Thus far, and so farewell.

Lucius.   Thanks, royal sir.
My emperor hath wrote: I must from hence,
And am right sorry that I must report ye
My master's enemy.

Cymbeline.   Our subjects, sir,
Will not endure his yoke, and for ourself   *5*
To show less sovereignty than they, must needs
Appear unkinglike.

Lucius.   So, sir. I desire of you
A conduct° overland to Milford Haven.
Madam, all joy befall your Grace, and you.°

Cymbeline. My lords, you are appointed for that office;°   *10*

---

182 **even** keep pace with   184 **soldier to** brave enough for   184
abide face   188 **Your carriage** removing you   192 **distemper** illness   3.5.8 **conduct** escort   9 **you** Cymbeline   10 **office** duty

The due of honor in no point omit.
So farewell, noble Lucius.

Lucius.   Your hand, my lord.

Cloten. Receive it friendly, but from this time forth
 I wear it as your enemy.

Lucius.   Sir, the event°
15 Is yet to name the winner. Fare you well.

Cymbeline. Leave not the worthy Lucius, good my lords,
 Till he have crossed the Severn. Happiness!
                    Exeunt Lucius et ceteri.°

Queen. He goes hence frowning, but it honors us
 That we have given him cause.

Cloten.   'Tis all the better;
20 Your valiant Britons have their wishes in it.

Cymbeline. Lucius hath wrote already to the Emperor
 How it goes here. It fits us therefore ripely°
 Our chariots and our horsemen be in readiness.
 The pow'rs that he already hath in Gallia
25 Will soon be drawn to head,° from whence he moves
 His war for Britain.

Queen.   'Tis not sleepy business,
 But must be looked to speedily and strongly.

Cymbeline. Our expectation that it would be thus
 Hath made us forward. But, my gentle queen,
30 Where is our daughter? She hath not appeared
 Before the Roman, nor to us hath tendered
 The duty of the day. She looks° us like
 A thing more made of malice than of duty.
 We have noted it.—Call her before us, for
 We have been too slight in sufferance.°
                    [*Exit Messenger.*]

35 *Queen.*   Royal sir,

14 **event** outcome 17s.d. **et ceteri** and others (Attendants and Lords)
22 **fits . . . ripely** behooves us therefore strongly 25 **drawn to
head** gathered into an army 32 **looks** seems to 35 **slight in sufferance** remiss in permissiveness

Since the exile of Posthumus, most retired
Hath her life been; the cure whereof, my lord,
'Tis time must do. Beseech your Majesty,
Forbear sharp speeches to her. She's a lady
So tender of° rebukes that words are strokes,   40
And strokes death to her.

Enter Messenger.

Cymbeline.   Where is she, sir? How
Can her contempt be answered?°

Messenger.   Please you, sir,
Her chambers are all locked, and there's no answer
That will be given to th' loud of noise we make.

Queen. My lord, when last I went to visit her,   45
She prayed me to excuse her keeping close;°
Whereto constrained by her infirmity,
She should that duty leave unpaid to you
Which daily she was bound to proffer. This
She wished me to make known, but our great court°   50
Made me to blame in memory.°

Cymbeline.   Her doors locked?
Not seen of late? Grant, heavens, that which I fear
Prove false!   *Exit.*

Queen.   Son, I say, follow the King.

Cloten. That man of hers, Pisanio, her old servant,
I have not seen these two days.

Queen.   Go, look after. *Exit* [*Cloten*].   55
Pisanio, thou that stand'st so for° Posthumus—
He hath a drug of mine. I pray his absence
Proceed by° swallowing that, for he believes
It is a thing most precious. But for her,
Where is she gone? Haply despair hath seized her,   60
Or, winged with fervor of her love, she's flown
To her desired Posthumus. Gone she is

40 **tender of** sensitive to   42 **answered** accounted for   46 **close** to
herself   50 **our great court** i.e., state affairs   51 **to blame in
memory** fail to remember   56 **stand'st so for** so much supportest
58 **Proceed by** result from

To death or to dishonor, and my end
Can make good use of either. She being down,
65   I have the placing of the British crown.

Enter Cloten.

How now, my son?

Cloten.   'Tis certain she is fled.
Go in and cheer the King. He rages; none
Dare come about him.

Queen. [*Aside*]   All the better. May
This night forestall° him of the coming day!

                           Exit Queen.

70 *Cloten.* I love and hate her, for° she's fair and royal,
And that° she hath all courtly parts° more exquisite
Than lady, ladies, woman. From every one
The best she hath, and she, of all compounded,
Outsells° them all. I love her therefore, but
75 Disdaining me and throwing favors on
The low Posthumus slanders° so her judgment
That what's else rare is choked; and in that point
I will conclude to hate her, nay, indeed,
To be revenged upon her. For, when fools
Shall—

Enter Pisanio.

80   Who is here? What, are you packing,° sirrah?°
Come hither. Ah, you precious pander! Villain,
Where is thy lady? In a word, or else
Thou art straightway with the fiends.

Pisanio.   O good my lord!

Cloten. Where is thy lady? Or, by Jupiter,
85 I will not ask again. Close° villain,
I'll have this secret from thy heart or rip
Thy heart to find it. Is she with Posthumus?

---

69 **forestall** deprive 70 **for** because 71 **that** because 71 **parts**
qualities 74 **Outsells** outvalues 76 **slanders** denigrates 80
packing plotting 80 **sirrah** (term of address to an inferior) 85
Close secretive

From whose so many weights of baseness cannot
  A dram of worth be drawn.

Pisanio.   Alas, my lord,
  How can she be with him? When was she missed?   90
  He is in Rome.

Cloten.   Where is she, sir? Come nearer.°
  No farther halting. Satisfy me home°
  What is become of her.

Pisanio. O my all-worthy lord!

Cloten.   All-worthy villain!
  Discover° where thy mistress is at once,   95
  At the next word. No more of "worthy lord"!
  Speak, or thy silence on the instant is
  Thy condemnation and thy death.

Pisanio.   Then, sir,
  This paper° is the history of my knowledge
  Touching her flight.   [*Presenting a letter*]

Cloten.   Let's see't. I will pursue her   100
  Even to Augustus' throne.

Pisanio. [*Aside*]   Or° this, or perish.
  She's far enough, and what he learns by this
  May prove his travel, not her danger.

Cloten.   Hum!

Pisanio. [*Aside*] I'll write to my lord she's dead. O
    Imogen,
  Safe mayst thou wander, safe return again!   105

Cloten. Sirrah, is this letter true?

Pisanio. Sir, as I think.

Cloten. It is Posthumus' hand, I know't. Sirrah, if thou
    wouldst not be a villain, but do me true service, undergo°
    those employments wherein I should have cause to use   110
    thee with a serious industry—that is, what villainy soe'er

_____

91 **nearer** to the point   92 **home** thoroughly   95 **Discover** reveal
99 **This paper** (cf. line 128 and 5.5.279)   101 **Or** either   109 **undergo** undertake

I bid thee do, to perform it directly and truly—I would
think thee an honest man. Thou shouldst neither want my
means for thy relief nor my voice for thy preferment.°

115 *Pisanio.* Well, my good lord.

Cloten. Wilt thou serve me? For since patiently and constantly thou hast stuck to the bare fortune of that beggar
Posthumus, thou canst not, in the course of gratitude,
but be a diligent follower of mine. Wilt thou serve me?

120 *Pisanio.* Sir, I will.

Cloten. Give me thy hand. Here's my purse. Hast any of
thy late master's garments in thy possession?

Pisanio. I have, my lord, at my lodging the same suit he
wore when he took leave of my lady and mistress.

125 *Cloten.* The first service thou dost me, fetch that suit hither. Let it be thy first service. Go.

Pisanio. I shall, my lord.   *Exit.*

Cloten. Meet thee at Milford Haven! I forgot to ask
him one thing; I'll remember't anon. Even there, thou
130 villain Posthumus, will I kill thee. I would these garments were come. She said upon a time—the bitterness
of it I now belch from my heart—that she held the very
garment of Posthumus in more respect than my noble
and natural person, together with the adornment of my
135 qualities. With that suit upon my back will I ravish her;
first kill him, and in her eyes. There shall she see my
valor, which will then be a torment to her contempt. He
on the ground, my speech of insultment° ended on his
dead body, and when my lust hath dined—which, as I
140 say, to vex her I will execute in the clothes that she so
praised—to the court I'll knock her back,° foot° her
home again. She hath despised me rejoicingly, and I'll
be merry in my revenge.

                    Enter Pisanio [with the clothes].

Be those the garments?

---

114 **preferment** advancement   138 **insultment** scornful triumph
141 **knock her back** beat her home   141 **foot** kick

Pisanio. Ay, my noble lord. 145

Cloten. How long is't since she went to Milford Haven?

Pisanio. She can scarce be there yet.

Cloten. Bring this apparel to my chamber; that is the second thing that I have commanded thee. The third is that
thou wilt be a voluntary mute to my design. Be but du- 150
teous, and true preferment shall tender itself to thee. My
revenge is now at Milford. Would I had wings to follow
it! Come, and be true. *Exit.*

Pisanio. Thou bid'st me to my loss,° for true to thee
Were to prove false, which I will never be, 155
To him° that is most true. To Milford go,
And find not her whom thou pursuest. Flow, flow,
You heavenly blessings, on her. This fool's speed
Be crossed° with slowness; labor be his meed.° *Exit.*

Scene 6. [*Wales.*]

Enter Imogen alone [*in boy's clothes*].

Imogen. I see a man's life is a tedious one.
I have tired myself, and for two nights together
Have made the ground my bed. I should be sick
But that my resolution helps me. Milford,
When from the mountain-top Pisanio showed thee, 5
Thou wast within a ken.° O Jove, I think
Foundations° fly the wretched—such, I mean,
Where they should be relieved. Two beggars told me
I could not miss my way. Will poor folks lie,
That have afflictions on them, knowing 'tis 10
A punishment or trial? Yes. No wonder,
When rich ones scarce tell true. To lapse in fulness°
Is sorer° than to lie for need, and falsehood
Is worse in kings than beggars. My dear lord,
Thou art one o' th' false ones. Now I think on thee 15

---

154 **loss** i.e., of honor 156 **him** Posthumus 159 **crossed**
thwarted 159 **meed** reward 3.6.6 **a ken** view 7 **Foundations**
security (quibble on "hospitals") 12 **lapse in fulness** i.e., lie when
prosperous 13 **sorer** worse

My hunger's gone, but even° before, I was
At point° to sink for° food. But what is this?
Here is a path to't. 'Tis some savage hold.°
I were best not call; I dare not call. Yet famine,
20   Ere clean° it o'erthrow nature, makes it valiant.
Plenty and peace breeds cowards; hardness° ever
Of hardiness is mother. Ho! Who's here?
If anything that's civil,° speak; if savage,
Take or lend.° Ho! No answer? Then I'll enter.
25   Best draw my sword, and if mine enemy
But fear the sword like me, he'll scarcely look on't.
Such a foe,° good heavens!   *Exit.*°

Enter Belarius, Guiderius, and Arviragus.

Belarius. You, Polydore, have proved best woodman°
      and
      Are master of the feast. Cadwal and I
30   Will play the cook and servant; 'tis our match.°
The sweat of industry would dry and die
But for the end it works to. Come, our stomachs
Will make what's homely° savory. Weariness
Can snore upon the flint when resty° sloth
35   Finds the down pillow hard. Now peace be here,
Poor house, that keep'st thyself.

Guiderius.   I am throughly weary.

Arviragus. I am weak with toil, yet strong in appetite.

Guiderius. There is cold meat i' th' cave. We'll browse on
      that
      Whilst what we have killed be cooked.

Belarius. [*Looking through door*]   Stay, come not in.
40   But that it eats our victuals, I should think
      Here were a fairy.

16 **even** just 17 **At point** about 17 **for** for lack of 18 **hold**
stronghold 20 **clean** completely 21 **hardness** hardship 23
civil civilized 24 **Take or lend** take (what I have) or give (what you
will) 27 **Such a foe** i.e., may I have (if any) such a foe 27s.d **Exit**
(at this point, since the stage is cleared, F marks a new scene) 28
woodman hunter 30 **match** agreement 33 **homely** plain 34
resty lazy

Guiderius.   What's the matter,° sir?

Belarius. By Jupiter, an angel; or, if not,
  An earthly paragon. Behold divineness
  No elder than a boy.

                    Enter Imogen.

Imogen. Good masters, harm me not.   45
  Before I entered here, I called and thought
  To have begged or bought what I have took. Good
      troth,°
  I have stol'n naught, nor would not, though I had found
  Gold strewed i' th' floor. Here's money for my meat.
  I would have left it on the board so soon   50
  As I had made my meal, and parted
  With pray'rs for the provider.

Guiderius.   Money, youth?

Arviragus. All gold and silver rather turn to dirt,
  As 'tis no better reckoned but of those
  Who worship dirty gods.

Imogen.   I see you're angry.   55
  Know, if you kill me for my fault, I should
  Have died had I not made it.

Belarius.   Whither bound?

Imogen. To Milford Haven.

Belarius. What's your name?

Imogen. Fidele, sir. I have a kinsman who   60
  Is bound for Italy; he embarked at Milford;
  To whom being going, almost spent with hunger,
  I am fall'n in this offense.

Belarius.   Prithee, fair youth,
  Think us no churls, nor measure our good minds
  By this rude place we live in. Well encountered!   65
  'Tis almost night; you shall have better cheer°
  Ere you depart, and thanks° to stay and eat it.
  Boys, bid him welcome.

41 **matter** subject (of your remark)   47 **Good troth** in truth   66
cheer entertainment   67 **thanks** i.e., our thanks

Guiderius.   Were you a woman, youth,
I should woo hard but be° your groom in honesty.
I'ld bid for you as I do buy.°

70 *Arviragus.*   I'll make't my comfort
He is a man. I'll love him as my brother,
And such a welcome as I'ld give to him
After long absence, such is yours. Most welcome.
Be sprightly,° for you fall 'mongst friends.

Imogen.   'Mongst friends?
—If brothers.° [*Aside*] Would it had been so that
75   they
Had been my father's sons! Then had my prize°
Been less,° and so more equal ballasting°
To thee, Posthumus.

Belarius.   He wrings° at some distress.

Guiderius. Would I could free't!

Arviragus.   Or I, whate'er it be,
What pain it cost, what danger. Gods!

80 *Belarius.*   Hark, boys. [*Whispers.*]

Imogen. Great men
That had a court no bigger than this cave,
That did attend themselves° and had the virtue
Which their own conscience sealed them,° laying by°
85   That nothing-gift° of differing° multitudes,
Could not outpeer° these twain. Pardon me, gods,
I'ld change my sex to be companion with them,
Since Leonatus false.

Belarius.   It shall be so.
Boys, we'll go dress our hunt.° Fair youth, come in.

---

69 **but be** ere I should fail to be (E. Dowden)   70 **I'ld bid ... buy**
i.e., I'd seek your hand in earnest   74 **sprightly** in good spirits   75
If brothers i.e., yes, if we were indeed brothers   76 **prize** price,
value (quibble on "captured ship")   77 **less** (since then she would
not be heir apparent)   77 **ballasting** weight   78 **wrings** writhes
83 **attend themselves** i.e., get along without attendants   84 **sealed
them** authenticated for them (as in affixing a waxen seal to a legal
document)   84 **laying by** setting aside   85 **nothing-gift** worthless
gift (flattery)   85 **differing** fickle   86 **outpeer** surpass   89 **hunt**
quarry

Discourse is heavy, fasting. When we have supped, 90
We'll mannerly demand thee of thy story,
So far as thou wilt speak it.

Guiderius.   Pray draw near.

Arviragus. The night to th' owl and morn to th' lark less
   welcome.

Imogen. Thanks, sir.

Arviragus. I pray draw near.   *Exeunt.* 95

Scene 7. [*Rome.*]

Enter two Roman Senators and Tribunes.

First Senator. This is the tenor of the Emperor's writ:°
   That since the common men are now in action
   'Gainst the Pannonians and Dalmatians,
   And that the legions now in Gallia are
   Full weak to undertake our wars against   5
   The fall'n-off° Britons, that we do incite
   The gentry to this business. He creates
   Lucius proconsul, and to you the tribunes,
   For this immediate levy, he commends°
   His absolute commission.° Long live Caesar!   10

Tribune. Is Lucius general of the forces?

Second Senator.   Ay.

Tribune. Remaining now in Gallia?

First Senator.   With those legions
   Which I have spoke of, whereunto your levy
   Must be supplyant.° The words of your commission
   Will tie you to° the numbers and the time   15
   Of their dispatch.

Tribune.   We will discharge our duty. *Exeunt.*

3.7.1 **writ** dispatch 6 **fall'n-off** revolted 9 **commends** entrusts
10 **absolute commission** full authority 14 **supplyant** supplemen-
tary 15 **tie you to** confirm for you

ACT 4

Scene 1. [*Wales.*]

Enter Cloten alone.

Cloten. I am near to th' place where they should meet,
if Pisanio have mapped it truly. How fit° his garments serve me! Why should his mistress, who was
made by him that made the tailor, not be fit° too?
5 The rather, saving reverence of° the word, for° 'tis said
a woman's fitness° comes by fits. Therein I must play
the workman. I dare speak it to myself, for it is not
vainglory for a man and his glass° to confer in his own
chamber—I mean, the lines of my body are as well
10 drawn as his; no less young, more strong, not beneath
him in fortunes, beyond him in the advantage of the
time,° above him in birth, alike conversant in general°
services, and more remarkable in single oppositions.°
Yet this imperceiverant° thing loves him in my despite.
15 What mortality° is! Posthumus, thy head, which now is
growing upon thy shoulders, shall within this hour be
off, thy mistress enforced,° thy garments cut to pieces
before her face; and all this done, spurn her home to
her father, who may haply be a little angry for my so
20 rough usage; but my mother, having power of° his
testiness, shall turn all into my commendations. My
horse is tied up safe. Out, sword, and to a sore° purpose!

4.1.2 **fit** suitably   4 **fit** suitable   5 **saving reverence of** begging
pardon for   5 **for** since   6 **fitness** sexual inclination   8 **glass**
looking-glass   11–12 **advantage of the time** social opportunities
12 **general** i.e., military   13 **single oppositions** duels   14 **imper-
ceiverant** imperceptive   15 **mortality** life   17 **enforced** raped
20 **power of** control over   22 **sore** causing suffering (quibble on
"wound," i.e., vagina)

284

Fortune put them into my hand. This is the very description of their meeting place, and the fellow dares not deceive me.   *Exit.*   25

Scene 2. [*Wales.*]

*Enter Belarius, Guiderius, Arviragus, and Imogen from
   the cave.*

Belarius. You are not well. Remain here in the cave;
   We'll come to you after hunting.

Arviragus.   Brother, stay here.
   Are we not brothers?

Imogen.   So man and man should be,
   But clay and clay° differs in dignity,°
   Whose dust° is both alike. I am very sick.   5

Guiderius. Go you to hunting, I'll abide with him.

Imogen. So sick I am not, yet I am not well,
   But not so citizen° a wanton° as
   To seem to die ere sick. So please you, leave me;
   Stick to your journal° course; the breach of custom   10
   Is breach of all. I am ill, but your being by me
   Cannot amend° me; society is no comfort
   To one not sociable. I am not very sick,
   Since I can reason of it. Pray you trust me here—
   I'll rob none but myself—and let me die,   15
   Stealing so poorly.°

Guiderius.   I love thee—I have spoke it—
   How much° the quantity, the weight as much
   As I do love my father.

Belarius.   What? How, how?

Arviragus. If it be sin to say so, sir, I yoke me

4.2.4 **clay and clay** one person and another   4 **dignity** rank   5
dust remains after death   8 **citizen** city-bred, bourgeois   8 **wanton** spoilt child   10 **journal** daily   12 **amend** cure   16 **poorly**
i.e., from myself only   17 **How much** as much

20   In my good brother's fault. I know not why
    I love this youth, and I have heard you say
    Love's reason's without reason. The bier at door,
    And a demand who is't shall die, I'ld say
    "My father, not this youth."

Belarius. [*Aside*]   O noble strain!°
25   O worthiness of nature, breed of greatness!
    Cowards father cowards and base things sire base;
    Nature hath meal and bran, contempt and grace.
    I'm not their father; yet who this should be
    Doth miracle itself, loved before me.°—
    'Tis the ninth hour o' th' morn.

30 *Arviragus.*   Brother, farewell.

Imogen. I wish ye sport.

Arviragus.   You health.—So please you,° sir.

Imogen. [*Aside*] These are kind creatures. Gods, what
    lies I have heard!
    Our courtiers say all's savage but at court.
    Experience, O, thou disprov'st report!
35   Th' imperious° seas breeds monsters; for the dish
    Poor tributary rivers as° sweet fish.
    I am sick still, heartsick. Pisanio,
    I'll now taste of thy drug.

Guiderius.   I could not stir him.°
    He said he was gentle,° but unfortunate;
40   Dishonestly afflicted, but yet honest.

Arviragus. Thus did he answer me, yet said hereafter
    I might know more.

Belarius.   To th' field, to th' field.—
    We'll leave you for this time; go in and rest.

Arviragus. We'll not be long away.

Belarius.   Pray be not sick,
    For you must be our housewife.

---

24 **strain** heredity   28–29 **who this . . . before me** that this person,
whoever he is, should be loved more than I is miraculous   31 **So
please you** at your service   35 **imperious** imperial   36 **as** just as
38 **stir him** move him (to tell his story)   39 **gentle** well-born

Imogen.　　　　　　　　　Well or ill,　　　　45
　I am bound° to you.　　　　　　　　　*Exit.*

Belarius.　　　　　And shalt be ever.
　This youth, howe'er distressed, appears° he hath had
　Good ancestors.

Arviragus.　　　　How angellike he sings!

Guiderius. But his neat° cookery! He cut our roots in
　　characters,°
　And sauced our broths as Juno had been sick　　50
　And he her dieter.

Arviragus.　　　　　Nobly he yokes
　A smiling with a sigh, as if the sigh
　Was that° it was for not being such a smile;
　The smile mocking the sigh that it would fly
　From so divine a temple to commix　　55
　With winds that sailors rail at.

Guiderius.　　　　　　　I do note
　That grief and patience, rooted in them both,
　Mingle their spurs° together.

Arviragus.　　　　　　Grow patience,
　And let the stinking elder,° grief, untwine
　His perishing° root with° the increasing vine.　　60

Belarius. It is great morning.° Come away.—Who's there?

Enter Cloten.

Cloten. I cannot find those runagates.° That villain
　Hath mocked me. I am faint.

Belarius.　　　　　　"Those runagates"?
　Means he not us? I partly know him. 'Tis
　Cloten, the son o' th' Queen. I fear some ambush.　　65
　I saw him not these many years, and yet
　I know 'tis he. We are held as outlaws. Hence!

46 **bound** indebted (Belarius quibbles on "tied by affection") 47
appears appears as though 49 **neat** elegant 49 **characters** designs 53 **that** what 58 **spurs** chief roots 59 **elder** elder tree 60
perishing destructive 60 **with** from 61 **great morning** broad
daylight 62 **runagates** runaways

Guiderius. He is but one. You and my brother search
　What companies° are near. Pray you, away.
　Let me alone with him.°

　　　　　　　　　[*Exeunt Belarius and Arviragus.*]

70　*Cloten.*　　　　　　Soft,° what are you
　That fly me thus? Some villain° mountaineers?
　I have heard of such. What slave art thou?

Guiderius.　　　　　　　　　　　　A thing
　More slavish did I ne'er than answering
　A "slave" without a knock.

Cloten.　　　　　　　Thou art a robber,
75　A lawbreaker, a villain. Yield thee, thief.

Guiderius. To who? To thee? What art thou? Have not I
　An arm as big as thine? A heart as big?
　Thy words, I grant, are bigger, for I wear not
　My dagger in my mouth. Say what thou art,
　Why I should yield to thee.

80　*Cloten.*　　　　　　　Thou villain base,
　Know'st me° not by my clothes?

Guiderius.　　　　　　　No, nor thy tailor, rascal,
　Who is thy grandfather. He made those clothes,
　Which, as it seems, make thee.

Cloten.　　　　　　　Thou precious varlet,°
　My tailor made them not.

Guiderius.　　　　　　Hence then, and thank
85　The man that gave them thee. Thou art some fool;
　I am loath to beat thee.

Cloten.　　　　　　Thou injurious° thief,
　Hear but my name and tremble.

Guiderius.　　　　　　　　What's thy name?

Cloten. Cloten, thou villain.

---

69 **companies** companions　70 **Let … him** leave him to me　70
Soft wait　71 **villain** low-born　81 **me** i.e., my rank　83 **precious
varlet** egregious knave　86 **injurious** insulting

Guiderius. Cloten, thou double villain, be thy name,
　I cannot tremble at it. Were it Toad, or Adder, Spider, 　90
　'Twould move me sooner.

Cloten.　　　　　　　　To thy further fear,
　Nay, to thy mere° confusion, thou shalt know
　I am son to th' Queen.

Guiderius.　　　　　I am sorry for't; not seeming°
　So worthy as thy birth.

Cloten.　　　　　　Art not afeard?

Guiderius. Those that I reverence, those I fear—the
　　wise; 　95
　At fools I laugh, not fear them.

Cloten.　　　　　　　Die the death!
　When I have slain thee with my proper° hand,
　I'll follow those that even now fled hence
　And on the gates of Lud's Town set your heads.
　Yield, rustic mountaineer.　　　*Fight and exeunt.* 　100

　　　　　Enter Belarius and Arviragus.

Belarius. No company's abroad?°

Arviragus. None in the world. You did mistake him sure.

Belarius. I cannot tell. Long is it since I saw him,
　But time hath nothing blurred those lines of favor°
　Which then he wore. The snatches° in his voice, 　105
　And burst of speaking, were as his. I am absolute°
　'Twas very Cloten.°

Arviragus.　　　　In this place we left them.
　I wish my brother make good time° with him,
　You say he is so fell.°

Belarius.　　　　　Being scarce made up,°
　I mean to man, he had not apprehension 　110

---

92 **mere** utter　93 **not seeming** since you do not seem　97 **proper**
own　101 **abroad** about　104 **lines of favor** contours of his face
105 **snatches** hesitations　106 **absolute** certain　107 **very Cloten**
Cloten himself　108 **make good time** have good fortune　109 **fell**
fierce　109 **made up** grown

Of roaring terrors; for defect of judgment
Is oft the cause of fear.°

Enter Guiderius [with Cloten's head].

But see, thy brother.

Guiderius. This Cloten was a fool, an empty purse;
There was no money in't. Not Hercules
115   Could have knocked out his brains, for he had none.
Yet I not doing this, the fool had borne
My head as I do his.

Belarius.   What hast thou done?

Guiderius. I am perfect° what: cut off one Cloten's head,
Son to the Queen, after his own report;
120   Who called me traitor, mountaineer, and swore
With his own single hand he'ld take us in,°
Displace our heads where—thank the gods—they grow,
And set them on Lud's Town.

Belarius.   We are all undone.

Guiderius. Why, worthy father, what have we to lose
125   But that° he swore to take, our lives? The law
Protects not us. Then why should we be tender
To° let an arrogant piece of flesh threat us,
Play judge and executioner all himself,
For° we do fear the law? What company
Discover you abroad?

130 *Belarius.*   No single soul
Can we set eye on, but in all safe reason
He must have some attendants. Though his humor°
Was nothing but mutation—ay, and that
From one bad thing to worse—not frenzy, not
135   Absolute madness could so far have raved
To bring him here alone. Although perhaps
It may be heard at court that such as we

111–12 **for defect . . . fear** (sense unclear and frequently emended;
Belarius seems to be saying that Cloten lacked the intelligence to be
frightened) 118 **perfect** well aware 121 **take us in** overcome us
125 **that** what 126–27 **tender/To** so considerate as to 129 **For**
because 132 **humor** chief characteristic

Cave here, hunt here, are outlaws, and in time
May make° some stronger head;° the which he
　hearing—
As it is like him—might break out, and swear　　　　140
He'ld fetch us in; yet is't not probable
To come° alone, either he so undertaking,
Or they so suffering.° Then on good ground we fear,
If we do fear this body hath a tail°
More perilous than the head.

Arviragus.　　　　　　　　Let ordinance°　　　　145
Come as the gods foresay° it. Howsoe'er,
My brother hath done well.

Belarius.　　　　　　　　I had no mind
To hunt this day. The boy Fidele's sickness
Did make my way long forth.°

Guiderius.　　　　　　　　With his own sword,
Which he did wave against my throat, I have ta'en　　150
His head from him. I'll throw't into the creek
Behind our rock, and let it to the sea
And tell the fishes he's the Queen's son, Cloten.
That's all I reck.°　　　　　　　　　　　　Exit.

Belarius.　　　　　　　I fear 'twill be revenged.
Would, Polydore, thou hadst not done't, though valor　155
Becomes thee well enough.

Arviragus.　　　　　　　Would I had done't,
So° the revenge alone pursued° me. Polydore,
I love thee brotherly, but envy much
Thou hast robbed me of this deed. I would revenges
That possible° strength might meet would seek us
　through°　　　　　　　　　　　　　　　160
And put us to our answer.

Belarius.　　　　　　　Well, 'tis done.

---

139 **make** make up　139 **head** force　142 **To come** for him to
come　143 **suffering** allowing　144 **tail** i.e., followers　145 **ordinance** whatever is ordained　146 **foresay** foretell, determine　149
way long forth i.e., way forth seem long　154 **reck** care　157 **So**
so that　157 **pursued** would have pursued　160 **possible** our available　160 **seek us through** search thoroughly for us

We'll hunt no more today, nor seek for danger
Where there's no profit. I prithee, to our rock;
You and Fidele play the cooks. I'll stay
165 Till hasty Polydore return, and bring him
To dinner presently.

Arviragus.   Poor sick Fidele,
I'll willingly to him. To gain° his color
I'ld let a parish of such Clotens blood°
And praise myself for charity.   *Exit.*

Belarius.   O thou goddess,
170 Thou divine Nature, thou thyself thou blazon'st°
In these two princely boys! They are as gentle
As zephyrs blowing below the violet,
Not wagging his sweet head; and yet as rough,
Their royal blood enchafed,° as the rud'st wind
175 That by the top doth take the mountain pine
And make him stoop to th' vale. 'Tis wonder
That an invisible instinct should frame° them
To royalty° unlearned, honor untaught,
Civility° not seen from other, valor
180 That wildly grows° in them but yields a crop
As if it had been sowed. Yet still it's strange
What Cloten's being here to us portends,
Or what his death will bring us.

Enter Guiderius.

Guiderius.   Where's my brother?
I have sent Cloten's clotpoll° down the stream
185 In embassy to his mother; his body's hostage
For his return.   *Solemn music.*

Belarius.   My ingenious° instrument!
Hark, Polydore, it sounds. But what occasion
Hath Cadwal now to give it motion? Hark!

Guiderius. Is he at home?

---

167 **gain** restore   168 **let . . . blood** kill a parish-full of Clotens
170 **blazon'st** proclaimest   174 **enchafed** heated   177 **frame** dispose   178 **royalty** regal conduct   179 **Civility** civilized behavior
180 **wildly grows** grows wild   184 **clotpoll** blockhead   186 **ingenious** skillfully constructed

Belarius.   He went hence even now.

Guiderius. What does he mean? Since death of my dear'st
    mother   190
  It did not speak before. All solemn things
  Should answer° solemn accidents.° The matter?
  Triumphs° for nothing and lamenting toys°
  Is jollity for apes and grief for boys.
  Is Cadwal mad?

    Enter Arviragus with Imogen, dead, bearing her
                in his arms.

Belarius.   Look, here he comes,   195
  And brings the dire occasion in his arms
  Of what we blame him for.

Arviragus.   The bird is dead
  That we have made so much on.° I had rather
  Have skipped from sixteen years of age to sixty,
  To have turned my leaping time into a crutch,   200
  Than have seen this.

Guiderius.   O sweetest, fairest lily!
  My brother wears thee not the one half so well
  As when thou grew'st thyself.

Belarius.   O Melancholy,
  Who ever yet could sound thy bottom, find
  The ooze, to show what coast thy sluggish crayer°   205
  Might eas'liest harbor in? Thou blessèd thing,
  Jove knows what man thou mightst have made; but
    I,°
  Thou diedst, a most rare boy, of melancholy.
  How found you him?

Arviragus.   Stark,° as you see,
  Thus smiling, as° some fly had tickled slumber,   210
  Not as Death's dart being laughed at;° his right cheek
  Reposing on a cushion.

---

192 **answer** correspond to   192 **accidents** events   193 **Triumphs**
public festivities   193 **lamenting toys** lamenting over trifles   198
on of   205 **crayer** small trading vessel   207 **I** i.e., what I know is
209 **Stark** stiff (as in death)   210 **as** as if   211 **as . . . at** as if
laughing at Death's arrow

Guiderius.   Where?

Arviragus.   O' th' floor;
His arms thus leagued.° I thought he slept, and put
My clouted brogues° from off my feet, whose rudeness°
Answered my steps too loud.

215 *Guiderius.*   Why, he but sleeps.
If he be gone, he'll make his grave a bed;
With female fairies will his tomb be haunted,
And worms will not come to thee.

Arviragus.   With fairest flowers,
Whilst summer lasts and I live here, Fidele,
220 I'll sweeten thy sad grave. Thou shalt not lack
The flower that's like thy face, pale primrose; nor
The azured harebell,° like thy veins; no, nor
The leaf of eglantine,° whom not to slander,
Outsweet'ned not thy breath. The ruddock° would
225 With charitable bill—O bill sore shaming
Those rich-left heirs that let their fathers lie
Without a monument!—bring thee all this;
Yea, and furred moss besides, when flow'rs are none,
To winter-ground° thy corse—

Guiderius.   Prithee have done,
230 And do not play in wenchlike words with that
Which is so serious. Let us bury him,
And not protract with admiration what
Is now due debt. To th' grave.

Arviragus.   Say, where shall's° lay him?

Guiderius. By good Euriphile, our mother.

Arviragus.   Be't so.
235 And let us, Polydore, though now our voices
Have got the mannish crack, sing him to th' ground,
As once to our mother; use like note and words,
Save that Euriphile must be Fidele.

Guiderius. Cadwal,

213 **leagued** folded   214 **clouted brogues** heavy, nail-studded
shoes   214 **rudeness** roughness   222 **azured harebell** sky-blue
wild hyacinth   223 **eglantine** sweetbriar   224 **ruddock** robin
229 **winter-ground** protect in winter (?)   233 **shall's** shall us (we)

    I cannot sing. I'll weep, and word° it with thee,   240
    For notes of sorrow out of tune are worse
    Than priests and fanes° that lie.

Arviragus.   We'll speak it then.

Belarius. Great griefs, I see, med'cine° the less, for Cloten
    Is quite forgot. He was a queen's son, boys,
    And though he came our enemy, remember   245
    He was paid° for that. Though mean and mighty, rotting
    Together, have one dust, yet reverence,
    That angel of the world, doth make distinction
    Of place 'tween high and low. Our foe was princely,
    And though you took his life as being° our foe,   250
    Yet bury him as° a prince.

Guiderius.   Pray you fetch him hither.
    Thersites'° body is as good as Ajax'°
    When neither are alive.

Arviragus.   If you'll go fetch him,
    We'll say our song the whilst. Brother, begin.

                            [*Exit Belarius.*]

Guiderius. Nay, Cadwal, we must lay his head to th'
    east;°   255
    My father hath a reason for't.

Arviragus.   'Tis true.

Guiderius. Come on then and remove him.

Arviragus.   So. Begin.

                 Song.

Guiderius.   Fear no more the heat o' th' sun
          Nor the furious winter's rages;
       Thou thy worldly task hast done,
          Home art gone and ta'en thy wages.   260
       Golden lads and girls all must,
       As° chimney-sweepers, come to dust.

---

240 **word** speak 242 **fanes** temples 243 **med'cine** cure 246
paid punished 250 **as being** because he was 251 **as** as being, because he was 252 **Thersites** (the vituperative Greek warrior of the
Trojan War) 252 **Ajax** (one of the Greek heroes at Troy) 255 **to
th' east** (the reverse of Christian practice) 263 **As** like

Arviragus.	Fear no more the frown o' th' great;
265	Thou are past the tyrant's stroke.
	Care no more to clothe and eat;
	To thee the reed is as the oak.
	The scepter, learning, physic,° must
	All follow this and come to dust.

270	*Guiderius.*	Fear no more the lightning flash,
	Arviragus.	Nor th' all-dreaded thunder-stone;
	Guiderius.	Fear not slander, censure rash;
	Arviragus.	Thou hast finished joy and moan.
	Both.	All lovers young, all lovers must
275		Consign to° thee and come to dust.
	Guiderius.	No exorciser° harm thee,
	Arviragus.	Nor no witchcraft charm thee.
	Guiderius.	Ghost unlaid forbear thee;°
	Arviragus.	Nothing ill come near thee.
280	*Both.*	Quiet consummation° have,
		And renownèd be thy grave.

Enter Belarius with the body of Cloten.

Guiderius. We have done our obsequies. Come, lay him
down.

Belarius. Here's a few flowers, but 'bout midnight, more.
The herbs that have on them cold dew o' th' night
285   Are strewings fitt'st for graves. Upon their faces.°
You were as flow'rs, now withered; even so
These herblets shall° which we upon you strew.
Come on, away; apart upon our knees.
The ground that gave them first has them again.
290   Their pleasures here are past, so is their pain.
                    Exeunt [Belarius, Guiderius, and Arviragus].

268 **scepter, learning, physic** i.e., kings, scholars, physicians   275
Consign to co-sign with (i.e., meet the same fate)   276 **exorciser**
spirit-raiser   278 **forbear thee** let thee alone   280 **consummation**
fulfillment, end   285 **faces** fronts   287 **shall** shall be

Imogen. (Awakes) Yes, sir, to Milford Haven. Which is the
    way?
  I thank you. By yond bush? Pray, how far thither?
  'Ods pittikins,° can it be six mile yet?
  I have gone° all night. Faith, I'll lie down and sleep.
                             [*Seeing Cloten*]
  But, soft, no bedfellow! O gods and goddesses!   *295*
  These flow'rs are like the pleasures of the world;
  This bloody man, the care on't. I hope I dream,
  For so° I thought I was a cave-keeper
  And cook to honest creatures. But 'tis not so;
  'Twas but a bolt° of nothing, shot at nothing,   *300*
  Which the brain makes of fumes.° Our very eyes
  Are sometimes like our judgments, blind. Good faith,
  I tremble still with fear, but if there be
  Yet left in heaven as small a drop of pity
  As a wren's eye, feared gods, a part° of it!   *305*
  The dream's here still. Even when I wake it is
  Without me, as within me; not imagined, felt.
  A headless man? The garments of Posthumus?
  I know the shape of's leg; this is his hand,
  His foot Mercurial,° his Martial° thigh,   *310*
  The brawns° of Hercules; but his Jovial° face—
  Murder in heaven? How? 'Tis gone. Pisanio,
  All curses madded° Hecuba° gave the Greeks,
  And mine to boot, be darted on thee! Thou,
  Conspired° with that irregulous° devil Cloten,   *315*
  Hath here cut off my lord. To write and read
  Be henceforth treacherous! Damned Pisanio
  Hath with his forgèd letters—damned Pisanio—
  From this most bravest vessel of the world
  Struck the maintop. O Posthumus, alas,   *320*
  Where is thy head? Where's that? Ay me, where's that?
  Pisanio might have killed thee at the heart

---

293 **'Ods pittikins** God's little pity, God have mercy   294 **gone**
walked   298 **so** i.e., while dreaming   300 **bolt** arrow   301 **fumes**
bodily vapors thought to rise to the brain and cause dreams   305 **a
part** i.e., grant me a part   310 **Mercurial** quick (like Mercury's)
310 **Martial** powerful (like Mars's)   311 **brawns** muscles   311
Jovial majestic (like Jove's)   313 **madded** maddened   313
Hecuba (wife of Priam, king of Troy)   315 **Conspired** having conspired   315 **irregulous** lawless

And left this head on. How should this be? Pisanio?
'Tis he and Cloten. Malice and lucre° in them
325 Have laid this woe here. O, 'tis pregnant,° pregnant!
The drug he gave me, which he said was precious
And cordial° to me, have I not found it
Murd'rous to th' senses? That confirms it home.°
This is Pisanio's deed, and Cloten.° O,
330 Give color to my pale cheek with thy blood,
That we the horrider may seem to those
Which° chance to find us. O my lord, my lord!
                    [*Falling on the body.*]

Enter Lucius and Captains; a Soothsayer to them.°

Captain. The legions garrisoned in Gallia
After° your will have crossed the sea, attending°
335 You here at Milford Haven with your ships.
They are in readiness.

Lucius.   But what from Rome?

Captain. The Senate hath stirred up the confiners°
And gentlemen of Italy, most willing spirits
That promise noble service, and they come
340 Under the conduct of bold Iachimo,
Siena's° brother.

Lucius.   When expect you them?

Captain. With the next benefit o' th' wind.

Lucius.   This forwardness°
Makes our hopes fair. Command our present numbers
Be mustered; bid the captains look to't.—Now, sir,
345 What have you dreamed of late of this war's purpose?

Soothsayer. Last night the very gods showed me a vision—
I fast° and prayed for their intelligence°—thus:

---

324 **lucre** greed   325 **pregnant** evident   327 **cordial** restorative
328 **home** thoroughly   329 **Cloten** i.e., Cloten's   332 **Which** who
332 s.d. **to them** (presumably the Soothsayer enters, a moment later, at
another door)   334 **After** according to   334 **attending** waiting for
337 **confiners** inhabitants   341 **Siena's** i.e., the Duke of Siena's
342 **forwardness** promptness   347 **fast** fasted   347 **intelligence**
communication

I saw Jove's bird, the Roman eagle, winged
From the spongy° south to this part of the west,
There vanished in the sunbeams; which portends,   350
Unless my sins abuse° my divination,
Success to th' Roman host.

Lucius.   Dream often so,
And never false.° Soft, ho, what trunk is here?
Without his top? The ruin speaks that sometime°
It was a worthy building. How, a page?   355
Or° dead or sleeping on him? But dead rather,
For nature doth abhor° to make his bed
With the defunct or sleep upon the dead.
Let's see the boy's face.

Captain.   He's alive, my lord.

Lucius. He'll, then, instruct us of this body. Young one, 360
Inform us of thy fortunes, for it seems
They crave to be demanded. Who is this
Thou mak'st thy bloody pillow? Or who was he
That, otherwise than noble nature did,°
Hath altered that good picture? What's thy interest   365
In this sad wrack?° How came't? Who is't? What art
thou?

Imogen. I am nothing, or if not,
Nothing to be were better. This was my master,
A very valiant Briton and a good,
That here by mountaineers lies slain. Alas,   370
There is no more such masters. I may wander
From east to occident, cry out for service,
Try many, all good, serve truly, never
Find such another master.

Lucius.   'Lack, good youth,
Thou mov'st no less with thy complaining than   375
Thy master in bleeding. Say his name, good friend.

---

349 **spongy** damp   351 **abuse** render inaccurate   353 **false** falsely
354 **sometime** once   356 **Or** either   357 **nature doth abhor** man
naturally abhors (Heilman)   364 **did** i.e., painted (J. C. Maxwell)
366 **wrack** ruin of a man

Imogen. Richard du Champ. [*Aside*] If I do lie and do
    No harm by it, though the gods hear, I hope
    They'll pardon it.—Say you, sir?

Lucius.   Thy name?

Imogen.   Fidele, sir.

380 *Lucius.* Thou dost approve° thyself the very same;
    Thy name well fits thy faith, thy faith thy name.
    Wilt take thy chance with me? I will not say
    Thou shalt be so well mastered, but be sure
    No less beloved. The Roman emperor's letters
385   Sent by a consul to me should not sooner
    Than thine own worth prefer° thee. Go with me.

Imogen. I'll follow, sir. But first, and't please the gods,
    I'll hide my master from the flies, as deep
    As these poor pickaxes° can dig; and when
    With wild wood-leaves and weeds I ha' strewed his
390   grave
    And on it said a century of° prayers,
    Such as I can,° twice o'er, I'll weep and sigh,
    And leaving so his service, follow you,
    So° please you entertain° me.

Lucius.   Ay, good youth,
395   And rather father thee than master thee.
    My friends,
    The boy hath taught us manly duties. Let us
    Find out the prettiest daisied plot we can
    And make him with our pikes and partisans°
400   A grave. Come, arm° him. Boy, he's preferred°
    By thee to us, and he shall be interred
    As soldiers can. Be cheerful; wipe thine eyes.
    Some falls are means the happier to arise.   *Exeunt.*

---

380 **approve** prove   386 **prefer** recommend   389 **pickaxes** i.e.,
fingers   391 **century of** hundred   392 **can** know   394 **So** if it
394 **entertain** employ   399 **partisans** halberds   400 **arm** carry
400 **preferred** recommended

Scene 3. [*Britain.*]

Enter Cymbeline, Lords, and Pisanio.

Cymbeline. Again, and bring me word how 'tis with her.
[*Exit a Lord.*]
A fever with° the absence of her son,
A madness, of which her life's in danger. Heavens,
How deeply you at once do touch° me! Imogen,
The great part of my comfort, gone; my queen   5
Upon a desperate bed,° and in a time
When fearful wars point at me; her son gone,
So needful for this present. It strikes me past
The hope of comfort.—But for thee, fellow,
Who needs must know of her departure and   10
Dost seem so ignorant, we'll enforce it from thee
By a sharp torture.

Pisanio.   Sir, my life is yours,
I humbly set it at your will; but for my mistress,
I nothing° know where she remains, why gone,
Nor when she purposes return. Beseech your Highness,   15
Hold me your loyal servant.

Lord.   Good my liege,
The day that she was missing he was here.
I dare be bound he's true and shall perform
All parts of his subjection° loyally. For Cloten,
There wants no diligence in seeking him,   20
And will° no doubt be found.

Cymbeline.   The time is troublesome.°
[*To Pisanio*] We'll slip you° for a season, but our
  jealousy°
Does yet depend.°

4.3.2 **with** resulting from   4 **touch** wound   6 **Upon ... bed** i.e.,
desperately ill   14 **nothing** not at all   19 **subjection** duty as a subject   21 **will** he will   21 **troublesome** full of troubles   22 **slip**
you let you go free   22 **jealousy** suspicion   23 **depend** remain

Lord.   So please your Majesty,
The Roman legions, all from Gallia drawn,
25   Are landed on your coast, with a supply
Of Roman gentlemen by the Senate sent.

Cymbeline. Now for° the counsel of my son and queen!
I am amazed with matter.°

Lord.   Good my liege,
Your preparation° can affront no less°
Than what you hear of. Come more,° for more you're
30   ready.
The want is but° to put those pow'rs in motion
That long to move.

Cymbeline.   I thank you. Let's withdraw,
And meet the time as it seeks us. We fear not
What can from Italy annoy° us, but
35   We grieve at chances here. Away.
                    Exeunt [all but Pisanio].

Pisanio. I heard no letter° from my master since
I wrote him Imogen was slain. 'Tis strange.
Nor hear I from my mistress, who did promise
To yield me often tidings. Neither know I
40   What is betid° to Cloten, but remain
Perplexed in all. The heavens still must work.
Wherein I am false I am honest; not true, to be true.
These present wars shall find I love my country,
Even to the note° o' th' King, or I'll fall in them.
45   All other doubts, by time let them be cleared;
Fortune brings in some boats that are not steered.
                              Exit.

27 **Now for** would I had   28 **amazed with matter** confounded by
business   29 **preparation** armed forces   29 **affront no less** i.e.,
face larger forces   30 **Come more** if more come   31 **The want is
but** the only thing needed is   34 **annoy** harm   36 **no letter** i.e., not
at all   40 **is betid** has happened   44 **note** knowledge

Scene 4. [*Wales.*]

Enter Belarius, Guiderius, and Arviragus.

Guiderius. The noise is round about us.

Belarius.   Let us from it.

Arviragus. What pleasure, sir, find we in life, to lock° it
    From action and adventure?

Guiderius.   Nay, what hope
    Have we in hiding us? This way° the Romans
    Must or° for Britons slay us or receive us   5
    For barbarous and unnatural revolts°
    During their use,° and slay us after.

Belarius.   Sons,
    We'll higher to the mountains, there secure us.
    To the King's party there's no going. Newness
    Of Cloten's death—we being not known, not mustered   10
    Among the bands—may drive us to a render°
    Where we have lived, and so extort from's that
    Which we have done, whose answer° would be death
    Drawn on° with torture.

Guiderius.   This is, sir, a doubt
    In such a time nothing becoming you   15
    Nor satisfying us.

Arviragus.   It is not likely
    That when they hear the Roman horses neigh,
    Behold their quartered fires,° have both their eyes
    And ears so cloyed importantly° as now,
    That they will waste their time upon our note,°   20
    To know from whence we are.

4.4.2 **lock** preclude   4 **This way** i.e., if we do so   5 **Must or** must
either   6 **revolts** rebels   7 **During their use** while they have use
for us   11 **render** account   13 **answer** requital   14 **Drawn on**
brought about   18 **quartered fires** camp fires   19 **cloyed impor-
tantly** burdened with important matters   20 **upon our note** on
noticing us

Belarius.   O, I am known
Of many in the army. Many years,
Though Cloten then° but young, you see, not wore him
From my remembrance. And besides, the King
25   Hath not deserved my service nor your loves,
Who find in my exile the want of breeding,°
The certainty° of this hard life; aye hopeless
To have the courtesy your cradle promised,
But to be still hot summer's tanlings° and
The shrinking slaves of winter.

30   *Guiderius.*   Than be so
Better to cease to be. Pray, sir, to th' army.
I and my brother are not known; yourself
So out of thought, and thereto so o'ergrown,°
Cannot be questioned.

Arviragus.   By this sun that shines,
35   I'll thither. What thing is't that I never
Did see man die, scarce ever looked on blood
But that of coward hares, hot° goats, and venison!
Never bestrid a horse, save one that had
A rider like myself, who ne'er wore rowel°
40   Nor iron on his heel! I am ashamed
To look upon the holy sun, to have
The benefit of his blest beams, remaining
So long a poor unknown.

Guiderius.   By heavens, I'll go.
If you will bless me, sir, and give me leave,
45   I'll take the better care, but if you will not,
The hazard therefore due° fall on me by
The hands of Romans!

Arviragus.   So say I. Amen.

Belarius. No reason I, since of your lives you set
So slight a valuation, should reserve

---

23 **then** i.e., was then   26 **Who ... breeding** you who through
sharing my exile experience a lack of education   27 **certainty** in-
escapability   29 **tanlings** tanned persons   33 **o'ergrown** replaced
in their thoughts   37 **hot** lecherous   39 **rowel** the wheel on a spur
46 **hazard therefore due** risk attendant upon being unblessed

My cracked° one to more care. Have with you, boys!   50
If in your country° wars you chance to die,
That is my bed too, lads, and there I'll lie.
Lead, lead. [*Aside*] The time seems long; their blood
    thinks scorn
Till it fly out and show them princes born.   *Exeunt.*

ACT 5

Scene 1. [*Britain.*]

Enter Posthumus alone [with a bloody handkerchief].

Posthumus. Yea, bloody cloth, I'll keep thee, for I wished
    Thou shouldst be colored thus. You married ones,°
    If each of you should take this course, how many
    Must murder wives much better than themselves
5   For wrying° but a little! O Pisanio,
    Every good servant does not all commands;
    No bond but° to do just ones. Gods, if you
    Should have ta'en vengeance on my faults, I never
    Had lived to put on this;° so had you saved
10   The noble Imogen to repent, and struck
    Me, wretch more worth your vengeance. But alack,
    You snatch some hence for little faults; that's love,
    To have them fall° no more; you some permit
    To second° ills with ills, each elder° worse,
15   And make them° dread it,° to the doers' thrift.°
    But Imogen is your own. Do your best wills,
    And make me blest to obey. I am brought hither
    Among th' Italian gentry, and to fight
    Against my lady's kingdom. 'Tis enough
20   That, Britain, I have killed thy mistress; peace,
    I'll give no wound to thee. Therefore, good heavens,
    Hear patiently my purpose. I'll disrobe me
    Of these Italian weeds and suit myself

5.1.2 **You married ones** (he addresses the audience)   5 **wrying** deviating, going wrong   7 **No bond but** i.e., he is bound only   9 **put on this** instigate this crime   13 **fall** i.e., from virtue   14 **second** follow up   14 **elder** i.e., later   15 **them** the doers   15 **dread it** repent the evil course   15 **thrift** profit

As does a Briton peasant. So I'll fight
Against the part° I come with; so I'll die   25
For thee, O Imogen, even for whom my life
Is every breath a death; and thus, unknown,
Pitied nor hated, to the face of peril
Myself I'll dedicate. Let me make men know
More valor in me than my habits° show.   30
Gods, put the strength o' th' Leonati in me.
To shame the guise° o' th' world, I will begin
The fashion, less without and more within.   *Exit.*

Scene 2. [*Britain.*]

*Enter Lucius, Iachimo, and the Roman Army at one door,
and the Briton Army at another, Leonatus Posthumus
following like a poor soldier. They march over and go
out.° Then enter again in skirmish Iachimo and Posthumus. He vanquisheth and disarmeth Iachimo and then
leaves him.*

Iachimo. The heaviness and guilt within my bosom
Takes off° my manhood. I have belied° a lady,
The princess of this country, and the air on't°
Revengingly enfeebles me; or° could this carl,°
A very drudge of nature's, have subdued me   5
In my profession? Knighthoods and honors, borne
As I wear mine, are titles but of scorn.
If that thy gentry, Britain, go before°
This lout as he exceeds our lords, the odds
Is that we scarce are men and you are gods.   *Exit.*   10

*The battle continues. The Britons fly; Cymbeline is taken.
Then enter to his rescue Belarius, Guiderius, and Arviragus.*

Belarius. Stand, stand! We have th' advantage of the
      ground.

25 **part** side   30 **habits** clothes   32 **guise** custom   5.2.s.d. **They
march . . . go out** (each group marches about the stage and exits by
the other door)   2 **Takes off** destroys   2 **belied** slandered   3 **on't**
of it   4 **or** otherwise   4 **carl** churl   8 **go before** excell

The lane is guarded. Nothing routs us but
The villainy of our fears.

Guiderius, Arviragus.   Stand, stand, and fight!

*Enter Posthumus and seconds the Britons. They rescue
Cymbeline and exeunt. Then enter Lucius, Iachimo, and
Imogen.*

Lucius. Away, boy, from the troops, and save thyself,
15   For friends kill friends, and the disorder's such
As War were hoodwinked.°

Iachimo.   'Tis their fresh supplies.

Lucius. It is a day turned strangely; or betimes°
Let's reinforce or fly.   *Exeunt.*

Scene 3. [*Britain.*]

Enter Posthumus and a Briton Lord.

Lord. Cam'st thou from where they made the stand?

Posthumus.   I did;
Though you, it seems, come from the fliers.

Lord.   I did.

Posthumus. No blame be to you, sir, for all was lost,
But that the heavens fought. The King himself
5   Of his wings destitute, the army broken,
And but the backs of Britons seen, all flying
Through a strait° lane; the enemy full-hearted,°
Lolling the tongue with slaught'ring, having work
More plentiful than tools to do't, struck down
10   Some mortally, some slightly touched,° some falling
Merely through fear, that the strait pass was dammed
With dead men hurt behind,° and cowards living
To die with lengthened shame.

Lord.   Where was this lane?

16 **hoodwinked** blindfolded   17 **or betimes** either quickly   5.3.7
strait narrow   7 **full-hearted** full of courage   10 **touched**
wounded   12 **behind** i.e., while running away

Posthumus. Close by the battle, ditched, and walled with
    turf;
  Which gave advantage to an ancient soldier,   15
  An honest one I warrant, who deserved
  So long a breeding as his white beard came to,°
  In doing this for's country. Athwart the lane
  He with two striplings—lads more like to run
  The country base° than to commit such slaughter;   20
  With faces fit for masks,° or rather fairer
  Than those for preservation cased or shame°—
  Made good the passage, cried to those that fled,
  "Our Britain's harts die flying, not our men.
  To darkness fleet° souls that fly backwards. Stand,   25
  Or we are Romans° and will give you that
  Like beasts which you shun beastly,° and may save
  But to look back in frown.° Stand, stand!" These three,
  Three thousand confident, in act as many—
  For three performers are the file° when all   30
  The rest do nothing—with this word "Stand, stand,"
  Accommodated by the place, more charming°
  With their own nobleness, which could have turned
  A distaff to a lance, gilded° pale looks,
  Part° shame, part spirit renewed; that some, turned
    coward   35
  But by example°—O, a sin in war,
  Damned in the first beginners!—gan to look
  The way that they° did and to grin° like lions
  Upon the pikes o' th' hunters. Then began
  A stop i' th' chaser,° a retire; anon°   40
  A rout, confusion thick. Forthwith they fly
  Chickens, the way which they stooped° eagles; slaves,

---

17 **So long ... came to** i.e., to live (renowned) as long after this day
as he had lived before in growing his beard   19–20 **run/The country
base** play the game of prisoner's base   21 **masks** for protection from
sunburn (so used by ladies)   22 **for preservation ... shame** covered
for protection or modesty   25 **fleet** are wafted   26 **are Romans** i.e.,
will behave like Romans   27 **beastly** i.e., like cowards   27–28
save/But to look back in frown i.e., prevent only by looking back de-
fiantly   30 **file** whole force   32 **more charming** i.e., winning over
others   34 **gilded** brought color to   35 **Part** some   36 **by example** by imitating others   38 **they** the three men   38 **grin** bare the
teeth   40 **stop ... chaser** sudden check (as of a horse) on the part of
the pursuer   40 **anon** soon   42 **stooped** swooped (hawking term)

The strides they victors made; and now our cowards,
Like fragments° in hard voyages, became
45 The life o' th' need.° Having found the back door open
Of the unguarded hearts, heavens, how they wound!
Some slain before,° some dying, some° their friends
O'erborne i' th' former wave, ten chased by one
Are now each one the slaughterman of twenty.
50 Those that would die or ere° resist are grown
The mortal bugs° o' th' field.°

Lord.   This was strange chance:
A narrow lane, an old man, and two boys.

Posthumus. Nay, do not wonder at it. You are made
Rather to wonder at the things you hear
55 Than to work any.° Will you rhyme upon't
And vent it° for a mock'ry? Here is one:
"Two boys, an old man twice a boy, a lane,
Preserved the Britons, was the Romans' bane."

Lord. Nay, be not angry, sir.

Posthumus.   'Lack, to what end?
60 Who dares not stand° his foe, I'll be his friend;
For if he'll do as he is made° to do,
I know he'll quickly fly my friendship too.
You have put° me into rhyme.

Lord.   Farewell. You're angry. *Exit.*

Posthumus. Still going?° This is a lord! O noble misery,°
65 To be i' th' field, and ask "What news?" of me!
Today how many would have given their honors
To have saved their carcasses, took heel to do't,
And yet died too! I, in mine own woe charmed,°
Could not find Death where I did hear him groan

---

44 **fragments** scraps (of food) 45 **life o' th' need** a source of life in
time of need 47 **slain before** i.e., who had feigned death 47 **some
some of** 50 **or ere** before 51 **mortal bugs** deadly terrors 51
field battle 55 **work any** perform any such deeds 56 **vent it** make
it known 60 **stand** withstand 61 **made** naturally inclined 63 **put**
forced 64 **going** running away 64 **noble misery** wretchedness of
false nobility 68 **charmed** preserved as by a charm

Nor feel him where he struck. Being an ugly monster,   70
'Tis strange he hides him in fresh cups, soft beds,
Sweet words, or hath moe ministers than we
That draw his knives i' th' war. Well, I will find him,
For being now a favorer to° the Briton,
No more a Briton.° I have resumed again   75
The part I came in. Fight I will no more,
But yield me to the veriest hind° that shall
Once touch my shoulder.° Great the slaughter is
Here made by th' Roman; great the answer° be
Britons must take. For me, my ransom's death.   80
On either side I come to spend my breath,°
Which neither here I'll keep nor bear again,
But end it by some means for Imogen.

Enter two [Briton] Captains and Soldiers.

First Captain. Great Jupiter be praised, Lucius is taken.
'Tis thought the old man and his sons were angels.   85

Second Captain. There was a fourth man, in a silly habit,°
That gave th' affront° with them.

First Captain.   So 'tis reported,
But none of 'em can be found. Stand, who's there?

Posthumus. A Roman,
Who had not now been drooping here if seconds°   90
Had answered him.°

Second Captain.   Lay hands on him. A dog,
A leg of Rome shall not return to tell
What crows have pecked them here. He brags his
     service
As if he were of note.° Bring him to th' King.

*Enter Cymbeline, Belarius, Guiderius, Arviragus, Pisanio,
and Roman Captives [guarded]. The Captains present
Posthumus to Cymbeline, who delivers him over to a
Jailer.*   *[Exeunt.]*

74 **being ... favorer to** since he now favors   75 **No more a Briton**
i.e., I will seek Death among the Romans   77 **hind** peasant   78
touch my shoulder as in a formal arrest   79 **answer** retaliation   81
spend my breath give up my life   86 **a silly habit** lowly clothing
87 **affront** attack   90 **seconds** supporters   91 **answered him**
acted as he did   94 **note** reputation

Scene 4. [*Britain.*]

Enter° Posthumus and [two] Jailers.

First Jailer. You shall not now be stol'n; you have locks
    upon you.
    So graze as you find pasture.

Second Jailer.   Ay, or a stomach.°

                        [*Exeunt Jailers.*]

Posthumus. Most welcome, bondage, for thou art a way,
    I think, to liberty. Yet am I better
5   Than one that's sick o' th' gout, since he had rather
    Groan so in perpetuity than be cured
    By th' sure physician, Death, who is the key
    T' unbar these locks. My conscience, thou art fettered
    More than my shanks and wrists. You good gods,
        give me
10   The penitent instrument to pick that bolt,°
    Then free° for ever. Is't enough I am sorry?
    So children temporal fathers do appease;
    Gods are more full of mercy. Must I repent,
    I cannot do it better than in gyves,°
15   Desired more than constrained.° To satisfy,°
    If of my freedom 'tis the main part,° take
    No stricter render° of me than my all.°
    I know you are more clement than vile men,
    Who of their broken debtors take a third,
20   A sixth, a tenth, letting them thrive again

5.4.s.d. **Enter** (the action may be continuous from 5.3, Posthumus
and the Jailers remaining on stage after the exit of Cymbeline at the
end of that scene; in any case at the beginning of 5.4 the locale of
the action changes from open country to a prison) 2 **stomach** appetite (for grazing) 10 **penitent . . . bolt** tool of repentance which
will unfetter my conscience 11 **free** i.e., in death 14 **gyves** fetters 15 **constrained** forced upon me 15 **satisfy** make atonement 16 **If . . . main part** i.e., if atonement is essential to my
freedom of conscience 17 **stricter render** sterner repayment 17
all i.e., life

On their abatement.° That's not my desire.
For Imogen's dear life take mine; and though
'Tis not so dear,° yet 'tis a life; you coined it.
'Tween man and man they weigh not every stamp;°
Though light, take pieces for the figure's° sake;   25
You rather mine, being yours.° And so, great pow'rs,
If you will take this audit,° take this life
And cancel these cold bonds.° O Imogen,
I'll speak to thee in silence.   [*Sleeps.*]

Solemn music. Enter, as in an apparition, Sicilius Leona-
tus, father to Posthumus, an old man attired like a war-
rior; leading in his hand an ancient Matron, his wife and
mother to Posthumus with Music° before them. Then, af-
ter other Music, follows the two young Leonati, brothers
to Posthumus, with wounds as they died in the wars.
They circle Posthumus round as he lies sleeping.

Sicilius. No more, thou Thunder-master,° show thy spite
on mortal flies.   30
With Mars fall out, with Juno chide, that thy adulteries
Rates° and revenges.
Hath my poor boy done aught but well, whose face I
never saw?
I died whilst in the womb he stayed attending° Nature's
law;
Whose father then, as men report thou orphans' father
art,   35
Thou shouldst have been, and shielded him from this
earth-vexing smart.°

Mother. Lucina° lent not me her aid, but took me in my
throes,

---

21 **abatement** reduced amount   23 **dear** valuable   24 **stamp** coin
25 **figure** the ruler's image stamped on the "piece" (coin)   26
You . . . being yours i.e., you should take my life the sooner since
(though light coin) it is at least stamped in your image   27 **take this**
audit accept this account   28 **cancel . . . bonds** i.e., remove
(through letting me die) these iron shackles (quibble on "void these
worthless contracts")   29s.d. **Music** musicians   30 **Thunder-master**
Jupiter   32 **Rates** scolds   34 **attending** awaiting   36 **earth-**
vexing smart suffering which plagues the life of man   37 **Lucina**
Juno Lucina (goddess of childbirth)

That from me was Posthumus ripped, came crying
    'mongst his foes,
        A thing of pity.

Sicilius. Great Nature like his ancestry moulded the stuff°
40   so fair
    That he deserved the praise o' th' world, as great
        Sicilius' heir.

First Brother. When once he was mature for man,°
    in Britain where was he
    That could stand up his parallel, or fruitful° object be
    In eye of Imogen, that best could deem his dignity?°

Mother. With marriage wherefore was he mocked, to be
45   exiled and thrown
    From Leonati seat and cast from her his dearest one,
        Sweet Imogen?

Sicilius. Why did you° suffer Iachimo, slight° thing of
    Italy,
    To taint his nobler heart and brain with needless
       jealousy,
    And to become the geck° and scorn o' th' other's vil-
50   lainy?

Second Brother. For this from stiller seats° we come, our
    parents and us twain,
    That striking in our country's cause fell bravely and
       were slain,
    Our fealty and Tenantius'° right with honor to maintain.

First Brother. Like hardiment° Posthumus hath to
    Cymbeline performed.
    Then, Jupiter, thou King of gods, why hast thou thus
55   adjourned°
    The graces for his merits due, being all to dolors
       turned?

---

40 **stuff** substance   42 **mature for man** fully matured   43 **fruitful** ripe, mature   44 **deem his dignity** judge his worth   48 **you**
Jupiter   48 **slight** worthless   50 **geck** dupe   51 **stiller seats** qui-
eter abodes (in the Elysian Fields)   53 **Tenantius** Sicilius   54
hardiment bold exploits   55 **adjourned** deferred

Sicilius. Thy crystal window ope; look out. No longer exercise
  Upon a valiant race thy harsh and potent injuries.

Mother. Since, Jupiter, our son is good, take off his miseries.

Sicilius. Peep through thy marble mansion. Help, or we poor ghosts will cry   60
  To th' shining synod of the rest° against thy deity.

Brothers. Help, Jupiter, or we appeal and from thy justice fly.

Jupiter descends° in thunder and lightning, sitting upon an eagle. He throws a thunderbolt. The Ghosts fall on their knees.

Jupiter. No more, you petty spirits of region low,°
  Offend our hearing. Hush! How dare you ghosts
Accuse the Thunderer, whose bolt, you know,   65
  Sky-planted,° batters all rebelling coasts?
Poor shadows of Elysium, hence, and rest
  Upon your never-withering banks of flow'rs.
Be not with mortal accidents° opprest.
  No care of yours it is; you know 'tis ours.   70
Whom best I love I cross;° to make my gift,
  The more delayed, delighted. Be content.
Your low-laid son our godhead will uplift;
  His comforts thrive, his trials well are spent.°
Our Jovial star° reigned at his birth, and in   75
  Our temple was he married. Rise, and fade.
He shall be lord of Lady Imogen,
  And happier much by his affliction made.
This tablet lay upon his breast, wherein
  Our pleasure his full fortune doth confine.°   80
And so, away; no farther with your din
  Express impatience, lest you stir up mine.
  Mount, eagle, to my palace crystalline.   *Ascends.*

---

61 **the rest** the other gods   62s.d. **descends** (Jupiter is lowered by suspension-gear from stage cover to stage)   63 **region low** Hades
66 **Sky-planted** based in the sky   69 **accidents** occurrences   71
cross thwart   74 **spent** ended   75 **Jovial star** the planet Jupiter
80 **confine** i.e., state precisely

Sicilius. He came in thunder; his celestial breath
85   Was sulphurous to smell; the holy eagle
        Stooped, as to foot us.° His ascension is
        More sweet° than our blest fields;° his royal bird
        Prunes° the immortal wing and cloys° his beak,
        As when his god is pleased.

All.   Thanks, Jupiter.

90 *Sicilius.* The marble pavement closes;° he is entered
        His radiant roof. Away, and, to be blest,
        Let us with care perform his great behest.
                                [*The Ghosts*] *vanish.*°

Posthumus. [*Waking*] Sleep, thou hast been a grandsire and
        begot
        A father to me, and thou hast created
95   A mother and two brothers; but, O scorn,°
        Gone! They went hence so soon as they were born.
        And so I am awake. Poor wretches that depend
        On greatness' favor, dream as I have done,
        Wake, and find nothing. But, alas, I swerve.°
100   Many dream not to find, neither deserve,
        And yet are steeped in favors. So am I,
        That have this golden chance and know not why.
        What fairies haunt this ground? A book? O rare one,
        Be not, as is our fangled° world, a garment
105   Nobler than that it covers. Let thy effects
        So follow to° be most unlike our courtiers,
        As good as promise.   *Reads.*
        "Whenas° a lion's whelp shall, to himself unknown,
        without seeking find, and be embraced by a piece of ten-
110   der air; and when from a stately cedar shall be lopped
        branches which, being dead many years, shall after re-
        vive, be jointed to the old stock, and freshly grow; then
        shall Posthumus end his miseries, Britain be fortunate
        and flourish in peace and plenty."

---

86 **Stooped . . . us** swooped (hawking term) as if to seize us in his
talons   87 **More sweet** (in contrast to his angry, sulphurous descent)
87 **our blest fields** the Elysian Fields   88 **Prunes** preens   88
cloys claws   90 **closes** (apparently in allusion to the trap door in the
underside of the stage cover through which Jupiter has ascended)
92s.d. **vanish** i.e., exit rapidly   95 **scorn** mockery   99 **swerve** err
104 **fangled** addicted to finery   106 **to** as to   108 **Whenas** when

'Tis still a dream, or else such stuff as madmen   *115*
Tongue,° and brain° not; either, both, or nothing;
Or senseless° speaking, or a speaking such
As sense° cannot untie. Be what it is,
The action of my life is like it,° which
I'll keep, if but for sympathy.°   *120*

Enter Jailer.

Jailer. Come, sir, are you ready for death?

Posthumus. Over-roasted rather; ready long ago.

Jailer. Hanging° is the word, sir. If you be ready for that, you are well cooked.

Posthumus. So, if I prove a good repast to the spectators, *125* the dish pays the shot.°

Jailer. A heavy reckoning for you, sir. But the comfort is, you shall be called to no more payments, fear no more tavern bills, which are as often the sadness of parting as the procuring of mirth. You come in faint for want of *130* meat, depart reeling with too much drink; sorry that you have paid too much, and sorry that you are paid too much;° purse and brain both empty; the brain the heavier for being too light, the purse too light, being drawn° of heaviness. O, of this contradiction you shall now be *135* quit. O, the charity of a penny cord! It sums up thousands in a trice. You have no true debitor and creditor° but it; of what's past, is, and to come, the discharge.° Your neck, sir, is pen, book, and counters;° so the acquittance° follows.   *140*

Posthumus. I am merrier to die than thou art to live.

Jailer. Indeed, sir, he that sleeps feels not the toothache; but

_____

116 **Tongue** speak   116 **brain** understand   117 **Or senseless** either irrational   118 **sense** the power of reason   119 **like it** i.e., without meaning or incapable of understanding   120 **sympathy** the resemblance   123 **Hanging** (the Jailer, picking up the metaphor in "Over-roasted," quibbles on "hanging of meat")   126 **the dish . . . shot** i.e., the excellence of the food justifies its cost   132–33 **are paid too much** have been subdued by too much liquor   134 **drawn** emptied   137 **debitor and creditor** account book   138 **discharge** payment   139 **counters** (used for reckoning)   139–40 **acquittance** receipt

a man that were° to sleep your sleep, and a hangman to
help him to bed, I think he would change places with his
145 officer;° for, look you, sir, you know not which way you
shall go.

Posthumus. Yes indeed do I, fellow.

Jailer. Your death has eyes in's head° then. I have not seen
him so pictured.° You must either be directed by some
150 that take upon them to know, or to take upon yourself
that which I am sure you do not know, or jump° the
after-inquiry on your own peril. And how you shall
speed in° your journey's end, I think you'll never return
to tell on.°

155 *Posthumus.* I tell thee, fellow, there are none want eyes to
direct them the way I am going but such as wink° and
will not use them.

Jailer. What an infinite mock is this, that a man should
have the best use of eyes to see the way of blindness! I
160 am sure hanging's the way of winking.

Enter a Messenger.

Messenger. Knock off his manacles; bring your prisoner to
the King.

Posthumus. Thou bring'st good news; I am called to be
made free.°

165 *Jailer.* I'll be hanged then.

Posthumus. Thou shalt be then freer than a jailer. No bolts
for the dead.

[*Exeunt Posthumus and Messenger.*]

Jailer. Unless a man would marry a gallows and beget young
gibbets, I never saw one so prone.° Yet, on my con-
170 science, there are verier knaves desire to live, for all° he

143 **a man that were** i.e., if a man were destined   145 **officer** executioner   148 **Your death . . . head** i.e., you seem to be informed
about what will happen to you after death   149 **pictured** (in the traditional skull or death's head)   151 **jump** gamble on   153 **speed
in** fare at   154 **on** of   156 **wink** close   164 **made free** i.e., by
death   169 **prone** eager   170 **for all** even though

be a Roman; and there be some of them° too that die
against their wills. So should I, if I were one. I would
we were all of one mind, and one mind good. O, there
were desolation of jailers and gallowses! I speak
against my present profit, but my wish hath a prefer-   *175*
ment° in't.   *Exit.*

Scene 5. [*Britain.*]

Enter Cymbeline, Belarius, Guiderius, Arviragus,
Pisanio, and Lords.

Cymbeline. Stand by my side, you whom the gods have
    made
Preservers of my throne. Woe is my heart
That the poor soldier that so richly fought,
Whose rags shamed gilded arms, whose naked
    breast
Stepped before targes of proof,° cannot be found.   *5*
He shall be happy that can find him, if
Our grace can make him so.

Belarius.   I never saw
Such noble fury in so poor a thing,
Such precious deeds in one that promised naught
But beggary and poor looks.

Cymbeline.   No tidings of him?   *10*

Pisanio. He hath been searched among the dead and living,
But no trace of him.

Cymbeline.   To my grief, I am
The heir of his reward, which I will add
To you, the liver, heart, and brain° of Britain,
By whom I grant she lives. 'Tis now the time   *15*
To ask of whence you are. Report it.

Belarius.   Sir,
In Cambria are we born, and gentlemen.

---

171 **them** Romans   175–76 **preferment** promotion (for myself)
5.5.5 **targes of proof** shields of proven strength   14 **liver, heart,
and brain** (the vital parts—Belarius, Guiderius, and Arviragus)

Further to boast were neither true nor modest,
Unless I add we are honest.

Cymbeline.   Bow your knees.
20   Arise my knights o' th' battle;° I create you
Companions to our person and will fit° you
With dignities becoming your estates.°

Enter Cornelius and Ladies.

There's business in these faces. Why so sadly
Greet you our victory? You look like Romans
And not o' th' court of Britain.

25   *Cornelius.*   Hail, great King!
To sour your happiness I must report
The Queen is dead.

Cymbeline.   Who worse than a physician
Would this report become? But I consider
By med'cine life may be prolonged, yet death
30   Will seize the doctor too. How ended she?

Cornelius. With horror, madly dying, like her life,
Which, being cruel to the world, concluded
Most cruel to herself. What she confessed
I will report, so please you. These her women
35   Can trip me° if I err, who with wet cheeks
Were present when she finished.

Cymbeline.   Prithee say.

Cornelius. First, she confessed she never loved you, only
Affected° greatness got by you, not you;
Married your royalty, was wife to your place,
Abhorred your person.°

40   *Cymbeline.*   She alone knew this,
And but° she spoke it dying, I would not
Believe her lips in opening° it. Proceed.

Cornelius. Your daughter, whom she bore in hand° to love

20 **knights o' th' battle** knights created on the battlefield   21 **fit** equip   22 **estates** ranks   35 **trip me** expose inaccuracy   38 **Affected** loved   40 **your person** you as a person   41 **but** except that   42 **opening** disclosing   43 **bore in hand** pretended

With such integrity, she did confess
Was as a scorpion to her sight, whose life,   45
But that her flight prevented it, she had
Ta'en off° by poison.

Cymbeline.   · O most delicate° fiend!
Who is't can read a woman? Is there more?

Cornelius. More, sir, and worse. She did confess she had
For you a mortal mineral,° which, being took,   50
Should by the minute° feed on life and, ling'ring,
By inches waste you. In which time she purposed,
By watching, weeping, tendance,° kissing, to
O'ercome you with her show° and, in time,
When she had fitted you° with her craft, to work   55
Her son into th' adoption of the crown;
But failing of her end by his strange absence,
Grew shameless desperate, opened, in despite
Of heaven and men, her purposes, repented
The evils she hatched were not effected, so   60
Despairing died.

Cymbeline.   Heard you all this, her women?

Ladies. We did, so please your Highness.

Cymbeline.   Mine eyes
Were not in fault, for she was beautiful;
Mine ears, that heard her flattery; nor my heart,
That thought her like her seeming.° It had been
     vicious°   65
To have mistrusted her. Yet, O my daughter,
That it° was folly in me thou mayst say,
And prove it in thy feeling.° Heaven mend all!

*Enter Lucius, Iachimo, [the Soothsayer,] and other Roman
     Prisoners, [guarded; the Messenger and Posthumus]
     Leonatus behind;° and Imogen.*

47 **Ta'en off** destroyed   47 **delicate** subtle   50 **mortal mineral**
deadly poison   51 **by the minute** minute by minute   53 **tendance**
attention   54 **show** simulation (of devotion)   55 **fitted you** shaped
you to her purpose   65 **seeming** appearance   65 **had been vicious**
would have been morally wrong   67 **it** trusting her   68 **prove . . .**
feeling experience the effect of my folly in your suffering 68s.d. **be-**
hind (Posthumus remains apart from the main group of players till
line 209)

         Thou com'st not, Caius, now for tribute. That
70   The Britons have razed out,° though with the loss
         Of many a bold one; whose kinsmen have made suit
         That their° good souls may be appeased with slaughter
         Of you their captives, which ourself have granted.
         So think of your estate.°

75 *Lucius.* Consider, sir, the chance of war. The day
         Was yours by accident; had it gone with us,
         We should not, when the blood was cool, have
              threatened
         Our prisoners with the sword. But since the gods
         Will have it thus, that nothing but our lives
80   May be called ransom, let it come. Sufficeth
         A Roman with a Roman's heart can suffer.
         Augustus lives to think on't—and so much
         For my peculiar° care. This one thing only
         I will entreat: my boy, a Briton born,
85   Let him be ransomed. Never master had
         A page so kind, so duteous, diligent,
         So tender over his occasions,° true,
         So feat,° so nurselike. Let his virtue join
         With my request, which I'll make bold your Highness
90   Cannot deny. He hath done no Briton harm,
         Though he have served a Roman. Save him, sir,
         And spare no blood beside.

    Cymbeline.   I have surely seen him;
         His favor° is familiar to me. Boy,
         Thou hast looked thyself into° my grace
95   And art mine own. I know not why, wherefore,
         To say° "Live, boy." Ne'er thank thy master. Live,
         And ask of Cymbeline what boon thou wilt,
         Fitting my bounty and thy state; I'll give it,
         Yea, though thou do demand a prisoner,
         The noblest ta'en.

100 *Imogen.*   I humbly thank your Highness.

───

70 **razed out** erased   72 **their** i.e., of those slain in battle   74
your estate the condition of your souls   83 **peculiar** individual   87
tender over his occasions sensitive to his wants   88 **feat** dexterous
93 **favor** face   94 **looked thyself into** gained by thy looks   96 **To
say** I am saying

Lucius. I do not bid thee beg my life, good lad,
    And yet I know thou wilt.

Imogen.   No, no, alack,
    There's other work in hand. I see a thing°
    Bitter to me as death; your life, good master,
    Must shuffle° for itself.

Lucius.   The boy disdains me;   105
    He leaves me, scorns me. Briefly° die their joys
    That place them on the truth° of girls and boys.
    Why stands he so perplexed?

Cymbeline.   What wouldst thou, boy?
    I love thee more and more. Think more and more
    What's best to ask. Know'st him thou look'st on?
        Speak.   110
    Wilt have him live? Is he thy kin? Thy friend?

Imogen. He is a Roman, no more kin to me
    Than I to your Highness; who, being born your vassal,
    Am something nearer.

Cymbeline.   Wherefore ey'st him so?

Imogen. I'll tell you, sir, in private, if you please   115
    To give me hearing.

Cymbeline.   Ay, with all my heart,
    And lend my best attention. What's thy name?

Imogen. Fidele, sir.

Cymbeline.   Thou'rt my good youth, my page;
    I'll be thy master. Walk with me; speak freely.

Belarius. Is not this boy revived from death?

Arviragus.   One sand another   120
    Not more resembles that sweet rosy lad
    Who died, and was Fidele. What think you?

Guiderius. The same dead thing alive.

Belarius. Peace, peace, see further. He eyes us not;
        forbear.

103 **thing** the ring on Iachimo's finger   105 **shuffle** shift   106
Briefly quickly   107 **truth** loyalty

125   Creatures may be alike. Were't he, I am sure
        He would have spoke to us.

    Guiderius.   But we saw him dead.

    Belarius. Be silent, let's see further.

    Pisanio. [*Aside*]   It is my mistress.
        Since she is living, let the time run on
        To good or bad.

    Cymbeline.   Come, stand thou by our side;
130   Make thy demand aloud.—Sir, step you forth,
        Give answer to this boy, and do it freely;
        Or, by our greatness and the grace of it,
        Which is our honor, bitter torture shall
        Winnow the truth from falsehood.—On, speak to him.

135 *Imogen.* My boon is that this gentleman may render°
        Of whom he had this ring.

    Posthumus. [*Aside*]   What's that to him?

    Cymbeline. That diamond upon your finger, say
        How came it yours.

    Iachimo. Thou'lt torture me to leave° unspoken that
        Which to be spoke would torture thee.

140 *Cymbeline.*   How? Me?

    Iachimo. I am glad to be constrained to utter that
        Which torments me to conceal. By villainy
        I got this ring. 'Twas Leonatus' jewel,
        Whom thou didst banish, and—which more may grieve
            thee,
145   As it doth me—a nobler sir ne'er lived
        'Twixt sky and ground. Wilt thou hear more, my lord?

    Cymbeline. All that belongs to this.

    Iachimo.   That paragon, thy daughter,
        For whom my heart drops blood and° my false spirits
        Quail to remember—Give me leave, I faint.

    135 **render** state   139 **to leave** for leaving   148 **and** and whom

Cymbeline. My daughter? What of her? Renew thy
    strength. 150
  I had rather thou shouldst live while nature will°
  Than die ere I hear more. Strive, man, and speak.

Iachimo. Upon a time—unhappy was the clock
  That struck the hour!—it was in Rome—accursed
  The mansion where!—'twas at a feast—O, would 155
  Our viands had been poisoned, or at least
  Those which I heaved to head!°—the good Posthumus—
  What should I say? He was too good to be
  Where ill men were, and was the best of all
  Amongst the rar'st of good ones—sitting sadly, 160
  Hearing us praise our loves of Italy
  For beauty that made barren the swelled boast
  Of him that best could speak; for feature,° laming
  The shrine° of Venus or straight-pight° Minerva,
  Postures° beyond brief nature;° for condition,° 165
  A shop° of all the qualities that man
  Loves woman for; besides that hook° of wiving,
  Fairness which strikes the eye—

Cymbeline.   I stand on fire.
  Come to the matter.°

Iachimo.   All too soon I shall,
  Unless thou wouldst grieve quickly. This Posthumus, 170
  Most like a noble lord in love and one
  That had a royal lover, took his hint,°
  And not dispraising whom we praised—therein
  He was as calm as virtue—he began
  His mistress' picture; which by his tongue being
    made, 175
  And then a mind put in't,° either our brags

---

151 **while nature will** i.e., the rest of your natural life   157 **heaved
to head** lifted to mouth   163 **feature** shapeliness   163–64
laming/The shrine making deformed (by comparison) the image
164 **straight-pight** tall, erect   165 **Postures** forms   165 **beyond
brief nature** i.e., more richly endowed than mortal beings   165
condition character   166 **shop** repository   167 **hook** fishhook
169 **matter** point   172 **hint** opportunity   176 **And then ... in't**
i.e., added to which was a good mind

Were cracked° of kitchen trulls, or his description
Proved us unspeaking sots.°

Cymbeline.   Nay, nay, to th' purpose.

Iachimo. Your daughter's chastity—there it begins.
180   He spake of her as° Dian had hot dreams
And she alone were cold;° whereat I, wretch,
Made scruple of° his praise and wagered with him
Pieces of gold 'gainst this which then he wore
Upon his honored finger, to attain
185   In suit° the place of's bed and win this ring
By hers and mine adultery. He, true knight,
No lesser of her honor confident
Than I did truly find her, stakes this ring;
And would so, had it been a carbuncle°
190   Of Phoebus' wheel,° and might so safely had it
Been all the worth of's car. Away to Britain
Post I in this design. Well may you, sir,
Remember me at court, where I was taught
Of° your chaste daughter the wide difference
195   'Twixt amorous° and villainous. Being thus quenched
Of hope, not longing,° mine Italian brain
Gan in your duller Britain operate
Most vilely; for my vantage,° excellent.
And, to be brief, my practice° so prevailed
200   That I returned with simular° proof enough
To make the noble Leonatus mad
By wounding his belief in her renown°
With tokens thus and thus; averring° notes
Of chamber hanging, pictures, this her bracelet—
205   O cunning, how I got it!—nay, some marks
Of secret on her person, that he could not
But think her bond of chastity quite cracked,

---

177 **cracked** boasted 178 **unspeaking sots** inarticulate fools
180 **as** as if 181 **cold** chaste 182 **Made scruple of** expressed
doubt about, disputed 185 **suit** amorous solicitation (Maxwell)
189 **carbuncle** red precious stone 190 **Of Phoebus' wheel** (deco-
rating the sun-god's chariot) 194 **Of** by 195 **amorous** i.e., faithful 195–96 **Being thus . . . longing** the fire of hope (though not of
desire) being thus put out 198 **vantage** profit 199 **practice** plot
200 **simular** simulated, specious 202 **renown** good name 203
averring avouching

I having ta'en the forfeit.° Whereupon—
Methinks I see him now—

Posthumus. [*Advancing*]   Ay, so thou dost,
Italian fiend! Ay me, most credulous fool,   210
Egregious murderer, thief, anything
That's due° to all the villains past, in being,
To come! O, give me cord or knife or poison,
Some upright justicer!° Thou, King, send out
For torturers ingenious. It is I   215
That all th' abhorrèd things o' th' earth amend°
By being worse than they. I am Posthumus,
That killed thy daughter—villainlike, I lie—
That caused a lesser villain than myself,
A sacrilegious thief, to do't. The temple   220
Of Virtue was she; yea, and she herself.°
Spit, and throw stones, cast mire upon me, set
The dogs o' th' street to bay me; every villain
Be called Posthumus Leonatus, and
Be villainy less° than 'twas! O Imogen!   225
My queen, my life, my wife! O Imogen,
Imogen, Imogen!

Imogen.   Peace, my lord. Hear, hear—

Posthumus. Shall's° have a play of this? Thou scornful
    page,
There lie thy part.°   [*Striking her; she falls.*]

Pisanio.   O gentlemen, help!
Mine and your mistress! O my lord Posthumus,   230
You ne'er killed Imogen till now. Help, help!
Mine honored lady!

Cymbeline.   Does the world go round?

Posthumus. How comes these staggers° on me?

Pisanio.   Wake, my mistress!

---

208 **forfeit** that which was forfeited for breach of contract   211–12
anything/That's due i.e., any word that's appropriate   214 **justicer**
judge   216 **amend** make better (by contrast)   221 **she herself**
Virtue herself   225 **less** i.e., by comparison with my villainy   228
Shall's shall us (we)   229 **There lie thy part** play your role lying
there   233 **staggers** dizziness

Cymbeline. If this be so, the gods do mean to strike me
    To death with mortal° joy.

235 *Pisanio.*   How fares my mistress?

Imogen. O, get thee from my sight;
    Thou gav'st me poison. Dangerous fellow, hence;
    Breathe not where princes are.

Cymbeline.   The tune° of Imogen!

Pisanio. Lady,
240   The gods throw stones of sulphur° on me if
    That box I gave you was not thought by me
    A precious° thing; I had it from the Queen.

Cymbeline. New matter still.

Imogen.   It poisoned me.

Cornelius.   O gods!
    I left out one thing which the Queen confessed,
245   Which must approve° thee honest. "If Pisanio
    Have," said she, "given his mistress that confection°
    Which I gave him for cordial, she is served
    As I would serve a rat."

Cymbeline.   What's this, Cornelius?

Cornelius. The Queen, sir, very oft importuned me
250   To temper° poisons for her, still pretending°
    The satisfaction of her knowledge only
    In killing creatures vile, as cats and dogs
    Of no esteem.° I, dreading that her purpose
    Was of more danger, did compound for her
255   A certain stuff which, being ta'en, would cease°
    The present pow'r of life, but in short time
    All offices of nature° should again
    Do their due functions. Have you ta'en of it?

Imogen. Most like° I did, for I was dead.°

235 **mortal** deadly, fatal   238 **tune** voice   240 **stones of sulphur**
thunderbolts   242 **precious** i.e., beneficial   245 **approve** prove
246 **confection** drug   250 **temper** mix   250 **still pretending** always alleging as her purpose   253 **esteem** value   255 **cease** sus-
pend   257 **offices of nature** bodily parts   259 **like** probably   259
dead as if dead

Belarius.   My boys,
There was our error.

Guiderius.   This is sure Fidele.   260

Imogen. Why did you throw your wedded lady from you?
Think that you are upon a rock,° and now
Throw me again.   [*Embracing him*]

Posthumus.   Hang there like fruit, my soul,
Till the tree die!

Cymbeline.   How now, my flesh, my child?
What, mak'st thou me a dullard° in this act?°   265
Wilt thou not speak to me?

Imogen. [*Kneeling*]   Your blessing, sir.

Belarius. Though you did love this youth, I blame ye not;
You had a motive° for't.

Cymbeline.   My tears that fall
Prove holy water on thee. Imogen,
Thy mother's° dead.

Imogen.   I am sorry for't, my lord.   270

Cymbeline. O, she was naught,° and long of° her it was
That we meet here so strangely; but her son
Is gone, we know not how nor where.

Pisanio.   My lord,
Now fear is from me, I'll speak troth.° Lord Cloten,
Upon my lady's missing, came to me   275
With his sword drawn, foamed at the mouth, and swore,
If I discovered° not which way she was gone,
It was my instant death. By accident
I had a feignèd letter of my master's
Then in my pocket, which directed him   280
To seek her on the mountains near to Milford;
Where, in a frenzy, in my master's garments,

262 **upon a rock** (sense unclear; "rock" is sometimes emended to
"lock," a hold in wrestling)   265 **mak'st ... dullard** treat me like a
fool (by ignoring me)   265 **act** action, scene   268 **motive** cause
270 **mother** step-mother   271 **naught** wicked   271 **long of** because of   274 **troth** truth   277 **discovered** revealed

Which he enforced from me, away he posts
With unchaste purpose and with oath to violate
285 My lady's honor. What became of him
I further know not.

Guiderius.   Let me end the story:
I slew him there.

Cymbeline.   Marry,° the gods forfend!°
I would not thy good deeds° should from my lips
Pluck a hard sentence. Prithee, valiant youth,
Deny't again.°

290 Guiderius.   I have spoke it, and I did it.

Cymbeline. He was a prince.

Guiderius. A most incivil° one. The wrongs he did me
Were nothing princelike, for he did provoke me
With language that would make me spurn the sea
295 If it could so roar to me. I cut off's head,
And am right glad he is not standing here
To tell this tale of mine.

Cymbeline.   I am sorry for thee.
By thine own tongue thou art condemned and must
Endure our law. Thou'rt dead.

Imogen.   That headless man
I thought had been my lord.

300 Cymbeline.   Bind the offender
And take him from our presence.

Belarius.   Stay, sir King.
This man is better than the man he slew,
As well descended as thyself, and hath
More of thee merited than a band of Clotens
305 Had ever scar for.°—Let his arms alone;
They were not born for bondage.

---

287 **Marry** indeed (by the Virgin Mary)   287 **forfend** forbid   288
thy good deeds i.e., in view of thy good deeds (in battle) that thou
290 **Deny't again** speak again and deny what you have said (Nosworthy)   292 **incivil** unmannerly   305 **Had ever scar for** ever
earned by wounds

Cymbeline.   Why, old soldier:
   Wilt thou undo the worth thou art unpaid for°
   By tasting of our wrath? How of descent
   As good as we?

Arviragus.   In that he spake too far.

Cymbeline. And thou° shalt die for't.

Belarius.   We will die all three   *310*
   But I will prove° that two on's° are as good
   As I have given out him. My sons, I must
   For mine own part unfold a dangerous speech,
   Though haply well for you.

Arviragus.   Your danger's ours.

Guiderius. And our good his.

Belarius.   Have at it then. By leave,°   *315*
   Thou hadst, great King, a subject who
   Was called Belarius.

Cymbeline.   What of him? He is
   A banished traitor.

Belarius.   He it is that hath
   Assumed° this age; indeed a banished man,
   I know not how a traitor.

Cymbeline.   Take him hence.   *320*
   The whole world shall not save him.

Belarius.   Not too hot.°
   First pay me for the nursing of thy sons,
   And let it° be confiscate all, so soon
   As I have received it.

Cymbeline.   Nursing of my sons?

Belarius. I am too blunt and saucy; here's my knee.   *325*
   Ere I arise I will prefer° my sons;

---

307 **the worth ... for** thy not yet rewarded esteem (?)   310 **thou**
Belarius   311 **But I will prove** if I do not prove (Maxwell)   311
on's of us   315 **By leave** by your permission   319 **Assumed** attained to   321 **hot** fast   323 **it** the payment   326 **prefer** promote
(in rank)

Then spare not the old father. Mighty sir,
These two young gentlemen that call me father
And think they are my sons are none of mine;
330   They are the issue of your loins, my liege,
And blood of your begetting.

Cymbeline.   How? My issue?

Belarius. So sure as you your father's. I, old Morgan,
Am that Belarius whom you sometime° banished.
Your pleasure was my mere° offense, my punishment
335   Itself, and all my treason; that I suffered
Was all the harm I did. These gentle princes—
For such and so they are—these twenty years
Have I trained up; those arts° they have as I
Could put into them. My breeding was, sir, as
340   Your Highness knows. Their nurse, Euriphile,
Whom for the theft I wedded, stole these children
Upon my banishment. I moved° her to't,
Having received the punishment before
For that which I did then. Beaten° for loyalty
345   Excited me to treason. Their dear loss,
The more of° you 'twas felt, the more it shaped
Unto° my end of stealing them. But, gracious sir,
Here are your sons again, and I must lose
Two of the sweet'st companions in the world.
350   The benediction of these covering heavens
Fall on their heads like dew, for they are worthy
To inlay heaven with stars.

Cymbeline.   Thou weep'st and speak'st.
The service° that you three have done is more
Unlike° than this thou tell'st. I lost my children;
355   If these be they, I know not how to wish
A pair of worthier sons.

Belarius.   Be pleased awhile.
This gentleman whom I call Polydore,
Most worthy prince, as yours, is true Guiderius;
This gentleman, my Cadwal, Arviragus,

333 **sometime** once   334 **mere** entire   338 **arts** accomplishments
342 **moved** incited   344 **Beaten** my having been beaten   346 **of**
by   346–47 **shaped/Unto** served   353 **service** i.e., in battle   354
Unlike improbable

Your younger princely son. He, sir, was lapped° 360
In a most curious° mantle, wrought by th' hand
Of his queen mother, which for more probation°
I can with ease produce.

Cymbeline.   Guiderius had
Upon his neck a mole, a sanguine° star;
It was a mark of wonder.

Belarius.   This is he, 365
Who hath upon him still that natural stamp.
It was wise Nature's end° in the donation
To be his evidence now.

Cymbeline.   O, what am I?
A mother to the birth of three? Ne'er mother
Rejoiced deliverance more. Blest pray you be, 370
That, after this strange starting from your orbs,°
You may reign in them now! O Imogen,
Thou hast lost by this a kingdom.

Imogen.   No, my lord,
I have got two worlds by't. O my gentle brothers,
Have we thus met? O, never say hereafter 375
But I am truest speaker. You called me brother
When I was but your sister, I you brothers
When ye were so indeed.

Cymbeline.   Did you e'er meet?

Arviragus. Ay, my good lord.

Guiderius.   And at first meeting loved,
Continued so until we thought he died. 380

Cornelius. By the Queen's dram she swallowed.

Cymbeline.   O rare instinct!
When shall I hear all through? This fierce° abridgment
Hath to it circumstantial° branches, which
Distinction should be rich in.° Where, how lived you?

---

360 **lapped** wrapped   361 **curious** elaborately wrought   362 **pro-
bation** proof   364 **sanguine** blood-red   367 **end** purpose   371
orbs spheres, orbits (of planets)   382 **fierce** drastic   383 **circum-
stantial** detailed   383–84 **which . . . rich in** which deserves to be
elaborately discriminated (Maxwell)

385   And when came you to serve our Roman captive?
How parted with your brothers? How first met them?
Why fled you from the court? And whither? These,
And your three motives° to the battle, with
I know not how much more, should be demanded,
390   And all the other bye-dependences°
From chance° to chance; but nor° the time nor place
Will serve our long inter'gatories. See,
Posthumus anchors upon Imogen,
And she like harmless lightning throws her eye
395   On him, her brothers, me, her master, hitting
Each object with a joy; the counterchange°
Is severally in all.° Let's quit this ground
And smoke° the temple with our sacrifices.
Thou° art my brother; so we'll hold thee ever.

400 *Imogen.* You° are my father too, and did relieve° me
To see this gracious season.°

Cymbeline.   All o'erjoyed
Save these in bonds; let them be joyful too,
For they shall taste our comfort.°

Imogen.   My good master,
I will yet do you service.

Lucius.   Happy be you!

405 *Cymbeline.* The forlorn° soldier, that so nobly fought,
He would have well becomed this place and graced
The thankings of a king.

Posthumus.   I am, sir,
The soldier that did company these three
In poor beseeming;° 'twas a fitment° for
410   The purpose I then followed. That I was he,

---

388 **your three motives** the motives of you three   390 **bye-dependences** connected circumstances   391 **chance** event   391 **but nor** but neither   396 **counterchange** exchange   397 **severally in all** in each and in all   398 **smoke** fill with smoke   399 **Thou** Belarius   400 **You** Belarius   400 **relieve** aid   401 **gracious season** joyful occasion   403 **taste our comfort** share in our joy   405 **forlorn** lost, missing   409 **beseeming** appearance, clothing   409 **fitment** suitable device

Speak, Iachimo. I had you down and might
Have made you finish.°

Iachimo. [*Kneeling*]   I am down again,
But now my heavy conscience sinks° my knee,
As then your force did. Take that life, beseech you,
Which I so often° owe; but your ring first,   *415*
And here the bracelet of the truest princess
That ever swore her faith.

Posthumus.   Kneel not to me.
The pow'r that I have on you is to spare you;
The malice towards you to forgive you. Live,
And deal with others better.

Cymbeline.   Nobly doomed!°   *420*
We'll learn our freeness° of a son-in-law:
Pardon's the word to all.

Arviragus.   You holp us, sir,
As° you did mean indeed to be our brother.
Joyed are we that you are.

Posthumus. Your servant, princes. Good my lord of Rome,   *425*
Call forth your soothsayer. As I slept, methought
Great Jupiter, upon his eagle backed,°
Appeared to me, with other spritely° shows
Of mine own kindred. When I waked, I found
This label° on my bosom, whose containing°   *430*
Is so from° sense in hardness that I can
Make no collection of° it. Let him show
His skill in the construction.°

Lucius.   Philharmonus!

Soothsayer. Here, my good lord.

Lucius.   Read, and declare the meaning.

Soothsayer. (*Reads*) "Whenas a lion's whelp shall, to him-   *435*
self unknown, without seeking find, and be embraced by

412 **finish** die   413 **sinks** lowers   415 **often** many times over
420 **doomed** judged   421 **freeness** generosity   423 **As** as if   427
upon his eagle backed upon the back of his eagle   428 **spritely**
ghostly   430 **label** piece of paper   430 **containing** contents   431
from remote from   432 **collection of** conclusion about   433 **construction** interpretation

a piece of tender air; and when from a stately cedar shall
be lopped branches which, being dead many years, shall
after revive, be jointed to the old stock, and freshly
440 grow; then shall Posthumus end his miseries, Britain be
fortunate and flourish in peace and plenty."
Thou, Leonatus, art the lion's whelp;
The fit and apt construction of thy name,
Being *Leo-natus*,° doth import so much.—
445 The piece of tender air, thy virtuous daughter,
Which we call *mollis aer*,° and *mollis aer*
We term it *mulier*.°—Which *mulier* I divine
Is thy most constant wife, who° even now
Answering the letter of the oracle,
450 Unknown to you, unsought, were clipped° about
With this most tender air.

Cymbeline.   This hath some seeming.°

Soothsayer. The lofty cedar, royal Cymbeline,
Personates° thee, and thy lopped branches point
Thy two sons forth; who, by Belarius stol'n,
455 For many years thought dead, are now revived,
To the majestic cedar joined, whose issue
Promises Britain peace and plenty.

Cymbeline.   Well,
My peace we will begin. And, Caius Lucius,
Although the victor, we submit to Caesar
460 And to the Roman empire, promising
To pay our wonted tribute, from the which
We were dissuaded by our wicked queen,
Whom° heavens in justice, both on her and hers,°
Have laid most heavy hand.

465 *Soothsayer.* The fingers of the pow'rs above do tune
The harmony of this peace. The vision
Which I made known to Lucius ere the stroke
Of this yet scarce-cold battle, at this instant
Is full accomplished; for the Roman eagle,

---

444 **Leo-natus** lion-born   446 **mollis aer** tender air   447 **mulier**
woman (thought to derive from *mollis,* soft)   448 **who** thou who
(Posthumus)   450 **clipped** embraced   451 **seeming** plausibility
453 **Personates** represents   463 **Whom** on whom   463 **hers** i.e.,
Cloten

From south to west on wing soaring aloft, 470
Lessened herself and in the beams o' th' sun
So vanished; which foreshowed our princely eagle,
Th' imperial Caesar, should again unite
His favor with the radiant Cymbeline,
Which shines here in the west.

Cymbeline. Laud we the gods, 475
And let our crooked° smokes climb to their nostrils
From our blest altars. Publish we this peace
To all our subjects. Set we forward;° let
A Roman and a British ensign wave
Friendly together. So through Lud's Town march, 480
And in the temple of great Jupiter
Our peace we'll ratify, seal it with feasts.
Set on there!° Never was a war did cease,
Ere bloody hands were washed, with such a peace.

Exeunt.

FINIS

---

476 **crooked** curling   478 **Set we forward** let us march   483 **Set on there** begin marching

Textual Note

There is only one "substantive" edition of *Cymbeline*, the Shakespeare Folio of 1623. Because of incomplete notation of properties and music in the stage directions of F, it seems clear that the printer's copy for F was not a promptbook or the faithful transcript of one; and several directions are phrased in the "fictive" language characteristic of an author writing his own stage directions. Probably therefore the copy for F consisted of an authorial manuscript or the faithful transcript of one: either (1) "foul papers" (the author's last working draft of the play before preparation of a promptbook) in unusually clean condition (like the copy for *Antony and Cleopatra*); (2) authorial "fair copy" (the author's faithful transcript of his own foul papers); or (3) a faithful scribal transcript of foul papers or authorial fair copy. The type for F was set by a single compositor, Jaggard's Compositor B. (See Charlton Hinman, *The Printing and Proof-Reading of the First Folio of Shakespeare,* 1963.) F provides, in general, a good text, correctly lined and with relatively few corruptions. In the present edition "accidental" errors in F have been emended silently; "substantive" errors requiring emendation are listed at the end of this note.

F is divided into acts and scenes. Division into acts presumably derives from original production of the play with four intervals for nondramatic music. (Cf. Wilfred T. Jewkes, *Act Division in Elizabethan and Jacobean Plays,* 1958.) Division into scenes presumably derives from annotation of the printer's copy by a Folio editor wishing to give the text a semblance of neoclassical style. The present edition follows the act divisions of F and, for convenience of reference, the scene divisions of the Globe edition, although at three points these vary (both correctly and incorrectly) from those of F. Globe 1.1 combines F 1.1 and 2, incorrectly since the stage (despite notice by players going off of those coming on) is technically clear at 1.1.69 (the "overlap" of players is paralleled at 1.2.118 of *Measure for Measure*). Globe 2.4 and 5 divide F 2.4, correctly since the stage is clear at 2.4.152. And Globe 3.6 combines F 3.6 and 7, incorrectly since the stage is clear at 3.6.27. Both Globe and F fail to mark a new scene at 4.2.100, incorrectly since the stage is clear at that point.

F contains no place headings, for the reason that the play was originally produced without changeable scenery. (Cf. Richard Southern, *Changeable Scenery: Its Origin and Development in the British Theatre,* 1952.) Place headings have been added to the present edition in accordance with a general requirement of the Signet Classic Shakespeare Series, but such headings designate only the three general locales of the action, Britain, Rome, and Wales. A more specific designation is impossible in at least three instances (1.2, 2.1, 2.5); and in any case specific designations are misleading since they suggest a change of scenery for each scene with a particular locale different from that of the preceding scene.

In the following list of substantive emendations the reading of the present edition is given in italic type, that of F in roman type.

1.1.4 *First Gentleman* 1 [so throughout balance of scene]   10 *Second Gentleman* 2 [so throughout balance of scene]   158 *Exeunt* Exit

1.2.1 *First Lord* 1 [so throughout balance of scene and in 2.1 and 2.3]   7 *Second Lord* 2 [so throughout balance of scene and in 2.1 and 2.3]

1.3.9 *this* his

1.4.41 *not* [not in F]   65 *Britain* Britanie   67 *but believe* beleeue   76–77 *purchase* purchases   119 *thousand* thousands

1.5.3s.d. *Exeunt* Exit   75s.d. [occurs after 1.74 in F]   85s.d. *Exeunt* Exit

1.6.7 *desire* desires   28 *takes* take   104 *Fixing* Fiering   109 *illustrous* illustrious   168 *men's* men   169 *descended* defended

2.1.25 *your* you   32 *tonight* night   49s.d. *Exeunt* Exit   59 *husband, than* Husband. Then   60 *make. The* make the   63s.d. *Exit* Exeunt

2.2.49 *bare* beare   51s.d. *Exeunt* Exit

2.3.7 *Cloten* [not in F]   28 *Cloten* [not in F]   29 *vice* voyce   43 *out* on't   47 *solicits* solicity   137 *garment* Garments   154 *you* your

2.4.6 *hopes* hope   18 *legions* Legion   24 *mingled* wing-led   47 *not* note   100–01 *that. She* that She   135 *the* her

2.5.16 *German* Iarmen   27 *have a* [not in F]

3.1.19 *ribbèd . . . palèd* ribb'd . . . pal'd   20 *rocks* Oakes   52 *he. We do say* be, we do. Say

3.2.67 *score* store   78 *here, nor* heere, not

3.3.2 *Stoop* Sleepe   23 *bribe* Babe   28 *know* knowes   83 *wherein they* whereon the

3.4.79 *afore't* a-foot   90 *make* makes   102 *out* [not in F]   124 *courtesan.* Curtezan?   148 *haply* happily

3.5.17s.d. *Exeunt* Exit   32 *looks* looke   40 *strokes* stroke   41s.d. *Messenger* a Messenger   55s.d. [occurs after "days" in F]   138 *insultment* insulment

3.6.70 *I'ld* I

3.7.9 *commends* commands

4.1.19 *her* thy   19 *haply* happily

4.2.49 [speech heading Arui. precedes "He" in F]   58 *patience* patient   122 *thank* thanks   132 *humor* Honor   186 *ingenious* ingenuous   205 *crayer* care   206 *Might* Might'st   290 *is* are   332s.d.–33 *Enter Lucius and Captains; a Soothsayer to them. Captain. The legions* Enter Lucius, Captaines, and a Soothsayer. Cap. To them, the Legions   336 *are in* are heere in

4.4.2 *find we* we finde   8 *us* v.   17 *the* their   27 *hard* heard

5.1.1 *wished* am wisht

5.3.24 *harts* hearts   42 *stooped* stopt   43 *they* the   84 *First Captain* 1 [so throughout balance of scene]   86 *Second Captain* 2 [so throughout balance of scene]

5.4.s.d. *Jailers* Gaoler   1 *First Jailer* Gao   51 *come* came   57 *look* looke, looke   129 *are as often* are often   139 *sir* Sis   154 *on* one   176s.d. *Exit* Exeunt

5.5.62 *Ladies* La   64 *heard* heare   126 *saw* see   134 *On* One   205 *it* [not in F]   297 *sorry* sorrow   334 *mere* neere   378 *ye* we   386 *brothers* Brother   392 *inter'gatories* Interrogatories   405 *so* no   435 *Soothsayer* [not in F]   444 *Leo-natus* Leonatus   448 *thy* this   468 *this yet* yet this

The Sources of Cymbeline

The sources of *Cymbeline* are discussed in the Introduction. The ninth novella of the Second Day of Boccaccio's *Decameron* is reprinted here in the anonymous translation of 1620. *Frederick of Jennen* is reprinted in an appendix to the New Arden edition of *Cymbeline* (1955). *The Rare Triumphs of Love and Fortune* is edited by W. W. Greg in the Malone Society Reprints (1931), *Clyomon and Clamydes* by Betty Littleton (1968). The *Ethiopica* of Heliodorus has been translated by Moses Hadas: *Heliodorus: An Ethiopian Romance* (1957). Relevant parts of the *History of England* and the *History of Scotland* in Holinshed's *Chronicles* (1587) are reprinted here. Blenerhasset's "Guidericus" and Higgins's "Guiderius" have been edited by Lily B. Campbell, in *Parts Added to the Mirror for Magistrates* (1946).

GIOVANNI BOCCACCIO

From The Decameron
The Second Day . . . ,
The Ninth Novel.

Wherein is declared that by over-liberal commending the chastity of women it falleth out (oftentimes) to be very dangerous, especially by the means of treacherers,* who yet (in the end) are justly punished for their treachery. . . .

There was a fair and good inn in Paris much frequented by many great Italian merchants according to such variety of occasions and business as urged their often resorting thither. One night among many other, having had a merry supper together, they began to discourse on divers matters, and, falling from one relation to another, they commoned† in very friendly manner concerning their wives left at home in their houses. Quoth the first: "I cannot well imagine what my wife is now doing, but I am able to say for myself that if a pretty female should fall into my company, I could easily forget my love to my wife and make use of such an advantage offered."

A second replied: "And, trust me, I should do no less, because I am persuaded that if my wife be willing to wander, the law is in her own hand and I am far enough from home. Dumb walls blab no tales and offenses unknown are seldom or never

---

*deceivers.
†talked.
From *The Decameron, Containing an Hundred Pleasant Novels*, translator unknown, vol. I, fols. 68–73v. London: Isaac Jaggard, 1620. In the present edition the traditional forms *Bernabò* (from *Bernardobuono*), *Ambrogiuolo* (English *Ambrose*), and *Zinevra* are substituted for the variant forms of 1620: *Bernardo*, *Ambroginolo* (a textual error), and *Genevra* (a linguistic variant). Spelling and punctuation are modernized, and a few necessary emendations are indicated in footnotes.

called in question." A third man was apt* in censure† with his former fellows of the jury; and it plainly appeared that all the rest were of the same opinion, condemning their wives over-rashly and alleging that, when husbands strayed so far from home, their wives had wit enough to make use of their time.

Only one man among them all, named Bernabò Lomellino and dwelling in Genoa, maintained the contrary, boldly avouch-ing that by the especial favor of Fortune he had a wife so per-fectly complete in all graces and virtues as any lady in the world possibly could be and that Italy scarcely contained her equal. For she was goodly of person and yet very young, quick, quaint,‡ mild, and courteous, and not anything appertaining to the office of a wife either for domestic affairs or any other em-ployment whatsoever but in womanhood she went beyond all other. No lord, knight, esquire, or gentleman could be better served at his table than himself daily was with more wisdom, modesty, and discretion. After all this, he praised her for riding, hawking, hunting, fishing, fowling, reading, writing, endit-ing,** and most absolute keeping his books of accounts that neither himself or any other merchant could therein excel her. After infinite other commendations he came to the former point of their argument concerning the easy falling of women into wantonness, maintaining with a solemn oath that no woman possibly could be more chaste and honest†† than she. In which respect he was verily persuaded that if he stayed from her ten years' space, yea, all his lifetime out of his house, yet never would she falsify her faith to him or be lewdly allured by any other man.

Among these merchants thus commoning together, there was a young proper man named Ambrogiuolo‡‡ of Piacenza who be-gan to laugh at the last praises which Bernabò had used of his wife and, seeming to make a mockery thereat, demanded if the Emperor had given him this privilege above all other married men. Bernabò, being somewhat offended, answered: "No em-peror hath done it but the especial blessing of heaven, exceeding

---

*For "was apt" 1620 has "unapt."
†opinion.
‡clever.
**composing.
††chaste.
‡‡pronounced *Ambroj-wolo*.

all the emperors on the earth in grace, and thereby have [I] received this favor." Whereto Ambrogiuolo presently* thus replied: "Bernabò, without all question to the contrary I believe that what thou hast said is true, but for aught I can perceive thou hast slender judgment in the nature of things, because if thou didst observe them well thou couldst not be of so gross understanding. For, by comprehending matters in their true kind and nature, thou wouldst speak of them more correctly than thou dost. And, to the end thou mayst not imagine that we who have spoken of our wives do think any otherwise of them than as well and honestly as thou canst of thine, nor that anything else did urge these speeches of them or falling into this kind of discourse but only by a natural instinct and admonition, I will proceed familiarly a little further with thee upon the matter already propounded.

"I have evermore understood that man was the most noble creature formed by God to live in this world, and woman in the next degree to him. But man, as generally is believed and as is discerned by apparent effects, is the most perfect of both. Having then the most perfection in him, without all doubt he must be so much the more firm and constant. So in like manner it hath been and is universally granted that woman is more various and mutable, and the reason thereof may be approved† by many natural circumstances which were needless now to make any mention of. If a man then be possessed of the greater stability and yet cannot contain himself from condescending‡—I say not to one that entreats him—but to desire any other that may please him and, beside, to covet the enjoying of his own pleasing contentment (a thing not chancing to him once in a month but infinite times in a day's space), what can you then conceive of a frail woman, subject by nature to entreaties, flatteries, gifts, persuasions, and a thousand other enticing means which a man that is affected to** her can use? Dost thou think then that she hath any power to contain?†† Assuredly, though thou shouldst rest so resolved, yet cannot I be of the same opinion. For I am sure thou believest and must needs confess it that

---

*immediately.
†proven.
‡restrain himself from falling.
**in love with.
††be continent.

thy wife is a woman, made of flesh and blood as other women are. If it be so, she cannot be without the same desires and the weakness or strength as other women have to resist such natural appetites as her own are. In regard whereof it is merely* impossible, although she be most honest, but she must needs do that which other women do, for there is nothing else possible either to be denied or affirmed to the contrary as thou most unadvisedly hast done."

Bernabò answered in this manner: "I am a merchant and no philosopher, and like a merchant I mean to answer thee. I am not to learn that these accidents by thee related may happen to fools who are void of understanding or shame, but such as are wise and endued with virtue have always such a precious esteem of their honor that they will contain those principles of constancy which men are merely careless of, and I justify† my wife to be one of them." "Believe me, Bernabò," replied Ambrogiuolo, "if, so often as thy wife's mind is addicted to wanton folly, a badge of scorn should arise on thy forehead to render testimony of her female frailty, I believe the number of them would be more than willingly you would wish them to be. And among all married men in every degree the notes are so secret of their wives' imperfections that the sharpest sight is not able to discern them, and the wiser sort of men are willing not to know them because shame and loss of honor is never imposed but in cases evident and apparent.

"Persuade thyself then, Bernabò, that what women may accomplish in secret they will rarely fail to do, or if they abstain, it is through fear and folly. Wherefore hold it for a certain rule that that woman is only chaste that never was solicited personally, or if she endured any such suit, either she answered yea or no. And, albeit I know this to be true by many infallible and natural reasons, yet could I not speak so exactly as I do if I had not tried experimentally the humors and affections of divers women. Yea, and let me tell thee more, Bernabò, were I in private company with thy wife, howsoever pure and precise‡ thou presumest her to be, I should account it a matter of no impossibility to find in her the selfsame frailty."

Bernabò's blood began now to boil and, patience being a little

---

*absolutely.
†affirm.
‡strict.

put down by choler,* thus he replied: "A combat of words requires overlong continuance, for I maintain the matter which thou deniest and all this sorts to nothing in the end. But seeing thou presumest that all women are so apt and tractable and thyself so confident of thine own power, I willingly yield for the better assurance of my wife's constant loyalty to have my head smitten off if thou canst win her to any such dishonest act by any means whatsoever thou canst use unto her; which if thou canst not do thou shalt only lose a thousand ducats of gold." Now began Ambrogiuolo to be heated with these words, answering thus: "Bernabò, if I had won the wager, I know not what I should do with thy head; but, if thou be willing to stand upon the proof,† pawn down five thousand ducats of gold, a matter of much less value than thy head, against a thousand ducats of mine, granting me a lawful limited time which I require to be no more than the space of three months after the day of my departing hence. I will stand bound‡ to go for Genoa and there win such kind consent of thy wife as shall be to mine own content.** In witness whereof, I will bring back with me such private and especial tokens as thou thyself shalt confess that I have not failed, provided that thou do first promise upon thy faith to absent thyself thence during my limited time and be no hindrance to me by thy letters concerning the attempt by me undertaken."

Bernabò said: "Be it a bargain. I am the man that will make good my five thousand ducats." And albeit the other merchants then present earnestly labored to break the wager, knowing great harm must needs ensue thereon, yet both the parties were so hot and fiery as all the other men spoke to no effect but writings were made, sealed,†† and delivered under either of their hands, Bernabò remaining at Paris and Ambrogiuolo departing for Genoa. There he remained some few days to learn the street's name where Bernabò dwelt as also the conditions and qualities of his wife; which scarcely pleased him when he heard them because they were far beyond her husband's relation and she reputed to be the only wonder of women, whereby

*anger.
†put the matter to a test.
‡ready.
**1620 has "consent."
††confirmed by the attaching of waxen seals.

he plainly perceived that he had undertaken a very idle enterprise. Yet would he not give it over so but proceeded therein a little further.

He wrought such means that he came acquainted with a poor woman who often frequented Bernabò's house and was greatly in favor with his wife; upon whose poverty he so prevailed by earnest persuasions but much more by large gifts of money that he won her to further him in this manner following. A fair and artificial* chest he caused to be purposely made wherein himself might be aptly contained and so conveyed into the house of Bernabò's wife under color† of a formal excuse that the poor woman should be absent from the city two or three days and she must keep it safe till she‡ return. The gentlewoman, suspecting no guile but that the chest was the receptacle of all the woman's wealth, would trust it in no other room than her own bedchamber, which was the place where Ambrogiuolo most desired to be.

Being thus conveyed into the chamber, the night going on apace and the gentlewoman fast asleep in her bed, a lighted taper stood burning on the table by her as in her husband's absence she ever used to have. Ambrogiuolo softly opened the chest according as cunningly he had contrived it and, stepping forth in his socks made of cloth, observed the situation of the chamber, the paintings, pictures, and beautiful hangings, with all things else that were remarkable; which perfectly he committed to his memory. Going near to the bed, he saw her lie there sweetly sleeping and her young daughter in like manner by her, she seeming then as complete and pleasing a creature as when she was attired in her best bravery.** No especial note or mark could he descry whereof he might make credible report but only a small wart upon her left pap with some few hairs growing thereon appearing to be as yellow as gold.

Sufficient had he seen and durst presume no further, but, taking one of her rings which lay upon the table, a purse of hers hanging by on the wall, a light-wearing robe of silk, and her girdle,†† all which he put into the chest and, being in himself,

*skillfully designed.
†pretense.
‡1620 has "he."
**finery.
††sash.

closed it fast as it was before; so continuing there in the chamber two several nights, the gentlewoman neither mistrusting or missing anything. The third day being come, the poor woman according as formerly was concluded came to have home her chest again and brought it safely into her own house, where Ambrogiuolo, coming forth of it, satisfied the poor woman to her own liking, returning with all the forenamed things so fast as conveniently he could to Paris.

Being arrived there long before his limited time, he called the merchants together who were present at the passed words and wager, avouching before Bernabò that he had won his five thousand ducats and performed the task he undertook. To make good his protestation, first he described the form of the chamber, the curious pictures hanging about it, in what manner the bed stood, and every circumstance else beside. Next he showed the several things which he brought away thence with him, affirming that he had received them of herself. Bernabò confessed that his description of the chamber was true and acknowledged moreover that these other things did belong to his wife. "But," quoth he, "this may be gotten by corrupting some servant of mine, both for intelligence of the chamber as also of the ring, purse, and what else is beside, all which suffice not to win the wager without some other more apparent and pregnant token." "In troth," answered Ambrogiuolo, "methinks these should serve for sufficient proofs, but seeing thou art so desirous to know more, I plainly tell thee that fair Zinevra thy wife hath a small round wart upon her left pap and some few little golden hairs growing thereon."

When Bernabò heard these words, they were as so many stabs to his heart, yea, beyond all compass of patient sufferance, and by the changing of his color it was noted manifestly (being unable to utter one word) that Ambrogiuolo had spoken nothing but the truth. Within a while after, he said: "Gentlemen, that which Ambrogiuolo hath said is very true. Wherefore let him come when he will and he shall be paid." Which accordingly he performed on the very next day, even to the utmost penny, departing then from Paris towards Genoa with a most malicious intention to his wife. Being come near to the city, he would not enter it but rode to a country house of his standing about ten miles distant thence. Being there arrived, he called a servant in whom he reposed especial trust, sending him to Genoa with two horses, writing to his wife that he was returned and she should come thither to see him. But secretly he charged his servant that, so soon as he had brought her to a convenient place, he should there kill her without any pity or compassion and then return to him again.

When the servant was come to Genoa and had delivered his letter and message, Zinevra gave him most joyful welcome and, on the morrow morning, mounting on horseback, with the servant rode merrily towards the country house. Divers things she discoursed on by the way, till they descended into a deep solitary valley, very thickly beset with high and huge spreading trees, which the servant supposed to be a meet place for the execution of his master's command. Suddenly drawing forth his sword and holding Zinevra fast by the arm, he said: "Mistress, quickly commend your soul to God, for you must die before you pass any further." Zinevra, seeing the naked sword and hearing the words so peremptorily delivered, fearfully answered: "Alas, dear friend, mercy for God's sake, and before thou kill me tell me wherein I have offended thee and why thou must kill me." "Alas, good mistress," replied the servant, "you have not any way offended me, but in what occasion you have displeased your husband, it is utterly unknown to me, for he hath strictly commanded me, without respect of pity or compassion, to kill you by the way as I bring you, and if I do it not, he hath sworn to hang me by the neck. You know, good mistress, how much I stand obliged to him and how impossible it is for me to contradict anything that he commandeth. God is my witness that I am truly compassionate of you, and yet by no means may I let you live."

Zinevra, kneeling before him weeping, wringing her hands, thus replied: "Wilt thou turn monster and be a murderer of her that never wronged thee, to please another man and on a bare command? God, who truly knoweth all things, is my faithful witness that I never committed any offense whereby to deserve the dislike of my husband, much less so harsh a recompense as this is. But, flying from mine own justification and appealing to thy manly* mercy, thou mayst (wert thou but so well pleased) in a moment satisfy both thy master and me in such manner as I will make plain and apparent to thee. Take thou my garments; spare me only thy doublet and such a bonnet as is fitting for a

---

*human.

man. So return with my habit to thy master, assuring him that the deed is done. And here I swear to thee by that life which I enjoy but by thy mercy, I will so strangely* disguise myself and wander so far off from these countries as neither he or thou nor any person belonging to these parts shall ever hear any tidings of me."

The servant, who had no great good will to kill her, very easily grew pitiful, took off her upper† garments, and gave her a poor ragged doublet, a silly chaperon,‡ and such small store of money as he had, desiring her to forsake that country, and so left her to walk on foot out of the valley. When he came to his master and had delivered him her garments, he assured him that he had not only accomplished his command but also was most secure from any discovery because he had no sooner done the deed but four or five very ravenous wolves came presently running to the dead body and gave it burial in their bellies. Bernabò, soon after returning to Genoa, was much blamed for such unkind** cruelty to his wife. But his constant avouching of her treason to him, according then to the country's custom, did clear him from all pursuit of law.

Poor Zinevra was left thus alone and disconsolate, and, night stealing fast upon her, she went to a silly†† village near adjoining where, by the means of a good old woman, she got such provision as the place afforded, making the doublet fit to her body and converting her petticoat to a pair of breeches according to the mariners' fashion. Then, cutting her hair and quaintly‡‡ disguised like to a sailor, she went to the seacoast. By good fortune she met there with a gentleman of Catalonia whose name was Signior Encararch who came on land from his ship, which lay hulling there about Alba*** to refresh himself at a pleasant spring. Encararch taking her to be a man, as she appeared no otherwise by her habit, upon some conference passing between them, she was entertained††† into his service, and, being brought aboard the ship, she went under the name of

---

*i.e., completely.
†outer.
‡simple hood.
**unnatural.
††humble.
‡‡cleverly.
***1620 has "Albagia."
†††hired.

Sicurano da Finale. There she had better apparel bestown on her by the gentleman, and her service proved so pleasing and acceptable to him that he liked her care and diligence beyond all comparison.

It came to pass within a short while after that this gentleman of Catalonia sailed with some charge* of his into Alexandria, carrying thither certain peregrine falcons which he presented to the Sultan, who oftentimes welcomed this gentleman to his table, where he observed the behavior of Sicurano attending on his master's trencher and therewith was so highly pleased that he requested to have him from the gentleman, who for his more advancement willingly parted with his so lately entertained servant. Sicurano was so ready and discreet in his daily services that he grew in as great grace with the Sultan as before he had done with Encararch.

At a certain season in the year, as customary order (there observed) had formerly been in the city of Acre, which was under the Sultan's subjection, there yearly met a great assembly of merchants, as Christians, Moors, Jews, Saracens, and many other nations beside, as at a common mart or fair. And to the end that the merchants, for the better sale of their goods, might be there in the safer assurance, the Sultan used to send thither some of his ordinary† officers, and a strong guard of soldiers beside, to defend them from all injuries and molestation; because he reaped thereby no mean‡ benefit. And who should be now sent about this business but his new-elected favorite, Sicurano, because she was skillful and perfect in the languages.

Sicurano, being come to Acre as lord and captain of the guard for the merchants and for the safety of their merchandises, she discharged her office most commendably, walking with her train through every part of the fair where she observed a worthy company of merchants, Sicilians, Pisans, Genoese, Venetians, and other Italians, whom the more willingly she noted in remembrance of her native country. At one especial time among other, chancing into a shop or booth belonging to the Venetians, she espied hanging up with other costly wares a purse and a girdle which suddenly she remembered to be

*cargo, merchandise.
†regular.
‡inconsiderable.

sometime* her own; whereat she was not a little abashed in her
mind. But, without making any such outward show, courteously
she requested to know whose they were and whether they
should be sold or no.

Ambrogiuolo of Piacenza was likewise come thither, and
great store of merchandises he had brought with him in a car-
rack appertaining to the Venetians, and he, hearing the Captain
of the Guard demand whose they were, stepped forth before
him and, smiling, answered that they were his, but not to be
sold, yet if he liked them, gladly he would bestow them on him.
Sicurano, seeing him smile, suspected lest himself had by some
unfitting behavior been the occasion thereof, and therefore,
with a more settled countenance, he said: "Perhaps thou smilest
because I that am a man, professing arms, should question after
such womanish toys?" Ambrogiuolo replied: "My lord, pardon
me; I smile not at you or your demand but at the manner how I
came by these things."

Sicurano upon this answer was ten times more desirous than
before and said: "If Fortune favored thee in friendly manner by
the obtaining of these things, if it may be spoken, tell me how
thou hadst them." "My lord," answered Ambrogiuolo, "these
things, with many more beside, were given me by a gentlewoman of Genoa named Madam Zinevra, the wife to one Bernabò Lomellino, in recompense of one night's lodging with her,
and she desired me to keep them for her sake. Now, the main
reason of my smiling was the remembrance of her husband's
folly in waging five thousand ducats of gold against one thousand of mine that I should not obtain my will of his wife, which
I did and thereby won the wager. But he, who better deserved to
be punished for his folly than she who was but sick of all
women's disease, returning from Paris to Genoa, caused her to
be slain, as afterward it was reported by himself."

When Sicurano heard this horrible lie, immediately she con-
ceived† that this was the occasion of her husband's hatred to her
and all the hard haps which she had since suffered. Whereupon
she reputed it for more than a mortal sin if such a villain should
pass without due punishment. Sicurano seemed to like well this
report and grew into such familiarity with Ambrogiuolo that, by

*once.
†understood.

her persuasions, when the fair was ended, she took him higher*
with her into Alexandria and all his wares along with him, fur-
nishing him with a fit and convenient shop where he made great
benefit of his merchandises, trusting all his moneys in the Captain's custody because it was the safest course for him; and so
he continued there with no mean contentment.

Much did she pity her husband's perplexity, devising by what
good and warrantable means she might make known her inno-
cency to him, wherein her place and authority did greatly stead
her; and she wrought with divers gallant merchants of Genoa
that then remained in Alexandria, and by virtue of the Sultan's
friendly letters beside, to bring him thither upon an especial occasion. Come he did, albeit in poor and mean order, which soon
was better altered by her appointment and he very honorably
though in private entertained† by divers of her worthy friends
till time did favor what she further intended.

In the expectation of Bernabò's arrival, she had so prevailed
with Ambrogiuolo that the same tale which he formerly told to
her he delivered again in presence of the Sultan, who seemed to
be well pleased with it. But after she had once seen her husband, she thought upon her more serious business, providing
herself of an apt opportunity when she entreated such favor of
the Sultan that both the men might be brought before him
where, if Ambrogiuolo would not confess without constraint
that which he had made his vaunt of concerning Bernabò's
wife, he might be compelled thereto perforce.

Sicurano's word was a law with the Sultan, so that, Ambrogiuolo and Bernabò being brought face to face, the Sultan
with a stern and angry countenance, in the presence of a most
princely assembly, commanded Ambrogiuolo to declare the
truth, yea, upon peril of his life, by what means he won the wager of the five thousand golden ducats he received of Bernabò.
Ambrogiuolo, seeing Sicurano there present, upon whose favor
he wholly relied, yet perceiving her looks likewise to be as
dreadful as the Sultan's and hearing her threaten him with most
grievous torments except he revealed the truth indeed, you may
easily guess, fair company, in what condition he stood at that instant.

*farther inland.
†welcomed.

Frowns and fury he beheld on either side, and Bernabò standing before him (with a world of famous witnesses) to hear his lie confounded by his own confession and his tongue to deny what it had before so constantly avouched. Yet, dreaming on no other pain or penalty but restoring back the five thousand ducats of gold and the other things by him purloined, truly he revealed the whole form of his falsehood. Then Sicurano, according as the Sultan had formerly commanded him, turning to Bernabò, said: "And thou, upon the suggestion of this foul lie, what didst thou to thy wife?" "Being," quoth Bernabò, "overcome with rage for the loss of my money and the dishonor I supposed to receive by my wife, I caused a servant of mine to kill her, and, as he credibly avouched, her body was devoured by ravenous wolves in a moment after."

These things being thus spoken and heard in the presence of the Sultan, and no reason as yet made known why the case was so seriously urged and to what end it would succeed, Sicurano spoke in this manner to the Sultan. "My gracious lord, you may plainly perceive in what degree that poor gentlewoman might make her vaunt, being so well provided both of a loving friend and a husband. Such was the friend's love that in an instant and by a wicked lie he robbed her both of her renown and honor and bereft her also of her husband. And her husband, rather crediting another's falsehood than the invincible truth whereof he had faithful knowledge by long and very honorable experience, caused her to be slain and made food for devouring wolves. Beside all this, such was the good will and affection borne to that woman both by friend and husband that the longest continuer of them in her company makes them alike in knowledge of her. But, because your great wisdom knoweth perfectly what each of them have worthily deserved, if you please, in your ever-known gracious benignity, to permit the punishment of the deceiver and pardon the party so deceived, I will procure such means that she shall appear here in your presence and theirs."

The Sultan, being desirous to give Sicurano all manner of satisfaction, having followed the course so industriously, bade him to produce the woman and he was well contented. Whereat Bernabò stood much amazed because he verily believed that she was dead. And Ambrogiuolo, foreseeing already a preparation for punishment, feared that the repayment of the money would not now serve his turn, not knowing also what he should further hope or suspect if the woman herself did personally appear, which he imagined would be a miracle. Sicurano, having thus obtained the Sultan's permission, in tears humbling herself at his feet, in a moment she lost her manly voice and demeanor as knowing that she was now no longer to use them but must truly witness what she was indeed; and therefore thus spoke:

"Great Sultan, I am the miserable and unfortunate Zinevra, that for the space of six whole years have wandered through the world in the habit of a man, falsely and most maliciously slandered by this villainous traitor Ambrogiuolo, and by this unkind, cruel husband betrayed to his servant to be slain and left to be devoured by savage beasts." Afterward, desiring such garments as better fitted for her and showing her breasts, she made it apparent before the Sultan and his assistants that she was the very same woman indeed. Then, turning herself to Ambrogiuolo with more than manly courage, she demanded of him when and where it was that he lay with her, as villainously he was not ashamed to make his vaunt. But he, having already acknowledged the contrary, being stricken dumb with shameful disgrace, was not able to utter one word.

The Sultan, who had always reputed Sicurano to be a man, having heard and seen so admirable an accident,* was so amazed in his mind that many times he was very doubtful whether this was a dream or an absolute relation of truth. But, after he had more seriously considered thereon and found it to be real and infallible, with extraordinary gracious praises he commended the life, constancy, conditions, and virtues of Zinevra, whom till that time he had always called Sicurano. So, committing her to the company of honorable ladies to be changed from her manly habit, he pardoned Bernabò her husband according to her request formerly made, although he had more justly deserved death; which likewise himself confessed and, falling at the feet of Zinevra, desired her in tears to forgive his rash transgression; which most lovingly she did, kissing and embracing him a thousand times.

Then the Sultan strictly commanded that on some high and eminent place of the city Ambrogiuolo should be bound and impaled on a stake, having his naked body anointed all over with honey and never to be taken off until of itself it fell in pieces, which according to the sentence was presently† performed.

* so wondrous an event.
† immediately.

Next, he gave express charge that all his money and goods should be given to Zinevra; which valued above ten thousand double ducats. Forthwith* a solemn feast was prepared wherein much honor was done to Bernabò, being the husband of Zinevra; and to her, as to a most worthy woman and matchless wife, he gave in costly jewels as also vessels of gold and silver plate so much as amounted to above ten thousand double ducats more.

When the feasting was finished, he caused a ship to be furnished for them, granting them license to depart for Genoa when they pleased, whither they returned most rich and joyfully, being welcomed home with great honor; especially Madam Zinevra, whom everyone supposed to be dead. And always after, so long as she lived, she was most famous for her manifold virtues. But as for Ambrogiuolo, the very same day that he was impaled on the stake, anointed with honey, and fixed in the place appointed to his no mean† torment, he not only died but likewise was devoured to the bare bones by flies, wasps, and hornets, whereof the country notoriously aboundeth. And his bones in full form and fashion remained strangely black for a long while after, knit together by the sinews; as a witness, to many thousands of people which afterward beheld the‡ carcass, of his wickedness against so good and virtuous a woman that had not so much as a thought of any evil towards him. And thus was the proverb truly verified that shame succeedeth after ugly sin and the deceiver is trampled and trod by such as himself hath deceived.

---

*1620 has "Forth-with with."
†inconsiderable.
‡1620 has "his."

RAPHAEL HOLINSHED

From The Chronicles of England, Scotland, and Ireland (1587)

[32]* "Kymbeline" or "Cymbeline," the son of Theomantius, was of the Britons made king after the decease of his father in the year of the world 3944, after the building of Rome 728, and before the birth of our Saviour 33. This man (as some write) was brought up at Rome and there made knight by Augustus Caesar, under whom he served in the wars, and was in such favor with him that he was at liberty to pay his tribute or not. Little other mention is made of his doings, except that during his reign the Saviour of the world, our Lord Jesus Christ the only son of God, was borne of a virgin about the twenty-third year of the reign of this Cymbeline. . . . Touching the continuance of the years of Cymbeline's reign, some writers do vary, but the best approved affirm that he reigned thirty-five years and then died, and was buried at London, leaving behind him two sons Guiderius and Arviragus.

But here is to be noted that, although our histories do affirm that as well this Cymbeline as also his father Theomantius lived in quiet with the Romans, and continually to them paid the tributes which the Britons had covenanted with Julius Caesar to pay, yet we find in the Roman writers that after Julius Caesar's death, when Augustus had taken upon him the rule of the empire, the Britons refused to pay that tribute. Whereat, as Cornelius Tacitus reporteth, Augustus (being otherwise occupied)

From *Shakespeare's Holinshed*, edited by Richard Hosley. New York: G. P. Putnam's Sons, 1968, pp. 4–8. Copyright © 1968 by Richard Hosley. Reprinted by permission of the publisher.
*Vol. 1, *History of England.* [References at heads of paragraphs are to pages of the appropriate volume of Holinshed (editor's note).]

was contented to wink. Howbeit, through earnest calling upon to recover his right by such as were desirous to see the uttermost of the British kingdom, at length, to wit in the tenth year after the death of Julius Caesar, which was about the thirteenth year of the said Theomantius, Augustus made provision to pass with an army over into Britain, and was come forward upon his journey into Gallia Celtica or, as we may say, into these hither parts of France.

But here receiving advertisements that the Pannonians, which inhabited the country now called Hungary, and the Dalmatians, whom now we call Slavonians, had rebelled, he thought it best first to subdue those rebels near home rather than to seek new countries and leave such in hazard whereof he had present possession. And so, turning his power against the Pannonians and Dalmatians, he left off for a time the wars of Britain. . . . But whether this controversy, which appeareth to fall forth betwixt the Britons and Augustus, was occasioned by Cymbeline or some other prince of the Britons, I have not to avouch. For that by our writers it is reported that Cymbeline, being brought up in Rome and knighted in the court of Augustus, ever showed himself a friend to the Romans, and chiefly was loath to break with them because* the youth of the Briton nation should not be deprived of the benefit to be trained and brought up among the Romans; whereby they might learn both to behave themselves like civil† men and to attain to the knowledge of feats of war.

[33] But whether for this respect or for that it pleased the almighty God so to dispose the minds of men at that present, not only the Britons but in manner all other nations were contented to be obedient to the Roman Empire. That this was true in the Britons, it is evident enough by Strabo's words, which are in effect as followeth. At this present (saith he) certain princes of Britain, procuring by ambassadors and dutiful demeanors the amity of the Emperor Augustus, have offered in the Capitol unto the gods presents or gifts, and have ordained the whole isle in a manner to be appertinent, proper, and familiar to the Romans. They are burdened with sore customs which they pay for wares, either to be sent forth into Gallia or brought from thence, which are commonly ivory vessels,

*So that.
†Educated.

shears, ouches* or earrings, and other conceits† made of amber and glasses, and suchlike manner of merchandise. So that now there is no need of any army or garrison of men-of-war to keep the isle, for there needeth not past one legion of footmen, or some wing of horsemen, to gather up and receive the tribute. . . .

Guiderius, the first son of Cymbeline (of whom Harrison saith nothing), began his reign in the seventeenth year after the incarnation of Christ. This Guiderius, being a man of stout courage,‡ gave occasion of breach of peace betwixt the Britons and Romans, denying to pay them tribute and procuring the people to new insurrections which by one mean or other made open rebellion, as Gyldas saith.

* * *

[154]** From thence the army of the Danes passed through Angus unto the river of Tay, all the people of the countries by which they marched fleeing afore them. King Kenneth [of Scotland] at the same time lay at Stirling, where, hearing of these grievous news, he determined forthwith to raise his people and to go against his enemies. . . .

[155] The Danes, being backed with the mountain, were constrained to leave the same and with all speed to come forward upon their enemies, that by joining, they might avoid the danger of the Scottishmen's arrows and darts. By this means therefore they came to hand strokes, in manner before the sign was given on either part to the battle. The fight was cruel on both sides; and nothing hindered the Scots so much as going about to cut off the heads of the Danes, ever as they might overcome them. Which manner being noted of the Danes, and perceiving that there was no hope of life but in victory, they rushed forth with such violence upon their adversaries that first the right and then after the left wing of the Scots was constrained to retire and flee back, the middleward†† stoutly yet keeping their ground; but the same stood in such danger, being now left naked on the sides, that the victory must needs have remained with the Danes had not a renewer of the battle come in time by the appointment (as is to be thought) of almighty God.

*Brooches.
†Fancy articles.
‡Brave spirit.
**Vol. 2, *History of Scotland*.
††Main body of soldiers.

For as it chanced, there was in the next field at the same time an husbandman, with two of his sons busy about his work, named Hay; a man strong and stiff in making and shape of body but endued with a valiant courage [5.3.15]. This Hay, beholding the King with the most part of the nobles fighting with great valiancy in the middleward, now destitute of the wings and in great danger to be oppressed by the great violence of his enemies, caught a ploughbeam in his hand and, with the same exhorting his sons to do the like, hasted toward the battle, there to die rather amongst other in defense of his country than to remain alive after the discomfiture, in miserable thralldom and bondage, of the cruel and most unmerciful enemies. There was near to the place of the battle a long lane fenced on the sides with ditches and walls made of turf, through the which the Scots which fled were beaten down by the enemies on heaps.

Here Hay with his sons supposing they might best stay the flight, placed themselves overthwart the lane, beat them back whom they met fleeing, and spared neither friend nor foe; but down they went, all such as came within their reach, wherewith divers hardy personages cried unto their fellows to return back unto the battle, for there was a new power of Scottishmen come to their succors by whose aid the victory might be easily obtained of their most cruel adversaries the Danes. Therefore might they choose whether they would be slain of their own fellows coming to their aid, or to return again to fight with the enemies. The Danes, being here stayed in the lane by the great valiancy of the father and the sons, thought verily there had been some great succors of Scots come to the aid of their King and, thereupon, ceasing from further pursuit, fled back in great disorder unto the other of their fellows fighting with the middleward of the Scots.

The Scots also that before was chased, being encouraged herewith, pursued the Danes unto the place of the battle right fiercely. Whereupon Kenneth, perceiving his people to be thus recomforted, and his enemies partly abashed,* called upon his men to remember their duties; and now, sith their adversaries' hearts began (as they might perceive) to faint, he willed them to follow upon them manfully, which if they did he assured them that the victory undoubtedly should be theirs. The Scots, encouraged with the King's words, laid about them so earnestly

*Put to confusion.

that in the end the Danes were constrained to forsake the field, and the Scots, eagerly pursuing in the chase, made great slaughter of them as they fled. This victory turned highly to the praise of the Scottish nobility, the which, fighting in the middleward, bore still the brunt of the battle, continuing manfully therein even to the end. But Hay, who in such wise (as is before mentioned) stayed them that fled, causing them to return again to the field, deserved immortal fame and commendation, for by his means chiefly was the victory achieved. And therefore, on the morrow after, when the spoil of the field and of the enemies' camp (which they had left void) should be divided, the chiefest part was bestowed on him and his two sons, by consent of all the multitude; the residue being divided amongst the soldiers and men-of-war, according to the ancient custom used amongst this nation.

Commentaries

G. WILSON KNIGHT

From The Crown of Life

The Vision dramatizes a choral prayer imploring the divinity to relieve the unjust sufferings of Posthumus. We shall next notice . . . the relation here of humanity to the divine, with especial regard to prayer. . . .

The Vision of Jupiter certainly occurs in a work saturated with religious suggestion. The people are not only vengeful; they can also repent. There is the forgiveness of both Posthumus and Imogen of each other before they learn of Iachimo's plot. Posthumus' remorse, as in the soliloquy just noticed, is powerful and joined with the truly remarkable thought—considering Shakespeare's usual attitude—that Imogen's unfaithfulness is a mere slip (5.1.12). We have Iachimo's summoning conscience (5.2.1) and later repentance, with Posthumus' finely worded forgiveness (5.5.417–20). Cymbeline himself finally realizes how he has been deceived, and forgives everyone, saying, "Pardon's the word to all" (422). The main people are shown as drawing towards a more godlike understanding.

The gods are even more frequently mentioned than in *King Lear*; and, as in *King Lear*, they are entwined with meditations

From *The Crown of Life: Essays in Interpretation of Shakespeare's Final Plays*, by G. Wilson Knight. London: Methuen, 1948, pp. 176, 179–81, 183–86, 189–90, 201–02. Reprinted by permission of the publisher.

on human justice or injustice. When Iachimo says it is "an office of the gods to venge" Posthumus' betrayal (1.6.92), the thought is a weaker version of Albany's two pronouncements on divine interposition in *King Lear* (4.2.46–50, 78–80). More directly comparable is Cymbeline's comment on the death of his wicked Queen, on whom, he says, the heavens "in justice, both on her and hers/Have laid most heavy hand" (5.5.463–64). The theology in *Cymbeline* is both more optimistic and more insistent than in *Lear*. There is a belief in "heaven's bounty" (1.6.78), in gracious (1.4.80) powers from whom good things come: Imogen is "the gift of the gods" (78), they made her sweet disposition (1.6.177), "the gods" make Belarius and the two boys "preservers" of Cymbeline's throne (5.5.1). If things go wrong, the people accept misfortune with a stoic faith in the guiding powers: Imogen accepts Pisanio's advice, recognizing that it is "all the comfort/The gods will diet" her with (3.4.180–81); "Let ordinance," says Arviragus, "Come as the gods foresay it" (4.2.145–46); Pisanio, baffled by many complications, contents himself with "The heavens still must work" (4.3.41); Lucius faces death in stoic resignation to the will of "the gods" (5.5.78); even men's "bloods," that is their physical life, are said to "obey the heavens" (1.1.1, 2). Britain would have lost "But that the heavens fought" (5.3.4). Man is here utterly dependent, more so than in *King Lear*, on the "gods" or "heavens" whose creature he is. That is why the people talk so naturally to them. Imogen half speaks to "Jove" as to a companion (3.6.6); when she wakes beside a dead body, her immediate cry is, "O gods and goddesses!" (4.2.295); there is her typical and pretty oath in misfortune "'Ods pittikins" (293). When she introduces herself to Caius Lucius as the servant of "Richard du Champ," she wryly hopes that the gods, if they happen to hear her falsehood, will forgive it (379): the gods are always, as it were, just round the corner, listening, likely to interrupt. The tendency is yet stronger with Posthumus, as we shall see. Guiderius and Arviragus have an equivalent sense of divine nearness though with them it is, aptly, felt most strongly through the sun (4.4.34, 41).

This prevailing sense of heaven's nearness shapes itself naturally into blessings and prayers, such as "The gods protect you" (1.1.128), "May the gods/Direct you to the best" (3.4.193–94), "Flow, flow,/You heavenly blessings, on her" (3.5.157–58), and "The benediction of these covering heavens/Fall on their heads like dew" (5.5.350–51). The gods are normally kind, and sus-

ceptible to pleading. When the possibility of a second love is
suggested to him, Posthumus exclaims:

> You gentle gods, give me but this I have,
> And sear up my embracements from a next
> With bonds of death!

(1.1.115–17)

Imogen, receiving his letter, slips naturally into

> You good gods
> Let what is here contain'd relish of love . . .

(3.2.29–30)

Or, when things are cruel:

> But if there be
> Yet left in heaven as small a drop of pity,
> As a wren's eye, fear'd gods, a part of it!

(4.2.303–05)

More formal, and Christian, prayers are involved when she
wishes she had charged the absent Posthumus

> At the sixth hour of morn, at noon, at midnight,
> To encounter me with orisons, for then
> I am in heaven for him.

(1.3.31–33)

We see her actually praying in her chamber:

> To your protection I commend me, gods!
> From fairies and the tempters of the night
> Guard me, beseech ye!

(2.2.8–10)

* * *

. . . The gods have been drawing nearer and nearer; and we
are prepared for the Ghosts' final invocation and the logical
though startling climax of Jupiter's appearance. If he does not
appear, to what do these tormented soliloquies lead?

The Vision is exactly in tone with the play's theological

impressionism, which, though a continuation of normal Shake-spearian thought, is, in its peculiar emphasis, new; recalling *King Lear* most, but with something of the religious optimism of *Pericles* and *The Winter's Tale*, though to be subtly distinguished nevertheless from the "fortune" of the one and the nature, in association with Apollo, of the other.

But, it may be said, the many appearances of "gods" and "heavens" in the text must be distinguished from a mythological deity such as Jupiter. Is there, it will be asked, a soil, as it were, of classical mythology rich enough to bear this staggering *deus ex machina?* The answer is that *Cymbeline,* whose purpose is in part to emphasize the importance of ancient Rome in Britain's history, probably exceeds any other Shakespearian play in its fecundity of classical, and especially mythological, reference.

Imogen is compared to "th' Arabian bird" (1.6.17) or Phoenix; Iachimo sees himself as Tarquin (2.2.12) and Imogen's bracelet as "the Gordian knot" (34); Imogen in bed reads the story of Philomel and Tereus (45), while her tapestry shows Cleopatra on Cydnus (2.4.69–72). Slander, says Pisanio "out-venoms all the worms of Nile" (3.4.35); Imogen refers to Aeneas and Sinon (3.4.58, 59); "not Hercules," says Guiderius, "could have knocked out" Cloten's brains, since "he had none" (4.2.114–15); he refers later to Thersites and Ajax (253). Imogen, for once stung to violence, imprecates "all curses madded Hecuba gave the Greeks" (313) on the supposed murderer of her lord. As for deities, no other play is so rich in Roman gods and goddesses: they are, moreover, presented with a peculiar feeling for their particular natures, they are *intimately* discerned. The comparison of Imogen to "Cytherea" is vividly conceived:

> Cytherea
> How bravely thou becom'st thy bed! fresh lily
> And whiter than the sheets.
>
> (2.2.14–16)

Britain's coasts stand "as Neptune's park" (3.1.19), the roaring waters being carefully realized. Juno's irascible jealousy is assumed (as, too, in our Vision) in Pisanio's remark that Imogen's beauty "made great Juno angry" (3.4.166); so is her regal dignity in the thought that Imogen's skill in cookery "sauc'd our broths as Juno had been sick, and he her dieter" (4.2.50–51). Two aspects of the sun god are presented: one in "the greedy touch/Of common-kissing Titan" (3.4.163–64); the other, in suggestion of his resplendent chariot, "had it been a carbuncle/Of Phoebus' wheel" (5.5.189–90) and the thought of "Phoebus" arising and watering his heavenly "steeds" in Cloten's serenade (2.3.21). There are the "two winking"—i.e. blind—"Cupids of silver" in Imogen's chamber (2.4.89), while a love-letter is called "young Cupid's tables" (3.2.39). Imogen shows

> A pudency so rosy the sweet view on't
> Might well have warm'd old Saturn.
>
> (2.5.11–12)

Diana gets a recurring notice. To preserve chastity is to "live like Diana's priest, betwixt cold sheets" (1.6.133); gold makes "Diana's rangers false" (2.3.69); Posthumus' mother seemed "the Dian of that time" (2.5.7); Posthumus speaks of his lady "as Dian had hot dreams" (5.5.180). Imogen's chamber aptly has a carving showing "chaste Dian bathing" (2.4.82). The eternity of art is well hinted in report of ladies

> . . . for feature laming
> The shrine of Venus or straight-pight Minerva,
> Postures beyond brief nature.
>
> (5.5.163–65)

The list is itself significant, but the degree of intimacy, the use of adjectives and reference to the typical behaviour or duties of the divinities concerned is even more so; mythology is felt as coming alive as we read. The Ghosts' references to Mars and Juno ("that thy adulteries rates and revenges," 5.4.31–32) is in keeping; and Sicilius' intimately realized comment later (84–89) on Jupiter's, and his eagle's, typical behavior a natural culmination.

Apart from Jupiter, the deities most honored here are (1) Diana, the goddess who actually appears in *Pericles*, and (2) Phoebus-Apollo, who rules in *The Winter's Tale*. But in this peculiarly Roman play, the main emphasis naturally falls on Jupiter, who is, as one expects, mentioned most frequently of all, the words, "Jove" or "Jupiter" recurring about a dozen times outside the Vision. "Jove" is exclamatory at 3.3.88; and part of a tiny prayer at 2.4.98 and 3.6.6. "By Jupiter" occurs twice at a central moment in the action (2.4.121, 122; and again at 3.5.84 and 3.6.42). Elsewhere we have "Jove knows what man thou

mightst have made" (4.2.207), and "Wert thou the son of Jupiter"
(2.3.125). Lucius cries "Great Jupiter be prais'd" (5.3.84). Imogen describes Posthumus as Hamlet describes his father:

> I know the shape of 's leg, this is his hand,
> His foot Mercurial, his Martial thigh,
> The brawns of Hercules, but his Jovial face. . . .
>
> (4.2.309–11)

Jupiter moreover contributes dramatically to the play's unfold-
ing purpose in the Soothsayer's earlier vision:

> *Lucius.*   . . . Now, sir,
>   What have you dream'd of late of this war's
>   purpose?
> *Soothsayer.* Last night the very gods show'd me a vision—
>   I fast and prayed for their intelligence—thus:
>   I saw Jove's bird, the Roman eagle, wing'd
>   From the spongy south to this part of the west,
>   There vanish'd in the sunbeams; which portends,
>   Unless my sins abuse my divination,
>   Success to the Roman host
>
> (344–52)

We accordingly have Jupiter's eagle already associated with a
prophecy outside our main Vision. The Soothsayer's vision
forms a miniature of what is shortly to be dramatized: both are
dreams; both suggest a transference of power, or virtue, in the
one personal, or matrimonial, and in the other national, from
Rome to Britain. Posthumus later reports his experience:

>   As I slept, methought,
> Great Jupiter, upon his eagle back'd,
> Appear'd to me, with other spritely shows
> Of mine own kindred.
>
> (5.5.426–29)

Jupiter, Rome's chief god, naturally dominates the play's conclusion, where the Soothsayer, after remarking that "the fingers of
the powers above do tune/The harmony of this peace" (465–66),
recounts and reinterprets his own dream, relating the eagle to
Rome; Cymbeline carrying on with "Laud we the gods" (475) and

deciding to ratify the peace "in the temple of great Jupiter" (481).

No other play gives Jupiter quite such honor, but he is Shakespeare's most frequent and most powerful god throughout; and after the parts played by the less important Diana and Apollo in *Pericles* and *The Winter's Tale,* one surely here expects Jupiter, who seems to have been reserved for the purpose, to do something spectacular.

Here is our stage-direction:

Jupiter descends in thunder and lightning, sitting upon an eagle. He throws a thunderbolt. The Ghosts fall on their knees.

Thunder and lightning are usual in Shakespeare's directions and both are imagistically associated with Jupiter; indeed, we find yet another example of the process already observed, whereby old tragic imagery becomes new dramatic actuality, Jupiter's appearance corresponding to Pericles' entry on a tempest-tossed ship, the throwing of Thaisa, as a-jewel-in-a-casket, overboard and the appearance of a bear during storm in *The Winter's Tale.* One is scarcely surprised to find yet another important tragic impression brought similarly to life. Is Jupiter's appearance any more surprising, or technically weak, than that of the bear? Shakespeare has made peace with one of his two main tempest-gods, Neptune and Jupiter (compactly presented together at *Coriolanus,* 3.1.255–6), at *Pericles,* 5.1 (direction); it is natural that he should now make peace with the other.

* * *

... How exactly these optimistic miniatures ... reflect, in Shakespeare's usual manner, our central symbolism, wherein the god, descending to thunder and lightning and throwing his dreaded bolt, proceeds to announce a reversal of the hero's suffering and a general happiness.

This is, of course, precisely what one would expect. Jupiter functions here as does Diana in *Pericles.* The theophany is there less powerful, the play's most potent moments concerning the actual resurrection and reunions; the same happens in *The Winter's Tale,* where Apollo remains a background, though appallingly potent, deity. In *Cymbeline* the poet attempts to make his theophany central and dominating. You can feel a progress from the rather pale figure of Diana through Apollo to Jupiter. Indeed, the description of Apollo's oracle directly forecasts *Cymbeline*:

Dion.   . . . O, the sacrifice!
How ceremonious, solemn and unearthly
It was i' the offering!
Cleomenes.   But of all, the burst
And the ear-deafening voice o' the oracle,
Kin to Jove's thunder, so surpris'd my sense,
That I was nothing.

(The Winter's Tale, 3.1.6–11)

Apollo's answer is in the exact style of Jupiter's tablet. Later we have fearful evidence of the god's powers in the trial scene and Antigonus' account of his dream-vision of Hermione, attributed to Apollo (3.3.15–45). It is natural that *Cymbeline*, whose Jupiter corresponds to Diana and Apollo in the sister-plays, should offer something even bolder to correspond to its greater stress on classical deities. *The Tempest* contains a masque where Juno, Ceres and Iris appear; while Ariel's thunderous appearance as a Harpy pronouncing judgment and conditional mercy is a close equivalent to Jupiter's appearance and actions. Finally *Henry VIII* contains Queen Katherine's vision of angels, introduced by an elaborately ritualistic direction in a style exactly recalling that in *Cymbeline*. Posthumus' and the Queen's reactions are similar. Compare

Posthumus.   But—O scorn!—
Gone! they went hence as soon as they were born:
And so I am awake. Poor wretches, that depend
On greatness' favor, dream as I have done;
Wake, and find nothing.

(5.4.95–99)

with

Q. Katherine. Spirits of peace, where are ye? Are ye all gone,
And leave me here in wretchedness behind ye?

(Henry VIII, 4.2.83–84)

* * *

The Vision is, indeed, purest Shakespeare, from whatever aspect we regard it. Here is a miniature of its main associations neatly compacted in Shakespeare's early work:

Thus yields the *cedar* to the axe's edge,
Whose arms gave shelter to the *princely eagle*,
Under whose shade the ramping *lion* slept,
Whose top branch over peer'd *Jove's* spreading tree,
And kept low shrubs from winter's powerful *wind*.

                                    (*3 Henry VI*, 5.2.11–15)

The Final Plays, with great consistency, rely on an expansion of earlier imagery and attendant symbolism as a basis for dramatic action; and what truth they reveal is accordingly a truth lying near to the heart of poetry.

Therefore our acceptance or rejection of this crucial scene is of primary importance. More even is at stake than our understanding of Shakespeare's reading of his country's destiny. We have regarded Jupiter as preeminently the Romans' god; but he is, throughout Shakespeare, more than that, and may often be best rendered "God," a word Shakespeare was diffident of using on the stage, though it occurs at *King Lear*, 5.3.17. The puritanical Malvolio thanks "Jove" for his good fortune (*Twelfth Night*, 2.5.195); while at *Measure for Measure*, 2.2.111, the Deity serves powerfully (in passages already quoted) to extend some of Shakespeare's purest and most fervent passages of Christian doctrine, explicitly referring, through the pronoun "He" (2.2.74–76), to the Christian God. We may practically equate Shakespeare's Jove with Jehovah, whilst also observing that, since representation of the supreme deity cannot be completely successful (as Milton also found), Shakespeare probably gains rather than loses in *Cymbeline* by reliance on a semifictional figure allowing a maximum of dignity with a minimum of risk. So, within a plot variously concerned with the building up and dispelling of deceptive appearance, we find, at its heart, this vivid revelation of a kindly Providence behind mortality's drama. Our apocalypse accordingly stands central among Shakespeare's last plays; study of it radiates out first into *Cymbeline*, next into the final group, and lastly into the mass of Shakespeare's work. It is our one precise anthropomorphic expression of that beyond-tragedy recognition felt through the miracles and resurrections of sister-plays and reaching Christian formulation in *Henry VIII*.

BERTRAND EVANS

From Shakespeare's Comedies

Though winds and waves, tempests and seas are absent from it, the world of *Cymbeline,* too, presents a lasting storm; what is more, it offers even less assurance than was ours during *Pericles* that the storm will ever blow to a happy ending. Whereas in *Pericles,* through such signs as the billow that saves Thaisa, we sensed a force, blurred but benign, protecting the royal family, and knew during the latter half of the action that Thaisa and Marina were merely lost, not dead—in *Cymbeline* we must scrutinize the face of the universe intently in order to discern the slightest sign of comfort. In the wisdom of the physician Cornelius and the loyalty of the servant Pisanio we have signs that goodness and truth at least have allies; but these are mainly bystanders to the torrent that sweeps Posthumus and Imogen along, and though they mean well we cannot suppose that their utmost will prevail against the great odds. Moreover, even as late as 4.3, when Pisanio hopefully ventures that "Fortune brings in some boats that are not steered" (46), we lack evidence that any "outside" intelligence, for good or ill, watches over man; and Pisanio's comment, besides coming later in the action, is not even so reassuring as the giant billow of *Pericles.* We do not learn until Posthumus's vision in 5.4, when Jupiter claims the credit for the conduct and control of everything—

> Be not with mortal accidents opprest.
> No care of yours it is; you know 'tis ours.
> Whom best I love I cross; to make my gift,
> The more delayed, delighted.   (5.4.69–72)

From *Shakespeare's Comedies,* by Bertrand Evans. Oxford: The Clarendon Press, 1960, pp. 247–48, 252–58, 277–78, 283–89. Reprinted by permission of the publisher.

—that any hand holds the rudder of man's ship. In this respect, then, *Cymbeline* resembles *Pericles* but goes much farther in the same direction—away from the old, insistent reassurance, toward fear that all can never be well.

But though the worlds represented are thus alike, the workmanship of representation differs as ineptness from virtuosity. On the evidence of *Pericles* and *Troilus and Cressida* alone, it would be necessary to conclude that when Shakespeare attempted to depict a world lacking design and purpose, uncontrolled by either man's will or external force, his own art caught the disorder of the world represented. *Cymbeline* is the contradiction of this evidence: as an exhibition of technical skill in the management of the dramatic devices he had favored from the first, it has no equal. *The Merry Wives of Windsor,* which put on an earlier dazzling display, is only a finger exercise beside *Cymbeline*.

To master the representation of his new world, Shakespeare called on all the old devices—but especially on those most useful in creating and exploiting discrepant awarenesses.* Whereas in *Pericles* the high proportion of scenes in which we hold advantage resulted mainly from use of extradramatic features, in *Cymbeline* it results entirely from dramatic devising. In managing the discrepant awarenesses of this one play, Shakespeare calls upon all the means he had found useful from *The Comedy of Errors* through *Measure for Measure.* As a result we hold advantage over some or all participants in twenty-three of twenty-seven scenes; advantage at some time over every named person; and simultaneous, multiple advantages over all persons in many scenes.

These facts would not alone make *Cymbeline* exceptional: even in *The Comedy of Errors* we held advantage in all scenes except the first and over all persons except Emilia, and in all of the mature romantic comedies multiplicity of discrepancies created by multiple dramatic devices, and multiplicity of effects resulting from exploitation of these discrepancies are the rule rather than the exception. What does make *Cymbeline* extraordinary is at once the fantastic complexity of its uses of discrepant awarenesses and the consummate skill with which its

---

*That is, dramatic ironies; compare Evans, p. vii: "Between the awareness that packs our minds and the ignorance that afflicts the participants lies a crucial—and highly exploitable—discrepancy" [editor's note].

intricacies are managed: with greater finality than does any
other play, it evinces Shakespeare's mastery of infinitely complex art. From the first his methods made heavy demands on
our minds in requiring them to accept, hold, and actively use
the advantages provided; but the tasks imposed by our advantages in *Cymbeline* are unprecedented. Here the uses of awareness are fairly gymnastic; our awareness is compelled through
a harder course of exercises than ever. From the point of view
of the creation, maintenance, and exploitation of discrepant
awarenesses—considered both quantitatively and artistically—
Cymbeline is Shakespeare's greatest achievement.

* * *

. . . Iachimo is unique outside of tragedy—a villain whose
vantage point is above that of other participants, and over
whom we ourselves have no advantage. In earlier plays some
benevolent force has stood guard over villainy, eyeing its
passes, ready to check it at need. The highest awareness has always belonged to good people. Don John of *Much Ado,* Shylock
of *The Merchant of Venice,* Angelo of *Measure for Measure* are
prevented not only from doing harm but even from appearing
really dangerous; at last, because of Prospero, the monsters of
The Tempest are pitiful even in their most swaggering moments.
But no force—*to our knowledge while action continues*—
watches Iachimo as Vincentio and Prospero watch Angelo and
Caliban.

The scene (1.4) of Posthumus and Iachimo's wager on Imogen's virtue gives us advantage over the heroine when she next
appears; henceforth she is never again mistress of her situation
and partner in our awareness. No heroine in the comedies is
cast in such a role—kept unaware so long, ignorant of so many
secrets, abused by so many practices, endangered from so many
quarters. Only Isabella of *Measure for Measure* spends nearly
as long in ignorance—but the cases are not comparable, for the
fact unknown to Isabella is the most comforting in her world,
the fact that her friendly "friar" is the all-powerful Duke. Beside Imogen's, the unknowing moments of earlier heroines
seem blessed, brief, trivial: those of Viola, unaware that Sebastian lives, and that the fierce duelist confronting her is a great
booby who wants only to make peace or run away; of Hero, unaware that cruel denunciation waits at the altar—but unaware
also that her name is already in process of being cleared; even

of Marina—after she has escaped the assassin's blow—unaware that forces of her "lasting storm" are converging on general re-union. If much that Imogen does not know is better than she supposes, yet much also is worse—and, worst of all, uncertain. "I see before me, man," she says ecstatically to Pisanio, setting off for Milford Haven to meet her banished husband; "nor here, nor here,/Nor what ensues, but have a fog in them/That I cannot look through" (3.2.78–80). But in truth she cannot see even straight ahead: not only will Posthumus not be at Milford Haven, but he has ordered her to be murdered on the road.

But Imogen is a deeply unaware heroine only because she is cast into an uncertain universe, too large for its puny inhabitants, where a lasting storm whirs friend from friend and all events "have a fog in them/That I cannot look through." Her unawareness is itself a sign of the fearsome world; for Imogen is anything but naïve, anything but naturally incompetent. She has no trace of that congenital affliction of persons who need no deceiving to be deceived—Bottom, Dogberry, Aguecheek, Malvolio: yet not even one of these remains so long ignorant of so much. The fact is that she is keen and capable. She looks through and through the Queen and Cloten; and her analysis of the situation in which we first find her and Posthumus is brilliant; so is her analysis of her circumstances after Posthumus has gone:

> A father cruel, and a stepdame false;
> A foolish suitor to a wedded lady
> That hath her husband banished. . . .
>
> (1.6.1–3)

If she lacks the aggressive self-sufficiency of Rosalind, yet she would have had no difficulty managing Rosalind's world. She would have managed Viola's tangled affairs with far less than Viola's distress. She would have failed at Helena's task—but, then, she would never have wished to succeed at it! She is approximately as able as Marina, who talks brothel keepers into giving her more congenial work, converts brothel habitués to churchgoers, and so far transforms one of these as to make him a proper husband. Neither Imogen nor Marina shows a decline in heroinely competence; *they are lost in their worlds only because their worlds are as they are.* Isabella of *Measure for Measure,* whose perspective is less true than Imogen's and whose

capability of dealing with life is inferior, is never so lost and
abused as Imogen; but her wicked world has Vincentio, without
whom she would have either to escape to the nunnery or be destroyed. Imogen strives alone in a world which has at least as
dire a need for a Vincentio, and in which there seems to be
none.

It is certainly not a sign of incompetence that Imogen falls
victim to Iachimo's practice. She is quick to recognize and
denounce his first attempt, when he makes a false report of
Posthumus's behavior in Rome and urges her to reciprocate:

> I dedicate myself to your sweet pleasure,
> More noble than that runagate to your bed,
> And will continue fast to your affection,
> Still close as sure.
>
> (136–39)

"Away," replies Imogen; "I do condemn mine ears that have/So
long attended thee" (141–42). Both her virtue and her rare
acumen speak here. There was every cause for her to be taken
in by Iachimo's report: she knows nothing of the wager; she
has perfect faith in Iachimo, who comes introduced by Posthumus himself as "one of the noblest note, to whose kindnesses I
am most infinitely tied"(22–23); she has heard of such Italian
temptations as might have overcome her own or any husband,
as she shows later in referring to "Some jay of Italy,/Whose
mother was her painting" (3.4.49–50).

But more than all is the reason of Iachimo himself, with
his subtle persuasiveness, the representation of which excels
the best of the kind that Shakespeare had achieved or would
achieve again. Iachimo works like Iago, seeming preoccupied
with his own musings while, as though unintentionally, he teases
on the mind of the victim; thus, with an apparent disregard of
Imogen, as though she should not hear, he debates with himself
how Posthumus could ever have been induced to change mis-
tresses:

> It cannot be i' th' eye, for apes and monkeys,
> 'Twixt two such shes, would chatter this way and
> Contemn with mows the other; nor i' th' judgment,
> For idiots, in this case of favor, would
> Be wisely definite; nor i' th' appetite—

> Sluttery, to such neat excellence opposed,
> Should make desire vomit emptiness,
> Not so allured to feed.

(1.6.39–46)

Not at all the meanest, Iachimo is the smoothest of Shakespeare's villains. Iago's front of a plain, blunt man is adequate to deceive Othello and everyone else in Venice and Cyprus; Iachimo's front is silken smooth, his persuasive charm irresistible. By all odds his is the finest language in the play. Shakespeare gives him the poet's tongue and the artist's eye: "On her left breast/A mole cinque-spotted, like the crimson drops/I' th' bottom of a cowslip" (2.2.37–38). The forty lines he speaks while Imogen lies asleep, "her sense but as a monument,/Thus in a chapel lying" (32–33), have a hypnotic fascination beyond any other passage in Shakespeare. It does not at all diminish Imogen that she is briefly spellbound by this villain's tongue; she is the more remarkable for having the strength to break the spell: "Away, I do condemn mine ears that have/So long attended thee" (1.6.141–42).

Shakespeare does not with Iachimo, as with Iago, cause him to expose to us in advance the devices of his cunning mind— and there is reason. Imogen's intellectual prestige is thus further protected: when she consents to receive the trunk in her own chamber "And pawn mine honor" (194) for the safety of its contents, we, too, are ignorant that the contents will be Iachimo himself. Perhaps we may guess; but the dramatist gives us no help in guessing. When his first attempt has failed, we have no way of knowing that Iachimo will try again. Never shrewder in all his shrewd management of our awareness than now, the dramatist gives him no private word with us, but allows us to hear exactly what Imogen hears:

> *Iach.* I have spoke this to know if your affiance
>   Were deeply rooted, and shall make your lord
>   That which he is, new o'er; and he is one
>   The truest mannered, such a holy witch
>   That he enchants societies into him;
>   Half all men's hearts are his.
> *Imo.*   You make amends.
> *Iach.* He sits 'mongst men like a descended god.
>   He hath a kind of honor sets him off
>   More than a mortal seeming. Be not angry,

Most mighty Princess, that I have adventured
To try your taking of a false report, which hath
Honored with confirmation your great judgment
In the election of a sir so rare,
Which you know cannot err.

(163–76)

Iachimo is cunning past men's thought: though we know of the
wager, whereas Imogen does not, we have no cause to doubt
that he has forfeited. When he turns as with an afterthought—"I
had almost forgot" (180)—to the next piece of business, it is
made to appear *to us as to Imogen* that his new request has no
possible connection with what has just passed. He does not immediately mention a trunk, but describes with fine circumstan-
tial detail—not neglecting, as if incidentally, to lavish more
praise on Posthumus—the occasion of his journey and the character of his purchase:

'Tis plate of rare device, and jewels
Of rich and exquisite form, their values great,
And I am something curious, being strange,
To have them in safe stowage. May it please you
To take them in protection?

(189–93)

"I will keep them/In my bedchamber," says Imogen, and then
Iachimo: "They are in a trunk,/Attended by my men" (195–97).
There is no more discussion of the matter, the subject being
suddenly changed to the question of Iachimo's return to Rome.
Only at the tag end of the scene is the trunk mentioned again—
and now without reference to the bedchamber. Thus, the last
idea left in our minds is of no possible trick of Iachimo's, but of
Imogen's responsibility to guard the plate and jewels: ". . . it
shall safe be kept/And truly yielded you" (209–10). If we have
any anxious thought, it is only that she may somehow fail in this
responsibility.

Since we are not to see Iachimo again until he emerges from
the trunk beside Imogen's bed, we should ordinarily expect him
to linger at the end of this scene in order to explain his intention.
But he leaves with Imogen, without so much as a smirk for our
advisement. The omission contradicts Shakespeare's method
in every play until now. Usually we would have been advised

explicitly even earlier—when Iachimo seemed to give up his hope of winning the wager—that he would shift from an honest test of Imogen's virtue to some treacherous device; next, as he continued to talk with Imogen about the plate and the jewels, the outline of his device would have taken definite shape in our minds; next, at the conclusion of the scene with Imogen, he would have remained for a moment to tell us plainly that he would enter the bedchamber in the trunk. There would have been even more: the bedchamber scene would not open as it now does—Imogen reading in bed, attended by her maid, the trunk resting to one side—but with the trunk being brought in, the bearers leaving, Iachimo then lifting the lid to glance around and speak a word to us: all this before Imogen should enter and go to bed. There would have followed Imogen's conversation with the maid—probably with some ironic allusions to the trunk and its precious contents—and then sleep, and only thereafter the emergence of Iachimo.

As the scenes are actually devised, however, not only is the usual care to make assurance double sure omitted, but the least suggestion that Iachimo will enter in the trunk is avoided. We may have guessed the truth, of course, or even have worked it out by reasoning that Iachimo's story of his mission to France to buy a present for the Emperor must be false, since Posthumus, whom he mentions as one of the contributors, would not have joined a group with Iachimo as "the factor for the rest." Yet so finely detailed is Iachimo's account of the mission, the jewels, and the "plate of rare device" that even after the incident is past we may wonder, at one level of consciousness, just where Iachimo temporarily hid these jewels and plate while he occupied their place in the trunk during the night!

The point, in any event, is that Shakespeare has not told us what to expect. He has not even told us that Iachimo is a villain; we cannot know that he is dishonorable until he emerges from the trunk. Though the wager he proposed to Posthumus was insulting, yet Posthumus accepted it—and Posthumus is a paragon. His first test of Imogen, though deceitful, is quite within the terms of the wager, hence no proof of villainy. When his first attempt fails, we have been given no reason to doubt that, finding Imogen's virtue so far incorruptible as to make further trial absurd, he simply abandons his attempt to win Posthumus's ring. We have been given no reason to know, therefore, while Imogen lies reading, attended by her maid, that the trunk beside the bed contains other than jewels and plate. We have been given no reason to suppose but that Iachimo lies in his own room, sleeping or contemplating his return to Rome and his admission of failure. ·

By denying us the usual advance notice, Shakespeare prevents our gaining advantage over his heroine during the part of the action which is most vital for what follows. We are less likely to think her naïve in being deceived by the trunk when we ourselves have been deceived. It is the perfection of Shakespeare's management of the awarenesses during this central incident that he has at once made it convincing that Iachimo's trick should succeed, and avoided dimming Imogen's heroinely luster. Once Iachimo has gained access to the chamber, the problem of protecting Imogen from seeming too easily "taken in" vanishes—for she is now asleep, "her sense but as a monument,/Thus in a chapel lying" (2.2.32–33), while Iachimo greedily—yet somehow worshipfully, with an aesthete's relish—stores his, mind with the evidence of precise detail. In short, Imogen is a truly great person, as brilliant as Rosalind and Portia, even more than worthy of the paragon Posthumus, and Shakespeare has taken pains to keep us in that opinion of her. We gain advantage over her only when and because she is asleep.

* * *

For where is Iachimo? From nothing that Shakespeare has told, shown, or hinted since 2.4 can we think other than that the partner in our black secret has vanished from the earth, leaving no means by which truth can be exposed. . . .

And yet none of it is so: our facts contradict her beliefs at every point. Moreover—again as in *Pericles*—it is in this darkest moment just at the ending of Imogen's soliloquy—

> O,
> Give color to my pale cheek with thy blood,
> That we the horrider may seem to those
> Which chance to find us. O my lord, my lord!
> 　　　　　(*Falls on the body.*)
> 　　　　　　　　　　　(4.2.329–32)

that we catch our first glimpse of dawn through a sudden sign of a kind that has been denied until now. Says the First Captain to Lucius, as they approach the spot where Imogen lies with headless Cloten:

> ... gentlemen of Italy, most willing spirits
> That promise noble service, and they come
> Under the conduct of bold Iachimo. ...

(338–40)

"Bold Iachimo": the bare mention is nearly worth actual sight. While Iachimo was lost in silence an element indispensable to the clearing of multiple errors was missing; notification of his return from oblivion is notification that all can yet be well. This hint of hope comes just after Imogen, in a gesture marking total defeat, has fallen upon the headless body and daubed her face with its blood.

* * *

... It is a fact that until 5.4 Shakespeare has exhibited only an uncontrolled universe the character of which is summed up by Pisanio's statement in the last line of 4.3: "Fortune brings in some boats that are not steered." By the time of this summation we have been shown some inconclusive signs that the drift of events may be toward a happy ending: the death of Cloten; the mention of the imminent arrival in Britain of Iachimo; the report of the Queen's illness. Finally, the summation is itself reassuring, for surely, no matter what force or lack of force brings them in, it is better that boats come in than that they be lost.

But though these signs are reassuring, *they are only signs of favorable chance*. There has been no hint of existence of any directing force: indeed, Pisanio's summation argues that there is none. So far as our awareness was advised, the world of *Pericles,* too, until Act 3, lacked a controlling force; then the dramatist—plainly dissatisfied with Gower's whim-directed universe—introduced the extraordinary billow that brought Thaisa's body to Cerimon, and from that point on, by various means, implied the existence of a benevolent intelligence behind the erstwhile seemingly unruled winds and waves. Gower's world of the first two acts of *Pericles* is extended through the first four and a half acts of *Cymbeline*—with nothing even so inconclusive as an extraordinary billow to suggest that any force is in control. Though we finally perceive an auspicious drift, yet we do so with the sense that things might as easily go ill as well. Nevertheless, 5.3 makes it plain that *Cymbeline* could now end happily without the services of a controlling force, for all the persons needed to disentangle truth are assembled. The dénouement of 5.5, that is to say, could follow immediately after 5.3, without 5.4.

But a chance ending, for artistic if not philosophical reasons, was manifestly intolerable to Shakespeare: always, everywhere, he must have a divinity—either within or without man—that shapes the ends of action. Hence in 5.4 Jupiter advises us of what we could not have guessed during the first four and a half acts—that the world of *Cymbeline* has been under control all the while; says Jupiter to the spirits of the four Leonati, Posthumus's kin:

> Be not with mortal accidents opprest.
> No care of yours it is; you know 'tis ours.
> Whom best I love I cross; to make my gift,
> The more delayed, delighted. Be content.
> Your low-laid son our godhead will uplift.
>
> (5.4.69–73)

This is more than a promise that all will be well: *it is an assertion that all has been well all the while*. During those four and a half acts when we feared that nobody knew the troubles we saw, the action lay in fact in Jupiter's palm—as that of *Measure for Measure* in Vincentio's and that of *The Tempest* in Prospero's.

But the difference is vast: we knew at once about Vincentio and Prospero, and we were left ignorant of Jupiter. So far as the dramatic effect during the first four and a half acts is concerned, Jupiter had as well not have been, since he was not in our awareness. Yet on the evidence of Shakespeare's usual method, the reason for his introduction of Jupiter is apparent: he would not tolerate action that stumbles to one ending but could have stumbled to another. His means of avoiding an accidental ending is always some controlling force, mortal or immortal: a fairy king, a brilliant heroine in disguise, an all-powerful duke—or a Jupiter. The great question, then, is not why he introduced Jupiter, but why he left us unaware of him until the dénouement.

A possible answer is that both *Pericles* and *Cymbeline* are deliberate experiments with the dramatic effects of uncertainty. This answer would make it appear that the dramatist toys with us during the first four and a half acts just as Jupiter toyed with Imogen and Posthumus, and for the same reason: "Whom best I love I cross; to make my gift,/The more delayed, delighted."

One formula, at least, is common to *Pericles* and *Cymbeline*: it is to make good people—Pericles, Thaisa, Marina; Cymbeline, Imogen, Posthumus—believe at first that they have suffered irreparable loss in an indifferent universe, and then to restore all. Applied to our own awareness, the formula is not quite so severe in these plays: though we are long denied the comforting knowledge that the world is benevolently controlled and are therefore subjected to the anxiety that comes of uncertainty, we are not made to believe that anyone has suffered irrecoverable loss. We know that death has not claimed Pericles' Thaisa and Marina, Imogen's Posthumus, or Posthumus's Imogen. But in the third romance, *The Winter's Tale,* as will be seen, the dramatist, *progressively deepening our anxiety* in the plays of the lasting storm, applies the same formula to our awareness as to that of Leontes: we, too, are made to believe that Hermione is dead. After reaching this extremity, Shakespeare returns to his old, habitual way: we are advised of Prospero immediately after the opening scene of *The Tempest,* and thereafter misgivings are impossible. If, therefore, the withholding of reassurance was a deliberate experiment, it was followed by quick, absolute repudiation. There are some objections to regarding it so, however, and there are other possible answers; but these must wait on the evidence of *The Winter's Tale* and *The Tempest.*

In any event, the introduction of Jupiter, however belated, serves unqualified notice that all now not only will but must be, and in fact always has been, well. It thus prevents the appearance of adventitious action running to adventitious ending. It enables us to watch the tortuous dénouement with minds free from anxiety. From this point of view it is an artistic masterstroke.

But it is also an artistic fraud. The fact is that at the end of 5.3 all lines of action have converged and all elements needed for a happy ending have been assembled; but more, it is a fact that to the dénouement of 5.5 the eagle-borne Jupiter of 5.4 actually contributes nothing but a riddling prophecy for the Soothsayer to interpret—and even this comes late, after all the secrets have been opened, and serves only to seem to prove Jupiter's earlier claim that he knew and controlled all, all the while. It is not Jupiter—nor is it Posthumus, to whom Jupiter appeared and on whose breast the prophetic tablet was laid—*but the bright-eyed heroine herself* who, having glimpsed a ring on the captive Iachimo's finger, finds her way up through mountains of error to the truth. So Jupiter is an artistic fraud—but perhaps the shrewdest in the plays. For while he gives the look of intention to what would otherwise seem accident, he actually does nothing, but leaves the participants to find their own way. As *deus ex machina* he is thus at once indispensable and superfluous.

The dénouement, then, runs from 5.3 to the end, with Jupiter serving only as a reassuring illusion. This is Shakespeare's longest final scene, and all but the very first and very last lines bustle with the exposure of secrets—for the preceding acts have buried more truths more deeply than in any other play. The opening of no other final scene finds our awareness so laden with secrets; no other finds the vision of so many participants so limited to small corners and pockets. The *King* is ignorant (1) that the Queen contrived the separation of Imogen and Posthumus for her own and Cloten's gain; (2) that Imogen lives and is present as the Roman page; (3) that the heroes who rescued him are his sons and his old servant; (4) that the prisoner he has handed over to the Jailer is Posthumus; (5) that this same prisoner was the fourth hero of the narrow lane. *Imogen* is ignorant (1) that both she and Posthumus were abused by Iachimo; (2) that Posthumus lives and is present; (3) that Pisanio was and is loyal; (4) that the rustics are her brothers; (5) that the drug given her by Pisanio was intended by the Queen to be fatal; (6) that she escaped death only by virtue of the physician's counter-practice. *Posthumus* is ignorant (1) that he and Imogen were abused by Iachimo; (2) that Pisanio deceived him with a false token of Imogen's death; (3) that Imogen is present as the Roman page; (4) that the mountaineers with whom he saved the kingdom are his brothers-in-law. *Arviragus* and *Guiderius* are ignorant (1) that they are princes; (2) that "Fidele" was their sister; (3) that she yet lives and is present as the Roman page; (4) that their heroic assistant in the battle of the narrow lane was their brother-in-law and that he is present now in Roman dress. *Belarius* is ignorant (1) that "Fidele" was sister to the King's sons; (2) that she is alive and present as the Roman page. *Iachimo* is ignorant that both his victims are present. *Lucius* is ignorant that his page is Cymbeline's daughter—and of all that led to her final masquerade. *Pisanio* is ignorant (1) that the drug given him by the Queen was meant to kill him; (2) that both his master and his mistress are present.

At the same time that each is ignorant of others' secrets, most participants are also either proprietors of current practices or secret-sharers of past practices that contributed to the present condition. Only Cymbeline and Lucius are denied the privilege of holding any secrets. *Cornelius* alone knows that the Queen—whose death and true character are quickly reported—intended murder, and that the drug with which he provided her was capable of producing only the appearance of death. *Iachimo* alone bears the secret of the "proofs" of Imogen's infidelity. *Pisanio* alone holds the secret of his deception of Posthumus in Imogen's "death," and of Cloten's practice in dressing himself as Posthumus. *Imogen* holds the secret of her own identity and of her former role as "Fidele." *Posthumus* holds the secret of his double masquerade—as the heroic Briton, and, just now, as the Roman prisoner. *Belarius* alone holds the secret of the rustic youths' identities. *Arviragus* and *Guiderius,* with Belarius, hold the secret of Cloten's disappearance. Such is the general disposition of awarenesses at the opening of the most elaborate final scene in Shakespeare. What is most remarkable is that, though the strands are many and marvelously intertwined, nothing snarls, and no loose end remains at last.

Jupiter being absent, no participant knows all that we know, but each fact of ours is known to some participant. Our vantage point is perfect; as usual the dénouement has nothing to expose to us. For us, then, the experience of the closing scene is that of witnessing the revelation of secrets that have been locked in our minds, and of observing the effects of their revelation upon the persons who have been ignorant of them and to whom they are of most concern; of being at hand when Imogen learns that Posthumus lives, when Posthumus learns that Imogen lives and is chaste, when Cymbeline learns that the heroes who saved his kingdom are his own sons and his son-in-law. The process of making everything known is extended and exploited as nowhere else in Shakespeare. The release of each secret accomplishes a welcome reduction, degree by degree, of the pressure that has been mounting in our minds since error first began to pile on error; one effect of the scene, thus, is the relief of overmuch understanding, painful because it has been unsharable.

From the first comedies Shakespeare has concentrated exploitative efforts upon two great moments: *that in which ignorance has achieved greatest depth and universality, and that in which persons who have acted in ignorance learn of their errors.* Cymbeline surpasses all other plays in the celebration of these contrasting moments—the first, already examined, "Fidele's" funeral and Imogen's soliloquy over "Posthumus's" body; and the second, now, the explosion of secrets in the closing scene. Never one to surrender a secret until he has exhausted its potentiality, Shakespeare relieves pressures on our awareness only after a last intensification which raises them to the bursting point. Thus when Iachimo has told how he destroyed Posthumus's faith in Imogen, the hero advances, identifies himself, curses Iachimo, and falls to berating himself for the Imogen he supposes dead. There is willful cruelty to us in this last-minute exploitation of the space between Posthumus's ignorance and our awareness that Imogen stands within arm's length! Posthumus's speech raises the pressure to where the pain of the unsharable becomes excruciating. But Shakespeare is not yet through with us. Since the pressure can be raised no further by verbal exploitation, he raises it by physical action to the level of bursting:

> *Post.*   Imogen,
>   Imogen, Imogen!
> *Imo.*   Peace, my lord; hear, hear—
> *Post.* Shall's have a play of this? Thou scornful page,
>   There lie thy part.   (*Striking her; she falls.*)
>   (5.5.226–29)

This is a final turn of the screw. The physical blow, the ultimate expression of Posthumus's unawareness, is followed instantly by relief, with Pisanio's "O my Lord Posthumus!/You ne'er killed Imogen till now" (230–31).

This effective, if cruel, formula the dramatist repeats in yielding the last great secret. Guiderius grandly announces that it was he who slew Cloten: "I have spoke it, and I did it" (290). Cymbeline, who earlier had knighted Belarius and the unknown youths for their heroic stand that saved his kingdom, now condemns Guiderius: "Thou'rt dead" (299). Through forty lines, from Guiderius's confession until Belarius makes known the youths' royalty, Shakespeare sustains the painful pressure of our awareness by exploiting the King's unawareness that he has condemned his own son. Though no blow like that which felled

Imogen is struck, yet physical action again pushes pressure to the bursting point when Guiderius is roughly seized by guards. This time it is Belarius whose word releases the pressure: "Let his arms alone;/They were not born for bondage" (305–06).

NORTHROP FRYE

From A Natural Perspective

Cymbeline, a play that might have been subtitled "Much Ado About Everything," is the apotheosis of the problem comedies: it combines the *Much Ado* theme of the slandered heroine, the *All's Well* theme of the expulsion of the hero's false friend, the *Measure for Measure* theme of the confusion and clarifying of government, and many others. There are even some curious echoes of names from *Much Ado:* in *Cymbeline* we have Posthumus Leonatus betrothed to Imogen, whose name is Innogen in Shakespeare's sources; in *Much Ado* we have Leonato, Governor of Messina in Sicily, whose wife's name, though she has no speaking part, is Innogen. The former name goes on echoing in *The Winter's Tale* as Leontes, King of Sicilia. The repetition may mean very little itself, but we notice in the romances a technique of what might be called spatial anachronism, in which Mediterranean and Atlantic settings seem to be superimposed on top of each other, as Bermudan imagery is superimposed on the island in *The Tempest*. In particular, there is a convention, referred to in the Prologue to Jonson's *Sad Shepherd* and prominent in *Comus* and *Lycidas,* of mixing British with Sicilian and Arcadian imagery in the pastoral.

The same technique of superimposition is used temporally as well, binding together primitive Wales, Roman Britain, and Italian Rome. *Cymbeline* has at least a token connection with the history plays of some significance. History is a prominent genre in Shakespeare until *Henry V,* when it seems to disappear and revive only in the much suspected *Henry VIII* at the end of

From *A Natural Perspective: The Development of Shakespearean Comedy and Romance,* by Northrop Frye. New York: Columbia University Press, 1965, pp. 65–70. Reprinted by permission of the publisher.

the canon. Yet the history of Britain to Shakespeare's audience began with the Trojan War, the setting of *Troilus and Cressida,* and included the story of Lear as well as the story of Macbeth. Even *Hamlet* is dimly linked with the period of Danish ascendancy over England. Alternating with these plays of a Britain older than King John are the Roman or Plutarchan plays, dealing with what, again, to Shakespeare's audience was the history of a cousin nation, another descendant of Troy. In *Cymbeline* the theme of reconciliation between the two Trojan nations is central, as though it were intended to conclude the double series started by *Troilus and Cressida.*

The reason for the choice of the theme may be partly that Cymbeline was king of Britain at the time of Christ. The sense of a large change in human fortunes taking place offstage has to be read into *Cymbeline,* and as a rule reading things into Shakespeare in the light of some external information is a dubious practice. Still, we notice the curiously oracular Jailer, who speaks for a world that knows of no other world, and yet can say: "I would we were all of one mind, and one mind good." We notice, too, the word "peace" at the end of the play, and the way that the promise to pay tribute to Augustus fits into that emperor's decree that all the world should be taxed, the decree that begins the story of the birth of Christ. But *Cymbeline* is not, to put it mildly, a historical play: it is pure folk tale, featuring a cruel stepmother with her loutish son, a calumniated maiden, lost princes brought up in a cave by a foster father, a ring of recognition that works in reverse, villains displaying false trophies of adultery and faithful servants displaying equally false trophies of murder, along with a great firework display of dreams, prophecies, signs, portents, and wonders.

What strikes one at once about the play is the extraordinary blindness of the characters in it. Imogen begins her journey to Milford Haven by saying:

> I see before me, man: nor here, nor here,
> Nor what ensues, but have a fog in them,
> That I cannot look through.

(3.2.78–80)

Lucius, after the battle he was so confident of winning has gone so awry, says:

> For friends kill friends, and the disorder's such
> As War were hoodwinked

(5.2.15–16)

and the Jailer tells Posthumus how little he knows of where he is
going. Posthumus replies that "none want eyes to direct them
the way I am going, but such as wink and will not use them."
Yet Posthumus himself has believed an even sillier story than
Claudio does in *Much Ado*. The crafty Queen wastes her energies trying to teach Cloten the subtleties of courtship; Belarius
tries to persuade his adopted sons to be disillusioned about a
world they have never seen. The word "election," implying free
choice, is used several times, but no one's choice seems very
well considered; the word "note," meaning distinction or prestige, also echoes, but distinctions are difficult to establish when
"Reverence,/The angel of the world" is compelled to focus on
the idiot Cloten, stepson of the weak and deluded Cymbeline.
In *Cymbeline*, as in all romances, there is a scaling down of the
human perspective. Posthumus is peevishly and querulously
jealous, he is no Othello; the Queen is squalidly unscrupulous,
and is no Lady Macbeth.

Imogen is by long odds the most intelligent character in the
play, and Imogen throughout is surrounded by a kind of atmos-
pheric pressure of unconsciousness. The emotional climaxes of
the play are the two great songs of the awakening and the laying
to rest of Imogen, and in neither of them has she any notion of
the context. The aubade is sung to her indifferent ear by the
agency of Cloten after she has unknowingly spent a night with
Iachimo; the obsequy is sung to her unconscious body by two
boys whom she does not know to be her brothers while the
headless Cloten is being laid beside her in the clothes of
Posthumus. We feel in *Pericles* that Marina's magical chastity
will get her safely through the peril of the brothel, but at least
she knows it is a peril: in other words, there is much less dramatic irony in *Pericles* than in *Cymbeline*. The ironic complications of *Cymbeline* are in themselves, of course, the customary
conventions of pastoral romance, where the simple childlike
pleasure of knowing more than the characters do is constantly
appealed to by the author. But there also seems to be a strong
emphasis on the misdirection of human will, which culminates
in the prison scene.

In this scene a number of characters appear who are new to

us but are older than the action of the play. They speak in a naïve doggerel verse not unlike in its dramatic effect to the verse of Gower in *Pericles,* and like it they are a sign that we are being confronted with something traditional and archaic. They are ghosts from the world of the dead, who have been invisible spectators of the action and now come to speak for us as spectators, impeaching the wisdom of Jupiter for allowing things to get in such a muddle. Jupiter tells them what, in fact, we have been seeing all along, that a skillful and quite benevolent design is being woven of the action despite all the efforts of human folly to destroy it. This scene is soon followed by the great contrapuntal tour de force of the recognition scene, when the truth is torn out of a score of mysteries, disguisings, and misunderstandings; when out of all the confusion of action a very simple conclusion is reached, and one which sounds very like peace on earth, good will toward men. The difference between *Cymbeline* and the earlier problem comedies, then, is that the counterproblem force, so to speak, which brings a festive conclusion out of all the mistakes of the characters, is explicitly associated with the working of a divine providence, here called Jupiter. Jupiter is as much a projection of the author's craftsmanship as the Duke in *Measure for Measure:* that is, the difference between *Cymbeline* and the problem comedies is not that *Cymbeline* is adding a religious allegory to the dramatic action. What it is adding to the dramatic action is the primitive mythical dimension which is only implicit in the problem comedies. *Cymbeline* is not a more religious play than *Much Ado:* it is a more academic play, with a greater technical interest in dramatic structure.

BRUCE R. SMITH

Eyeing and Wording in *Cymbeline*

How you *feel* about a Shakespeare play depends a lot on the physical circumstances in which you take it in. Holding this printed Signet Classics edition of *Cymbeline* in your hands, you have an experience of the play that is primarily visual. You see the words, you may even sound them out in your head, but any actual sounds that reach your eardrums are likely to be random noises in the room around you. What you feel is primarily the texture of macerated wood chips that have been turned into paper. Watching *Cymbeline* on DVD, on your laptop or in a classroom adds fictional space and actors' bodies to the experience and endows space and bodies with audible words—sounds that you hear at relatively close range, whether they come out of your laptop speakers or through earphones or through speakers attached to the classroom DVD player. Feeling has now got more complicated. It involves the vibration of sound waves in your ears, the stimulation of the retinas in your eyes, electrical impulses coursing through your nerves, and your subjective experience of those physical sensations. See and hear *Cymbeline* in a live performance in a theater and you might expect that the visceral sensations would be more intense and more intimate still. Intense, perhaps. Performance in a theater, as enthralling as it may be, inevitably distances you from what you are seeing. The words striking your ears may have a presence that no amplification equipment can ever match, in nuance if not in volume, but what you see is going to be farther away. The 1599 Globe Theatre, a cylinder three stories tall and ninety-nine feet in diameter, was an acoustically live space and relatively inti-

This essay, written for the Signet Classics edition of *Cymbeline*, is reprinted with the author's permission.

mate, too, with no spectator more than fifty feet from the actors onstage, but that fifty feet introduces a disjunction between vision and words.

Shakespeare seems to capitalize on that effect in the last scene of *Cymbeline*. Act 5, scene 5, does go on. At 484 lines, it ranks as the longest recognition scene in all of Shakespeare's scripts. What the onstage spectator-listeners witness during this protracted period is a disjunction between vision and words. Names do not match bodies; stories do not match actions. The onstage spectators *see* Posthumus strike to the ground a British traitor; the onstage audience *hears* a different story from Pisanio: "O my lord Posthumus,/You ne'er killed Imogen till now" (5.5.230–31). The effect of putting the right name to the body, the right story to the action, is to set the visible world in motion and make the onlookers dizzy:

> Cymbeline. Does the world go round?
> Posthumus. How comes these staggers on me?
>
> (232–33)

Spectator/listeners in the yard and the galleries did not, of course, experience this vertigo. Standing or sitting at a distance, they got to enjoy the congruity between vision and words that they had seen coming—but not before they had enjoyed the *in*congruity to the absolute limit of possibility. They had seen one image, one sequence of actions, even as they had heard two different stories *about* that sequence of actions. Posthumus's violent gesture threatens to obliterate one of the competing stories, the "right" one. It is a dangerous moment in the move toward narrative closure, in the way it recapitulates all of the play's misalignments of things heard with things seen, above all Iachimo's nefarious inventory of Imogen's bedchamber. Iachimo's slanders turn Posthumus the idolator of Imogen into Posthumus the iconoclast. Faced with an incongruity between words and image, Posthumus would reconcile the two, not by questioning the words, but by destroying the image: "O that I had her here, to tear her limb-meal!" (2.4.147). That act of violence he finally does commit in the play's last scene, mistaking his wife for the British traitor just as he has mistaken her earlier for Iachimo's whore.

No less palpable in *Cymbeline* 5.5 is the sense that seeing constitutes a way of knowing quite apart from words, whether those words be true or false. The violence of Posthumus's attack on the supposed British traitor is anticipated earlier in the scene when Imogen, still in disguise, sees her husband for the first time since he ordered her murder. The very sight of him rivets her: "I see a thing/Bitter to me as death," she tells Lucius (5.5.103–04). Everyone notices the effect. "Wherefore ey'st him so?" (114) the king asks her. Morgan (Belarius in disguise) and his sons go unremarked by their erstwhile housekeeper. "He eyes us not," Morgan tells the boys (124). To eye, "to direct the eyes to, fix the eyes upon, look at or upon, behold, observe" (*OED* 1.2.a), is an outward-directed action that, in this play, carries physical power. Even as the king turns the spectacle of reconciled husband and wife, father and brothers, into words, he testifies to a power in Imogen's gaze that defies language. "See," he begins, in one of the play's many commands to "look," "see," "behold":

> Posthumus anchors upon Imogen,
> And she like harmless lightning throws her eye
> On him, her brothers, me, her master, hitting
> Each object with a joy; the counterchange
> Is severally in all.
>
> (393–97)

"Throw," "hit," "counterchange": these words invest Imogen's looks specifically with the power to *touch*. The "harmless lightning" that she casts about the stage recalls the more dangerous "*thunder and lightning*" (5.4.62s.d.) with which Jupiter made his descent in the previous scene—effects that were likely realized with squibs or other fireworks thrown about the stage by the actor playing Jupiter. In those fireworks the spectators could actually see the beams of light that Cymbeline later attributes to Imogen. According to Joseph Roach, such eyeing was part of an early modern actor's stock-in-trade: "his motions could transform the air through which he moved, animating it in waves of force rippling outward from a center in his soul. His passions, irradiating the bodies of spectators through their eyes and ears, could literally transfer the contents of his heart to theirs, altering their moral natures."* In sum, it seems fair to

---

*Joseph Roach, *The Player's Passion: Scenes in the Science of Acting* (Newark: University of Delaware Press, 1985), p. 27.

say that vision in *Cymbeline* 5.5 stands in a dubious place vis-a-vis language: vision *against* language in the case of Posthumus's violence on the British traitor, vision *before* language in the case of Imogen's first sight of her husband, perhaps vision *beyond* language in the case of Imogen's lightninglike gazes.

What are we to make of these disjunctions between the visual and the verbal? What is it about that separation that seems to have kept Shakespeare's spectator-listeners watching and listening during the two hours' traffic of the stage—and then some? Five explanations suggest themselves. Genre theory, first of all, would find in the irony of visual appearance versus verbal reality the very thing that makes comedy comedy and tragedy tragedy. A discrepancy between image and word can be funny (comedy) or disastrous (tragedy) or in the case of *Cymbeline* a sequential combination of the two (tragicomedy). Deconstruction would find in the gap between image and word an example writ large of *the* fundamental fact about human language: Words, after all, have no necessary relationship with the things they purport to name. In more technical language, $s \neq S$, the signifier does not equal the Signified. The many discrepancies in *Cymbeline* between vision and word would, for a student of Lacan's psychoanalytical theory, provide evidence of the existential lack that all human subjects experience through the imposition of language. A reading informed by Renaissance humanism would be equally positivist. The confirmation of *opsis*, knowing-through-sight, in *logos*, knowing-through-words, would be regarded as the end toward which the entire play moves. Beyond genre theory, beyond deconstruction, beyond Lacanian psychoanalytical theory, beyond Renaissance humanism there is a fifth explanation that takes into account early modern ideas about the physiology and physics of vision.

Iacomo begins his attempted seduction of Imogen in 1.6 obliquely, with admiration of how men's eyes can discriminate between stars and grains of sand, how they can "Partition make with spectacles so precious/'Twixt fair and foul" (1.6.37–38). When Imogen fails to catch the compliment, Iachimo offers a textbook explanation of early modern theories of perception, as he moves from eye (39) to judgment (41) to appetite (43) to will (47). The very sight of Imogen—"this object which,/Takes prisoner the wild motion of mine eye,/Fixing it only" (102–04)—has worked just such an effect on *his* will. Eye + judgment + appetite + will + physical possession: each of these elements figured in what early modern men and women told themselves was happening when they eyed another person. Thomas Wright, in his self-help book *The Passions of the Mind in General* (1601, rev. 1604), describes the way sight sensations get fused with other sensations in the imagination and then get communicated, via aerated spirits that rush through the nerves, to the heart, where contraction or dilation activates all the body's fluids. Only *then* is the whole experience referred to judgment in the brain—and to the naming of the experience in words. Imagination, the collecting of experience from all the senses, *precedes* judgment in Wright's account—and judgment happens, not in the brain, but in the heart.

Although Aristotle had argued that vision happens when light reflected from objects enters the human eye, many early modern men and women still adhered to the opinion of Plato, Cicero, Euclid, and Ptolemy that it's the other way around: vision happens when beams of fire are projected outward from the human eye. Certainly that is what vision *feels* like. We experience vision as being directed *at* or *to* something: we decide (or so we think) where to cast our gaze. Even a thorough-going Aristotelian like Helkiah Crooke in his medical encyclopedia *Microcosmographia* (1616, 1631) has to give the so-called "extramission theory" some credit. "Visive spirits" in the eye are drawn to light, Crooke says, so that the presence of "lucid and white objects" can strike the viewer blind,

> because the visive spirits being drawn out, and as it were enticed by that which is like unto them, do break forth of the Eye with so great a violence and force, that by such irruption, either the substance of the crystalline humor, or the coat thereof, or something else in the eye (which hath many tender parts) is either broken, or at least suffers some notable alteration.*

Testimonials like Wright's and Crooke's tell us what eyeing *felt like* to early modern men and women, at least to early modern men and women who tried to put the experience into words. Common to all these accounts are force, violence, lightness, quickness, touch. Jupiter's fireworks in 5.4 illustrate the very

---

*Helkiah Crooke, *Microcosmographia* (London: Jaggard, 1631), p. 669, orthography modernized.

qualities that Wright and other early modern writers attempt to describe. These qualities of seeing call into question the efficacy of words. Language is deliberate in pace and linear in direction; vision is quick and multidirectional. Part of what makes the extramission theory of vision so puzzling to us is the huge gap between the vocabulary we have for specifying visual experience—how much of our lexicon is a catalogue of objects out there in the world?—and our vocabulary for talking about tactile experience. Our vocabulary directs us to *what* we see, not *how* we see it. Early modern understandings of vision suggest that the real issue in the final scene of *Cymbeline* may not be appearance versus reality, as modern criticism would have it, but the volatility of vision versus the words that would fix those sensations. Violence as well as pleasure attends the convergence of those two quite distinct ways of apprehending the world.

RICHARD HOSLEY AND SYLVAN BARNET

Cymbeline on Stage and Screen

Our earliest record of *Cymbeline* is an account by Simon Forman, who saw the play performed by the King's Men at their open-air or "public" playhouse, the First Globe, shortly before his death in September of 1611. Forman provides a synopsis of the plot but, unfortunately, no information about the staging. The play was presumably performed also by the King's Men at their indoor or "private" playhouse, the Blackfriars. The original performance took place sometime between December of 1609 and the end of 1610, though we do not know at which playhouse. This question, however, is of historical interest only, since the two playhouses had essentially the same stage facilities: at the rear of the stage and running its full width, an "attiring house" with three doorways, one of which, fitted out with curtains or hangings, might serve as a shallow "discovery space" some five or six feet wide; in the second story of the tiring house, a row of spectators' "rooms" or "boxes" whose front openings were occasionally used for framed action above; in the middle of the stage, a trapdoor; and, directly over the stage, a ceiling trap in the "heavens" housing descent machinery. Apparently the staging of *Cymbeline* was conceived with the generally similar stage structures of both playhouses in mind.

Staging facilities essentially like those at the Globe and the Blackfriars were presumably available for the only other early performance of which we have record, by the King's Men at Whitehall Palace before Charles I on January 1, 1634. This performance was probably at the small indoor playhouse the Cockpit-in-Court, the usual venue at Whitehall for the production of plays without changeable scenery. The play was "well-liked by the King."

The original staging of *Cymbeline* calls for the bringing on-stage of a bed and for the use of descent machinery. Otherwise, the staging is quite simple, the play not requiring a stage trap, an "above," or a discovery space. Thus the "cave" of Acts 3 and 4 is not a three-dimensional space (which might be thought to require representation by an alcove or by a structure standing upon the stage); rather, it is represented only in the two dimensions of its entrance, presumably one of the tiring-house doorways. Accordingly, players enter "from" and exit "to" the "cave"—an offstage presence suggested to the spectator's imagination by an open doorway representing the cave's mouth.

Imogen's bed, in accordance with contemporary staging convention, is "drawn in" to the stage (or "put forth" from the tiring house) by supernumerary players functioning as stagehands: *"Enter Imogen in her bed, and a Lady. . . . Iachimo [comes] from the trunk"* (2.2). Presumably the bed was a small curtained four-poster. The trunk containing Iachimo is also carried onstage by players, who of course must return to remove both bed and trunk at the end of the scene. This standard technique of the "open" or "thrust" stage can be seen also in the carrying on of the supposedly dead Imogen and in the carrying on and off of the body of Cloten (4.2).

The play requires descent machinery in order to manage a complex and spectacular flight by the god Jupiter riding upon an eagle: *"Jupiter descends in thunder and lightning, sitting upon an eagle. He throws a thunderbolt. . . ."* Jupiter then speaks twenty-one lines, ending with "Mount, eagle, to my palace crystalline." A stage direction follows, *"Ascends,"* and (after some other dialogue) Sicilius says, "The marble pavement closes; he is entered/His radiant roof " (5.4). Thus Jupiter astride his eagle is lowered to the stage and then later winched up through the trapdoor in the stage ceiling and back into the playhouse heavens.

In 1642 the performance of plays in England was forbidden by an act of Parliament, the prohibition lasting until 1660 when Charles II was restored to the throne. Shortly thereafter, a new kind of playhouse came into existence, combining stage features of nonscenic indoor playhouses like the Blackfriars with stage features of scenic court playhouses like the Great Hall Playhouse at Whitehall. In order to accommodate the apparatus of changeable scenery on the rear half of the new stage, the stage doors and the windows over the stage of the old tiring-house front were rotated ninety degrees on a vertical axis and positioned on either side of the forward part of the new stage. Thus the three doors at the rear of the old stage became one or two doors on each side of the new, and the three boxes above and behind the old stage became one or two upper-story boxes directly above the shifted doors.

Changeable scenery involved, most notably, three or four pairs of frame-and-canvas "backshutters" which slid in grooves across the rear part of the stage. Each pair of shutters was painted so as to constitute the two halves of a "scene." When "closed," the two shutters were drawn together at midstage (in the manner of a pair of sliding doors being closed) so as to display a single complete scene only slightly marred by the vertical seam which necessarily cut the picture in half. And, when "opened," the shutters were drawn apart toward the sides of the stage, where they were masked from the audience's view by a system of wings and a stage "frontispiece" remotely resembling the modern proscenium arch. (Most of the action of the play was performed on the front half of the stage, forward of the frontispiece and flanked by the stage doors.) The opening of the shutters might discover another pair of closed shutters displaying a second picture (the "scene" having thus, in theatrical language, been "changed"); or the opening of the shutters might discover, in the space immediately behind, an actor or actors together with appropriate stage properties. Thus a good-sized discovery space, a kind of "inner stage" large enough to contain a bed and other props, was available at the rear of the scenic part of the stage.

Cymbeline, although assigned as an old Blackfriars play to the King's Company in 1668, appears not to have been performed during the two decades after 1660. Then, in 1682, an adaptation of the play by Thomas Durfey entitled *The Injured Princess* (variously subtitled *The Fatal Wager* and *The Unequal Match* and in one instance titled *Eugenia*) was performed by the King's Company under Davenant's management at the Theatre Royal in Drury Lane and published in the same year. A facsimile of the 1682 edition has been published by the Cornmarket Press (1970), introduction by T. P. Matheson.

Durfey changes the names of several characters: Imogen to Eugenia, Iachimo to Shatillion (now "an opinionated Frenchman"), Posthumus to Ursaces, and Helen to Clarina. He retains the general structure of Shakespeare's play and the essential nature and function of most of the characters. Two characters, however, are amplified and altered in the service of a new sub-plot. Clarina is now the confidante of Eugenia and the daughter of Pisanio. And Pisanio, while retaining most of the functions of his original role, has become a heroic old soldier and the confidant of Ursaces. (Durfey's Pisanio is rather unpleasant in that, unlike Shakespeare's character, he has little faith in Eugenia's innocence.) Clarina, suspected of complicity in the flight of Eugenia, is abducted by Cloten, threatened with rape by his companion Jachimo (an added character with a borrowed name), and rescued by Pisanio, who kills Jachimo and is then blinded by Cloten (pp. 38–39). Durfey makes many other changes. In revising 4.2 he has Arviragus bring the head of Cloten onstage (p. 41), and he omits both Shakespeare's dirge "Fear no more the heat o' th' sun" and Imogen's lament over the decapitated body of Cloten. In one of the battle scenes Durfey expands Shakespeare's brief wordless skirmish between Posthumus and Iachimo (5.2) into a dialogue of some eighty lines in which Shatillion, after being mortally wounded by Ursaces, confesses his slander against Eugenia (pp. 48–50). Durfey omits the imprisonment of Posthumus, the dream theophany, the comic dialogue between Posthumus and the Jailer (5.4), and the soothsayer (4.2 and 5.5). And he shortens the dénouement to about half its original length. His dénouement is, however, impoverished by the poetic justice earlier meted out to Shatillion, for, as Matheson suggests, that character's death "moderates the mood of harmony and forgiveness essential to the conclusion in *Cymbeline*." The dénouement is also weakened by Durfey's elimination of one of Shakespeare's most provocative symbols—Posthumus's striking of Imogen.

The Injured Princess is an unhappy piece of work—melodramatic, ranting, sentimental, moralistic, overblown in style, cliché-ridden. Durfey rewrites Shakespeare wholesale, here introducing or substituting a new passage, there modifying the language of a phrase or sentence, here changing an individual word. In the process he frequently adulterates the tapestry of Shakespeare's mythical and legendary allusions, as in Iachimo's soliloquy in the bedroom scene (2.2), where Durfey (pp. 20–21) retains the reference to Tarquin but omits Cytherea (line 14), the Gordian knot (line 34), and the leaf turned down where Philomel gave up (line 45). He also tends to sacrifice Shakespeare's concrete visual images: although the candle is still available as a property that might be referred to, Durfey discards the bold conceit of the flame's seeking to underpeep Imogen's eyelids and the attendant metaphoric language (lines 19–23). By contrast, a fair example of Durfey's poetry is afforded by Pisanio's observation that, if Eugenia ever once becomes fickle, "Like a huge stone she rolls the steepy hill, / Not to be stopped by conscience, force, or skill" (p. 20).

As we should expect, *The Injured Princess* was performed with changeable scenery. In the bedroom scene we find: "Scene IV discovers Eugenia in bed; a Lady [Clarina] waiting; a chest standing by. . . . /Enter Shatillion from the chest; . . . /Gets into the chest" (p. 20). Here both bed and chest are evidently discovered by an opening of the scenic backshutters. And, in the scene corresponding to Shakespeare's 4.2 in which Cloten's body is carried offstage, the shutters are again used, this time for a "concealment" which replaces the carry-off of Shakespeare's text: "*Arviragus*. . . . his body lies/In yonder thicket. . . . /*Exeunt [Lucius, Eugenia, Soldiers]. Scene shuts upon Cloten's dead body*" (pp. 42–44).

Further, *The Injured Princess* calls for an action above that is not required in *Cymbeline,* in the scene of Cloten's morning serenade to Eugenia (Shakespeare's 2.3): "*Flutes and a song here; a Lady [Lelia] looks out [above]./Lelia.* My lady is rising, sir, she hears your music./*Cloten.* Ud so, she peeps through the window yonder now. . . . /*Enter Eugenia and Clarina [below]*" (p. 21). At the Theatre Royal the "window" was presumably represented by the front opening of a box over one of the side-stage doors.

The Injured Princess held the stage for more than sixty years, performances by the King's Company (under the title of *Cymbeline or The Fatal Wager* or simply *Cymbeline*) being recorded at Lincoln's Inn Fields during the first two decades of the eighteenth century and at Covent Garden during the 1730s. Shakespeare's *Cymbeline,* after an abortive attempt by Theophilus Cibber to present it at the New Haymarket in 1744, was finally restored to the stage by the King's Company at Covent Garden in 1746, Hannah Pritchard taking the role of Imogen, Lacy Ryan that of Posthumus, and a Mr. Hale that of Iachimo. (Presumably the text was cut and rearranged, but we do not know how or by whom.) Thus Shakespeare's play was apparently not performed for more than a century after the closing of the Caroline playhouses in 1642. But if it *had* been performed during the late seventeenth or early eighteenth century, stage directions supplied by the early editors of Shakespeare indicate that it would have been performed with changeable scenery. Rowe (1709) provides the following directions in the bedroom scene: *"Scene II a magnificent bedchamber, in one part of it a large trunk. Imogen is discovered reading in her bed, a Lady attending. . . . /Iachimo rises from the trunk. . . . /He goes into the trunk. The scene closes"* (p. 2771). (The term "magnificent" here is doubtless more fictive than theatrical, and in any case the opulence of Imogen's bedchamber as depicted in Rowe's frontispiece must be a flight of fantasy little related to stage practice.) Pope (1723), Theobald (1733), and most succeeding editors of the eighteenth, nineteenth, and early twentieth centuries give us more or less elaborate versions essentially of Rowe's staging. A vestige of his influence is apparent in the acceptance of his inappropriate stage direction *"The scene closes"* by the New Arden editor in 1955 and by the New Cambridge editor in 1960.

Pope, believing that the dream theophany of 5.4 (lines 30–92) was not written by Shakespeare but "plainly foisted in afterwards for mere show," relegated it, in his edition of 1723, to a four-page footnote along with the ensuing dialogue between Posthumus and the Jailer (lines 93–176). He did retain the imprisonment of Posthumus (lines 1–29). However, in 5.5 he again footnoted the Soothsayer's interpretation of Jupiter's prophecy (lines 425–57). In taking this position, Pope encouraged two later eighteenth-century editors (Hanmer, 1744, and Warburton, 1747) to reject Shakespeare's authorship of those actions; and he may also, if only indirectly, have given some support to the eighteenth- and nineteenth-century traditions of omitting them from performance.

Early in the 1750s Charles Marsh, a London bookseller, undertook to prepare an adaptation of *Cymbeline* which, as he tells us in his preface to the edition of 1759 (Cornmarket facsimile, 1969), was several times rehearsed for performance at the Theatre Royal in Covent Garden. The parts of Imogen, Posthumus, and Iachimo were to be taken by Susanna Cibber, Spranger Barry, and Charles Macklin; and Marsh was to have an author's benefit if the play ran nine nights. In the sequel, however, the play never opened.

Marsh's text is a straightforward and capable version, commendable alike for the adapter's good judgment in cutting and his reluctance to improve the texture of Shakespeare's verse. He changes none of the characters' names and introduces no new characters. (In this respect the full extent of his adventuring is to assign the name Trebonius to Lucius's Captain in Shakespeare's 4.2, and to identify the two Gentlemen of 1.1 as Trebonius and Pisanio.) Marsh makes three significant changes. He limits the general locale to Britain by the expedient of endowing Lucius with a house in Britain and then transferring the two Roman scenes (Shakespeare's 1.4 and 2.4) to the specific locale of that house, where Posthumus, having been granted asylum by his newly acquired patron Lucius, is introduced by Philario to Iachimo as in Shakespeare. Marsh also causes Imogen to keep the trunk overnight in her closet, so that in the bedroom scene (Shakespeare's 2.2) only the bed is discovered, Iachimo entering from and exiting to the "closet" by way of a stage door. And Marsh, like Durfey in *The Injured Princess*, eliminates Posthumus's imprisonment, the dream theophany, the comic Jailer (Shakespeare's 5.4), and the Soothsayer (4.2 and 5.5). And since he transposes none of his retained scenes, Marsh's version of *Cymbeline* is structurally even closer to Shakespeare's play than Garrick's.

Another adaptation of *Cymbeline*, by William Hawkins, "late professor of poetry in the University of Oxford," was also published in 1759 (Cornmarket facsimile, 1969). In that year the play had a run of six nights at Covent Garden and a command performance for the Prince of Wales. Imogen was played by the accomplished Mrs. Vincent, Posthumus by David Ross.

Hawkins, like Marsh, restricts the general locale to Britain. His first act begins *in medias res* with the arrival from Rome of the saber-rattling Lucius and proceeds immediately to Imogen's flight to join Leonatus at Milford Haven (Shakespeare's 3.1 and 2). Cloten is now Cymbeline's adopted son and in treasonous communication with Caesar Augustus; the Queen has recently died; and Pisanio (as Iachimo is now called) has already while in Rome succeeded in poisoning Leonatus's mind against Imogen. Leonatus himself does not appear until Act 4, when he rescues Cymbeline on the field of battle. Most of the material of Shakespeare's Act 5 is retained, with the exception of the dream theophany and the Jailer. Thus Hawkins's version is a dramatization of most of the last three acts of Shakespeare's *Cymbeline*, running to a bit more than half the length of the original play. And the story becomes a kind of pastoral, in part because

Hawkins omits Shakespeare's Acts 1 and 2 with their court and urban locales, in part because he locates his dénouement not at the palace or at Cymbeline's tent (Rowe's guess) but in the Welsh countryside of Belarius and the princes: *"Scene the forest and cave"* (p. 76).

Hawkins's attempt to conform to the unities of time and place has the effect of eliminating the four most dramatic scenes of Shakespeare's play: the wager scene (1.4), the attempted-seduction scene (1.6), the bedroom scene (2.2), and the scene in which Posthumus is convinced of Imogen's infidelity (2.4). Thus the essentials of the plot against Imogen and Posthumus are boiled down to a nine-line report by Hawkins's Pisanio to Cloten:

> First, roundly I described her bedchamber,
> The arras, ceiling, pictures (for of these
> I took most faithful inventory when
> I lay concealèd there); then I produced
> The bracelet that I ravished from her arm
> As sleep, the ape of death, lay dull upon her;
> And last I quoted [= noted] the cinque-spotted mole
> That richly stains her breast like crimson drops
> I' th' bottom of a cowslip. (p. 12)

Then in Act 4 it becomes clear, from the surfacing of an incriminating letter written by Cloten to Pisanio, that Cloten, as a spurned suitor of Imogen, has vengefully instigated the intrigue against her and Leonatus (Pisanio, the Iachimo character, thus being demoted from intriguer to cat's paw): "I have bought the fidelity of the princess's woman with my gold; she will give thee admittance into her chamber, . . . enough where thou mayst make such note as will be sufficient to the madding of the abhorred Leonatus" (p. 69). Thus Hawkins, in dropping the bedroom scene, also eliminates the device of the trunk which enables Iachimo to spend the night concealed in Imogen's bedchamber as she sleeps. And, in dropping the wager along with the wager scene, he creates a Leonatus who, though still guilty in other respects, is free of the blame he bears in Shakespeare's play for agreeing to a wager on his wife's chastity.

Still another adaptation of *Cymbeline*, by David Garrick, was produced by him at Drury Lane in 1761 and published in 1762 (Cornmarket facsimile, 1969). Garrick played Posthumus; a

Miss Bride, Imogen; and Charles Holland, Iachimo. This "acting version" (as it is sometimes called) was phenomenally successful, enjoying more than 130 performances between 1761 and 1766, when Garrick retired. In general it may be said that Garrick restored a majority of the essentials of Shakespeare's text to the stage.

He unquestionably deserves praise for making very few changes in or omissions from, and no additions to, Shakespeare's text of the four great scenes developing Iachimo's intrigue. Here and there Garrick trims away a bit of fat, his only dubious cuts being the Parthian at 1.6.20, "sluttery" and "vomit" some twenty-five lines later, Cleopatra and her Roman at 2.4.69–72, and the two winking Cupids serving as Imogen's andirons at lines 88–91. In these cuts Garrick evinces a certain fastidiousness, a moralistic bias reluctant to emphasize adultery and sexual love, and, in his suppressing Shakespeare's "story" of Imogen's tapestry (in Garrick's version Imogen's bedchamber is "hanged" only with "richest stuff, the colors blue and silver"), a tendency to prefer the abstract to the concrete.

Elsewhere, although he is generally more willing to make do with the original text than Durfey or Hawkins, Garrick makes frequent cuts and intermittently rewrites Shakespeare's verse, almost always for the worse. Thus Belarius's reference to Arviragus's carrying Fidele onstage, "Look, here he comes,/And brings the dire occasion in his *arms*/Of what we blame him for" (4.2.195), is thriftily rewritten through the change of only one word when Garrick omits the carry-on but retains Arviragus's entrance, the text becoming: "Look, here he comes,/And brings the dire occasion in his *looks*/Of what we blame him for" (p. 55).

Garrick also frequently transposes scenes and parts of scenes, though not, as is sometimes said, for the purpose of reducing the number of scene changes. In one instance a transposition becomes necessary in order to accommodate an altered staging: Garrick splits Shakespeare's 4.2 into two parts at line 291, inserting 4.3 (Cymbeline, Lords, and Pisanio) between them. In the first part of the split scene he keeps the body of Fidele offstage and causes that of Cloten to be carried off. Then, immediately following the transposed 4.3, he begins the second part of the split 4.2 with a discovery of the bodies of Fidele and Cloten "*on a bank strewed with flowers./Imogen (awakes).* Yes, sir, to Milford Haven. Which is the way?" (p. 57). Further, Garrick introduces "*A dance*" (noticed in the dialogue and well ad-

vertised in the playbill) in the scene of Cloten's morning serenade to Imogen (2.3; p. 28); a short passage praising the newly
crowned King George III (2.4; p. 31); and, in the dénouement,
some forty lines of bathetic verse in which Cornelius and the
Queen's Ladies explain what manner of person the Queen really was and how she died (5.5; pp. 64–65). (This sequence was
omitted from performances after the first night, but Garrick
printed it anyway.) Finally, it need hardly be mentioned that
Garrick omits Posthumus's imprisonment, the dream theophany, the Jailer, and the Soothsayer.

John Philip Kemble first produced *Cymbeline* in 1785 at
Drury Lane, two years later staging an extremely successful
benefit at that playhouse for his sister Sarah Siddons, who
played Imogen to his Posthumus. Mrs. Siddons was a very fine
Imogen in the first half of the play, but her great beauty and majestic style seem to have made her less effective in the later
scenes requiring transvestite disguise.

Kemble mounted several other productions of *Cymbeline*
over the next four decades, some of them with opulent scenery.
A critic of his production at Drury Lane in 1801 complains that
"the bed on which Imogen reclines was out of all proportion; so
much so that even Barrymore himself [as Iachimo], though of
the order of tall proportions, stood almost in need of a ladder to
take a view of Imogen's person" (quoted by George Odell).
And the playbill for Kemble's production at Covent Garden in
1827 boasts that the play will be performed "with new scenery,
dresses, and decorations, executed from the best authorities and
displaying, as accurately as stage effect will permit, the habits,
weapons, and buildings of the Gaulish and Belgic colonists of
the southern counties of Britain before their subjugation by the
Romans" (quoted by Odell). In accordance with the fashion of
his day, Kemble omitted the dream theophany from his productions.

William Charles Macready produced *Cymbeline* in 1838 at
Covent Garden and in 1843 at Drury Lane. The latter production is well documented through the survival of copies both of
Macready's promptbook and of the designs for scenes and costumes. He used twelve sets in twenty scenes, cutting more than
a third of the text and, as usual, omitting the dream theophany.

Macready, who had earlier played both Posthumus and
Iachimo, developed in his production of 1843 an untraditional
interpretation of Iachimo, giving that character a "convincing

air of frankness instead of the sly, insinuating manner" usually associated with the part (Carol Carlisle). The innovation was successful. Helen Faucit played Imogen as "a dignified, intelligent woman with noble ideals; her strength of character gave additional effectiveness to her normal gentleness of manner and explained her occasional abandonment of that manner" (Carlisle). The production is historically significant in that Macready staged the bedroom scene in an early kind of box set.

Henry Irving produced *Cymbeline* at the Lyceum Theatre in London in 1896, Ellen Terry playing Imogen to his Iachimo. Since he was using thirteen sets in eighteen scenes, Irving cut the text to about half its original length, omitting, of course, the dream theophany. The result was a ponderous production, Miss Terry noting in her diary, "Everything is so slow, so slow!" (quoted by William Winter).

Irving's interpretation of Iachimo was sentimental and perverse, whereas Ellen Terry's of Imogen was passionate and mercurial; indeed, her special talents as an actress for that part were apparently Irving's chief reason for putting on the play. Despite her personal success as Imogen, however, the production was a failure. Irving blamed the play, complaining that "*Cymbeline*, except for Imogen, isn't worth a damn for the stage" (quoted by Winter). The *Times* critic, on the other hand, blamed the overelaborate scenery, posing the question whether for such plays as *Cymbeline* "it would not be well to adopt on the stage a more or less fantastic setting, with something of that indefiniteness of place, period, and costume which the modern stage manager for some reason will only allow to comic opera" (quoted by Odell). This interesting suggestion was to be, in effect, acted upon by the inspired designer of a production of *Cymbeline* some sixty years later.

In 1913 the producer Edwin Thanhouser made a two-reel silent film of *Cymbeline* directed by Frederic Sullivan. Imogen was played by Flo La Badie and Posthumus by James Cruze. The film was made apparently in Hollywood and screened both in the United States and England. It survives in a single print, which has been studied by Robert Hamilton Ball.

The first reel begins with a scene showing Belarius, Guiderius, and Arviragus (identified as "the King's sons") before their cave and continues with the story of Imogen and Posthumus as far as her departure with Pisanio for Milford Haven. Imogen and Posthumus are shown courting in a garden, and their secret marriage is shown in an outdoor setting. The second reel deals with Imogen's sojourn with her lost brothers and the war against the invading Romans. However, Cloten, dropped from the action after 2.1, is of course not beheaded, and Imogen is not found apparently dead, the Queen and her "poison" intrigue having also been dropped after a scene based on 1.1. In addition, the imprisonment of Posthumus is eliminated along with the dream theophany.

The bedroom scene, praised by contemporary reviewers, involves a curious distortion of the trunk device. Imogen and her lady attendant pass through the antechamber to her bedroom, where the waiting woman begins to prepare Imogen for bed. Iachimo steals into the antechamber, peeks into the bedchamber, disappears as the attendant comes and leaves. He emerges from a trunk which he has not been shown entering, and which is a part of the furniture of the room, not as in Shakespeare his own device for concealment. He goes to the sleeping "Imogen, puts her hair away from her neck and shoulders (if there is a mole it is decorously above a tight bodice), takes the bracelet from her wrist, and departs exultant."

Shakespeare's five acts of dialogue are reduced to thirty subtitles. A few retain some of the poetry: "Hang there like fruit my soul/Till the tree die!" Others, however, like Belarius's explanation to Cymbeline, are (to put it tactfully) prosaic: "Sir, I stole your sons as babes—I give them back to you."

Ball considers the acting to be "better than might be expected, no worse than in similar films of 1913." And he gives the director and producer credit for appropriate exploitation of the potentialities of the new dramatic medium: ". . . it is the outdoor scenery which lends the film a kind of charm. . . . Most of the pictures are outdoors where garden, sea coast, open country, mountains and rocks are attractively photographed, sometimes at long range. Most of the shots, however, are medium to close with a few closeups to emphasize Imogen's bracelet or give the final clinch."

In 1937 George Bernard Shaw wrote a shortened version (some 300 lines) of the fifth act of *Cymbeline* (about 800 lines) which he later published with an explanatory foreword as *Cymbeline Refinished* (1946). He offered this "variation on Shakespeare's ending" to both Stratford and the Old Vic, but neither management was interested; and he then offered it to André van Gyseghem, who used it in the production he directed at the Embassy Theatre in London late in 1937.

In his rewriting of Act 5, Shaw omits the staging of the battle (Scene 2), instead describing it retrospectively in an opening dialogue between Philario and a Roman Captain. He then uses, practically verbatim, the whole of Posthumus's soliloquy before the battle (Scene 1), adjusting the tenses and omitting Posthumus's short prayer (lines 21–22), so that the soliloquy looks backward toward rather than forward to the battle. Further, he omits Posthumus's lengthy and overdetailed descriptions of the battle to a Briton Lord (Scene 3). He omits also the imprisonment of Posthumus, the dream theophany, and Posthumus's dialogue with the Jailer (Scene 4). And in the dénouement he cuts or drastically condenses Shakespeare's systematic revelations that reveal only what we already know (Scene 5).

In his foreword Shaw writes about his developing attitude toward Act 5. When he first considered rewriting it, he concurred in the received opinion of his day: namely that "it was a cobbled-up affair by several hands, including a vision in prison accompanied by scraps of quite ridiculous doggerel." (The "doggerel" consists of Shakespeare's Elizabethan fourteeners, old-fashioned to spectators in 1610, which he deploys in an elegant stanzaic form in order to give an antique formality to the ghostly speeches of Sicilius, the Mother, and the two Brothers.) But after rereading the act for the first time in many years Shaw discovered that this notion had been "an unpardonable stupidity. The act is genuine Shakespeare to the last full stop, and late-phase Shakespeare in point of verbal workmanship." Further, "the doggerel is not doggerel: it is a versified masque. . . . Performed as such, with suitable music and enough pictorial spendor, it is not only entertaining on the stage, but, with the very Shakespearian feature of a comic Jailer which [accompanies] it, just the thing to save the last act." However, despite the sensitive and accurate perceptions of this modified judgment, Shaw then proceeded to omit from his variation both the dream theophany and the Jailer. He does not explain why.

A likely explanation may be found in Shaw's desire "to rewrite the act as Shakespeare might have written it if he had been post-Ibsen and post-Shaw instead of post-Marlowe." Thus Shaw altered the basic nature of Shakespeare's characters, giving them a pronounced likeness to those of his own twentieth-century drawing-room comedies. And in the process, of course, he necessarily altered the way the characters think and the style in which they speak. For example, when Posthumus recognizes that Fidele (whom he has just struck) is in actuality Imogen, Shakespeare's Imogen utters a sad but magnanimous reproach: "Why did you throw your wedded lady from you?/Think that you are upon a rock, and now/Throw me again" (5.5.261–63). Shaw's Imogen (whom Posthumus has just knocked down *"with a blow of his fist"*) is both resentful and scornful: "You dare pretend you love me. . . . /You made this wager! And I'm married to you!" And Iachimo becomes a jazz-age sophisticate: "I think, madam, you do forget that chest./*Imogen.* I forget nothing. . . . /Subtle Italian villain! I would that chest had smothered you./ *Iachimo.* Dear lady,/It very nearly did./*Imogen.* I will not laugh." Clearly the altered tone of the refashioned characterization is completely at odds with the tone of Shakespeare's play. Shaw of course knew this; and he knew also that his variation was incompatible with the supernaturalism of the dream theophany and the rude philosophy of the Jailer's comedy. So, serving himself instead of Shakespeare, he left them out.

Cymbeline Refinished appears to have been revived only once or twice in the professional theater, presumably because directors recognize that it is an impertinent joke—a sort of burlesque in which "high" people of the European Renaissance use the (as it were) "low" language of twentieth-century middle-class liberals. Further, a proper solution of the problem posed by the inordinate length and occasional tedium of Shakespeare's last act lies not in rewriting but in judicious pruning of the battle scenes and the dénouement and in restoring the dream theophany and the Jailer. Something like this solution, including a new tradition of shortening the battle and presenting it symbolically in slow motion, has been adopted by most directors in the second half of the twentieth century.

Three of the most notable modern productions were mounted on the stage of the Shakespeare Memorial Theatre in Stratford-upon-Avon. The directors were Peter Hall (1957), William Gaskill (1962), and John Barton (1974).

In Hall's production Dame Peggy Ashcroft played Imogen, triumphantly repeating the success she had enjoyed in the role twenty-five years earlier in 1932 at the Old Vic. She was ably supported by Geoffrey Keen as Iachimo, Richard Johnson as Posthumus, and Clive Revill as Cloten.

The set, designed by the Italian painter Lila de Nobili, consisted of an upstage row of some half-dozen scenic locales, squeezed together so that only a single characteristic detail of each structure was visible, the several details being lined up cheek by jowl in a solid mass. Muriel St. Clare Byrne describes the set as follows: "Instead of being set round a deep stage like the units of an Hôtel de Bourgogne *décor simultané*, the typical delights of our eighteenth-century romantic landscape poets were combined in one gloriously fantastic 'Gothic' background—the boskage of dark woods, the horrid steeps (practicable) of wild scenery, mysterious archways and twisting staircases, the pillars and fan vaulting of a ruined abbey, the square tower of a village church, a minaret, and a glimpse of a handsome Renaissance interior, all framed in a proscenium of giant oaks." Such an unconventional and exotic set inevitably displeased some members of the audience; others, however, found it stunningly effective and exactly right for *Cymbeline*. A good photograph of the set is reproduced in *Shakespeare in the Theatre* by Richard David, p. 230.

In the bedroom scene the bed and trunk were not brought on- and offstage by stagehands or extras in the manner of the open stage; nor were they discovered and concealed by a front curtain or curtains in the usual manner of the proscenium-arch stage. Rather, the director used the alternative technique of proscenium-arch staging, initially revealing the bed and trunk by lightup and concealing them at the end of the action by blackout. Immediately after Imogen was seized wholly by sleep, a small door in the side of the trunk popped open and Iachimo's hand came sinuously through the hole in order to open the latch of the trunk. This gadgety business provoked laughter, but the authority of the actor and the power of Shakespeare's lines enabled Geoffrey Keen quickly to reestablish the appropriate atmosphere of menace and evil.

Hall's production marks a milestone in that it appears to be the first major production to restore Posthumus's dream vision and the theophany of Jupiter. Byrne writes that the director "shirked none of the production difficulties of the last act. We had all four Ghosts, and rumor says that the full treatment, complete with eagle, was intended, but that the bird of Jove proved too heavy to fly and now lies abandoned in the basement. Be this as it may, the voice of the Thunderer, plus a handsome gold backcloth of divinity, emblems and clouds, completed the vision and the revelation. *And* we had the Jailer." To this account one may add that the "gold backcloth of divinity" was a very large and very beautiful rendering of Inigo Jones's design for

Aurelian Townshend's masque *Tempe Restored* (1632), in which Jupiter is depicted brandishing a handful of thunderbolts while astride his imperial eagle in full flight.

In William Gaskill's production of 1962, Imogen was played by Vanessa Redgrave, Iachimo by Eric Porter, Posthumus by Patrick Allen, and Cloten by Clive Swift. Miss Redgrave's performance was highly praised by most critics.

J. C. Trewin commends the production as a complicated example of "something to look at"—a production "over which the shadow of Brecht hovered. The stage was framed in an off-white fish-net mesh that resembled rough and rucked knitting. Against it the designer, René Allio, either assembled bits and pieces of scenery or swung down a symbolic device from the flies. The battle was stylized. Posthumus was caged in a kind of chicken-coop. Among the artifices there were such streaks of naturalism as the carrying on of Cloten's severed head and Imogen's later mourning over a headless body grimly ensanguined." The bringing on of Cloten's head appears to echo the staging of Durfey's *Injured Princess*.

Miss Redgrave, according to John Russell Brown, dealt superbly with the very real difficulties facing the actress of Imogen in 4.2: ". . . although Cloten's headless body was an object which raised nervous laughter, the audience was then held in rapt belief and concern as Imogen was roused from her drugged sleep to feel it at her side. Miss Redgrave carried this scene boldly, by accepting the improbability and absurdity of her expression of half-conscious thoughts. . . . [She] accepted both fantasy and pathos as manifestations of a mind overmastered by feeling, and her performance had the strength and simplicity to carry conviction."

Gaskill's production marks a second milestone in that it appears to be the first major production to restore the flight of Jupiter. Brown writes that "the broadest stroke in the text of the play, the appearance of Jupiter, was notably well done: John Corvin, in gold costume and make-up, descended on a wide-winged copper eagle and spoke his lines with deliberate force." The eagle "was supported on a solid and obvious steel pole . . . , but this did not detract from his supernatural reality because the actor's firm and simple acceptance of unhurried formal speech carried a strong conviction and awakened forward interest." A photograph of the descent is reproduced opposite p. 191 of Brown's book.

In John Barton's production of 1974, Imogen was played by Susan Fleetwood, Iachimo by Ian Richardson, Posthumus by Tim Piggott-Smith, and Cloten by Charles Keating. This was an exciting production, sensitive to the needs of the play, though one may question the wisdom of expanding Cornelius's role into that of a Jacobean "presenter" or commentator (akin to Gower in *Pericles*), armed with a knowledge of Shakespeare's sources and quoting the Folio stage directions. The set, designed by John Napier, was spare and emblematic, essentially an empty box with curtains at the rear; the design for Wales was described by Peter Thomson as "lunar." Thomson writes further that "the abiding memories are of the staging of the bedroom scene, the audience's applause at the descent of Jupiter's eagle, and the kneeling downstage center of Imogen and Posthumus Leonatus in a reunion that was genuinely touching."

Barton's production marks yet a third milestone in the restoration of the original staging of *Cymbeline* in that the bed was brought onstage in full view of the audience by stagehands or actors using the open-stage technique of Shakespeare's day: "A big white bed is wheeled down to dominate the center of the stage."

Thomson discusses another aspect of Barton's staging of the bedroom scene: "Imogen reads and sleeps, and the lid of the trunk is pushed up to form a headboard upstage of the bed. The picture [on the raised lid] is of a headless, hairy, male nude [who is also obese], and suddenly Richardson's head is on the neck. The violation of the white room is obscene." Richard David, on the other hand, felt that this tricky business lowered the tone: "The placing of the trunk at the bed's head, so that Iachimo pops up above the sleeping Imogen like a bad fairy and eventually, as the clock strikes three, disappears again centrally as if through a trap, had all the air of pantomime." A photograph of the scene is reproduced opposite p. 136 of Thomson's review.

Thomson also records that the flight of Jupiter was enhanced by the introduction of "a great golden egg, which opened out to form an eagle's wings and reveal the gold-painted god." Since several later directors have now followed suit in staging the descent of Jupiter, it seems clear that Gaskill and Barton have succeeded in restoring a vital Jacobean stage tradition after a hiatus of more than three hundred years.

In 1983 the BBC Television Shakespeare series aired a production of *Cymbeline* directed by Elijah Moshinsky. Imogen

was played by Helen Mirren, Posthumus by Michael Penning-
ton, and Iachimo by Robert Lindsay. All three give capable and
interesting performances, but Claire Bloom's characterization
of the Queen is a minor masterpiece in its successful avoidance
of the stereotype of the Wicked Stepmother. As Roger Warren
writes, Miss Bloom is "no melodramatic villainess, but a striking Medici Queen Mother, maintaining her smilingly aristocratic manner even when planning to poison Imogen."

Katherine Duncan-Jones notes that Moshinsky, in creating a
visual style for the play, imposes on "the cluttered world of
Shakespeare's Ancient Britain the lucid visual images of the
great Dutch Masters. . . . Imogen sitting alone waiting for news
of her exiled husband is a Van Dyck beauty in a Vermeer interior." But another visual style is less successful. "The mountains of Wales are for some reason presented as the steppes of
Russia. Instead of a cave, the Welsh exiles inhabit a comfortable if plain dacha, so the vital contrast between the court and
the pastoral world is lost. The most painful casualty is Fidele's
funeral, which happens inside the dacha with the princes squat-
ting uncomfortably over the corpse."

The production is occasionally marred by acting or business
conveying sexual implications that are unsupported by the text.
In 1.6 we see a closeup of Imogen and Iachimo face-to-face in
profile, she absently and with closed eyes moving her slightly
parted lips toward his as he offers to kiss her. Apparently this
Imogen, unlike the one who oft restrained Posthumus from his
lawful pleasure, represses a strong libido. Again, in the bedroom scene Iachimo comes from the trunk in a state of utter
nakedness. Questions arise like a flock of frightened birds. Is he
cold? Did he undress while in the trunk or before entering it?
Does he perhaps intend the supreme brutality (and folly) of
jumping into bed with Imogen? And if Iachimo is naked without warrant of the text, why is not Imogen also naked when the
text requires her to be so? For how otherwise can he see the
mole "under" her breast? And again, in 5.3 Posthumus impul-
sively plants a kiss on the cheek of the Briton Lord to whom he
has reported the conduct of the battle. Is Posthumus then perhaps a closet homosexual? As Duncan-Jones rightly observes,
"Moshinsky seems at times intent on adding more puzzles to an
already puzzling text."

Jupiter is preserved but his descent is not. "Posthumus's vision comes over as a fragment from *Ruddigore*; Jove . . . has no

eagle and looks like a shabby old clergyman" (Duncan-Jones). "Posthumus's family merely gathered round the chair in which he slept, while Jupiter stood looking down on them in the foreground of the shot" (Warren). In an apparent attempt to compensate for the loss of Jupiter's eagle, Moshinsky provides three brief shots of a real eagle towering in his pride of place: before and after the first cave scene (3.3) and again at 4.2.96 where, in a piece of transparent symbolism, he shows the eagle being ineffectually attacked by a hawk. At this point the picture cuts to Cloten insolently bullying Guiderius; and then cuts again (with strong musical emphasis) to a screen-filling closeup of the severed head of Cloten held aloft by a foreshortened Guiderius. Again we have an echo of *The Injured Princess*.

In discussing the mock burial of Fidele, Warren makes an important suggestion. He notes that the dirge of 4.2 is not spoken but sung—"to magical effect, though clearly against the implications of the text. The passage containing those implications was one of several drastic and regrettable cuts that not only diminished the play's effectiveness but seemed quite unnecessary, since the scenes which were virtually uncut, notably those between Iachimo, Posthumus, and Imogen early on, had worked so well in television terms." To this criticism may be added another, namely that the director's elaborate rearrangements of the text in the last three acts gain little in theatrical effect and do nothing to clarify the action.

A final point on the cutting of *Cymbeline*. Frank Kermode, writing on the John Barton production of 1974, suggests that many of Mr. Barton's cuts (for example, whole swatches of text in 1.6, the attempted-seduction scene) "were made to get rid of very obscure and difficult passages; but these may be necessary superfluities, and their absence in a measure falsifies the play." Kermode's essay is a cogent and strongly argued plea for retaining in production the cruxes and angularities of Shakespeare's text. "No one would dream of cutting *The Ring*; should our Shakespearians not at least consider playing all the notes?"

Before we turn to productions from the last decade and a half of the twentieth century and the first half decade of the twenty-first, we can remind ourselves that *Cymbeline* is a play with many difficulties. In the eighteenth century Samuel Johnson put the matter in a characteristically uncompromising way:

To remark the folly of the fiction, the absurdity of the conduct, the confusion of the names and manners of different times, and the impossibility of the events in any system of life, were to waste criticism upon unresisting imbecility, upon faults too evident for detection, and too gross for exaggeration.

This is strong stuff, but we can at least agree that the language is sometimes clotted—viewers and readers often must wonder if perhaps they have not been paying adequate attention—as, for instance, in the opening speech:

> *First Gentleman.* You do not meet a man but frowns. Our bloods
> No more obey the heavens than our courtiers
> Still seem as does the King's.

In fact, in its original printing in the first Folio (1623) the speech is even less intelligible:

> You do not meet a man but Frownes.
> Our bloods no more obey the Heauens
> Then our Courtiers:
> Still seemes, as do's the Kings.

Various modern editors treat these lines variously, but no matter how one punctuates them they remain hard to grasp. Like Pisanio in a later scene, we are "perplexed," and like Posthumus speaking of a prophecy, we can "make no collection of it." Still, for a director, perhaps the biggest problem is how to think of the play as a whole. The editors of the first Folio classified it as a tragedy, perhaps thinking of the resemblance of King Cymbeline to King Lear, each of whom rejects a virtuous daughter with unfortunate consequences. Also approaching tragedy is Posthumus's Othello-like rejection of his beloved, but of course *Cymbeline* ends happily. If the editors had established a group called "Romances" or "Tragicomedies," there would have been no problem, but aside from tragedy, there were comedy and history, and *Cymbeline* does not sit easily within any of these three genres. Shall one emphasize the play's historical aspects, with its implications concerning Britain's imperial destiny? (Probably its first viewers did take this theme very seriously, in the context of the aspirations of James I in the early seventeenth century, but a director working for today's audiences can hardly take this line.) Shall one—guided by the fact that the first editors called it a tragedy—treat the play seriously, as a serious work about a serious matter? (Hard to do.) Given the Folio's three categories, that leaves the option of comedy, but, alas, there are no funny scenes and very few funny lines in the play, though as we shall see, at least one modern production has played it for laughs. Beyond this matter of the sometimes clotted language and the genre of the play, with its glimpses of the pseudohistory of ancient Celtic Britain and ancient Rome and the intrigue of Medieval/Renaissance Italy, we must recognize that the play is very long (some three and a half hours in the theater, if it is uncut), that the hero is a most unattractive fellow (actors much prefer the role of the villainous Iachimo), and that the closing scene is monstrously long with its nearly five hundred lines of explanation, recognition, and prophecy; at least two dozen revelations are made to the characters on the stage, though only one of these revelations (the death of the queen) is new to the audience.

In 1988 Peter Hall returned to *Cymbeline*—we have already glanced at his 1957 production—at the National Theatre in London. The audience saw a Jacobean facade with a central doorway, a silhouette of a great tree on the floor, and above the doorway a gold disk painted to represent the Copernican heaven; in the prison scene the disk opened to permit Jupiter to descend, classically garbed and seated on an eagle. When Imogen set out for Milford Haven in Wales, a circular section of the planked floor rose and pivoted, creating a sloping surface of rocks and grass, and an area at the back of the stage became a cave from which Belarius and the two princes emerged. Costumes were mid-seventeenth century (lace collars for men, ringlets for women), and the production on the whole was serious.

And now (in the words of *Monty Python*) for something completely different: With the 1989 version directed by JoAnne Akalaitis for the New York Shakespeare Festival we get to a production that must be characterized as postmodern. Postmodernism subscribes to an aesthetic of fragmentation (think of *Monty Python*): It dismisses concepts of unity, consistency, and clarity as illusions, and it emphasizes contradictions, ironic juxtapositions, ambiguous incongruities, and what the director Peter Sellars has called "visual counterpoint," the use of visual imagery (for example a film clip) that ironically contradicts the action that the audience sees being performed. Thus, if *Cymbeline* is puzzling to many traditional directors and scholars partly because it does not seem to fit the classification of "Tragedies," where the editors of the first Folio put it in 1623, this very fact makes it especially interesting to postmodern directors. In Akalaitis's playbill the production was described as a "Romantic fantasy set in Victorian England," but this was only a starting point. Shakespeare's early-seventeenth-century play was staged not with Jacobean costumes of the period nor (given the period in which *Cymbeline* is set) with some sort of approximation of ancient British costumes; rather, the British army wore kilts and pith helmets, and the Roman army wore Victorian military garb with plumed helmets, with the result that both armies seemed to be made up of toy soldiers. Cymbeline's kidnapped sons, living in rural conditions, wore loin cloths and war paint that supposedly evoked American Indians of the eighteenth or nineteenth century. Casting was color blind: Imogen was white, one of her brothers was black and the other was Hispanic. Reviews were almost uniformly hostile, but several writers in *American Theatre* (December 1989) vigorously responded, arguing that the journalists did not understand what was going on. Thus, Elinor Fuchs, in a piece entitled "Misunderstanding Postmodernism," explained to the benighted reviewers that the new aesthetic gives value to "a multiple and decentered way of understanding the world and our own subjectivity" and it requires us to "respond to many 'texts' at once" (p. 25).

We will meet postmodernism again when we look at Danny Scheie's 2000 production in Santa Cruz, but first we should consider some imaginative yet less extreme productions. In 1997 Adrian Noble presented a fairly heavily cut *Cymbeline* at Stratford (also in London the next year). He chose to evoke the Asian theater, dressing his warriors rather like samurai and his courtiers rather like Asian scholars with skull caps and long black jackets—and thereby he eradicated whatever political implications the play may have concerning Britain's imperial destiny. His set—a blue cube with an orange moon, and a white saillike cloth suspended that swooped forward or backward to change the scene—evoked much favorable comment. Actors entered the stage via a walkway through the audience, rather as in some Japanese drama. When the first spectators entered the theater, they saw a white-garbed hooded figure seated by a fire. Additional performers, also dressed in white, joined him by ones and twos, until there were perhaps twenty or twenty-five seated figures. A performer in reddish-orange then entered, and—in place of the opening expository dialogue between a nameless First Gentleman and a nameless Second Gentleman— this figure narrated a history about a king named Cymbeline. Each seated character rose when he or she was mentioned, and took on the role. In addition to helping the audience to grasp a complicated plot, this device helped to establish the play as a sort of folk tale, a story whose improbabilities somehow have a universal or archetypal significance. Benedict Nightingale in the *London Times* (28 February 1997) called Noble's version "superb."

A production by Andrei Serban in 1998, at the New York Shakespeare Festival, did not attract much attention, in contrast to Danny Scheie's production staged in 2000 in Santa Cruz. Members of the audience who had already read or seen the play must have been amazed to find that Scheie treated it as a comedy. He neglected no opportunity to get a laugh, often undercutting the stage action by showing on six video monitors images from old Hollywood films, newsreels, and animations. Such notables as the Beatles, Elizabeth Taylor as Cleopatra, and Edward VIII and Mrs. Simpson appeared on the monitors, and the audience saw and heard the news in Italian when Posthumus was in Rome but the sound shifted to Latin when the Romans arrived in Britain. On the stage proper, the audience saw the two anonymous Gentlemen of the first scene represented by a ventriloquist and his dummy; Belarius and the two kidnapped sons of Cymbeline lived in a pup tent and wore boy scout garb; the first scene in Italy was set in a mafioso pool hall, where the denizens wore dark suits and let cigarettes dangle from their mouths. Running gags were used. Whenever the name "Fidele" was spoken, the audience heard a motif from the overture of Beethoven's *Fidele*. The patriotic themes within the play were spoofed, not least by a Union Jack painted on the chest of Posthumus—he is, after all, a British hero—who in one scene was totally nude for some ten minutes. At the end of the play the cast lined up on the stage and sang a patriotic hymn by Cecil Spring-Rice, "I Vow to Thee My Country." The effect doubtless was intended to be ironic, but here the director may have miscalculated; the audience, joining in, seemed moved. Stephen Orgel, in a long and essentially sympathetic review of the production, says the production as a whole "had a Monty

Pythonish energy and wit, but the larger point pretty much got lost" (*Shakespeare Quarterly* 52 [2001]: 285).

In 2001, a year after Danny Scheie's Santa Cruz production, Mike Alfreds directed a minimalist production of *Cymbeline* at the Globe on the South Bank of the Thames, and in 2002 at the Brooklyn Academy of Music. The play was performed by only six actors—four men and two women—accompanied by two musicians, who used Asian musical instruments (chiefly percussion) to set the moods for various scenes. (Mark Rylance, artistic director of the Globe, introduced the actors, told the audience to turn off cell phones and not to rustle candy wrappers, and then in the course of the evening played the parts of Cloten, Posthumus, and the Queen's physician.) This skeleton cast even managed to represent such a stage direction as "Enter Lucius, Iachimo, and the Roman army at one door, and the Briton army at another, Leonatus Posthumus following like a poor soldier. They march over and go out" (5.1). All six actors wore pajama-like off-white tunics, trousers, and shoes, and when they were not playing a role they remained visible to the audience. Indeed, an actor not at the moment performing a role often handed a necessary prop to a performer. The props were not realistic; thus, when Iachimo took notes in Imogen's bedroom, he scratched with a stylus on a miniature washboard. To indicate a change of scene, a musician sounded a gong and an actor proclaimed the name of the new locale. When Imogen enters disguised as a boy in 3.6, the performer (Jane Arnfield) said "Enter Imogen dressed as a man" and that was that: The audience accepted the pajamas as a fresh disguise. Much was ingenious and highly engaging but Charles Isherwood, in a review in *Variety* (18 March 2002), may have put his finger on the weakness of Alfreds's production:

The choice of *Cymbeline* for the less-is-more treatment works against the play's strengths. Unlike many another Shakespeare play, *Cymbeline* does not derive its energies primarily from the beauty of its language or the depth of its characterizations: instead, it is the colorful machinery of the plot and the wealth of exotic incident that provide the dramatic momentum. The Globe's production, which smoothed out the exotic colors of the play through its ascetic approach, thus emphasized its weak points and downplayed its strengths. The result was a bit wan, like a tapestry left in the sun too long that has been bleached of color and definition.

In 2002 New Yorkers could also see a production directed by Bartlett Sher, where Cymbeline's court was dressed in what passes for samurai garb, the Italians in what passes for Elizabethan garb, and the two abducted sons in what passes for cowboy garb. The Wild West was thus conceived as a sort of equivalent to rural Wales, and the boys sang country-western music. Two performers who clarified the plot by serving as narrators acted also as prop men and musicians.

A year later, Dominic Cooke directed a production of the Royal Shakespeare Company at the Swan Theatre in Stratford-upon-Avon. Except for some large shutters leaning against the back wall, the stage was relatively bare. Rome was a table, and Milford Haven was established by pulling a fake sheep onto the stage. Dress was a mixed bag: primitive furs and feathers for the ancient Brits, but top-hats for Cymbeline's bodyguards and a tight-fitting dress and snakeskin boots for the wicked queen; white suits and sunglasses for the pasta-eating Italians; and period armor for the Roman soldiers in Britain. Preparing for battle, the Britons performed a ritual dance; Cloten's marvelous aubade (the wake-up song in 2.3, "Hark, hark, the lark at heaven's gate sings") was sung by bird-headed performers, who at the last "arise" were accompanied by ringing alarm clocks.

In this brief survey we have seen a staggering variety of productions, and a reader may wonder, "Why can't they just do the play straight?" The answer is obvious: One cannot do it "straight" because there is no essential *Cymbeline*, no text that can be performed without interpretation. Would a "straight" performance be one that (as in Shakespeare's day) took place only in daylight or, if indoors, with candles for illumination, on a stage like Shakespeare's, with boys playing female roles, and with performers costumed in the way that we think Shakespeare's actors probably were costumed? Such a production would have more than a whiff of "museum theater" about it. It would be an interesting experiment, but no more. And, given the improbabilities of the plot and the evident theatricality of some of its episodes (most notably the appearance of Jupiter), the play invites a self-conscious or "metatheatrical" presentation. True, some of the productions that we have surveyed have striven so hard to be interesting—so hard to be part of a "living theater"—that they have lost sight of the text, but most of them have played a significant role in the history of the productions of *Cymbeline*. They have entertained their audiences—and

surely that counts for something!—and they have made at least
some of their audiences think further about the play and perhaps also about life. Some viewers and readers doubtless have
concluded that the play is a delightful fairy tale and nothing
more; some have concluded that like a delightful fairy tale it
touches on archetypal issues, and it speaks meaningfully to the
imagination and it in some mysterious way tells us something
about our lives. Perhaps we can say of this play, which takes us
to Renaissance Rome and to ancient Britain and which shows
us the spiritual journeys of Imogen and Posthumus, what G. K.
Chesterton said about traveling: "The whole object of travel is
not to set foot in foreign land; it is at last to set foot on one's
own country as a foreign land."

Bibliographic note: Martin Butler has a useful survey of the history of productions in his edition of *Cymbeline* (2005). Roger
Warren discusses productions in two books: *Cymbeline* (in a
series called "Shakespeare in Performance," 1989) and (Peter
Hall's production of 1988) *Staging Shakespeare's Late Plays*
(1990). Ros King, in *Cymbeline: Constructions of Britain*
(2005), devotes a chapter to "Constructing Production," in
which he raises many interesting issues and then concentrates on
versions by Durfey, Garrick, Kemble, Barton, Dorn (in Mu-
nich), and Scheie's production (2000) in Santa Cruz. King's
book grew out of his work as dramaturg for Scheie's production.
  The open-stage production techniques of the First Globe and
the Blackfriars are discussed by Richard Hosley in *The Revels
History of Drama in English: III 1575–1613* (1975). The techniques of early scenic production are treated by Richard Southern in *Changeable Scenery* (1952) and by Stephen Orgel and
Roy Strong in *Inigo Jones: The Theatre of the Stuart Court*
(1973). (Jones's scenic design for *Tempe Restored* showing a
descent of Jupiter is reproduced by Orgel and Strong at *II*, 478.)
Reconstruction drawings of English scenic playhouses from the
Caroline period to the twentieth century have been published by
Richard Leacroft in *The Development of the English Playhouse*
(1973).
  C. B. Young has a short historical account of productions of
Cymbeline in the New Cambridge edition, ed. J. C. Maxwell
(1960). More detailed treatments are provided by William Win-
ter, *Shakespeare on Stage* (third series, 1916) and George C. D.
Odell, *Shakespeare from Betterton to Irving* (1920). A detailed

synopsis of Durfey's *Injured Princess* is supplied by Hazelton Spencer in *Shakespeare Improved* (1927). Garrick's adaptation of *Cymbeline* is discussed by George Winchester Stone in *Philological Quarterly* 54 (1975). William Charles Macready's production of 1843 is treated in detail by Carol Carlisle in *Shakespeare and the Victorian Stage,* ed. Richard Foulkes (1986). George Bernard Shaw's *Cymbeline Refinished* and its foreword are available in *The Complete Plays* (1962).

The Peter Hall production of 1957 is reviewed by Muriel St. Clare Byrne in *Shakespeare Quarterly* 8 (1957) and Richard David in *Shakespeare in the Theatre* (1978); the William Gaskill production of 1962, by J. C. Trewin in *Shakespeare's Plays Today* (1971) and John Russell Brown in *Shakespeare's Plays in Performance* (1966); the John Barton production of 1974, by Peter Thomson in *Shakespeare Survey* 28 (1975), Richard David in *Shakespeare in the Theatre,* and Frank Kermode in *The Times Literary Supplement* (July 5, 1974).

Among useful comments on fairly recent productions are: On Adrian Noble's production of 1997, Robert Smallwood in *Shakespeare Survey* 51 (1998): 228–30; on Mike Alfreds (2001), Michael Dobson in *Shakespeare Survey* 55 (2002): 314–16, and Charles Isherwood, *Variety,* March 18, 2002; on Bartlett Sher (2002), Charles Isherwood in *Variety,* January 28, 2002; on Dominic Cooke (2003), Russell Jackson in *Shakespeare Quarterly* 55 (2004): 189–90, and Katherine Duncan-Jones in *The Times Literary Supplement,* August 15, 2003; on Danny Scheie (2000), Stephen Orgel in *Shakespeare Quarterly* 52 (2001): 277–85.

Edwin Thanhouser's film of 1913 is described by Robert Hamilton Ball in *Shakespeare on Silent Film* (1968). Elijah Moshinsky's videotape production of 1983 is discussed in Susan Willis, *The BBC Shakespeare* (1991), and is reviewed by Katherine Duncan-Jones in *The Times Literary Supplement* (July 22, 1983) and Roger Warren in *Shakespeare Quarterly* 29 (1983). Moshinsky's videotape is available in the BBC/Time-Life Shakespeare Series.

The four operas based on *Cymbeline* are discussed by Winton Dean in "Shakespeare in the Opera House," *Shakespeare Survey* 18 (1965).

The Two Noble Kinsmen

THE TWO NOBLE KINSMEN:

Presented at the Blackfriers by the Kings Maiesties servants, with great applause:

Written by the memorable Worthies of their time;
{ Mr. *John Fletcher*, and } Gent.
{ Mr. *William Shakspeare*. }

Printed at *London* by *Tho. Cotes*, for *Iohn Waterson*: and are to be sold at the signe of the *Crowne* in *Pauls* Church-yard. 1 6 3 4.

Frontispiece to the first published version of *The Two Noble Kinsmen.*

Introduction

The Two Noble Kinsmen was first published in a quarto edition of 1634, with statements on its title page that it had been "Presented at the Blackfriers by the Kings Maiesties servants, with great applause" and that it was "Written by the memorable Worthies of their time; Mr. *John Fletcher,* and Mr. *William Shakespeare,* Gent." The publisher was John Waterson, a reputable figure who brought out other plays belonging to the King's Men, the company with which Shakespeare and Fletcher had been intimately associated. Although in 1646, when Waterson assigned to Humphrey Moseley his rights in the play, it was included with two others as simply the work of "Mr. Flesher," there is an immediately strong case for accepting the title page's statement of authorship. If Waterson were looking for a way of attracting custom, it would have been at least as effective in 1634 to attribute the play to Beaumont and Fletcher. Moreover, it appears that the manuscript from which he printed had been used in the theater itself* and that Waterson had bought it from the players in the normal way of business. And we shall see that the probable date of composition and first performance was 1613, when we have other evidence that Shakespeare and Fletcher were working in close association.

*See Textual Note.

It is true, on the other hand, that Heminges and Condell did not include *The Two Noble Kinsmen* in the Shakespeare Folio of 1623, where in the preliminary address *"To the great Variety of Readers"* there is an implication that all of Shakespeare's plays were being published in the collection. But it appears that *Timon of Athens* was not originally included in their plans for the volume, and we know that *Troilus and Cressida,* probably through difficulties over copyright, was almost left out. And they did omit *Pericles.* That *The Two Noble Kinsmen* was included in the 1679 Folio of "Beaumont and Fletcher" plays is also not substantial evidence against Shakespeare's part-authorship, for that volume brought together many plays in which Fletcher collaborated with various dramatists of his time, the linking of his name with Beaumont's on the title page (as in the earlier Beaumont and Fletcher Folio of 1647) being merely a tribute to the brief association of the two men which laid the basis for Fletcher's fame and established a mode of dramatic writing which was long influential in the English theater.

Nevertheless, the publishing history of the play belongs far more with Beaumont and Fletcher than with Shakespeare. It has been regularly included in collected editions of Beaumont and Fletcher since their Folio of 1679, from Tonson's edition of 1711 to the Cambridge edition of Arnold Glover and A. R. Waller of 1905–12. It did not appear in a collected Shakespeare until 1841, when Charles Knight (who believed that Fletcher's collaborator here was George Chapman) yielded to the extent of including it in a volume of "Doubtful Plays" appended to his Pictorial Shakespeare. By then, though dissentient voices were not infrequently raised, the case for Shakespeare's part-authorship had become more than formidable. Pope, in his Shakespeare of 1725, thought the play contained "more of our author than some of those which have been received as genuine," and Lamb and Coleridge and De Quincey were all convinced of Shakespeare's presence, though Hazlitt and Shelley could find nothing of it. William Spalding, however, in his *Letter on Shakspere's Authorship of The Two Noble Kinsmen* (Edinburgh, 1833; reprinted in the *Transactions of the New Shakspere Society,* 1874), Samuel Hickson in his article "The Shares of Shakspere and Fletcher in 'The Two Noble Kinsmen'" (*Westminster Review,* 1847; reprinted in the *Transactions of the New Shakspere Society,* 1874), and above all Harold Littledale in the introduction to his edition of the play for the New Shakspere Society (1876–85) brought the techniques of nineteenth-century scholarship to bear on the problem and, though they differed to some extent in assigning to the two dramatists their respective shares, they left little doubt in most readers' minds that here we have a collaboration between the leading dramatist of the King's Men and the writer who succeeded him in that role in 1613.

The elder dramatist's authorship is commonly recognized most surely in the first and fifth acts, particularly in the first three scenes of Act 1 and the first, third, and fourth scenes of Act 5: that is, the solemn approach of the three Queens to Theseus on his wedding day, the conversation of Palamon and Arcite while they are still in Thebes, the scene where Emilia and Hippolyta talk of friendship, the invocations addressed to Mars and Venus and Diana, and the conclusion of the whole story in Arcite's victory and death. In addition, Shakespeare has been generally found in the opening lines of 2.1, where the Jailer's Daughter makes her first appearance, and in 3.1, where the escaped Palamon meets the disguised Arcite. In the rest of the play there are frequent echoes of other plays by Shakespeare: the madness of the Jailer's Daughter has obvious associations with Ophelia's, and in the later pages of this Introduction it will be suggested that Fletcher for special purposes was drawing upon his intimate knowledge of his collaborator's work. If we accept the commonly held view of the two writers' shares (and there is little reason to be skeptical about it), it was Shakespeare who wrote the beginning and the ending and introduced all the major characters and strands of action. But by the time this play was composed he may have been less regularly in attendance at the playhouse than formerly, and it seems likely enough that the final putting together of the manuscript was left to Fletcher. Indeed, more than one scholar has come to the conclusion that he made some insertions in the Shakespeare scenes.

It will be convenient to set out the probable authorship of the play's various scenes thus:

Prologue .... Fletcher?

Act 1, sc. 1–3 .... Shakespeare
      sc. 4–5 .... Shakespeare?

Act 2, sc. 1 (lines 1–59) .... Shakespeare
      sc. 1 (remainder), 2–5 .... Fletcher

The dividing of the play between Shakespeare and Fletcher has been worked out by scholars primarily on the basis of the stylistic differences between their writing. Certainly even a casual reading of the play will show that certain scenes have a complex, "knotted" verse that is close to Shakespeare's in his later years, while others belong clearly with the open-textured, casual style that Beaumont and Fletcher developed in manifest reaction against the involutions of the earliest Jacobeans. The difference has been brought home forcibly to the present editor through the process of annotation. If one compares the scenes where Palamon and Arcite talk together, putting 1.2 and 3.1 on one side and 2.1 (from the exit of the Jailer, his Daughter, and her Wooer), 3.3, and 3.6 on the other, one sees immediately that the first group requires continuous attention from the reader, and probably frequent recourse to the annotations, while the second group has nearly the familiarity of the English now current. When the editor was preparing the annotations, it was with no thought of giving fuller comment on Shakespeare's portion than on Fletcher's, but in the event it proved that in Shakespeare's the proportion of notes to lines was 51% in the scenes just indicated while in Fletcher's the proportion of notes to lines was 25%. Elsewhere in Fletcher's part of the play the figure is higher, as the terms used in connection with the morris dance of 3.5 needed comment, and Fletcher can use a more elaborate vocabulary for special purposes (as in the description of the knights in 4.2 and in the account of madness in 4.3). Nevertheless, the presence of the two hands is obvious almost throughout, and evident at a glance in scenes where the basic material (Palamon and Arcite talking together) is similar.

The time of composition is hardly in dispute. The entertainment which the country Schoolmaster presents to Theseus and his court in 3.5 is taken over from an antimasque in Francis Beaumont's *Masque of the Inner Temple and Gray's Inn*, presented at Whitehall on 20 February 1613. In the published book of the masque we learn that this part of the entertainment was so well liked by the King that he asked to have it danced again at the end of the whole performance. Such antimasques at court were commonly entrusted to professional players, and it would be an easy matter for Fletcher, with his friend and former collaborator Beaumont's permission, to make further use of what had already proved successful. But clearly this would not be likely except soon after the original performance. The date 1613 for *The Two Noble Kinsmen* is confirmed by the reference in Jonson's *Bartholomew Fair* (1614) to "Palamon" as a character in a play (4.3): this is not certain evidence, for the name also occurs in Samuel Daniel's *The Queen's Arcadia* (1605), but Daniel's work was a university play and was already some years old in 1614; Jonson is far more likely to have had a recent and better-known play in mind. Moreover, 1613 was the year in which a lost play called *Cardenio** (which in 1653 was attributed to Fletcher and Shakespeare by the publisher Humphrey Moseley) was twice acted at court, and it was the year too in which *Henry VIII* was almost certainly acted for the first time. Although by no means all Shakespeare scholars are agreed on the double authorship of *Henry VIII*, there is strong cumulative evidence that in 1613, after Shakespeare had come to the end of his series of "romances" and was about to retire from the stage, and when Beaumont on his marriage had broken with the theater and thus terminated the short but highly profitable collaboration that he and Fletcher had known for some five years, a new and brief association was established between Fletcher and Shakespeare, and that *The Two Noble Kinsmen* was one of its fruits.

In these circumstances, and with the assumption that the main planning of the play was, as it has seemed likely, Shakespeare's, we should expect to find a clear enough relationship to the "romances" which Shakespeare had been writing since *Pericles* (c. 1609) and which he had brought to a conclusion in *The Tempest* (1611). And resemblances are hardly to be missed. In *Pericles* he had gone to Gower's *Confessio Amantis* for his

---

*It may exist in an altered form in Lewis Theobald's version of the story, called *Double Falsehood* and published in 1728.

story: here he goes to Gower's contemporary, Chaucer. *Pericles* and *The Winter's Tale* have Hellenistic settings: *The Two Noble Kinsmen* takes us to Athens and briefly to Thebes. The "romances" present a world where the gods are freely invoked and where they play a direct part in the action—Diana appearing to Pericles in a dream and sending him to Ephesus so that he may find his lost wife, Thaisa, Jupiter appearing to Posthumus Leonatus in prison and offering a riddling promise of good fortune to him and of a happy ending to the strife between Rome and Britain, Apollo being consulted on the question of Hermione's guilt and striking dead Mamillius when his father, Leontes, rejects the message from the oracle. In *The Tempest* there are, it is true, no gods—they would be out of place in a drama where a human character has unlimited control over events (though not over the human will)—but there are spirits who represent Juno and Ceres and Iris and who offer divine blessings and admonitions. *The Two Noble Kinsmen* keeps the gods off the stage too, but their altars are there, they are solemnly invoked, and tokens of their favor are given. At the play's end Theseus marvels how the apparently contradictory promises of Mars and Venus have both been fulfilled. More obviously, more disturbingly indeed, than in the previous plays the human characters of *The Two Noble Kinsmen* are subject to divine power. Theseus can devise a plan for finding out Emilia's husband and for ending the strife between the knights, but it is the gods who circuitously determine things, to the wonder and embarrassment of those concerned.

In some striking features this play has a special relationship with *Pericles*. That had a detachable first act (which was omitted at a Stratford-on-Avon revival in 1947), with formal speechmaking in a context of love and death: so has *The Two Noble Kinsmen*, which could easily have been adjusted to begin with Palamon and Arcite already in prison. Then Arcite's encounter in 2.2 with the countrymen who will take part in the games for Emilia's birthday resembles Pericles' encounter with the fishermen in 2.1, where he learns there are games to be held in Thaisa's honor: both Pericles and Arcite are victors and are received into the lady's favor. But in *Pericles* the games are a formal tournament, which takes place in an atmosphere of high ceremonial, while in *The Two Noble Kinsmen* it is a matter of simple running and wrestling. The tournament, however, is not forgotten and occurs offstage in the final encounter between Palamon and Arcite, each aided by his three knights. The cry of "The mean knight!" which indicates at the end of 2.2 that Pericles has been victorious anticipates the cries of "Palamon!" and "Arcite!" and "Victory!" that Emilia hears in 5.3. Here the influence of one of Shakespeare's romances is seen operative on a Fletcher portion of the later play.

But there is a more subtle echo of *The Winter's Tale*. Commentators have sometimes seen there a suggestion that Leontes, believing his wife is being unfaithful to him with his best friend, is unconsciously more deeply outraged by the breach in friendship than by the breach in marriage. Certainly the nostalgic reminiscences of Leontes and Polixenes in 1.2, their sense that an Eden was lost when they grew up and took wives, is to be linked with the passage in *The Two Noble Kinsmen*, 1.3, where Emilia and Hippolyta talk of the friendship between Theseus and Pirithous and the friendship between Emilia and the dead girl Flavina: Hippolyta is not sure that even now she has the first place in Theseus' heart, Emilia has no thought that a husband can be as near to her as Flavina was. In the center of the later play, moreover, there is the friendship of Palamon and Arcite: it is broken when they both love Emilia, but even as they plan to fight to the death (in 3.3) they look back with some longing on their earlier and lighter loves which did not harm their friendship. That is a brief respite, for Palamon is soon asserting his claim again, but the scene where they help to arm each other (3.6) is strong in its suggestion of enduring affection. They embrace solemnly before the invocation of their respective divine patrons (5.1), and Arcite's words to Emilia when he appears to have won her are heavily charged with a sense of the price he has paid:

> Emily,
> To buy you I have lost what's dearest to me
> Save what is bought, and yet I purchase cheaply
> As I do rate your value.
>
> (5.3.111–14)

Shakespeare's "romances" are, among other things, love stories, but they are not simple exaltations of the bond which ties most men to women.

This indeed suggests a connection with his earliest plays. *The Two Gentlemen of Verona* was also a play about friendship, and it is difficult not to believe that its very title was echoed in that of *The Two Noble Kinsmen*. There Valentine and Proteus were firm friends until Proteus fell in love with the girl his friend loved. The right and wrong of the matter were simple: Proteus is thoroughly treacherous and gets to the point of attempting rape. When he repents, Valentine has so high a sense of what friendship demands that he is willing to let Proteus have the girl, not thinking even of consulting her. At that time Shakespeare could make discreet fun of the friendship-idea and could quickly make all things come right. Moreover, it was Proteus' villainy and Valentine's simple faith that caused the trouble, while in *The Two Noble Kinsmen* Palamon and Arcite love Emilia because they have to, and Arcite dies because the gods have determined so. That Shakespeare thought back to *The Two Gentlemen* is, I think, indubitable, just as he thought back to *The Comedy of Errors* in the final turn of events in *Pericles*, just as he remembered the rambling romantic plays of the popular theater he first knew when he wrote *Pericles* and *Cymbeline* and *The Winter's Tale*. In going back to beginnings, *The Two Noble Kinsmen* is of a piece with the "romances," though it has a formality of structure, as we shall see, that links it with *The Tempest* more than with the plays that immediately preceded that.

It is, however, another early play that is here most prominently in his mind, and again the resemblance goes along with contrast and deliberate reconsideration. Like *The Two Noble Kinsmen, A Midsummer Night's Dream* begins with preparations for the wedding of Theseus and Hippolyta, it is partly concerned with an amateur performance given before the Duke by his subjects, and it shows the court during a May-morning ceremony coming upon two men who have fallen out through rivalry in love. In the earlier play the wedding is not interrupted, there being merely a planned delay before it takes place; the play-within-the-play occurs at the end, not the middle; the rivals in love have had their quarrel already sorted out by Puck and Oberon before Theseus arrives. And it is not quite the same Theseus in the two plays. The earlier Duke has the authority of the later one, but he is ever sanguine and relaxed: he will not believe the "story of the night," he is patronizing toward play-acting and somewhat ill-mannered during the performance. The Duke of *The Two Noble Kinsmen* may finally attempt to console himself by marveling at the divine legerdemain, but there is an unrelaxed seriousness in him and a continuing puzzlement. The man who at first decrees perpetual imprisonment for Palamon and Arcite, and later death for them both, and after that death for the loser (and his supporters) in the tournament, is a shrewd realist very different from the man who told Hermia he could not bend the law for her sake—her father's authority being supreme—and finally acquiesced in her marriage with Lysander and told Egeus he must accept the situation. We can see a similar change, along with a resemblance, in the later play's echoing of Helena's account of her girlhood friendship with Hermia (3.2): when Emilia speaks of the relationship between herself and Flavina, Shakespeare is no longer offering a merely gentle picture of two girls together.

Shakespeare, then, using a well-known story that had been prominently in his mind when he wrote *A Midsummer Night's Dream* (c. 1595–96), helped to compose a play that had strong links both with the late "romances" and with early comedies that he had already shown a disposition to recall and to look upon with a changed vision. The reunions at the ends of *The Comedy of Errors* and *Pericles* are as different as we can imagine; the spanning of the years in *Pericles* and *The Winter's Tale* does not make those plays similar in spirit to the romances of the 1570's (and the following decade or so) that Sidney made fun of in *An Apology for Poetry;* magic has a different look in *The Tempest* when we compare that play with *A Midsummer Night's Dream*. There is a certain casualness of manner in *The Two Noble Kinsmen*, such indeed as Lytton Strachey saw in the late "romances" as a whole, but it goes along with a reserving of judgment about human beings and the conditions under which they live.

And in this situation Fletcher was no longer with Beaumont but with an elder dramatist whose plays were always strongly in his mind, to the point where he would deliberately modify an initial Shakespeare-situation and then work out the pattern of event that would result. He and Beaumont had done that with *Philaster* (c. 1609), taking the *Hamlet*-situation without the ghost, as later—on his own—he was to write a sequel to *The Taming of the Shrew* in *The Woman's Prize, or The Tamer Tamed*

(c. 1611) and, probably along with Massinger, to invert the *Lear*-situation in *Thierry and Theodoret* (c. 1617). With Beaumont he had shared a lodging and had developed a dramatic mode in which their two minds functioned, it seemed, as one: though we may perhaps be able to differentiate his verse from Beaumont's, we do not get the feeling in their joint plays that two diverse attitudes are alternating as each in his turn pushes his pen. Fletcher's later collaboration with Massinger resembles his collaboration with Shakespeare in *The Two Noble Kinsmen* to the extent that we feel the characterization and the march of event are seen through different eyes in different parts of the play. If we are correct, as many people have thought, in assuming that Shakespeare put his scenes into Fletcher's hands and let him do the job of conflating the two shares, this was a situation new to this dramatist. That the story would have attracted him is understandable: the clash between love and friendship in Palamon and Arcite has some similarity to that between friendship and honor in Melantius and Amintor in *The Maid's Tragedy* (c. 1610) and would similarly lend itself to the patterned alternations of conduct that Fletcher delighted in; and there must have been a piquancy in working in association with Shakespeare, to whom he owed much, whose work, however, must have seemed old-fashioned, imperfectly sophisticated. He and Beaumont had pulled Hamlet down to the comic level of Philaster; now Shakespeare's Palamon and Arcite could be irreverently handled in the same play as Shakespeare was presenting them.

It is not that Fletcher makes the kinsmen directly absurd (though coming near it in their exchange of sentiments, followed at once by their quarrel, in 2.1), and he clearly has some partiality for Arcite; but he does take a feline pleasure in the way love holds them, in the way they try to live up to the friendship code at the same time as they are protesting their separate devotions to Emilia. And this goes along with a special fluency in his writing (seen, for example, in the prison-and-garden sequence of 2.1), and a fondness for setting the story in brakes and flowers. Nature is never ominous for Fletcher, but its presence as a framework for strife is always ironic.

In one place the work of Fletcher's deflating hand reminds us of an effect found in Shakespeare's own *The Winter's Tale*, 5.2, and in scenes frequently ascribed to Fletcher in *Henry VIII* (2.1, 4.1). The Messenger in *The Two Noble Kinsmen*, 4.2, seems to

the present editor's ear to be intentionally comic, with his ec-
static praise of the attendant knights, his overreadiness to speak
at line 72, his general extravagance of imagery, and in particular the doting on one knight's freckles and the ludicrous comparison of his sinews to the bodily shape of a pregnant woman
(lines 128–29). Here I believe we have Fletcher taking up what
he found in *The Winter's Tale*, and pushing it much further both
in *Henry VIII* and in *The Two Noble Kinsmen*.

If general opinion is right in assigning the opening of 2.1 to
Shakespeare, it was he who introduced the Jailer's Daughter.
But the use made of her is characteristically Fletcher's. First we
should note his boldness in giving her so many scenes alone
(2.3, 2.5, 3.2, 3.4): the contrast with Emilia's safe establishment
in Theseus' court is striking; and while Emilia is always herself,
never in love, protesting yet acquiescent, grieved rather than
disturbed, the Jailer's Daughter moves from light-hearted romance:

> Out upon't,
> What pushes are we wenches driven to
> When fifteen once has found us!
>
> (2.3.5–7)

to fear and hunger, and thence to a sense of exposure:

> I am very cold, and all the stars are out too,
> The little stars and all, that look like aglets.
> The sun has seen my folly.
>
> (3.4.1–3)

and thence to madness. The descent is not merely pathetic: it is
comic, as we see in her taking part in the morris dance of 3.5,
and it is powerfully suggestive of the casual destructiveness of
the love-impulse. Aspatia in *The Maid's Tragedy* is too often
seen as a merely pathetic figure: there is destructiveness there
too, for herself and for Amintor. Fletcher had a strong sense of
how disintegration worked, most brilliantly realized in his Max-
imus in *Valentinian* (c. 1614). And we may, I think, assume that
it was Fletcher's idea to have the girl in *The Two Noble Kinsmen*
"cured" by making her take her humble Wooer for Palamon,
and thus in imagination lie with the man she loved. At the end

of the play Emilia is almost on the point of marrying Arcite: the gods intervene, and she is in Palamon's arms. Neither girl has choice, neither girl has, ultimately it seems, the power to differentiate. Moreover, they are linked in that the Jailer's Daughter has to play her part in the morris dance, her madness making her, in the opinion of the Countrymen, the more apt for the grotesque gambols required, while Emilia, trying to preserve neutrality and sobriety, is nevertheless shuttled from one knight's arms to the other's. This gives to the country entertainment of 3.5 a function in the play: it is a comic counterpart to, and an anticipation of, the final tournament, and their respective roles in the two spectacles bring together the girl who loves Palamon and the girl who weds him. In his development of the subplot, Fletcher seems thus to have continued his work of deflation.

Here, however, it is necessary to distinguish with some care. Shakespeare's handling of Palamon and Arcite and Theseus and Emilia is no simple romancing, as we have seen. They are powerless human beings manipulated by the gods, and in a measure comic in their subjection. But the comedy is wry and serious, nowhere more so than in Palamon's invocation of Venus in 5.1.* Fletcher's comedy is much more self-conscious, more obviously grotesque, and though it too is wry there is laughter in it.

Not only deflation of the elder dramatist can be seen, but a measure of parody too. The Jailer's Daughter echoes Ophelia; Emilia brooding over the pictures of Palamon and Arcite in 4.2 echoes the Gertrude who was made to look on pictures of Claudius and the elder Hamlet; even the Doctor's bed-trick in 5.2 (for it is substantially that) may echo Shakespeare's elaborate employments of the device. And again and again there are tricks of wording—e.g., the Doctor's "I think she has a perturbed mind, which I cannot minister to" (4.3.60–61)—which take up phrases which Fletcher knew from Shakespeare. The parodying is not hostile or unadmiring. We can remember that in 1613 Shakespeare was forty-nine and Fletcher thirty-four, that we have strong evidence that they worked together on two, perhaps on three, plays: the relationship must have been a complex one. Through the remaining twelve years of Fletcher's career his predecessor's work was never far from his mind, but he

*See "A Note on the Source."

enjoyed it without a total reverence. That in writing his share of *The Two Noble Kinsmen* he made the play something of a medley would not deeply disturb him. He did not bring to the writing of any play a sense of full commitment.

A court record suggests that Shakespeare and Fletcher's play was given there in 1619,* and the occurrence in the text of two actors' names† enables us to deduce that the play was revived about 1625–26. The title page of 1634 is perhaps deliberately ambiguous in its "Presented at the Blackfriers": this could imply, but need not, that the play was still in the repertory. But after 1642 for a very long time the stage had almost no use for the play.‡ In 1664 Pepys saw at Lincoln's Inn Fields Theatre *The Rivals* (not a new play then), which is a free adaptation of *The Two Noble Kinsmen* and, though it was published anonymously in 1668, can be safely attributed to Sir William Davenant. He was a dramatist of experience and some note in Charles I's reign, he was largely responsible for the restarting of theater performances in London during the Interregnum (his operatic *The Siege of Rhodes* being acted in 1656), and he was one of the two London theater managers in the earliest Restoration years. He made free use of pre-1642 drama, adapting *Macbeth* and (with Dryden) *The Tempest* for current taste. In *The Rivals* he contrived a version of the story he found in Shakespeare and Fletcher, with no Theseus, no petitioning Queens, no invocation of the gods, no tournament, and a happy ending. Though he occasionally keeps to the words he found,

---

*E. K. Chambers, *William Shakespeare: A Study of Facts and Problems*, Oxford, 1930, II, p. 346.

†See Textual Note, p. 575.

‡The almost complete disregard of our play in the late seventeenth century is indicated by Dryden's failure to mention it in his Preface to his volume of *Fables* (1700) or to give in his *Palamon and Arcite* included in that volume any clear indication that he had read it. He does, when writing of Emilia at Book I, line 175, use the phrase "To do the observance due to sprightly May," which is a little nearer to "to do observance/To flow'ry May" (*The Two Noble Kinsmen*, 2.4.50–51) than to Chaucer's "to have remembraunce/To don honour to May" (*The Knight's Tale*, lines 188–89), but Chaucer in another context has "to doon his observaunce to May" (line 642). Dryden also makes a little more of the freckled face of one of the kinsmen's supporters (Book III, lines 76, 475) than Chaucer does (lines 1311–12), which could be due to the stress on this feature in *The Two Noble Kinsmen*, 4.2.120–23. Neither of these points can make us firmly deduce that Dryden gave the play a thought as he adapted Chaucer.

he uses none of the old names and changes the place of action to Arcadia. Heraclea, corresponding to Emilia, cannot make up her mind between Theocles and Philander, but finds that Philander is loved by Celania, the daughter of the Provost (no mere jailer): therefore she decides to take Theocles, and Philander consents to love Celania. Davenant wanted to make a refined comedy, and to do it he had to remove most of the action and all the grossness. Celania does go distracted for a while, but only in a polite way. The play is of no importance, but so far as is known it provided the occasion for the only contact with the stage that *The Two Noble Kinsmen* had between the early seventeenth century and the early twentieth century. Not even William Poel is on record as having thought of a revival.

Then in March 1928 the Old Vic staged it, with Ernest Milton as Palamon, Eric Portman as Arcite, Jean Forbes-Robertson as the Jailer's Daughter, and Barbara Everest as Emilia. Writing in *The London Mercury* for April 1928, A. G. MacDonell praised Jean Forbes-Robertson, and noted that Palamon was done comically, in a red wig. This reviewer was much taken with the realistic playing of the mad scenes, and grateful that he did not have to endure simple nobility in two kinsmen. The only other production I have been able to trace is that at the Antioch Area Theatre, Antioch College, Ohio, which was given eight times in August and September 1955 under the direction of Arthur Lithgow. I am most grateful to Mr. Lithgow, now of the McCarter Theatre at Princeton, and to Miss Marcia Overstreet and Miss Ernestine C. Brecht of Antioch College, for writing to me about this production. Mr. Lithgow reports that the play proved "very stage-worthy," particularly the scenes involving the Jailer's Daughter, and that Mr. Ellis Rabb was "very grand" as Palamon. Some cutting had to be done of "repetitive passages," but Shakespeare's hand was felt in the "high imagery."

This is a relatively inglorious stage history for a play in which Shakespeare was concerned, and we must honor the Old Vic and Antioch College for going against the current. Despite the coldness of the London reviewers (MacDonell was typical), it is evident that something happened to the Jailer's Daughter scenes when they got on the stage, and this was confirmed at Antioch College, where indeed the play as a whole seems to have found itself at home. It is more than time that a further attempt was made to see it in action. It does, after all, contain the invocations to the gods in 5.1, passages of dramatic verse outstanding even in 1613, a good time for dramatic verse; it contains some of Fletcher's most skillful and characteristic writing; it will one day, perhaps, come to be recognized as throwing a new kind of light on Shakespeare's concluding work in the theater. It needs a large and flexible stage: there is a most suitable one at Stratford, Ontario, another at Chichester in England, and others—both indoor and outdoor—easily found in the United States. One of these might well meet the challenge of what was perhaps Shakespeare's (though only partly Shakespeare's) last play.

It has some good verse and a fairly realistic picture of the onset of madness, but the director contemplating a revival will want to be assured of more than that. It is true that he must face difficulties. The play has the appearance of a romantic story, as Beaumont and Fletcher's *Philaster* has, but in neither instance does the romantic effect properly work. With *Philaster* that was because Beaumont and Fletcher were determined on a sophisticated undercutting of the romantic gesture; with *The Two Noble Kinsmen* there is the complication that two men of widely differing temperaments shared the writing. Shakespeare had used "romance" with high authority in *The Winter's Tale* and *The Tempest*, involving his audience in a love story in a setting that was both natural and strange, and at the same time making them feel that they were in the presence of stern and unknowable powers. But now he was working with Fletcher, whose sights were lower, essentially those that had characterized *Philaster*. For Shakespeare, we can assume it was the sense of the inscrutable that made the story attractive to him; for Fletcher, it was its essential, often painful, but never overwhelming, absurdity. Because it seems likely that Fletcher had the task of putting together his and Shakespeare's work on the play, the overriding effect is Fletcherian: we are taken to high realms of thought, and deliberately let down, as we are so often, but less extravagantly, in the other plays in which Fletcher had a main hand. It is a paradox that Shakespeare seems to have planned *The Two Noble Kinsmen* and that Fletcher gave it its dominant tone. But that tone is dominant, not exclusive: from Shakespeare we get the solemn pageant of the Queens' mission in 1.1,

the sage talk of Emilia and Hippolyta in 1.3, the sharp magnil-
oquence of the prayers in 5.1; and Fletcher's deflations do not
take them from our memory.

But what has probably put off most readers and potential
directors has been the nature of the characterization. Shakespeare's handling of character from *Pericles* onwards was lacking in the complexity and verisimilitude that had marked the
comedies and frequently the tragedies of his middle and mature
years. But audiences have been ready to accept Leontes in place
of Othello, Miranda in place of Rosalind, Prospero in place of
Hamlet, because in these plays they are led consistently toward
the idea of "great creating Nature," toward a sense of epiphany,
toward an austere assertion that to accept what is remains the
best hope, the highest wisdom, we have. But Fletcher has been
little more successful on the stage from the eighteenth to the
twentieth century, either alone or in collaboration with Beaumont, than he has been in association with Shakespeare. Reviewing the Old Vic performance of *The Two Noble Kinsmen* in
1928, James Agate asked how any actress could make anything
of Emilia, passed from hero to hero as from pillar to post.*
A. G. MacDonell, we have seen, found even one manifestly noble kinsman enough to bear. Fletcher offers nothing in the way
of obvious compensation for his stereotyping of human characters: these are, he suggests, the types that men fall into, or imagine they fall into, or try to live up to the idea of falling into. The
Fletcherian drama is a drama about men's refusal to live as individuals. In his plays, men avoid nakedness by doing what
they feel the codes and traditions of society demand from them.
We may differentiate Palamon from Arcite: one is more rough,
the other ready to see himself as sinning because he devoted
himself to Emilia a few seconds after his friend did. But each
keeps within a stereotype, a notion that belongs to the playhouse of the mind that men are always imagining for themselves: they are alike victims and worshipers of Bacon's Idols
of the Theater. It is a kind of characterization that in recent years
Brecht has familiarized us with, and we should now therefore
be the more fitted to respond to the mode and to see what the
play as a whole is saying.

It is indeed a well-arranged play, despite the duality of authorship and the dichotomy of attitude that in this instance is thus

Brief Chronicles, London, 1943, pp. 53–56.

imposed. Instead of the loose story-telling we might expect, we have a fairly tight structure, and in A Note on the Source we shall see that this has been achieved partly through the changes made in adapting Chaucer. The action involves three inter-woven strands: (1) the prologue-action, as we may call it, con-cerning the conflict between Athens and Thebes; (2) the story of the rivalry for Emilia; (3) the story of the Jailer's Daughter. The first makes the play begin in a manner of high seriousness and formal rhetoric, and it is in manifest contrast with the slighter, more personal stories of the knights and the girls. The subplot, as we have seen, reflects ironically on the plot of the knights.

The act division throughout is firm, and is related to the play's changes of locality. Act 1 concerns itself with the con-flict between Athens (chivalrous) and Thebes (ignoble), ending with the imprisonment of the nearly dead Palamon and Arcite (noble on the wrong side). Act 2 gives us their falling in love and release from prison, and introduces the subplot. Act 3 is wholly outside the town: it shows how Palamon and Arcite meet again, how the Jailer's Daughter loses Palamon, how The-seus and his court are entertained by a group of rustics includ-ing the Daughter, and finally how the Duke comes upon the kinsmen and decrees their final trial. Act 4, which is briefly and quietly indeterminate, makes toward the cure of the Daughter and emphasizes the perplexity of Emilia: it is, as often with a fourth act, a halting place before the catastrophe. Act 5 gives us the tournament and its curious consequences, with both girls in some sense pledged to Palamon. Athens and Thebes are the localities of Act 1, Athens and the country nearby those of Act 2; the country consistently is the place of action in Act 3, the city of Athens (but alternating between palace and prison) in Acts 4 and 5. As the play progresses its range of locality shrinks, so that what begins as an opposition of Thebes and Athens ends as an opposition of palace and prison within a single city. The point of rest toward which we move is marked by death and bereavement and acquiescence: the Jailer who freed Arcite in Act 2, and put Palamon under further restraint, is prominently in the stage picture when Palamon is prepared for execution and then, at the news of Arcite's death, for marriage.

The play's recurrent irony is supported by other details of the planning. Theseus is ceremoniously petitioned by the Queens in 1.1 and by Hippolyta, Emilia, and Pirithous in 3.6: he yields in both instances, though with eloquence in the earlier, Shakespearian passage and with the cleverness of compromise in Fletcher's 3.6. The talk between Palamon and Arcite in 1.2, where they show their wish to leave a corrupt Thebes, becomes ironic when in fighting for Thebes they come near death and are sentenced to life imprisonment. The discussion of friendship by Hippolyta and Emilia in 1.3 not only anticipates the dominant friendship motif in the play as a whole, but casts an ironic light on the knights' subsequent devotion to Emilia. And just as the subplot as a whole reflects on Emilia and her ultimate disposal, so the entertainment devised by the Schoolmaster, which brings Theseus and the Jailer's Daughter together on the stage for the only time, is not only a contrast to and an anticipation of the wryly presented tournament of Act 5: it also gives a distorted image of the entertainment that the kinsmen and the Duke and his ladies offer to the audience in the theater.

Of course, this is a Blackfriars play. The King's Men had taken over that "private" theater (previously used by the child actors) around 1610 and had begun by using it as their winter house, keeping the Globe for the summer. The title page of 1634 mentions only the Blackfriars, and we may assume that at least by the 1620's this play had found its right home there. It is a sophisticated—even, we have seen, a dislocated—play, not firm, ultimately, in its implications but surely fascinating, if disturbing and at times irritating, to watch. Its epilogue calls it "the tale we have told—/For 'tis no other." That was what Shakespeare had insistently, in the text as well as in the title, called *The Winter's Tale*. *The Two Noble Kinsmen*, like that earlier "romance," is a strange story with many reversals of fortune, but like that too it has its unromantic aftertaste and is more carefully structured than a casual glance suggests. The Blackfriars audience was at times most gullible, ready to lose itself in a merely romanticized wonderland, but it could rise to the appreciation of something complex: it welcomed Fletcher's masterpiece in comedy, *The Humorous Lieutenant* (c. 1619–20), and, though we cannot be sure that it much liked the experience, it saw Ford's *The Broken Heart* some dozen years after that. There were doubtless moments of puzzlement with *The Two Noble Kinsmen* in 1613 and the following years, but some at least of the spectators must have noticed that the supreme dramatist and his more than clever successor were not failing them.

Nor would they, I think, fail us now if we put their joint play
again on the stage.*

CLIFFORD LEECH

*Since this Introduction was written, Paul Bertram has published a substantial book with the title *Shakespeare and The Two Noble Kinsmen* (New
Brunswick, 1965), arguing that Shakespeare was the sole author of the play.
It is a piece of well-informed writing, and Bertram has scored some good
points in showing how the nineteenth-century scholars seized on the idea
of dual authorship because of a reluctance to imagine Shakespeare writing
the franker sections of the play. He argues, moreover, that the play has unity
in its plotting (as indeed it has) and that throughout there is the same full
use of Chaucer. Less successfully, he disposes of the evidence of verse tests
by insisting that some of the scenes treated by the editors as verse are really in prose (as they are presented in the quarto): this is, I think, to disregard the strong blank-verse character of much of the writing. The reader of
the present edition will be able to decide whether the scenes involving the
Countrymen and the Jailer and his Daughter (apart from the beginning of
2.1 and the whole of 4.3) are legitimately printed as verse. Moreover,
Bertram is one of the, alas, many who have a low regard for Fletcher: he
insists on Shakespeare's sole authorship of *Henry VIII* and *The Two Noble
Kinsmen*, but will let Fletcher have *Cardenio*, which seems to him of minor
weight. And he does not successfully meet the evidence of the 1634 title
page. It is possible to quote, as he does, the statement of Leonard Digges,
in the 1640 edition of Shakespeare's *Poems*, that Shakespeare did not beg
"from each witty friend a Scene/To peece his Acts with," but that is another matter than the frank and equal sharing of a play with his obvious
successor in 1613. It used to be necessary to argue for Shakespeare's participation in *The Two Noble Kinsmen*: now we have to safeguard Fletcher's
right to a part of it. And the argument of this Introduction is that there are,
despite close cooperation, a difference of view and a difference of style
which indicate two authors, one of them supreme and the other at least major in his time.

Addendum: Brian Vickers, in *Shakespeare, Co-Author* (2002), admirably
sets forth a convincing case for dual authorship [SB].

Theseus, Duke of Athens
Pirithous, friend to Theseus
Artesius, an Athenian
Palamon ⎫ kinsmen, nephews to Creon, King
Arcite ⎭ of Thebes
Valerius, a Theban
Six Knights
Jailer
Wooer to the Jailer's Daughter
Doctor
Brother ⎫ to the Jailer
Two Friends ⎭
Schoolmaster
A Herald, Messengers, Countrymen, Hymen,
    a Boy, an Executioner, Guard, Taborer,
    Bavian or Fool, Lords, and Attendants
Hippolyta, an Amazon, bride to Theseus
Emilia, her sister
Three Queens
The Jailer's Daughter
Waiting-woman to Emilia
Maids, Country Wenches, and Nymphs

Scene: Athens and the country nearby; Thebes]

The Two Noble Kinsmen

PROLOGUE

Flourish.°*

New plays and maidenheads are near akin:
Much followed° both, for both much money gi'en,
If they stand sound and well. And a good play—
Whose modest scenes blush on his marriage day,
And shake to lose his honor—is like her   5
That after holy tie and first night's stir
Yet still is modesty, and still retains
More of the maid to sight than husband's pains.°
We pray our play may be so, for I am sure
It has a noble breeder, and a pure,   10
A learnèd, and a poet never went
More famous yet 'twixt Po and silver Trent.
Chaucer, of all admired, the story gives:
There constant to eternity it lives.
If we let fall° the nobleness of this,°   15
And the first sound this child hear be a hiss,
How will it shake the bones of that good man,
And make him cry from under ground, "O fan
From me the witless chaff of such a writer°

---

*The degree sign (°) indicates a footnote, which is keyed to the text
by line number. Text references are printed in **boldface** type; the annotation follows in roman type.
Prologue s.d. **Flourish** i.e., of trumpets 2 **followed** pursued, culti-
vated 8 **pains** endeavors 15 **let fall** fail to maintain 15 **this** i.e.,
Chaucer's poem 19 **such a writer** (the singular is notable, but by no
means decisive on the question of authorship)

449

20   That blasts my bays, and my famed works makes lighter
        Than Robin Hood!" This is the fear we bring;
        For, to say truth, it were an endless° thing,
        And too ambitious, to aspire to him.
        Weak as we are, and almost breathless swim
25   In this deep water, do but you hold out
        Your helping hands, and we shall tack about,°
        And something do to save us. You shall hear
        Scenes, though below his art, may yet appear
        Worth two hours' travail.° To his bones sweet sleep;
30   Content to you. If this play do not keep
        A little dull time from us, we perceive
        Our losses fall so thick we must needs leave.°

                                                    Flourish.

22 **endless** purposeless, vain   26 **tack about** change direction   29
travail labor (with a suggestion of "travel," as the play's action moves
from place to place)   32 **leave** give up acting

ACT 1

[Scene 1. *Athens. Before a temple.*]

Enter Hymen° with a torch burning; a boy in a white robe before, singing and strewing flowers; after Hymen, a nymph, encompassed in her tresses,° bearing a wheaten garland;° then Theseus between two other nymphs with wheaten chaplets° on their heads; then Hippolyta the bride, led by Pirithous, and another holding a garland over her head, her tresses likewise hanging; after her, Emilia holding up her train [; Artesius and Attendants].

Music.

The Song

Roses, their sharp spines being gone,
Not royal in their smells alone,
    But in their hue;
Maiden pinks, of odor faint,
Daisies smell-less, yet most quaint,°   5
    And sweet thyme true;

Primrose, first-born child of Ver,°
Merry spring-time's harbinger,
    With harebells dim;
Oxlips, in their cradles growing,   10
Marigolds, on death-beds blowing,°
    Lark's-heels trim;°

All dear Nature's children sweet
Lie 'fore bride and bridegroom's feet,   *Strew flowers.*

1.1.s.d. **Hymen** god of marriage **encompassed in her tresses** with hair loose, in token of virginity **wheaten garland** a symbol of fertility and peace **chaplets** wreaths **5 quaint** pretty **7 Ver** spring **11 on death-beds blowing** blooming on graves **12 trim** neat

15   Blessing their sense;
        Not an angel° of the air,
        Bird melodious, or bird fair,
        Is° absent hence;

        The crow, the sland'rous cuckoo, nor
20   The boding raven, nor chough hoar,
        Nor chatt'ring pie,
        May on our bridehouse° perch or sing,
        Or with them any discord bring,
        But from it fly.

        *Enter three Queens in black, with veils stained, with
        imperial crowns. The first Queen falls down at the foot of
        Theseus; the second falls down at the foot of Hippolyta;
                  the third before Emilia.*

25   *First Queen.* For pity's sake and true gentility's,°
        Hear and respect° me.

        Second Queen.   For your mother's sake,
        And as you wish your womb may thrive with fair ones,
        Hear and respect me.

        Third Queen. Now for the love of him whom Jove hath
                  marked
30   The honor of your bed,° and for the sake
        Of clear° virginity, be advocate
        For us, and our distresses. This good deed
        Shall raze you° out o' th' Book of Trespasses°
        All you are set down there.

        Theseus. Sad lady, rise.

        Hippolyta.   Stand up.

35   *Emilia.*   No knees to me.
        What woman I may stead° that is distressed
        Does bind me to her.

---

16 **angel** here a synonym for "bird"   18 **Is** (often emended to "Be,"
but the indicative seems acceptable)   22 **bridehouse** house where a
wedding is celebrated   25 **gentility** nobleness   26 **respect** give attention to   29–30 **whom . . . bed** for whom Jove has destined the honor of
wedding you   31 **clear** pure   33 **raze you** delete for you   33 **Book
of Trespasses** recording angel's register of sins   36 **stead** help

Theseus. What's your request? Deliver you for all.

First Queen. We are three queens, whose sovereigns fell
    before
  The wrath of cruel Creon;° who endured°   40
  The beaks of ravens, talons of the kites,
  And pecks of crows, in the foul fields of Thebes.
  He will not suffer us to burn their bones,
  To urn their ashes, nor to take th' offense
  Of mortal loathsomeness from the blest eye   45
  Of holy Phoebus,° but infects the winds
  With stench of our slain lords. O pity, duke,
  Thou purger of the earth, draw thy feared sword
  That does good turns to th' world; give us the bones
  Of our dead kings, that we may chapel° them;   50
  And of thy boundless goodness take some note
  That for our crownèd heads we have no roof,
  Save this which is the lion's and the bear's,
  And vault° to everything.

Theseus.   Pray you kneel not.
  I was transported with your speech, and suffered   55
  Your knees to wrong themselves. I have heard the
    fortunes
  Of your dead lords, which gives me such lamenting
  As wakes my vengeance and revenge for 'em.
  King Capaneus° was your lord. The day
  That he should° marry you, at such a season   60
  As now it is with me, I met your groom.
  By Mars's altar, you were that time fair:
  Not Juno's mantle° fairer than your tresses,
  Nor in more bounty spread her; your wheaten wreath
  Was then nor threshed° nor blasted;° Fortune at you   65

---

40 **Creon** king of Thebes after Oedipus   40 **endured** have endured
45–46 **blest eye/Of holy Phoebus** i.e., the sun   50 **chapel** bury in a
chapel   54 **vault** arched roof (here the sky)   59 **Capaneus** (here
four syllables, though classically three)   60 **should** was to   63
Juno's mantle (Juno was goddess of marriage and her mantle is described in *Iliad*, XIV; but the peacock was sacred to Juno, and "mantle" also suggests the bird's spread tail)   65 **threshed** beaten so as to
separate grain from husks (here an image for fertilizing: cf. 1.1 opening s.d.)   65 **blasted** i.e., by widowhood

Dimpled her cheek with smiles. Hercules our kins-
        man,°
Then weaker than your eyes, laid by his club:
He tumbled down upon his Nemean hide°
And swore his sinews thawed. O grief and time,
70   Fearful consumers, you will all devour.

First Queen. O I hope some god,
Some god hath put his mercy in your manhood,
Whereto he'll infuse pow'r, and press you forth
Our undertaker.°

Theseus.   O no knees, none, widow,
75   Unto the helmeted Bellona° use them,
And pray for me your soldier.
Troubled I am.   *Turns away.*
                              [*The Queens rise.*]

Second Queen.   Honored Hippolyta,
Most dreaded Amazonian, that hast slain
The scythe-tusked boar, that with thy arm as strong
80   As it is white, wast near to make the male
To thy sex captive, but that this thy lord,
Born to uphold creation in that honor
First Nature 'stilled it in,° shrunk thee into
The bound° thou wast o'erflowing, at once subduing
85   Thy force and thy affection; soldieress,
That equally canst poise° sternness with pity,
Whom° now I know hast much more power on him
Than ever he had on thee, who ow'st° his strength
And his love too, who is a servant for
90   The tenor of thy speech;° dear glass of° ladies,

---

66 **kinsman** (according to Plutarch's "Life of Theseus," both he and
Hercules were descended on their mothers' side from Pelops; moreover, Theseus as alleged son of Poseidon could claim kinship with
Hercules, son of Zeus)   68 **Nemean hide** (Hercules customarily
wore the hide of the lion of Nemea, which he had slain)   73–74
press you forth/Our undertaker impel you to champion our cause
75 **Bellona** goddess of war   83 **'stilled it in** instilled in it   84
bound limit, as bank of a river   86 **equally canst poise** canst justly
balance   87 **Whom** (usual in seventeenth century before a paren-
thetic clause)   88 **ow'st** possessest   89–90 **who . . . speech** who is
obedient to everything you say   90 **glass of** mirror for (as in "mirror
for magistrates," etc.)

Bid him that we whom flaming war doth scorch
Under the shadow of his sword may cool us;
Require him he advance it o'er our heads;
Speak't in a woman's key, like such a woman
As any of us three; weep ere you fail;   95
Lend us a knee;
But° touch the ground for us no longer time
Than a dove's motion when the head's plucked off;
Tell him if he i' th' blood-sized° field lay swoll'n,
Showing the sun his teeth, grinning at the moon,   100
What you would do.

Hippolyta.   Poor lady, say no more.
I had as lief tracc° this good action with you
As that whereto I am going, and never yet
Went I so willing way.° My lord is taken
Heart-deep with your distress. Let him consider.   105
I'll speak anon.

Third Queen. (*Kneel[s] to Emilia*) O my petition was
Set down in ice, which by hot grief uncandied°
Melts into drops, so sorrow wanting form
Is pressed with deeper matter.°

Emilia.   Pray stand up,
Your grief is written in your cheek.

Third Queen.   O woe,   110
You cannot read it there; there through my tears,°
Like wrinkled pebbles in a glassy stream
You may behold 'em.° Lady, lady, alack!
He that will all the treasure know o' th' earth
Must know the center° too; he that will fish   115
For my least minnow, let him lead his line°
To catch one at my heart. O pardon me,

97 **But** only   99 **blood-sized** spread with blood   102 **trace** pursue
104 **so willing way** any way so willingly   106–09 **O my . . .
deeper matter** i.e., the formality of her previous speech (lines 29–34)
now melts into tears, but grief in its formlessness can receive the imprint of a "deeper matter" (in this instance the desire for funeral rites
and vengeance)   107 **uncandied** dissolved   111 **there through
my tears** i.e., in her eyes   113 **'em** i.e., her eyes, where her grief is
imaged   115 **center** i.e., of the earth   116 **lead his line** weight it
with lead

Extremity that sharpens sundry wits
Makes me a fool.   [*She rises.*]

Emilia.   Pray you say nothing, pray you.
120   Who cannot feel nor see the rain, being in't,
Knows neither wet nor dry. If that you were
The ground-piece° of some painter, I would buy you
T' instruct me 'gainst a capital grief indeed
Such heart-pierced° demonstration.° But alas,
125   Being a natural sister of our sex,°
Your sorrow beats so ardently upon me
That it shall make a counter-reflect° 'gainst
My brother's heart, and warm it to some pity
Though it were made of stone. Pray have good comfort.

130   *Theseus.* Forward to th' temple, leave not out a jot
O' th' sacred ceremony.

First Queen.   O this celebration
Will long last, and be more costly than
Your suppliants' war. Remember that your fame
Knolls in the ear o' th' world; what you do quickly
135   Is not done rashly; your first thought is more
Than others' labored meditance,° your premeditating
More than their actions. But O Jove, your actions,
Soon as they move, as ospreys do the fish,°
Subdue before they touch. Think, dear duke, think
What beds our slain kings have.

140   *Second Queen.*   What griefs our beds
That our dear lords have none.

Third Queen.   None fit for th' dead.
Those that with cords, knives, drams' precipitance,°
Weary of this world's light, have to themselves

---

122 **ground-piece** flat representation (?)   124 **heart-pierced** heart-piercing   124 **demonstration** i.e., your demonstration of grief would instruct me how to bear any great grief   125 **Being ... sex** since you are a woman like me (but "sifter" may be the right reading: see Textual Note)   127 **counter-reflect** reflection   136 **meditance** meditation, planning   138 **ospreys do the fish** (the osprey was believed to fascinate the fish before catching it)   142 **drams' precipitance** suicide by taking poison

Been death's most horrid agents, human grace°
Affords them dust and shadow.°

First Queen.   But our lords   145
Lie blist'ring 'fore the visitating° sun,
And were good kings when living.

Theseus.   It is true,
And I will give you comfort, to give° your dead lords
      graves.
The which to do, must make some work with Creon.

First Queen. And that work presents itself to th' doing.°   150
Now 'twill take form,° the heats are gone tomorrow.
Then bootless toil must recompense itself
With its own sweat. Now he's secure,°
Not dreams we stand before your puissance,
Rinsing our holy begging in our eyes   155
To make petition clear.

Second Queen.   Now you may take him,
Drunk with his victory.

Third Queen.   And his army full
Of bread° and sloth.

Theseus.   Artesius, that best knowest
How to draw out° fit to this enterprise
The prim'st for this proceeding, and the number   160
To carry° such a business, forth and levy
Our worthiest instruments, whilst we dispatch
This grand act of our life, this daring deed
Of fate° in wedlock.

First Queen.   Dowagers, take hands,
Let us be widows to our woes,° delay   165
Commends us to a famishing hope.

---

144 **grace** mercy 145 **shadow** shelter 146 **visitating** inflicting
harm (?) 148 **to give** by giving 150 **presents itself to th' doing**
offers itself to be done at once 151 **form** shape 153 **secure** confident 158 **bread** food, feasting 159 **draw out** select 161
carry carry out 163–64 **daring deed/Of fate** deed challenging fate
165 **be widows to our woes** live with our woes like widows (as
we are)

All [Queens].   Farewell.

Second Queen. We come unseasonably, but when could
    grief
  Cull forth,° as unpanged° judgment can, fitt'st time
  For best solicitation?

Theseus.   Why, good ladies,
170 This is a service whereto I am going
  Greater than any was; it more imports me
  Than all the actions that I have foregone°
  Or futurely° can cope.

First Queen.   The more proclaiming
  Our suit shall be neglected. When her arms,
175 Able to lock Jove from a synod,° shall
  By warranting° moonlight corslet thee, O when
  Her twining cherries shall their sweetness fall°
  Upon thy tasteful° lips, what wilt thou think
  Of rotten kings or blubbered queens, what care
180 For what thou feel'st not, what thou feel'st being able
  To make Mars spurn his drum? O if thou couch
  But one night with her, every hour in't will
  Take hostage of thee for a hundred,° and
  Thou shalt remember nothing more than what
  That banquet bids thee to.

185 *Hippolyta.* [*Kneels*]   Though much unlike
  You should be so transported, as much sorry
  I should be such a suitor;° yet I think,
  Did I not by th' abstaining of my joy,
  Which breeds a deeper longing, cure their surfeit
190 That craves a present med'cine, I should pluck
  All ladies' scandal° on me. Therefore, sir,
  As I shall here make trial of my pray'rs,
  Either presuming them to have some force

---

168 **Cull forth** choose   168 **unpanged** untormented   172 **fore-
gone** previously experienced   173 **futurely** in the future   175
synod council   176 **warranting** authorizing   177 **fall** let fall
178 **tasteful** tasting   183 **Take . . . hundred** i.e., you will feel committed to spend a hundred more with her   185–87 **Though . . .
suitor** i.e., my reluctance to ask this is as great as my doubt that you
would be so moved by our lovemaking   191 **scandal** disgrace

Or sentencing for aye their vigor dumb,°
Prorogue° this business we are going about, and hang   *195*
Your shield afore your heart, about that neck
Which is my fee,° and which I freely lend
To do these poor queens service.

All Queens. [To Emilia]   O help now,
Our cause cries for your knee.

Emilia. [Kneels]   If you grant not
My sister her petition in that force,°   *200*
With that celerity and nature which
She makes it in,° from henceforth I'll not dare
To ask you anything, nor be so hardy°
Ever to take a husband.

Theseus.   Pray stand up.
            [Hippolyta and Emilia rise.]
I am entreating of myself to do   *205*
That which you kneel to have me. Pirithous,
Lead on the bride; get you and pray the gods
For success, and return; omit not anything
In the pretended° celebration. Queens,
Follow your soldier, as before.° *[To Artesius]* Hence
    you,   *210*
And at the banks of Aulis° meet us with
The forces you can raise, where we shall find
The moiety of a number for a business
More bigger-looked.°   *[Exit Artesius.]*
                Since that our theme is haste,
I stamp this kiss upon thy current° lip.   *215*

194 **sentencing ... dumb** declaring that they shall never be uttered
again 195 **Prorogue** postpone 197 **fee** property 200 **in that
force** with that vigor 201–02 **nature which/She makes it in** condition of mind in which she makes it 203 **hardy** bold 209 **pretended** intended 210 **as before** as I have already declared myself
211 **banks of Aulis** (see Textual Note: Aulis was a seaport, but
"banks" could refer to the shore; however, this was an odd way to proceed from Athens to Thebes) 212–14 **where ... bigger-looked**
while I shall gather the other half of a force that would serve for a
larger undertaking than this 215 **current** fleeting (transferred from
Theseus, who is in haste), with a suggestion also of putting his royal
stamp on her lip as on a coin

Sweet, keep it as my token. [*Kisses Hippolyta.*] Set you
    forward,
For I will see you gone.

   [*Hippolyta, Emilia, Pirithous and Attendants begin
       to move*] *towards the temple.*

Farewell, my beauteous sister. Pirithous,
Keep the feast full,° bate not an hour on't.

Pirithous.   Sir,
220   I'll follow you at heels. The feast's solemnity
    Shall want° till your return.

Theseus.   Cousin, I charge you
    Budge not from Athens. We shall be returning
    Ere you can end this feast, of which I pray you
    Make no abatement. Once more, farewell all.
                [*The procession enters the temple.*]

First Queen. Thus dost thou still make good the tongue
225   o' th' world.°

Second Queen. And earn'st a deity equal with Mars.

Third Queen. If not above him, for
    Thou being but mortal makest affections bend
    To godlike honors.° They themselves,° some say,
    Groan under such a mast'ry.°

230 *Theseus.*   As we are men,
    Thus should we do. Being sensually subdued,
    We lose our human title.° Good cheer, ladies.
    Now turn we towards your comforts.

                      Flourish. Exeunt.

---

219 **full** fully   221 **want** be incomplete   225 **make good the
tongue o' th' world** justify what the world says of you   228–29
makest . . . honors turn your natural inclinations toward the winning
of divine honors   229 **They themselves** i.e., the gods   230 **mast'ry**
i.e., as yours   231–32 **Being . . . title** by yielding to our senses we
lose our claim to be considered men

Scene 2. [*Thebes.*]

Enter Palamon and Arcite.

Arcite. Dear Palamon, dearer in love than blood°
   And our prime° cousin, yet° unhardened in
   The crimes of nature, let us leave the city
   Thebes, and the temptings in't, before we further
   Sully our gloss of youth;   5
   And here to keep in abstinence we shame
   As in incontinence:° for not to swim
   I' th' aid o'° th' current were almost to sink,
   At least to frustrate striving;° and to follow
   The common stream, 'twould bring us to an eddy   10
   Where we should turn° or drown; if labor through,
   Our gain but life and weakness.

Palamon.   Your advice
   Is cried up° with example: what strange ruins
   Since first we went to school may we perceive
   Walking in Thebes? Scars and bare weeds   15
   The gain o' th' Martialist,° who did propound
   To his bold ends honor and golden ingots,
   Which though he won he had not, and now flirted°
   By peace for whom he fought: who then shall offer
   To Mars's so scorned altar? I do bleed   20
   When such I meet, and wish great Juno would
   Resume her ancient fit of jealousy°
   To get the soldier work, that peace might purge
   For her repletion,° and retain° anew

1.2.1 **blood** kinship   2 **prime** closest   2 **yet** as yet   6–7 **here . . .
incontinence** here it is as shameful to abstain from vice as (elsewhere) to indulge in it   8 **I' th' aid o'** i.e., with   9 **frustrate striving** make our efforts useless   11 **turn** i.e., turn and begin to swim
with the current   13 **cried up** supported   16 **Martialist** follower
of Mars (i.e., soldier)   18 **flirted** mocked   21–22 **Juno . . . jealousy** (Juno's jealousy was a contributing factor to the Trojan War)
23–24 **peace might purge/For her repletion** (a common image: war
was seen as a recurrent necessity so that society might "purge" itself
of the results of too self-indulgent living: "for" here means "as a remedy for")   24 **retain** take into service

25   Her charitable heart, now hard and harsher
      Than strife or war could be.

      Arcite.   Are you not out?°
      Meet you no ruin but the soldier in
      The cranks and turns° of Thebes? You did begin
      As if you met decays of many kinds.
30   Perceive you none that do arouse your pity
      But th' unconsidered° soldier?

      Palamon.   Yes, I pity
      Decays where'er I find them, but such most
      That sweating in an honorable toil
      Are paid with ice° to cool 'em.

      Arcite.   'Tis not this
35   I did begin to speak of: this is virtue
      Of no respect in Thebes. I spake of Thebes,
      How dangerous if we will keep our honors
      It is for our residing, where every evil
      Hath a good color,° where every seeming good's
40   A certain evil, where not to be ev'n jump°
      As they° are, here were to be° strangers, and
      Such things to be,° mere° monsters.

      Palamon.   'Tis in our power
      (Unless we fear that apes can tutor's) to
      Be masters of our manners. What need I
45   Affect° another's gait, which is not catching
      Where there is faith, or to be fond upon
      Another's way of speech, when by mine own
      I may be reasonably conceived°—saved too,
      Speaking it truly?° Why am I bound
50   By any generous bond° to follow him
      Follows his tailor,° haply so long until

26 **Are you not out?** are you not mistaking the matter?   28 **cranks
and turns** winding streets and passages   31 **unconsidered** neglected   34 **Are paid with ice** i.e., are treated coolly (ironically appropriate, because they have been sweating)   39 **color** appearance
40 **jump** exactly   41 **they** i.e., the Thebans   41 **were to be** would
be   42 **Such things to be** to be such things as they (the Thebans) are
42 **mere** absolute   45 **Affect** imitate   48 **conceived** understood
49 **Speaking it truly** i.e., if I speak the truth   50 **generous bond**
nobleman's obligation   50–51 **follow him/Follows his tailor** imitate a man who takes instruction about conduct from his tailor

The followed make pursuit?° Or let me know
Why mine own barber is unblest, with him
My poor chin too, for° 'tis not scissored just
To such a favorite's glass.° What canon° is there   55
That does command my rapier from my hip
To dangle't in my hand, or to go tiptoe
Before the street be foul?° Either I am
The fore-horse in the team, or I am none
That draw i' th' sequent trace.° These poor slight
     sores   60
Need not a plantain.° That which rips my bosom
Almost to th' heart's—

Arcite.   Our uncle Creon.

Palamon.   He,
A most unbounded tyrant, whose successes
Makes heaven unfeared, and villainy assured
Beyond its power there's nothing; almost puts   65
Faith in a fever, and deifies alone
Voluble° chance; who° only attributes
The faculties of other instruments
To his own nerves and act;° commands men service,
And what they win in't, boot° and glory; one   70
That fears not to do harm; good, dares not.° Let
The blood of mine that's sib° to him be sucked
From me with leeches, let them break and fall
Off me with that corruption.

Arcite.   Clear-spirited° cousin,
Let's leave his court, that we may nothing share   75

51–52 **until/The followed make pursuit** until the tailor, not having
been paid, pursues his client to dun him   54 **for** because   54–55
just/To such a favorite's glass exactly in the fashion affected by such-
and-such a favored person   55 **canon** law (particularly divine or
ecclesiastical law)   57–58 **go tip-toe/Before the street be foul** (suggestive either of a mincing gait or of a way of walking so as to avoid
noise, for purposes of surprise attack)   58–60 **Either . . . trace** either
I shall lead or I shall refuse to be one that merely follows (the image
being from a team of horses)   61 **plantain** (the leaves of the plantain
herb were much used for treating wounds, stanching blood, etc.)   67
Voluble inconstant   67 **who** i.e., the "tyrant" of line 63   67–69
who . . . act i.e., who takes what his subjects do as his own achievement   70 **boot** profit, booty   71 **good, dares not** dares not do good
72 **sib** related   74 **Clear-spirited** noble-spirited

Of his loud infamy; for our milk
Will relish of the pasture,° and we must
Be vile or disobedient, not his kinsmen
In blood unless in quality.°

Palamon.   Nothing truer.
80   I think the echoes of his shames have deafed
The ears of heav'nly justice: widows' cries
Descend again into their throats, and have not
Due audience of° the gods.

Enter Valerius.

Valerius!

Valerius. The king calls for you; yet be leaden-footed°
85   Till his great rage be off him. Phoebus, when
He broke his whipstock° and exclaimed against
The horses of the sun, but whispered to°
The loudness of his fury.

Palamon.   Small winds shake him,
But what's the matter?°

Valerius. Theseus, who where he threats appalls, hath
90   sent
Deadly defiance to him and pronounces
Ruin to Thebes, who is at hand to seal
The promise of his wrath.°

Arcite.   Let him approach.
But that we fear the gods in him,° he brings not
95   A jot of terror to us. Yet what° man
Thirds° his own worth (the case is each of ours)

76–77 **our milk/Will relish of the pasture** i.e., what we produce
will be affected by our environment   78–79 **not his kinsmen . . .
quality** i.e., we must not hold the position of members of his family
unless we are like him in character   83 **Due audience of** fitting attention from   84 **be leaden-footed** do not hasten   86 **whipstock**
(here) whip   87 **to** in comparison with   89 **the matter** the cause of
disturbance   92–93 **seal/The promise of his wrath** confirm what
his angry words have spoken   94 **fear the gods in him** fear him as
an emissary of the gods   95 **what** here equivalent to "every"   96
Thirds reduces to a third of its former strength

When that his action's dregged,° with mind assured
'Tis bad he goes about.

Palamon.   Leave that unreasoned.°
Our services stand now for Thebes, not Creon.
Yet to be neutral to him were dishonor,   100
Rebellious to oppose: therefore we must
With him stand to the mercy of our Fate,
Who hath bounded our last minute.°

Arcite.   So we must.
Is't said this war's afoot, or it shall be
On fail of some condition?°

Valerius.   'Tis in motion: 105
The intelligence of state came in the instant
With the defier.°

Palamon.   Let's to the king, who were he
A quarter carrier of that honor which
His enemy come in, the blood we venture
Should be as for our health, which were not spent,   110
Rather laid out for purchase.° But alas,
Our hands advanced before our hearts,° what will
The fall o' th' stroke do damage?

Arcite.   Let th' event,°
That never erring arbitrator, tell us
When we know all ourselves, and let us follow   115
The becking of our chance.   *Exeunt.*

---

97 **dregged** accompanied by dross matter   98 **unreasoned** unspo-
ken, not argued about   103 **Who hath bounded our last minute**
who has already settled the time when our lives end   105 **On fail of
some condition** if stated terms of peace are not agreed to   106–07
The intelligence . . . defier i.e., the news that the war had started
came at the same time as the declaration   111 **laid out for purchase**
invested for profit   112 **Our hands advanced before our hearts**
i.e., our hands being engaged rather than our desires   113 **event**
result

Scene 3. [*Athens*.]

Enter Pirithous, Hippolyta, Emilia.

Pirithous. No further.

Hippolyta.   Sir, farewell. Repeat my wishes
To our great lord, of whose success I dare not
Make any timorous question, yet I wish him
Excess and overflow of power, and't might be
5   To dure° ill-dealing Fortune. Speed° to him:
Store never hurts good governors.°

Pirithous.   Though I know
His ocean needs not my poor drops, yet they
Must yield their tribute there. [*To Emilia*] My precious
        maid,
Those best affections° that the heavens infuse
10 In their best-tempered pieces,° keep enthroned
In your dear heart.

Emilia.   Thanks, sir. Remember me
To our all-royal brother, for whose speed°
The great Bellona I'll solicit; and
Since in our terrene° state petitions are not
15 Without gifts understood, I'll offer to her
What I shall be advised° she likes: our hearts
Are in his army, in his tent.

Hippolyta.   In's bosom.
We have been soldiers, and we cannot weep
When our friends don their helms, or put to sea,
20 Or tell of babes broached on the lance, or women
That have sod° their infants in—and after eat them—

1.3.4–5 **and't might be/To dure** in case it were necessary to undergo
5 **Speed** hasten   6 **Store never hurts good governors** plenty is never
a handicap to good leaders   9 **affections** inclinations   10 **best-
tempered pieces** most harmoniously wrought creatures   12 **speed**
success   14 **terrene** earthly   16 **shall be advised** am told   21 **sod**
boiled

The brine they wept at killing 'em.° Then if
You stay to see of us such spinsters,° we
Should hold you here forever.

Pirithous.   Peace be to you
As I pursue this war, which shall be then   25
Beyond further requiring.°   *Exit Pirithous.*

Emilia.   How his longing
Follows his friend! Since his depart,° his sports,
Though craving seriousness and skill, passed slightly
His careless execution,° where nor gain
Made him regard, or loss consider, but   30
Playing one business in his hand, another
Directing in his head—his mind nurse equal
To these so diff'ring twins.° Have you observed him,
Since our great lord departed?

Hippolyta.   With much labor;°
And I did love him for't. They two have cabined°   35
In many as dangerous as poor a corner,
Peril and want contending.° They have skiffed
Torrents whose roaring tyranny and power
I' th' least of these° was dreadful; and they have
Fought out together where Death's self was lodged,   40
Yet Fate hath brought them off.° Their knot of love,
Tied, weaved, entangled, with so true, so long,
And with a finger of so deep a cunning,
May be outworn, never undone.° I think
Theseus cannot be umpire to himself,   45
Cleaving his conscience° into twain and doing

---

22 **brine they wept at killing 'em** tears they shed as they killed
them   23 **spinsters** i.e., weak women   25–26 **which . . . requiring** i.e., peace will be ensured   27 **depart** departure   28–29
passed slightly/His careless execution i.e., were given only slight
and careless attention   32–33 **his mind . . . twins** i.e., his mind was
equally concerned with what he was doing and with what he was
imagining (fighting with Theseus)   34 **labor** attention   35 **cab-
ined** lodged together   37 **contending** i.e., being comparable in degree   39 **I' th' least of these** (referring either to "Peril and want,"
line 37, or to "tyranny and power," line 38)   41 **brought them off**
brought them to safety   44 **May be outworn, never undone** i.e.,
may be worn out by death, not unknotted before   46 **conscience**
consciousness

Each side like° justice, which he loves best.°

Emilia.   Doubtless
　　There is a best, and Reason has no manners
　　To say it is not you.° I was acquainted
50　Once with a time when I enjoyed a playfellow.
　　You were at wars, when she the grave enriched
　　Who made too proud the bed, took leave o' th' moon
　　(Which then looked pale at parting) when our count°
　　Was each eleven.

Hippolyta.   'Twas Flavina.

Emilia.   Yes.
55　You talk of Pirithous' and Theseus' love.
　　Theirs has more ground,° is more maturely seasoned,
　　More buckled° with strong judgment, and their
　　　　needs
　　The one of th' other may be said to water
　　Their intertangled roots of love. But I
60　And she I sigh and spoke of were things innocent,
　　Loved for we did,° and like the elements
　　That know not what, nor why, yet do effect
　　Rare issues by their operance,° our souls
　　Did so to one another: what she liked
65　Was then of me approved, what not condemned—
　　No more arraignment;° the flow'r that I would pluck
　　And put between my breasts, O then but beginning
　　To swell about the blossom, she would long
　　Till she had such another, and commit it
70　To the like innocent cradle, where phoenixlike

---

47 **like** equal　45–47 **Theseus ... best** i.e., even Theseus cannot judge whether he loves best himself or Pirithous　49 **To say it is not you** (Emilia, taking Hippolyta's remark in a different way from that intended, suggests that Theseus must love Hippolyta best of all; lines 95–96 make it less likely that "you" is indefinite, meaning that Theseus must in reason love himself better than his friend)　53 **our count** the number of our years　56 **ground** foundation　57 **buckled** supported　61 **for we did** merely because we did　62–63 **effect/Rare issues by their operance** produce strange happenings through their operation　65–66 **what not condemned—/No more arraignment** what she did not like was condemned by me, without further consideration of the case

They died in perfume;° on my head no toy°
But was her pattern;° her affections°—pretty
Though happily her careless were°—I followed
For my most serious decking;° had mine ear
Stol'n some new air, or at adventure hummed on   75
From musical coinage,° why, it was a note
Whereon her spirits would sojourn, rather dwell on,
And sing it in her slumbers. This rehearsal,°
Which—every innocent° wots well—comes in
Like old importment's bastard,° has this end   80
That the true love 'tween maid and maid may be
More than in sex dividual.°

Hippolyta.   Y' are out of breath,
And this high-speeded pace is but to say
That you shall never, like the maid Flavina,
Love any that's called man.

Emilia.   I am sure I shall not.   85

Hippolyta. Now alack, weak sister,
I must no more believe thee in this point,
Though in't I know thou dost believe thyself,
Than I will trust a sickly appetite
That loathes even as it longs. But sure, my sister,   90
If I were ripe for your persuasion, you
Have said enough to shake me from the arm
Of the all-noble Theseus, for whose fortunes
I will now in and kneel, with great assurance
That we, more than his Pirithous, possess   95
The high throne in his heart.

Emilia.   I am not against
Your faith, yet I continue mine.

                                        Exeunt.

70–71 **phoenixlike/They died in perfume** (referring to the legendary phoenix, from whose fragrant funeral pyre the next phoenix was born)   71 **toy** trifling ornament   72 **pattern** i.e., for imitation   72 **affections** inclinations, preferences   73 **Though happily her careless were** though her preferences might be carelessly made   74 **decking** adornment   75–76 **hummed on/From musical coinage** i.e., improvised   78 **rehearsal** recital   79 **innocent** child   80 **Like old importment's bastard** like a feeble imitation of the experience itself   81–82 **That ... dividual** i.e., that their love may be greater than the love of those different in sex

Scene 4. [*Thebes.*]

Cornets. A battle struck° within. Then a retreat.
Flourish. Then enter Theseus (victor) [with a Herald,
Lords and Attendants and with Palamon and Arcite
carried on hearses].° The three Queens meet him, and
fall on their faces before him.

First Queen. To thee no star be dark!°

Second Queen.   Both heaven and earth
    Friend° thee forever!

Third Queen.   All the good that may
    Be wished upon thy head, I cry "amen" to't!

Theseus. Th' impartial gods, who from the mounted°
    heavens
5   View us their mortal herd, behold who err
    And in their time chastise. Go and find out
    The bones of your dead lords, and honor them
    With treble ceremony; rather than a gap
    Should be in their dear° rites, we would supply't.
10   But those we will depute which shall invest
    You in your dignities, and even° each thing
    Our haste does leave imperfect. So adieu,
    And heaven's good eyes look on you.

                           Exeunt Queens.
                      What are those?

Herald. Men of great quality, as may be judged
15   By their appointment.° Some of Thebes have told's
    They are sisters' children, nephews to the king.

1.4.s.d. **struck** sounded **hearses** carriages   1 **To thee no star be
dark** let all stars be favorable to you   2 **Friend** befriend   4
mounted high (with a suggestion of the gods on horseback looking
down on men as beasts under their control)   9 **dear** valued   11
even make right   15 **appointment** accouterment

Theseus. By th' helm of Mars, I saw them in the war,
    Like to a pair of lions smeared with prey,
    Make lanes in troops aghast. I fixed my note°
    Constantly on them, for they were a mark   20
    Worth a god's view. What prisoner was't that told me°

    When I enquired their names?

Herald.   We 'lieve° they're called
    Arcite and Palamon.

Theseus.   'Tis right: those, those;
    They are not dead?

Herald. Nor in a state of life: had they been taken   25
    When their last hurts were given, 'twas possible
    They might have been recovered. Yet they breathe
    And have the name of men.°

Theseus.   Then like men use 'em.
    The very lees of such—millions of rates°—
    Exceed the wine of others. All our surgeons   30
    Convent° in their behoof, our richest balms,
    Rather than niggard, waste. Their lives concern us
    Much more than Thebes is worth. Rather than have 'em
    Freed of this plight and in their morning state,°
    Sound and at liberty, I would 'em dead,°   35
    But forty-thousandfold we had rather have 'em
    Prisoners to us than Death.° Bear 'em speedily
    From our kind air, to them unkind,° and minister
    What man to man may do—for our sake more,
    Since I have known frights, fury, friends' behests,   40
    Love's provocations, zeal, a mistress' task,
    Desire of liberty, a fever, madness,

19 **fixed my note** directed my attention   21 **What . . . me** i.e., what
was it that a prisoner told me   22 **'lieve** believe   28 **have the name
of men** can still be called men   29 **millions of rates** millions of
times   31 **Convent** summon   34 **in their morning state** as they
were this morning   35 **would 'em dead** would rather they were dead
37 **Death** i.e., prisoners to Death   38 **kind air, to them unkind** i.e.,
the open air is healthy to us but not to them

Hath set a mark which Nature could not reach to
Without some imposition—sickness in will
45   O'er-wrestling strength in reason.° For our love
And great Apollo's° mercy, all our best
Their best skill tender.° Lead into the city,
Where, having bound things scattered, we will post
To Athens 'fore our army.   *Flourish. Exeunt.*

Scene 5. [*Thebes.*]

*Music. Enter the Queens with the hearses of their knights,
in a funeral solemnity, &c.*

[*Song*]

Urns and odors bring away,°
Vapors, sighs, darken the day;
Our dole more deadly looks than dying:
Balms and gums° and heavy cheers,°
5   Sacred vials filled with tears,
And clamors through the wild air flying.

Come, all sad and solemn shows
That are quick-eyed Pleasure's foes:
We convent° nought else but woes,
10   We convent, &c.

Third Queen. [*To Second Queen*] This funeral path brings°
to your household's grave.
Joy seize on you again. Peace sleep with him.

Second Queen. [*To First Queen*] And this to yours.°

40–45 **Since . . . reason** i.e., since I have known cases where unusual
physical or emotional disturbance has produced results that Nature
could not produce without some special stimulus ("imposition"), this
disturbance being able to overcome what could be reasonably expected
46 **Apollo** as god of healing   47 **tender** minister   1.5.1 **bring
away** accompany us   4 **gums** (used for perfume at the funeral rites)
4 **heavy cheers** sad faces   9 **convent** summon, bring together   11
brings leads   13 **this to yours** (the Queens now take their different
paths home)

First Queen. [*To Third Queen*] Yours this way. Heavens lend°
  A thousand differing ways to one sure end.   15

Third Queen. This world's a city full of straying° streets,
  And death's the market place where each one meets.
                         Exeunt severally.

14 **lend** provide   16 **straying** winding

ACT 2

Scene 1. [*Athens. A garden with a room in a prison above.*]

Enter Jailer and Wooer.

Jailer. I may depart with° little while I live: something I
may cast to you, not much. Alas, the prison I keep,
though it be for great ones, yet they seldom come. Before one salmon you shall take a number of minnows.
5   I am given out to be better lined than it can appear to me
report is a true speaker.° I would I were really that I
am delivered° to be. Marry,° what I have, be it what it
will, I will assure° upon my daughter at the day of my
death.

10 *Wooer.* Sir, I demand no more than your own offer, and I
will estate° your daughter in what I have promised.

Jailer. Well, we will talk more of this when the solemnity°
is passed. But have you a full promise of her?

Enter Daughter.

When that shall be seen, I tender my consent.

15 *Wooer.* I have, sir. Here she comes.

Jailer. Your friend and I have chanced to name you here,
upon the old business; but no more of that now. So soon
as the court-hurry° is over, we will have an end of it.

2.1.1 **depart with** give   5–6 **I am … speaker** I am generally believed to be better off than there seems to me cause for rumor to assert
7 **delivered** said   7 **Marry** indeed   8 **assure** i.e., bestow   11 **estate** endow   12 **solemnity** i.e., wedding   18 **court-hurry** celebra-
tions at court (?)

I' th' meantime look tenderly to the two prisoners. I can
tell you they are princes.   20

Daughter. These strewings° are for their chamber. 'Tis pity
they are in prison, and 'twere pity they should be out. I
do think they have patience to make any adversity
ashamed: the prison itself is proud of 'em, and they have
all the world in their chamber.°   25

Jailer. They are famed to be a pair of absolute° men.

Daughter. By my troth, I think Fame but stammers 'em:°
they stand a grize° above the reach of report.

Jailer. I heard them reported in the battle to be the only
doers.°   30

Daughter. Nay, most likely, for they are noble suff'rers. I
marvel how they would have looked had they been victors, that with such a constant nobility enforce a freedom out of bondage, making misery their mirth, and
affliction a toy to jest at.   35

Jailer. Do they so?

Daughter. It seems to me they have no more sense of their
captivity than I of ruling Athens. They eat well, look
merrily, discourse of many things, but nothing of their
own restraint° and disasters. Yet sometime a divided°   40
sigh, martyred as 'twere i' th' deliverance, will break
from one of them—when the other presently° gives it so
sweet a rebuke that I could wish myself a sigh to be so
chid, or at least a sigher to be comforted.

Wooer. I never saw 'em.   45

Jailer. The duke himself came privately in the night, and so
did they:° what the reason of it is I know not.

21 **strewings** rushes   24–25 **they . . . chamber** their nobility
makes their chamber into a whole world (?), everyone visits them (?)
26 **absolute** complete   27 **Fame but stammers 'em** i.e., their reputation falls short of their worth   28 **grize** step   29–30 **only doers**
unique performers   40 **restraint** imprisonment   40 **divided** broken off   42 **presently** at once   46–47 **The duke . . . they** i.e., Theseus brought the princes secretly to the prison

Enter Palamon and Arcite above.

Look, yonder they are. That's Arcite looks out.

Daughter. No, sir, no! That's Palamon! Arcite is the lower°
50 of the twain. You may perceive a part of him.

Jailer. Go to, leave your pointing. They would not make us
their object.° Out of their sight!

Daughter. It is a holiday to look on them. Lord, the diff-
'rence of men!

Exeunt [Jailer, Wooer, Daughter].

Palamon. How do you, noble cousin?

55 *Arcite.*   How do you, sir?

Palamon. Why, strong enough to laugh at misery,
And bear the chance of war. Yet we are prisoners
I fear forever, cousin.

Arcite.   I believe it,
And to that destiny have patiently
Laid up my hour to come.°

60 *Palamon.*   O cousin Arcite,
Where is Thebes now? Where is our noble country?
Where are our friends, and kindreds?° Never more
Must we behold those comforts, never see
The hardy youths strive for the games of honor,
65 Hung with the painted favors of their ladies,
Like tall ships under sail; then start amongst 'em
And as an east wind leave 'em all behind us,
Like lazy clouds, whilst Palamon and Arcite,
Even in the wagging of a wanton leg,°
70 Outstripped the people's praises, won the garlands
Ere they have time to wish 'em ours. O never
Shall we two exercise, like twins of Honor,
Our arms again, and feel our fiery horses

---

49 **lower** shorter   51–52 **They would not make us their object** they
would not point at us   60 **Laid up my hour to come** i.e., resolved
myself   61–62 **Where is Thebes ... kindreds** (these references to
Thebes are very different from those in the princes' conversation of 1.2)
69 **Even ... leg** as quickly as a leg might be wantonly or idly moved

Like proud seas under us! Our good swords now—
Better the red-eyed god of war ne'er wore!—   75
Ravished our sides, like age must run to rust
And deck the temples of those gods that hate us.
These hands shall never draw 'em out like lightning
To blast whole armies more.

Arcite.   No, Palamon,
Those hopes are prisoners with us: here we are   80
And here the graces of our youths must wither
Like a too timely° spring; here age must find us,
And which is heaviest, Palamon, unmarried;
The sweet embraces of a loving wife,
Loaden with kisses, armed with thousand Cupids,   85
Shall never clasp our necks, no issue° know us,
No figures of ourselves shall we e'er see,
To glad our age, and like young eagles teach 'em
Boldly to gaze against bright arms,° and say:
"Remember what your fathers were, and conquer."   90
The fair-eyed maids shall weep our banishments,
And in their songs curse ever-blinded Fortune
Till she for shame see what a wrong she has done
To youth and nature. This is all our world:
We shall know nothing here but one another,   95
Hear nothing but the clock that tells° our woes.
The vine shall grow, but we shall never see it;
Summer shall come, and with her all delights;
But dead-cold winter must inhabit here still.

Palamon. 'Tis too true, Arcite. To our Theban hounds,   100
That shook the agèd forest with their echoes
No more now must we halloo, no more shake
Our pointed javelins, whilst the angry swine°
Flies like a Parthian quiver° from our rages,
Struck with our well-steeled darts. All valiant uses,°   105

---

82 **too timely** too early   86 **issue** children   89 **arms** weapons and armor (with an allusion to the eagle's ability to look directly at the sun)   96 **tells** counts   103 **angry swine** wild boar   104 **Parthian quiver** (the Parthian bowman was famed for shooting his arrows while retreating: here the fleeing boar, with the arrows stuck in it, is seen as the Parthian's quiver)   105 **uses** customs, practices

The food and nourishment of noble minds,
In us two here shall perish. We shall die—
Which is the curse of honor—lastly,°
Children of grief and ignorance.

Arcite.   Yet, cousin,
110 Even from the bottom of these miseries,
From all that Fortune can inflict upon us,
I see two comforts rising, two mere° blessings,
If the gods please: to hold here a brave patience,
And the enjoying of our griefs together.
115 Whilst Palamon is with me, let me perish
If I think this our prison.

Palamon.   Certainly,
'Tis a main° goodness, cousin, that our fortunes
Were twined together. 'Tis most true, two souls
Put in two noble bodies, let 'em suffer
120 The gall of hazard,° so° they grow together,
Will never sink; they must not, say° they could.
A willing man dies sleeping, and all's done.°

Arcite. Shall we make worthy uses of this place
That all men hate so much?

Palamon.   How, gentle cousin?

125 *Arcite.* Let's think this prison holy sanctuary,
To keep us from corruption of worse men.
We are young and yet desire the ways of honor
That liberty and common conversation,
The poison of pure spirits, might like women
130 Woo us to wander from. What worthy blessing
Can be but our imaginations
May make it ours? And here being thus together,
We are an endless mine° to one another;
We are one another's wife, ever begetting
New births of love; we are father, friends, acquain-
135   tance;

---

108 **lastly** (three syllables)   112 **mere** pure   117 **main** principal
120 **The gall of hazard** the bitterness of misadventure   120 **so** provided that   121 **say** even if   122 **A willing . . . done** a man resigned to his fate dies as gently as falling asleep (but the tone of this
line is not resigned)   133 **mine** source of wealth

We are in one another families;
I am your heir, and you are mine. This place
Is our inheritance; no hard oppressor
Dare take this from us; here with a little patience
We shall live long, and loving; no surfeits seek us;   140
The hand of war hurts none here, nor the seas
Swallow their youth. Were we at liberty,
A wife might part us lawfully, or business,
Quarrels consume us, envy of ill men
Crave our acquaintance.° I might sicken, cousin,   145
Where you should never know it, and so perish
Without your noble hand to close mine eyes,
Or prayers to the gods. A thousand chances,
Were we from hence, would sever us.

Palamon.   You have made me—
I thank you, cousin Arcite—almost wanton°   150
With my captivity. What a misery
It is to live abroad, and everywhere!
'Tis like a beast, methinks. I find the court here,
I am sure a more content,° and all those pleasures
That woo the wills of men to vanity   155
I see through now, and am sufficient°
To tell the world 'tis but a gaudy shadow
That old Time, as he passes by, takes with him.
What had we been old° in the court of Creon,
Where sin is justice, lust and ignorance   160
The virtues of the great ones! Cousin Arcite,
Had not the loving gods found this place for us,
We had died as they do, ill old men, unwept,
And had their epitaphs, the people's curses.
Shall I say more?

Arcite.   I would hear you still.

Palamon.   Ye shall.   165
Is there record of any two that loved
Better than we do, Arcite?

---

145 **Crave our acquaintance** i.e., contaminate by impact on us (editors have variously emended, e.g., to "Grave"=bury, "Cleave"=separate) 150 **wanton** i.e., delighted 154 **a more content** i.e., a court more contented than the real one 156 **sufficient** able 159 **What had we been old** what if we had been old (editors have emended to "What had we been, old . . .")

Arcite.   Sure there cannot.

Palamon. I do not think it possible our friendship
  Should ever leave us.

Arcite.   Till our deaths it cannot,

  Enter Emilia and her Woman [below].

170 And after death our spirits shall be led
  To those that love eternally.° Speak on, sir.

                    [*Palamon sees Emilia.*]

Emilia. This garden has a world of pleasures in't.
  What flow'r is this?

Woman.   'Tis called Narcissus, madam.

Emilia. That was a fair boy certain, but a fool
175 To love himself:° were there not maids enough?

Arcite. Pray, forward.°

Palamon.   Yes.

Emilia.   Or were they all hard-hearted?

Woman. They could not be to one so fair.

Emilia.   Thou wouldst not.

Woman. I think I should not, madam.

Emilia.   That's a good wench;
  But take heed to your kindness, though.

Woman.   Why, madam?

Emilia. Men are mad things.

180 *Arcite.*   Will ye go forward, cousin?

Emilia. Canst not thou work such flowers in silk,
  wench?

Woman.   Yes.

170–71 **our ... eternally** our souls shall be with famous lovers in
Elysium 173–75 **Narcissus ... himself** (Narcissus fell in love with
his own reflection in water, and drowned in trying to embrace it) 176
forward i.e., continue

Emilia. I'll have a gown full of 'em and of these.
   This is a pretty color, will't not do
   Rarely upon a skirt, wench?

Woman.   Dainty, madam.

Arcite. Cousin, cousin, how do you, sir? Why, Palamon!   185

Palamon. Never till now I was in prison, Arcite.

Arcite. Why, what's the matter, man?

Palamon.   Behold, and wonder.
   By heaven, she is a goddess.

Arcite. [*Seeing Emilia*]   Ha!

Palamon.   Do reverence.
   She is a goddess, Arcite.

Emilia.   Of all flow'rs
   Methinks a rose is best.

Woman.   Why, gentle madam?   190

Emilia. It is the very emblem of a maid.
   For when the west wind courts her gently°
   How modestly she blows,° and paints° the sun
   With her chaste blushes! When the north comes near
     her,
   Rude and impatient, then like chastity   195
   She locks her beauties in her bud again,
   And leaves him to base briers.°

Woman.   Yet, good madam,
   Sometimes her modesty will blow so far
   She falls for't:° a maid,
   If she have any honor, would be loath   200
   To take example by her.

Emilia.   Thou art wanton.

Arcite. She is wondrous fair.

---

192 **gently** (three syllables)   193 **blows** opens into flower   193
paints gives an image of   197 **leaves him to base briers** leaves
only base briers for him   199 **for't** as a result of it

Palamon.   She is all the beauty extant.°

Emilia. The sun grows high, let's walk in. Keep these
     flowers:
     We'll see how mere art can come near their colors.
205 I am wondrous merry-hearted, I could laugh now.

Woman. I could lie down,° I am sure.

Emilia.   And take one with you?°

Woman. That's as we bargain,° madam.

Emilia.   Well, agree° then.
                         Exeunt Emilia and Woman.

Palamon. What think you of this beauty?

Arcite.   'Tis a rare one.

Palamon. Is't but a rare one?

Arcite.   Yes, a matchless beauty.

Palamon. Might not a man well lose himself and love
210 her?

Arcite. I cannot tell what you have done. I have.
     Beshrew mine eyes for't, now I feel my shackles.

Palamon. You love her, then?

Arcite.   Who would not?

Palamon.   And desire her?

Arcite. Before my liberty.

Palamon.   I saw her first.

Arcite. That's nothing.

Palamon.   But it shall be.

215 *Arcite.*   I saw her too.

Palamon. Yes, but you must not love her.

---

202 **extant** in existence   205–06 **laugh ... lie down** (the waiting-
woman turns Emilia's merriment into an allusion to the proverb
"laugh and lie down")   206 **And take one with you** i.e., lie down
with a (male) companion   207 **bargain, agree** come to terms

Arcite. I will not as you do, to worship her,
    As she is heavenly and a blessèd goddess:
    I love her as a woman, to enjoy her.
    So both may love.   220

Palamon. You shall not love at all.

Arcite.   Not love at all?
    Who shall deny me?

Palamon. I that first saw her, I that took possession
    First with mine eye of all those beauties
    In her revealed to mankind. If thou lov'st her,   225
    Or entertain'st a hope to blast my wishes,
    Thou art a traitor, Arcite, and a fellow°
    False as thy title to her. Friendship, blood°
    And all the ties between us I disclaim
    If thou once think upon her.

Arcite.   Yes, I love her,   230
    And if the lives of all my name° lay on it,
    I must do so, I love her with my soul.
    If that will lose ye,° farewell, Palamon:
    I say again, I love, and in loving her maintain
    I am as worthy and as free a lover   235
    And have as just a title to her beauty
    As any Palamon or any living
    That is a man's son.

Palamon.   Have I called thee friend?

Arcite. Yes, and have found me so; why are you
    moved thus?
    Let me deal coldly° with you: am not I   240
    Part of your blood, part of your soul? You have told me
    That I was Palamon and you were Arcite.

Palamon. Yes.

Arcite.   Am not I liable to those affections,°
    Those joys, griefs, angers, fears, my friend shall
    suffer?

---

227 **fellow** (often used contemptuously at this time)   228 **blood**
kinship   231 **name** family   233 **lose ye** make me lose you   240
coldly rationally   243 **affections** emotions

Palamon. Ye may be.

245 *Arcite.*   Why then would you deal so cunningly,
So strangely, so unlike a noble kinsman,
To love alone? Speak truly, do you think me
Unworthy of her sight?

Palamon.   No, but unjust,
If thou pursue that sight.

Arcite.   Because another
250 First sees the enemy, shall I stand still
And let mine honor down, and never charge?

Palamon. Yes, if he be but one.

Arcite.   But say that one
Had rather combat me?

Palamon.   Let that one say so,
And use thy freedom; else if thou pursuest her,
255 Be as that cursèd man that hates his country,
A branded villain.

Arcite.   You are mad.

Palamon.   I must be,
Till thou art worthy, Arcite: it concerns me.°
And in this madness if I hazard thee°
And take thy life, I deal but truly.

Arcite.   Fie, sir.
260 You play the child extremely. I will love her,
I must, I ought to do so, and I dare,
And all this justly.

Palamon.   O that now, that now
Thy false self and thy friend had but this fortune
To be one hour at liberty, and grasp
Our good swords in our hands, I would quickly teach
265   thee
What 'twere to filch affection from another.
Thou art baser in it than a cutpurse.

257 **it concerns me** it is of importance to me   258 **hazard thee** put
your life in danger (?), risk losing your friendship (?)

Put but thy head out of this window more,
And as I have a soul, I'll nail thy life to't.

Arcite. Thou dar'st not, fool, thou canst not, thou art
    feeble.   270
Put my head out? I'll throw my body out,
And leap° the garden, when I see her next

               Enter Jailer [above].

And pitch° between her arms to anger thee.

Palamon. No more; the keeper's coming; I shall live
    To knock thy brains out with my shackles.

Arcite.   Do.   275

Jailer. By your leave, gentlemen.

Palamon.   Now, honest keeper?

Jailer. Lord Arcite, you must presently° to th' duke;
    The cause I know not yet.

Arcite.   I am ready, keeper.

Jailer. Prince Palamon, I must awhile bereave you
    Of your fair cousin's company.

                  Exeunt Arcite and Jailer.

Palamon.   And me too,   280
Even when you please, of life. Why is he sent for?
It may be he shall marry her, he's goodly,°
And like enough the duke hath taken notice
Both of his blood and body. But his falsehood—
Why should a friend be treacherous? If that   285
Get him a wife so noble and so fair,
Let honest men ne'er love again. Once more
I would but see this fair one. Blessed garden,
And fruit, and flowers more blessed that still° blos-
    som
As her bright eyes shine on ye! Would I were   290

---

272 **leap** leap down into   273 **pitch** plant myself   277 **presently**
immediately   282 **goodly** handsome   289 **still** ever

For° all the fortune of my life hereafter
Yon little tree, yon blooming apricock!
How I would spread, and fling my wanton arms
In at her window! I would bring her fruit
295   Fit for the gods to feed on; youth and pleasure
Still as she tasted should be doubled on her,
And if she be not heavenly I would make her
So near the gods in nature, they should fear her.

Enter Jailer [above].

And then I am sure she would love me. How now, keeper,
Where's Arcite?

300   *Jailer.*   Banished. Prince Pirithous
Obtained his liberty; but never more
Upon his oath and life must he set foot
Upon this kingdom.

Palamon. [Aside]   He's a blessed man,
He shall see Thebes again, and call to arms
305   The bold young men, that when he bids 'em charge
Fall on like fire. Arcite shall have a fortune,°
If he dare make himself a worthy lover,
Yet in the field to strike a battle° for her,
And if he lose her then, he's a cold coward.
310   How bravely may he bear himself to win her
If he be noble Arcite! Thousand ways.°
Were I at liberty, I would do things
Of such a virtuous greatness that this lady,
This blushing virgin, should take manhood to her
And seek to ravish me.

315   *Jailer.*   My lord, for you
I have this charge too.

Palamon.   To discharge my life?

Jailer. No, but from this place to remove your lordship:
The windows are too open.°

---

291 **For** in exchange for   306 **a fortune** a chance   308 **strike a
battle** sound a call to battle   311 **Thousand ways** i.e., there are a
thousand ways in which he may show himself brave   318 **open** easy
to escape from

Palamon.   Devils take 'em
    That are so envious° to me! Prithee kill me.

Jailer. And hang for't afterward.

Palamon.   By this good light,   320
    Had I a sword I would kill thee.

Jailer.   Why, my lord?

Palamon. Thou bring'st such pelting° scurvy news
        continually
    Thou art not worthy life. I will not go.

Jailer. Indeed you must, my lord.

Palamon.   May I see the garden?

Jailer. No.

Palamon.   Then I am resolved, I will not go.   325

Jailer. I must constrain you then; and for you are danger-
        ous,
    I'll clap more irons on you.

Palamon.   Do, good keeper.
    I'll shake 'em so, ye shall not sleep,
    I'll make ye a new morris.° Must I go?

Jailer. There is no remedy.

Palamon.   Farewell, kind window.   330
    May rude wind never hurt thee. O my lady,
    If ever thou hast felt what sorrow was,
    Dream how I suffer. Come; now bury me.
                        Exeunt Palamon and Jailer.

319 **envious** malicious 322 **pelting** paltry, contemptible 329
make ye a new morris dance a new morris dance for you (in which
bells would jingle on the dancer's coat)

Scene 2. [*The open country.*]

Enter Arcite.

Arcite. Banished the kingdom! 'Tis a benefit,
   A mercy I must thank 'em for; but banished
   The free enjoying of that face I die for,
   O 'twas a studied punishment, a death
5   Beyond imagination! Such a vengeance
   That, were I old and wicked, all my sins
   Could never pluck upon me. Palamon,
   Thou has the start now, thou shalt stay and see
   Her bright eyes break each morning 'gainst thy
      window,
10   And let in life into thee; thou shalt feed
   Upon the sweetness of a noble beauty
   That Nature ne'er exceeded, nor ne'er shall.
   Good gods! What happiness has Palamon!
   Twenty to one, he'll come to speak to her,
15   And if she be as gentle as she's fair,
   I know she's his: he has a tongue will tame
   Tempests, and make the wild rocks wanton. Come what
      can come,
   The worst is death. I will not leave the kingdom.
   I know mine own° is but a heap of ruins,
20   And no redress there. If I go, he has her.
   I am resolved another shape° shall make me,°
   Or end my fortunes. Either way I am happy:
   I'll see her and be near her, or no more.

*Enter four country people, and one with a garland
before them.*

First Countryman. My masters, I'll be there, that's certain.

25 *Second Countryman.* And I'll be there.

2.2.19 **mine own** i.e., Thebes   21 **another shape** a disguise   21
make me bring good fortune to me

Third Countryman. And I.

Fourth Countryman. Why, then, have with ye,° boys. 'Tis
but a chiding.°
Let the plough play today; I'll tickle't out
Of the jades'° tails tomorrow.

First Countryman.   I am sure
To have my wife as jealous as a turkey,   30
But that's all one.° I'll go through,° let her mumble.

Second Countryman. Clap her aboard° tomorrow night,
and stow° her,
And all's made up again.

Third Countryman.   Aye, do but put
A fescue in her fist,° and you shall see her
Take a new lesson out° and be a good wench.   35
Do we all hold,° against° the Maying?

Fourth Countryman.   Hold?
What should ail us?°

Third Countryman.   Arcas will be there.

Second Countryman.   And Sennois
And Rycas, and three better lads ne'er danced
Under green tree; and ye know what wenches, ha?
But will the dainty dominie,° the schoolmaster,   40
Keep touch,° do you think? For he does all,° ye know.

Third Countryman. He'll eat a hornbook° ere he fail.
Go to,

---

27 **have with ye** i.e., I'll be there too   27 **'Tis but a chiding** the
worst that can happen is a chiding   29 **jades'** nags'   31 **that's all
one** that's a matter of indifference   31 **go through** i.e., go through
with it   32 **Clap her aboard** board her (as a conquered ship)   32
stow fill the hold with cargo (continuing the metaphor)   33–34
put/A fescue in her fist (a "fescue" was a small stick, etc., which a
teacher used as a pointer: here it indicates a penis, the idea being
"give *her* something to point with")   35 **Take a new lesson out**
learn a new lesson (continuing the metaphor)   36 **hold** hold to our
purposes   36 **against** in regard to   37 **ail us** make us incapable
40 **dainty dominie** fine schoolmaster   41 **Keep touch** hold to his
word   41 **does all** i.e., is indispensable   42 **hornbook** sheet of paper protected by a sheet of transparent horn, used in teaching the al-
phabet, etc.

The matter's too far driven between
Him and the tanner's daughter to let slip now,°
45   And she must see the duke, and she must dance too.

Fourth Countryman. Shall we be lusty!°

Second Countryman. [*Dances*]   All the boys in Athens
Blow wind i' th' breech on's,° and here I'll be
And there I'll be, for our town, and here again
And there again! Ha, boys, hey for the weavers!°

First Countryman. This must be done i' th' woods.

50   *Fourth Countryman.*   O pardon me.°

Second Countryman. By any means.° Our thing of learning°
says so,
Where he himself will edify the duke
Most parlously° in our behalfs. He's excellent i' th'
woods;
Bring him to th' plains,° his learning makes no cry.°

Third Countryman. We'll see the sports, then every man
55   to's tackle.°
And, sweet companions, let's rehearse by any means
Before the ladies see us, and do sweetly,°
And God knows what may come on't.

Fourth Countryman.   Content;
The sports once ended, we'll perform. Away, boys, and
hold!°

43–44 **The matter's . . . slip now** i.e., their love affair cannot fail to
lead to marriage   46 **lusty** vigorous   46–47 **All . . . breech on's**
i.e., all the boys in Athens are supporting us (literally, are helping us
to dance by blowing us from the ground)   49 **hey for the weavers**
(the Second Countryman, like Bottom, is a weaver and will dance in
honor of his craft)   50 **pardon me** (indicating dissent)   51 **By any
means** in any case   51 **Our thing of learning** i.e., the schoolmaster
53 **parlously** amazingly   53–54 **He's excellent . . . plains** (a double entendre is fairly obvious, implying that the schoolmaster is better
in the earlier than in the later stages of sexual activity)   54 **makes
no cry** wins no applause (and, continuing the metaphor, he will
not make a girl cry out)   55 **every man to's tackle** let every man
keep his engagement   57 **sweetly** delectably   59 **hold** hold to your
purposes

Arcite. [*Comes forward*] By your leaves, honest friends.
    Pray you, whither go you?   60

Fourth Countryman. Whither? Why, what a question's
    that!

Arcite. Yes, 'tis a question to me that know not.

Third Countryman. To the games, my friend.

Second Countryman. Where were you bred you know
    it not?

Arcite.   Not far, sir.
    Are there such games today?

First Countryman.   Yes, marry are there,   65
    And such as you never saw. The duke himself
    Will be in person there.

Arcite.   What pastimes are they?

Second Countryman. Wrestling and running. [*Aside*] 'Tis
    a pretty fellow.

Third Countryman. Thou wilt not go along?

Arcite.   Not yet, sir.

Fourth Countryman.   Well, sir,
    Take your own time. Come, boys.

First Countryman.   My mind misgives me.   70
    This fellow has a vengeance° trick o' th' hip:
    Mark how his body's made for't.°

Second Countryman.   I'll be hanged, though,
    If he dare venture. Hang him! Plum porridge,°
    He wrestle? He roast eggs!° Come, let's be gone, lads.
                    Exeunt [*the*] *four* [*Countrymen*].

Arcite. This is an offered opportunity   75
    I durst not wish for. Well, I could have wrestled,°

---

71 **vengeance** confounded   72 **for't** i.e., for wrestling   73 **Plum
porridge** dish made of plums thickened with barley, etc. (here used as
a term of contempt for one not likely to excel in wrestling)   74 **He
roast eggs** i.e., he would be more capable of cooking an egg   76
could have wrestled used to be able to wrestle

The best men called it excellent, and run
Swifter than wind upon a field of corn,
Curling the wealthy ears, never flew.° I'll venture,
80　　And in some poor disguise be there. Who knows
Whether my brows may not be girt with garlands,
And happiness° prefer me to a place
Where I may ever dwell in sight of her?　　　*Exit Arcite.*

Scene 3. [*The prison.*]

Enter Jailer's Daughter alone.

Daughter. Why should I love this gentleman? 'Tis odds
He never will affect° me; I am base,°
My father the mean keeper of his prison,
And he a prince; to marry him is hopeless,
5　　To be his whore is witless. Out upon't,
What pushes° are we wenches driven to
When fifteen once has found us!° First I saw him;
I, seeing, thought he was a goodly man:
He has as much to please a woman in him,
10　　If he please to bestow it so, as ever
These eyes yet looked on. Next, I pitied him,
And so would any young wench o' my conscience
That ever dreamed, or vowed her maidenhead
To a young handsome man. Then I loved him,
15　　Extremely loved him, infinitely loved him.
And yet he had a cousin, fair as he too.
But in my heart was Palamon, and there,
Lord, what a coil he keeps!° To hear him
Sing in an evening, what a heaven it is!
20　　And yet his songs are sad ones. Fairer spoken
Was never gentleman. When I come in

78–79 **Swifter . . . flew** swifter than wind . . . ever flew (the illogical
negative "never" is idiomatic in the seventeenth century, but editors
have frequently emended) 82 **happiness** good fortune 2.3.2 **affect** love 2 **base** of low birth 6 **pushes** shifts 7 **When fifteen
once has found us** when we have reached the age of fifteen 18 **coil
he keeps** disturbance he makes

To bring him water in a morning, first
He bows his noble body, then salutes me thus:
"Fair, gentle maid, good-morrow, may thy goodness
Get thee a happy husband." Once he kissed me.   25
I loved my lips the better ten days after—
Would he would do so ev'ry day! He grieves much,
And me as much to see his misery.
What should I do to make him know I love him,
For I would fain enjoy him? Say I ventured   30
To set him free? What says the law then? Thus
    much
For law, or kindred!° I will do it,
And this night, or tomorrow, he shall love me.   *Exit.*

Scene 4. [*At the games.*]

*Short flourish of cornets,° and shouts within. Enter
Theseus, Hippolyta, Pirithous, Emilia, Arcite [disguised]
with a garland, &c.*

Theseus. You have done worthily. I have not seen,
  Since Hercules, a man of tougher sinews.
  Whate'er you are, you run the best and wrestle
  That these times can allow.°

Arcite.   I am proud to please you.

Theseus. What country bred you?

Arcite.   This; but far off, prince.   5

Theseus. Are you a gentleman?

Arcite.   My father said so,
  And to those gentle uses gave me life.°

Theseus. Are you his heir?

Arcite.   His youngest, sir.

31–32 **Thus much/For law, or kindred** (we can imagine her click-
ing her fingers, thus filling out line 32)   2.4.s.d. **cornets** hunting
horns   4 **allow** acknowledge, praise   7 **to those gentle uses gave
me life** brought me up to practice such noble customs

Theseus.   Your father
   Sure is a happy sire, then. What proves you?°

10 *Arcite.* A little of all noble qualities:°
   I could have kept° a hawk, and well have halloo'd
   To a deep cry° of dogs; I dare not praise
   My feat in horsemanship, yet they that knew me
   Would say it was my best piece;° last, and greatest,
   I would be thought a soldier.

15 *Theseus.*   You are perfect.

Pirithous. Upon my soul, a proper man.

Emilia.   He is so.

Pirithous. How do you like him, lady?

Hippolyta.   I admire° him:
   I have not seen so young a man so noble,
   If he say true, of his sort.

Emilia.   I believe
20   His mother was a wondrous handsome woman:
   His face methinks goes that way.°

Hippolyta.   But his body
   And fiery mind illustrate° a brave father.

Pirithous. Mark how his virtue,° like a hidden sun,
   Breaks through his baser garments.

Hippolyta.   He's well got,° sure.

Theseus. What made you seek this place, sir?

25 *Arcite.*   Noble Theseus,
   To purchase name,° and do my ablest service
   To such a well-found° wonder as thy worth,
   For only in thy court, of all the world,
   Dwells fair-eyed Honor.

---

9 **What proves you** what can you show for yourself   10 **qualities** abilities   11 **could have kept** was able to keep   12 **deep cry** loud pack   14 **piece** feature, accomplishment   17 **admire** wonder at   21 **goes that way** suggests that   22 **illustrate** confer honor on (stressed on second syllable)   23 **virtue** nobility   24 **well got** nobly descended   26 **purchase name** win reputation   27 **well-found** well-reputed

Pirithous.   All his words are worthy.

Theseus. Sir, we are much indebted to your travel,°   30
    Nor shall you lose your wish. Pirithous,
    Dispose of° this fair gentleman.

Pirithous.   Thanks, Theseus.
    [*To Arcite*] Whate'er you are y' are mine, and I shall
      give you
    To a most noble service, to this lady,
    This bright young virgin; pray observe her goodness;   35
    You have honored her fair birthday with your virtues,
    And as your due y' are hers. Kiss her fair hand, sir.

Arcite. Sir, y' are a noble giver. Dearest beauty,
    Thus let me seal my vowed faith. [*Kisses her hand.*]
      When your servant,
    Your most unworthy creature, but offends you,   40
    Command him die: he shall.

Emilia.   That were too cruel.
    If you deserve well, sir, I shall soon see't.
    Y' are mine, and somewhat better than your rank
      I'll use you.

Pirithous. I'll see you furnished,° and because you say
    You are a horseman, I must needs entreat you   45
    This afternoon to ride, but 'tis a rough one.°

Arcite. I like him better, prince: I shall not then
    Freeze in my saddle.

Theseus.   Sweet, you must be ready,
    And you, Emilia, and you, friend, and all,
    Tomorrow by the sun° to do observance   50
    To flow'ry May in Dian's wood. Wait well, sir,
    Upon your mistress. Emily, I hope
    He shall not go afoot.

Emilia.   That were a shame, sir,
    While I have horses. [*To Arcite*] Take your choice, and
      what

---

30 **travel** journey (or, perhaps, labor)   32 **Dispose of** take charge of
44 **furnished** provided (with what you need)   46 **a rough one** i.e.,
an untrained or unruly horse   50 **by the sun** by sunrise

55   You want at any time, let me but know it.
      If you serve faithfully, I dare assure you
      You'll find a loving mistress.

Arcite.   If I do not,
      Let me find that my father ever hated,
      Disgrace and blows.

Theseus.   Go, lead the way: you have
          won it.°
60   It shall be so; you shall receive all dues
      Fit for the honor you have won; 'twere wrong else.
      Sister, beshrew my heart, you have a servant
      That, if I were a woman, would be master.
      But you are wise.

Emilia.   I hope too wise for that,° sir.
                              Flourish. Exeunt omnes.

              Scene 5. [*The prison.*]

              Enter Jailer's Daughter alone.

Daughter. Let all the dukes, and all the devils, roar:
      He is at liberty. I have ventured for him,
      And out I have brought him to a little wood
      A mile hence. I have sent him where a cedar,
5   Higher than all the rest, spreads like a plane
      Fast by a brook, and there he shall keep close°
      Till I provide him files and food, for yet
      His iron bracelets are not off. O Love,
      What a stout-hearted child thou art! My father
10   Durst better have endured cold iron° than done it.
      I love him, beyond love and beyond reason,
      Or wit,° or safety: I have made him know it.
      I care not, I am desperate. If the law
      Find me,° and then condemn me for't, some wenches,

59 **you have won it** i.e., your success in the games makes you deserve
to lead the way   64 **I hope too wise for that** (Emilia rejects Theseus'
suggestion of marriage)   2.5.6 **keep close** stay in hiding   10 **endured cold iron** suffered death with sword or ax   12 **wit** good sense
14 **Find me** bring me to judgment

Some honest-hearted maids, will sing my dirge,   15
And tell to memory my death was noble,
Dying almost a martyr. That way he takes
I purpose is my way too. Sure he cannot
Be so unmanly as to leave me here.
If he do, maids will not so easily   20
Trust men again. And yet he has not thanked me
For what I have done—no, not so much as kissed me,
And that methinks is not so well. Nor scarcely
Could I persuade him to become a freeman,
He made such scruples of the wrong he did   25
To me, and to my father. Yet I hope,
When he considers more, this love of mine
Will take more root within him. Let him do
What he will with me, so he use me kindly,
For use me so he shall, or I'll proclaim him,   30
And to his face, no man.° I'll presently°
Provide him necessaries, and pack my clothes up,
And where there is a path of ground° I'll venture,
So° he be with me. By him, like a shadow,
I'll ever dwell. Within this hour the hubbub   35
Will be all o'er the prison: I am then
Kissing the man they look for. Farewell, father;
Get many more such prisoners, and such daughters,
And shortly you may keep yourself.° Now to him.

                                                          [*Exit.*]

---

31 **no man** impotent   31 **presently** at once   33 **path of ground**
way through woods, etc. (some editors emend to "patch of ground")
34 **So** provided that   39 **shortly you may keep yourself** i.e., you
will lose all of them and will have only yourself to look after

ACT 3

Scene 1. [*The open country.*]

*Cornets in sundry places. Noise and hallooing° as
people a-Maying. Enter Arcite alone.*

Arcite. The duke has lost Hippolyta; each took
    A several° laund.° This is a solemn rite
    They owe bloomed May, and the Athenians pay it
    To th' heart of ceremony.° O Queen Emilia,
5   Fresher than May, sweeter
    Than her gold buttons° on the boughs or all
    Th' enameled knacks° o' th' mead or garden—yea,
    We challenge too the bank of any nymph
    That makes the stream seem flowers!° Thou, O jewel
10   O' th' wood, o' th' world, hast likewise° blest a place
    With thy sole presence, in thy rumination,°
    That I, poor man, might eftsoons° come between
    And chop on some cold thought.° Thrice blessed
      chance
    To drop on° such a mistress, expectation
15   Most guiltless on't!° Tell me, O lady Fortune,

3.1.s.d. **hallooing** cries of people calling to each other from a distance, or urging dogs in the chase 2 **several** different 2 **laund**
open space among woods (obsolete form of "lawn") 4 **To th'
heart of ceremony** most ceremoniously 6 **buttons** buds 7
enameled knacks trifles of various colors 8–9 **the bank . . .
flowers** i.e., by the stream reflecting the flowers on its bank 10
likewise like the "nymph" of line 8 11 **in thy rumination** as you
meditate there 12 **eftsoons** quickly 12–13 **come . . . thought**
("chop" was a hunting term meaning to seize prey before it was
away from cover: here the idea is apparently that Arcite hopes
merely to come into Emilia's chaste ["cold"] thoughts) 14 **drop
on** come upon 14–15 **expectation/Most guiltless on't** i.e., without at all expecting it

Next after Emily my sovereign, how far
I may be proud. She takes strong note of° me,
Hath made me near her;° and this beauteous morn,
The prim'st° of all the year, presents me with
A brace of horses: two such steeds might well   20
Be by a pair of kings backed, in a field
That their crowns' titles tried.° Alas, alas,
Poor cousin Palamon, poor prisoner, thou
So little dream'st upon my fortune that
Thou think'st thyself the happier thing, to be   25
So near Emilia! Me thou deem'st at Thebes,
And therein wretched, although free. But if
Thou knew'st my mistress breathed on me, and that
I eared° her language, lived in her eye°—O coz,
What passion would enclose thee!°

Enter Palamon as out of a bush, with his shackles.
[He] bends his fist at Arcite.

Palamon.   Traitor kinsman,   30
Thou shouldst perceive my passion, if these signs
Of prisonment were off me, and this hand
But owner of a sword. By all oaths in one,
I and the justice of my love would make thee
A confessed traitor, O thou most perfidious   35
That ever gently° looked, the void'st of honor
That e'er bore gentle token!° Falsest cousin
That ever blood made kin, call'st thou her thine?
I'll prove it in my shackles, with these hands
Void of appointment,° that thou liest, and art   40
A very thief in love, a chaffy° lord,
Nor worth the name of villain—had I a sword,
And these house-clogs° away.

---

17 **takes strong note of** observes closely   18 **made me near her** made me attend on her   19 **prim'st** supreme   22 **That their crowns' titles tried** where their claims to the crowns were being decided   29 **eared** listened to, with also a suggestion of "ear"=to plow   29 **in her eye** where she can see me, but with the suggestion of being so close as to see his reflection in her eye   30 **enclose thee** i.e., imprison you (doubly ironic in that Arcite thinks Palamon physically in prison while he is actually free but is "enclosed" by the passion indicated)   36 **gently** nobly   37 **bore gentle token** showed outward sign of nobility   40 **Void of appointment** without weapons to fight with   41 **chaffy** worthless   43 **house-clogs** i.e., his shackles

Arcite.   Dear cousin Palamon—

Palamon. Cozener Arcite, give me language such
    As thou hast showed me feat.°

45 *Arcite.*   Not finding in
    The circuit of my breast any gross stuff
    To form me like your blazon,° holds me to
    This gentleness of answer: 'tis your passion
    That thus mistakes, the which to you being enemy
50 Cannot to me be kind:° honor and honesty
    I cherish, and depend on, howsoe'er
    You skip° them in me, and with them, fair coz,
    I'll maintain my proceedings. Pray be pleased
    To show in generous° terms your griefs,° since that
55 Your question's° with your equal, who professes
    To clear his own way,° with the mind and sword
    Of a true gentleman.

Palamon.   That thou durst, Arcite!

Arcite. My coz, my coz, you have been well advertised°
    How much I dare. Y' have seen me use my sword
60 Against th' advice° of fear. Sure° of another
    You would not hear me doubted, but your silence
    Should break out, though i' th' sanctuary.°

Palamon.   Sir,
    I have seen you move in such a place° which well
    Might justify your manhood: you were called
    A good knight and a bold. But the whole week's not
65   fair
    If any day it rain. Their valiant temper°

44–45 **give . . . feat** i.e., let your language correspond with your actions   47 **your blazon** your description of me   49–50 **the
which . . . kind** as your passion is your enemy, it cannot be kind to
me, your friend and other self   52 **skip** overlook   54 **generous** noble   54 **griefs** grievances   55 **question's** quarrel's   55–56 **pro-
fesses/To clear his own way** claims to justify his conduct   58
advertised informed (stressed on second syllable)   60 **advice** warning   60 **Sure** surely   62 **i' th' sanctuary** in a church, but also with
the suggestion of breaking out of "sanctuary" (a place of safety) for
the sake of righting his friend   63 **in such a place** i.e., in battle or
tournament   66 **temper** character

Men lose when they incline° to treachery,
And then they fight like compelled° bears, would fly
Were they not tied.

Arcite.   Kinsman, you might as well
Speak this and act it in your glass, as to   70
His ear which now disdains you.

Palamon.   Come up to me,
Quit me of these cold gyves,° give me a sword,
Though it be rusty, and the charity
Of one meal lend me. Come before me then,
A good sword in thy hand, and do but say   75
That Emily is thine, I will forgive
The trespass thou hast done me, yea my life
If then thou carry't;° and brave souls in shades
That have died manly, which will seek of me
Some news from earth, they shall get none but this,   80
That thou art brave and noble.

Arcite.   Be content.
Again betake you to your hawthorn house.°
With counsel of the night,° I will be here
With wholesome viands. These impediments°
Will I file off. You shall have garments, and   85
Perfumes to kill the smell o' th' prison. After,
When you shall stretch yourself and say but "Arcite,
I am in plight,"° there shall be at your choice
Both sword and armor.

Palamon.   O you heavens, dares any
So noble bear° a guilty business? None   90
But only Arcite. Therefore none but Arcite
In this kind is so bold.

Arcite.   Sweet Palamon!

---

67 **incline** yield   68 **compelled** i.e., in bear-baiting (stressed on first
syllable here)   72 **gyves** fetters   78 **If then thou carry't** i.e., if
you then kill me   82 **hawthorn house** shelter in the hawthorn bush
83 **With counsel of the night** with only night as my confidant   84
These impediments Palamon's shackles   88 **in plight** in good condition, ready   90 **bear** carry out

Palamon. I do embrace you and your offer. For
　　Your offer do't I only, sir. Your person
95　Without hypocrisy I may not wish

　　　　　　　　　　　　　　　　Wind horns off.

　　More than my sword's edge on't.

　　Arcite.　　　　　　　　　You hear the horns.
　　Enter your musit° lest this match between's
　　Be crossed ere met.° Give me your hand. Farewell.
　　I'll bring you every needful thing. I pray you
　　Take comfort and be strong.

100　*Palamon.*　　　　　　　Pray hold your promise,
　　And do the deed with a bent brow°—most certain
　　You love me not; be rough with me, and pour
　　This oil° out of your language. By this air,
　　I could for each word give a cuff,° my stomach°
　　Not reconciled by reason.

105　*Arcite.*　　　　　　　　Plainly spoken,
　　Yet pardon me hard language.° When I spur

　　　　　　　　　　　　　　　　Wind horns.

　　My horse, I chide him not. Content and anger
　　In me have but one face.° Hark, sir, they call
　　The scattered to the banquet:° you must guess
　　I have an office° there.

110　*Palamon.*　　　　　　　Sir, your attendance
　　Cannot please heaven, and I know your office
　　Unjustly is achieved.°

　　Arcite.　　　　　If a good title°—
　　I am persuaded this question, sick between's,
　　By bleeding must be cured.° I am a suitor

---

97 **musit** gap in a hedge through which a hare, etc., might pass when
hunted　98 **crossed ere met** i.e., prevented before begun　101 **with
a bent brow** sternly　103 **oil** courtesy, gentleness　104 **cuff** blow
104 **stomach** anger　106 **pardon me hard language** allow me not to
use hostile language　108 **one face** the same outward manifestation
109 **banquet** light repast, as for a hunting party　110 **office** duty to
perform　112 **Unjustly is achieved** has been unfairly won　112 **If a
good title** (either Arcite interrupts himself or, as some editors have
done, we should emend "If" to "I've")　113-14 **this question . . .
cured** (Arcite sees the quarrel as a sick person standing between them:
they must cure the sickness by letting blood from it)

That to your sword you will bequeath this plea,°   *115*
And talk of it no more.

Palamon.   But this one word:
You are going now to gaze upon my mistress,
For, note you, mine she is.

Arcite.   Nay, then.

Palamon.   Nay, pray you,
You talk of feeding me to breed me strength.
You are going now to look upon a sun   *120*
That strengthens what it looks on: there you have
A vantage o'er me, but enjoy't till
I may enforce my remedy. Farewell.

          Exeunt [severally].

Scene 2. [*The open country.*]

Enter Jailer's Daughter alone.

Daughter. He has mistook the brake° I meant, is gone
After his fancy.° 'Tis now well nigh morning.
No matter, would it were perpetual night,
And darkness lord o' th' world. Hark! 'Tis a wolf!
In me hath grief slain fear, and but for one thing   *5*
I care for nothing, and that's Palamon.
I reck not if the wolves would jaw me, so
He had this file. What if I halloo'd for him?
I cannot halloo. If I whooped, what then?
If he not answered, I should call a wolf   *10*
And do him but that service.° I have heard
Strange howls this live-long night: why may't not be
They have made prey of him? He has no weapons,
He cannot run, the jingling of his gyves
Might call fell° things to listen, who have in them   *15*
A sense to know a man unarmed, and can
Smell where resistance° is. I'll set it down°

115 **plea** lawsuit 3.2.1 **brake** thicket 2 **After his fancy** where
his fancy has led him 11 **do him but that service** i.e., (ironically)
bring a wolf to him 15 **fell** savage 17 **resistance** the power to resist 17 **set it down** take it as settled

He's torn to pieces: they howled many together
And then they fed on him. So much for that;
20   Be bold to ring the bell.° How stand I then?
All's chared° when he is gone. No, no, I lie.
My father's to be hanged for his escape,
Myself to beg, if I prized life so much
As to deny my act, but that I would not,
25   Should I try death by dozens.° I am moped:°
Food took I none these two days,
Sipped some water. I have not closed mine eyes
Save when my lids scoured off their brine.° Alas,
Dissolve my life, let not my sense unsettle,
30   Lest I should drown, or stab, or hang myself.
O state of nature,° fail together° in me,
Since thy best props are warped! So which way now?
The best way is the next° way to a grave:
Each errant step beside° is torment. Lo,
The moon is down, the crickets chirp, the screech-
35   owl
Calls in° the dawn. All offices° are done
Save what I fail in. But the point is this:
An end, and that is all.°   *Exit.*

Scene 3. [*The open country.*]

Enter Arcite, with meat, wine, and files.

Arcite. I should be near the place. Ho, cousin Palamon!

Enter Palamon.

Palamon. Arcite?

---

20 **ring the bell** i.e., toll the bell for his death   21 **All's chared** all
tasks are ended   25 **Should I try death by dozens** should I have to
die many times or in many ways   25 **moped** bewildered, numbed
28 **when my lids scoured off their brine** when I closed them to get
rid of my tears   31 **state of nature** condition of being alive   31 **together** altogether   33 **next** nearest   34 **Each errant step beside**
i.e., each step that does not lead directly to my grave   36 **Calls in**
summons (the owl, doing duty for the cock, indicates the upside-
downness of her world)   36 **offices** tasks   38 **An end, and that is
all** i.e., only death is to come

Arcite.　　　　　　The same. I have brought you food and
　　files.
　　Come forth and fear not; here's no Theseus.

Palamon. Nor none so honest, Arcite.

Arcite.　　　　　　　　That's no matter,
　　We'll argue that hereafter. Come, take courage,　　　　　　5
　　You shall not die thus beastly;° here, sir, drink,
　　I know you are faint; then I'll talk further with you.

Palamon. Arcite, thou mightst now poison me.

Arcite.　　　　　　　　　　I might;
　　But I must° fear you first. Sit down, and good now,°
　　No more of these vain parleys: let us not,　　　　　　　10
　　Having our ancient reputation with us,
　　Make talk for fools and cowards.° To your health, &c.
　　　　　　　　　　　　　　　　　[*He drinks.*]

Palamon. Do.°

Arcite.　　　Pray sit down then, and let me entreat you,
　　By all the honesty and honor in you,
　　No mention of this woman, 'twill disturb us;　　　　　　15
　　We shall have time enough.

Palamon.　　　　　　Well, sir, I'll pledge you.
　　　　　　　　　　　　　　　　　[*He drinks.*]

Arcite. Drink a good hearty draught, it breeds good blood,
　　man.
　　Do not you feel it thaw you?

Palamon.　　　　　　　　Stay, I'll tell you
　　After a draught or two more.

Arcite.　　　　　　　Spare it not,
　　The duke has more, coz. Eat now.

Palamon.　　　　　　Yes.　　　[*He eats.*]

3.3.6 **thus beastly** in your present beastlike condition　9 **must**
should have to　9 **good now** please　12 **Make talk for fools and
cowards** give matter for fools and cowards to talk about　13 **Do** i.e.,
do drink

20 *Arcite.*   I am glad
      You have so good a stomach.°

      Palamon.   I am gladder
      I have so good meat to't.

      Arcite.   Is't not mad° lodging
      Here in the wild woods, cousin?

      Palamon.   Yes, for them
      That have wild° consciences.

      Arcite.   How tastes your victuals?
      Your hunger needs no sauce, I see.

25 *Palamon.*   Not much.
      But if it did, yours° is too tart. Sweet cousin,
      What is this?

      Arcite.   Venison.

      Palamon.   'Tis a lusty° meat.
      Give me more wine. [*Arcite gives him the wine.*] Here,
          Arcite, to the wenches
      We have known in our days. The Lord Steward's
          daughter,
      Do you remember her?

                              [*He offers the wine to Arcite.*]

30 *Arcite.*   After you, coz.

      Palamon. She loved a black-haired man.

      Arcite.   She did so. Well, sir?

      Palamon. And I have heard some call him Arcite, and—

      Arcite. Out with't, 'faith.

      Palamon.   She met him in an arbor:
      What did she there, coz? Play o' th' virginals?°

21 **stomach** appetite 22 **mad** fantastic 24 **wild** disordered 26
yours i.e., the sauce you bring in your words and presence 27 **lusty**
hearty, invigorating 34 **Play o' th' virginals** ("virginals" was the
name of a small instrument like a spinet: here punningly used with
reference to sexual intercourse)

Arcite. Something she did, sir.

Palamon.   Made her groan a month for't;   35
  Or two, or three, or ten.°

Arcite.   The Marshal's sister
  Had her share too, as I remember, cousin,
  Else there be tales° abroad. You'll pledge her?

Palamon.   Yes.
                                          [*He drinks.*]

Arcite. A pretty brown wench 'tis. There was a time
  When young men went a-hunting—and a wood,   40
  And a broad beech, and thereby hangs a tale.
  Heigh ho!

Palamon.   For Emily, upon my life! Fool,
  Away with this strained mirth! I say again
  That sigh was breathed for Emily. Base cousin,
  Dar'st thou break° first?

Arcite.   You are wide.°

Palamon.   By heaven and earth,   45
  There's nothing in thee honest.

Arcite.   Then I'll leave you:
  You are a beast° now.

Palamon.   As thou mak'st me, traitor.

Arcite. There's all things needful: files and shirts and
      perfumes.
  I'll come again some two hours hence, and bring
  That that shall quiet all.

Palamon.   A sword and armor?   50

Arcite. Fear me not; you are now too foul;° farewell.
  Get off your trinkets,° you shall want nought.

35–36 **groan . . . ten** (Palamon leads archly to the idea of gestation)
38 **tales** false reports   45 **break** break our agreement not to refer to
Emilia (but also with a suggestion of emotion breaking out)   45 **wide**
wide of the mark   47 **beast** i.e., not fit for conversation   51 **foul** un-
washed, etc.   52 **trinkets** i.e., shackles

Palamon.   Sirrah°—

Arcite. I'll hear no more.   *Exit.*

Palamon.   If he keep touch,° he dies for't.
                                               Exit.

Scene 4. [*The open country.*]

Enter Jailer's Daughter.

Daughter. I am very cold, and all the stars are out too,
 The little stars and all, that look like aglets.°
 The sun has seen my folly. Palamon!
 Alas, no, he's in heaven. Where am I now?
5 Yonder's the sea, and there's a ship: how't tumbles,
 And there's a rock lies watching under water;
 Now, now, it beats upon it;° now, now, now!
 There's a leak sprung, a sound° one; how they cry!
 Spoon° her before the wind, you'll lose all else!
10 Up with a course° or two, and tack about,° boys!
 Good night, good night, y' are gone. I am very hungry.
 Would I could find a fine frog; he would tell me
 News from all parts o' th' world; then would I make
 A carack° of a cockleshell, and sail
15 By east and north-east to the King of Pigmies,
 For he tells fortunes rarely. Now my father
 Twenty to one is trussed up in a trice°
 Tomorrow morning. I'll say never a word.

 (*Sing[s]*) For I'll cut my green coat, a foot above my
    knee,
    And I'll clip my yellow locks, an inch below
20   mine eye.

52 **Sirrah** (contemptuous form of address)   53 **keep touch** keep his
promise   3.4.2 **aglets** jewels used as hair ornaments and for tags to
laces   7 **it beats upon it** i.e., the ship strikes the rock   8 **sound** great
9 **Spoon** scud   10 **course** sail attached to the lower yards of a ship
10 **tack about** change direction   14 **carack** ship of large burden   17
trussed up in a trice hanged immediately

> Hey, nonny, nonny, nonny!
> He's° buy me a white cut,° forth for to ride,
> And I'll go seek him, through the world
>   that is so wide.
>   Hey, nonny, nonny, nonny!

O for a prick now like a nightingale,   25
To put my breast against!° I shall sleep like a top else.
>   *Exit.*

Scene 5. [*The open country.*]

*Enter a Schoolmaster, four Countrymen and Bavian,° five
wenches, with a Taborer.°*

Schoolmaster. Fie, fie,
  What tediosity and disensanity°
  Is here among ye? Have my rudiments
  Been labored so long with ye, milked unto ye,
  And, by a figure,° even the very plumbroth°   5
  And marrow of my understanding laid upon ye?
  And do you still cry "where" and "how" and "where-
      fore"?
  You most coarse frieze° capacities, ye jean° judgments,
  Have I said "thus let be," and "there let be,"
  And "then let be," and no man understand me?   10
  Proh deum, medius fidius,° ye are all dunces!
  For why, here stand I. Here the duke comes; there are
      you
  Close° in the thicket; the duke appears; I meet him
  And unto him I utter learnèd things,

---

22 **He's** (vulgar form of "He'll")   22 **cut** laboring horse, so called
because either with docked tail or gelded   25–26 **prick . . . against**
(alluding to the common belief that the nightingale presses against a
thorn in order to stay awake and sing)   3.5.s.d. **Bavian** the fool in the
morris dance (the word signifying either "driveler" or "baboon") **Taborer** one who plays a small drum   2 **disensanity** insanity ("dis-"
here being intensive)   5 **figure** i.e., of speech   5 **plumbroth** (as
"plum porridge," 2.2.73)   8 **frieze** rough woollen cloth   8 **jean** a
kind of fustian (also spelled "jane")   11 **Proh deum, medius fidius**
O God, most certainly (Latin)   13 **Close** secretly

15   And many figures; he hears, and nods, and hums,
      And then cries "Rare!", and I go forward; at length
      I fling my cap up—mark there—then do you,
      As once did Meleager and the boar,°
      Break comely° out before him—like true lovers,°
20   Cast yourselves in a body° decently,
      And sweetly, by a figure, trace and turn,° boys.

First Countryman. And sweetly we will do it, Master
   Gerald.

Second Countryman. Draw up the company. Where's
   the taborer?

Third Countryman. Why, Timothy!

Taborer.   Here, my mad boys, have at ye!°

Schoolmaster. But, I say, where's their women?

25 *Fourth Countryman.*   Here's Friz and Maudlin.

Second Countryman. And little Luce with the white
   legs, and bouncing° Barbary.

First Countryman. And freckled Nell, that never failed
   her master.°

Schoolmaster. Where be your ribands, maids? Swim°
      with your bodies,
      And carry it° sweetly and deliverly,°
30   And now and then a favor,° and a frisk.°

Nell. Let us alone,° sir.

Schoolmaster.   Where's the rest o' th' music?°

Third Countryman. Dispersed° as you commanded.

18 **Meleager and the boar** (alluding to Meleager's killing the Caly-
donian boar, and his bringing the boar's head to Atalanta)   19
comely fittingly   19 **lovers** i.e., of Theseus   20 **Cast yourselves
in a body** arrange yourselves in a group for the dance   21 **trace
and turn** dance and revolve   24 **have at ye** i.e., I am ready for you
26 **bouncing** large of body   27 **that never failed her master** i.e.,
did whatever he wanted of her   28 **Swim** move flowingly   29
carry it i.e., perform the dance   29 **deliverly** nimbly   30 **favor**
(presumably a kiss)   30 **frisk** caper   31 **Let us alone** leave it to us
31 **music** musicians   32 **Dispersed** i.e., scattered in arranged
places

Schoolmaster.   Couple° then,
And see what's wanting. Where's the Bavian?
My friend, carry your tail without offense
Or scandal to the ladies; and be sure   35
You tumble with audacity, and manhood,
And when you bark do it with judgment.

Bavian.   Yes, sir.

Schoolmaster. Quo usque tandem?° Here is a woman
     wanting.°

Fourth Countryman. We may go whistle.° All the fat's
     i' th' fire.

Schoolmaster. We have,   40
As learnèd authors utter, washed a tile,°
We have been *fatuus,*° and labored vainly.

Second Countryman. This is that scornful piece,° that
     scurvy hilding,°
That gave her promise faithfully she would be here,
Cicely the sempster's° daughter.   45
The next gloves that I give her shall be dogskin.
Nay, and° she fail me once! You can tell, Arcas,°
She swore by wine and bread she would not break.°

Schoolmaster. An eel and woman,
A learnèd poet says,° unless by th' tail   50
And with thy teeth thou hold, will either° fail.
In manners this was false position.°

First Countryman. A fire ill° take her! Does she flinch
     now?

---

32 **Couple** take your partners   38 **Quo usque tandem** how long
now (Latin)   38 **wanting** missing   39 **We may go whistle** we
have occupied ourselves to no purpose   41 **washed a tile** labored
in vain (Latin "*laterem lavare*")   42 **fatuus** foolish (Latin)   43
piece creature   43 **hilding** good-for-nothing   45 **sempster's** probably here=sempstress's   47 **and** if   47 **Arcas** (the name of one
of the Countrymen: cf. 2.2.37)   48 **break** break her word   50 **A
learnèd poet says** (no one has identified the "poet," if he existed;
but Fletcher used the proverb in other plays)   51 **either** both   52
position statement of a proposition, affirmation (the Schoolmaster
means that Cicely's breaking her word was the equivalent in manners to the stating of a false proposition in logic)   53 **fire ill** (perhaps equivalent to "pox," or "ill" may be adverbial)

Third Countryman.   What
    Shall we determine,° sir?

Schoolmaster.   Nothing.
55   Our business is become a nullity,
    Yea, and a woeful, and a piteous nullity.

Fourth Countryman. Now when the credit of our town lay
    on it,
    Now to be frampel,° now to piss o' th' nettle!°
    Go thy ways, I'll remember thee, I'll fit thee!°

          Enter Jailer's Daughter.

Daughter.

60   [*Sings*] The George Alow° came from the south,
        From the coast of Barbary-a,
    And there he met with brave gallants of war,
        By one, by two, by three-a.
    Well hailed, well hailed, you jolly gallants,
65   And whither now are you bound-a?
    O let me have your company
        Till we come to the sound-a.

There was three fools fell out about an owlet.

    The one said it was an owl;
70   The other he said nay;
    The third he said it was a hawk,
    And her bells° were cut away.

Third Countryman. There's a dainty° mad woman,
    master,
    Comes i' th' nick,° as mad as a march hare.
75   If we can get her dance, we are made again:°
    I warrant her, she'll do the rarest° gambols.

---

54 **determine** decide to do   58 **frampel** peevish, froward   58 **piss
o' th' nettle** give herself occasion to show bad temper   59 **fit thee**
punish you as you deserve   60 **George Alow** (this was the name of a
ship in a ballad published in 1611)   72 **bells** (used on a hawk for
ease in tracing it)   73 **dainty** fine   74 **i' th' nick** i.e., just when we
need her   75 **we are made again** our fortune is once more secure
76 **rarest** finest

First Countryman. A mad woman? We are made, boys.

Schoolmaster. And are you mad, good woman?

Daughter.   I would be sorry else.
  Give me your hand.

Schoolmaster.   Why?

Daughter.   I can tell your fortune.
  You are a fool. Tell ten. I have posed him.° Buzz.°   80
  Friend, you must eat no white bread; if you do,
  Your teeth will bleed extremely. Shall we dance, ho?
  I know you, y' are a tinker: sirrah tinker,
  Stop no more holes but what you should.°

Schoolmaster.   Dii boni!°
  A tinker, damsel?

Daughter.   Or a conjuror.   85
  Raise me a devil now, and let him play
  Qui passa,° o' th' bells and bones.°

Schoolmaster.   Go take her,
  And fluently° persuade her to a peace.
  Et opus exegi, quod nec Iovis ira, nec ignis.°
  Strike up,° and lead her in.°

Second Countryman.   Come, lass, let's trip it.   90

Daughter. I'll lead.

Third Countryman. Do, do.

---

80 **Tell ten. I have posed him** (counting on one's fingers was a common method of testing idiocy: the Jailer's Daughter decides the Schoolmaster cannot pass the test) 80 **Buzz** (exclamation commanding
silence) 84 **Stop . . . should** (alluding to the proverb "A tinker stops
one hole and makes others"; but with an obvious double meaning here)
84 **Dii boni** good gods (Latin) 87 **Qui passa** (the song "Chi passa
per questa strada") (Italian) 87 **bells and bones** (similar to Bottom's
"the tongs and the bones," *A Midsummer Night's Dream,* 4.1.32:
"bones" were bone clappers held between the fingers) 88 **fluently**
quickly 89 **Et . . . ignis** I have achieved something which neither
Jove's anger nor fire . . . (from Ovid's *Metamorphoses,* 15.871, where it
reads *"Iamque opus . . . nec ignes"*) (Latin) 90 **Strike up** begin the
music 90 **in** offstage, into the thicket where the dancers will wait

   Schoolmaster.   Persuasively, and cunningly!°
                                            Wind horns.

     Away, boys! I hear the horns.
     Give me some meditation,° and mark your cue.
                        Exeunt all but Schoolmaster.

     Pallas° inspire me!

     Enter Theseus, Pirithous, Hippolyta, Emilia, Arcite,
        and train. [A chair and stools are brought out.]°

   Theseus.   This way the stag took.

   Schoolmaster. Stay, and edify!°

95   *Theseus.*   What have we here?

   Pirithous. Some country sport, upon my life, sir.

   Theseus. Well, sir, go forward, we will edify.
     Ladies, sit down; we'll stay it.°   *[They sit.]*

   Schoolmaster. Thou doughty duke, all hail! All hail,
     sweet ladies!

100 *Theseus.* This is a cold beginning.°

   Schoolmaster. If you but favor, our country pastime made is.
     We are a few of those collected here
     That ruder tongues distinguish° villager.
     And to say verity, and not to fable,
105   We are a merry rout, or else a rabble
     Or company, or by a figure *Chorus,*°
     That 'fore thy dignity will dance a morris.
     And I that am the rectifier° of all,
     By title Pedagogus, that let fall
110   The birch upon the breeches of the small ones,
     And humble with a ferula° the tall ones,

---

91 **cunningly** skillfully   93 **meditation** time for meditation (?), attention (?)   94 **Pallas** as goddess of learning   94s.d. **A chair and stools are brought out** (see Textual Note for lines 65–67)   95 **edify** (the Schoolmaster's English for "profit mentally," "be edified")   98 **stay it** wait here for it   100 **cold beginning** (deliberately taking "hail" for a reference to the weather)   103 **distinguish** classify   106 **by a figure Chorus** (the Schoolmaster's "figure" allows him to compare the morris dancers with the chorus of a classical play)   108 **rectifier** (pedant's word for "director")   111 **ferula** cane

Do here present this machine,° or this frame;°
And dainty duke, whose doughty dismal fame
From Dis to Daedalus,° from post to pillar°
Is blown abroad, help me, thy poor well-willer,   115
And with thy twinkling eyes look right and straight
Upon this mighty "Morr," of mickle weight;
"Is" now comes in—which being glued together
Makes "Morris,"° and the cause that we came hither,
The body of our sport of no small study.   120
I first appear, though rude, and raw, and muddy,
To speak before thy noble grace this tenor,°
At whose great feet I offer up my penner;°
The next° the Lord of May, and Lady bright,
The Chambermaid and Servingman by night   125
That seek out silent hanging;° then mine Host
And his fat Spouse, that welcomes to their° cost
The gallèd° Traveler, and with a beck'ning
Informs the Tapster to inflame the reck'ning;
Then the beest-eating° Clown, and next the Fool,   130
The Bavian with long tail, and eke long tool,°
Cum multis aliis° that make a dance.
Say "Aye," and all shall presently advance.

Theseus. Aye, aye, by any means, dear dominie.

Pirithous.   Produce.°

Schoolmaster. Intrate, filii!° Come forth and foot it.   135

---

112 **machine** structure, device (stressed on first syllable)   112
frame contrivance   114 **Dis to Daedalus** (Dis was the Greek god of
the underworld, Daedalus the maker of the Labyrinth in Crete: the
Schoolmaster's use of learning is indiscriminate)   114 **from post to
pillar** from one resource to another (the Schoolmaster is desperate for
a rhyme)   117–19 **Morr ... Morris** (perhaps the Schoolmaster
holds up two boards in turn, with the syllables "Morr" and "is" on
them, and then puts them together; but the first board could show a
picture of a Moor)   122 **tenor** properly, the wording of a document;
drift   123 **penner** pen case (offered as a token of his services to
Theseus)   124 **next** i.e., next to appear   126 **seek out silent hanging** i.e., seek out a curtain or tapestry behind which they can make
love   127 **their** (perhaps plural because "Traveler" is so understood)
128 **gallèd** distressed   130 **beest-eating** (probably indicates the
Clown's partiality for "beest," the milk of a cow soon after calving,
used in making puddings)   131 **tool** sexual organ   132 **Cum multis aliis** with many others (Latin)   134 **Produce** bring forth   135
Intrate, filii enter, my sons (Latin)

Knock.° Enter the Dance. Music. [They] dance.

    Ladies, if we have been merry
    And have pleased ye with a derry,
    And a derry, and a down,
    Say the Schoolmaster's no Clown.
140   Duke, if we have pleased thee too
    And have done as good boys should do,
    Give us but a tree or twain
    For a maypole, and again,
    Ere another year run out,
145   We'll make thee laugh and all this rout.°

Theseus. Take twenty, dominie. [*To Hippolyta*] How does
    my sweetheart?

Hippolyta. Never so pleased, sir.

Emilia.   'Twas an excellent dance,
    And for a preface I never heard a better.

Theseus. Schoolmaster, I thank you. One see 'em all re-
    warded.

Pirithous. [*Gives money.*] And here's something to paint
150   your pole withal.

Theseus. Now to our sports again.

Schoolmaster. May the stag thou hunt'st stand° long,
    And thy dogs be swift and strong,
    May they kill him without lets,°
155   And the ladies eat his dowsets!°   *Wind horns.*
    [*To the dancers*] Come, we are all made. *Dii deaeque*
      omnes!°
    Ye have danced rarely, wenches.   *Exeunt.*

135s.d. **Knock** (the Schoolmaster gives a signal for the entry: but see
Textual Note, pp. 576–77)   145 **rout** company   152 **stand** endure
154 **lets** hindrances   155 **dowsets** testicles   156 **Dii deaeque
omnes** all gods and goddesses (Latin)

Scene 6. [*The open country.*]

Enter Palamon from the bush.

Palamon. About this hour my cousin gave his faith
  To visit me again, and with him bring
  Two swords and two good armors: if he fail,
  He's neither man nor soldier. When he left me,
  I did not think a week could have restored   *5*
  My lost strength to me, I was grown so low
  And crestfall'n with my wants. I thank thee, Arcite,
  Thou art yet a fair foe, and I feel myself,
  With this refreshing, able once again
  To outdure° danger. To delay it longer   *10*
  Would make the world think when it comes to hearing
  That I lay fatting like a swine to fight,°
  And not a soldier. Therefore this blest morning
  Shall be the last; and that sword he refuses,°
  If it but hold,° I kill him with: 'tis justice.   *15*
  So love and Fortune for me!

Enter Arcite with armors and swords.

                                  O good-morrow!

Arcite. Good-morrow, noble kinsman.

Palamon.   I have put you
  To too much pains, sir.

Arcite.   That too much, fair cousin,
  Is but a debt to honor, and my duty.

Palamon. Would you were so in all, sir! I could wish ye   *20*
  As kind a kinsman as you force me find
  A beneficial foe, that my embraces
  Might thank ye, not my blows.

3.6.10 **outdure** survive   12 **fatting like a swine to fight** being fattened to fight as a swine is fattened to be eaten   14 **that sword he refuses** (Palamon will give Arcite his choice)   15 **If it but hold** if it does not break

Arcite.   I shall think either,
  Well done, a noble recompense.

Palamon.   Then I shall quit° you.

25   *Arcite.* Defy me in these fair terms, and you show°
  More than a mistress to me. No more anger,
  As you love anything that's honorable!
  We were not bred° to talk, man. When we are armed
  And both upon our guards, then let our fury,
30   Like meeting of two tides, fly strongly from us,
  And then to whom the birthright° of this beauty
  Truly pertains—without upbraidings, scorns,
  Despisings of our persons, and such poutings
  Fitter for girls and schoolboys—will be seen,
35   And quickly, yours or mine. Will't please you arm, sir?
  Or if you feel yourself not fitting yet
  And furnished with your old strength, I'll stay,° cousin,
  And ev'ry day discourse you into health,
  As I am spared.° Your person I am friends with,
40   And I could wish I had not said I loved her,
  Though I had died.° But loving such a lady
  And justifying° my love, I must not fly from't.

Palamon. Arcite, thou art so brave an enemy
  That no man but thy cousin's fit to kill thee.
  I am well and lusty.° Choose your arms.

45   *Arcite.*   Choose you, sir.

Palamon. Wilt thou exceed in all, or dost thou do it
  To make me spare thee?

Arcite.   If you think so, cousin,
  You are deceived, for as I am a soldier
  I will not spare you.

Palamon.   That's well said.

Arcite.   You'll find it.°

---

24 **quit** requite   25 **show** appear   28 **bred** brought up   31 **birth-right** the right to possess her, given to one of us at birth   37 **stay** wait   39 **As I am spared** as long as I am alive   41 **Though I had died** i.e., as a result of my silence   42 **justifying** affirming, defending   45 **lusty** vigorous   49 **find it** i.e., find it so

Palamon. Then as I am an honest man and love,   50
  With all the justice of affection°
  I'll pay thee soundly.° This I'll take.

                              [*Chooses an armor.*]

Arcite.   That's mine then.
                              [*Takes the other.*]
  I'll arm you first.

Palamon.   Do. [*Arcite arms him.*] Pray thee tell
    me, cousin,
  Where gott'st thou this good armor?

Arcite.   'Tis the duke's,
  And to say true, I stole it. Do I pinch you?   55

Palamon. No.

Arcite.   Is't not too heavy?

Palamon.   I have worn a lighter,
  But I shall make it serve.

Arcite.   I'll buckle't close.

Palamon. By any means.°

Arcite.   You care not for a grand guard?°

Palamon. No, no, we'll use no horses. I perceive
  You would fain be at that fight.°

Arcite.   I am indifferent.°   60

Palamon. 'Faith, so am I. Good cousin, thrust the buckle
  Through far enough.

Arcite.   I warrant you.

Palamon.   My casque° now.

Arcite. Will you fight bare-armed?

Palamon.   We shall be the nimbler.

---

51 **justice of affection** justice administered by one who loves the offender   52 **soundly** fully, strongly   58 **By any means** i.e., please
do   58 **grand guard** part of armor worn by knight on horseback
60 **at that fight** i.e., fight on horseback   60 **indifferent** i.e., as to
how we fight   62 **casque** helmet

Arcite. But use your gauntlets, though. Those are o' th'
    least:°
    Prithee take mine, good cousin.

65 *Palamon.*   Thank you, Arcite.
    How do I look, am I fall'n much away?°

Arcite. 'Faith, very little: love has used you kindly.

Palamon. I warrant thee, I'll strike home.

Arcite.   Do, and spare not;
    I'll give you cause, sweet cousin.

Palamon.   Now to you, sir.
                        [*He arms Arcite.*]

70 Methinks this armor's very like that, Arcite,
    Thou wor'st that day the three kings fell, but lighter.

Arcite. That was a very good one, and that day
    I well remember you outdid me, cousin.
    I never saw such valor: when you charged
75 Upon the left wing of the enemy,
    I spurred hard to come up, and under me
    I had a right good horse.

Palamon.   You had indeed:
    A bright bay, I remember.

Arcite.   Yes, but all
    Was vainly labored in me: you outwent me,
80 Nor could my wishes reach you.° Yet a little
    I did by imitation.

Palamon.   More by virtue;°
    You are modest, cousin.

Arcite.   When I saw you charge first,
    Methought I heard a dreadful clap of thunder
    Break from the troop.

Palamon.   But still before that flew

---

64 **Those are o' th' least** i.e., those you have are the smallest possible
66 **am I fall'n much away** have I got much thinner   80 **Nor could
my wishes reach you** i.e., my wish to be by your side could not put
me there   81 **virtue** natural talent

The lightning of your valor. Stay a little,   85
Is not this piece too strait?°

Arcite.   No, no, 'tis well.

Palamon. I would have nothing hurt thee but my sword,
A bruise would be dishonor.

Arcite.   Now I am perfect.°

Palamon. Stand off° then.

Arcite.   Take my sword, I hold° it better.

Palamon. I thank ye. No, keep it, your life lies° on it.   90
Here's one: if it but hold, I ask no more
For all my hopes. My cause and honor guard me!

Arcite. And me my love!

    They bow several ways;° then advance and stand.

                    Is there ought else to say?

Palamon. This only, and no more. Thou art mine aunt's
    son,
And that blood we desire to shed is mutual,
In me thine, and in thee mine. My sword   95
Is in my hand, and if thou kill'st me
The gods and I forgive thee. If there be
A place prepared for those that sleep in honor,
I wish his weary soul that falls may win it.
Fight bravely, cousin. Give me thy noble hand.   100

Arcite. Here, Palamon. [*They take hands.*] This hand shall
    never more
Come near thee with such friendship.

Palamon.   I commend° thee.

Arcite. If I fall, curse me, and say I was a coward,
For none but such dare die in these just trials.
Once more farewell, my cousin.   105

---

86 **strait** tight   88 **perfect** ready   89 **Stand off** stand away   89
hold think   90 **lies** depends   93s.d. **bow several ways** bow formally in different directions, as in the lists   103 **commend** praise,
honor

Palamon.   Farewell, Arcite.
                        [They] fight.
               Horns within; they stand.

Arcite. Lo, cousin, lo, our folly has undone us.

Palamon. Why?

Arcite. This is the duke, a-hunting as I told you:
110   If we be found, we are wretched. O retire
     For honor's sake, and safety, presently°
     Into your bush again. Sir, we shall find
     Too many hours to die in, gentle cousin.
     If you be seen, you perish instantly
115   For breaking prison, and I, if you reveal me,
     For my contempt;° then all the world will scorn us,
     And say we had a noble difference,°
     But base disposers° of it.

Palamon.   No, no, cousin,
     I will no more be hidden, nor put off
120   This great adventure to a second trial.
     I know your cunning, and I know your cause.°
     He that faints° now, shame take him: put thyself
     Upon thy present guard.°

Arcite.   You are not mad?

Palamon. Or I will make th' advantage of this hour
125   Mine own, and what to come shall threaten me
     I fear less than my fortune.° Know, weak cousin,
     I love Emilia, and in that I'll bury
     Thee, and all crosses° else.

Arcite.   Then come what can come,
     Thou shalt know, Palamon, I dare as well
130   Die as discourse or sleep. Only this fears me:°
     The law will have the honor of our ends.
     Have at thy life!

---

111 **presently** at once   116 **contempt** i.e., of Theseus' banishment
of him   117 **difference** quarrel   118 **disposers** controllers   121
your cause i.e., why you wish to postpone the fight   122 **faints**
draws back   123 **Upon thy present guard** on guard at once   126
my fortune i.e., my fortune in this fight   128 **crosses** obstacles
130 **fears me** makes me fear

Palamon.   Look to thine own well, Arcite.
                    [*They*] *fight again. Horns.*

Enter Theseus, Hippolyta, Emilia, Pirithous and train.

Theseus. What ignorant and mad malicious° traitors
    Are you, that 'gainst the tenor° of my laws
    Are making battle, thus like knights appointed,   *135*
    Without my leave, and officers of arms?°
    By Castor,° both shall die.

Palamon.   Hold° thy word, Theseus.
    We are certainly both traitors, both despisers
    Of thee, and of thy goodness. I am Palamon
    That cannot love thee, he that broke thy prison: *140*
    Think well what that deserves; and this is Arcite:
    A bolder traitor never trod thy ground,
    A falser ne'er seemed friend. This is the man
    Was begged° and banished, this is he contemns thee
    And what thou dar'st do; and in this disguise   *145*
    Against thy own edict follows thy sister,
    That fortunate bright star,° the fair Emilia,
    Whose servant—if there be a right in seeing,
    And first bequeathing of the soul to—justly
    I am, and which is more, dares think her his.   *150*
    This treachery, like a most trusty lover,
    I called him now to answer. If thou be'st
    As thou art spoken, great and virtuous,
    The true decider of all injuries,
    Say "Fight again," and thou shalt see me, Theseus,   *155*
    Do such a justice thou thyself wilt envy.
    Then take my life, I'll woo thee to't.

Pirithous.   O heaven,
    What more than man is this!

Theseus.   I have sworn.

Arcite.   We seek not
    Thy breath of mercy, Theseus: 'tis to me

---

133 **malicious** evilly disposed   134 **tenor** purport   136 **officers of arms** officials formally appointed to supervise a fight   137 **Castor** (son of Zeus by Leda, twin brother to Pollux)   137 **Hold** keep   144 **begged** petitioned for   147 **fortunate bright star** star bringing good fortune

160   A thing as soon to die as thee to say it,
       And no more moved. Where° this man calls me traitor,
       Let me say thus much: if in love be treason
       In service of so excellent a beauty,
       As I love most, and in that faith will perish,
165   As I have brought my life here to confirm it,
       As I have served her truest, worthiest,
       As I dare kill this cousin that denies it,
       So let me be most traitor, and ye please me.
       For° scorning thy edict, duke, ask that lady
170   Why she is fair, and why her eyes command me
       Stay here to love her; and if she say "traitor,"
       I am a villain fit to lie unburied.

Palamon. Thou shalt have pity of us both, O Theseus,
       If unto neither thou show mercy. Stop,
175   As thou art just, thy noble ear against us;
       As thou art valiant, for thy cousin's soul
       Whose twelve strong labors crown his memory,°
       Let's die together, at one instant, duke:
       Only a little let him fall before me,
180   That I may tell my soul he shall not have her.

Theseus. I grant your wish, for to say true your cousin
       Has ten times more offended, for I gave him
       More mercy than you found, sir, your offenses
       Being no more than his. None here speak for 'em,
185   For ere the sun set both shall sleep forever.

Hippolyta. Alas the pity! Now or never, sister,
       Speak not to be denied: that face of yours
       Will bear the curses else of after ages
       For these lost cousins.

Emilia.   In my face, dear sister,
190   I find no anger to 'em, nor no ruin:
       The misadventure of their own eyes kill° 'em.
       Yet that I will be woman, and have pity,
       My knees shall grow to th' ground but° I'll get mercy.

---

161 **Where** whereas   169 **For** as for   176–77 **thy cousin's...
memory** i.e., the soul of Hercules, who legendarily performed twelve
great labors   191 **kill** (plural verb through association with "eyes,"
despite the singular subject)   193 **but** unless (or until)

Help me, dear sister; in a deed so virtuous
The powers of all women will be with us.   195

                                    [*They kneel.*]
Most royal brother!

Hippolyta.   Sir, by our tie of marriage!

Emilia. By your own spotless honor!

Hippolyta.   By that faith,
That fair hand, and that honest heart you gave me!

Emilia. By that you would have pity° in another,
By your own virtues infinite!

Hippolyta.   By valor,   200
By all the chaste nights I have ever pleased you!

Theseus. These are strange conjurings.°

Pirithous.   Nay, then I'll in too:
                                    [*He kneels.*]
By all our friendship, sir, by all our dangers,
By all you love most—wars, and this sweet lady!

Emilia. By that you would have trembled to deny   205
A blushing maid!°

Hippolyta.   By your own eyes; by strength,
In which you swore I went beyond all women,
Almost all men, and yet I yielded, Theseus.

Pirithous. To crown all this: by your most noble soul,
Which cannot want° due mercy! I beg first.   210

Hippolyta. Next hear my prayers.

Emilia.   Last let me entreat, sir.

Pirithous. For mercy!

Hippolyta.   Mercy!

Emilia.   Mercy on these princes!

199 **By that you would have pity** by whatever you would have pity
on   202 **conjurings** conjurations   205–06 **By that … maid** presumably, the love the maid asked for   210 **want** fail to get (?), lack
the power to feel (?)

Theseus. Ye make my faith° reel. [*They rise.*] Say I felt
    Compassion to 'em both, how would you place it?°

215 *Emilia.* Upon their lives—but with their banishments.

Theseus. You are a right° woman, sister. You have pity,
    But want the understanding where to use it.
    If you desire their lives, invent a way
    Safer than banishment. Can these two live
220   And have the agony of love about 'em,
    And not kill one another? Every day
    They'd fight about you, hourly bring your honor
    In public question with their swords. Be wise then,
    And here forget 'em. It concerns your credit,
225   And my oath equally. I have said they die:
    Better they fall by th' law than one another.
    Bow° not my honor.

Emilia.   O my noble brother,
    That oath was rashly made, and in your anger;
    Your reason will not hold° it. If such vows
230   Stand for express will,° all the world must perish.
    Beside, I have another oath, 'gainst yours,
    Of more authority, I am sure more love,
    Not made in passion neither, but good heed.

Theseus. What is it, sister?

Pirithous.   Urge it home, brave lady.

235 *Emilia.* That you would ne'er deny me anything
    Fit for my modest suit, and your free granting.
    I tie you to your word now: if ye fall in't,°
    Think how you maim your honor—
    For now I am set a-begging, sir, I am deaf
240   To all but your compassion—how their lives
    Might breed the ruin of my name, opinion.°
    Shall anything that loves me perish for me?

---

213 **faith** i.e., in his own judgment   214 **how would you place it** i.e., in what way would you have it bestowed   216 **right** true, typical   227 **Bow** humiliate, bring disgrace on   229 **hold** hold to   230 **express will** unshakable resolve   237 **fall in't** renege on it   240–41 **how . . . opinion** i.e., how the taking away of their lives might lead to the ruin of my name and reputation (some editors emend to "name's opinion"; some take "opinion" as an exclamation of contempt)

That were a cruel wisdom. Do men prune
The straight young boughs that blush with thousand
   blossoms
Because they may be rotten?° O duke Theseus,   245
The goodly mothers that have groaned for these,
And all the longing maids that ever loved,
If your vow stand, shall curse me and my beauty,
And in their funeral songs for these two cousins
Despise my cruelty, and cry woe worth° me,   250
Till I am nothing but the scorn of women.
For heaven's sake save their lives, and banish 'em.

Theseus. On what conditions?

Emilia.   Swear 'em never more
To make me their contention, or to know me,°
To tread upon thy dukedom, and to be,   255
Wherever they shall travel, ever strangers
To one another.

Palamon.   I'll be cut a-pieces
Before I take this oath: forget I love her?
O all ye gods despise me then! Thy banishment
I not mislike, so° we may fairly carry   260
Our swords and cause along. Else never trifle,
But take our lives, duke: I must love and will,
And for that love must and dare kill this cousin
On any piece° the earth has.

Theseus.   Will you, Arcite,
Take these conditions?

Palamon.   He's a villain then.   265

Pirithous. These are men.°

Arcite. No, never, duke. 'Tis worse to me than begging
To take my life so basely. Though I think
I never shall enjoy her, yet I'll preserve
The honor of affection, and die for her,   270
Make° death a devil.

---

245 **Because they may be rotten** because they may later become
rotten   250 **woe worth** woe befall   254 **know me** hold me in their
minds   260 **so** provided that   264 **piece** i.e., of ground   266 **men**
i.e., complete men   271 **Make** though you make

Theseus. What may be done? For now I feel compassion.

Pirithous. Let it not fall° again, sir.

Theseus.   Say, Emilia,
　　If one of them were dead, as one must, are you
275　Content to take th' other to your husband?
　　They cannot both enjoy you. They are princes
　　As goodly as your own eyes, and as noble
　　As ever Fame yet spoke of. Look upon 'em,
　　And if you can love, end this difference.
280　I give consent; are you content too, princes?

Both [*Cousins*]. With all our souls.

Theseus.   He that she refuses
　　Must die then.

Both [*Cousins*].   Any death thou canst invent, duke.

Palamon. If I fall from that mouth,° I fall with favor,
　　And lovers yet unborn shall bless my ashes.

285 *Arcite.* If she refuse me, yet my grave will wed me,
　　And soldiers sing my epitaph.

Theseus.   Make choice, then.

Emilia. I cannot, sir, they are both too excellent:
　　For me, a hair shall never fall of these men.°

Hippolyta. What will become of 'em?

Theseus.   Thus I ordain it,
290　And by mine honor, once again, it stands,
　　Or both shall die. You shall both to your country,
　　And each within this month, accompanied
　　With three fair knights, appear again in this place,
　　In which I'll plant a pyramid;° and whether,°
295　Before us that are here, can force his cousin
　　By fair and knightly strength to touch the pillar,
　　He shall enjoy her; the other lose his head,
　　And all his friends.° Nor shall he grudge to fall,

273 **fall** weaken   283 **from that mouth** i.e., the sentence being
spoken by her   288 **For . . . men** it will not be from me that a hair of
either shall perish   294 **pyramid** obelisk   294 **whether** which of
the two   298 **And all his friends** i.e., they shall lose their heads too

Nor think he dies with interest in this lady.
Will this content ye?

Palamon.   Yes. Here, cousin Arcite,   *300*
I am friends again, till that hour.

Arcite.   I embrace ye.

Theseus. Are you content, sister?

Emilia.   Yes, I must, sir,
Else both miscarry.

Theseus.   Come, shake hands again, then,
And take heed, as you are gentlemen, this quarrel
Sleep till the hour prefixed,° and hold your course.°   *305*

Palamon. We dare not fail thee, Theseus.

Theseus.   Come, I'll give ye
Now usage like to princes, and to friends.
When ye return, who wins I'll settle here,°
Who loses°—yet I'll weep upon his bier.   *Exeunt.*

---

305 **prefixed** arranged   305 **hold your course** keep to your resolve
308 **settle here** give him a home in Athens   309 **Who loses**—
(Theseus, by changing the construction, shows his realization that the
second half of the antithesis must be anticlimactic)

ACT 4

Scene 1. [*The prison.*]

Enter Jailer and his friend.

Jailer. Hear you no more, was nothing said of me
Concerning the escape of Palamon?
Good sir, remember.

First Friend.   Nothing that I heard,
For I came home before the business°

5   Was fully ended. Yet I might perceive,
Ere I departed, a great likelihood
Of both their pardons. For Hippolyta
And fair-eyed Emily upon their knees
Begged with such handsome pity that the duke

10   Methought stood staggering, whether he should follow
His rash oath or the sweet compassion
Of those two ladies; and to second them
That truly noble prince Pirithous,
Half his own heart,° set in too,° that° I hope

15   All shall be well. Neither heard I one question
Of your name, or his 'scape.

Enter Second Friend.

Jailer.   Pray heaven it hold so.

Second Friend. Be of good comfort, man; I bring you
news,
Good news.

Jailer.   They are welcome.

4.1.4 **business** (three syllables)   14 **Half his own heart** i.e., the
possessor of half of Theseus' heart   14 **set in too** joined in as well
14 **that** so that

Second Friend.   Palamon has cleared you,
  And got your pardon, and discovered° how
  And by whose means he escaped, which was your
      daughter's,   20
  Whose pardon is procured too, and the prisoner,
  Not to be held ungrateful to her goodness,
  Has given a sum of money to her marriage,
  A large one I'll assure you.

Jailer.   Ye are a good man
  And ever bring good news.

First Friend.   How was it ended?   25

Second Friend. Why, as it should be: they that never
      begged
  But they prevailed had their suits fairly granted.
  The prisoners have their lives.

First Friend.   I knew 'twould be so.

Second Friend. But there be new conditions, which you'll
      hear of
  At better time.

Jailer.   I hope they are good.

Second Friend.   They are honorable;   30
  How good they'll prove I know not.

                        Enter Wooer.

First Friend.   'Twill be known.

Wooer. Alas, sir, where's your daughter?

Jailer.   Why do you ask?

Wooer. O sir, when did you see her?

Second Friend.   How he looks!

Jailer. This morning.

Wooer.   Was she well? Was she in health?
  Sir, when did she sleep?

19 **discovered** revealed

35 *First Friend.*   These are strange questions.

Jailer. I do not think she was very well, for now
    You make me mind her,° but° this very day
    I asked her questions, and she answered me
    So far from what she was, so childishly,
40   So sillily, as if she were a fool,
    An innocent,° and I was very angry.
    But what of her, sir?

Wooer.   Nothing but my pity;°
    But you must know it, and as good by me
    As by another that less loves her.

Jailer.   Well, sir?

First Friend. Not right?°

Second Friend.   Not well?

45 *Wooer.*   No, sir, not well.
    'Tis too true, she is mad.

First Friend.   It cannot be.

Wooer. Believe you'll find it so.

Jailer.   I half suspected
    What you have told me: the gods comfort her!
    Either this was her love to Palamon,
50   Or fear of my miscarrying° on his 'scape,
    Or both.

Wooer.   'Tis likely.

Jailer.   But why all this haste,° sir?

Wooer. I'll tell you quickly. As I late was angling
    In the great lake that lies behind the palace,
    From the far shore, thick set with reeds and sedges,
55   As patiently I was attending sport,
    I heard a voice, a shrill one, and attentive
    I gave my ear, when I might well perceive
    'Twas one that sung, and by the smallness of it

---

37 **mind her** call her to mind   37 **but** only   41 **innocent** idiot
42 **Nothing but my pity** it is only pity that makes me speak   45
Not right i.e., in the head   50 **miscarrying** dying   51 **haste** (the
Wooer's haste in coming to tell the Jailer)

A boy or woman. I then left my angle
To his own skill, came near, but yet perceived not   60
Who made the sound, the rushes and the reeds
Had so encompassed it.° I laid me down
And listened to the words she sung, for then,
Through a small glade cut by the fishermen,
I saw it was your daughter.

Jailer.   Pray go on, sir.   65

Wooer. She sung much, but no sense. Only I heard her
Repeat this often: "Palamon is gone,
Is gone to th' wood to gather mulberries;
I'll find him out tomorrow."

First Friend.   Pretty soul!

Wooer. "His shackles will betray him, he'll be taken,   70
And what shall I do then? I'll bring a bevy,
A hundred black-eyed maids, that love as I do,
With chaplets° on their heads of daffadillies,
With cherry lips, and cheeks of damask roses,
And all we'll dance an antic° 'fore the duke,   75
And beg his° pardon." Then she talked of you, sir,
That you must lose your head tomorrow morning,
And she must gather flowers to bury you,
And see the house made handsome. Then she sung
Nothing but "Willow, willow, willow,"° and between   80
Ever was "Palamon, fair Palamon,"
And "Palamon was a tall young man."° The place
Was knee-deep where she sat; her careless tresses
A wreath of bullrush rounded; about her stuck
Thousand fresh water flowers of several colors—   85
That methought she appeared like the fair nymph
That feeds the lake with waters, or as Iris°
Newly dropped down from heaven. Rings she made
Of rushes that grew by, and to 'em spoke
The prettiest posies:° "Thus our true love's tied,"   90

---

62 **it** i.e., the place   73 **chaplets** wreaths   75 **antic** grotesque
dance, as in an antimasque   76 **his** i.e., Palamon's   80 **Willow,
willow, willow** (Desdemona's song in *Othello*, 4.3)   82 **Palamon
was a tall young man** (a variant of the song "When Samson was a tall
young man," possibly referred to in *Love's Labor's Lost*, 1.2.171)   87
Iris goddess of the rainbow   90 **posies** mottoes engraved on rings

"This you may loose,° not me," and many a one.
And then she wept, and sung again, and sighed,
And with the same breath smiled, and kissed her hand.

Second Friend. Alas, what pity it is!

Wooer.   I made in to her.°
95 She saw me, and straight sought the flood; I saved her,
And set her safe to land—when presently°
She slipped away, and to the city made,
With such a cry, and swiftness, that believe me
She left me far behind her. Three or four
100 I saw from far off cross° her: one of 'em
I knew to be your brother; where she stayed,°
And fell, scarce to be got away. I left them with her,

Enter Brother, Daughter, and others.

And hither came to tell you. Here they are.

Daughter.

[*Sings*] May you never more enjoy the light, &c.
Is not this a fine song?

105 *Brother.*   O, a very fine one.

Daughter. I can sing twenty more.

Brother.   I think you can.

Daughter. Yes, truly can I. I can sing "The Broom"°
And "Bonny Robin."° Are not you a tailor?

Brother. Yes.

Daughter.   Where's my wedding gown?

Brother.   I'll bring it tomorrow.

91 **loose** (may have the meaning "lose," the two words being commonly spelled "loose")   94 **made in to her** i.e., forced my way through the rushes to her   96 **presently** at once   100 **cross** intercept   101 **stayed** stopped   107 **The Broom** (a popular song quoted in W. Wager's play *The Longer thou livest the more Fool thou art* [c. 1559] and elsewhere: "broom" here is the shrub of that name)   108 **Bonny Robin** (a song preserved in Queen Elizabeth's Virginal Book and in William Ballet's Lute Book: Ophelia sings a line of it in *Hamlet*, 4.5, where, as here, it may imply a sexual meaning for "Robin")

Daughter. Do, very rearly,° I must be abroad else°   110
  To call the maids, and pay the minstrels,
  For I must lose my maidenhead by cocklight:°
  'Twill never thrive else.°

  (*Sings*) O fair, O sweet,° &c.

Brother. You must e'en take it patiently.

Jailer.   'Tis true.   115

Daughter. Good e'en, good men, pray did you ever hear
  Of one young Palamon?

Jailer.   Yes, wench, we know him.

Daughter. Is't not a fine young gentleman?

Jailer.   'Tis, love.

Brother. By no mean cross her, she is then distempered
  Far worse than now she shows.

First Friend.   Yes, he's a fine man.   120

Daughter. O, is he so? You have a sister?

First Friend.   Yes.

Daughter. But she shall never have him, tell her so,
  For a trick that I know.° Y' had best look to her,
  For if she see him once, she's gone, she's done,
  And undone in an hour. All the young maids   125
  Of our town are in love with him, but I laugh at 'em
  And let 'em all alone.° Is't not a wise course?

First Friend.   Yes.

Daughter. There is at least two hundred now with child
  by him,
  There must be four; yet I keep close° for all this,

---

110 **rearly** early   110 **I must be abroad else** otherwise I shall be
away from home   112 **by cocklight** before dawn   113 **'Twill
never thrive else** otherwise things will never prosper with me   114
O fair, O sweet (a song included among "Certaine Sonets" in Sidney's 1598 Folio)   123 **For a trick that I know** because of a stratagem that I know   127 **let 'em all alone** pay no attention to them
129 **keep close** maintain secrecy

130   Close as a cockle;° and all these must be boys—
He has the trick° on't—and at ten years old
They must be all gelt for musicians,
And sing the wars of Theseus.

Second Friend.   This is strange.

Daughter. As ever you heard, but say nothing.

First Friend.   No.

Daughter. They come from all parts of the dukedom to
135   him.
I'll warrant ye, he had not so few last night
As twenty to dispatch: he'll tickle 't up°
In two hours, if his hand be in.°

Jailer.   She's lost
Past all cure.

Brother.   Heaven forbid, man.

Daughter. Come hither, you are a wise man.

140 *First Friend.*   Does she know him?

Second Friend. No, would she did.

Daughter.   You are master of a ship?°

Jailer. Yes.

Daughter. Where's your compass?

Jailer.   Here.

Daughter.   Set it to th' north.
And now direct your course to th' wood, where Palamon
Lies longing for me. For the tackling let me alone.

---

130 **Close as a cockle** (the proverb occurs also in Shirley's *The
School of Compliment* [1625]: "cockle" here indicates "cockle-shell,"
formerly used for the shells of mollusks generally)   131 **trick**
method   137 **tickle 't up** i.e., finish the task (with a strong suggestion of sexual pleasure)   138 **if his hand be in** if he is in good form
141 **master of a ship** (the Daughter has taken the Schoolmaster for a
tinker, 3.5.83, and the Brother for a tailor, 4.1.108: Palamon is always
a soldier, and she completes the proverbial four occupations by taking
her father for a sailor)

Come° weigh, my hearts, cheerly all! O, O, O, 'tis up!° 145
The wind's fair: top the bowling!° Out with the main-
   sail!
Where's your whistle, master?

Brother.   Let's get her in.

Jailer. Up to the top, boy!

Brother.   Where's the pilot?

First Friend.   Here.

Daughter. What ken'st° thou?

Second Friend.   A fair wood.

Daughter.   Bear for° it, master! Tack about!

(*Sings*) When Cynthia with her borrowed light, &c.   150

                                        Exeunt.

                  Scene 2. [*The palace of Theseus.*]

                  Enter Emilia alone, with two pictures.

Emilia. Yet I may bind those wounds up,° that must open
   And bleed to death for my sake else: I'll choose,
   And end their strife. Two such young handsome men
   Shall never fall for me; their weeping mothers,
   Following the dead cold ashes of their sons,   5
   Shall never curse my cruelty. Good heaven,
   What a sweet face has Arcite! If wise Nature
   With all her best endowments, all those beauties
   She sows into the births of noble bodies,
   Were here a mortal woman, and had in her   10

145 **Come** (lines 145–49 are hardly verse, and the 1634 quarto prints
mainly as prose; but a faint sense of line breaks seems to lie behind
the Daughter's staccato phrases) 145 **'tis up** (i.e., the tackling: the
"O, O, O" indicating the Daughter's imaginary exertions) 146 **top
the bowling** slant the bowline (rope run from the middle of the per-
pendicular of the weather side of a sail to the larboard or starboard
bow, for the purpose of keeping the sail steady in a wind) 149
ken'st seest 149 **Bear for** sail toward 4.2.1 **bind those wounds
up** (proleptic for "prevent those wounds from being given")

The coy denials of young maids, yet doubtless
She would run mad for this man. What an eye,
Of what a fiery sparkle, and quick° sweetness,
Has this young prince! Here° Love himself sits smiling:
15   Just such another° wanton Ganymede
Set Jove a-fire with and enforced the god
Snatch up the goodly boy° and set him by him,
A shining constellation. What a brow
Of what a spacious majesty he carries—
20   Arched like the great-eyed Juno's, but far sweeter,
Smoother than Pelops' shoulder!° Fame and Honor
Methinks from hence,° as from a promontory
Pointed° in heaven, should clap their wings and sing
To all the under-world° the loves and fights
25   Of gods and such men near 'em.° Palamon
Is but his foil, to him a mere dull shadow:
He's swarth,° and meager, of an eye as heavy
As if he had lost his mother; a still temper,°
No stirring in him, no alacrity,
30   Of all this spritely sharpness not a smile.°
Yet these that we count errors may become him:
Narcissus° was a sad boy, but a heavenly.
O who can find the bent of woman's fancy?
I am a fool, my reason is lost in me,
35   I have no choice,° and I have lied so lewdly°
That women ought to beat me. On my knees
I ask thy pardon, Palamon: thou art alone,°
And only beautiful, and these the eyes,
These the bright lamps of beauty, that command
And threaten Love, and what young maid dare cross°
40   'em?
What a bold gravity, and yet inviting,

13 **quick** vital   14 **Here** i.e., in his eye   15 **another** i.e., another
smile (or eye?)   17 **the goodly boy** i.e., Ganymede   21 **Pelops'
shoulder** (Pelops was son of Tantalus and father of Atreus: Marlowe,
Hero and Leander, 1.65, mentions his shoulder as a standard of white-
ness)   22 **from hence** i.e., from Arcite's brow   23 **Pointed** coming
to its point   24 **the under-world** the earth   25 **such men near
'em** demigods, etc.   27 **swarth** dark-complexioned   28 **still temper** placid disposition   30 **smile** trace (with an echo of Arcite's
smiling mentioned in lines 14–15)   32 **Narcissus** (cf. 2.1.173–75)
35 **choice** ability to choose   35 **lewdly** grossly   37 **alone** unique,
supreme   40 **cross** gainsay

Has this brown manly face! O Love, this only
From this hour is complexion.° Lie there, Arcite,
Thou art a changeling° to him, a mere gipsy,
And this the noble body. I am sotted,°   45
Utterly lost, my virgin's faith has fled me!
For if my brother but even now had asked me
Whether° I loved, I had run mad for Arcite;
Now if my sister, more for Palamon.
Stand both together:° now come ask me, brother.   50
Alas, I know not. Ask me now, sweet sister.
I may go look.° What a mere child is Fancy,
That having two fair gawds° of equal sweetness
Cannot distinguish, but must cry for both!

                    Enter [a] Gentleman.

How now, sir?

Gentleman.   From the noble duke your brother,   55
    Madam, I bring you news: the knights are come.

Emilia. To end the quarrel?

Gentleman.   Yes.

Emilia.   Would I might end first!
    What sins have I committed, chaste Diana,°
    That my unspotted youth must now be soiled
    With blood of princes, and my chastity   60
    Be made the altar where the lives of lovers,
    Two greater and two better never yet
    Made mothers joy, must be the sacrifice
    To my unhappy beauty?

        Enter Theseus, Hippolyta, Pirithous and Attendants.

Theseus.   Bring 'em in
    Quickly: by any means,° I long to see 'em.   65
    Your two contending lovers are returned,

42–43 **this only/From this hour is complexion** i.e., only this complexion is acceptable   44 **changeling** child left by the fairies in place of another   45 **sotted** reduced to stupidity   48 **Whether** which of the two   50 **Stand both together** (she puts the two pictures side by side)   52 **I may go look** i.e., I may go seek (for I do not yet know)   53 **gawds** toys, trifles   58 **Diana** (appropriately invoked by Emilia, as in 5.1, as Diana was the patron of Amazons)   65 **by any means** indeed

And with them their fair knights. Now, my fair sister,
You must love one of them.

Emilia.   I had rather both,
So° neither for my sake should fall untimely.

Enter [a] Messenger.

Theseus. Who saw 'em?

Pirithous.   I a while.°

70   *Gentleman.*   And I.

Theseus. From whence come you, sir?

Messenger.   From the knights.

Theseus.   Pray speak,
You that have seen them, what they are.

Mesenger.   I will, sir,
And truly what I think. Six braver spirits
Than these they have brought, if we judge by the out-
        side,
75   I never saw nor read of. He that stands
In the first place with Arcite, by his seeming
Should be a stout° man, by his face a prince.
His very looks so say him: his complexion
Nearer a brown than black; stern, and yet noble,
80   Which shows him hardy, fearless, proud of dangers;
The circles of his eyes show fire within him,
And as a heated° lion so he looks;
His hair hangs long behind him, black and shining
Like ravens' wings; his shoulders broad and strong,
85   Armed long and round,° and on his thigh a sword
Hung by a curious baldric,° when he frowns
To seal his will with:° better o' my conscience
Was never soldier's friend.°

Theseus. Thou hast well described him.

---

69 **So** provided that   70 **a while** briefly   77 **stout** bold, strong
82 **heated** enraged (with perhaps a suggestion of "in heat")   85
Armed long and round with long, round arms   86 **baldric** belt
86–87 **when he frowns/To seal his will with** to effect his desire with
when he is angry   87–88 **better . . . friend** i.e., no soldier has had a
better, more trustworthy sword

Pirithous.   Yet a great deal short,
 Methinks, of him that's first with Palamon.   90

Theseus. Pray speak him, friend.

Pirithous.   I guess he is a prince too,
 And if it may be, greater;° for his show°
 Has all the ornament of honor in't.
 He's somewhat bigger than the knight he° spoke of,
 But of a face far sweeter. His complexion   95
 Is, as a ripe grape, ruddy. He has felt
 Without doubt what he fights for,° and so apter
 To make this cause his own. In's face appears
 All the fair hopes of what he undertakes,°
 And when he's angry, then a settled° valor,   100
 Not tainted with extremes, runs through his body
 And guides his arm to brave things. Fear he cannot,
 He shows no such soft temper. His head's yellow,
 Hard-haired, and curled, thick twined like ivy tods,°
 Not to undo° with thunder. In his face   105
 The livery of the warlike maid° appears,
 Pure red and white, for yet no beard has blest him;
 And in his rolling eyes sits Victory,
 As if she ever meant to court his valor.°
 His nose stands high, a character° of honor;   110
 His red lips, after fights,° are fit for ladies.

Emilia. Must these men die too?

Pirithous.   When he speaks, his tongue
 Sounds like a trumpet. All his lineaments
 Are as a man would wish 'em, strong and clean.
 He wears a well-steeled ax, the staff of gold. 115
 His age some five and twenty.

Messenger.   There's another,

92 **greater** i.e., more than a prince 92 **show** appearance 94 **he** i.e., the Messenger 97 **what he fights for** i.e., love 98–99 **In's face ... undertakes** i.e., he shows great hope of success 100 **settled** steady 104 **ivy tods** ivy bushes 105 **Not to undo** not to be undone, not disheveled 106 **the warlike maid** (the goddess of war, Bellona) 109 **court his valor** (if "court" is right—see Textual Note—the image is strained: the look in his eyes seems in love with his own valor) 110 **character** token 111 **after fights** when fighting is over

A little man, but of a tough soul, seeming
As great as any; fairer promises
In such a body yet I never looked on.

Pirithous. O, he that's freckle-faced?

120 *Messenger.*   The same, my lord.
Are they° not sweet ones?

Pirithous.   Yes, they are well.

Messenger.   Methinks,
Being so few and well disposed,° they show
Great and fine art in nature. He's white-haired,°
Not wanton white, but such a manly color
125 Next to an auburn;° tough, and nimble set,
Which shows an active soul. His arms are brawny,
Lined with strong sinews: to the shoulder-piece
Gently they swell, like women new-conceived,°
Which speaks him prone to labor,° never fainting
130 Under the weight of arms; stout-hearted, still,°
But when he stirs, a tiger. He's gray-eyed,
Which yields compassion where he conquers;° sharp
To spy advantages, and where he finds 'em
He's swift to make 'em his. He does no wrongs,
135 Nor takes none.° He's round-faced, and when he smiles
He shows° a lover, when he frowns a soldier.
About his head he wears the winner's oak,°
And in it stuck the favor of his lady.
His age some six and thirty. In his hand
140 He bears a charging staff,° embossed with silver.

Theseus. Are they all thus?

Pirithous.   They are all the sons of Honor.

---

121 **they** i.e., the freckles   122 **disposed** arranged   123 **white-haired** blond   125 **auburn** yellowish white   128 **new-conceived** recently made pregnant   129 **labor** toil (but continuing the image of "new-conceived")   130 **still** quiet   131–32 **gray-eyed . . . conquers** (apparently gray eyes were considered a sign of mercy)   134–35 **He does no wrongs,/Nor takes none** he neither inflicts nor submits to an unfair attack   136 **shows** appears   137 **winner's oak** wreath of oak leaves bestowed for valor   140 **charging staff** spear used in charging an enemy

Theseus. Now as I have a soul I long to see 'em!
　　Lady, you shall see men fight now.°

Hippolyta.　　　　　　　　　　I wish it,
　　But not the cause, my lord. They would show
　　Bravely about the titles of two kingdoms;°　　　　　145
　　'Tis pity Love should be so tyrannous.
　　O my soft-hearted sister, what think you?
　　Weep not till they weep blood. Wench, it must be.

Theseus. You have steeled 'em with your beauty.
　　　Honored friend,
　　To you I give the field:° pray order it　　　　　　150
　　Fitting the persons that must use it.

Pirithous.　　　　　　　　　　Yes, sir.

Theseus. Come, I'll go visit 'em: I cannot stay,°
　　Their fame has fired me so. Till they appear,
　　Good friend, be royal.°

Pirithous.　　　　　　There shall want no bravery.°

Emilia. Poor wench, go weep, for whosoever wins　　155
　　Loses a noble cousin, for thy sins.　　　　　*Exeunt.*

Scene 3. [*The prison.*]

Enter Jailer, Wooer, Doctor.

Doctor. Her distraction is more at some time of the moon
　　than at other some, is it not?

Jailer. She is continually in a harmless distemper, sleeps
　　little, altogether without appetite, save often drinking,
　　dreaming of another world, and a better; and what　　5
　　broken° piece of matter soe'er she's about, the name

---

143 **you shall see men fight now** (Hippolyta, as an Amazon, would
have a prejudice in favor of women as fighters: Theseus assures her
she will now see fighting on a higher level than she has known)
144–45 **would ... kingdoms** i.e., would be good to watch if they
were fighting to win each other's kingdoms　150 **give the field** assign the task of arranging the tournament　152 **stay** wait　154 **be
royal** make the arrangements with magnificence　154 **bravery**
splendor　4.3.6 **broken** disconnected

Palamon lards it,° that she farces° ev'ry business withal,
fits it to every question.

Enter Daughter.

Look where she comes, you shall perceive her behavior.

10 *Daughter.* I have forgot it quite. The burden° on't was
"Down-a down-a," and penned by no worse man than
Geraldo, Emilia's schoolmaster.° He's as fantastical°
too, as ever he may go upon's legs,° for in the next world
will Dido see Palamon, and then will she be out of love
15 with Aeneas.°

Doctor. What stuff's here? Poor soul!

Jailer. E'en thus all day long.

Daughter. Now for this charm that I told you of, you must
bring a piece of silver on the tip of your tongue, or no
20 ferry.° Then if it be your chance to come where the
blessed spirits—as there's a sight now°—we maids that
have our livers perished,° cracked to pieces with love,
we shall come there, and do nothing all day long but
pick flowers with Proserpine.° Then will I make Pala-
25 mon a nosegay, then let him mark me°—then!

Doctor. How prettily she's amiss! Note her a little further.

Daughter. 'Faith, I'll tell you, sometime we go to barley-
break,° we of the blessed. Alas, 'tis a sore life they
have i' th' other place, such burning, frying, boiling, hiss-
30 ing, howling, chatt'ring, cursing—O they have shrewd

---

7 **lards it** fills it (is rubbed into it like lard)   7 **farces** stuffs   10
burden refrain   12 **Emilia's schoolmaster** (the Daughter is of
course mistaken)   12 **fantastical** fanciful   13 **as ever he may go
upon's legs** i.e., as he could possibly be   13–15 **for . . . Aeneas** (she
imagines that the Schoolmaster has taught her a song about Dido after
death loving Palamon, now dead too, instead of Aeneas)   19–20 **no
ferry** (Charon, the ferryman of the underworld, will not take you
across the Styx)   21 **as there's a sight now** i.e., as I can see them
now ("as" may be merely exclamatory, and possibly "sight" here
means "great number")   22 **perished** shriveled up (the liver was believed to be the seat of the affections)   24 **pick flowers with Proserpine** (Proserpine was picking flowers when Pluto carried her off to
be queen of the underworld)   25 **mark me** pay attention to me
27–28 **barley-break** (a game played by six persons in couples, in
which one couple occupies a marked space called "hell")

measure;° take heed! If one be mad, or hang or drown themselves, thither they go, Jupiter bless us, and there shall we be put in a cauldron of lead and usurers' grease,° amongst a whole million of cutpurses, and there boil like a gammon of bacon that will never be enough.°   *Exit.*   35

Doctor. How her brain coins!°

[*Enter Daughter.*]

Daughter. Lords and courtiers, that have got maids with child, they are in this place, they shall stand in fire up to the navel, and in ice up to th' heart, and there th' offend- ing part burns, and the deceiving part freezes: in troth a very grievous punishment, as one would think, for such a trifle. Believe me, one would marry a leprous witch to be rid on't, I'll assure you.   40

Doctor. How she continues this fancy! 'Tis not an engraffed° madness, but a most thick and profound melancholy.°   45

Daughter. To hear there a proud lady, and a proud city wife, howl together! I were a beast and° I'd call it good sport. One cries "O this smoke!", another "This fire!" One cries "O that ever I did it behind the arras!" and then howls; th' other curses a suing fellow° and her gar- den house.°   50

(*Sings*) I will be true, my stars, my fate, &c.

Exit Daughter.

Jailer. What think you of her, sir?   55

Doctor. I think she has a perturbed mind, which I cannot minister to.

Jailer. Alas, what then?

30–31 **shrewd measure** harsh punishment   33–34 **usurers' grease** fat sweated by usurers   36 **enough** done, cooked   37 **coins** spins fancies   46 **engraffed** implanted, firmly planted   46–47 **thick and profound melancholy** (morbid condition known as "melancholy," to be distinguished from the normal "melancholy" humor)   49 **and** if   52 **suing fellow** persistent wooer   52–53 **garden house** (notoriously used for assignations)

Doctor. Understand you she ever affected any man ere she
60   beheld Palamon?

Jailer. I was once, sir, in great hope she had fixed her liking
on this gentleman my friend.

Wooer. I did think so too, and would account I had a great
penn'orth° on't, to give half my 'state° that both she and
65   I at this present stood unfeignedly on the same terms.

Doctor. That intemperate surfeit of her eye° hath distempered the other senses: they may return and settle again
to execute their preordained faculties, but they are now
in a most extravagant vagary. This you must do: confine
70   her to a place where the light may rather seem to steal in
than be permitted; take upon you, young sir her friend,
the name of Palamon; say you come to eat with her, and
to commune of love. This will catch her attention, for
this her mind beats upon:° other objects that are inserted
75   'tween her mind and eye become the pranks and
friskins° of her madness. Sing to her such green° songs
of love as she says Palamon hath sung in prison. Come
to her, stuck in° as sweet flowers as the season is mistress of, and thereto make an addition of some other
80   compounded° odors, which are grateful° to the sense.
All this shall become° Palamon, for Palamon can sing,
and Palamon is sweet and ev'ry good thing. Desire to eat
with her, carve her,° drink to her, and, still among,° in-
termingle your petition of grace and acceptance into her
85   favor. Learn what maids have been her companions and
play-feres,° and let them repair to her with "Palamon" in
their mouths, and appear with tokens, as if they sug-
gested° for him. It is a falsehood she is in, which is with
falsehoods to be combated. This may bring her to eat, to
90   sleep, and reduce° what's now out of square° in her into
their former law and regiment.° I have seen it approved,°

64 **penn'orth** bargain   64 **'state** property   66 **intemperate surfeit
of her eye** i.e., by seeing Palamon   74 **beats upon** is preoccupied with
76 **friskins** vagaries   76 **green** youthful   78 **stuck in** adorned with
80 **compounded** mixed   80 **grateful** pleasing   81 **become** be suitable for   83 **carve her** carve for her   83 **still among** ever between-
whiles   86 **play-feres** playfellows   87–88 **suggested** interceded
90 **reduce** bring back   90 **out of square** irregular   91 **regiment**
government, order   91 **approved** confirmed

how many times I know not, but to make the number
more I have great hope in this. I will between the pas-
sages° of this project come in with my appliance.° Let
us put it in execution and hasten the success,° which   95
doubt not will bring forth comfort.   *Exeunt.*

93–94 **passages** separate stages 94 **appliance** device, stratagem
(presumably his device of making the disguised Wooer sleep with
her) 95 **success** result

ACT 5

Scene 1. [*Before the altars of Mars, Venus and Diana.*]

Flourish. Enter Theseus, Pirithous, Hippolyta,
Attendants.

Theseus. Now let 'em enter, and before the gods
    Tender their holy prayers. Let the temples
    Burn bright with sacred fires, and the altars
    In hallowed clouds commend their swelling incense°
5   To those above us. Let no due be wanting:
    They have a noble work in hand, will honor°
    The very powers that love 'em.

Flourish of cornets. Enter Palamon and Arcite and their
Knights.

Pirithous.   Sir, they enter.

Theseus. You valiant and strong-hearted enemies,
    You royal german-foes,° that this day come
10   To blow that nearness° out that flames between ye,
    Lay by your anger for an hour, and dovelike
    Before the holy altars of your helpers,
    The all-feared gods, bow down your stubborn bodies.
    Your ire is more than mortal: so your help be;
15   And as the gods regard ye,° fight with justice.
    I'll leave you to your prayers, and betwixt ye
    I part° my wishes.

5.1.4. **swelling incense** incense that swells into clouds 6 **will honor**
i.e., which will honor 9 **german-foes** foes who are of the same
family 10 **nearness** kinship and friendship (editors have suggested
"furnace" and "fierceness" as emendations) 15 **as the gods regard
ye** i.e., as they are just to you 17 **part** divide

Pirithous.   Honor crown the worthiest!
                         Exit Theseus and his train.

Palamon. The glass° is running now that cannot finish
  Till one of us expire. Think you but thus,
  That were there ought in me which strove to show°   20
  Mine enemy in this business, were't one eye
  Against another, arm oppressed by arm,°
  I would destroy th' offender, coz, I would
  Though parcel° of myself. Then from this gather
  How I should tender° you.

Arcite.   I am in labor°   25
  To push your name, your ancient love, our kindred
  Out of my memory, and i' th' self same place
  To seat something I would confound.° So hoist we°
  The sails that must these vessels° port° even where
  The heavenly limiter° pleases.

Palamon.   You speak well.   30
  Before I turn,° let me embrace thee, cousin.
                         [They embrace.]

  This I shall never do again.

Arcite.   One farewell.

Palamon. Why, let it be so: farewell, coz.
                Exeunt Palamon and his Knights.

Arcite.   Farewell, sir.
  Knights, kinsmen, lovers, yea my sacrifices,
  True worshippers of Mars—whose spirit in you   35
  Expels the seeds of fear, and th' apprehension,
  Which still is farther off it°—go with me
  Before the god of our profession. There
  Require of him the hearts of lions, and

---

18 **glass** hourglass   20 **show** i.e., show itself   22 **arm oppressed by arm** if one of my arms were tyrannized over by the other   24 **parcel** part   25 **tender** treat (with an ironical suggestion of the adjectival sense)   25 **in labor** endeavoring (as a woman in childbed endeavors to give birth)   28 **confound** destroy   28 **hoist we** let us hoist   29 **these vessels** our fortunes and persons   29 **port** bring to port   30 **limiter** (the god who sets limits to things)   31 **turn** turn away   37 **farther off it** (the idea of fear is farther from fear itself than its "seeds," or first beginnings, are)

40   The breath of tigers, yea the fierceness too,
        Yea the speed also—to go on,° I mean,
        Else wish we to be snails. You know my prize
        Must be dragged out of blood, force and great feat
        Must put my garland on, where she sticks
45   The queen of flowers:° our intercession then
        Must be to him that makes the camp a cistern
        Brimmed with the blood of men. Give me your aid
        And bend your spirits towards him.

*They [prostrate themselves and then] kneel [before Mars's
altar].*

        Thou mighty one, that with thy power hast turned
50   Green Neptune° into purple, [whose approach]
        Comets prewarn,° whose havoc in vast field
        Unearthèd skulls proclaim, whose breath blows down
        The teeming Ceres' foison,° who dost pluck
        With hand armipotent from forth blue clouds°
55   The masoned turrets, that both mak'st and break'st
        The stony girths° of cities! Me thy pupil,
        Youngest follower of thy drum, instruct this day
        With military skill, that to thy laud
        I may advance my streamer,° and by thee
60   Be styled the lord o' th' day! Give me, great Mars,
        Some token of thy pleasure.

*Here they fall on their faces as formerly,° and there is heard
clanging of armor, with a short thunder as the burst of a
battle, whereupon they all rise and bow to the altar.*

        O great corrector of enormous° times,
        Shaker of o'er-rank° states, thou grand decider
        Of dusty and old titles, that heal'st with blood
65   The earth when it is sick, and cur'st the world

41 **go on** advance   44–45 **where she sticks/The queen of flowers**
where Emilia places her favor (the queen of flowers because it is hers)
50 **Green Neptune** i.e., the sea (as the Textual Note explains, the
bracketed words at the end of this line are not in the quarto, but some
such words seem necessary)   51 **prewarn** give warning of   53
The teeming Ceres' foison the harvest (whose goddess Ceres was)
54 **from forth blue clouds** from their height in the sky   56 **stony
girths** walls   59 **streamer** banner, pennon   61s.d. **as formerly**
(suggesting they had done so at line 48)   62 **enormous** monstrous,
degenerate   63 **o'er-rank** overripe

O' th' plurisy° of people! I do take
Thy signs auspiciously and, in thy name,
To my design° march boldly. Let us go.   *Exeunt.*

*Enter Palamon and his Knights, with the former obser-
vance.°*

Palamon. Our stars must glister with new fire, or be
    Today extinct. Our argument is love,   70
    Which if the goddess of it grant, she gives
    Victory too: then blend your spirits with mine,
    You whose free nobleness do make my cause
    Your personal hazard; to the goddess Venus
    Commend we our proceeding, and implore   75
    Her power unto our party.

        Here they kneel as formerly° [to Venus's altar].

    Hail sovereign queen of secrets, who hast power
    To call the fiercest tyrant from his rage
    And weep unto a girl;° that hast the might
    Even with an eye-glance to choke Mars's drum   80
    And turn th' alarm to whispers; that canst make
    A cripple flourish with° his crutch, and cure him
    Before Apollo;° that may'st force the king
    To be his subject's vassal, and induce
    Stale Gravity to dance: the pollèd° bachelor   85
    Whose youth like wanton boys through bonfires
    Have° skipped thy flame, at seventy thou canst catch
    And make him, to the scorn of his hoarse throat,°
    Abuse° young lays of love; what godlike power
    Hast thou not power upon? To Phoebus° thou   90
    Add'st flames, hotter than his; the heavenly fires
    Did scorch his mortal son,° thine him;° the huntress,°

66 **plurisy** plethora   68 **design** goal   68s.d. **former observance**
(the prostration and kneeling used by Arcite and his Knights, but paid
now to Venus's altar, at line 76)   76s.d. **as formerly** (again referring
to Arcite and his Knights)   79 **weep unto a girl** i.e., make him weep
like a girl   82 **flourish with** brandish   83 **Before Apollo** sooner
than Apollo (the god of healing)   85 **pollèd** bald   87 **Have** (plural
through the influence of "boys")   88 **to the scorn of his hoarse
throat** so that his hoarseness is mocked   89 **Abuse** employ in a ludicrous fashion   90 **Phoebus** (as sun god)   92 **his mortal son**
Phäethon, who was destroyed when Phoebus allowed him to drive the
sun chariot   92 **thine him** (Phoebus was made to feel the heat of
love)   92 **huntress** (Diana, who loved Endymion)

All moist and cold, some say began to throw
Her bow away, and sigh. Take to thy grace
95   Me thy vowed soldier, who do bear thy yoke
As 'twere a wreath of roses, yet is heavier
Than lead itself, stings more than nettles.
I have never been foul-mouthed against thy law,
Ne'er revealed secret, for I knew none; would not,
100   Had I kenned all that were;° I never practiced°
Upon man's wife, nor would the libels read
Of liberal wits;° I never at great feasts
Sought to betray a beauty,° but have blushed
At simp'ring sirs that did. I have been harsh
105   To large confessors,° and have hotly asked them
If they had mothers: I had one, a woman,
And women 'twere they wronged. I knew a man
Of eighty winters, this I told them, who
A lass of fourteen brided. 'Twas thy power
110   To put life into dust: the aged cramp
Had screwed his square foot round,°
The gout had knit his fingers into knots,
Torturing convulsions from his globy eyes
Had almost drawn their spheres,° that what was life
115   In him seemed torture. This anatomy°
Had by his young fair fere° a boy, and I
Believed it was his, for she swore it was,
And who would not believe her? Brief,° I am
To those that prate and have done no companion;
120   To those that boast and have not a defier;
To those that would and cannot a rejoicer.
Yea him I do not love, that tells close offices°
The foulest way, nor names concealments° in

---

100 **all that were** all secrets in existence 100 **practiced** entered
into designs 101–02 **the libels read/Of liberal wits** read the abu-
sive writings of licentious wits 103 **betray a beauty** i.e., reveal her
frailty 105 **large confessors** those who boasted much of their love
conquests 111 **screwed his square foot round** (the play on
"square" and "round" makes the image more grotesque) 113–14
globy . . . spheres ("globy" suggests "swollen," and here "spheres"
must be the eyes themselves, drawn from their sockets; but there is a
suggestion of the spheres of the Ptolemaic universe being distorted
through pain) 115 **anatomy** skeleton 116 **fere** mate 118 **Brief**
in brief 122 **close offices** secret actions 123 **concealments**
things that should be concealed

　　The boldest language. Such a one I am,
　　And vow that lover never yet made sigh　　　　　　125
　　Truer than I. O then most soft sweet goddess,
　　Give me the victory of this question, which
　　Is true love's merit,° and bless me with a sign
　　Of thy great pleasure.

Here music is heard, doves° are seen to flutter; they fall
*　　again upon their faces, then on their knees.*

　　O thou that from eleven to ninety reign'st　　　　130
　　In mortal bosoms, whose chase° is this world
　　And we in herds thy game,° I give thee thanks
　　For this fair token, which being laid unto
　　Mine innocent true heart, arms in assurance
　　My body to this business. Let us rise　　　　　　135
　　And bow before the goddess.　　　　　*They bow.*
　　　　　　　　Time comes on.　　　　*Exeunt.*

Still° music of records.° Enter Emilia in white, her hair
*　　about her shoulders, a wheaten wreath;° one in white*
*　　holding up her train, her hair stuck° with flowers; one*
*　　before her carrying a silver hind,° in which is conveyed*
*　　incense and sweet odors, which being set upon the altar*
*　　[of Diana], her maids standing aloof, she sets fire to it;*
*　　then they curtsy and kneel.*

Emilia. O sacred, shadowy, cold and constant queen,
　　Abandoner of revels, mute contemplative,
　　Sweet, solitary, white as chaste, and pure
　　As wind-fanned snow, who to thy female knights　　140
　　Allow'st no more blood than will make a blush,
　　Which is their order's robe! I here thy priest
　　Am humbled 'fore thine altar. O vouchsafe
　　With that thy rare green eye, which never yet
　　Beheld thing maculate, look on thy virgin;　　　145
　　And sacred silver mistress, lend thine ear—
　　Which ne'er heard scurrile term, into whose port°

128 **merit** reward　129s.d. **doves** (birds sacred to Venus)　131 **chase**
place of hunting　132 **in herds thy game** (cf. the similar image at
1.4.5)　136s.d. **Still** soft **records** recorders　**her hair about her**
shoulders, a wheaten wreath (cf. 1.1s.d.) **stuck** adorned **hind** female red deer, emblem of virginity, sacred to Diana　147 **port** portal

Ne'er entered wanton sound—to my petition
Seasoned with holy fear. This is my last
150 Of vestal office: I am bride-habited,
But maiden-hearted; a husband I have 'pointed,°
But do not know him; out of two I should
Choose one, and pray for his success, but I
Am guiltless of election.° Of mine eyes
155 Were I to lose one, they are equal precious,
I could doom neither: that which perished should
Go to't unsentenced. Therefore, most modest queen,
He of the two pretenders° that best loves me
And has the truest title° in't, let him
160 Take off my wheaten garland, or else grant
The file and quality° I hold I may
Continue° in thy band.

*Here the hind vanishes under the altar, and in the place
ascends a rose tree, having one rose upon it.*

See what our general of ebbs and flows°
Out from the bowels of her holy altar
165 With sacred act advances: but one rose.
If well inspired,° this battle shall confound°
Both these brave knights, and I a virgin flow'r
Must grow alone, unplucked.

*Here is heard a sudden twang of instruments, and the rose
falls from the tree.*

The flow'r is fall'n, the tree descends. O mistress,
170 Thou here dischargest me, I shall be gathered.
I think so, but I know not thine own will:
Unclasp thy mystery.
I hope she's pleased, her signs were gracious.
                                   They curtsy and exeunt.

---

151 **'pointed** had appointed for me   154 **Am guiltless of election**
have made no choice (with the suggestion that she would betray Diana
if she made a choice)   158 **pretenders** claimants   159 **truest title**
best claim   161 **file and quality** station and character   162 **Continue** continue to have   163 **general of ebbs and flows** (Diana as
goddess of the moon)   166 **well inspired** prompted by the goddess
166 **confound** destroy

Scene 2. [*The prison.*]

Enter Doctor, Jailer, and Wooer (in habit of Palamon).

Doctor. Has this advice I told you done any good upon
    her?

Wooer. O very much. The maids that kept her company
    Have half-persuaded her that I am Palamon.
    Within this half-hour she came smiling to me,
    And asked me what I would eat, and when I would kiss
        her.
    I told her presently,° and kissed her twice.   5

Doctor. 'Twas well done. Twenty times had been far better,
    For there the cure lies mainly.

Wooer.   Then she told me
    She would watch° with me tonight, for well she knew
    What hour my fit would take me.

Doctor.   Let her do so,   10
    And when your fit comes, fit her home,° and presently.

Wooer. She would have me sing.

Doctor. You did so?

Wooer.   No.

Doctor.   'Twas very ill done, then:
    You should observe° her ev'ry way.

Wooer.   Alas,
    I have no voice, sir, to confirm° her that way.   15

Doctor. That's all one,° if ye make a noise.
    If she entreat again, do anything:
    Lie with her if she ask you.

5.2.6 **presently** at once   9 **watch** stay awake   11 **fit her home**
give her the right treatment (lie with her)   14 **observe** humor   15
confirm convince   16 **That's all one** that is a matter of indifference

Jailer.   Ho° there, doctor!

Doctor. Yes, in the way of cure.

Jailer.   But first, by your leave,
   I' th' way of honesty.°

20 *Doctor.*   That's but a niceness:°
   Ne'er cast your child away for honesty;
   Cure her first this way, then if she will be honest,
   She has the path before her.°

Jailer.   Thank ye, doctor.

Doctor. Pray bring her in and let's see how she is.

25 *Jailer.* I will, and tell her her Palamon stays for her.
   But, doctor, methinks you are i' th' wrong still.

                                        Exit Jailer.

Doctor.   Go, go.
   You fathers are fine fools! Her honesty?
   And° we should give her physic till we find that—

Wooer. Why, do you think she is not honest, sir?

Doctor. How old is she?

Wooer.   She's eighteen.

30 *Doctor.*   She may be,
   But that's all one, 'tis nothing to our purpose.
   Whate'er her father says, if you perceive
   Her mood inclining that way that I spoke of,
   Videlicet,° the way of flesh—you have me?°

Wooer. Yet very well, sir.

35 *Doctor.*   Please her appetite
   And do it home:° it cures her° *ipso facto*°
   The melancholy humor that infects her.

Wooer. I am of your mind, doctor.

---

18 **Ho** hold, stop   20 **honesty** chastity (i.e., in marriage)   20 **niceness** overscrupulousness   23 **has the path before her** i.e., can marry afterwards   28 **And** if   34 **Videlicet** namely (Latin)   34 **have me** understand me   36 **do it home** do it thoroughly   36 **her** (an "ethic" dative)   36 **ipso facto** in itself, through its own power (Latin)

Enter Jailer, Daughter, Maid.

Doctor. You'll find it so. She comes: pray humor her.

Jailer. Come, your love Palamon stays° for you, child,   40
And has done this long hour, to visit you.

Daughter. I thank him for his gentle patience.
He's a kind gentleman, and I am much bound to him.
Did you ne'er see the horse he gave me?

Jailer.   Yes.

Daughter. How do you like him?

Jailer.   He's a very fair° one.   45

Daughter. You never saw him dance?

Jailer.   No.

Daughter.   I have often.
He dances very finely, very comely,
And for a jig°—come cut and long tail to him°—
He turns ye like a top.

Jailer.   That's fine indeed.

Daughter. He'll dance the morris twenty mile an hour,   50
And that will founder the best hobby-horse,
If I have any skill,° in all the parish;
And gallops to the tune of "Light o' Love."°
What think you of this horse?

Jailer.   Having these virtues,
I think he might be brought to play at tennis.   55

Daughter. Alas, that's nothing.

Jailer.   Can he write and read too?

Daughter. A very fair hand, and casts° himself th' accounts
Of all his hay and provender: that ostler

---

40 **stays** waits   45 **fair** fine   48 **jig** (a boisterous dance, often accompanied by song and used after a play)   48 **come cut and long tail to him** i.e., whatever the competition ("cut and long tail," derived from the practice of docking horses' and dogs' tails, means "all kinds," "everybody")   52 **have any skill** know anything about it   53 **Light o' Love** (a well-known song, referred to in *The Two Gentlemen of Verona*, 1.2.83)   57 **casts** makes up

Must rise betime that cozens him. You know
The chestnut mare the duke has?

60 *Jailer.*   Very well.

Daughter. She is horribly in love with him, poor beast,
But he is like his master, coy and scornful.

Jailer. What dowry has she?

Daughter.   Some two hundred bottles,°
And twenty strike° of oats; but he'll ne'er have her.
65 He lisps in's neighing able to entice
A miller's mare:° he'll be the death of her.°

Doctor. What stuff she utters!

Jailer. Make curtsy, here your love comes.

Wooer. [*Comes forward.*]   Pretty soul,
How do ye? That's a fine maid! There's a curtsy!

70 *Daughter.* Yours to command i' th' way of honesty.
How far is't now to th' end o' th' world, my masters?

Doctor. Why, a day's journey, wench.

Daughter. [*To Wooer*]   Will you go with me?

Wooer. What shall we do there, wench?

Daughter.   Why, play at stool-ball.°
What is there else to do?

Wooer.   I am content,
If we shall keep our wedding there.

75 *Daughter.*   'Tis true,
For there, I will assure you, we shall find
Some blind° priest for the purpose, that will venture
To marry us, for here they are nice° and foolish.

---

63 **bottles** bundles   64 **strike** (measure usually equivalent to the
bushel)   66 **miller's mare** (a mare used for turning a mill wheel
would be the least likely to behave wantonly)   66 **he'll be the death
of her** (this passage on a wonderful horse, lines 44–66, looks back to
the famous horse of John Banks, whose tricks and apparent intelligence
are frequently referred to in Elizabethan literature: it performed at least
between 1588 and 1600, and was remembered)   73 **stool-ball** (ball
game played most often by women, and requiring a stool or stools)   77
blind (so that he should not recognize them)   78 **nice** overscrupulous

Besides, my father must be hanged tomorrow,
And that would be a blot i' th' business.   80
Are not you Palamon?

Wooer.   Do not you know me?

Daughter. Yes, but you care not for me. I have nothing
   But this poor petticoat and two coarse smocks.°

Wooer. That's all one, I will have you.

Daughter.   Will you surely?

Wooer. Yes, by this fair hand will I.

                                   [*Takes her hand.*]

Daughter.   We'll to bed, then.   85

Wooer. E'en when you will.   [*Kisses her.*]

Daughter.   O sir, you would fain be nibbling.

Wooer. Why do you rub my kiss off?

Daughter.   'Tis a sweet one,
   And will perfume me finely against the wedding.
   Is not this your cousin Arcite?

Doctor.   Yes, sweetheart,
   And I am glad my cousin Palamon   90
   Has made so fair a choice.

Daughter.   Do you think he'll have me?

Doctor. Yes, without doubt.

Daughter.   Do you think so too?

Jailer.   Yes.

Daughter. We shall have many children. [*To the Doctor*]
   Lord, how y' are grown!°
   My Palamon I hope will grow, too, finely
   Now he's at liberty. Alas, poor chicken,°   95
   He was kept down with hard meat° and ill lodging,
   But I'll kiss him up again.°

83 **smocks** undergarments, shifts   93 **how y' are grown** (she noted
that Arcite was shorter than Palamon at 2.1.49–50)   95 **chicken** child
96 **hard meat** coarse food   97 **kiss him up again** make him grow
with kissing (with a phallic suggestion)

Enter a Messenger.

Messenger. What do you here? You'll lose the noblest sight
    That e'er was seen.

Jailer.   Are they i' th' field?

Messenger.   They are.
    You bear a charge° there, too.

100 *Jailer.*   I'll away straight.
    I must e'en leave you here.

Doctor.   Nay, we'll go with you:
    I will not lose the fight.°

Jailer.   How did you like her?°

Doctor. I'll warrant you within these three or four days
    I'll make her right again. [*To Wooer*] You must not from
      her,
    But still preserve her in this way.

105 *Wooer.*   I will.

Doctor. Let's get her in.

Wooer.   Come, sweet, we'll go to dinner,
    And then we'll play at cards.

Daughter.   And shall we kiss too?

Wooer. A hundred times.

Daughter.   And twenty?

Wooer.   Aye, and twenty.

Daughter. And then we'll sleep together?

Doctor.   Take her offer.

Wooer. Yes, marry will we.

110 *Daughter.*   But you shall not hurt me.

---

100 **bear a charge** have a duty   102 **fight** (the emendation "sight"
has been suggested and may be right: cf. line 98 and 5.3.1)   102
How did you like her what did you think of her condition

Wooer. I will not, sweet.

Daughter.   If you do, love, I'll cry.   *Exeunt.*

Scene 3. [*Near the place of the tournament.*]

*Flourish. Enter Theseus, Hippolyta, Emilia, Pirithous, and
    some Attendants.*

Emilia. I'll no step further.

Pirithous.   Will you lose this sight?

Emilia. I had rather see a wren hawk at a fly
    Than this decision: ev'ry blow that falls
    Threats a brave life, each stroke laments the place
    Whereon it falls, and sounds more like a bell°   5
    Than blade. I will stay here. It is enough
    My hearing shall be punishèd with what
    Shall happen, 'gainst the which there is
    No deafing°—but to hear, not taint mine eye
    With dread sights it may shun.

Pirithous.   Sir, my good lord,   10
    Your sister will no further.

Theseus.   O she must.
    She shall see deeds of honor in their kind,°
    Which sometime show well, penciled.° Nature now
    Shall make and act the story, the belief
    Both sealed with eye and ear.° [*To Emilia*] You must be
        present.   15
    You are the victor's meed,° the price,° and garland
    To crown the question's title.°

Emilia.   Pardon me.
    If I were there, I'd wink.°

5.3.5 **bell** i.e., a bell that tolls for the dead   9 **deafing** i.e., closing
the ear   12 **in their kind** in their true shape   13 **penciled** when
portrayed in art   14–15 **the belief/Both sealed with eye and ear**
i.e., so that we both see and hear the action, while a painting merely
gives us the dumb sight   16 **meed** reward   16 **price** prize   17
crown the question's title bestow the title which is in question   18
wink close my eyes

Theseus.   You must be there:
This trial is as 'twere i' th' night, and you
The only star to shine.

20   *Emilia.*   I am extinct.°
There is but envy° in that light which shows
The one the other: Darkness, which ever was
The dam° of Horror, who does stand accursed
Of many mortal millions, may even now,
25   By casting her black mantle over both,
That° neither could find other, get herself
Some part of a good name,° and many a murder
Set off° whereto she's guilty.

Hippolyta.   You must go.

Emilia. In faith, I will not.

Theseus.   Why, the knights must kindle
30   Their valor at your eye. Know of this war
You are the treasure, and must needs be by
To give the service pay.°

Emilia.   Sir, pardon me,
The title of a kingdom may be tried
Out of itself.°

Theseus.   Well, well, then, at your pleasure.
35   Those that remain with you could wish their office
To any of their enemies.

Hippolyta.   Farewell, sister.
I am like to know your husband 'fore yourself
By some small start of time. He whom the gods
Do of the two know best,° I pray them he
40   Be made your lot.
                    Exeunt Theseus, Hippolyta, Pirithous, &c.

Emilia. Arcite is gently visaged; yet his eye

20 **extinct** no longer shining (continuing the image of the star)   21
envy malice   23 **dam** mother   26 **That** so that   27 **Some part of
a good name** a partly good reputation   28 **Set off** atone for   32
give the service pay reward the service   33–34 **The title . . . itself** a
claim to a kingdom may be settled in a battle fought outside the kingdom   38–39 **He . . . best** the one known by the gods to be best

Is like an engine° bent, or a sharp weapon
In a soft sheath: mercy and manly courage
Are bedfellows in his visage. Palamon
Has a most menacing aspect,° his brow   45
Is graved,° and seems to bury what it frowns on;
Yet sometime 'tis not so, but alters to
The quality of his thoughts:° long time his eye
Will dwell upon his object; melancholy
Becomes him nobly. So does Arcite's mirth,   50
But Palamon's sadness is a kind of mirth,
So mingled° as if mirth did make him sad,
And sadness merry. Those darker humors that
Stick misbecomingly on others, on him
Live in fair dwelling.   55
             Cornets. Trumpets sound as to a charge.
Hark how yon spurs to spirit do incite
The princes to their proof!° Arcite may win me,
And yet may Palamon wound Arcite to
The spoiling of his figure.° O what pity
Enough for such a chance?° If I were by,   60
I might do hurt, for they would glance their eyes
Toward my seat, and in that motion might
Omit a ward,° or forfeit an offense°
Which craved that very time. It is much better
I am not there. O better never born   65
Than minister to such harm!

Cornets. A great cry and noise within, crying "A Pala-
mon!" Enter [a] Servant.

                              What is the chance?

Servant. The cry's "A Palamon!"

Emilia. Then he has won: 'twas ever likely.
He looked all grace° and success, and he is

---

42 **engine** instrument (here suggesting "bow")   45 **aspect** (stressed
on second syllable)   46 **graved** engraved, furrowed (with the play
on "grave," suggesting that he kills)   47–48 **alters to/The quality
of his thoughts** changes according to the character of his thoughts
52 **mingled** complex   57 **proof** test   59 **figure** body   59–60 **O
what . . . chance** i.e., how much pity would be sufficient for such a
happening   63 **ward** pass of defense   63 **forfeit an offense** lose
the opportunity of making an attack   69 **grace** favor

70   Doubtless the prim'st of men. I prithee run
     And tell me how it goes.
                         Shout, and cornets. Crying "A Palamon!"

     Servant.   Still "Palamon!"

     Emilia. Run and inquire. [*Exit Servant.*] Poor servant,°
          thou hast lost!
     Upon my right side still° I wore thy picture,
     Palamon's on the left. Why so I know not,
75   I had no end in't else:° chance would have it so.
     On the sinister° side the heart lies: Palamon
     Had the best boding chance.°
                         Another cry, and shout within, and cornets.
                                   This burst of clamor
     Is sure th' end o' th' combat.

                         Enter Servant.

     Servant. They said that Palamon had Arcite's body
80   Within an inch o' th' pyramid, that the cry
     Was general "A Palamon!" But anon
     Th' assistants° made a brave redemption,° and
     The two bold titlers° at this instant are
     Hand-to-hand at it.

     Emilia.   Were° they metamorphosed
85   Both into one! O why? There were no woman
     Worth so composed a man:° their single share,°
     Their nobleness peculiar to them, gives
     The prejudice of disparity, value's shortness,°
     To any lady breathing.
                         Cornets. Cry within: "Arcite! Arcite!"
                                   More exulting?
     "Palamon" still?

90   *Servant.*   Nay, now the sound is "Arcite!"

---

72 **Poor servant** i.e., Arcite   73 **still** always   75 **no end in't else**
no purpose at all in it   76 **sinister** left   77 **the best boding chance**
i.e., the most favorable omen   82 **assistants** i.e., Arcite's knights
82 **redemption** rescue   83 **titlers** claimants to the title   84 **Were**
O that they were   86 **so composed a man** a man so compounded
86 **their single share** the share of virtue that each has singly   88
The prejudice . . . shortness i.e., the disadvantage of inequality, the
state of inferiority

Emilia. I prithee lay attention to the cry.
  Set both thine ears to th' business.

Cornets. A great shout and cry: "Arcite! Victory!"

Servant.   The cry is
  "Arcite!" and "Victory!" Hark! "Arcite! Victory!"
  The combat's consummation is proclaimed
  By the wind instruments.

Emilia.   Half-sights° saw   95
  That Arcite was no babe. God's lid,° his richness
  And costliness° of spirit looked through him:° it could
  No more be hid in him than fire in flax,
  Than humble banks can go to law° with waters
  That drift° winds force to raging. I did think   100
  Good Palamon would miscarry, yet I knew not
  Why I did think so: our reasons are not prophets
  When oft our fancies are. They are coming off.°
  Alas, poor Palamon!

*Cornets. Enter Theseus, Hippolyta, Pirithous, Arcite as
    victor, and Attendants, &c.*

Theseus. Lo, where our sister is in expectation,   105
  Yet quaking and unsettled!° Fairest Emily,
  The gods by their divine arbitrament
  Have given you this knight: he is a good one
  As ever struck at head. Give me your hands.
  Receive you her, you him; be plighted with   110
  A love that grows as you decay.

Arcite.   Emily,
  To buy you I have lost what's dearest to me
  Save what is bought, and yet I purchase cheaply
  As I do rate your value.

Theseus.   O loved sister,
  He speaks now of as brave a knight as e'er   115
  Did spur a noble steed. Surely the gods
  Would have him die a bachelor, lest his race

---

95 **Half-sights** glimpses   96 **lid** eyelid   97 **costliness** rareness
97 **looked through him** was apparent in him   99 **go to law** engage
in conflict   100 **drift** driving   103 **coming off** leaving the place of
tournament   106 **unsettled** uncertain, still disturbed

Should show i' th' world too godlike! His behavior
So charmed me that methought Alcides° was
120   To him a sow° of lead. If I could praise
Each part of him to th' all I have spoke,° your Arcite
Did° not lose by't, for he that was thus good
Encount'red yet his better. I have heard
Two emulous Philomels° beat the ear o' th' night
125   With their contentious throats, now one the higher,
Anon the other, then again the first,
And by and by outbreasted,° that the sense°
Could not be judge between 'em: so it fared
Good space between these kinsmen, till heavens did
130   Make hardly° one the winner. Wear the garland
With joy that you have won. For the subdued,
Give them our present justice,° since I know
Their lives but pinch° 'em. Let it here be done.
The scene's not for our seeing: go we hence
Right joyful, with some sorrow. [*To Arcite*] Arm your
135   prize:°
I know you will not loose her. Hippolyta,
I see one eye of yours conceives a tear
The which it will deliver.   *Flourish.*

Emilia.   Is this winning?
O all you heavenly powers, where is your mercy?
140   But that your wills have said it must be so,
And charge me live to comfort this unfriended,
This miserable prince, that cuts away
A life more worthy from him than all women,
I should, and would, die too.

Hippolyta.   Infinite pity
145   That four such eyes should be so fixed on one
That two must needs be blind for't!°

Theseus.   So it is.   *Exeunt.*

119 **Alcides** Hercules   120 **sow** mass of solidified metal taken from
a furnace   120–21 **If . . . spoke** if I were to praise his every quality
in the same way as I have praised him in general terms   122 **Did**
would   124 **Philomels** nightingales   127 **outbreasted** outsung
127 **that the sense** so that the hearing   130 **hardly** with difficulty
132 **present justice** i.e., immediate execution   133 **pinch** irk   135
Arm your prize i.e., take Emilia to your arms   146 **That two must
needs be blind for't** i.e., that one of the men must die

Scene 4. [*The same.*]

Enter Palamon and his Knights pinioned, Jailer, Executioner, &c., Guard.

Palamon. There's many a man alive that hath outlived
  The love o' th' people, yea i' th' self same state°
  Stands many a father with his child: some comfort
  We have by so considering. We expire,
  And not without men's pity; to live still   5
  Have their good wishes;° we prevent
  The loathsome misery of age, beguile
  The gout and rheum that in lag° hours attend
  For gray approachers.° We come towards the gods
  Young and unwappered,° not halting under crimes   10
  Many and stale:° that sure shall please the gods
  Sooner than such,° to give° us necctar with 'em,
  For we are more clear° spirits. My dear kinsmen,
  Whose lives for this poor comfort° are laid down,
  You have sold 'em too too cheap.

First Knight.   What ending could be   15
  Of more content? O'er us the victors have
  Fortune, whose title° is as momentary
  As to us death is certain. A grain of honor
  They not o'er-weigh us.

Second Knight.   Let us bid farewell,
  And with our patience anger tott'ring Fortune,   20
  Who at her certain'st° reels.

Third Knight.   Come, who begins?

5.4.2 **state** condition 5–6 **to live still/Have their good wishes** have their good wishes that we should still live 8 **lag** last 9 **gray approachers** gray-haired men approaching death 10 **unwappered** unwearied (perhaps with a suggestion of sexual excess) 11 **stale** of long standing 12 **such** i.e., men such as described 12 **to give** so that they will give 13 **clear** noble, unstained 14 **this poor comfort** (Palamon admits the puniness of his own consolation) 17 **title** i.e., favor 21 **at her certain'st** when she seems most stable

Palamon. E'en he that led you to this banquet shall
    Taste to you all.° [*To Jailer*] Ah, ha, my friend, my
    friend,
    Your gentle daughter gave me freedom once:
25   You'll see't done now forever.° Pray, how does she?
    I heard she was not well. Her kind of ill°
    Gave me some sorrow.

Jailer.   Sir, she's well restored,
    And to be married shortly.

Palamon.   By my short life,
    I am most glad on't: 'tis the latest thing
30   I shall be glad of, prithee tell her so.
    Commend me to her, and to piece° her portion
    Tender her this.   [*Gives him a purse.*]

First Knight.   Nay, let's be offerers all.

Second Knight. Is it a maid?

Palamon.   Verily I think so,
    A right good creature, more to me° deserving
    Than I can 'quite° or speak of.

35 *All Knights.*   Commend us to her.
                        They give their purses.

Jailer. The gods requite you all, and make her thankful.

Palamon. Adieu; and let my life be now as short
    As my leave-taking.   *Lies on the block.*

First Knight.   Lead, courageous cousin.

Second and Third Knights. We'll follow cheerfully.

A great noise within, crying "Run! Save! Hold!" Enter in
    haste a Messenger.

Messenger.   Hold, hold, O hold, hold, hold!

---

23 **Taste to you all** act as taster at a banquet for you   25 **You'll
see't done now forever** i.e., you will see me win a final freedom   26
kind of ill i.e., madness   31 **piece** contribute to   34 **to me** i.e.,
from me   35 **'quite** requite

Enter Pirithous in haste.

Pirithous. Hold, ho! It is a cursèd haste you made   40
    If you have done° so quickly. Noble Palamon,
    The gods will show their glory in a life°
    That thou art yet to lead.

Palamon.   Can that be,
    When Venus I have said° is false? How do things fare?°

Pirithous. Arise, great sir, and give the tidings ear   45
    That are most dearly° sweet and bitter.

Palamon.   What
    Hath waked us from our dream?°

Pirithous.   List then. Your cousin,
    Mounted upon a steed that Emily
    Did first bestow on him, a black one, owing°
    Not a hair-worth of white, which some will say   50
    Weakens his price, and many will not buy
    His goodness with this note°—which superstition
    Here finds allowance°—on this horse is Arcite
    Trotting the stones of Athens, which the calkins°
    Did rather tell° than trample, for the horse   55
    Would make his length a mile,° if 't pleased his rider
    To put pride in him. As he thus went counting
    The flinty pavement, dancing as 'twere to th' music
    His own hoofs made—for as they say from iron
    Came music's origin—what envious flint,   60
    Cold as old Saturn, and like him possessed
    With fire malevolent, darted a spark,
    Or what fierce sulphur else to this end made,
    I comment not: the hot horse, hot as fire,
    Took toy° at this, and fell to what disorder   65
    His power could give his will, bounds, comes on end,

41 **done** finished   42 **show their glory in a life** i.e., through your life (as their creature) their glory will be manifested   44 **I have said** i.e., as I have said   44 **How do things fare** what has happened   46 **dearly** intensely   47 **dream** i.e., of death   49 **owing** possessing   52 **with this note** because of this peculiarity   53 **Here finds allowance** is here confirmed   54 **calkins** (parts of a horseshoe turned down to prevent slipping)   55 **tell** count   56 **make his length a mile** take mile-long paces   65 **toy** fright, exception

Forgets school-doing,° being therein trained
And of kind manage;° piglike he whines
At the sharp rowel, which he frets at rather
70   Than any jot obeys; seeks all foul means
Of boist'rous and rough jadery to dis-seat
His lord, that kept it° bravely. When nought served,
When neither curb would crack, girth break, nor
    diff'ring° plunges
Dis-root his rider whence he grew, but that
75   He kept him 'tween his legs, on his hind hoofs
On end he stands,
That Arcite's legs being higher than his head
Seemed with strange art to hang; his victor's wreath
Even then fell off his head; and presently°
80   Backward the jade comes o'er, and his full poise°
Becomes the rider's load. Yet is he living,
But such a vessel 'tis that floats but for
The surge that next approaches. He much desires
To have some speech with you. Lo, he appears.

Enter Theseus, Hippolyta, Emilia, Arcite in a chair.

85   *Palamon.* O miserable end of our alliance!
The gods are mighty! Arcite, if thy heart,
Thy worthy, manly heart be yet unbroken,
Give me thy last words: I am Palamon,
One that yet loves thee dying.

Arcite.   Take Emilia,
90   And with her all the world's joy. Reach° thy hand.
Farewell. I have told° my last hour. I was false,
Yet never treacherous.° Forgive me, cousin.
One kiss from fair Emilia. [*She kisses him.*] 'Tis
done.
Take her. I die.   [*Dies.*]

Palamon.   Thy brave soul seek Elysium!

---

67 **school-doing** training 68 **of kind manage** well disciplined
72 **it** i.e., his seat 73 **diff'ring** varying 79 **presently** at once
80 **poise** weight 90 **Reach** i.e., give me 91 **told** counted, lived
through 91–92 **false./Yet never treacherous** (Arcite admits Palamon's greater right to Emilia in seeing her first, but declares he took
no unfair advantage)

Emilia. I'll close thine eyes, prince. Blessed souls be with
     thee!°   95
  Thou art a right good man, and while I live
  This day° I give to tears.

Palamon.   And I to honor.°

Theseus. In this place first you fought: e'en very here
  I sund'red you. Acknowledge to the gods
  Our thanks that you are living.°   100
  His part is played, and though it were too short
  He did it well. Your day is lengthened, and
  The blissful dew of heaven does arrouse° you.
  The powerful Venus well hath graced her altar,
  And given you your love. Our master Mars   105
  Hath vouched his oracle, and to Arcite gave
  The grace of the contention.° So the deities
  Have showed due justice. Bear this° hence.

Palamon.   O cousin,
  That we should things desire which do cost us
  The loss of our desire!° That nought could buy   110
  Dear love but loss of dear love!°

Theseus.   Never Fortune
  Did play a subtler game. The conquered triumphs,
  The victor has the loss; yet in the passage°
  The gods have been most equal.° Palamon,
  Your kinsman hath confessed the right o' th' lady   115
  Did lie in you, for you first saw her, and
  Even then proclaimed your fancy. He restored her
  As your stol'n jewel, and desired your spirit
  To send him hence forgiven. The gods my justice
  Take from my hand,° and they themselves become   120

---

95 **Blessed souls be with thee** i.e., may you be with the blessed souls
97 **This day** i.e., the anniversaries of this day   97 **to honor** i.e., to
honoring Arcite's memory   99–100 **Acknowledge . . . living** declare to the gods that we rejoice in your being alive (the emendation of
"Our" to "Your" has been suggested)   103 **arrouse** sprinkle   107
grace of the contention i.e., good fortune in the contest   108 **this**
i.e., Arcite's body   109–10 **That we . . . desire** i.e., alas that the
winning of what we want takes away our desire for it   110–11 **That
nought . . . dear love** i.e., that one love (Emilia) could be won only by
losing another (Arcite)   113 **passage** course of events   114 **equal**
just   120 **Take from my hand** i.e., take away from me

The executioners. Lead your lady off,
And call your lovers° from the stage of death,°
Whom I adopt my friends. A day or two
Let us look sadly, and give grace unto
125   The funeral of Arcite, in whose end°
The visages of bridegrooms we'll put on
And smile with Palamon; for whom an hour,
But one hour since, I was as dearly sorry
As glad of Arcite; and am now as glad
130   As for him sorry. O you heavenly charmers,°
What things you make of us! For what we lack,
We laugh;° for what we have, are sorry;° still
Are children in some kind. Let us be thankful
For that which is, and with you leave° dispute
135   That are above our question. Let's go off,
And bear us like the time.°   *Flourish. Exeunt.*

---

122 **lovers** i.e., his Knights   122 **stage of death** scaffold   125 **in whose end** at the conclusion of which   130 **you heavenly charmers** the Fates (who control us with their charms or magic)   131–32 **For what we lack,/We laugh** we feel pleasure at the thought of the thing we do not possess   132 **for what we have, are sorry** we are sad to have what we do possess   134 **leave** cease to   136 **bear us like the time** conduct ourselves appropriately to the occasion

EPILOGUE

I would now ask ye how ye like the play,
But, as it is with schoolboys, cannot say.°
I am cruel° fearful. Pray yet stay a while,
And let me look upon ye. No man smile?
Then it goes hard, I see. He that has   *5*
Loved a young handsome wench, then, show his face—
'Tis strange if none be here—and if he will
Against his conscience, let him hiss, and kill
Our market. 'Tis in vain, I see, to stay° ye.
Have at the worst can come,° then! Now what say ye?   *10*
And yet mistake me not: I am not bold;
We have no such cause. If the tale° we have told—
For 'tis no other—any way content ye,
For to that honest purpose it was meant ye,°
We have our end; and ye shall have ere long   *15*
I dare say many a better, to prolong
Your old loves to us. We, and all our might,
Rest at your service. Gentlemen, good night.

Flourish.

FINIS

Epilogue   2 **say** speak   3 **cruel** dreadfully   9 **stay** i.e., try to prevent   10 **Have at the worst can come** let us face the worst event possible   12 **tale** (alluding to the title of the source)   14 **meant ye** intended for you

Textual Note

There is no doubt that the text used by the printer of the quarto of 1634 had been in the hands of a prompter (presumably of the Blackfriars Theatre). The most obvious evidence of this is the appearance in the margin of three "warnings"—i.e., reminders that preparation must be made for an ensuing entry. These are noted below in the list of places where the present edition varies from the quarto, but it will be useful to bring them together here:

(1) On C3▼ of the quarto, in the left margin opposite 1.3.58–64:

> 2. Hearses rea-/dy with Pala-/mon: and Arci-/te: the 3./ Queenes./ Theseus: and/ his Lordes/ ready.

At this point the scene has more than thirty lines to run: the "warning" is of what will be required at the beginning of 1.4, which comes on C4▼.

(2) On C4▼, in the left margin opposite 1.4.26–27:

> 3. Hearses rea-/dy.

These hearses are for the bodies of the three kings slain at Thebes and will be brought on at the beginning of 1.5 twenty lines later, on the same page of the quarto.

(3) On G2▼, in the left margin opposite 3.5.65–66:

> Chaire and/ stooles out.

These properties are required for Theseus and his company to sit on to watch the Schoolmaster's entertainment: the dialogue indicates that they sit some thirty lines later, at 3.5.98.

Further evidence of theater use of the copy behind the quarto is in the appearance of actors' names in the entries. At 4.2.69 the quarto stage direction reads *"Enter Messengers. Curtis."* (*"Messengers"* being clearly an error for *"Messenger"*), and the entry which opens 5.3 reads *"... and/ some Attendants, T. Tucke: Curtis."* The actors referred to can be identified as Curtis Greville, who was a hired man in the King's Company in 1626, probably having joined them the preceding year, and Thomas Tuckfield, whose name appears in a list of "Musitions and other necessary attendantes" of the King's Company in 1624.* From these dates it is clear that the actors' names were inserted on the occasion of a revival in the 1620's, not for the original performance of 1613.

Actors' names appearing in a text may be due to an author who has a particular member of the company in mind for a part, but this could not be the case with the two names in *The Two Noble Kinsmen.* For one thing, Greville and Tuckfield were not with the company when Shakespeare and Fletcher were writing the play; for another, the messenger of 4.2 and the attendants of 5.3 are characterless parts: an author would have no views on who should play them, but a prompter might wish to remind himself of the actors' identities.

The quarto contains further indications of playhouse use. Act 4 ends with the stage direction *"Florish. Exeunt."*, the *"Florish"* obviously being wrongly placed: it is needed for the entry of Theseus and the rest at the beginning of Act 5. The same thing occurs at the end of 5.2. In these instances we can deduce that "Florish" was added in the margin between 4.3 and 5.1 and between 5.2 and 5.3 respectively, and the printer took it as going with the exits and not with the following entries. Then we have several marginal stage directions printed, like the "warnings" noted above, in roman type—one at the beginning of 2.4:

This short flo-/rish of Cor-/nets and/ Showtes with-/in.

and another opposite the heading *"Actus Tertius.":*

Cornets in/ sundry places./ Noise and/ hallowing as/ people a May-/ing:

The marginal placing, the use of roman type, and the curious phrasing "This short florish" all suggest that here we have prompter's additions to the manuscript. A third instance of this is at 3.5.134–37, where the text in the quarto is as follows:

	Per. Produce.	*Musicke Dance.*
Knocke for	*Intrate filij,* Come forth, and foot it,	
Schoole. Enter	*Ladies, if we have been merry*	
The Dance.	*And have pleased thee with a derry.*	

*Gerald Eades Bentley, *The Jacobean and Caroline Stage,* II (Oxford, 1941), pp. 451–52, 606–07.

The italic stage direction can be taken as authorial. In the original manuscript we can assume there was a space after the one-word speech of Pirithous, and this could explain the omission of a speech heading before the next line, which is clearly the beginning of a speech by the Schoolmaster after the dance. But a prompter would see no clearly marked entry and would want one. Moreover, he might feel it necessary to indicate a signal to be given by the Schoolmaster, and therefore insert "Knocke for Schoole[master]"—i.e., the Schoolmaster should strike the floor of the stage with a staff. But at 3.5.17 the agreed signal was to be his flinging up his cap: the author of the scene would not be likely to forget this so quickly, but a prompter might at first reading. Like the two previously noted stage directions, this one is in roman.

One other stage direction is marginal and in roman. This occurs at 3.6.93:

They bow se-/verall wayes:/ then advance/ and stand.

An asterisk is inserted in 3.6.93 after Arcite has said "And me my love:" and before he continues "Is there ought else to say?" This is, I think, likely to be an authorial addition: it is literary in character, and the placing of the asterisk looks like an author's wish to indicate that the action must come between the two halves of Arcite's speech. But for the printer it would appear in the margin along with the prompter's additional stage directions and warnings, so he has used roman type for this as for those.

Even so, the evidence for the presence of the prompter's hand is fairly plentiful, and he may also have been responsible for all the indications of sound effects (horns, cornets, flourishes), not merely for those noted above. Yet it does not seem very likely that in 1634 the printer had in front of him a prompt-book actually used in performance. Sir Walter Greg drew attention to the possibility that even "warnings" could appear in a manuscript which was merely annotated by a prompter before the promptbook itself was made.* And it is evident that the "warnings" here given are not complete: an executioner's block would be needed for 5.4, and a chair for Arcite at 5.4.86. Also, some of the entries are incomplete: Artesius and Attendants

---

*The Shakespeare First Folio (Oxford, 1955), p. 141.

must be added at 1.1.1 (though we can assume that the printer is responsible for the apparent omission of Pirithous); a Herald, Lords, Attendants, Palamon and Arcite must be added at 1.4.1; at 3.5.1 the entry includes "2. *or* 3 *wenches*", but five are needed for the dance; at 4.1.102 the vague *"and others"*, though possible in a prompt copy, may be an additional sign of authorial inexactitude.

Our text also contains certain things that might well have been eliminated in a prompt copy. At 1.1.217 there is the stage direction *"Exeunt towards the Temple."* This indicates that Hippolyta, Emilia, Pirithous and the Attendants begin to move toward the stage door that here represents the temple entrance, but Theseus has still an exchange with Pirithous (lines 219–24) before the procession has left the stage. This is clear enough to a reader, but a prompter would be likely to tidy it up. Then at 2.1.47 there is the direction *"Enter Palamon and Arcite, above."* The Jailer and his Daughter comment from below and then leave the stage. The quarto marks a general *"Exeunt."* and then gives a new scene heading:

The action is surely continuous, and in the present edition a new scene is not started at this point. The kinsmen need to remain above, as the later part of the scene will be more effective if they look down to the garden to see Emilia, as they do in Chaucer: moreover, the "leap the garden . . . and pitch between her arms" of 2.1.277–78 strongly suggests that Arcite is above. The explanation of the condition of the text here is probably that 2.1.1–59 are by Shakespeare and the rest of the scene by Fletcher: they had worked out in advance that Shakespeare would introduce the new characters (Jailer, Daughter, Wooer) and Fletcher would do the kinsmen's first encounter with Emilia. So the two sections of the scene would be separate: 2.1.60 would start a new sheet of paper. In other words, this suggests that the printer in 1634 had in front of him either the holograph manuscript of Shakespeare and Fletcher or a transcript faithful to it. It should also be noted that the quarto is unusual in its indications of locality: in addition to the *"Temple"* and *"prison"* already noted, we have *"Enter Palamon as out of a Bush"* at 3.1.30 and *"Enter Palamon from the Bush"* at 3.6.1. Such indications of locality are of course rare in seventeenth-century play texts: those in our play are similar to *"Enter Timon in the woods"* and *"Enter Timon from his Caue"* in the Folio text *Timon of Athens*, 4.3.1 and 5.1.30. *Timon* was almost certainly printed either from Shakespeare's own manuscript or from a faithful transcript of it.

Now it must be remembered that we know of performances of *The Two Noble Kinsmen* in 1613, probably in 1619, and around 1625.* The printer's copy in 1634 has some relation to the last of these (from the evidence of the two actors' names), but it is puzzling to think of the prompter on that occasion annotating the authors' original manuscript if a prompt copy for 1613 (and 1619) were available. It could of course have been lost or not immediately available. And we cannot be sure that all the prompter's additions were made at the same time: the "warnings" and additional stage directions could have been inserted in 1613 and the actors' names in 1625. Nevertheless, there is a good case for believing that the quarto is directly based on the author's manuscript (or a faithful transcript of it), which the prompter had annotated before the making of a promptbook. When the play came to be printed, the company would be more likely to give such a manuscript to the publisher rather than the promptbook itself, which would be needed at the theater if the play were to be acted again.[†]

When the play was reprinted in the Beaumont and Fletcher Folio of 1679, the text was based on that of the quarto. This is firmly established not only by the statement in the Folio itself but by the frequent agreement between the texts in accidentals. Although the 1679 printing shows a considerable number of variants, they have no independent authority and are mainly corrections of misprints, new misprints, and casual changes in accidentals. For the present edition, therefore, the Folio readings have been treated in the same way as those of all subsequent texts: that is, they have been regarded as editorial emendations or errors, to be taken into account in emending the quarto text but not recorded where they have not been accepted by the present editor.

*See Introduction.
[†]F. O. Waller in his article "Printer's Copy for *The Two Noble Kinsmen*," *Studies in Bibliography*, XI (1958), 61–84, has argued along these lines. This article incorporates material in Waller's unpublished Chicago dissertation of 1958, *A Critical, Old-spelling Edition of "The Two Noble Kinsmen":* the fullest textual studies so far made of the play are to be found in this thesis and in Paul Bertram's *Shakespeare and The Two Noble Kinsmen* (New Brunswick, 1965). Bertram, however, takes the view that the printer in 1634 had before him a holograph Shakespeare manuscript which had been used as a prompt book.

All substantive departures from the quarto are recorded below, with the reading of the present edition in italic followed by the quarto reading in roman. It will be seen that the prompter's "warnings" have been transposed into stage directions and inserted in square brackets at the appropriate places. The stage directions which have been noted above as almost certainly the prompter's are, however, printed in this edition in the same way as other stage directions (which may of course be either author's or prompter's).

It may be noted that, unlike most of his predecessors, the present editor accepts Skeat's emendation "harebells" at 1.1.9, and that he is the first to take the quarto speech heading *"All"* at 4.1.146 as part of the Jailer's Daughter's speech.

In this edition italic type is used for speech headings and stage directions, as generally in the quarto, and roman type is used for all dialogue and songs (in place of the quarto's italic for proper names in the dialogue and for the songs). Punctuation and spelling have been modernized, obvious typographical errors have been silently corrected, and the quarto's Latin headings for acts and scenes are given in English. The quarto's "nev'r," "ev'r," "ev'n" spellings are here rendered as "ne'er," "e'er," "e'en," whenever the meter seems to require a monosyllable; elsewhere the full spellings of these words are used. When a quarto reading exists in two states, corrected and uncorrected, the list below indicates the uncorrected state by a raised "a" after the reading given, the corrected state by a raised "b."

In a number of places the quarto prints lines as prose which there seems to be good reason to take as blank verse. Decisions in such cases are always difficult, but the present edition follows several of its predecessors in printing as verse where a blank verse rhythm seems to underlie, and sometimes clearly to emerge from, the fairly free dialogue pattern.

In conformity with the practice of this series, localities have been inserted in scene headings, but these and all other editorial additions to the quarto are given in square brackets.

Prologue 19 *writer* wrighter 25 *water, do* water. Do 26 *tack* take 29 *travail* travell

1.1. s.d. *Pirithous* Theseus 9 *harebells* her bels 16 *angel* angle 20 *chough hoar* Clough hee 59 *lord. The day* Lord the day 61 *groom.* Groome, 68 *Nemean* Nenuan 83 *'stilled* stilde (Folio "stil'd") 90 *thy* the 99 *blood-sized* blood cizd 112 *glassy* glasse 125 *sister* sifter 138 *move* mooves 155 *Rinsing* Wrinching 210 *soldier, as before.* Soldier (as before) 211 *Aulis* Anly 217 s.d. *Hippolyta . . . towards* Exeunt towards

1.2.65 *power there's nothing; almost puts* power: there's nothing, almost puts   70 *glory; one* glory on;[b] glory on[a]

1.3.22 *brine* brine,   31 *one* ore   54 *eleven* a eleven   54 *Flavina* Flauia   58–64 (note in quarto margin: "2. Hearses rea-/dy with Palamon: and Arci-/te: the 3./ Queenes./ Theseus: and/ his Lordes/ ready.")   79 *every innocent* fury-innocent 82 *dividual* individuall

1.4.18 *smeared* smeard[b] succard[a]   22 *We 'lieve* We leave   26–27 (note in quarto margin: "3. Hearses rea-/dy.")   40 *friends' behests* friends, beheastes   41 *Love's provocations* Loves, provocations   45 *O'er-wrestling* Or wrastling   49 *'fore* for

2.1.1 *little . . . live:* little, . . . live,   17 *that now. So* that. Now, so   47s.d. (in quarto, after "night" in line 46) 53 (in quarto, new scene heading: "Scæna 2. Enter Palamon, and Arcite in prison.")   57 *war. Yet* warre yet,   75 *wore* were   76 *Ravished* Bravishd   121 *could.* could,   172 (quarto makes this the last line of Arcite's speech)   204 *mere* neere   211 *have.* have,   256 *be,* be.   257 *Arcite:* Arcite,   272s.d. (and throughout rest of scene) *Jailer* Keeper   316 *life?* life.

2.2 (quarto marks as "Scæna 3.")   39 *ye* yet   51 *means.* meanes   51 *says* sees   73 *him!* him

2.3 (quarto marks as "Scæna 4.")

2.4s.d. *Short . . . within.* This short . . . within (in margin) 19 *I believe* Beleeve,

2.5 (quarto marks as "Scæna 6.")

3.1s.d. *Cornets . . . a-Maying* (in quarto, in margin)   2 *laund* land   2 *rite* Right   10 *place* pace   36 *looked, the void'st* lookd the voydes   94 *only, sir. Your* onely, Sir your   95s.d. *Wind horns off* Winde hornes of Cornets   97 *musit* Musicke   107 *not.* nor;

3.2.1 *brake* Beake   7 *reck* wreake   19 *fed* feed   28 *brine* bine

3.3.23 *them* then   50 *armor?* Armour.

3.4.9 *Spoon* Vpon   10 *tack* take

3.5 (quarto marks as "Scæna 6.") s.d. *Bavian* Baum five [italic]   2. or 3.   8 *jean* jave   47 *once! You can tell, Arcas,* once, you can tell Arcas   65–67 (note in quarto margin: "Chaire and/stooles out.")   67 *till we* till   91s.d. *Wind horns* (in quarto after "I'll lead")   93s.d. *Exeunt . . . Schoolmaster* (in quarto, after "boys," line 92)   97 *Theseus* Per. 135s.d. *Knock* Knocke for Schoole (in margin)   135 (quarto omits speech heading)   137 *ye* thee   140 *thee* three   155s.d. *Wind horns* (in quarto, after "made," line 156)

3.6 (quarto marks as "Scæna 7.")   28 *man. When* man, when   39 *spared. Your* spard, your   68 *I warrant* Ile warrant   86 *strait* streight   111 *safety,*

safely   146 *thy* this   175 *us;* us,   176 *valiant,* valiant;   243 *prune* proyne
290 *again, it* againe it

4.1.45–46 *Wooer. No, sir . . .'Tis*—Wooer, [italic] No Sir not well. / Woo.
[speech heading] Tis   48 *have told* told   84 *wreath* wreake   110 *rearly*
rarely   120 *Far* For   141 *Second Friend* 1. Fr.   145 *cheerly all! O, O, O*
cheerely./ All. [speech heading] Owgh, owgh, owgh   149 *Tack* take

4.2.16 *Jove* Love   37 *pardon, Palamon:* pardon: Palamon,   54s.d. *Enter
a Gentleman* Enter Emil. and Gent.   69s.d. *Enter a Messenger* Enter
Messengers. Curtis   76 *first* fitst   81 *fire* faire   86–87 *baldric, . . . with:*
Bauldricke; . . . with,   104 *tods* tops   109 *court* corect

4.3.8s.d. (in quarto, after "business," line 8)   29 *i' th' other* i'th/Thother
83 *carve* crave

5.1.s.d. *Flourish* (in quarto, precedes "*Exeunt.*" of 4.3)   7s.d. *Flourish of
cornets* (in quarto, at line 5)   50 *whose approach* (first added by Seward in
1750: the words, or something like them, seem necessary)   54 *armipotent*
armenypotent   68 *design march boldly.* designe; march boldly,   91 *his;*
his 118–21 *Brief, I . . . done no companion;/ To . . . not a defier;/ To . . . rejoicer.* briefe I . . . done; no Companion/ To . . . not; a defyer/ To . . . cannot; a Rejoycer,   130 (quarto inserts speech heading "Pal.")   136s.d. *They
bow* (in quarto, after line 134)   151 *'pointed* pointed   152 *him; out of two*
him out of two,   154 *election. Of mine eyes* election of mine eyes,

5.2.34 *Videlicet, the way of flesh* (quarto has "Videlicet" in roman and "way
of flesh" in italic, doubtless through a casual error)   39 *humor* honour   53
tune turne

5.3.s.d. *Flourish* (in quarto, precedes "*Exeunt*" of 5.2) *Attendants* (quarto
adds: "T. Tucke: Curtis.")   13 *well, penciled* well pencild   54 *him* them
66s.d. *Cornets . . . "A Palamon!"* (in quarto, at line 64) *Enter a Servant*
(may be erroneous, as there were attendants on stage, and the servant brings
no news)   75 *in't else:* in't; else   77 s.d. (in quarto, at line 75)   92s.d. (in
quarto, at line 91)   121 *to th' all I* to'th all; I

5.4.1 (quarto omits speech heading)   5–6 *pity; to live still . . . wishes;*
pitty. To live still, . . . wishes,   39 *Second and Third Knights* 1. 2. K 46
dearly early   76 *On end he stands* (in quarto, printed at the end of the line,
perhaps indicating that it was preceded by some illegible words in the manuscript   78 *victor's* victoros   86–87 *mighty! . . . unbroken,* mightie . . .
unbroken: 106 *Hath* Hast   132 *sorry; still* sorry still,

A Note on the Source of
The Two Noble Kinsmen

The play's source, we have seen, is *The Knight's Tale*, which was most easily available to the collaborators in Speght's edition of Chaucer published in 1598 (reprinted three times by 1602). In the dramatization a considerable number of changes were made. We may notice them under several heads:

(1) The action throughout is compressed. In Chaucer there is a time lapse between the first seeing of Emilia by the kinsmen and the release of Arcite. Then Arcite spends some years in Thebes before returning to Athens to see Emilia again. Meanwhile Palamon has seven years in prison. When Theseus has arranged the tournament, the kinsmen are to return to Athens in a year's time. Arcite takes some time to die after the horse has thrown him, and it is a matter of years before Emilia brings herself to marry Palamon. In the play we are not told how long Palamon and Arcite are in prison, but there is no suggestion that it is a great while. Clearly Palamon escapes soon after Arcite has entered Emilia's service. The time lapse before the tournament is a single month. Arcite dies almost immediately, and Emilia is to marry Palamon, it appears, the next day.

These changes are partly to give an effect of tighter structure to what is in Chaucer a diffuse narrative, but they also increase the sense of divine manipulation. The kinsmen in 2.1 look forward to a slow lifetime in prison: instead, they are whirled through a series of events, and at the end of the play Emilia is passed from arm to arm in a manner that suggests no cosmic concern for her dignity.

(2) There are also changes for the sake of obvious dramatic effectiveness. In the poem Theseus' wedding is not interrupted by the mission of the Queens. There are not three Queens but a crowd of queens and duchesses. Emilia has no attendant in the garden with whom she can talk informally and lightly. Palamon

is not removed from the garden-room after Arcite's departure. At the tournament each of the kinsmen is to be accompanied by a hundred knights. The invocations to the gods are in the order Venus, Diana, Mars, which has not the climactic effect secured in the play by Emilia's prayer coming last. The falling of the single rose from the tree brings the whole scene to a striking (and disturbing) conclusion.

(3) Other changes increase this sense of disturbance. Most obvious among these is the decree of Theseus that the knights defeated in the tournament shall die. Of course, this allows the theatrically effective saving of Palamon from the block, and it puts more at stake than the disposal of Emilia's person. Shakespeare may have thought of this change because in *Pericles* the unsuccessful suitors of Antiochus' daughter were similarly vowed to death. In any event, it is an element in the play that links it with the dangers and actual deaths that are found in the preceding "romances." Moreover, there is nothing in the invocation of Venus in *The Knight's Tale* that resembles the words on the goddess' power that Palamon speaks. He hails her as

> sovereign queen of secrets, . . .
>   that canst make
> A cripple flourish with his crutch, and cure him
> Before Apollo; that may'st force the king
> To be his subject's vassal, and induce
> Stale Gravity to dance: the pollèd bachelor
> Whose youth like wanton boys through bonfires
> Have skipped thy flame, at seventy thou canst catch
> And make him, to the scorn of his hoarse throat,
> Abuse young lays of love.
>
>   (5.1.77, 81–89)

The images of the cripple grotesquely cured, of authority submissive and dancing, of old age straining its throat with a love song, contribute powerfully to that harsh strain in Shakespeare's section of the play that has been noted in the Introduction. And then we find Palamon seeking favor by boasting of his own credulity, and doing it in terms that, for an audience, are surely meant to be repellent:

>   I knew a man
> Of eighty winters, this I told them, who
> A lass of fourteen brided. 'Twas thy power

> To put life into dust: the aged cramp
> Had screwed his square foot round,
> The gout had knit his fingers into knots,
> Torturing convulsions from his globy eyes
> Had almost drawn their spheres, that what was life
> In him seemed torture. This anatomy
> Had by his young fair fere a boy, and I
> Believed it was his, for she swore it was,
> And who would not believe her?

(107–18)

We may think back to Antony's concern with his gray hairs, to Leontes' finding wrinkles in what he thinks is Hermione's statue, but the degree of frankness is new. Palamon, the servant of Venus, puts himself side by side with the other victims he describes.*

(4) Nothing in Chaucer corresponds to the Jailer's Daughter plot. We are simply told that Palamon escaped with the help of a friend. In the Introduction (pp. 438–40) we have seen how Shakespeare and Fletcher use the subplot to affect the audience's response to the story of the knights and their love.

(5) In Chaucer the gods are at odds with each other, and the quarrel is settled by the ingenuity of Saturn, so that all promises can be kept. In the play we are rather made to feel that a single power speaks through the gods, that the matter is predetermined, that all that the gods do is to give hints of a future which neither prayer nor divine intervention can modify.

In a few places the play includes some quite incidental echoes of Chaucer. Thus Arcas, one of the Countrymen named at 2.2.37 and 3.5.47, is the name of the son of Callisto, who, as "Calystope," is referred to in *The Knight's Tale,* line 1198. The Schoolmaster mentions the story of Meleager and Atalanta at 3.5.18: Chaucer mentions it at *The Knight's Tale,* lines 1212–13. In the play the tournament is held in the place where Theseus found the knights fighting (3.6.293): in *The Knight's Tale,* lines 1999–2006, we learn that it is Arcite's funeral pyre that is to be erected in that place. The consolation that Palamon offers to his friends as they are about to submit themselves to the

---

*In his introduction to the Signet edition of Shakespeare's *Sonnets* (1964), W. H. Auden has commented on this passage's choice of "humiliating or horrid" examples of the power of Venus and on "the intensity of the disgust at masculine sexual vanity."

block (5.4.1–13), although altogether sharper in its comments on the nature of life, bears an obvious relation to the arguments that Theseus uses in *The Knight's Tale,* lines 2189–98, in order to persuade Palamon and Emilia to give up their mourning for Arcite and enter into marriage. Such points of casual resemblance between play and poem, with the dramatists freely manipulating the words and images they found in Chaucer, show the intimacy of their acquaintance with the source.

The Knight's Tale had been twice dramatized before 1613. In 1566 Richard Edwardes' *Palamon and Arcite* was acted at Christ Church, Oxford, before Elizabeth, and Henslowe's *Diary* registers a *Palamon and Arcite* acted in 1594, probably as a new play. Neither of these is extant, but there is no reason to believe that they had any connection with *The Two Noble Kinsmen.*

In the Introduction we have seen that Shakespeare and Fletcher were dependent also on their memories of several earlier Shakespeare plays, ranging from *The Two Gentlemen of Verona* to the late "romances," and that this has helped to make the play into something very different from a straightforward dramatization of Chaucer.

Commentaries

GERALD EADES BENTLEY

Shakespeare and the Blackfriars Theatre

It is necessary at the outset in a discussion of this sort to place Shakespeare in what seems to me his proper context—a context which none but the Baconians and Oxfordians deny, but which most scholars and critics tend to ignore. That context is the London commercial theatre and the organized professional acting troupe.

Shakespeare was more completely and continuously involved with theatres and acting companies than any other Elizabethan dramatist whose life we know. Most Elizabethan dramatists had only their writing connection with the theatres, but Shakespeare belonged to the small group which both wrote and acted. In this small group of actor-dramatists, the best-known names are those of Heywood, Rowley, Field and Shakespeare. Of this thoroughly professionalized band, Shakespeare is the one most closely bound to his company and his theatre, for he is the only one of the four who did not shift about from company to company but maintained his close association with a single acting troupe for more than twenty years. Besides this, he was bound to theatres and actors in still another fashion which makes him unique among all Elizabethan dramatists: he

From *Shakespeare Survey* I (1948): 38–50. Reprinted by permission of the author and the editor.

is the only dramatist we know who owned stock in theatre buildings over an extended period. His income was derived from acting, from writing plays, from shares in dramatic enterprises, and from theatre rents. From the beginning to the end of his writing career we must see him in a theatrical context if we are not to do violence to the recorded facts. At the beginning is our first reference to him in Greene's allusion to the "Tygers hart wrapt in a Players hyde"; at the end are his own last words, so far as we know them, in his will. This will is mostly concerned with Stratford affairs, but when he does turn to the years of his London life and his many London associates, he singles out only three for a last remembrance. These men are John Heminges, Henry Condell, and Richard Burbage—all three actors, all three fellow-sharers in the acting company of the King's men, all three fellow-stock-holders in the Globe and the Blackfriars. If Shakespeare's proper context is not the London commercial theatres and the professional troupes, then evidence has no meaning, and one man's irresponsible fancies are as good as another's.

Now in spite of all the evidence that Shakespeare's dominant preoccupation throughout his creative life was the theatre, most scholars and critics of the last 150 years have written of him as the professional poet and not as the professional playwright. For the most part he has been studied as Spenser and Milton and Keats are studied. For a century and a half the great majority of studies of Shakespeare's genius and development have been concerned with literary influences and biographical influences and not with theatrical influences.* We have studied his sources and his text, his indebtedness to Ovid and Holinshed and Montaigne and Plutarch. Even in biographical studies the preference has always been for the nontheatrical aspects of Shakespeare's life—his boyhood in the woods and fields about Stratford, his marriage and his wife, the death of his son Hamnet, his relations with Southampton and Essex, his supposed

---

The Cambridge Bibliography of English Literature will serve as an example. The bibliography of Shakespeare fills 136 columns, of which one half-column is devoted to "The Influence of Theatrical Conditions." This is not to say, of course, that there have been no proper studies of the theatres and acting companies of Shakespeare's time. There are many. But there are comparatively few books and articles devoted to the examination of Shakespeare's work in the light of this knowledge or to a consideration of the specific influence such matters had on his methods and development.

breakdown, his retirement to Stratford. Now any or all of these facts, or alleged facts, no doubt had an influence on the great creations of Shakespeare. I do not suggest that our study of them should be discontinued. But given the verified documentary evidence which we have, is it not dubious practice to devote a large part of our investigations to the more or less problematical influences in Shakespeare's career and to devote a very small part of our efforts to that enormously significant influence which dominated the majority of his waking hours for the twenty-odd years of his creative maturity? A dozen or more unquestioned documents show that Shakespeare's daily concern was the enterprise of the Lord Chamberlain-King's company. Shakespeare had obviously read Ovid and Holinshed and Lord North's *Plutarch;* surely he must have mourned for the untimely death of his only son; but none of these can have occupied his mind for so long as his daily association with the enterprise of the Lord Chamberlain-King's men. Of the factors in his life and development which we can now identify, this was surely the most important.

Now what are the events in his long and absorbing association with this troupe which we can expect to have influenced his work? One of the first must have been the protracted plague closings of 1593 and 1594, for out of this disaster to all London players the Lord Chamberlain's company apparently rose.* Another must have been the assembling of the players and the drawing up of the agreement for the formal organization of the Lord Chamberlain's company. The record suggests that Shakespeare was one of the leaders in this organization, for when the new company performed before the court in the Christmas season of 1594–95, payment was made to Richard Burbage, the principal actor, Will Kemp, the principal comedian, and William Shakespeare.† How did the great possibilities offered by this new troupe, destined to become the most famous and most successful in the history of the English theatre, affect the writing of its chief dramatist?

In the winter of 1598–99 occurred another event which must have been of absorbing interest for all members of the company. This was of course the building of the Globe on the Bankside.

---

*E. K. Chambers, *The Elizabethan Stage,* pp. 2, 192–93 and 4, 348–49; *William Shakespeare,* pp. 1, 27–56.

†*The Elizabethan Stage,* pp. 4, 164.

Here was a theatre built for the occupancy of a particular company, and six of the seven owners were actors in the company. Assuredly it was built, so far as available funds would allow, to the specific requirements of the productions of the Lord Chamberlain's men. What facilities did Shakespeare get which he had not had before? How did he alter his composition to take advantage of the new possibilities? Can there be any doubt that as a successful man of the theatre he did so? Yet I know of no study which attempts to assess this vital new factor in relation to Shakespeare's development.

The next event which must have been of great importance for Shakespeare's company was its involvement in the Essex rebellion. This exceptional case has received the full attention of critics and scholars because of its supposed relation to a performance of Shakespeare's *Richard II*. Actually, however, the Essex rebellion, much though it must have excited the company for a few months, was the least influential of all these factors affecting the company's activities and Shakespeare's development. Apparently the company's innocence was established without much difficulty.* There is no indication that their later performances or Shakespeare's later writing were affected by the experience. Though the events were sensational, and though they must have caused great anxiety for a time, they cannot be thought of as events of long-term significance in the history of this group of men who were so important and influential in Shakespeare's career and development.

Of much more importance in the affairs of the company was their attainment of the patronage of James I less than two months after the death of Elizabeth.† This patronage and the King's livery certainly became one of the important factors in creating the great prestige of the company. In the ten years before they became the King's company, their known performances at court average about three a year; in the ten years after they attained their new service their known performances at court average about thirteen a year, more than those of all other London companies combined.‡ They were officially the premier company in London; a good part of their time must have been devoted to the preparation of command performances. Surely

---

William Shakespeare, 1, pp. 353–55; *The Elizabethan Stage*, pp. 2, 204–07.
†*The Elizabethan Stage*, 2, pp. 208–09.
‡*Ibid.*, 4, pp. 108–30.

this new status of the troupe must have been a steady and pervasive influence in the development of its principal dramatist, William Shakespeare.

The final event which I wish to mention in the affairs of the King's company was perhaps the most important of all. There is no doubt that it made a great change in the activities of the company, and I do not see how it can have failed to be a principal influence in Shakespeare's development as a dramatist. This event was the acquisition of the famous private theatre in Blackfriars. No adult company in London had ever before performed regularly in a private theatre. For thirty years the private theatres with their superior audiences, their concerts, their comfortable accommodations, their traffic in sophisticated drama and the latest literary fads, had been the exclusive homes of the boy companies, the pets of Society. Now for the first time a troupe of those rogues and vagabonds, the common players, had the temerity to present themselves to the sophisticates of London in a repertory at the town's most exclusive theatre. I suspect that this was one of the turning points in Tudor and Stuart dramatic history. Beaumont and Jonson and Fletcher had begun to make the craft of the playwright more socially respectable. The increasing patronage of the drama by the royal family, and the growing splendor and frequency of the court masques which were written by ordinary playwrights and performed in part by common players, were raising the prestige of the drama and the theatre from its Elizabethan to its Caroline state. The acquisition of the Blackfriars in 1608 by the King's company and the full exploitation of the new playhouse must have been the most conspicuous evidence to Londoners of the changing state of affairs. Surely it is impossible that the King's men and their principal dramatist, William Shakespeare, could have been unaware of this situation. Surely they must have bent all their efforts in the selection and performance of old plays and in the commissioning and writing of new ones to the full exploitation of this unprecedented opportunity. The new state of affairs must have been apparent in much that they did, and it must have influenced decidedly the dramatic compositions of Shakespeare.

So far, it has been my contention that all we know of William Shakespeare has shown him to be above all else a man of the theatre, that during the twenty years of his creative maturity most of his time was spent in closest association with members of the Lord Chamberlain-King's company and in thought about their needs and their interests, and that therefore in the affairs of this company we should seek one of the principal influences in his creative life. I have mentioned six events which (so far as we can tell through the mists of 350 years) seem to have been important in the affairs of that theatrical organization. These events are not all of equal importance, but each of them, except possibly the Essex rebellion, must have had a marked effect on the activities of Shakespeare's company and therefore on the dramatic creations of Shakespeare himself. Each one, it seems to me, deserves more study than it has received in its relation to the development of Shakespeare's work.

Let me invite your attention now to a fuller consideration of one of the most important of these events in the history of the Lord Chamberlain-King's company, namely the acquisition of the Blackfriars Theatre. What did this event mean in the history of the company, and how did it affect the writing of William Shakespeare?

Probably we should note first the time at which the Blackfriars would have begun to influence the company and the writing of Shakespeare. All the dramatic histories say that the King's men took over the Blackfriars Theatre in 1608, and this is true in a legal sense, for on 9 August 1608 leases were executed conveying the Blackfriars Playhouse to seven lessees: Cuthbert Burbage, Thomas Evans, and five members of the King's company—John Heminges, William Sly, Henry Condell, Richard Burbage, and William Shakespeare.* The few scholars who have examined in detail the history of the King's company have noted, however, that Shakespeare and his fellows probably did not begin to act at the Blackfriars in August of 1608. The plague was rife in London at that time; fifty plague deaths had been recorded for the week ending 28 July, and for a year and a half, or until December 1609, the bills of mortality show an abnormally high rate from the plague.† Though specific records about the closing of the theatres are not extant, we have definite statements that they were closed for part of this period, and comparison with other years suggests that there must have been

---

*The Elizabethan Stage, pp. 2, 509–10. Technically Richard Burbage leased one-seventh of the theatre to each of the other six.
†Ibid., 4, 351.

very little if any public acting allowed in London between the first of August 1608 and the middle of December 1609. Therefore, it has occasionally been said, the Blackfriars was not used by the King's men much before 1610, and no influence on their plays and their productions can be sought before that year.

This conclusion of little or no influence before 1610 is, I think, a false one. It is based on the erroneous assumption that the actors and playwrights of the King's company would have known nothing about the peculiarities of the Blackfriars and that they would have had no plays prepared especially for that theatre until after they had begun performing in it. Actors are never so stupid or so insular as this in any time. The King's men, we may be sure, were well aware of the Blackfriars and the type of performance it required, or specialized in, long before they came to lease the theatre. There must be many evidences of this, but three in particular come readily to mind.

Seven years before, in 1601, the King's men had been involved in the War of the Theatres, which was in part a row between the public theatres and the private theatres. The chief attack on the public theatres and adult actors was made in Jonson's *Poetaster,* performed at the Blackfriars. Certain actors of the Lord Chamberlain's company, and possibly Shakespeare himself, were ridiculed in this Blackfriars play. The reply, *Satiromastix,* was written by Thomas Dekker and performed by Shakespeare's company at the Globe.* Certainly in 1601 at least, the company was well aware of the goings on at Blackfriars.

A second piece of evidence pointing to their knowledge of the peculiar requirements of the Blackfriars is the case of Marston's *Malcontent.* Marston wrote this play for the boys at the Blackfriars, who performed it in that theatre in 1604. The King's men stole the play, as they admitted, and performed it at the Globe; the third edition, also 1604, shows the alterations they commissioned John Webster to make in order to adapt a Blackfriars script to a Globe performance, and in the induction to the play Richard Burbage, speaking in his own person, points out one or two of the differences between Blackfriars requirements and Globe requirements.†

---

*See J. H. Penniman, *The War of the Theatres,* and R. A. Small, *The Stage Quarrel.*
†F. L. Lucas, *The Works of John Webster,* pp. 3, 294–309.

Finally, and most familiar of all evidence that the King's men were quite alive to what went on at Blackfriars, is the "little eyases" passage in *Hamlet* and Shakespeare's rueful admission that, for a time at any rate, the competition of the Blackfriars was too much for the company at the Globe.

Clearly the King's men did not have to wait until their performances of 1610 at the Blackfriars to know how their plays needed to be changed to fit them to that theatre and its select audience. They had known for several years what the general characteristics of Blackfriars performances were. Indeed, the leading member of the company, Richard Burbage, had a double reason for being familiar with all the peculiarities of the Blackfriars, for since his father's death in 1597 he had been the owner of the theatre and the landlord of the boy company that made it famous.* We can be perfectly sure, then, that from the day of the first proposal that the King's men take over the Blackfriars they had talked among themselves about what they would do with it and had discussed what kinds of plays they would have to have written to exploit it. It is all too often forgotten that in all such discussions among the members of the King's company William Shakespeare would have had an important part. He had more kinds of connections with the company than any other man: he was actor, shareholder, patented member, principal playwright, and one of the house-keepers of the Globe; even Burbage did not serve so many functions in the company. Few men in theatrical history have been so completely and inextricably bound up with the affairs of an acting troupe.

When would the King's men have begun planning for their performances at the Blackfriars? We cannot, of course, set the exact date, but we can approximate it. There is one faint suggestion that consideration of the project may have started very early indeed. Richard Burbage said that Henry Evans, who had leased the theatre from him for the Children of the Queen's Revels, began talking to him about the surrender of his lease in 1603 or 1604.† These early discussions evidently came to nothing, for we know that the boys continued in the theatre for three or four years longer. Burbage's statement about Evans does sug-

---

*J. Q. Adams, *Shakespearean Playhouses*, pp. 199–223.
†"The Answers of Heminges and Burbage to Edward Kirkham," 1612, printed by F. G. Fleay, *A Chronicle History of the London Stage*, p. 235.

gest the interesting possibility that the King's men may have dallied with the project of leasing the Blackfriars Theatre as early as 1603 or 1604. This, however, is only the faintest of possibilities. The Blackfriars was tentatively in the market then, but all we know is that Burbage had to consider for a short time the possibility of getting other tenants for his theatre. Whether the King's men came to his mind and theirs as possible tenants, we do not know.

We can be sure that active planning for performances at the Blackfriars did get under way when Burbage, who was both the leading actor of the King's men and owner of the Blackfriars Theatre, knew for certain that the boy actors would give up their lease and that arrangements for a syndicate of King's men to take over the theatre could be made. Conferences among these men—the Burbages, Heminges, Condell, Shakespeare, and Sly—and probably preliminary financial arrangements would have been going on before a scrivener was called in to draw up a rough draft of the lease. Such preliminaries, which must come before a lease can be formally signed, often consume months. We know that the leases were formally executed on 9 August 1608;* therefore discussions in June and July or even in April and May are likely enough. We know that the Blackfriars Theatre was available as early as March 1608, for in a letter dated 11 March 1608 Sir Thomas Lake officially notified Lord Salisbury that the company of the Children of Blackfriars must be suppressed and that the King had vowed that they should never act again even if they had to beg their bread. General confirmation of this fact is found in a letter written two weeks later by the French ambassador.† Thus it is evident that in March of 1608 Richard Burbage knew his theatre was without a tenant. March to July 1608, then, are the months for discussions among the King's men of prospective performances at the Blackfriars.

What did this little group of Shakespeare and his intimate associates of the last fourteen years work out during their discussions in the months of March to July 1608?

One of the things they must have considered was alterations of their style of acting. As Granville-Barker has pointed out,‡ the acting in the new Blackfriars before a sophisticated audience

*William Shakespeare, pp. 2, 62–63.
†The Elizabethan Stage, pp. 2, 53–54.
‡Prefaces to Shakespeare, 2nd ser., pp. 249–50.

would have to be more quiet than in the large open-air Globe before the groundlings. It would be easier to emphasize points in the quiet candlelit surroundings, and "sentiment would become as telling as passion." There must also have been extended discussions of what to do about the repertory: which of the company's plays would be suitable for the elegant new theatre and which should be kept for the old audience at the Globe? Some of their decisions are fairly obvious. *Mucedorus,* which Rafe in *The Knight of the Burning Pestle* says he had played before the Wardens of his company and which went through fifteen editions before the Restoration, was clearly one of the Globe plays which might be laughed at by a Blackfriars audience. Similarly, *The Merry Devil of Edmonton* was not a good Blackfriars prospect. Certain other plays in the repertory might be expected to please at the Blackfriars; Marston's *Malcontent,* for instance, could easily be changed back to its original Blackfriars form, and Jonson's *Every Man in His Humour* and *Every Man out of His Humour,* though nine and ten years old, had been played by the company at court in the last three years and ought to be suitable for the Blackfriars.

These discussions of the old repertory, though no doubt important to the company then, are fruitless for us now. I know of no evidence as to their decisions. More important are the proposals for new plays for the Blackfriars, and I think we do have some evidence as to what these decisions were. The experienced members of the King's company were familiar with the fact so commonly recorded in the annals of the Jacobean theatre that new plays were in constant demand. With the acquisition of the new theatre they had an opportunity to claim for their own the most profitable audience in London. We know from the later Jacobean and Caroline records that this is just what they did.* It seems likely that one of the foundations of their later unquestioned dominance of the audiences of the gentry was their decision about plays and playwrights made in their discussions of March to July 1608.

One of their decisions, I suggest, was to get Jonson to write Blackfriars plays for them. He was a likely choice for three reasons. First, because he was developing a following among the courtly audience (always prominent at the Blackfriars) by his

*See Bentley, *The Jacobean and Caroline Stage,* Vol. 1, chap. 1 *passim*; pp. 2, 673–81.

great court masques. At this time he had already written his six early entertainments for King James—those at the Coronation, at the Opening of Parliament, at Althorp, at Highgate, and the two at Theobalds. He had written for performance at Whitehall *The Masque of Blackness, The Masque of Beauty, Hymenaei,* and the famous *Lord Haddington's Masque.* The sensational success of these courtly entertainments made Jonson a most promising choice to write plays for the courtly audience which the King's men did succeed in attracting to Blackfriars.

A second reason which would have led the King's men to Jonson as a writer for their new theatre was his great reputation among the literati and critics. In this decade from 1601 to 1610 the literary allusions to him are numerous, more numerous than to Shakespeare himself. The poems to Jonson and the long prose passages about him in this time are far more frequent than to Shakespeare; quotations from his work occur oftener, and I find three times as many literary and social references to performances of his plays and masques as to Shakespeare's. Poems about him or references to his work are written in these years by John Donne, Sir John Roe, Sir Dudley Carleton, the Venetian ambassador, John Chamberlain, Sir Thomas Lake, Sir George Buc, Sir Thomas Salusbury.* This is just the kind of audience which might be attracted to the Blackfriars, and which, eventually, the King's men did attract there.

There was a third reason which would have made Jonson seem to the King's men a very likely bet for their new theatre: he had already had experience in writing plays for this theatre when it was occupied by boys. Before the conferences of the King's men about their new project he had already had performed at Blackfriars *Cynthia's Revels, The Poetaster, The Case Is Altered,* and *Eastward Ho.* Possibly just before the time of the conferences of the King's men he had been writing for the Blackfriars another play, *Epicoene,* for he says in the Folio of 1616 that the play was performed by the Children of Blackfriars, but the date he gives for performance comes after their expulsion from the Blackfriars Theatre. Not only had Jonson had the valuable experience of writing four or five plays for the Blackfriars, but the Induction to *Cynthia's Revels* and his personal statements about boys of the company, like Nathan Field

*See Bentley, *Shakespeare and Jonson,* pp. 1, 38–41, 65–67, 73–79, 87–90, and Bradley and Adams, *The Jonson Allusin-Book, passim.*

and Salathiel, or Solomon, Pavy,* strongly suggest that he had directed them in their rehearsals. What valuable experience for the King's men planning their first performance in this new theatre!

Now all these qualifications of Jonson as a prospect for the King's men are, in sober fact, only speculations. Perhaps they simply show that if *I* had been participating in the conferences about the Blackfriars I should have argued long and lustily for Ben Jonson. Alas, I was not there! What evidence is there that they really did agree to secure his services for the company? The evidence is that before these conferences he had written only four plays for the Lord Chamberlain's or King's company— three, nine, and ten years before—nothing for the company in the years 1605–08. After these conferences, he wrote all his remaining plays for the company, with the exception of *Bartholomew Fair* six years later, a play which he gave to his good friend and protégé Nathan Field for the Lady Elizabeth's company at the Hope, and *A Tale of a Tub,* twenty-five years later, which he gave to Queen Henrietta's men. Jonson's first play after the reopening of Blackfriars was *The Alchemist;* it was written for the King's men, and numerous allusions show clearly that it was written for Blackfriars. So were *Catiline, The Devil Is an Ass, The Staple of News, The New Inn*, and *The Magnetic Lady.* Of course we lack the final proof of recorded reference to a definite agreement, but the evidence is such as to suggest that one of the decisions reached by the King's men in the reorganization of their enterprise to exploit the great advantages of their new theatre was to secure the services of Ben Jonson to write plays for the literate and courtly audience at Blackfriars.

Another decision, which I suggest the King's men made at these conferences, was to secure for their new theatre the services of the rising young collaborators, Francis Beaumont and John Fletcher. These gentlemen were younger than Jonson by about ten years, and as yet their reputations were distinctly inferior to his, but they had already displayed those talents which were to make their plays the stage favorites at Blackfriars for the next thirty-four years,† and were to cause Dryden to say

---

*See "A Good Name Lost," *Times Literary Supplement* (30 May 1942), p. 276.

†*The Jacobean and Caroline Stage,* pp. 1, 29 and 109–14.

sixty years later that "their plays are now the most pleasant and frequent entertainments of the stage."

One of the great assets of Beaumont and Fletcher was social. In the years immediately before and after 1608, the London theatre audience was developing the social cleavage which is such a marked characteristic of the Jacobean and Caroline drama and stage. In Elizabeth's time the London theatre was a universal one, in which a single audience at the Globe could embrace Lord Monteagle, Sir Charles Percy, city merchants, lawyers, Inns of Court students, apprentices, servants, beggars, pickpockets, and prostitutes. The later Jacobean and Caroline audience was a dual one. The gentry, the court, the professional classes, and the Inns of Court men went to the Blackfriars, the Phoenix, and later to the Salisbury Court; the London masses went to the larger and noisier Red Bull and Fortune and Globe. This new state of affairs was just developing when the King's men had their conferences about the Blackfriars in 1608. They evidently saw what was coming, however, for in the next few years they understood and exploited the situation more effectively than any other troupe in London. Indeed, the very acquisition of the Blackfriars and its operation in conjunction with the Globe was a device which had never been tried before in London and which is the clearest evidence that the King's men knew just what was happening.

Under these circumstances, then, the social status of Beaumont and Fletcher was an asset for the company in their new house. Francis Beaumont came of an ancient and distinguished Leicestershire family, with many connections among the nobility. John Fletcher was the son of a Lord Bishop of London and onetime favorite of Elizabeth. To a Blackfriars audience the social standing of these two young men would have been more acceptable than that of any other dramatist writing in London in 1608.

Another asset which made Beaumont and Fletcher valuable for the new enterprise of the King's men was their private theatre experience. So far as we can make out now, all their plays before this time had been written for private theatres and most of them for the Blackfriars. *The Woman Hater* had been prepared for the private theatre in St. Paul's, but *The Knight of the Burning Pestle, The Scornful Lady,* and *The Faithful Shepherdess* were Blackfriars plays. I think we can add to this list *Cupid's Revenge.* This play has been variously dated, but two forthcoming articles by James Savage* seem to me to offer convincing evidence that the play was prepared for Blackfriars about 1607 and that it displays a crude preliminary working out of much of the material which made *Philaster* one of the great hits of its time and one of the most influential plays of the seventeenth century. In any event, Beaumont and Fletcher were among the most experienced Blackfriars playwrights available in 1608. It is true that in 1608 none of their plays had been a great success; indeed the two best, *The Knight of the Burning Pestle* and *The Faithful Shepherdess,* are known to have been unsuccessful at first. The King's men, however, were experienced in the ways of the theatre; it does not seem rash to assume that at least one of them knew enough about audiences and about dramatic talents to see that these young men were writers of brilliant promise—especially since that one was William Shakespeare.

Beaumont and Fletcher, then, because of their experience and social standing were very desirable dramatists for the King's men to acquire in 1608 for their new private theatre. What is the evidence that they did acquire them? The evidence is that all the Beaumont and Fletcher plays of the next few years are King's men's plays, several of them famous hits—*Philaster, The Maid's Tragedy, A King and No King, The Captain, The Two Noble Kinsmen, Bonduca, Monsieur Thomas, Valentinian.* The dating of many of the Beaumont and Fletcher plays is very uncertain because of their late publication, and it may be that two or three of the later plays were written for other companies, but at least forty-five plays by Beaumont and Fletcher were the property of the Jacobean and Caroline King's men.† None of their plays before 1608, when Blackfriars was acquired, was, so far as we can find, written for the King's men. It seems a reasonable assumption, therefore, that another of the policies agreed upon at the conferences of 1608 was to secure the services of Beaumont and Fletcher for the company in its new enterprise at the Blackfriars.

The third of these three important changes in policy which I think the King's men agreed upon at their conferences about the new Blackfriars enterprise in 1608, is the most interesting of all

*"The Date of Beaumont and Fletcher's *Cupid's Revenge*" and "Beaumont and Fletcher's *Philaster* and Sidney's *Arcadia.*"

†*The Jacobean and Caroline Stage,* pp. 1, 109–15.

to us, but it was the easiest and most obvious for them. Indeed, it may well have been assumed almost without discussion. It was, of course, that William Shakespeare should write henceforth with the Blackfriars in mind and not the Globe.

Why was this decision an easy and obvious one? The company could assume, of course, that he would continue to write for them, since he was a shareholder and a patented member of the company and a housekeeper in both their theatres. Since the formation of the company, fourteen years before, all his plays had been written for performance by them, always, in the last ten years, for performance at the Globe. All his professional associations as well as his financial ones were with this company, and probably no one in the group even considered his defection. Burbage, Shakespeare, Heminges, and Condell were the real nucleus of the organization.

This new enterprise at the Blackfriars was a very risky business. As we have noted, no adult company had ever tried to run a private theatre before. The King's men not only proposed to make a heavy investment in this new departure, but they intended to continue running their old public theatre at the same time. Every possible precaution against failure needed to be taken. One such precaution would be the devotion of Shakespeare's full-time energies to the Blackfriars instead of the Globe. They could trust Shakespeare; he knew their potentialities and their shortcomings as no other dramatist did—indeed, few dramatists in the history of the English theatre have ever had such a long and intimate association with an acting company as William Shakespeare had had with these men. If anybody knew what Burbage and Heminges and Condell and Robert Armyn and Richard Cowley could do on the stage and what they should not be asked to do, that man was William Shakespeare. He could make them a success at the Blackfriars as they had been at the Globe if any one could.

Another reason for the transfer of Shakespeare's efforts was the fact that the Globe could be left to take care of itself with an old repertory as the Blackfriars could not. For one thing, there was no old repertory for the Blackfriars, since the departing boys appear to have held on to their old plays. For another thing, it was the Blackfriars audience which showed the greater avidity for new plays; the public theatre audiences were much more faithful to old favorites. They were still playing *Friar Bacon and Friar Bungay* at the Fortune in 1630 and Marlowe's

Edward II at the Red Bull in 1620 and *Dr. Faustus* at the Fortune in 1621 and *Richard II* and *Pericles* at the Globe in 1631.*
In the archives of the Globe at this time there must have been a repertory of more than a hundred plays, including at least twenty-five of Shakespeare's. Moreover, certain plays written for the Globe in the last few years, like Wilkins's *Miseries of Enforced Marriage* and the anonymous *Yorkshire Tragedy* and *The Fair Maid of Bristol* and *The London Prodigal*, had provided playwrights who might be expected to entertain a Globe audience with more of the same fare, but who could scarcely come up to the requirements of sophistication at Blackfriars. Altogether, then, the Globe repertory had much less need of Shakespeare's efforts in 1608 than did the Blackfriars repertory.

Why should Shakespeare have wanted to write for the Blackfriars, or at least have agreed to do so? The most compelling of the apparent reasons is that he had money invested in the project and stood to lose by its failure and gain by its success. He was one of the seven lessees of the new theatre; he had paid down an unknown sum and had agreed to pay £5. 14s. 4d. per year in rent.† He had at least a financial reason for doing everything he could to establish the success of the Blackfriars venture, and what Shakespeare could do most effectively was to write plays which would insure the company's popularity with the audience in its new private theatre.

A third reason for this postulated decision of the King's men in 1608 to have Shakespeare devote his entire attention to the Blackfriars and abandon the Globe was that the King's men saw that the real future of the theatrical profession in London lay with the court and the court party in the private theatres. Their receipts for performances at court showed them this very clearly. In the last nine years of Elizabeth, 1594–1602, they had received from court performances an average of £35 a year; in the first five years of the reign of the new king, 1603–07, they had averaged £131 per year in addition to their new allowances for liveries as servants of the King.‡ The Blackfriars and not the Globe was the theatre where they could entertain this courtly audience with commercial performances. There is no doubt that

*Ibid., pp. 1, 156, 174, 157, 24, 129.
†*Shakespearean Playhouses*, pp. 224–25.
‡*The Elizabethan Stage*, pp. 4, 164–75.

in the next few years after 1608 the Blackfriars did become the principal theatre of the company. In 1612 Edward Kirkham said they took £1,000 a winter more at the Blackfriars than they had formerly taken at the Globe.* When Sir Henry Herbert listed receipts from the two theatres early in the reign of King Charles, the receipts for single performances at the Globe averaged £6. 13s. 8d.; those for single performances at the Blackfriars averaged £15. 15s., or about two and one-half times as much.† In 1634 an Oxford don who wrote up the company simply called them the company of the Blackfriars and did not mention the Globe at all;‡ when the plays of the company were published in the Jacobean and Caroline period, the Blackfriars was mentioned as their theatre more than four times as often as the Globe was.** Such evidence proves that the Blackfriars certainly did become the principal theatre of the King's men. I am suggesting that in the conferences of 1608 the King's men had some intimation that it would, and accordingly they persuaded William Shakespeare to devote his attention to that theatre in the future instead of to the Globe.

So much for the reasons that Shakespeare might be expected to change the planning of his plays in 1608. What is the evidence that he did? The evidence, it seems to me, is to be seen in *Cymbeline, The Winter's Tale, The Tempest,* and *The Two Noble Kinsmen,* and probably it was to be seen also in the lost play, *Cardenio.* The variations which these plays show from the Shakespearian norm have long been a subject for critical comment. The first three of them in particular, since they are the only ones which have been universally accepted as part of the Shakespeare canon, have commonly been discussed as a distinct genre. Widely as critics and scholars have disagreed over the reasons for their peculiar characteristics, those peculiarities have generally been recognized, whether the plays are called Shakespeare's Romances, or Shakespeare's Tragi-Comedies, or his Romantic Tragi-Comedies, or simply the plays of the fourth period. No competent critic who has read carefully through the Shakespeare canon has failed to notice that there is something different about *Cymbeline, The Winter's Tale, The Tempest,* and *The Two Noble Kinsmen.*

*C. W. Wallace, *University of Nebraska Studies* 8 (1908): 36–37, n. 6.
†*The Jacobean and Caroline Stage,* pp. 1, 23–24.
‡*Ibid.,* pp. 1, 26, n. 5.
**Ibid.,* pp. 1, 30, n. 1.

When critics and scholars have tried to explain this difference between the plays of the last period and Shakespeare's earlier work, they have set up a variety of hypotheses. Most of these hypotheses have in common only the trait which I noted at the beginning of this paper—namely, they agree in considering Shakespeare as the professional poet and not the professional playwright. They turn to Shakespeare's sources, or to his inspiration, or to his personal affairs, or to the bucolic environment of his Stratford retirement, but not to the theatre which was his daily preoccupation for more than twenty years. Dowden called this late group in the Shakespeare canon "On the Heights," because he thought the plays reflected Shakespeare's new-found serenity. Such a fine optimism had, perhaps, something to recommend it to the imaginations of the Victorians, but to modern scholars it seems to throw more light on Dowden's mind than on Shakespeare's development. Dowden's explanation seemed utterly fatuous to Lytton Strachey, who thought that the plays of "Shakespeare's Final Period" were written by a Shakespeare far from serene, who was really "half enchanted by visions of beauty and loveliness and half bored to death." Violently as Dowden and Strachey differ, they agree in seeking subjective interpretations.

Best known of the old explanations of the peculiarities of the plays of this last period is probably Thorndike's:* the contention that the great success of *Philaster* caused Shakespeare to imitate it in *Cymbeline* and to a lesser extent in *The Winter's Tale* and *The Tempest*. In spite of the great horror of the Shakespeare idolaters at the thought of the master imitating superficial young whippersnappers like Beaumont and Fletcher, no one can read the two plays together without noting the striking similarities between them. The difficulty is that although the approximate dates of the two plays are clear enough, their *precise* dates are so close together and so uncertain that neither Thorndike nor any subsequent scholar has been able to prove that *Philaster* came before *Cymbeline,* and the Shakespeare idolaters have been equally unable to prove that *Cymbeline* came before *Philaster*.

I suggest that the really important point is not the priority of either play. The significant and revealing facts are that both

*Ashley H. Thorndike, *The Influence of Beaumont and Fletcher on Shakespeare*.

were written for the King's company; both were written, or at least completed, after the important decision made by the leaders of the troupe in the spring of 1608 to commission new plays for Blackfriars; and both were prepared to be acted in the private theatre in Blackfriars before the sophisticated audience attracted to that house. It is their common purpose and environment, not imitation of one by the other, which makes them similar. Both *Philaster* and *Cymbeline* are somewhat like Beaumont and Fletcher's earlier plays, especially *Cupid's Revenge,* because Beaumont and Fletcher's earlier plays had all been written for private theatres and all but one for Blackfriars. Both *Philaster* and *Cymbeline* are unlike Shakespeare's earlier plays because none of those plays had been written for private theatres. The subsequent plays of both Beaumont and Fletcher and Shakespeare resemble *Philaster* and *Cymbeline* because they too were written to be performed by the King's men before the sophisticated and courtly audience in the private theatre at Blackfriars.

So much I think we can say with some assurance. This explanation of the character of Shakespeare's last plays is in accord with the known facts of theatrical history; it accords with the biographical evidence of Shakespeare's long and close association with all the enterprises of the Lord Chamberlain's-King's men for twenty years; it is in accord with his fabulously acute sense of the theatre and the problems of the actor; and it does no violence to his artistic integrity or to his poetic genius.

May I add one further point much more in the realm of speculation? Since John Fletcher became a playwright for the King's men at this time and continued so for the remaining seventeen years of his life, and since the activities of the King's men had been one of Shakespeare's chief preoccupations for many years, is it not likely that the association between Fletcher and Shakespeare from 1608 to 1614 was closer than has usually been thought? Shakespeare was nearing retirement; after 1608 he wrote plays less frequently than before; Fletcher became his successor as chief dramatist for the King's company. In these years they collaborated in *The Two Noble Kinsmen, Henry VIII,* and probably in *Cardenio.* Is it too fantastic to suppose that Shakespeare was at least an adviser in the preparation of *Philaster, A King and No King,* and *The Maid's Tragedy* for his fellows? Is it even more fantastic to think that Shakespeare, the old public theatre playwright, preparing his first and crucial play for a private theatre, might have asked advice—or even taken it—from the two young dramatists who had written plays for this theatre and audience four or five times before?

Perhaps this is going too far. I do not wish to close on a note of speculation. My basic contention is that Shakespeare was, before all else, a man of the theatre and a devoted member of the King's company. One of the most important events in the history of that company was its acquisition of the Blackfriars Playhouse in 1608 and its subsequent brilliantly successful exploitation of its stage and audience. The company was experienced and theatre-wise; the most elementary theatrical foresight demanded that in 1608 they prepare new and different plays for a new and different theatre and audience. Shakespeare was their loved and trusted fellow. How could they fail to ask him for new Blackfriars plays, and how could he fail them? All the facts at our command seem to me to demonstrate that he did not fail them. He turned from his old and tested methods and produced a new kind of play for the new theatre and audience. Somewhat unsurely at first he wrote *Cymbeline* for them, then, with greater dexterity in his new medium, *The Winter's Tale,* and finally, triumphant in his old mastery, *The Tempest.*

THEODORE SPENCER

The Two Noble Kinsmen

For about a hundred years critical opinion has been divided as to whether Shakespeare did or did not write a large part of *The Two Noble Kinsmen*. The play was entered on the Stationers' Register in 1634 as "by John Fletcher and William Shakespeare," and the quarto was printed in the same year with their names on the title page. But the play does not occur in any of the Shakespeare folios, and though Fletcher's style is unmistakably present, in the so-called Shakespearean scenes there are characteristics which to many readers have seemed un-Shakespearean. Professor Tucker Brooke sums up the negative case: "When we consider individually the parts of *The Two Noble Kinsmen* which have been ascribed to Shakespeare, we find invariably that each act, scene or verse falls just short of what it should be. Always there is the strong Shakespearean reminiscence, but nowhere the full and perfect reality that we could swear to."* Consequently other authors, especially Massinger, have been suggested for these scenes, and the play is ordinarily omitted from Shakespeare's collected works.†

From *Modern Philology* 36 (1939): 255–76. Reprinted by permission of The University of Chicago Press.

*The *Shakespeare Apocrypha* (Oxford, 1908), p. xliii.

†There is a good summary of the history of the criticism of *The Two Noble Kinsmen* by Henry D. Gray. "Beaumont and *The Two Noble Kinsmen*," *PQ* 2 (1923): 112–31. Mr. Gray's own theory is, however, one of the most fantastic of the lot. He suggests that Fletcher timorously began the play alone, then got stuck and asked for Beaumont's help. Beaumont saw a chance of giving wider publicity to his recent *Masque of the Temple and Gray's Inn*, and started to assist Fletcher by inserting some of the characters from it in the third act; he also wrote a first draft of most of the other scenes. Before he finished, however, he got married and went to live in Kent, out of reach. Fletcher, in despair, and feeling quite unable to write the play alone, turned to Shakespeare. Shakespeare agreed to help, rewrote most of Act 3, scene 1, and brightened up the characters of Palamon and Arcite. But he too left town before he finished, going home to Stratford for good, and the play remained largely as Beaumont had drafted it.

But there is opinion of equal weight on the other side, and it is, I believe, now generally agreed that Shakespeare wrote Act 1, scenes 1–3; Act 3, scene 1; Act 5, except scene 2, and possibly more, and that he was equally responsible with Fletcher for the characterization and the plotting. To my mind the matter is clinched by a remarkably able and interesting article by Mr. Alfred Hart,* which analyzes the language of the Shakespearean scenes in the play in great detail, and by showing how closely it resembles that of Shakespeare's other plays, makes Shakespeare's authorship entirely convincing.

That the play was written in 1613 there can also be little doubt: the inclusion of the characters from Beaumont's masque of that date is strong evidence. As Professor Kittredge says, it "may be put immediately after *Henry VIII*."† Shakespeare's share in it, therefore, is the last thing he wrote, and it may be of considerable interest to study the play in the light of that fact. We may be able, as a result, to understand more clearly Shakespeare's latest style; we may be able to reach some conclusions as to why he ended his dramatic career when he did; and we may get a clearer picture not only of Jacobean drama at the end of Shakespeare's career, but of the different ways human experience can be represented on the stage.

II

The story of Palamon and Arcite, whether told by Boccaccio, Chaucer, or Shakespeare and Fletcher, is intrinsically feeble, superficial, and undramatic. For there is no real difference between Palamon and Arcite; they are both noble individuals, and the only reasons Palamon, rather than Arcite, wins the lady whom they both love are (*a*) that he saw her first and (*b*) that he had the sense to pray for success to Venus rather than to Mars. These reasons, to be sure, may have been more forceful in Chaucer's day, when the courtly ideal of love still had some literary vitality, than they were in Shakespeare's, but even in Chaucer they are entirely external; they have nothing to do with character; when Palamon finally wins the lady, he does so by

---

*"Shakespeare and the Vocabulary of *The Two Noble Kinsmen*," *RES 10* (1934): 274–87.
†*Complete Works of William Shakespeare* (Boston, 1936), p. 1409.

the help of a supernatural trick, not because he is the better man. Granted the outline of the story, anyone who tells it is forced to make the two heroes colorless and indistinguishable: should he do anything else, the story disappears. The same albinism extends to Emily, the heroine. She has no will of her own; if she should express a preference for either Arcite or Palamon, it would ruin the plot, which is based entirely on external motivation, and as a result she can be only a passive, if beautiful, doll, a shop-window dummy, forced to take whichever husband the gods decide. The whole thing is two-dimensional and unreal, a piece of tapestry, not, like the story of Troilus and Cressida, an active conflict.

Chaucer, however, makes it very appealing, and after reading *The Knight's Tale*, subdued by its grace and charm, we can see why an Elizabethan dramatist might think the story suitable for the stage. The opportunity, of which Chaucer takes such admirable advantage, for set speeches; the apparent, though superficial, conflict between the two heroes; the extension of their personal quarrel into a quarrel that involves the gods—all these things look like good dramatic material. Actually, of course, they are not, and I imagine that both Shakespeare and Fletcher, once they got started on their dramatization, realized that they were faced with a tough problem. They solved it very differently, and—as far as the immediate result was concerned, i.e., the writing of an effective play—Fletcher succeeded, and Shakespeare failed. The failure, to us, is more interesting than the success, but we must not be fooled by our idolatry of Shakespeare into taking credit away from Fletcher. The artificiality and spurious dramatic validity of the story offered a good opportunity for his accomplished and unscrupulous talent, and within his usual limits he made an expert job of it. The Fletcherian parts of the play are first-rate theater; their contrasts and conflicts make an immediate and successful impression. The Shakespearean parts, on the other hand, are static and, though with splendor, stiff. They are slow, and dense, compared with Fletcher's easy liquescence. They have a deliberate yet vague grandeur, a remote and half-exhausted exaltation; they are expressed through a clotted rhetoric that is the poetry of a man who has finished with action. Their style is the style of old age, and the imagery is an old man's imagery. Nevertheless, there is underneath a nobility, a control, a mastery of words, however fatigued, which make Fletcher's cleverness look cheap.* That mastery, and its peculiarity, its poetic success and its dramatic failure, its relation to Shakespeare's work as a whole, are worth careful study.

The play begins with an uninteresting prologue of a very conventional variety, a piece of hack writing (whoever wrote it) without significance. But the first scene of the first act, a scene which is unquestionably by Shakespeare, starts in a fashion as characteristic of Shakespeare's part in this play as it is uncharacteristic of nearly all his previous writing. It starts with a pageant: Hymen and a nymph symbolically attend the majestic entrance of Theseus, Hippolyta, and Emilia. It is processional, static, dignified, in the manner of a masque: the exact opposite to the opening of *The Tempest*, where all is action and excitement. It is the kind of thing that in an earlier play Shakespeare would have saved for a later scene, after the interest of the audience had been aroused by a personality or a conflict. And the entrance of these three chief characters is followed not by speech, but by a song:

> Roses, their sharp spines being gone,
> Not royal in their smells alone,
> But in their hue;
> Maiden pinks, of odor faint,
> Daisies smell-less, yet most quaint
> And sweet thyme true—

It is a song about flowers, echoing the subject matter of Perdita's flower speeches in the fourth act of *The Winter's Tale*, and with a reminiscence, it seems, of the tone of *The Phoenix and the Turtle*:

> The crow, the sland'rous cuckoo, nor
> The boding raven, nor chough hoar,
> Nor chatt'ring pie
> May on our bridehouse perch or sing,
> Or with them any discord bring,
> But from it fly!

*De Quincey (*Works*, ed. Black [1862], X, 49), in his essay on rhetoric, wrote of Shakespeare's part of the play as follows: "The first and the last acts of *The Two Noble Kinsmen*, which in point of composition, is perhaps the most superb work in the language . . . had been the most gorgeous rhetoric, had they not happened to be something far better."

Even when the song is over, and the semiritualistic, removed, pageantlike tone is established, the action does not begin vigorously: it still moves slowly, in a kind of dramatic pavane: "Enter three *Queens*, in black, with veils stain'd, with imperial crowns. The first *Queen* falls down at the foot of *Theseus;* the second falls down at the foot of *Hippolyta;* the third before *Emilia.*" And the three queens, thus disposed about the stage in a formal design, begin the dialogue rhythmically, almost in a chant:

1. *Queen:* For pity's sake and true gentility's,
        Hear and respect me!
2. *Queen:*   For your mother's sake,
        And as you wish your womb may thrive with
            fair ones,
        Hear and respect me!
3. *Queen:* Now for the love of him whom Jove hath mark'd
        The honor of your bed, and for the sake
        Of clear virginity, be advocate
        For us and our distresses!

Theseus, Hippolyta, and Emilia reply in turn, with the same formal grace, in slow rhythms, the courtly echoes of dramatic action.

The queens request Theseus to do justice to their dead lords, and Theseus, interrupted in his wedding ceremony, is "transported" by their words, being carried out of the action back into the past. His speech to the first queen (ll. 54ff.) illustrates one of the kinds of rhythm which seems to be natural to Shakespeare at the close of his career. The thought almost invariably stops, not at the end, but in the middle of the line, there is a striking reliance on strong verbs for descriptive effect, and the slow lines move like figures in heavy garments:

    King Capaneus was your lord. The day
    That he should marry you, at such a season
    As now it is with me, I met your groom
    By Mars's altar. You were that time fair;
    Not Juno's mantle fairer than your tresses,
    Nor in more bounty spread. Your wheaten wreath
    Was then nor thresh'd nor blasted; Fortune at you
    Dimpled her cheek with smile. Hercules our kinsman
    (Then weaker than your eyes) laid by his club;

> He tumbled down upon his Nemean hide,
> And swore his sinews thaw'd. O grief and time,
> Fearful consumers, you will all devour!

As usual with Shakespeare, the situation is generalized at the end. But the speech does not advance the action in any way: it is more like the comment of a chorus than the speech of a protagonist, it is melancholy and dreamlike. Theseus' reflections about the ravages made by grief and time on the queen's once beautiful face disturb him, and he turns aside—"Troubled I am"—abstracted by his thoughts of evanescence and decay.

The ritualistic movement proceeds, and the second queen appeals for help to Hippolyta. Her speech, too, has a tone which is characteristic of Shakespeare's final style. It is not, like the tone of Theseus' speech, the tone of remembrance, or of reverie, though it is related to that, being also "nonactive"; it is rather the tone of invocation, of apostrophe, of worship. It is again "removed," the tone of a looker-on, not a participant: appropriate as it is to the particular situation, it is also, one feels, appropriate to Shakespeare's own feeling about human experience at this last period in his life. Everyone who has written poetry knows that there are times when the tension of the immediate practical problem of composition is half-consciously resolved by a relapse or release into a semihypnotic incantation. The immature poet will fall into an incantation borrowed from someone else; the poet who is ripe and rich in technical experience discovers in words the beat of his own emotional vibration, and will produce, when set in his maturity at a particular job, the incantation, the tone, and the order which belong only to him. These may be different at different periods of his career, but to a sensitive reader they are unmistakable. And there are, in the Shakespearean parts of *The Two Noble Kinsmen*, an unmistakable incantation, tone, and order: the incantation which accepts illusion, the tone which has forgotten tragedy, and an order melted at the edges into a larger unity of acceptance and wonder. They appear again, in a tired fashion, in the long speech which Palamon makes to Venus in the first scene of the fifth act; in that speech, as in the speech of the second queen to Hippolyta, there is something trancelike and remote. In both speeches we feel a continuation of the mood of Miranda's "O brave, new world," and the rhythm of the queen's words is an adagio rhythm, haunting, invocatory, spoken, as it were, behind a veil.

As rhetoric, the speech is superb. It consists of a twenty-three-line sentence, the first nine lines invariably running over, to break in the middle, leading in the tenth line to a variation, with the pause at the end of the line for once, which alters the flow and hence commands attention. And yet, in spite of its excellence, the writing is tired, the muscles behind it seem slack and old, and, like the speech of Theseus I have already quoted, it ends unconvincingly.

> Honored Hippolyta,
> Most dreaded Amazonian, that hast slain
> The scythe-tusk'd boar; that with thy arm, as strong
> As it is white, was near to make the male
> To thy sex captive, but that this thy lord—
> Born to uphold creation in that honor
> First Nature styl'd it in—shrunk thee into
> The bound thou wast o'erflowing, at once subduing
> Thy force and thy affection; soldieress
> That equally canst poise sternness with pity:
> Who now, I know, hast much more power on him
> Than ever he had on thee; who ow'st his strength,
> And his love too, who is a servant for
> The tenor of thy speech; dear glass of ladies,
> Bid him that we, whom flaming War doth scorch,
> Under the shadow of his sword may cool us;
> Require him he advance it o'er our heads;
> Speak't in a woman's key, like such a woman
> As any of us three; weep ere you fail;
> Lend us a knee;
> But touch the ground for us no longer time
> Than a dove's motion when the head's plucked off;
> Tell him, if he i' th' blood-siz'd field lay swol'n,
> Showing the sun his teeth, grinning at the moon,
> What you would do.

To this prayer Hippolyta offers a consoling answer, and then the third queen turns to Emilia, with the same studied, elaborate, and removed kind of expression used by the other queens. Emilia replies at some length; her speeches are deliberately longer than those of Theseus and Hippolyta so that, being the heroine of the play, she may appear more prominent at the opening. When she has finished, Theseus starts abruptly out of his trance, and in a peremptory tone orders the wedding procession to proceed:

> Forward to th' temple! Leave not out a jot
> O' th' sacred ceremony.

But the queens delay him still further, in their eloquent speeches begging him to bury their slain husbands. At first Theseus continues to hold out against them:

> Why, good ladies,
> This is a service, whereto I am going,
> Greater than any war. It more imports me
> Than all the actions that I have foregone
> Or futurely can cope.

But they persuade him still. The rhythm of the first queen's speech on this occasion is again the rhythm of invocation, although she speaks in a different tone, and from a different angle than before. She still, however, describes experience contemplated from a distance; as, in a sense, the writing of Fletcher describes experience contemplated from a distance. But, as we shall see, the distance from which Fletcher contemplates is very different in altitude, and in direction, from Shakespeare's:

> 1. *Queen:*   The more proclaiming
>   Our suit shall be neglected. When her arms,
>   Able to lock Jove from a synod, shall
>   By warranting moonlight corslet thee—O, when
>   Her twinning cherries shall their sweetness fall
>   Upon thy tasteful lips, what wilt thou think
>   Of rotten kings or blubber'd queens? What care
>   For what thou feel'st not? What thou feel'st being able
>   To make Mars spurn his drum. O, if thou couch
>   But one night with her, every hour in't will
>   Take hostage of thee for a hundred, and
>   Thou shalt remember nothing more than what
>   That banquet bids thee to!*

---

*This speech illustrates a peculiarity of the Shakespearean parts of the play: the number of invocatory "O's." In this first scene, of 234 lines, there are 12 of such "O's"—a minor reflection of the general tone. In a typical Fletcher scene, 2, 2, of 277 lines, there are only 4 invocatory "O's."

Finally, Theseus succumbs; he will postpone his marriage and revenge the queens, and he ends by saying—it is the third example in this scene of an un-electrified platitude:

> As we are men,
> Thus should we do. Being sensually subdu'd,
> We lose our human title. Good cheer, ladies!
> Now turn we towards your comforts.

III

I have discussed the opening scene of this play at length because it has several striking characteristics. In the first place, it represents a great elaboration, on Shakespeare's part, of his source. Chaucer describes the supplication of the queens and Theseus' determination to help them in about eighty lines; there is no suggestion that they are appealing to Theseus on his marriage day, and there is no suggestion of the conflict in his mind between love and war. Chaucer is too anxious to get started on the story of Palamon and Arcite to waste time on any but the most necessary of preliminaries. Yet Shakespeare makes a great deal of the preliminaries: each of the queens speaks, each of the main characters responds, and there is an obvious, if incomplete, expression of a conflict in values. The value of war and the value of love, the standard of action and the standard of emotion, which, as Mr. Wilson Knight has observed, play so large a part in Shakespeare's work, are here, in the mind of Theseus, deliberately presented, and yet, dramatically speaking, they are the ghosts of themselves. For Theseus' queerly abstracted conflict between the joys of marriage and his responsibility to the queens has no real bearing on the course of the main events in the play, and the decisions he comes to are abrupt, apart from the action—if we can call it "action." It is as if Shakespeare had written the scene half automatically, recalling the kind of conflict which he had described earlier with passion and penetration, but which he was now using as merely the most convenient means for dramatic exposition; a remembered technique, with the emotional content forgotten. Technically, as I have tried to suggest, the scene is admirable. The first queen is set against Theseus, the second queen is set against Hippolyta, the third queen is set against Emilia: each responds to each, in a mounting rhythm, in a verbal counterpoint, like voices in a chorale; it is planned, deliberate and controlled. But it is not the technique of *Julius Caesar* or of *Lear*. If we imagine the scene on the stage, we see gesture rather than action. Drama has returned to its womb, and has once more become ritual. It is the dramatic writing of a man to whom action has lost importance, but who is trying to recapture, for the immediate necessity of writing a moneymaking play, the devices and the lost enthusiasm of a forgotten intensity. It is the writing of a man who has come out on the other side of human experience, and who, looking back, can no longer be interested in what he has once seen so vividly and so passionately felt. The figures still struggling in the *selva oscura* are the figures of a pageant or a dream.

IV

Fletcher's share in the play is very different. The emotional tone is not that of a man who has been *through* experience: it is the tone of a man who has never got there. His rhythms are the rhythms, not of remote or incandescent contemplation, but of the easy lullaby of sentiment. We are not abstracted or lifted up; there is no incantation. Instead we are soothed, smoothed, softened. And yet, theatrically speaking, it is a great success; and only when we reflect do we realize that we are in so much smaller a dimension. Act 2, scene 2 is a good example of Fletcher's ability.

Arcite and Palamon are in prison, having been captured by Theseus in his avenging war against Creon. They enter on the upper stage and begin discussing their situation. They are in prison for life, and all activity is over. "Here we are," says Arcite,

> And here the graces of our youth must wither
> Like a too timely spring. Here age must find us,
> And, which is heaviest, Palamon, unmarried.
> The sweet embraces of a loving wife,
> Loaden with kisses, arm'd with thousand Cupids,
> Shall never clasp our necks; no issue know us;
> No figures of ourselves shall we ev'r see
> To glad our age, and like young eagles teach 'em

> Boldly to gaze against bright arms, and say
> "Remember what your fathers were, and conquer!"

The technique and the tone are typically Fletcherian: the great majority of the lines end with an extra syllable; there are few of those heavy pauses in the middle of the lines which produce in Shakespeare's latest style so rich and full an effect; all is languorous and gentle. The tone, like Shakespeare's tone, might be called remote. Yet it is remote in a very different sense. If we compare what Arcite says about "The sweet embraces of a loving wife" with what Theseus has said earlier to the first queen (1.1.59ff.), we realize that what weakens Fletcher's writing is that he is describing something that has never happened. It is one of his favorite emotional tricks to project us into a fanciful future, and then to melt us by telling us what may go on there in relation to the character who is speaking. For example, in *Henry VIII* (3.1.431ff.) Wolsey speaks to Cromwell:

> And when I am forgotten, as I shall be,
> And sleep in dull cold marble, where no mention
> Of me more must be heard of, say I taught thee—
> Say Wolsey, that once trod the ways of glory
> And sounded all the depths and shoals of honor,
> Found thee a way (out of his wrack) to rise in—

There are a thousand examples of this kind of writing in Fletcher's plays; this emotional tone is perhaps the surest mark of his style, and the falling lines, with their lingering feminine endings, fit it very appropriately. But, as far as I am aware, it never occurs in Shakespeare; Shakespeare has too strong a sense of reality. To tease our feelings by summoning up melancholy pictures of how people are going to behave when a character is dead, or to lament the loss of imaginary blessings, are not devices which occur to his more robust and unsentimental temperament. Fletcher, on the other hand, could not write an emotional scene without using them. They make an immediate effect on the audience, and we are moved by a vague feeling of rather complacent pity as we listen. Such scenes seem to have caught the Elizabethan ear at once, and to have held the affection of audiences for nearly a century. The emotion is so much easier than Shakespeare's; it is no trouble to understand because there is no mental toughness or gristle combined with it. Fletcher's share in *The Two Noble Kins-men* is, as I have said, much better theater than Shakespeare's.*

The rest of this particular scene is very cleverly written. Palamon and Arcite console themselves for the prospect of their long imprisonment by thinking that they will at least have each other, and they work themselves up to vows of mutual affection:

> *Palamon:* Is there record of any two that lov'd
>   Better than we do, Arcite?
> *Arcite:*   Sure, there cannot.
> *Palamon:* I do not think it possible our friendship
>   Should ever leave us.
> *Arcite:*   Till our deaths, it cannot.

But then Emilia, who is to be the cause of their dissension, appears below with the waiting woman, talking about flowers. Palamon sees her first and stands transfixed. Arcite tries to urge him

---

*Once we become aware of this emotional habit of Fletcher's we can detect his hand where we might otherwise be uncertain. For example, the beginning of Act 3, scene 1, is unquestionably Shakespeare's; style, meter, tone, and vocabulary are firmly his. Yet all these begin to weaken as the scene progresses. We move from incantation to action, and Fletcher's hand becomes unmistakable. Palamon (ll. 72ff.) asks Arcite to fight with him for Emily, and the first thing he does is to project himself into an imaginary future, producing in the rhythm of the lines and in the minds of the audience that sentimental, unreal, and melting sensation which I have just tried to describe.

> Give me a sword . . .
> and do but say
>   That Emily is thine, I will forgive
>   That trespass thou hast done me, yea, my life,
>   If then thou carry't; and brave souls in shades,
>   That have died manly, which will seek of me
>   Some news from earth, they shall get none but this—
>   That thou art brave and noble.

Another sure sign of Fletcher's hand in the end of this scene is the way Palamon and Arcite use each other's names when they address each other:

> *Palamon:*   O you heavens, dares any
> So noble bear a guilty business? None
> But only Arcite; therefore none but Arcite
> In this kind is so bold.
> *Arcite:*   Sweet Palamon

There is something soft about this; it is the equivalent, in poetry, of the action of a man who, having mortally offended his wife, thinks that he can make up to her by stroking her cheek.

on to further protestations of friendship, but he can get nothing out of him, so he too looks down at the garden, is hopelessly smitten, and a very deftly managed series of interwoven short speeches follows, in which Arcite and Palamon comment on the beauty of Emilia while she and her woman go on talking about flowers. When Emilia leaves it is all over with the friendship between Palamon and Arcite; they are both in love up to the ears, they can think of nothing but Emilia, and the scene comes to an end with their mutual recriminations, an ironic and successful contrast to their feelings toward each other at the beginning.

This smooth and accomplished action is almost the reverse of Shakespeare's static pageantry. And the way Fletcher describes his two heroes is very different from the way Shakespeare had described them earlier, the first time we see them, in Act 1, scene 2. The words Shakespeare puts into their mouths are not the words of sentiment; Palamon and Arcite are not like two graceful saplings, swaying in unison in a sentimental moonlight. They are a pair of moralists, with a strong sense of evil and a strong sense of indignation at the corruption engendered in Thebes by their wicked uncle, Creon. What Fletcher tells us about them bears only on the immediate dramatic situation; they say no more than is necessary to put the particular scene across. But Shakespeare reveals their characters by their attitude to a general situation, and we are in a different, a wider world of perception. His Arcite and Palamon talk as follows:

> *Arcite:* Dear Palamon, dearer in love than blood,
> And our prime cousin, yet unhard'ned in
> The crimes of nature—let us leave the city
> Thebes and the temptings in't before we further
> Sully our gloss of youth.
> And here to keep in abstinence we shame
> As in incontinence; for not to swim
> I' th' aid o' th' current were almost to sink,
> At least to frustrate striving; and to follow
> The common stream, 'twould bring us to an eddy
> Where we should turn or drown; if labor through,
> Our gain but life and weakness.
>
> *Palamon:*   Your advice
> Is cried up with example. What strange ruins,
> Since first we went to school, may we perceive
> Walking in Thebes!

He goes on to describe how the soldier, dedicated to Mars, receives nothing but scars and rags for his reward. Arcite widens the application: in Thebes there is nothing good; it is a place

> where every evil
> Hath a good color; where ev'ry seeming good's
> A certain evil; where not to be ev'n jump
> As they are here, were to be strangers, and
> Such things to be mere monsters.

They talk in this style for some eighty lines, and it is only when they are told that they must fight for Thebes against Theseus that their sense of duty makes them cast off their bitter mood and find a solution in action.

Now this is a very extraordinary way of presenting a pair of romantic lovers to an audience. To be sure, it shows them as highly idealistic, but we have only to think of Romeo to realize that what they are being idealistic about has nothing to do with what is to be their predominant emotion in the action that follows. Romeo, when he is first presented to us, is an idealist; but he is a positive idealist in the sense that he is in a dream of illusion, and that his waking is the fulfillment of his dream. Palamon and Arcite are *dis*-illusioned; their view of the world they live in may be said to begin where the view of Shakespeare's tragic heroes leaves off: in an awareness of the evil which conditions their existence. Their speeches are haunted by the ghost of Timon. But Timon looks back at Athens and curses its vileness as a result of a disillusionment which has been led up to by the previous action. Palamon and Arcite look back in disgust at Thebes before we have been given any satisfactory reason for their disgust. One cannot help wondering why Shakespeare should have presented them in so remarkable a fashion. Was he relying, in a fatigued or bored state of mind, on a means of arousing interest which he had found useful in the past, and was here repeating half automatically because he could not think of anything else? This explanation is borne out by the fact that Palamon and Arcite use, in their disgusted speeches, a rather stock set of images and comparisons. The hard lot of the unrewarded soldier is an Elizabethan commonplace; so is the foolishness, described by Palamon, of contemporary fashions in dress; and the shocking difference between what seems and what is, which Palamon emphasizes in the speech I have just quoted, is one of the main themes in all of Shakespeare's mature work. In other words, just as we find, in the first scene of the play, the almost ritualistic manipulation of the ghosts of dramatic action, so we find here the ghosts of familiar themes, used as convenient means for exposition, but lacking, in the long run, the reality of conviction. Shakespeare, we feel, is looking back on what once mattered, but which matters no longer, and his description of the emotions of Palamon and Arcite about the world they live in does not quite convince us because it no longer seems necessary to Shakespeare to have those emotions explained: they can, undramatically, be taken for granted.

V

Yet the composition of Shakespeare's opening scenes consists by no means merely of repetitions or echoes of his earlier emotional grooves and dramatic triumphs; these scenes emphasize a positive value of their own—the value of loyalty. The queens are passionately loyal to their dead husbands; Palamon and Arcite, "dearer in love than blood," share a common view of their debased country; the intimate friendship of Theseus and Pirithous is richly described (1.3.41):

> Their knot of love
> Tied, weav'd, entangled, with so true, so long,
> And with a finger of so deep a cunning,
> May be outworn, never undone—

and the first (if only) human, individualizing fact we learn about Emilia is that she once had an intimate friendship of a similar kind with a girl named Flavina who died at the age of eleven.* "You talk," says Emilia (1.3.55ff.):

> You talk of Pirithous' and Theseus' love.
> Theirs has more ground, is more maturely season'd,
> More buckled with strong judgment, and their needs
> The one of th' other may be said to water
> Their intertangled roots of love, but I
> And she I sigh and spoke of, were things innocent,

---

*There is no hint of this in Chaucer.

Lov'd for we did, and like the elements
That know not what nor why, yet do effect
Rare issues by their operance, our souls
Did so to one another. What she lik'd
Was then of me approv'd; what not, condemn'd,
No more arraignment. The flow'r that I would pluck
And put between my breasts (then but beginning
To swell about the blossom) she would long
Till she had such another, and commit
To the like innocent cradle, where, phoenix-like,
They died in perfume. On my head no toy
But was her pattern; her affections (pretty,
Though happily her careless wear) I followed
For my most serious decking. Had mine ear
Stol'n some new air, or at adventure humm'd one
From musical coinage, why, it was a note
Whereon her spirits would sojourn (rather dwell on)
And sing it in her slumbers.

This charming, this delicious speech crowns the theme of
friendship, already so clearly illustrated by Theseus and Pirithous and by Palamon and Arcite. But the theme is to be dis-
rupted by the subsequent behavior of Palamon and Arcite; that
is one reason why it is so strongly emphasized at the start. One
of Shakespeare's favorite dramatic devices in his mature work
is to establish a set of values and then to show how it is vio-
lated by the individual action which follows. He does this in
Troilus and Cressida through the speeches of Ulysses; he does
it more indirectly in *Hamlet, Othello,* and *King Lear;* he
clearly had it in mind when planning *The Two Noble Kinsmen.*
But Fletcher, tied by temperament to the immediate and the obviously practical, was not concerned with such matters, and,
when he took charge of the situation after the first act, the
wider implication, the fundamental and general contrast which
the story, in Shakespeare's eyes, could be seen to illustrate, disappeared. It was not appropriate to Fletcher's romantic and
myopic vision.

That Shakespeare should have so strongly emphasized the
theme of union through friendship is as characteristic of the
tone of his final period as his habit of breaking the thought in
the middle of a line is characteristic of his final metrical technique. It is not, to be sure, quite the same as the theme of rec-

onciliation, which we find in all the plays from *Pericles* on. But it is the state of mind which occurs *after* reconciliation. And as the vile picture of Thebes given by Palamon and Arcite is different, not being the result of previous action, from the picture of Athens given by Timon, so Emilia's account of her friendship with Flavina is different from the reunion of Pericles with Marina or of Leontes with Hermione. The union of Emilia and Flavina did not come about as the result of a dramatic process. It just was. Such writing, as I have already observed, is the writing of a man who has been *through* experience, for whom process and movement are over, who does not care about how or why things happen, as long as they are. In such a state of mind one may plan dramatic action, in a routine, habitual way, but one cannot put one's heart into making it exciting. Another desire is much more important; the desire to contemplate—not turmoil, or contrast, or friction—which are dreams—but the beauty of the individual life itself, in a garland of flowers.

> O queen Emilia,
> Fresher than May, sweeter
> Than her gold buttons on the boughs or all
> Th' enamel'd knacks o' th' mead or garden! Yea;
> We challenge too the bank of any nymph,
> That makes the stream seem flowers! Thou, O jewel
> O' th' wood, o' the world, hast likewise bless'd a place
> With thy sole presence.*

There is some uncertainty in the phrasing of Arcite's speech; it has not the perfection of Perdita's flower speeches in *The Winter's Tale*; but the caught breath, the broken wonder, the magical invocation are still here, trembling through a shattered rhythm into words.

VI

There is one episode in the story of Arcite and Palamon which, unlike the previous parts, definitely demands the tone of invocation; it is the episode where the two lovers pray respectively to Mars and Venus for success in their combat. The scene,

*3.1.4ff.

as was to be expected, is obviously by Shakespeare; it was his meat exactly, and he does it handsomely, in a manner that repays close attention. The first speech (5.1.49ff.), that of Arcite before the altar of Mars, is a dignified and exalted piece of writing, and the familiar invocatory rhythms of Shakespeare's latest style are obvious throughout:

> O great corrector of enormous times,
> Shaker of o'er-rank states, thou grand decider
> Of dusty and old titles, that heal'st with blood
> The earth when it is sick, and cur'st the world
> O' th' plurisy of people! I do take
> Thy signs auspiciously, and in thy name
> To my design march boldly.

This is more or less what we would expect in an address to Mars, and it is not unlike what we find in Chaucer. But when Arcite leaves the stage, and Palamon takes his place to pray to Venus, we have a very remarkable speech indeed, so remarkable that it is odd that no one seems to have noticed its peculiarity. It is not in the least like the speech made by Chaucer's Palamon, who praises the goddess, and swears to serve her forever if she will give him Emily. Chaucer's Palamon is devoted and charming, his words are tender and youthful, full of graceful pleading. Shakespeare's Palamon addresses Venus in a different manner—I give the long speech entire:

> Hail, sovereign queen of secrets, who hast power
> To call the fiercest tyrant from his rage,
> And weep unto a girl; that hast the might,
> Even with an eye-glance, to choke Mars's drum
> And turn th' alarm to whispers; that canst make
> A cripple flourish with his crutch, and cure him
> Before Apollo; that mayst force the king
> To be his subject's vassal, and induce
> Stale gravity to dance; the polled bachelor—
> Whose youth, like wanton boys through bonfires,
> Have skipp'd thy flame—at seventy thou canst catch,
> And make him, to the scorn of his hoarse throat,
> Abuse young lays of love. What godlike power
> Hast thou not power upon? To Phoebus thou
> Add'st flames, hotter than his: the heavenly fires

Did scorch his mortal son, thine him. The huntress
All moist and cold, some say, began to throw
Her bow away, and sigh. Take to thy grace
Me thy vowed soldier, who do bear thy yoke
As 'twere a wreath of roses, yet is heavier
Than lead itself, stings more than nettles. I
Have never been foul-mouth'd against thy law;
Nev'r reveal'd secret, for I knew none—would not,
Had I learn'd all that were. I never practic'd
Upon man's wife, nor would the libels read
Of liberal wits. I never at great feasts
Sought to betray a beauty, but have blush'd
At simp'ring sirs that did. I have been harsh
To large confessors, and have hotly ask'd them
If they had mothers. I had one, a woman,
And women 'twere they wrong'd. I knew a man
Of eighty winters—this I told them—who
A lass of fourteen brided. 'Twas thy power
To put life into dust. The aged cramp
Had screw'd his square foot round,
The gout had knit his fingers into knots,
Torturing convulsions from his globy eyes
Had almost drawn their spheres, that what was life
In him seem'd torture. This anatomy
Had by his young fair fere a boy, and I
Believ'd it was his, for she swore it was,
And who would not believe her? Brief, I am
To those that prate and have done, no companion;
To those that boast and have not, a defier;
To those that would and cannot, a rejoicer.
Yea, him I do not love that tells close offices
The foulest way, nor names concealments in
The boldest language. Such a one I am,
And vow that lover never yet made sigh
Truer than I. O, then, most soft-sweet goddess,
Give me the victory of this question, which
Is true love's merit, and bless me with a sign
Of thy great pleasure.

    Here music is heard and doves are seen to flutter. They
    fall again upon their faces, then on their knees.
O thou that from eleven to ninety reign'st
In mortal bosoms, whose chase is this world,

And we in herds thy game, I give thee thanks
For this fair token; which being laid unto
Mine innocent true heart, arms in assurance
My body to this business.

I have quoted the whole of this speech because its peculiarity can only be fully seen if all of it is taken into account. It is divided into three main parts: the first describes the effects of Venus, the second describes the purity of Palamon, the third is a final invocation in (as usual) generalized terms, which unites the other two. But what extraordinary images, for a prayer to Venus, the speech contains! We are first told that love affects a man of seventy, then that it affects a man of eighty, and finally that it affects a man of ninety. The emphasis is, throughout, on old age, and the result is that what impresses us, after reading or hearing the speech, is not the power of love, but a series of images of decay. The speech accomplishes the reverse of what is intended; the negatives dominate the positives; it is, as it were, poetry inside out. The cripple and his crutch, the "polled bachelor" of seventy, his hoarse throat abusing "young lays of love," the gouty old man of eighty with his foot screwed around and his eyes convulsed—such are the vivid pictures that remain in the mind. And even if we think of these ancient wrecks as being rejuvenated by love, the process is not an agreeable one. The flames of love scorch more than the sun; the yoke of love, while it seems like a wreath of roses, is actually heavier than lead and stings more than nettles. And as Palamon goes on to describe his own purity, and his avoidance of the way society in general treats love, we notice, not his avoidance, but rather the things he avoids—the liberal wits, the simp'ring sirs, and the large confessors. So that when, toward the end of the speech, Palamon calls Venus a "soft-sweet goddess," we are surprised; hardly anything he has previously told us about her has prepared us for such a description.

This speech is interesting in yet another fashion. For it is a mixture, not quite fused, of the two moods which we have already seen as predominant in Shakespeare's part of the play: the invocatory mood of Arcite's speech in Act 3 to the imagined Emilia, and the satirical mood of Arcite's and Palamon's speeches about Thebes in Act 1. As it begins we are once more caught by the echo of that indescribable slow magic, that rich exalted wonder of the final style:

> who hast power
> To call the fiercest tyrant from his rage,
> And weep unto a girl.

But it is not sustained, and Shakespeare calls back, with a good deal of inappropriateness, the ghost of his almost forgotten mood of disillusionment to fill out the remaining lines. He does not seem, in other words, to be interested in writing for Palamon the kind of speech which Palamon—eager and ardent with young love—should speak. Writing rapidly, as it is likely he did, to get a job finished, he relied on habitual tones and habitual rhythms, using the artifice of long practice without the intensity of the appropriately dramatic emotion.

But Emilia's speech to Diana, which follows Palamon's to Venus, is eminently appropriate, and it is significant that Emilia must pray "bride-habited, but maiden-hearted," and without passion to her "sacred, silver mistress." Hers is a prayer with which reality has nothing to do, for it cannot, under the circumstances, be granted. And here Shakespeare's words fit their occasion admirably:

> O sacred, shadowy, cold, and constant queen,
> Abandoner of revels, mute, contemplative,
> Sweet, solitary, white as chaste, and pure
> As wind-fann'd snow. . . .
> > I here, thy priest,
> Am humbled fore thine altar.

VII

The rest of the play—the subplot of the jailer's daughter who goes mad for love of Palamon, the meeting of Palamon and Arcite in the forest, the entertainment given to Theseus by the yokels, and the denouement—all this moves competently and swiftly; situation rather than character is emphasized, the style is clear and easily understood, and it was doubtless entirely successful on the stage. Now and then we recognize Shakespeare's hand, as in the extremely vivid account, in the last scene, of the rearing horse that killed Arcite, but most of it is Fletcher's, and, for our present purposes, not worth careful analysis.

The Shakespearean parts of the play, however—as I hope

I have shown—*are* worth careful analysis, for they illustrate what was happening to Shakespeare at the end of his career more clearly than anything in *The Tempest* or *Henry VIII*. The most striking fact that stands out is that Shakespeare seems no longer to be interested in process or in change and hence is no longer interested in the development of character. Whether he wrote the lines or not, what is apparently his state of mind is summed up in Theseus' address to the gods in the last speech of the play:

> Let us be thankful
> For that which is, and with you leave dispute
> That are above our question.

And in this acceptance of "that which is," there is a mingling— it is of course inevitable—of an awareness of good and an awareness of evil, the one felt almost ecstatically, though never, as in *The Winter's Tale*, entirely so; the other felt as being continually in the background, though never pressing into the immediate situation. The speeches of Theseus, of the queens, of Palamon and Arcite are contemplative, not active, and what change occurs in the main characters is very superficial. The story itself, to be sure, demands remoteness, a pageantlike treatment, and a slighting of differences in character, but though Shakespeare must obviously have seen this, his seeing it does not satisfactorily account for the almost unnecessary *stasis* of his presentation. Nor does it account for the incompleteness of much of the actual writing. Professor Tucker Brooke is right when he speaks of each act, scene, or verse falling "just short of what it should be." Professor Brooke thinks that this means that Shakespeare could not have written those acts or scenes, but that is not a necessary conclusion. It means more probably that he was no longer fully interested in what he was doing. The style of the Shakespearean parts of *The Two Noble Kinsmen*, as Palamon's address to Venus so clearly shows, is the style of an old man, a style that reveals, to be sure, an expert technique in handling words, and a mastery of incantation, but which has little concern for the tricks that would please an audience, and which is, in a sense, dramatically stagnant. After studying Shakespeare's part of the play, we feel that his return to Stratford and his abandonment of writing were almost inevitable. In fact, it is possible to wonder whether his retirement was entirely voluntary. The shareholders in the Globe knew what the public wanted; the differences between Shakespeare's slow pageantry—its faded, difficult magnificence, its elaborate remoteness—and Fletcher's easy, accomplished manipulation, were clear enough to anyone with an eye on the box office: Fletcher's style was obviously much better adapted to the increasing superficiality of the popular taste. One can even imagine a deputation calling on Shakespeare—it is not an agreeable thought—to suggest that, all things considered, it would be wise to go home and write no more.

On the Design of
The Two Noble Kinsmen

I suspect that most readers of *The Two Noble Kinsmen* have at some time felt reluctant to acknowledge that Shakespeare had much to do with the play. No doubt they are put off because the work is so undramatic: the action, particularly in the "Shakespearian" first and last acts, is sluggish, and the whole plot, twice boiled down from Boccaccio's epic, remains essentially narrative; the characters lack the interest of real individuality, and, though a great deal happens to them, they do not grow, or alter, in a Shakespearian way. Yet we are prepared to accept much that is similarly "undramatic" as Shakespeare's, in the work of the five years or so between the time he engaged himself with *Pericles* and the writing of *The Two Noble Kinsmen*, probably in 1613. Again, the quality of the verse perplexes readers in search of Shakespeare; there is something wordy in those long speeches which fail to advance the action, something elaborate and self-conscious in the weighing of the rhythms, in the complex network of syntax, in the bold images; there seems a tendency to "write it up":

> O, when
> Her twining cherries shall their sweetness fall
> Upon thy tasteful lips, what wilt thou think
> Of rotten kings or blubber'd queens?

> (1.1.176–79)

When we come across a passage like that, we may feel some sympathy with Tucker Brooke: "Always there is the strong

From *A Review of English Literature* 5 (1964): 89–105. Reprinted by permission of the author and the editor.

Shakespearian reminiscence, but nowhere quite the full and perfect reality that we could swear to."* But it is not really debatable that the verse of part of *The Two Noble Kinsmen* is Shakespeare's, the rest being Fletcher's. Theodore Spencer, Marco Mincoff and Kenneth Muir have all written excellent essays, approaching the verse along different paths, which strongly back up the old evidence of the metrical tests.† The arguments for Shakespeare do not need rehearsing here.

The reluctance to believe that *The Two Noble Kinsmen*, even in part, is a product of Shakespeare's mind and art really comes, not from the feeling that the play is undramatic or that the verse cannot be his, but from a conviction that the play is inane. It is worth quoting Tucker Brooke again: "It contains no spark of psychological insight or philosophy of life which can in sober moments be thought either worthy of the mature Shakespeare or even suggestive of him."‡ I am sure that it is the seeming want of "idea" in the play that makes readers find fault with verse and dramaturgy which they would be content to accept as Shakespeare's if the play were, to them, more intellectually respectable. That rich fund of suggestion which sets us on to our theories of what Shakespeare *meant* by the Romances certainly seems absent from the play. Even Spencer, acknowledging Shakespeare's hand, and admiring so much in the verse, saw the Shakespeare of this play as an old man who had been *through* experience, no longer interested in process or in change, not caring how or why things happen, but speaking of "that which is"; and, working rapidly to get a job finished, giving us tired writing, the muscles behind it slack and old. So remote and so dramatically stagnant is the result, in Spencer's view, that he imagines a deputation calling on Shakespeare to suggest that "it would be wise to go home and write no more."

It seems to me that there is much more purposeful thought in the play than Brooke and Spencer saw; we really need not be ashamed of it. It is strange that the pensiveness of the play, in the first and last acts, has not aroused more interest: a pensive-

---

The Shakespeare Apocrypha (1908), p. xliii.
†*Modern Philology* 36 (1938–39): 255–76; *English Studies* 33 (1952): 97–115; *Shakespeare as Collaborator* (1960), pp. 98–147. See also A. Hart, *Shakespeare and the Homilies* (1934), pp. 242–56. Putting aside some scenes about which there *could* be debate, the Shakespearian portions are 1.1–3, 3.1, 5.1, 3, 4.
‡*op. cit.*, p. xliii.

ness which, through those slow-moving scenes, hatches an "idea" bewildering enough but subtle (however unsubtle it seems in the simplifications of one's commentary). So far as I know, Clifford Leech has been the only critic to remark on the curious division of view which belittles the love in the play, and on the insistence that "mature" love means abandoning something more worthwhile.* Though Leech finds a contradiction where I find consistency, and though the "totality of its effect" speaks to him of Fletcher and to me of Shakespeare, it was from his remarks that this small exploration began.

Spencer noted the strangeness of Palamon's address to Venus (5.1.77–136) in the ceremonial scene of prayer to the gods for divine aid before the great tournament. As seen by Palamon, the power of Venus is a power that changes her victims' natures, overturns them rather, that grips them the more the older they get, making them more and more ludicrous and grotesque. As the apparently sincere tribute to the might of Venus continues, the operations of almighty love seem more and more disgusting. The invocation is fairly harmless:

> Hail, sovereign queen of secrets, who hast power
> To call the fiercest tyrant from his rage,
> And weep unto a girl . . .

But before we reach the parallel invocation, "that may'st force the king/To be his subject's vassal," we hear the words, "that canst make/A cripple flourish with his crutch"; it is in this manner the address goes on:

> the poll'd bachelor—
> Whose youth, like wanton boys through bonfires,
> Have skipt thy flame—at seventy thou canst catch,
> And make him, to the scorn of his hoarse throat,
> Abuse young lays of love.

The "tributes" grow more satirical as the man of eighty takes the place of the man of seventy:

> I knew a man
> Of eighty winters—this I told them—who

*The John Fletcher Plays (1962), pp. 147–50.

> A lass of fourteen brided: 'twas thy power
> To put life into dust; the aged cramp
> Had screw'd his square foot round,
> The gout had knit his fingers into knots,
> Torturing convulsions from his globy eyes
> Had almost drawn their spheres, that what was life
> In him seem'd torture: this anatomy
> Had by his young fair fere a boy, and I
> Believ'd it was his, for she swore it was,
> And who would not believe her?

This emblem of the power of love is used in the address as a defense of the chastity of wives! Eighty does not see the end of Venus' power:

> O thou that from eleven to ninety reign'st
> In mortal bosoms, whose chase is this world,
> And we in herds thy game . . .

The long speech emphasizes not only the power of love to transform and to make the deformed more deformed, but also the surreptitious and clandestine. It is the close chamber work that is described, even if Palamon professes to reject it. As Muir mildly sums up, "The pleasanter side of love is not represented." Palamon, one of the victims of Venus, describes himself as:

> Thy vow'd soldier, who do bear thy yoke
> As 'twere a wreath of roses, yet is heavier
> Than lead itself, stings more than nettles.

Of this strange speech, Muir says it is absurd to think that Shakespeare "was putting his own personal sentiments into Palamon's mouth," and remarks that "Shakespeare was in danger of shattering the conventions in which the play was written," Muir makes a good justification of the speech in terms of Palamon's disillusioned temperament, the suffering and loss he has undergone through his love for Emilia, and the pains he has still to undergo—either to win the tournament and so cause the death of his blood-brother, Arcite, or else to lose, and so be executed. But perhaps Palamon is not meant to recognize the drift of his own speech; the cynicism *may* be not his, but Shakespeare's; I think we must consider what the conventions of this play are, before we say that this speech risks shattering them.

Both Spencer and Muir say that this address to Venus does not at all resemble the corresponding speech in Chaucer's *The Knight's Tale* (the source of the play). True, but in Chaucer's poem the walls of Venus' temple are painted with all the miseries of love:

> First in the temple of Venus maystow se,
> Wroght on the wal, ful pitous to biholde,
> The broken slepes, and the sikes colde,
> The sacred teeris, and the waymentynge,
> The firy strokes of the desirynge
> That loves servantz in this lyf enduren . . .
>
> (1918–23)*

The famous victims of love are also there, Solomon, Hercules, Medea and so on:

> Thus may ye seen that wysdom ne richesse,
> Beautee ne sleighte, strengthe ne hardyesse,
> Ne may with Venus holde champartie,
> For as hir list the world than may she gye.
> Lo, alle thise folk so caught were in hir las,
> Til they for wo ful ofte seyde 'allas!'
> Suffiseth heere ensamples oon or two,
> And though I koude rekene a thousand mo.
>
> (1947–54)

Chaucer's lines are an effective shortening of Boccaccio, and are central to his story. There is a corresponding mood in Theseus' derisive words as he finds the cousins, Arcite and Palamon, fighting to the death over a woman they have never spoken to, who knows nothing of their desire:

> Se how they blede! be they noght wel arrayed?
> Thus hath thir lord, the god of love, ypayed
> Hir wages and hir fees for hir servyse!
>
> (1801–03)

---

*Quotations from *The Knight's Tale* are taken from *The Works of Geoffrey Chaucer*, ed. F. N. Robinson, Cambridge, Mass. (1957).

The Knight's Tale is a magnificent study of human helplessness, of men and women floundering after happiness, but, being entirely at the mercy of love, of the mighty of this world,
and of the gods—or destiny—or fortune, moving steadily into
wretchedness. The image which comes out on top is the Boethian
image of the drunken man: every step he takes toward his house
is a step away from it.

> Infinite harmes been in this mateere.
> We witen nat what thing we preyen heere.
> We faren as he that dronke is as a mouse.
> A dronke man woot wel he hath an hous,
> But he noot which the righte wey is thider;
> And to a dronke man the wey is slider.
> And certes, in this world so faren we;
> We seken faste after felicitee,
> But we goon wrong ful often, trewely.

> (1259–67)

In the Prologue to *The Two Noble Kinsmen* is a tribute to
Chaucer, the seriousness of which is perhaps obscured by the
facetious tone of the opening lines and the conventional humility of the plea for sympathy. Twenty of the thirty-two lines keep
Chaucer in mind:

> Chaucer, of all admir'd, the story gives;
> There constant to eternity it lives . . .
> . . . to say truth, it were an endless thing,
> And too ambitious, to aspire to him,
> Weak as we are, and almost breathless swim
> In this deep water.

It seems to me that Shakespeare was fired by the dark
Chaucerian vision of what happened to two men pursuing
their desires, or being pursued by their desires. Emulation
would be the wrong word—the Prologue discounts it—but he
had his own dark vision to present of men moving into their
future as through a thick fog, and so slight a play as *The Two
Noble Kinsmen* is made much less slight when we understand
this vision, and realize that Palamon's address to Venus is
the center of the play. And what of Fletcher? According to
Spencer, Fletcher was congenitally incapable of appreciat-

ing the significance of the Shakespearian scenes. Certainly, Shakespeare's grand design sags when Fletcher takes over; but that he knew the design and tried to fill it out is inescapable.

To take simple matters first, the address to Venus is at all times relevant to the subplot of the jailer's daughter. She falls in love with Palamon, who is quite unaware of her passion during the whole of its wretched course. She acts to bind him to her, secretly letting him out of prison, but her action has no effect. She goes mad, her mind filled with images of sexual pleasure, and in the end she is brought towards a cure by her former wooer's pretending to be Palamon and going to bed with her. "For all the genuineness of her love," says Leech, "it is not proof against substitution," and he notices here an important link with Emilia's acquiescence in either of the two cousins as a husband. This we must look at later: at the moment, it is enough to say that the story of the jailer's daughter gives a particularly unpleasant picture of what happens when sexual desire gets hold of one:

> What pushes are we wenches driven to
> When fifteen once has found us!
>
> (2.3.6–7)

The idea of the play is very carefully worked into those first three slow-moving scenes which are unquestionably Shakespeare's. In the first scene, the solemn wedding of Theseus and Hippolyta is interrupted by the three widowed queens, who beseech Theseus to break off the wedding and go to war against Creon at Thebes; in the end he consents.

It is clear that Shakespeare is taking trouble to show us the marriage as a momentous change in Theseus' life. Before a word is spoken, there is the solemn ritual of the wedding procession, described in an elaborate stage direction. As the queens plead that he should turn aside, he insists on the magnitude of his resolution:

> This is a service, whereto I am going,
> Greater than any was; it more imports me
> Than all the actions that I have foregone
> Or futurely can cope.
>
> (1.1.170–73)

More portentously, he calls his marriage

> This grand act of our life, this daring deed
> Of fate in wedlock.

(163–64)

"This daring deed of fate" means, I think, "this deed which dares fate." Theseus sees himself as consciously bringing about, by marriage, an elemental change in his life. The sense of new life in marriage, of metempsychosis, almost, is seen more clearly in the appeal of one of the queens to Hippolyta:

> Honor'd Hippolyta,
> Most dreaded Amazonian, that hast slain
> The scythe-tusk'd boar; that, with thy arm as strong
> As it is white, wast near to make the male
> To thy sex captive, but that this thy lord—
> Born to uphold creation in that honor
> First Nature stilled it in—shrunk thee into
> The bound thou wast o'erflowing, at once subduing
> Thy force and thy affection . . .

(77–85)

Here, marriage is more than a change in a manner of life, it is the shaping of a new identity for Hippolyta. The images for this change of personality are startling. In making the Amazonian warrior a bride, Theseus is confirming the order of nature, but it is constriction and not release: "*shrunk* thee into/The bound thou wast o'erflowing"; "*subduing*/Thy force and thy affection." There is no sense here, of course, of crude subjugation; Hippolyta is more than acquiescent in her "shrinking": "never yet," she says, "went I so willing way" (103–04). Like Theseus, she moves by resolve into a new continent of her life; she moves also into a state which nature demands; but she moves also out of freedom into restriction.

By itself, this passing reference to Hippolyta's past life is nothing, and the images of containment might point only to the commonplace idea of there being truer fulfillment and freedom in the service and subordination of self in marriage. But the reference looks forward to the third scene, which elaborates, disconcertingly, the comparison between the two stages of life,

youth and the riper days of marriage. Hippolyta and Emilia
mention the former life of Theseus as they discuss the depth of
his friendship with Pirithous; Hippolyta appears to excuse herself from the charge of supplanting Pirithous:

> Their knot of love
> Tied, weav'd, entangled, with so true, so long,
> And with a finger of so deep a cunning,
> May be out-worn, never undone. I think
> Theseus cannot be umpire to himself,
> Cleaving his conscience into twain, and doing
> Each side like justice, which he loves best.

> (1.3.41–47)

To this, Emilia, all politeness, replies

> Doubtless
> There is a best, and reason has no manners
> To say it is not you.

> (47–49)

But her real reply follows at once in her very beautiful story of
her childhood love for Flavina, who died when she was eleven
("O thou that from eleven to ninety reign'st"). Theirs was a love
of absolute spontaneity and absolute Innocence:

> But I,
> And she I sigh and spoke of, were things innocent.
> Lov'd for we did, and like the elements
> That know not what nor why, yet do effect
> Rare issues by their operance, our souls
> Did so to one another: what she lik'd
> Was then of me approv'd; what not, condemn'd,
> No more arraignment; the flower that I would pluck
> And put between my breasts, O—then but beginning
> To swell about the blossom—she would long
> Till she had such another, and commit it
> To the like innocent cradle . . .

> (59–70)

The evocation of a state of happiness and innocent impulse is
wonderful, but Emilia calls it

> this rehearsal
> Which, every innocent wots well, comes in
> Like old importment's bastard.

(78–80)

This must mean (as Herford glimpsed) that words can give only the feeblest picture of what was once all-important. Finally, Emilia says she has told her story with this purpose, to show

> That the true love 'tween maid and maid may be
> More than in sex dividual.*

(81–82)

That Hippolyta is shaken by this firm belief that the second stage of life can yield nothing to compare with the spontaneous love of youth is clear from some asperity and assertiveness in her reply, which ends:

> But sure, my sister,
> If I were ripe for your persuasion, you
> Have said enough to shake me from the arm
> Of the all-noble Theseus; for whose fortunes
> I will now in and kneel, with great assurance
> That we, more than his Pirithous, possess
> The high throne in his heart.
>
> *Emilia.*   I am not
> Against your faith; yet I continue mine.

(90–97)

In these two scenes, there is the clearest presentation of three people conscious of the two major "ways of life" it is necessary to tread, innocence and experience, the impulsive life of youth with its friendship, and the more contained life of marriage. The first stage of each of the three characters has been shown to us: Hippolyta the "o'erflowing" Amazon, Theseus the warrior in firm bands of mutually supporting friendship with Pirithous, and, most fully, Emilia in childish love with Flavina. Theseus and Hippolyta have willingly moved to the second stage which Emilia refuses; she is sure she will not "love any that's call'd man" (85). The two ways of life have already been compared in

*"Individual" in the Quarto.

value; the poetic weight is obviously with innocence and Flavina.

The second scene of the play, introducing us to the noble kinsmen and having nothing to do with marriage, can now be seen to interlock. Palamon and Arcite, disgusted by the corruption of Thebes, dedicated to each other and to honor, resolve to break with their past and begin a new life elsewhere; they are prevented by the interruption of the news that Theseus is moving against Thebes; they decide that they must fight for their city in spite of their contempt for Creon. The course of this scene is parallel with the course of the first scene. In that first scene, Theseus, resolved to enter a new life, has to alter his resolution when the queens burst in on his wedding. Both Theseus and the cousins must put a good face on their being diverted from their intentions, justifying themselves as following the only honorable course, but the fact of diversion is underlined very strongly: the *action* of each scene is basically the action of change of cherished purpose under the pressure of unexpected events. It is, I think, a Chaucerian view of the frailty of our determinations which comes across, accompanied by the Chaucerian irony that the protagonists, accepting the change of purpose as being the only honorable choice, usher in the misery which follows. By supporting the queens, Theseus brings war to Thebes; by staying to fight in that war, Palamon and Arcite are captured and so brought to their fatal sight of Emily.

Palamon is troubled by the exigence of things pulling us aside from what we purpose; he knows it is his duty to fight under a man he despises, but will it not damage his soul? he asks:

> Our hands advanc'd before our hearts, what will
> The fall o' the stroke do damage?

Arcite's dour reply is deeper than it looks:

> Let th' event,
> That never-erring arbitrator, tell us
> When we know all ourselves; and let us follow
> The becking of our chance.

(1.2.112-16)

In other words, we shall know enough to comment on the morality of actions only when we see what the actions have led to; from that point of view, Palamon's question is idle, for we cannot judge beforehand the advisability of an action. That his question is idle from a second point of view is implied by Arcite's closing words; which suggest that we have little choice but to follow where chance beckons us. Perhaps I overinterpret, but I set these remarks, comments on the ignorance and ineffectiveness of man, by Theseus' famous remarks at the end of the play:

> O you heavenly charmers,
> What things you make of us! For what we lack
> We laugh, for what we have are sorry; still
> Are children in some kind. Let us be thankful
> For that which is, and with you leave dispute
> That are above our question.
>
> (5.4.130–35)

The first two scenes show the breaking of resolutions; the third scene stops short with a resolution—Emilia's, not to marry. Even if we did not know the story, we might guess the play would go on to tell us how she was proved wrong.

There is one more touch in these first three scenes which must be noted, Hippolyta's disbelief that Emilia will never "love any that's call'd man":

> I must no more believe thee in this point—
> Though in't I know thou dost believe thyself—
> *Than I will trust a sickly appetite,*
> *That loathes even as it longs.*
>
> (1.3.87–90)

We are here introduced to that division of the self, one of Venus' tortures, which has been seen in Palamon's invocation, when he spoke of himself bearing Venus' yoke as though it were a wreath of roses, "yet is heavier than lead itself." We seek what we know destroys. When a resolution means resisting a stage of life on which nature insists, the life of sexual relations, there will be more than unexpected happenings to fight against it, there will be one's own desires. In essence, Emilia's resolve is to live in the past, in the age before puberty; if the rest of the play is to show how vain such a resolve is, it is also going to show good grounds for that nostalgia for innocence.

We move from the first act with the themes of the play set out in full: a simplified division of life into the two stages of innocence and experience, the uncertainty of feeling with which one moves from one to another, a sense of how fragile our determinations are. We may well wish that Shakespeare had gone on to develop the themes and not left so much to Fletcher. But obviously Fletcher was working to Shakespeare's design (I hardly suppose it was Fletcher's in the first place).

In Act 2, scene 1, the imprisoned Palamon and Arcite talk about their predicament. The pleasures of their youth are ended, the pleasures of the future are closed to them:

> Here the graces of our youth must wither,
> Like a too timely spring; here age must find us,
> And which is heaviest, Palamon, unmarried.
>
> (2.1.81–83)

Arcite expatiates (it is too feeble to quote) on the pleasures of marriage and having children. He is thinking conventionally of the two stages of life, one kind of happiness following another in due season. But as the kinsmen try to rouse themselves from their dejection, they realize that the one thing which they can keep while they are in prison, their friendship and brotherhood, is in fact something finer than what marriage would bring:

> Here being thus together
> We are an endless mine to one another;
> We're one another's wife, ever begetting
> New births of love . . .
> Were we at liberty,
> A wife might part us lawfully, or business.
>
> (132–35; 142–43)

But almost at once they catch sight of Emilia, and, in wrangling over their "rights" to her love, their vaunted friendship and their vaunted superiority to the claims of women are alike shattered; the long and bitter rivalry begins.

Before Emilia walks in the garden, Arcite shows both a longing for marriage and an intenser clinging to a friendship which is above marriage. He is both the Theseus and the Emilia of the first act. But what are his divided sentiments worth? "Let us follow the becking of our chance"—even in prison. Once Emilia has walked beneath the window of their cell, there is no more basking in youthful friendship. They must take their future in the way in which chance and Venus insist upon it. It is a horrible enough future, because the Venus who debases them as they struggle with each other for Emilia is of course their own sexual nature.

It is interesting that Shakespeare and Fletcher, in handling the story, from the duel in the wood onwards, insist as Chaucer does not that whichever of the two cousins does *not* get Emily shall die. An extra incident is brought in (3.6.273–82) in which Emilia is given her choice of the two lovers, and the one not chosen is to die. In the deciding tournament, the dramatists leave out the ban on slaughter which Chaucer's Theseus pronounces. Not only do they leave it out, but they put in an extra scene of preparation for the execution of the loser, Palamon. One reason for this emphasis is, no doubt, to increase the painfulness of Emilia's position. But it is also a very strong way of indicating that to gain the new love is to destroy the old; it is the development of the theme played quietly in the first act, on the "rivalry" between Pirithous and Hippolyta for Theseus' affection. When Arcite is the victor in the lists, he says:

> Emily,
> To buy you I have lost what's dearest to me,
> Save what is bought.
>
> (5.3.111–13)

When Arcite has met with his fatal accident and Palamon is in turn received as husband, Palamon speaks to the dying man:

> O cousin,
> That we should things desire, which do cost us
> The loss of our desire! That naught could buy
> Dear love but loss of dear love.
>
> (5.4.108–11)

Emilia's role in both the old tale and in the play is central to the author's exhibition of the pains of love. In Chaucer, it is managed mainly by silence: Emily's passiveness and aloofness add much to the sense of the absurdity of the strife of the two cousins, and to the whole comment on human helplessness. Her prayer to Diana is that she be left alone:

Chaste goddesse, wel wostow that I
Desire to been a maiden al my lif,
Ne nevere wol I be no love ne wif.

(2304–06)

There is too little in this figure of silence and withdrawal to
make a character in a play; but up to the time of the tournament,
her role is amplified rather than changed. Her reasons for wishing to remain a maiden are magnificently filled out in the Flavina scene and though she plays a more active part in the scene in
which the cousins are discovered fighting in the wood, her answers are strictly neutral; she is moved by pity that these
young men should miscarry, not by affection or any desire for
a husband. But, from Act 4 onwards, Chaucer's Emily is completely altered and, in Fletcher's hands, immensely cheapened.
There is something missing in the play; we do not see her moving towards accepting her role as a wife; she is suddenly there,
trying to make up her mind which one of the cousins she likes
best. The design of the play has only temporarily disappeared.
When Shakespeare resumes with Emilia in Act 5, we can see
what was meant to happen; to romance a little, that Emilia
should move, listlessly and as in a dream, to abandon her old
resolution and accept "the becking of her chance":

This is my last
Of vestal office: I'm bride-habited,
But maiden-hearted: a husband I have 'pointed
But do not know him; out of two I should
Choose one, and pray for his success, but I
Am guiltless of election.

(5.1.149–54)

With the phrase, "I am guiltless of election," Emilia's indecision
over the merits of Palamon and Arcite, of which so much is made,
falls into place as a contrast with her relations with Flavina—
"Lov'd for we did." If we take Clifford Leech's hint, and link her
indecision with the willingness of the jailer's daughter to accept a
pseudo-Palamon as a lover, we can see more sharply the distinction between the two stages of love: the first all impulse and spontaneity, the second a forced movement into a love so half-hearted
that the object might be either of two cousins, a love so un-
centered that a substitute will do as well as the real thing. The

absurdity of the ending of the story—that Emilia should accept Arcite because he wins a fight, and then, when Arcite is killed, accept with equal readiness his cousin—is not "got round" by Shakespeare; it is the clinching of the case against Venus and the poverty of the relationships which she provides.

In this play, shared between two authors, the central idea is again and again approached from a different point; the idea is built up cumulatively by a series of comments and speeches which lie about the hub of the plot; the plot gets its true meaning by the reflected light of the surrounding meditations. We are given, clearly enough, a life in two stages: youth, in which the passion of spontaneous friendship is dominant, and the riper age in which there is a dominant sexual passion, leading to marriage where it can. The movement from one stage to the next, the unavoidable process of growth, is a movement away from innocence, away from joy. Theseus and Hippolyta apparently succeed in avoiding misery (are we meant to recall any of the tragic stories of love associated with the Theseus legend?), but the backward look to a fuller, richer youth is there for both; indeed, the lack of misery in Theseus and Hippolyta gives strength to a thesis of the loss of innocence which otherwise becomes too lurid.

The growth into experience I described as walking into the future as through a fog. Theseus goes forward boldly enough, but the postponement of the wedding by the three queens is an omen of the weakness of our powers. It is not our contriving that sends us steadily forward; we have to do what chance and circumstance and our own sexuality drive us to. The ingredients will differ. But, in the range between Emilia, with hardly any sexuality, and the jailer's daughter, all sexuality, there is not much free choice evident; the example of Palamon and Arcite is obviously meant to be the most striking. The irony of the way in which their course is shaped by chance and coincidence is harped on more by Chaucer than by Shakespeare, but it is in *The Two Noble Kinsmen*; what is most impressive is that every step, whether forced or free, in the course of that love which is the strongest thing in their lives, further disrupts the friendship which they know to be the finest thing in their lives. They are like men enchanted, gladly accepting what they are forced to do, yet knowing it to be ruin. The only arbitrator is "th' event."

If I see Shakespeare looking dim-eyed at innocence and seeing salvation disappear with puberty, I have to ask what relevance this "attack" on maturer life and love has to the portrayal of innocence in the earlier romances. There, sexual love may seem the natural and beautiful fulfillment of an otherwise immature innocence, particularly in Perdita and Miranda. But the idea of the deforming power of sexuality does exist in the romances; it is there in *Pericles,* when the youthful Pericles meets Antiochus' daughter and when Marina is in the brothel. It is there in *The Winter's Tale*; Clifford Leech most aptly cites (*op. cit.,* p. 149) Polixenes' recollection of his idyllic youth in friendship with Leontes:

> We were as twinn'd lambs that did frisk i' the sun,
> And bleat the one at the other: what we changed
> Was innocence for innocence; we knew not
> The doctrine of ill-doing, nor dream'd
> That any did. Had we pursued that life,
> And our weak spirits ne'er been higher rear'd
> With stronger blood, we should have answer'd heaven
> Boldly "not guilty"; the imposition clear'd,
> Hereditary ours.

(1.2.67–75)

There is no holding Shakespeare to one set of ideas; always, a new play releases a new evaluation; if we sense inconsistency it is generally because our vision is too myopic; we cannot hold such a range of focus as Shakespeare could. *The Two Noble Kinsmen* seems to me to give the most cynical assessment of the progress of life since the writing of *Troilus and Cressida.* It is a pity that Shakespeare did not write the whole of the play, but there is real intellectual substance in the work even as it is. Perhaps the flavor is unpalatable, still not the sort of thing one wants to associate Shakespeare with. Certainly, the vision is rather sweeping and careless of detail, but I believe it is Shakespearian.

LOIS POTTER

Tim Carroll's
The Two Noble Kinsmen, 2000

The Two Noble Kinsmen, directed by Tim Carroll, was the second production by the Red Company—without Vanessa Redgrave but with Yolanda Vasquez, who joined the company to play Hippolyta. Carroll trimmed the play not only of lines (particularly Shakespearean ones) but also of scenes (much of 1.1 and the whole of 1.2, which seems to have been a late decision) and of characters. The disappearance of the three knights who are supposed to support Palamon and Arcite in their combat meant that the heroes addressed to us, not to their followers, the speeches in the temple and (in Palamon's case) on the scaffold—a breaking of the dramatic illusion which the Chaucerian part of the play does not normally allow. At first viewing, I wondered how well the audience could understand what was going on, but I was in the yard on the second occasion and felt a remarkable degree of warmth toward the production. People were of course understanding what was there, not wondering about what wasn't. Though Carroll cut what he found boring, he did not remove what was merely difficult. Thus, Palamon retained his lines about the eighty-year-old man and his young bride, and Pirithous had most of his great final speech about the horse that goes mad. Moreover, the lines that did remain were given their full value, with, for example, beautiful orchestration of voices at antiphonal moments, as in 3.6 when Hippolyta, Emilia, and Pirithous were asking mercy for Palamon and Arcite.

From "Shakespeare at the Globe, 2000," *Shakespeare Quarterly* 52 (2001): 126–28 © Folger Shakespeare Library. Reprinted with permission of The Johns Hopkins University Press.

While most productions of this play go on the assumption that it was meant to be spectacular, Carroll opted for extreme simplicity. The "signs" given by the gods in the temple scene (5.1), for instance, were simple and unspectacular (a brief flare-up of flame for Arcite, smoke for Palamon, and, for Emilia, a rose whose petals crumble in her hand). The one scenic device was a structure suggesting a crude siege tower or catapult, topped with the giant skull of a horse and a tail. At times, it re-called the Greek theater's *ekkyklema,* a rolling platform appar-ently used to reveal characters who were unable to enter under their own power: the half-dead kinsmen were first seen lying at its base in 1.4. But it could also be representational: the prison of the kinsmen or a maypole in the morris dance scene, with red streamers emerging from its mouth. As something primitive and incomprehensible, like Peter Shaffer's *Equus,* it repre-sented the three gods who are addressed in the temple scene. In the final scene, it became both Palamon's scaffold and, by a turn as sudden as that of the story, the place where Arcite lay dying. It towered over Pirithous as he gave his famous speech, powerfully delivered by Jonathan Oliver, whose slow and pre-cise treatment of the climax left no doubt about exactly what had happened and how horrendous it was.

Because Carroll chose to cut 1.2, Jasper Britton and Will Keen, as Palamon and Arcite, first appeared in the prison scene, which was well balanced between idealism and egotism: Pala-mon's reaction to Arcite's declaration of love for Emilia—"I saw her first"—was so perfectly timed that it got not only laugh-ter but applause for the neatness with which it followed the vows of eternal friendship the two men had just been exchanging. Both characters easily established a good relationship with their audience—though I saw a few ominous signs that Britton might be planning to introduce more of the show-stealing behavior that had worked for his Caliban: there was a little too much giggling in 3.3, where the two men drink to "the wenches we have known" and the laughter at "How do I look?" in 3.6, where they arm each other for a fight that they don't really want nearly over-powering the pathos of the situation. But the remarkable mixture of comic and tragic in their relationship and its consequences was probably better judged than I have ever seen it before.

It helped that other characters treated them with sympathy. Martin Turner was an unusually likable and attractive Theseus, fully conscious of the cost of war (here made visible by the body bags for the three kings). When in 1.4 he announced his intention of posting back to Athens, the tone in which he named the city evoked not only Hippolyta's presence there but the extent to which Athens represented something valuable, the complete opposite of bloodstained, warlike Thebes. He was himself aware, rather than a butt, of the irony in his situation, as he was forced to modify his principles in the light of one complicated dilemma after another: "And, by my honor—*once again*—it stands." Carroll brought out his three-way relationship with Hippolyta and Pirithous (he danced with both of them in the forest), and Emilia's simple, lyrical speech about her eleven-year-old love for another girl, beautifully spoken by Geraldine Alexander, suggested that bisexuality was a natural state in the world of Athens. Emilia's reluctance to marry either kinsman was fully understandable in the context of her Amazonian background, which was more emphasized than usual. She kicked off her shoes with relief at the beginning of the garden scene (2.2) and put them on with reluctance in 4.2 when told to go meet her suitors.

The director intelligently gave Palamon a brief snatch of song at his first appearance to explain why the Jailer's Daughter later refers to his singing, and the young woman (who is never named) echoed it later, when she had gone mad for love of him. In this notoriously show-stealing role, which includes three consecutive soliloquies, Kate Fleetwood played to the whole house effectively but was admirably disciplined in avoiding the temptation to exploit her relationship with the audience. The fact that her madness made her so miserable gave her as much in common with Hamlet as with Ophelia and kept the part from becoming an occasion for cheap laughs about sex-starved women. Paul Chahidi, playing the wooer who impersonates Palamon out of a desperate desire to cure the Daughter's madness, said in a postperformance talk that the actors themselves had had no idea how the audience would take the play and were surprised at how many laughs they got. The basic question about all Fletcherian drama—"Just how funny is it supposed to be?"—is still being answered in different ways by different directors. This production was probably the most completely satisfactory that I have seen, though admittedly some of its success was the result of knowing what to cut. Despite its simplicity, it achieved some fine effects, as when the fragile beauty of the solo voice in the opening wedding song was followed by a chorus, placed all round the second gallery, scattering paper petals over the wedding

party as it entered through the yard. This procession was appropriately mirrored in Arcite's funeral procession at the end, which
took all the characters out of the yard; the Jailer's Daughter and
her Wooer brought up the rear, garlanded for their wedding but
sufficiently serious and perturbed to leave open the question of
her recovery.

SYLVAN BARNET

The Two Noble Kinsmen on Stage

The Two Noble Kinsmen has a surprisingly short stage history. Briefly, this history can be summarized thus:

1. Probably some performances in 1613, the date usually assigned to the composition of the play.
2. Possibly a performance at court around 1619.
3. Probably a revival around 1626.
4. Performances of William Davenant's much altered version, *The Rivals*, 1664–67.
5. Six performances by the Old Vic in 1928.
6. Eighteen or twenty productions, from 1954 to 2005.

But first, a disclaimer. The play's stage history may be a little richer than this outline suggests. For instance, although there is no hard evidence, it is entirely possible that the play was performed a number of times between 1613 and 1625. And although it is fairly certain that *The Two Noble Kinsmen* was not done (except in Davenant's drastic adaptation) later in the seventeenth century, and was not done again in any form until the Old Vic staged the original play in 1928, it is likely that in the last few decades some unrecorded performances have been given on college campuses. Still, even allowing for such productions, the record is extremely thin for a play associated with Shakespeare's name.

In his Introduction to the Signet edition, Clifford Leech sketches the evidence that the play was written around 1613 and staged in that year. It was not published until 1634, however, in a book whose title page says the play was "Presented at the Blackfriers," i.e., presented at the indoor theater that Shakespeare's company had fairly recently used for performances in the winter. Whether the play actually had remained in the regular repertory from the time of composition until 1634 is unknown, but may be doubted. There is not even indisputable evidence for a performance at Blackfriars or anywhere else in 1613. The evidence for a possible court performance around 1619 is also inconclusive, consisting only of the name of the play—along with the names of twenty-nine other plays—as a work under consideration for a court performance.

The evidence for a production in 1626, however, is fairly strong. As Leech points out in the Signet Classics edition the text includes the names of two actors who were with the company only around 1626. Presumably their names were inserted into a prompt copy prepared for a revival, and it was this copy which served as the source for the printed version of 1634.

Before turning to Davenant's reworking of the play and then to modern productions, we might spend a moment thinking about what an early seventeenth-century production of *The Two Noble Kinsmen* may have been like. Because of the title page's reference to Blackfriars, some scholars have perhaps overestimated the influence of this theater on the play, and on Shakespeare's other late plays, the plays that now are customarily called the romances. It has sometimes been said (without supporting evidence) that staging at Blackfriars was more elaborate, more spectacular, than at the Globe. The fact is that Shakespeare's *Pericles, Cymbeline*, and *The Winter's Tale*—three late plays with considerable spectacle—are known to have been staged at the Globe, and *The Tempest* may also have been staged there. Nothing in the staging of these plays, or of *The Two Noble Kinsmen*, was impossible for the Globe. A reader should understand, too, that such stage direction as

Enter Palamon as out of a bush [3.1.30]

and

Exeunt towards the temple [1.1.217]

do not require a bush or a temple. Such directions probably reflect the author's imagination rather than the stage's physical settings. In the second of these, for instance, the "temple" is probably no more than the stage door that is to be imagined as temple. On the other hand, some of the stage directions do give us a good idea of what the spectators saw, or what the playwright hoped they would see. For instance, after the prologue the play begins with this stage direction:

> *Enter Hymen with a torch burning; a boy in a white robe before, singing and strewing flowers; after Hymen, a nymph, encompassed in her tresses, bearing a wheaten garland; then Theseus between two other nymphs with wheaten chaplets on their heads; then Hippolyta the bride, led by Pirithous, and another holding a garland over her head, her tresses likewise hanging; after her, Emilia holding up her train. Music.*

There follows a song, and then we get this stage direction:

> *Enter three Queens in black, with veils stained, with imperial crowns. The first Queen falls down at the foot of Theseus; the second falls down at the foot of Hippolyta; the third before Emilia.*

Two other examples:

> *Here music is heard, doves are seen to flutter; they fall again upon their faces, then on their knees* [5.1.129]

And:

> *Still* [i.e., soft] *music of records* [i.e., recorders]. *Enter Emilia in white, her hair about her shoulders, a wheaten wreath; one in white holding up her train, her hair stuck with flowers; one before her carrying a silver hind* [i.e., a deer], *in which is conveyed incense and sweet odors, which being set up* [on the altar], *her maids standing, she sets fire to it; then they curtsy and kneel.* [5.1.136]

Most revivals of the play have tried to convey the rich formality of such scenes, though some have allowed humor to break in, and allowed audiences to smile (if not to laugh) at the courtesies of Palamon and Arcite.

Davenant's revival in the 1660s, really a play in its own right rather than a production of *The Two Noble Kinsmen*, may be briefly disposed of. Samuel Pepys, who saw it on September 10, 1664, remarked, "No excellent play, but good acting in it."

Pepys saw it again in December, and it seems to have held the stage at least until 1667. Davenant thoroughly revised Shakespeare's text, and altered all of the names of the characters, but he kept the rivalry of the two knights as the chief story, although Davenant's Arcite does not die at the end. Davenant omits the subplot of the Jailer's Daughter, and he invents a lady of status so that both knights can, at last, marry.

From 1667 until early 1928 the stage history of *The Two Noble Kinsmen* is a blank, but in the spring of 1928, the Old Vic company gave the play six performances. On the whole the critical reception was courteous—a few actors were praised and certain scenes were said to be effective—but there was little enthusiasm for the play, even though the company added some comic business (Palamon wore a red wig) in an effort to make the work acceptable. James Agate, probably the most influential critic of the day, in *Brief Chronicles* put it this way:

> After all, there must be a reason why a work of art should languish in oblivion, and three hundred years make a fairly conclusive test. Any play which is ever to come into its own should have done so in less than three hundred years; hence this play can have very little to come in to.
>
> The piece was most charmingly dressed and mounted in good Chaucerian vein, and one gathered that it was quite adequately acted. As Palamon Mr. Ernest Milton moped more than intelligently, and as Arcite Mr. Eric Portman wore with gusto the same romantic air and boots which he used for Juliet's lover. Miss Jean Forbes-Robertson lent her grave beauty to the Jailer's Daughter, and Miss Barbara Everett did her best with Emilia. But her best could not be good enough, since the art of acting has yet to be invented which shall cope successfully with a young woman allowing herself to be transferred—from one lover to another—like a sack of corn.

The next production seems not to have been given until 1954, when undergraduates at Harvard staged four performances. In the next thirty or so years it was performed by several college and regional theater groups, for instance the Reading University Dramatic Society (1959), the British Council (1970), and the Berkeley Shakespeare Festival (1985). After the Old Vic production in 1928, probably the first important production was at the York Theatre Royal in 1973, directed by Richard Digby. Although some reviewers fretted about the question of dual authorship, on the whole they enjoyed the production. The New Theatre Company's production in 1974, at Regents Park Open Air Theatre, received a few polite remarks and at least one commentator praised the stylized, ritualistic manner that is certainly appropriate for a play that begins with a procession headed by the god Hymen and that ends with the intervention of the gods. But the most memorable criticism was a brief dismissal made by a reviewer in *Drama* (Winter 1974).

> No amount of lesbianism, Fascist salutes or touches of Kabuki could breathe life into more than a passing phrase or two of this farrago.

The Cherub Company's 1979 production at Edinburgh and London, a heavily cut version initially performed on a stage only twelve feet square, was perhaps the most unusual revival. Directed by Andrew Visnevski, it was given by an all-male cast; the men who played men wore chains and leather pants with exaggerated codpieces, and those who played women had red and white circles painted around their nipples. The bare-chested hunky heroes, and especially their "tender ferocity" in the arming scene, strongly impressed one reviewer. Given Arcite's statement to Palamon, "We are one another's wife," today most viewers can hardly avoid seeing a homoerotic element in the play. Emilia's speech about "the true love 'tween maid and maid" is of course also relevant.

In 1979 Walter Scholz directed a Los Angeles production of the Shakespeare Society of America, which began with the entire cast onstage dancing while the Prologue was spoken and was highly praised for its effective use of dance and ritual; a 1985 heavily cut outdoor production at Berkeley, with Elizabethan costumes, was equally praised, especially for its willingness to allow the audience to be amused by some aspects of the play, including the death of Arcite. This Berkeley production, in which the director in his role as director spoke the Prologue and the Epilogue, is not to be confused with two earlier Berkeley productions—one in the open air—staged in 1979, nor with a later one, discussed below, staged in 2000.

In 1986 Barry Kyle directed the Royal Shakespeare Company in a somewhat abridged and in a few places rewritten version of *The Two Noble Kinsmen* at the Swan Theatre in Stratford-upon-Avon and later in London. (The Swan, a fairly small playhouse—in three tiers it seats 440 people, none farther than thirty feet from the stage—is devoted chiefly to performing relatively unfamiliar works of Shakespeare and his contemporaries.) This production caught much of the complexity or shifting styles of the play by combining the solemnity of ritual (parts of the play used conventions of the Japanese theater) with some folksy, rustic, Elizabethan humor and strong sexuality in the morris dance (a phallic maypole issued a stream of white silk aimed at female members of the cast). The Japanese elements, for instance samurai-like costumes, provided an interesting way of representing a remote code of honor. The two lovers, Palamon and Arcite, described in the play as " 'twins of honor' " and scarcely distinguishable to a reader, were in this production made distinct: Palamon was the fiery lover, Arcite the relatively cool soldier. (By the way, Palamon was played by a white actor, Gerard Murphy, and Arcite by a black, Hugh Quarshie.) Insofar as one can judge from reviews, this production seems to have been the best received of any production of the play in the twentieth century. In a review of Kyle's production, Roger Warren, in *Shakespeare Quarterly* 38 (Spring 1987), took the play seriously and saw it as a work about the terrible cost of love:

> Sexual love was linked repeatedly to destruction: the execution block was a pillow, and even the horse that kills Arcite was a gift from Emilia. At the close, Palamon knelt by Arcite, tears streaming down his face, clutching the rose that was the production's symbol of Venus and her destructive power; on either side of them stood Emilia, and the Jailer's Daughter, wearing identical veils, to bring out the bitter irony that either might have been his bride for all it mattered by comparison with what he had lost. It was a final image of the destructiveness of love in this play, a love that kills Arcite, deceives the Jailer's Daughter, and offers a bleak marriage prospect for Palamon and Emilia. (84)

In 1993 there were three productions. One, by Falstaff Productions, in New York, has been characterized as "postmodern," i.e., it was marked by ironies and discontinuities, though it must be said that even the straightest production of *The Two Noble Kinsmen* necessarily reveals ironic contrasts between, say, sanity and madness, and high ideals and savage behavior. Still, this version did what it could to dislocate the viewer. To take an almost trivial instance: The schoolmaster wore a red mortar-board and red shorts over what passed as an Elizabethan costume. Or, for a more significant instance: The singing of the mad daughter could be heard during the fight between Palamon and Arcite. A second production in 1993—this one very heavily cut, and acted by a small company, hence there was abundant doubling of roles—was given by the Red Heel Company in Philadelphia. Here, too, was a postmodern touch, since viewers were not always certain which role a given actor was performing. The third production of 1993 was given at the Ashland Shakespeare Festival in Oregon. It was set in the age of Chaucer, and throughout the performance a portrait of Chaucer hung above the stage. Costumes were a sort of fairy-tale medieval, and there was a great emphasis on spectacle. The most interesting production of the present century has been Tim Carroll's, at the Globe in London, in 2000. This production is discussed in a review by Lois Potter, which we print in this volume.

The Two Noble Kinsmen has rarely been staged—less often even than *Cymbeline* and *Pericles*—and, given Shakespeare's enormous popularity, the reasons probably are multiple. First, of course, is Fletcher's name; a coauthor's name is likely to diminish interest. But Lois Potter in *Shakespeare Quarterly* 47 (1996) offers additional reasons:

> Its collaborative nature is only part of the problem: when a play is successful, no one thinks of it as a collaboration anyway. More important is the fact that it does not lend itself to star casting, the theater's main way of selling an unusual revival; its central characters are young, and the plot demands that the two male leads be evenly balanced. The central female role, Emilia, is notoriously difficult to play. And although the subplot heroine, the Jailer's Daughter, invariably steals the show, and her soliloquies are now widely used as audition pieces, she, too, is young; and her role is more like to enable a star to be born . . . than to attract one already established. (198)

Bibliographic note: The editions of the play by Eugene Waith (1989) and by Lois Potter (1997) include useful stage histories, and Hugh Richmond has written a valuable essay on the topic in *Shakespeare, Fletcher, and "The Two Noble Kinsmen,"* ed. Charles Frey (1989). For twentieth-century productions through 1981, see G. Harold Metz, "*The Two Noble Kinsmen* on the Twentieth Century Stage," *Theatre History Studies* 4 (1984): 63–69. Most productions have been reviewed only very briefly, but some slightly longer reviews are of interest: On the Globe production in Los Angeles, see Joseph Stodder and Lillian Wilds in *Shakespeare Quarterly* 31 (1980): 254–74; on the all-male Cherub production of 1979, see Gerald M. Berkowitz in *Shakespeare Quarterly* 31 (1980): 163–67; on the Berkeley production of 1985, see *Shakespeare Quarterly* 37 (Autumn 1986): 396–97. On Barry Kyle's production of 1986, see *Shakespeare Quarterly* 38 (Spring 1987): 83–84; Nancy Klein Maguire in *Shakespeare Bulletin* 4:4 (July 1986): 8–9, and Nicholas Shrimpton in *Shakespeare Survey* 40 (1988): 175–77. Lois Potter, in *Shakespeare Quarterly* 47 (1996): 197–203, reviews three 1993 productions: Falstaff Productions, New York; Red Heel Theater Company, Walnut Studio, Philadelphia; Ashland Shakespeare Festival, Oregon; and in *Shakespeare Quarterly* 48 (1997): 225–27, Potter discusses a Japanese production of 1988. Potter's review of Tim Carroll's Royal Shakespeare Company production (2000) is reprinted above, in this volume.

Suggested References

The number of possible references is vast and grows alarmingly. (The *Shakespeare Quarterly* devotes one issue each year to a list of the previous year's work, and *Shakespeare Survey*—an annual publication—includes a substantial review of biographical, critical, and textual studies, as well as a survey of performances.) The vast bibliography is best approached through James Harner, *The World Shakespeare Bibliography on CD-Rom: 1900-Present*. The first release, in 1996, included more than 12,000 annotated items from 1990–93, plus references to several thousand book reviews, productions, films, and audio recordings. The plan is to update the publication annually, moving forward one year and backward three years. Thus, the second issue (1997), with 24,700 entries, and another 35,000 or so references to reviews, newspaper pieces, and so on, covered 1987–94.

For guidance to the immense amount that has been written, consult Larry S. Champion, *The Essential Shakespeare: An Annotated Bibliography of Major Modern Studies*, 2nd ed. (1993), which comments briefly on 1,800 publications.

Though no works are indispensable, those listed below have been found especially helpful. The arrangement is as follows:

1. Shakespeare's Times
2. Shakespeare's Life
3. Shakespeare's Theater
4. Shakespeare on Stage and Screen
5. Miscellaneous Reference Works
6. Shakespeare's Plays: General Studies
7. The Comedies
8. The Romances
9. The Tragedies
10. The Histories
11. *Pericles*
12. *Cymbeline*
13. *The Two Noble Kinsmen*

The titles in the first five sections are accompanied by brief explanatory annotations.

1. Shakespeare's Times

Andrews, John F., ed. *William Shakespeare: His World, His Work, His Influence*, 3 vols. (1985). Sixty articles, dealing not only with such subjects as "The State," "The Church," "Law," "Science, Magic, and Folklore," but also with the plays and poems themselves and Shakespeare's influence (e.g., translations, films, reputation).

Byrne, Muriel St. Clare. *Elizabethan Life in Town and Country* (8th ed., 1970). Chapters on manners, beliefs, education, etc., with illustrations.

Dollimore, John, and Alan Sinfield, eds. *Political Shakespeare: New Essays in Cultural Materialism* (1985). Essays on such topics as the subordination of women and colonialism, presented in connection with some of Shakespeare's plays.

Greenblatt, Stephen. *Representing the English Renaissance* (1988). New Historicist essays, especially on connections between political and aesthetic matters, statecraft and stagecraft.

Joseph, B. L. *Shakespeare's Eden: the Commonwealth of England 1558–1629* (1971). An account of the social, political, economic, and cultural life of England.

Kernan, Alvin. *Shakespeare, the King's Playwright: Theater in the Stuart Court 1603–1613* (1995). The social setting and the politics of the court of James I, in relation to *Hamlet, Measure for Measure, Macbeth, King Lear, Antony and Cleopatra, Coriolanus*, and *The Tempest*.

Montrose, Louis. *The Purpose of Playing: Shakespeare and the Cultural Politics of the Elizabethan Theatre* (1996). A poststructuralist view, discussing the professional theater "within the ideological and material frameworks of Elizabethan culture and society," with an extended analysis of *A Midsummer Night's Dream*.

Mullaney, Steven. *The Place of the Stage: License, Play, and Power in Renaissance England* (1988). New Historicist analysis, arguing that popular drama became a cultural institution "only by . . . taking up a place on the margins of society."

Schoenbaum, S. *Shakespeare: The Globe and the World* (1979). A readable, abundantly illustrated introductory book on the world of the Elizabethans.

Shakespeare's England, 2 vols. (1916). A large collection of scholarly essays on a wide variety of topics, e.g., astrology, costume, gardening, horsemanship, with special attention to Shakespeare's references to these topics.

2. Shakespeare's Life

Andrews, John F., ed. *William Shakespeare: His World, His Work, His Influence*, 3 vols. (1985). See the description above.

Bentley, Gerald E. *Shakespeare: A Biographical Handbook* (1961). The facts about Shakespeare, with virtually no conjecture intermingled.

Chambers, E. K. *William Shakespeare: A Study of Facts and Problems*, 2 vols. (1930). The fullest collection of data.

Fraser, Russell. *Young Shakespeare* (1988). A highly readable account that simultaneously considers Shakespeare's life and Shakespeare's art.

———. *Shakespeare: The Later Years* (1992).

Schoenbaum, S. *Shakespeare's Lives* (1970). A review of the evidence and an examination of many biographies, including those of Baconians and other heretics.

———. *William Shakespeare: A Compact Documentary Life* (1977). An abbreviated version, in a smaller format, of the next title. The compact version reproduces some fifty documents in reduced form. A readable presentation of all that the documents tell us about Shakespeare.

———. *William Shakespeare: A Documentary Life* (1975). A large-format book setting forth the biography with facsimiles of more than two hundred documents, and with transcriptions and commentaries.

3. Shakespeare's Theater

Astington, John H., ed. *The Development of Shakespeare's Theater* (1992). Eight specialized essays on theatrical companies, playing spaces, and performance.

Beckerman, Bernard. *Shakespeare at the Globe, 1599–1609* (1962). On the playhouse and on Elizabethan dramaturgy, acting, and staging.

Bentley, Gerald E. *The Profession of Dramatist in Shakespeare's Time* (1971). An account of the dramatist's status in the Elizabethan period.

———. *The Profession of Player in Shakespeare's Time, 1590–1642* (1984). An account of the status of members of London companies (sharers, hired men, apprentices, managers) and a discussion of conditions when they toured.

Berry, Herbert. *Shakespeare's Playhouses* (1987). Usefully emphasizes how little we know about the construction of Elizabethan theaters.

Brown, John Russell. *Shakespeare's Plays in Performance* (1966). A speculative and practical analysis relevant to all of the plays, but with emphasis on *The Merchant of Venice, Richard II, Hamlet, Romeo and Juliet,* and *Twelfth Night.*

———. *William Shakespeare: Writing for Performance* (1996). A discussion aimed at helping readers to develop theatrically conscious habits of reading.

Chambers, E. K. *The Elizabethan Stage,* 4 vols. (1945). A major reference work on theaters, theatrical companies, and staging at court.

Cook, Ann Jennalie. *The Privileged Playgoers of Shakespeare's London, 1576–1642* (1981). Sees Shakespeare's audience as wealthier, more middle-class, and more intellectual than Harbage (below) does.

Dessen, Alan C. *Elizabethan Drama and the Viewer's Eye* (1977). On how certain scenes may have looked to spectators in an Elizabethan theater.

Gurr, Andrew. *Playgoing in Shakespeare's London* (1987). Something of a middle ground between Cook (above) and Harbage (below).

———. *The Shakespearean Stage, 1579–1642* (3rd ed., 1992). On the acting companies, the actors, the playhouses, the stages, and the audiences.

———, and Mariko Ichikawa. *Staging in Shakespeare's Theatres* (2000). Like Alan C. Dessen's book, cited above, a careful analysis of what the Elizabethans saw on the stage.

Harbage, Alfred. *Shakespeare's Audience* (1941). A study of the size and nature of the theatrical public, emphasizing the representativeness of its working class and middle-class audience.

Hodges, C. Walter. *The Globe Restored* (1968). A conjectural restoration, with lucid drawings.

Hosley, Richard. "The Playhouses," in *The Revels History of Drama in English,* vol. 3, general editors Clifford Leech and T. W. Craik

(1975). An essay of a hundred pages on the physical aspects of the playhouses.

Howard, Jane E. "Crossdressing, the Theatre, and Gender Struggle in Early Modern England," *Shakespeare Quarterly* 39 (1988): 418–40. Judicious comments on the effects of boys playing female roles.

Orrell, John. *The Human Stage: English Theatre Design, 1567–1640* (1988). Argues that the public, private, and court playhouses are less indebted to popular structures (e.g., innyards and bear-baiting pits) than to banqueting halls and to Renaissance conceptions of Roman amphitheaters.

Slater, Ann Pasternak. *Shakespeare the Director* (1982). An analysis of theatrical effects (e.g., kissing, kneeling) in stage directions and dialogue.

Styan, J. L. *Shakespeare's Stagecraft* (1967). An introduction to Shakespeare's visual and aural stagecraft, with chapters on such topics as acting conventions, stage groupings, and speech.

Thompson, Peter. *Shakespeare's Professional Career* (1992). An examination of patronage and related theatrical conditions.

———. *Shakespeare's Theatre* (1983). A discussion of how plays were staged in Shakespeare's time.

4. Shakespeare on Stage and Screen

Bate, Jonathan, and Russell Jackson, eds. *Shakespeare: An Illustrated Stage History* (1996). Highly readable essays on stage productions from the Renaissance to the present.

Berry, Ralph. *Changing Styles in Shakespeare* (1981). Discusses productions of six plays (*Coriolanus, Hamlet, Henry V, Measure for Measure, The Tempest*, and *Twelfth Night*) on the English stage, chiefly 1950–1980.

———. *On Directing Shakespeare: Interviews with Contemporary Directors* (1989). An enlarged edition of a book first published in 1977, this version includes the seven interviews from the early 1970s and adds five interviews conducted in 1988.

Brockbank, Philip, ed. *Players of Shakespeare: Essays in Shakespearean Performance* (1985). Comments by twelve actors, reporting their experiences with roles. See also the entry for Russell Jackson (below).

Bulman, J. C., and H. R. Coursen, eds. *Shakespeare on Television* (1988). An anthology of general and theoretical essays, essays on individual productions, and shorter reviews, with a bibliography and a videography listing cassettes that may be rented.

Coursen, H. P. *Watching Shakespeare on Television* (1993). Analyses not only of TV versions but also of films and videotapes of stage presentations that are shown on television.

Davies, Anthony, and Stanley Wells, eds. *Shakespeare and the Moving Image: The Plays on Film and Television* (1994). General essays (e.g., on the comedies) as well as essays devoted entirely to *Hamlet, King Lear,* and *Macbeth.*

Dawson, Anthony B. *Watching Shakespeare: A Playgoer's Guide* (1988). About half of the plays are discussed, chiefly in terms of decisions that actors and directors make in putting the works onto the stage.

Dessen, Alan C. *Elizabethan Stage Conventions and Modern Interpretations* (1984). On interpreting conventions such as the representation of light and darkness and stage violence (duels, battles).

Donaldson, Peter. *Shakespearean Films/Shakespearean Directors* (1990). Postmodernist analyses, drawing on Freudianism, Feminism, Deconstruction, and Queer Theory.

Jackson, Russell, and Robert Smallwood, eds. *Players of Shakespeare 2: Further Essays in Shakespearean Performance by Players with the Royal Shakespeare Company* (1988). Fourteen actors discuss their roles in productions between 1982 and 1987.

———. *Players of Shakespeare 3: Further Essays in Shakespearean Performance by Players with the Royal Shakespeare Company* (1993). Comments by thirteen performers.

Jorgens, Jack. *Shakespeare on Film* (1977). Fairly detailed studies of eighteen films, preceded by an introductory chapter addressing such issues as music, and whether to "open" the play by including scenes of landscape.

Kennedy, Dennis. *Looking at Shakespeare: A Visual History of Twentieth-Century Performance* (1993). Lucid descriptions (with 170 photographs) of European, British, and American performances.

Leiter, Samuel L. *Shakespeare Around the Globe: A Guide to Notable Postwar Revivals* (1986). For each play there are about two pages of introductory comments, then discussions (about five hundred words per production) of ten or so productions, and finally bibliographic references.

McMurty, Jo. *Shakespeare Films in the Classroom* (1994). Useful evaluations of the chief films most likely to be shown in undergraduate courses.

Rothwell, Kenneth, and Annabelle Henkin Melzer. *Shakespeare on Screen: An International Filmography and Videography* (1990). A reference guide to several hundred films and videos produced between 1899 and 1989, including spinoffs such as musicals and dance versions.

Smallwood, Robert. *Players of Shakespeare 4* (1998). Like the volumes by Brockbank and Jackson, listed above, contains remarks by contemporary performers.

Sprague, Arthur Colby. *Shakespeare and the Actors* (1944). Detailed discussions of stage business (gestures, etc.) over the years.

Willis, Susan. *The BBC Shakespeare Plays: Making the Televised Canon* (1991). A history of the series, with interviews and production diaries for some plays.

5. Miscellaneous Reference Works

Abbott, E. A. *A Shakespearean Grammar* (new edition, 1877). An examination of differences between Elizabethan and modern grammar

Allen, Michael J. B., and Kenneth Muir, eds. *Shakespeare's Plays in Quarto* (1981). One volume containing facsimiles of the plays issued in small format before they were collected in the First Folio of 1623.

Blake, Norman. *Shakespeare's Language: An Introduction* (1983). On vocabulary, parts of speech, and word order.

Bullough, Geoffrey. *Narrative and Dramatic Sources of Shakespeare,* 8 vols. (1957–75). A collection of many of the books Shakespeare drew on, with judicious comments.

Campbell, Oscar James, and Edward G. Quinn, eds. *The Reader's Encyclopedia of Shakespeare* (1966). Old, and in some ways superseded by Michael Dobson's *Oxford Companion* (see below), but still highly valuable.

Cercignani, Fausto. *Shakespeare's Works and Elizabethan Pronunciation* (1981). Considered the best work on the topic, but remains controversial.

Champion, Larry S. *The Essential Shakespeare: An Annotated Bibliography of Major Modern Studies* (2nd ed., 1993). An invaluable guide to 1,800 writings about Shakespeare.

Dent, R. W. *Shakespeare's Proverbial Language: An Index* (1981). An index of proverbs, with an introduction concerning a form Shakespeare frequently drew on.

Dobson, Michael, ed. *The Oxford Companion to Shakespeare* (2001). Probably the single most useful reference work for information (arranged alphabetically) about Shakespeare and his works.

Greg, W. W. *The Shakespeare First Folio* (1955). A detailed yet readable history of the first collection (1623) of Shakespeare's plays.

Harner, James. *The World Shakespeare Bibliography.* See headnote to Suggested References.

Hosley, Richard. *Shakespeare's Holinshed* (1968). Valuable presentation of one of Shakespeare's major sources.

Kökeritz, Helge. *Shakespeare's Names* (1959). A guide to pronouncing some 1,800 names appearing in Shakespeare.

———. *Shakespeare's Pronunciation* (1953). Contains much information about puns and rhymes, but see Cercignani (above).

Muir, Kenneth. *The Sources of Shakespeare's Plays* (1978). An account of Shakespeare's use of his reading. It covers all the plays, in chronological order.

Miriam Joseph, Sister. *Shakespeare's Use of the Arts of Language* (1947). A study of Shakespeare's use of rhetorical devices, reprinted in part as *Rhetoric in Shakespeare's Time* (1962).

The Norton Facsimile: The First Folio of Shakespeare's Plays (1968). A handsome and accurate facsimile of the first collection (1623) of Shakespeare's plays, with a valuable introduction by Charlton Hinman.

Onions, C. T. *A Shakespeare Glossary,* rev. and enlarged by R. D. Eagleson (1986). Definitions of words (or senses of words) now obsolete.

Partridge, Eric. *Shakespeare's Bawdy,* rev. ed. (1955). Relatively brief dictionary of bawdy words; useful, but see Williams, below.

Shakespeare Quarterly. See headnote to Suggested References.

Shakespeare Survey. See headnote to Suggested References.

Spevack, Marvin. *The Harvard Concordance to Shakespeare* (1973). An index to Shakespeare's words.

Vickers, Brian. *Appropriating Shakespeare: Contemporary Critical Quarrels* (1993). A survey—chiefly hostile—of recent schools of criticism.

Wells, Stanley, ed. *Shakespeare: A Bibliographical Guide* (new edition, 1990). Nineteen chapters (some devoted to single plays, others devoted to groups of related plays) on recent scholarship on the life and all of the works.

Williams, Gordon. *A Dictionary of Sexual Language and Imagery in Shakespearean and Stuart Literature,* 3 vols. (1994). Extended discussions of words and passages; much fuller than Partridge, cited above.

6. Shakespeare's Plays: General Studies

Bamber, Linda. *Comic Women, Tragic Men: A Study of Gender and Genre in Shakespeare* (1982).

Barnet, Sylvan. *A Short Guide to Shakespeare* (1974).

Callaghan, Dympna, Lorraine Helms, and Jyotsna Singh. *The Weyward Sisters: Shakespeare and Feminist Politics* (1994).

Clemen, Wolfgang H. *The Development of Shakespeare's Imagery* (1951).

Cook, Ann Jennalie. *Making a Match: Courtship in Shakespeare and His Society* (1991).

Dollimore, Jonathan, and Alan Sinfield, eds. *Political Shakespeare: New Essays in Cultural Materialism* (1985).

Dusinberre, Juliet. *Shakespeare and the Nature of Women* (1975).

Granville-Barker, Harley. *Prefaces to Shakespeare,* 2 vols. (1946–47; volume 1 contains essays on *Hamlet, King Lear, Merchant of Venice, Antony and Cleopatra,* and *Cymbeline*; volume 2 contains essays on *Othello, Coriolanus, Julius Caesar, Romeo and Juliet, Love's Labor's Lost*).

———. *More Prefaces to Shakespeare* (1974; essays on *Twelfth Night, A Midsummer Night's Dream, The Winter's Tale, Macbeth*).

Harbage, Alfred. *William Shakespeare: A Reader's Guide* (1963).

Howard, Jean E. *Shakespeare's Art of Orchestration: Stage Technique and Audience Response* (1984).

Jones, Emrys. *Scenic Form in Shakespeare* (1971).

Lenz, Carolyn Ruth Swift, Gayle Greene, and Carol Thomas Neely, eds. *The Woman's Part: Feminist Criticism of Shakespeare* (1980).

Novy, Marianne. *Love's Argument: Gender Relations in Shakespeare* (1984).

Rose, Mark. *Shakespearean Design* (1972).

Scragg, Leah. *Discovering Shakespeare's Meaning* (1994).

————. *Shakespeare's "Mouldy Tales": Recurrent Plot Motifs in Shakespearean Drama* (1992).

Traub, Valerie. *Desire and Anxiety: Circulations of Sexuality in Shakespearean Drama* (1992).

Traversi, D. A. *An Approach to Shakespeare,* 2 vols. (3rd rev. ed. 1968–69).

Vickers, Brian. *The Artistry of Shakespeare's Prose* (1968).

Wells, Stanley. *Shakespeare: A Dramatic Life* (1994).

Wright, George T. *Shakespeare's Metrical Art* (1988).

7. The Comedies

Barber, C. L. *Shakespeare's Festive Comedy* (1959; discusses *Love's Labor's Lost, A Midsummer Night's Dream, The Merchant of Venice, As You Like It, Twelfth Night*).

Barton, Anne. *The Names of Comedy* (1990).

Berry, Ralph. *Shakespeare's Comedy: Explorations in Form* (1972).

Bradbury, Malcolm, and David Palmer, eds. *Shakespearean Comedy* (1972).

Bryant, J. A., Jr. *Shakespeare and the Uses of Comedy* (1986).

Carroll, William. *The Metamorphoses of Shakespearean Comedy* (1985).

Champion, Larry S. *The Evolution of Shakespeare's Comedy* (1970).

Evans, Bertrand. *Shakespeare's Comedies* (1960).

Frye, Northrop. *Shakespearean Comedy and Romance* (1965).

Leggatt, Alexander. *Shakespeare's Comedy of Love* (1974).

Miola, Robert S. *Shakespeare and Classical Comedy: The Influence of Plautus and Terence* (1994).

Nevo, Ruth. *Comic Transformations in Shakespeare* (1980).

Ornstein, Robert. *Shakespeare's Comedies: From Roman Farce to Romantic Mystery* (1986).

Richman, David. *Laughter, Pain, and Wonder: Shakespeare's Comedies and the Audience in the Theater* (1990).

Salingar, Leo. *Shakespeare and the Traditions of Comedy* (1974).

Slights, Camille Wells. *Shakespeare's Comic Commonwealths* (1993).

Waller, Gary, ed. *Shakespeare's Comedies* (1991).

Westlund, Joseph. *Shakespeare's Reparative Comedies: A Psychoanalytic View of the Middle Plays* (1984).

Williamson, Marilyn. *The Patriarchy of Shakespeare's Comedies* (1986).

8. The Romances (*Pericles, Cymbeline, The Winter's Tale, The Tempest, The Two Noble Kinsmen*)

Adams, Robert M. *Shakespeare: The Four Romances* (1989).
Felperin, Howard. *Shakespearean Romance* (1972).
Frye, Northrop. *A Natural Perspective: The Development of Shakespearean Comedy and Romance* (1965).
Mowat, Barbara. *The Dramaturgy of Shakespeare's Romances* (1976).
Warren, Roger. *Staging Shakespeare's Late Plays* (1990).
Young, David. *The Heart's Forest: A Study of Shakespeare's Pastoral Plays* (1972).

9. The Tragedies

Bradley, A. C. *Shakespearean Tragedy* (1904).
Brooke, Nicholas. *Shakespeare's Early Tragedies* (1968).
Champion, Larry S. *Shakespeare's Tragic Perspective* (1976).
Drakakis, John, ed. *Shakespearean Tragedy* (1992).
Evans, Bertrand. *Shakespeare's Tragic Practice* (1979).
Everett, Barbara. *Young Hamlet: Essays on Shakespeare's Tragedies* (1989).
Foakes, R. A. *Hamlet versus Lear: Cultural Politics and Shakespeare's Art* (1993).
Frye, Northrop. *Fools of Time: Studies in Shakespearean Tragedy* (1967).
Harbage, Alfred, ed. *Shakespeare: The Tragedies* (1964).
Mack, Maynard. *Everybody's Shakespeare: Reflections Chiefly on the Tragedies* (1993).
McAlindon, T. *Shakespeare's Tragic Cosmos* (1991).
Miola, Robert S. *Shakespeare and Classical Tragedy: The Influence of Seneca* (1992).
———. *Shakespeare's Rome* (1983).
Nevo, Ruth. *Tragic Form in Shakespeare* (1972).
Rackin, Phyllis. *Shakespeare's Tragedies* (1978).

Rose, Mark, ed. *Shakespeare's Early Tragedies: A Collection of Critical Essays* (1995).

Rosen, William. *Shakespeare and the Craft of Tragedy* (1960).

Snyder, Susan. *The Comic Matrix of Shakespeare's Tragedies* (1979).

Wofford, Susanne. *Shakespeare's Late Tragedies: A Collection of Critical Essays* (1996).

Young, David. *The Action to the Word: Structure and Style in Shakespearean Tragedy* (1990).

———. *Shakespeare's Middle Tragedies: A Collection of Critical Essays* (1993).

10. The Histories

Blanpied, John W. *Time and the Artist in Shakespeare's English Histories* (1983).

Campbell, Lily B. *Shakespeare's "Histories": Mirrors of Elizabethan Policy* (1947).

Champion, Larry S. *Perspective in Shakespeare's English Histories* (1980).

Grene, Nicholas. *Shakespeare's Serial History Plays* (2002).

Hodgdon, Barbara. *The End Crowns All: Closure and Contradiction in Shakespeare's History* (1991).

Holderness, Graham. *Shakespeare Recycled: The Making of Historical Drama* (1992).

———, ed. *Shakespeare's History Plays: "Richard II" to "Henry V"* (1992).

Jones, Robert C. *Those Valiant Dead: Reviving the Past in Shakespeare's Histories* (1991).

Knowles, Ronald. *Shakespeare's Arguments with History* (2002).

Leggatt, Alexander. *Shakespeare's Political Drama: The History Plays and the Roman Plays* (1988).

Levine, Nina S. *Women's Matters: Politics, Gender, and Nation in Shakespeare's Early History Plays* (1998).

Ornstein, Robert. *A Kingdom for a Stage: The Achievement of Shakespeare's History Plays* (1972).

Pugliatti, Paola. *Shakespeare the Historian* (1996).

Rackin, Phyllis. *Stages of History: Shakespeare's English Chronicles* (1990).

Reese, Max Meredith. *The Cease of Majesty: A Study of Shakespeare's History Plays* (1961).

Ribner, Irving. *The English History Play in the Age of Shakespeare* (rev. ed., 1965).

Saccio, Peter. *Shakespeare's English Kings* (2nd ed., 1999).

Spiekerman, Tim. *Shakespeare's Political Realism* (2001).

Tillyard, E.M.W. *Shakespeare's History Plays* (1944).

Velz, John W., ed. *Shakespeare's English Histories: A Quest for Form and Genre* (1996).

11. *Pericles*

Useful scholarly editions of *Pericles* have been prepared by Doreen DelVecchio and Antony Hammond (1998), Roger Warren (2003), and Susan Gossett (2004).

For a bibliographic guide covering the years 1940–85, see Nancy C. Michael's *Pericles,* listed below.

For readings concerned with stage and television productions, see the bibliographic note above, following *Pericles* on Stage and Screen, and see the material, also above, in Section 4 of this list of Suggested References. See also David Skeele's book, listed below.

For the play in the context of Shakespeare's other late plays, see above, Section 8.

Many important essays, on all aspects of the play (e.g., text, interpretation, production) are reprinted in volumes 2, 15, 36, 51, 66, 79, and 90 of *Shakespearean Criticism.* For a collection of critical essays, see (below) David Skeele's *Pericles.*

Danby, John F. *Poets on Fortune's Hill* (1952). A portion is reprinted above.

Edwards, Philip. "An Approach to the Problem of *Pericles.*" *Shakespeare Survey* 5 (1952): 25–49.

Ewbank, Inga-Stina. " 'My Name Is Marina': The Language of Recognition," in *Shakespeare's Styles.* Ed. Philip Edwards et al. (1980), pp. 111–30.

Frye, Northrop. *A Natural Perspective* (1965).

Helms, Lorraine. "The Saint in the Brothel: Or, Eloquence Rewarded." *Shakespeare Quarterly* 41 (1990): 319–32.

Hoeniger, F. David. "Gower and Shakespeare in *Pericles.*" *Shakespeare Quarterly* 33 (1982): 461–79.

Jackson, MacDonald P. *Defining Shakespeare: "Pericles" as a Test Case* (2003).

Knight, G. Wilson. *The Crown of Life* (1948). A portion is reprinted above.

Michael, Nancy C. *"Pericles": An Annotated Bibliography* (1987).

Muir, Kenneth. *Shakespeare as Collaborator* (1960). A portion is reprinted above.

Skeele, David. *Pericles: Critical Essays* (2000)

———. *Thwarting the Wayward Seas: A Critical and Theatrical History of Shakespeare's "Pericles" in the Nineteenth and Twentieth Centuries* (1998).

Taylor, Gary. "The Transmission of *Pericles*." *Papers of the Bibliographical Society of America* 80 (1986): 193–217.

Tillyard, E.M.W. *Shakespeare's Last Plays* (1938).

Traversi, D. A. *Shakespeare: The Last Phase* (1954).

Vickers, Brian. *Shakespeare, Co-Author* (2002).

12. *Cymbeline*

Useful scholarly editions of *Cymbeline* have been prepared by J. M. Nosworthy (1955) and by Martin Butler (2005).

For a bibliographic guide (covering material from 1864 to 2000) to all three of the romances, see *"Cymbeline," "The Winter's Tale," and "The Tempest,"* ed. John S. Mebane (2002).

For readings concerned with stage and television productions, see the bibliographic note above, following "*Cymbeline* on Stage and Screen," and see the material, also above, in Section 4 of this list of Suggested References.

For the play in the context of Shakespeare's other late plays, see above, Section 8.

Many important essays, on all aspects of the play (e.g., text, interpretation, production) are reprinted in volumes 4, 15, 36, 47, 61, 73, 84, and 93 of *Shakespearean Criticism.*

Brockbank, J. P. "History and Histrionics in *Cymbeline*." *Shakespeare Survey* 11 (1958): 42–49.

Crumley, J. Clinton. "Questioning History in *Cymbeline*." *Studies in English Literature 1500–1900* 41(2001): 297–316

Desmet, Christy. "Shakespearian Comic Character: Ethos and Epideictic in *Cymbeline*," in *Acting Funny: Comic Theory and Practice in Shakespeare's Plays.* Ed. Frances Teague (1994), pp. 123–41.

Dubrow, Heather. *Shakespeare and Domestic Loss: Forms of Deprivation, Mourning, and Recuperation* (1999).

Gajowski, Evelyn. "Sleeping Beauty, or 'What's the Matter?': Female Sexual Autonomy, Voyeurism, and Misogyny in *Cymbeline*, in *Re-Visions of Shakespeare: Essays in Honor of Robert Ornstein*. Ed. Evelyn Gajowski (2004), pp. 89–107.

Gesner, Carol. *"Cymbeline"* and the Greek Romance: A Study in Genre," in *Studies in English Renaissance Literature*. Ed. W. F. McNeir (1962), pp. 105–31.

Gibbons, Brian. *Shakespeare and Multiplicity* (1993).

King, Ros. *"Cymbeline": Constructions of Britain* (2005).

Mikalachki, Jodi. *The Legacy of Boadicea: Gender and Nation in Early Modern England* (1998).

Simonds, Peggy Muñoz. *Myth, Emblem, and Music in Shakespeare's "Cymbeline."* (1992).

13. *The Two Noble Kinsmen*

Useful scholarly editions of *The Two Noble Kinsmen* have been prepared by G. R. Proudfoot (1970), Eugene Waith (1989), and Lois Potter (1997).

For readings concerned with stage productions, see the bibliographic note above, following *The Two Noble Kinsmen* on Stage, and see the material, also above, in Section 4 of this list of Suggested References.

For the play in the context of Shakespeare's other romances, see above, Section 8.

Many important essays, on all aspects of the play (e.g., authorship, interpretation, production), are reprinted in volumes 9, 41, 50, 58, and 70 of *Shakespearean Criticism*.

Berggren, Paula. " 'For what we lack,/We laugh': Incompletion and *The Two Noble Kinsmen*." *Modern Language Studies* 14 (1984): 3–17.

Bertram, Paul. *Shakespeare and "The Two Noble Kinsmen"* (1965).

Bruster, Douglas. "The Jailer's Daughter and the Politics of Madwomen's Language." *Shakespeare Quarterly* 46 (1995): 277–300.

Donaldson, E. Talbot. *The Swan at the Well: Shakespeare Reading Chaucer* (1985).

Frey, Charles, ed. *Shakespeare, Fletcher, and "The Two Noble Kinsmen"* (1989).

Hillman, Richard. "Shakespeare's Romantic Innocents and the

Misappropriation of the Romantic Past: The Case of *The Two Noble Kinsmen.*" *Shakespeare Survey* 43 (1991): 69–79.

Leech, Clifford. *The John Fletcher Plays* (1962).

Muir, Kenneth. *Shakespeare as Collaborator* (1960).

Shannon, Laurie. *Sovereign Amity: Figures of Friendship in Shakespearean Contexts* (2002).

Sinfield, Alan. "Cultural Materialism and Intertextuality: The Limits of Queer Reading in *A Midsummer Night's Dream* and *The Two Noble Kinsmen.*" *Shakespeare Survey* 56 (2003): 67–78.

Sullivan, Garrett A. *The Drama of Landscape: Land, Property and Social Relations on the Early English Stage* (1998).

Thompson, Ann. *Shakespeare's Chaucer: A Study in Literary Origins* (1978).

Vickers, Brian. *Shakespeare, Co-Author* (2002).

The Signet Classics
Shakespeare Series:

The Histories

EXTENSIVELY REVISED AND UPDATED EXPERT
COMMENTARY PROVIDES MORE ENJOYMENT THROUGH
A GREATER UNDERSTANDING OF THE TEXTS

HENRY IV: PART I, Maynard Mack, ed.

HENRY IV: PART II, Norman Holland, ed.

HENRY V, John Russell Brown, ed.

HENRY VI: PARTS I, II, & III, Lawrence V. Ryan,
Arthur Freeman, & Milton Crane, ed.

RICHARD II, Kenneth Muir, ed.

RICHARD III, Mark Eccles, ed.

**Available wherever books are sold or at
signetclassics.com**